The Billboard Guide to Progressive Music

The Billboard Guide to Progressive Music

Bradley Smith

BILLBOARD BOOKS
An Imprint of Watson-Guptill Publications
New York

Senior Editor: Bob Nirkind
Edited by: Sylvia Warren
Book and cover design: Areta Buk
Production Manager: Ellen Greene

First published 1997 by Billboard Books, an imprint of Watson-Guptill Publications, a division of Billboard Productions, Inc., at 1515 Broadway, New York, NY 10036

Library of Congress Cataloging-in-Publication Data
Smith, Bradley.
The Billboard guide to progressive music / Bradley Smith.
p. cm.
ISBN 0-8230-7665-2
1. Popular music—Discography. 2. Progressive rock music—Discography. 3. Avant garde (Music)—Discography. I. Title.
ML 156.4.P6S6 1997
781.64—dc21
97-19899
CIP
MN

Manufactured in the United States of America

First printing, 1997

1 2 3 4 5 6 7 8 9 / 06 05 04 03 02 01 00 99 98 97

THIS BOOK IS DEDICATED TO MY DEAR AND BELOVED MOTHER,
WHO HAS BEEN MY GREATEST FRIEND AND TEACHER,
AND WHO HAS ALWAYS STOOD BY ME IN TIMES OF TRIAL.

ACKNOWLEDGMENTS

Thanks to Mark Olson and Ira Rosenblatt, for their valuable assistance in the digital realms and for finally giving up the attempt to get me to abandon my beloved typewriters.

Thanks to James Resemius, Mark Lillemoen, Gerald Bosch, Diane Rubright, and Linden Dahlstrom for their support and encouragement.

Thanks also to Brian Durham, for providing a constant source of inspiration.

I would also like to thank Alan Freeman, the writer and publisher of *Audion* magazine in the U.K., for beginning (in the 1980s) the all-important written record and dialogue about this wonderful music.

And thanks especially to all those at Billboard Books, for their commitment to this project and to the furtherance of the appreciation of progressive music.

Contents

Introduction

What is progressive music? It is, first and foremost, an art form, one that is concerned with abstraction and introspection, rather than with the commercially-driven trends and fashions that shape works created purely for entertainment. Progressive music always looks forward, striving to be new and different, dissenting vigorously from the current musical establishment. Like all serious art, it is a challenge to the senses, and like all serious music, it requires active listening. The term "progressive" was once applied to the avant-garde fringe of the popular music categories *rock* (prog rock), *jazz* (progressive jazz), and *new age*. However, in a development that has until recently completely escaped the attention of the mainstream media, progressive music has become a genre unto itself, with a large canon of titles.

It is universally accepted that when we listen to music, our responses are uniquely personal. All the elements of what we are listening to—harmonics, color, drama, narrative, mood—form impressions in our mind totally different from anyone else's. Yet neither the mainstream music industry nor music critics fully take into account the almost limitless possibilities inherent in the way that human beings process and react to sound. Progressive music, which began in the 1960s and has grown steadily since then, represents a demonstration of those possibilities.

Progressive music is about sound itself and all the diversity which that implies. It involves lengthy works of electronics, solo piano or guitar, sounds of nature, collage constructions, and dense conceptual pieces, as well as more familiar sounds such as band-oriented jams featuring the standard guitars, percussion, keyboards, and bass.

Today's media environment, with its aural bombardments and competing musical agendas, has fostered a "one mind" world of listener conformity. It is a world where people give lip service to music's vast imaginative dimensions, yet rarely celebrate such diversity when it appears. In other words, we either accept the music delivered to us via the narrow media pipelines, or we're judged to be "out of it." Most musical discussion (in the popular realm) is shackled and chained to a commercial and competitive perception of what is "in" and what is "out," who is up and who is down. Discussions among the musically "hip" are about styles, fashions, trends, personalities, technologies, instruments, and—above all—sales. But if we view music as art, even music in the popular realm, then we must deplore such a low level of debate, which deals in superficialities and has the effect of sucking the "art" right out of music. Unfortunately, this situation has existed for a long time, and the fact that it continues to flourish in what is alleged to be an enlightened age is a glaring failure of art education in general and music education in particular.

The popular styles of music (the nonclassical forms) that control most of the artillery in the media music wars have become, largely, commercial contrivances, and as such, are far too limiting. The now-generic forms of song length and structure as well as other formulaic techniques combine to create a conformity of expression and perception. The three- to five-minute vocal with an easily understood content and direction is the form preferred by the musical mainstream genres (pop, rock, jazz, country, blues, rap, folk, etc.). This popular formula looms over musicians like an autocratic dictator—those who fail to acknowledge its power face exclusion from the commercial realms and ridicule from the critical pulpits. Deviation from popular styles puts the music at risk of being perceived as unprofitable and unhip, or not being heard at all.

This is not to deny the validity of precedents set by popular musical forms. To appreciate what has gone before is essential. But precedents exist to be challenged or toppled utterly, and relying on precedent is not a progressive act. For those looking for the great leap forward in modern music, it is here, and it is the progressive music genre. Progressive music is breaking the chains that keep music bound to the popular genres, and is ready to topple the dictatorship of old formulas with a coup of new ideas.

In many ways, the artists and audiences of the progressive music movement have always operated as though they constituted a distinct genre, comparable to other genres, yet the music industry hasn't acknowledged this or given progressive music its blessing. Progressive music has been routinely ignored by radio, critics, video channels, and the media in general, and conspicuously absent from awards ceremonies. For too long now, the critical music establishment in the U.S. and U.K. have promulgated the notion that the artists deserving of the most attention are those who are the most profitable and fashionable. In this way, the function of the music critic has been perverted completely by market-driven concerns and trends, and the public's attention has long been diverted away from the innovators toward the mediocrities.

A strong and informed critical study of progressive music is long overdue. The music discussed in this book is essentially of a different form from popular music, and it has taken every conceivable critical hit for its deviation from the pursuit of the perfect rock song, pop song, or jazz standard. It has often been a convenient whipping boy. Critics and DJs presented with recordings such as Yes's *Tales from Topographic Oceans,* Mike Oldfield's *Tubular Bells,* Tangerine Dream's *Rubycon,* and others like them react negatively because they are looking for the next Elvis,

Madonna, Sex Pistols, Duke Ellington, or Buddy Guy. Similarly, longer works, more abstract works, complex hybrids, and instrumental music tend to be rejected in favor of briefer, simpler traditional styles. Thus even in this reputedly diverse age, where quality, not conformity, is supposed to count, progressive artists have rarely been given the powerful platforms the media could provide them with.

When progressive music *has* been critiqued, it has often been dismissed as too cerebral, too elitist, or unexciting. These uninformed assessments are blatantly untrue. Progressive music includes some of the most grooving, twisted, loopy, outside, mind-body-dissolving gyrations and emanations ever recorded.

Making things difficult for progressive music on the other side of the cultural fence is the view among many aesthetes that the better we understand the techniques—the details of the artist's craft—the more valid, and the richer, will be our reaction or response to the work. Although this seems to be a polar opposite view to the prevailing theory by academics and tech-heads that the public understands very little, so keep programming to that level, the result for progressive music is the same—it keeps progressive works from wide exposure.

Equating the true appreciation of music with mastery of the details of the craft contains an element of truth to it, but such mastery is not a panacea, and those who gravitate too far in that direction actually work against a wider enjoyment of progressive music. When listeners focus on music theory, notations, chord patterns, instruments and instrument technology, studio technology, and the like, all of which can be difficult to understand unless one is involved or specifically trained in those areas, it detracts from the music itself. To understand progressive music, we shouldn't need to consult a musicologist, instrument technician, studio engineer, or orchestra conductor. It shouldn't matter what the technical details are. Good musicians affect our emotions with the quality of their ideas, not simply with the quantity of notes or equipment they can manipulate in the service of those ideas. The only context that really matters is our own.

Also working against a mature appreciation of progressive music has been the tendency of a devoted few to slavishly accept as authentic any release whatsoever that even remotely resembles something progressive. This sort of fanaticism is counterproductive in any field, but especially in art, because it offers no useful criteria for inclusion. There will be no such rubber-stamping in this book.

There are very few artists who have consistently made successful contributions to the overall canon of progressive music. Most of the artists discussed in this book have at one point or another operated in other genres and have not solely concentrated on creating groundbreaking compositions with each release. There is no formula for divining progressive artists. There is no master list of progressive-only artists; one cannot simply point to an artist and say "Ah, progressive." Each recording is different, and should be evaluated on its own merits, removed from all the other recordings that may or may not be similar to it. Progressive music is about a body of separate recordings, not a set list of specific artists.

Thus, those seeking a full appraisal of every album by all artists who are even slightly progressive will have to look elsewhere. This is especially true of those artists in the progressive rock portion of the spectrum. Due to the evolutionary nature of progressive music over recent years, much of what was considered progressive rock in the early 1970s is now very simply just "rock." There is very little that can be defended as truly progressive today in the catalogs of many of the 1970s so-called prog rock groups. Many bands that were so labeled then have today reverted to the mainstream, their past innovations now fully integrated and accepted into the current popular notions of what constitutes rock and roll. In addition, while the 1970s were an era when new sounds did flourish, those sounds were not all from the rock end of the spectrum, and they did not vanish once the seventies ended. Nor is it true that progressive music has been produced only by the once-dominant roster of English and German artists.

Unfortunately, clinging to the 1970s as the only prog decade, to prog rock as the only form, or to English and German artists as the only representatives of the genre is akin to admitting that the era of progressive music had come and gone. Given such limited parameters, no other conclusion was possible. The artists and recordings which emerged in the 1980s and 1990s that continued the progressions were denied their proper place by such folly. They were held back from receiving their due attention by those who now confined their appreciation of the genre to completing their collections of (by now) pop crossover albums by many of the same English and German artists they had been originally attracted to because they weren't sellouts. When the media did begin to pay attention to progressive music in the 1980s, it was easy to declare the genre dead because the collectors—presumably those in the know—appeared much more interested in the older artists and older forms than in radical new progressive forms.

Progressive music deserves a clarity of coverage that it currently lacks. While there are precedents for what can be included, as a genre unto itself it has basically continued on through the years with few organized, formal studies of it. Progressive music has been peripherally included as footnotes in writings about rock, jazz, and new age music. Those recordings which would merit the most critical acclaim if they were identified as being examples of the progressive genre have often received the least attention.

It is time to rectify this situation, to begin to assemble a functional framework for evaluation of progressive music as a separate genre. Certainly not all readers will accept my views and positions entirely, but the positive critical framework that I have created can be used as a point of departure for future evaluation of progressive music.

Music is in our homes, our streets, our workplaces. It emanates from our radios, stereos, televisions, and computers. Music, by the mere fact of its ubiquity, is a crucial component of our environment and helps to define and shape our cultural ecology. And our culture and environment inevitably shape who we are as individuals. This musical ecology may either grow, or retard, our imagination, intelligence, sensitivity, happiness, and health. The question is, ought not the emphasis to be on growth rather than on formulas that have been left on autopilot?

This book, then, gives the reader an opportunity to make informed choices that lead to growth. I have chosen from an existing number of recordings, and made distinctions between them based on the strength of the music (composition, originality, performance, scope, etc.). In selecting the best of the lot, I have deliberately created a specific canon of progressive recordings, based on an aggressively high standard for quality rather than on sales, trends, or overly technical analysis.

There will be very little biographical information about the artists in this book. This volume is concerned with the features of their various works. And, although it is not a complete discography for these artists, you will find that the titles considered are truly representative. Modern classical music, or "new music," will not be a part of this book either, because the classical realm involves totally different structures from the music covered here.

This book is not intended to be an all-inclusive encyclopedia, a neutral compendium of everything available. That would be both impossible and undesirable. To be neutral is not only boring, but does an extreme disservice to the reader/listener/music consumer. Music listening requires time—so why waste it? Music purchasing requires money—so why waste it? The reader can use this book as a sort of arbiter of taste, or as a consumer guide—recommending some things over others so that he or she can avoid wasting valuable time and money on mediocre offerings.

Because in trying to successfully describe music with words, one eventually runs out of choices, especially in a volume of this size and scope, I apologize in advance for the repetition of certain words. Descriptions are somehow inherently inadequate when attempting to convey to others the sensation of a particular sound, and finding the right words is even more difficult with the newer forms and approaches of progressive music. The final judgment call, then, lies with you.

PART 1

An Overview of Progressive Music

A CONCISE HISTORY OF PROGRESSIVE MUSIC

What has come to be known as "progressive music" has its roots in the late 1960s, the era of psychedelia. The year 1967 was a critical coming-of-age-as-artists period for popular music, when musicians finally began to perform something other than the standard three-minute vocal love song. The pop music world had to play catch-up in a big hurry with the rest of the arts, as popular music had not really been taken seriously as an art form until this period.

Practically every performer in the rock world seemed to embrace the psychedelic community's fondness for surrealism, with its dreamy, improvisational free-form anything-goes attitude and its kaleidoscopic patterns and strong colors. Song lyrics became intentionally and ambitiously poetic in an obscure, occasionally nonlinear way, and were backed by a musical accompaniment that could reasonably be called avant-garde, albeit timid and brief.

The inspiration for much of the progressive movement (i.e., the meeting place between the pop music machine and the avant-garde) has been the pioneering leadership of the late 1960s rock artists. The Beatles, the Bonzo Dog Band, Country Joe and the Fish, the Doors, Fifty Foot Hose, the Great Society, the Jimi Hendrix Experience, Jefferson Airplane, the Moody Blues, the Mothers of Invention, Soft Machine, and the United States of America were all absolutely pivotal in paving the way for the artists that are covered in this book. The crucial significance of their actions was to break down the barriers to real artistry in the commercial popular music realm, and in many ways to define just what artistry in modern popular music is.

But from the vantage point of the current musical era, these artists and their innovations have been almost completely absorbed into mainstream consciousness, certainly in ways that many of their successors in progressive music have not yet been. In addition, the aforementioned artists, who led the now well-documented musical revolutions of 1967–1971 abdicated that leadership, so that by 1971 most were either no longer recording or had retrenched toward more traditional popular styles. The result was that the progressive styles these artists introduced were taken up by others and developed to a degree far beyond their original visions. However, many others in the rock and pop world never went past the initial tiptoe into progressive art during this period, and the work of those musicians is now all firmly consigned to the pop mainstream.

It must be noted that while the progressive music genre can be traced back to the psychedelic era, relatively few titles from that period can be considered as "hard core" progressive. It was not until the early 1970s that one could with any certainty identify a progressive music "movement" which was then at work within the popular genres of rock and jazz. It took several years for a core collection of artists and titles to converge and take a direction that could be called progressive.

By 1969, recording, tape, and home stereo technology was developing by leaps and bounds, and there emerged new and more serious listening habits among music fans. The stereo album-length format replaced the single 45-length mono format, and this changed radically the way audiences approached and listened to music. This new audience heard music in larger chunks, usually between 35 and 55 minutes per album. This made longer, more ambitious compositions viable and attractive. The near-infinite possibilities of recording sound in stereo placed the emphasis not only on compositions but on sound itself. This era of change was one of intense excitement regarding the diverse types of sounds and varieties of music available, much of it previously unrecorded music. This attention to sound and the possibilities of a newer, freer kind of music and recording spawned the progressive movement. The excitement over new sounds was evident not only in the rock and jazz realms, but was also marked by such forms as the "new electronic" by such composers as Wendy Carlos and Morton Subotnick and by the beginning of the *Environments* series (in 1969, on Atlantic Records, with a new title appearing yearly for the next decade), both of which contributed heavily to the progressive movement.

The diversity of the music industry between the years 1969 and 1972 made it possible for a broad range of unique and disparate artists to take advantage of this medium and the new atmosphere of experimentation. These artists were quick to explore totally new areas, appealing to initially small but growing audiences willing to digest these new musics in a quest to hear diverse sounds. Those audiences were almost solely made up of the so-called "counterculture" (and yes, the marijuana subculture), for whom extended instrumental voyages converged with meditation, awareness/consciousness raising, and dreamy space-out sessions. This explicit linking of the new music with specific personal acts of self-exploration has been of vital importance throughout the history of progressive music, and is as significant today as it was then.

Pink Floyd, Ron Geesin, the Third Ear Band, Terry Riley, Tangerine Dream, John McLaughlin, Bo Hansson, Popol Vuh, Deuter, and Wendy Carlos (whose 1972 *Sonic Seasonings,* currently out of print and not yet available on CD, was a release of fundamental importance within the progressive genre) were all pioneers of instrumental music produced for this new era. With this movement away from pop music forms and vocals toward abstraction and a focus on the music alone, progressive music as a genre began in earnest.

The breakthrough form that psychedelia had made possible was reinterpreted. Pop, folk, and blues elements were de-emphasized or eliminated, and the dreamier, free-form elements enhanced, thereby creating a new form—a progressive split from the earlier pop version of psychedelia. This split is obvious when one compares the so-called psychedelia of the San Francisco groups such as the Grateful Dead with that of more progressive artists. Whereas the San Francisco groups remained entrenched in the older styles, the progressive artists desperately wanted to move beyond those limitations.

While the new musical atmosphere of experimentation was heavily reported in the media, up until the early 1970s it was not attributed to any specific grouping of artists. When progressive styles and titles began appearing more frequently, by 1971–1972, it was the British and German artists who seemed to lead the way in the rock areas, while America provided the development of fusion, a critical element which in turn immediately influenced the European artists.

The instrumental jamming characteristic of fusion was imbued with a deeper meaning—a direct influence from jazz—that took on spiritual and metaphysical proportions. Soon the rock-oriented musicians took up this jazz aesthetic, creating a hybrid of the two genres where extended instrumental music was a necessary ingredient, essential to serious, exploratory new electrified music. Using the album-length stereo format, these extended instrumentals integrated the contemporary themes of self-exploration and seriousness into the very fiber of progressive music.

The composer/instrumentalist became a new kind of pop star, personified by emerging artists like John McLaughlin, Keith Emerson, Mike Oldfield, and Klaus Schulze, who had a glorious—even heroic—instrumental proficiency and who brought the musical values of the classical and jazz spheres into the popular realm. It was precisely at this point that segments of popular music left behind trendiness and disposability, moving instead toward the complex creation of personal and lasting art. For those in the establishment who had asked, "How can this new music by long-haired young hippies be serious?" progressive music, more than any other genre, had an answer.

In addition to the revolutionary change in the music were the sheer visual spectacle and aural bombast with which the new styles were presented. New recording techniques gave a more realistic volume to the music that was not possible a scant five years earlier. Albums were presented in lavish, colorful gatefold sleeves displaying artwork and lyrics. At live shows, sound systems were improving, sophisticated light shows were being developed, and some artists were beginning to wear bizarre makeup and costumes.

While all genres benefited from these new developments, the progressive genre perhaps benefited the most. Progressive groups used the new techniques to put across their abstract instrumental compositions and succeeded in making their revolutionary music stand out in the din of pop culture. Throughout the 1970s, audiences marveled at the sights and sounds from the likes of such supergroups as Pink Floyd, Yes, Emerson, Lake & Palmer, Mahavishnu Orchestra, Genesis, King Crimson, Tangerine Dream, Renaissance, Return To Forever, Jethro Tull, Gong, Camel, Curved Air, Focus, and Finch, each offering their own radically new sounds and presentations. Music this large and ambitious had not been seen before. It was a breakthrough explosion, one that emphasized the arena-level potency of the new progressive genre.

These larger-than-life supergroups provided progressive music with a popular aesthetic: a blend of classical and jazz styles with modern techniques; improvisation; avant-garde experimentation; high tech instrumentation and amplification; studio effects; wild album cover art; in-concert visuals; and explorations of philosophical and metaphysical concepts.

While the supergroups carved out their niches and solidified the audience base for progressive music, by the mid- to late-1970s there were rumblings of a fresh new energy and approach among emerging progressive artists, who opted for a more personal style rather than the bombast of the arena-touring supergroups. Audiences with eclectic tastes began to develop for the various strata of distinctive progressive styles. These splinter styles built upon the previous progressive precedents, then moved off into such individualistic realms that each was perceived as being a totally new experience. Included among the diverse artists in the 1970s who traveled this more personalized progressive path were Brand X, Bruford, Clearlight, Brian Eno, Gotic, Henry Cow, Steve Hillage, National Health, Sally Oldfield, Terje Rypdal, Shylock, Throbbing Gristle, and Eberhard Weber.

Progressive audiences reveled in this proliferation of musical styles, listeners built collections of many genres, from many countries, and artists produced some of their finest work. While the audiences were certainly there, this eclecticism was not embraced by FM radio the way the prog supergroups were. And as the supergroups disbanded or ran their course, progressive music was increasingly abandoned by radio and the music media. The pace of this trend quickened in the late 1970s, when many FM stations switched to slicker commercial formats, leaving behind the free-form anarchic approach essential to playing more lengthy progressive works. The literal forms and concise nature demanded by commercial radio necessitated the exclusion of progressive music.

At the same time that the demands of commercial radio were dictating what music got airtime, the emerging pop music critical establishment was aggressively pitting the new forms of punk and new wave musics against the progressive genre (especially progressive rock—the other styles were mainly ignored), setting up progressive music as the enemy of what these critics saw as the all-important cultural movement that punk and new wave represented. Without radio airplay or critical favor, record companies had little choice but to begin de-emphasizing progressive music. Promotion, budgets, and signings declined sharply, so that by 1981 progressive music was effectively no longer a significant player in the popular markets.

The result of this ironic turn of events was that progressive music, which had been seen as the vanguard of all that was radical in music in the early 1970s, had, by that decade's end, been rejected by the same people who had once regarded it as revolutionary. The overselling of punk and new wave and the perception of progressive music as the enemy both took place without any honest, straightforward critical analysis. With the popular music world relying primarily on trends, progressive music was "in" one day and "out" the next, with no explanation given other than the personal preferences of the critics and the commercial formats of FM radio. The fact that there were still a substantial number of high-quality progressive titles being recorded and released, and that the audiences and sales were there, didn't matter to critics or radio.

In the early 1980s, a highly narcissistic and meandering period in Western culture, the main pursuit of many in the media was the creation of something totally "different" for the "new" decade. In the music world, the reality was that "new" simply meant a return to existing pop forms, with glossed-up, synthed-up, and simplified forms dressed up in fast-paced high-tech presentations. The results for progressive music were mixed. Although the return to briefer, slicker forms gave progressive music renewed commitment to continue to innovate and to develop fresh approaches, in the 1980s many of the remaining prog rock groups and artists went along with the prevailing conformity, a trend that has continued on to the present day. Progressive audiences watched with confusion and revulsion as many of the prog rock artists from the previous decade "sold out." The rules of the music industry system worked against the rock-oriented artists who wanted to stay in the progressive spectrum. If they wrote and recorded genuine progressive rock, they had to go to a smaller label or act entirely independently (which would deny them a significant amount of distribution, promotion, and exposure); if they went pop, they could receive full backing from the industry. In this climate, progressive rock suffered, and as a result progressive music in general suffered further segmentation. A decade earlier the electronics of Pink Floyd and Tangerine Dream had not been seen as distinctly separate, nor had the rest of their compositional elements, and it was common to contextualize Gong, Klaus Schulze, Mike Oldfield, Camel, and Popol Vuh in the same general area. All that changed during the 1980s. Radio, the critics, and then the record companies actively avoided progressive music in favor of the commercial forms they believed would help the bottom line, and progressive music split off into many small, highly disparate groups. The emergence of a calmer, less rock- or band-oriented music—what has come to be known as "new age music"—further challenged the established notion of what progressive music was for many people. With the largely industry-driven segmentation of what had been the audience for progressive music came the splitting away of space music, electronic music, or "cosmic" music away from the more rock- or jazz-flavored styles.

The best of what has been termed new age music is only a continuation of the cosmic electronics and mellower psychedelic hybrid textures of the 1970s. The decision by the music industry to launch "new age" as a category unto itself in the 1980s only further fragmented and confused audiences as to what progressive music specifically consisted of. Promoters segregated music according to mood: if it was on the mellow side, it was known as new age; if it was more band-oriented, more rhythmic, it was jazz; if it included vocals, it was pop/rock. This meant that progressive music was scattered throughout the three very different industry categories, and this system lacked a framework which would emphasize similarities, preventing the emergence of any overall or unifying theme which could link all progressive styles.

Under the new age umbrella, progressive music continued its abstract goals and forms (serious instrumental music; lengthy pieces), although the rock-oriented factions were temporarily on hold or dead-ending. The quality of titles that originated in the early- and mid-1980s was exceptionally high. By then the inner-directed, spacey music created by the 1970s pioneers had produced a new wave of artists (e.g., Emerald Web, David Parsons, Constance Demby), who took these introspective musical voyages as their starting point. The highly individualistic, esoteric, and eclectic music made by these artists was so unique it could be produced only independently of the big labels and the mass media. Industry rules were bypassed, with artists recording and releasing the music themselves or on smaller labels. However, in the corporate-driven music business of the time, many of the older 1970s artists were no longer willing to maintain a commitment to making music regardless of trend or profit, a commitment which had always been a hallmark of the progressive movement.

In addition, the hype accompanying the marketing of new age music had, by the late 1980s, resulted in a flood of poor releases, overwhelming what progressive elements there were. Anyone with a keyboard, synth, flute, or harp could release an album—usually with a mystical title—that was simply endless twee tosh. The new age category, divorced from its avant-garde origins, became the ultimate nonthreatening, mindless music—soft sounds for relaxing at home without the individual really listening closely. This completely undermined the ability of novice listeners to differentiate instrumental music of high quality from the easy listening garbage. New age music, divorced from its avant-garde origins, became the ultimate bourgeois music category—nonthreatening, nonthinking soft sounds to relax at home with—a way for people to pretend they are appreciating instrumental music when in reality they are doing nothing of the sort. Certainly new age was not an appropriate vehicle for carrying the torch of progressive music, and its confines remain too narrow even today.

A key development for progressive music in the 1980s was the growing involvement of female artists. While the audiences for progressive music have generally been gender-neutral, in the 1970s progressive recording artists were almost all males. The list of progressive artists from the 1980s and 1990s, however, contains a large number of women. The work of artists such as Annette Peacock, Cosey Fanni Tutti, Kate Bush, Claire Hamill, Constance Demby, Danielle Dax, Annea Lockwood, Vicki Richards, and Fiorella Terenzi has been significant, as have the contributions of the female members of groups like Emerald Web, Solstice, Thistle, Dark, Voice of Eye, Anekdoten, Anglagard, Melting Euphoria, and White Willow.

Another critical development in progressive music in the CD age has been the advent of reissues of top-notch albums made by unsung independent musicians who attempted to bypass the commercial routes, but were not rewarded with any acclaim or exposure because their releases were minimally distributed when they first came out, and quickly lost. Many of these musicians are now getting the attention they deserve. The high-quality CD reissues, which have cleaner, superior sound than the vinyl pressings did, in addition to bonus tracks and extensive liner notes, are being reintroduced into the media pipeline to newer, more receptive audiences, and are kept in print much longer than the vinyl versions. The more well-known progressive artists have also received the finest remastering and reissue treatment. All the back-catalog titles by Chris and Cosey, Emerson, Lake and Palmer, Finch, Focus, Genesis, Bo Hansson, King Crimson, National Health, Pink Floyd, Popol Vuh, Renaissance, Schicke, Führs and Fröhling, Tangerine Dream, Throbbing Gristle, and Yes are available in the finest possible CD presentations.

These reissues are just one aspect of the 1990s renaissance for progressive music. The innovation and creativity that produced the revolutions of the early years, when a Tangerine Dream, Pink Floyd, or Throbbing Gristle record stood listeners on their heads and made them rethink their perceptions of music, never really went away, and they are now as much in evidence as they were in the 1970s. Artists such as Lightwave, Voice of Eye, and In Be Tween Noise have been consistently releasing works that are as much of a dislocating head-change as anything put out by the old masters.

The 1990s have also seen a return of the rock-based progressive hybrids—new fusions that are more driving and hard-hitting than ever before.

Generating the most excitement in years are groups which have reignited the progressive rock band ethic, such as Djam Karet, Ozric Tentacles, Happy Family, Boud Deun, Fire Merchants, Xaal, and Melting Euphoria. Vocal prog, too, seems in good hands, with Scandinavians White Willow and Anekdoten adding refreshing new twists to a style that is quite difficult to operate in, yet remaining resolutely progressive.

The return to adventurousness by composers such as Mike Oldfield, Ron Geesin, and Terje Rypdal, and the reunions of King Crimson, Brand X, and Gong, have further underscored the enduring strength of the progressive genre. Each of these artists was given a hero's welcome by audiences in the 1990s.

In addition, a host of progressive music publications, reissue labels, independent labels, and mail-order services abounds in countries from Japan to Italy to Sweden to the United States. In this way, progressive music has come full circle, returning to its devoted grassroots, where a wildly diverse group of sounds, styles, artists, and audiences exists almost entirely independently of the popular music industry. Progressive music, having withstood the harshest of market pressures and bucked many an industry-hyped trend, is now at last poised to take its place as a mature genre in its own right.

PROGRESSIVE MUSIC AS ACTIVE LISTENING MUSIC

The term "active listening" refers to a private process—a carefully thought out, purposeful approach toward hearing that involves all of the listener's sensory, cognitive, intellectual, emotional, and spiritual faculties at their peak. Having an open, informed, and willing mind, the active listener pays the closest possible attention, not tuning anything out, in order to extract everything possible from the stimuli presented. Logically, then, active listening music is the music that stimulates the senses, the intellect, and the spirit of the active listener to the greatest degree, leading to more intricate and sophisticated forms of sensation, pleasure, and awareness.

Active listening music has few apparent self-limitations. It is often characterized as avant-garde, and sometimes as "highbrow." Active listening music can be either wildly improvisational or painstakingly composed. It may contain references to previous artistic precedent or to art forms other than music. Due to the attention to sound, it is often well-engineered, recorded, and produced. Some general adjectives that can be used to describe active listening music are *abstract, ambitious, atmospheric, challenging, conceptual, difficult, distinguished, eclectic, experimental, intellectual, lyrical, poetic, varied,* and *weird*. Specific terms that have been applied to active listening music over the years, each of which delineates a particular aspect or style, are *acid rock, art rock, art song, classical rock, collage music, concept rock, drug music, electronic music, environmental music, fusion, "head" music, industrial, jazz rock, modern music, mood music, new age, opt-out music, progressive jazz, progressive rock, psychedelia, quiet music, space music,* and *trance music.*

Although active listening/progressive music operates, at least partially, within the framework of the modern popular commercial music industry, artistically and aesthetically it is quite different from popular music. In general terms, "popular" forms of music may be thought of as commercial, concise, conventional, danceable, entertaining, formalistic, literal, traditional, and trendy. The different forms of music usually labeled as popular are big band, blues, country-western, disco, easy listening, folk, funk, gospel, grunge/alternative rock, hard rock, hard-core, heavy metal, Muzak, punk, rap, rhythm and blues, religious music, soul, Top 40 pop, and traditional jazz. Whatever the form, the nature of popular music is essentially to take an already fixed musical style or form and then build on it or add to it (now increasingly possible via technological means) without radically deviating from the basic form of the original. The resulting product is slightly different from the models, yet intrinsically familiar at the same time. Progressive/active listening forms borrow sounds and structures from popular styles, so the relationship between the two is not mutually exclusive, but progressive forms are more complex hybrids than popular forms, hence the extra attention needed in listening to them. Progressive forms aim for sounds that are not only slightly different, but usually radically different.

A primary difference between the world of active listening/progressive music and the world of popular music involves the musicians. A fundamental belief of progressive musicians is that music is more than just a casual entertainment, hobby, or job. They strongly believe that their music is art, and that the creation of art that has integrity is in itself entertaining. These musician/artists may have an extensive interest in and knowledge of art, art history, music history, music theory, aesthetics, and perhaps even philosophy. They also have an extensive knowledge of various instruments and technologies. They are concerned with producing high-quality recordings because they want their music to be listened to closely.

Progressive musicians tend to be minimally concerned with trends, fashions, images, hype, ego, and celebrity. They have a strong desire to experiment, to evolve, to challenge themselves and their audiences, and to take the necessary risks in order to do so. Because of this, they generally operate with autonomy, not allowing interference from those who are concerned with market-driven decisions involving trends and greater profit schemes.

A second defining feature of active listening music is the listener. The active listener has a subtle and quite complex personal relationship with the music, one that goes far, far beyond merely turning on the radio or stereo set or purchasing a recording to play at weekend parties. Active listeners have specific listening habits, rituals, and activities. To them music is not a backdrop to something else. When they listen to music, other activities or distractions are avoided, preferably excluded. They will have a specific environment in which to listen to music, perhaps a special room or location, or a certain place in which to listen on headphones. Active listeners allow themselves enough time and space in which to listen closely. Some may set goals for their music listening, such as meditation, relaxation, creative visualization, and getting high.

Most active listeners are connoisseurs of above-average audio equipment and components. For some this becomes an obsession. Compact discs are now without a doubt the preferred format, and listeners always strive to hear high-quality "audiophile" recordings. They often have an extensive knowledge of various recordings, and the all-important willingness to search for particular hard-to-find recordings. Many acquire large collections.

Active listeners, like the musicians who create active listening music, tend to have a strong appreciation for other arts, such as painting, sculpture, film and video, and theater. Many have a strong dislike of the parade of trends and fashions in relation to the arts, and a few may even be openly hostile to popular culture in general.

THE SOCIAL, POLITICAL, AND CULTURAL CONTEXT

When compared with pop music's "chart toppers," progressive music hasn't enjoyed commercial or critical success, or media favor. Why is this so? To answer that question, one needs to look at the general sociopolitical and cultural context within which progressive music has developed and, in particular, at seven phenomena that were or are part of that context: the generation gap; the psychedelic experience; the counterculture versus the establishment; conformity; the abstract versus the literal; entertainment versus art; and parallels between progressive music and the world of speculative fiction.

The Generation Gap

Before 1967 there really was no avant-garde in the popular music realm, with the exception of certain jazz artists. The radical changes that took place in modern popular music, especially rock music, in the late 1960s were a reflection of that period's generation gap. To many of the youth at the time, and thereafter through the 1970s, 1980s, and 1990s, it was crucial to have music that reflected and fueled their rebellion from older generations—a rebellion that was inherently political.

In music, this rebellion required forms that the older generations not only disliked but couldn't understand. Volume, abstract lyrics, weird studio effects, new instruments, and lengthy jams were utilized in a conscious break with the past. To the most radical proponents of the new music the traditional song form—the easily understood 2- to 5-minute love song—became the enemy, representative of a repressive, ugly, ignorant society unable to deal honestly with its problems. Both the content (the lyrics) and the form (the music) had to change.

Throughout the many youth rebellions during and since the 1960s, young people, in an effort to forge something totally new to express themselves and to separate from their elders, have given birth to new musical forms. Those who veered toward abstraction (see below) became active listeners and practiced active listening music; those who veered toward literalism (such as punk rockers, rappers, etc.) did not.

The Psychedelic Experience

Over the last four decades, the effect of drugs such as marijuana and the so-called psychedelics (LSD, hashish, and psilocybin) both on individuals and on society has been enormous. These effects have been especially strong in the arts in general and in the world of music in particular. Psychedelic experiences—chemically induced voyages into altered brain states that may invoke dreams, hallucinations, out-of-body experiences, nightmares, and so on—have an obvious appeal to those who depend on the imagination. For them, the altered states, whether they are achieved chemically or through disciplined meditation, may not be undertaken for pure hedonism but as means to consciousness exploration. With these different brain states comes a very deeply felt perception of music as otherworldly, as a sacred realm, as an egoless space into which one can disappear. Each person who experiences music in this way has a different perception of it, and different uses for it, from the evocation of a tranquil, introspective thought-dream to the accompaniment for a wild, chaotic dance.

Historically, there is a rich tradition of using music itself as a means to achieve altered mental states, via mantras, chants, drumming, rhythm, and other rituals. Native American, African, and Oriental cultures all offer examples of such rituals, some of which include the use of psychedelics. In modern Western culture, active listening music, perhaps more than other types of music, can claim direct descent from this tradition. Indeed, active listening music is often viewed as "drug music" because those listening to it can attempt to reach an altered state of consciousness. Some of the effect is achieved simply by extending the length of the music beyond that offered by briefer, 2- to 3-minute, popular forms. With "space music," for example, extended length is critical to the goal of drawing the listener into a dream world. It is not only the listeners who strive toward altered states, but the musicians themselves. Creators of the more chaotic forms of music use the liberating sensations of the altered state to create wildly innovative sound-making, whether in the arena of consistency of rhythm or through improvised, Dadaesque found sounds. A free-form approach is encouraged. Thus both active listening musicians and audiences routinely explore many experiences directly related to psychedelia.

The Counterculture versus the Establishment

Rebellious youth—psychedelicized and politicized, and sexually, artistically, and spiritually hungry for more than the current structures can offer—is seen as an enormous threat by corporate capitalism, by the military, and by organized religion. To these representatives of "the establishment," it is evocative of socialism/communism/anarchism; it is too honest, too sexual, too individualistic, too unrestrained; it is the counterculture, where *counter* means "against."

Modern music is one area where art directly challenges the power of religion. Since the 1960s, even the pop mainstream of music has been promoted as existing on a spiritual realm, as meeting the spiritual needs of people. The artist/musician has become a sort of priest, the musical concert a sort of religious gathering for worship or prayer, and the recordings themselves sacred objects, or relics. The tribalism of the 1968-1972 period in modern music, with its large outdoor festivals where thousands of fans disrobed partially or completely and frolicked riotously before the spectacle of the music onstage, demonstrated the sheer power inherent in the new music, a power that could never have even been imagined by those who grew up listening to the older forms. Progressive music, which is druggy, abstract, weird, unique, and radical; which dissents; which does not fit in with the world of the emotionally repressed, shallow, or willfully ignorant, has been one of the preferred genres of the counterculture. It is totally outside the mainstream, and therefore totally hip.

Conformity

People seem to crave a collective experience, be it in art, sports, religion, politics, or hobbies. They have a strong craving to share their interests with a large group having the same interests. This fact is not lost on the media music machine, which creates music superstars who become a focal point for those desirous of a collectively shared musical experience. The fortunate few dominate radio, TV, and every other media outlet. The music superstars are like any other in-demand product, and the music industry thrives on the low-risk superstar + the familiar = profits formula. It gives listeners the popular music experience they expect—nothing too challenging, too controversial, or too unconventional.

The Abstract versus the Literal

Years ago, I played "Atom Heart Mother" by Pink Floyd for a friend. In the middle of the piece, he looked at me worriedly and said "I don't get it. What's this about? What am I supposed to think?" My friend was simply unable to appreciate a piece of music that wasn't like anything else he had heard. A literalist, he needed musical and cultural "facts" to which he could relate the sounds he was hearing. "Atom Heart Mother," a piece of abstract, progressive music, was not accessible to him.

Most popular forms of music are designed for people like my friend. Both lyrics and musical accompaniment are meant to have a specific, literal meaning that would be hard to miss by the target audience—people in pursuit of a collective experience. And there's absolutely nothing wrong with that. But it becomes impossible for many listeners to appreciate any other kind of music. Upon encountering abstraction (usually instrumental), those versed only in the literal modes of expression search desperately for the intended meaning, waiting to be told what the music is supposed to "mean," what the intended "message" is. Since they can't figure it out, and when no one tells them, they dismiss the music as too "intellectual," too "elitist," too "serious." But abstraction doesn't offer literal messages, or facts, or answers. It poses questions. And each individual's reactions will be complex, and totally different from anyone else's. In the sense that abstract music suggests many possibilities, rather than offering one or two clear messages that the listener is *supposed* to understand, is not just antiliteral but anti–authority.

Active listening music is that part of the popular music world which best represents and promotes abstraction. Its overall goal is to expand the palette of expression to include abstraction, and to promote understanding and tolerance of that expanded expression.

Entertainment versus Art

Until the 1960s, musicians were seen as mere entertainers, not artists. Only the classical composer was given the stature of true artist. Popular musicians had to content themselves with being faceless, clean-cut, uniformed accompaniments for current pop songs or vocalists. Seldom were they allowed to compose, and if they did, they did so according to the dictates of commercial demands from the industry bosses. In the late 1960s, the music industry, in a logical profit-seeking move, courted counterculture pop musicians who viewed themselves as artists. While this decision proved considerably irritating for conservative idealogues, it did widen the pop music mainstream so that it could include, at least in theory, pure "art."

But therein lies a problem. Art can work within the music entertainment world only if it is profitable. In entertainment, the value of a work, any work, is the profit that can be made by selling that work. Entertainment has only one agenda—to give pleasure, for a fee. Art has many agendas. Entertainment music is of a piece, easy to listen to, and usually uncontroversial, whereas art music is fragmented and often controversial. Any given work of art is a complex thing—appealing to some, but seldom to all. For these reasons, it is much easier to market entertainment music to the general public than it is to market art.

In the entertainment world, the best "art" is that which sells the most. What sells the most becomes the most important. In art, the criteria are totally different, and many artists are radical innovators who see their role as challenging societal norms. Yet freedom of artistic expression means that key assumptions (laws, rules, norms) can be openly challenged. This is threatening to any power structure. It is especially threatening to conservatives, who may lump all artists together as weird, dangerous, perhaps criminal. Businesspeople may make occasional alliances with artists, but only if they know it will work for them by making money.

But musicians have radically reorganized themselves since the 1960s in every sense. Empowered by spirituality, youth, rebellion, drugs, and new technology, they set themselves the ambitious goals of creating new compositional forms, bringing to the forefront their instrumental prowess, and developing a musical content that explored the full range of human emotions. The popular music world has fragmented enormously since the inception of these bold musical goals. While the revolutions in acceptable lyrical content and frankness continue, the revolutions in musical form have been pushed to the margins in favor of the traditional popular forms and progressive music has generally been relegated to the "avant-garde" shelf. There is nothing intrinsically wrong with this classification, except that the industry as a whole regards the avant-garde—the progressive elements—as nonentertainment, and therefore nonmarketable in any substantial way. This does not have to be, and it is dreadfully disappointing.

PARALLELS BETWEEN PROGRESSIVE MUSIC AND THE WORLD OF SPECULATIVE FICTION

In the purely cultural realm, the influence of speculative fiction, or science fiction, on progressive music has been present since the beginning, and in many ways the characteristics and development of speculative fiction parallel those of progressive music. By the late 1960s speculative fiction had outgrown its beginnings as juvenile comic book-level entertainment and was offering highly cerebral, poetic, experimental, and visionary forms.

This journey toward serious art in a genre that previously hadn't been taken seriously is similar to that made by progressive musicians of the same era. Progressive musicians and writers of speculative fiction both transcended the norms of their medium by creating personal, meaningful works of art, which were no longer disposable diversions but engaging forums for individual expression.

Some of the themes of speculative fiction can be found indirectly in progressive music works: allegorical themes such as the growth of self-awareness; the nature of freedom and conformity; technological development and its implications; the subtleties of political and social upheaval and conflict; visions of the future, both utopian and nightmarish; and complex imaginings of alien worlds, beings, and cultures.

The large quantity of highly dramatic and forward-looking speculative fiction that began appearing in the 1960s parallels the youth movements of our times, with their anarchic, rebellious, bohemian, and visionary agendas, including sexual liberation and political reform, all of which informed and influenced the music world just as it did the rest of the arts. The space program, especially in the wake of the 1969 moon landing and on through the 1970s, created an optimism about vast explorations of the unknown, igniting visionary imaginings of the future.

The musical soundtracks of science fiction films and TV series are an often uncredited influence on progressive music. These highly experimental (often musique concrète) works were surprisingly avant-garde, especially for the mainstream worlds of movies and television. The use of "space music" or "cosmic music" in progressive music circles goes hand in hand with that of science fiction soundtracks, and the imagery provided in films and TV for this music was certainly a factor in the creative process of making progressive space music.

An interesting example of space music from the television world is the soundtrack of a 1971 episode from the BBC series *Doctor Who,* entitled "Colony in Space" (aired well before the emergence of Tangerine Dream and Klaus Schulze as electronic music composers) some highly avant-garde electronic music is heard first when the character of the Doctor and his companion Jo Grant explore the surface of an alien planet and then later when they encounter the ancient culture of beings that live there. These ethereal new sounds of electronics were used to represent a voyage into the unknown. In fact the program's famous opening depicts a strange vanishing point while its theme music is playing, and a musical and visual vortex beckons the viewer to enter. Another curious use of music from this season was an episode entitled "The Mind of Evil," which actually used instrumental excerpts from the second King Crimson album.

Examples of progressive musicians exploring fantasy allegorical themes at length include: Jon Anderson's *Olias of Sunhillow;* Gong's *Radio Gnome Invisible* trilogy (*Flying Teapot, Angel's Egg, You);* Bo Hansson's *Lord of the Rings;* Jack Lancaster and Robin Lumley's *Marscape;* Sally Oldfield's *Water Bearer;* Pink Floyd's *The Piper at the Gates of Dawn* and *Animals;* and Tangerine Dream's *Alpha Centauri, Zeit,* and *Force Majeure.* Some of the prog rock supergroups' more well-known songs have been fantasy-themed, among them Genesis's "Watcher of the Skies," Pink Floyd's "Set the Controls for the Heart of the Sun," and Yes's "Starship Trooper."

Also reflecting fantasy influences in progressive music is the glorious album cover artwork. The choice of art is of vital importance because the cover art for a release should convey what moods the sounds are intended to conjure and will influence the impressions listeners have about the music before they have even heard it. The most famous works of fantasy in the world of progressive music cover art are by sleeve artists Roger Dean, Monique Froese, and the Hipgnosis company.

Hipgnosis was a very popular British operation specializing in highly kaleidoscopic, eye-catching sleeves. They are best known for their Pink Floyd album sleeves, beginning with 1968's *A Saucerful of Secrets* and continuing through the 1970s. Hipgnosis employed a bold technique for the Floyd's 1970 sleeve of *Atom Heart Mother.* The cover art was a set of photographs of cows on a farm; no photo of the musicians and—more importantly—no words appeared (except on the spine). This abstract approach to sleeve art, which allows the listener to interpret the artwork personally, underlines the fundamentally abstract nature of progressive music.

Perhaps the most celebrated fantasy-oriented Hipgnosis/Floyd cover was the one for the epic release *Dark Side of the Moon,* which depicted just a prism of colored streams of light moving across a black background over the length of a gatefold sleeve. Equally compelling was the poster inside, which showed a barren desert landscape tinted a deep green. The listener could not help feeling when unwrapping and examining such albums that he or she was indeed about to step into a mysterious vortex and emerge in an alien world (just like Doctor Who), with the music as accompaniment.

Artist Roger Dean is celebrated for his sleeves for Yes. His first Yes cover was *Fragile* in 1972, followed by extravagant paintings for *Yessongs, Tales from Topographic Oceans, Relayer, Yesterdays,* and *Drama.* Dean devised the Yes logo, and also designed the group's superb stage objects during their mid-1970s tours. These sci-fi creations of Dean's can be glimpsed in the *Live At Q.P.R. 1975* concert discs.

Dean's art is strongly in the realm of fantasy. His forte is colorful, friendly alien landscapes which hint at exciting adventures taking place within and which are reminiscent of many covers of sci-fi/fantasy novels. Dean's art for Jon Anderson's *Olias Of Sunhillow* concept album in 1976 illustrates an entire narrative, creating a spiky, spindly world, in contrast to the rounded, expansive designs he is most known for.

The art of Monique Froese for Tangerine Dream's and Edgar Froese's sleeves is breathtaking. Unfortunately not all of her art appears intact on the CD reissues, and anyone who wants a full appreciation of her creations must track down the vinyl gatefold sleeves.

Monique Froese utilized both painting and photography, and later, computer art. Her sleeves are the essence of atmosphere and mystery—evocative of space, alien worlds, and strange encounters—and also themes of nature—waterscapes and forests where intense meditation, contemplation, or new experiences take place. Her brilliant visuals were a perfect match to the highly abstract space music of Tangerine Dream. Their long compositions (often 10 to 20 minutes in length) are paralleled by the cover imagery, which evokes a journey of some sort—either outward, through space and toward alien worlds, or inward, toward new feelings, thoughts, and sensations.

Froese's finest artwork are the original gatefold covers for Tangerine Dream's *Alpha Centauri, Zeit, Atem, Phaedra, Rubycon, Stratosfear,* and *Force Majeure,* plus Edgar Froese's *Aqua* and *Epsilon in Malaysian Pale.*

PART 2

Key Recordings in Progressive Music

This book is about organizing information. Since it is as impossible to cover everything as it is to like everything, determining what recordings to include becomes a matter of subjective differentiation. Clearly, however, some artists and recordings are simply better than others in one way or another, and there has been no hesitation in making such distinctions when choosing which titles to review here. This book is essentially a consumer guide intended to point the reader toward the good and away from the bad or mediocre. It is neither a history nor a discography. The final selection of the titles reviewed here was painstakingly made. Everything that might have been included was in fact considered, and the fact that roughly 330 recordings were chosen is just how it turned out. More could have been added, but 330 seemed about right, and quality was more important than quantity.

Those who prefer a more concise overview can consult Appendix 1, The Canon: 100 Classic Progressive Recordings, then refer back to the alphabetical listing for further elaboration from the reviews. Three other appendixes offer more specialized listings: Appendix 2, Five Progressive Music Styles; Appendix 3, The Top 30 Space Music Discs; and Appendix 4, The Top 30 Sound Quality Discs. Finally, Appendix 5 lists selected additional titles of albums that are on the periphery of the genre.

The artists are arranged alphabetically, and specific recordings by that artist are listed chronologically. Each listing begins with the artist's name, followed by the title of the release, the release date (down to the month wherever possible), the label it currently appears on, and the format and import status if applicable. All titles are U.S. releases, unless otherwise stated.

Clearly, many of the artists listed made recordings that are not included here. Recordings that are not part of the progressive/active listening universe, are just plain lousy releases, or represent something done better elsewhere are not included. With prolific artists, such lesser work can be as much as one-fourth to one-half of their output. For the purposes of this guide, it is neither necessary nor desirable to review all of the recordings ever released by progressive music artists. Also not included are titles currently out of print. Fortunately, only a handful of key progressive titles fall into this category.

Because a visual performance of music is often preferable to the music alone, some video releases have been included. Those listed are excellent, high-quality releases that are key to a complete understanding of progressive music. Many are available on laser disc, often only as imports, and some are difficult to locate. While some of the video titles are available on VHS, readers should consider investing in a laser disc player for a stronger visual and sound reproduction that avoids the gradual erosion of videotape.

A deliberate decision was made to include imports, as limiting the reviews to domestically available discs would yield an incomplete picture of progressive music. Those who want a true appreciation of progressive music will make the necessary investment of time and money to track down and purchase imports, independent label titles, videos, and laser discs. Appendix 6, Obtaining the Music, provides assistance on where to go when buying by mail.

In addition to the historical notes and detailed music analysis, the quality of the sound is discussed for virtually every recording included here. After all, music is about sound, and if the sound isn't up to par, then what's the point?

Also, special attention is paid to the cover art, which is an often-neglected but extremely important facet of progressive music. Cover art imagery—the listener's visual introduction to the abstract and sometimes mysterious realms of avant-garde and instrumental music—can be an essential factor in the totality of the listening experience. Cover art should be selected with great care, and thus the reviews note when the artwork accurately represents the music, as well as when the artwork does nothing of the sort.

Finally, of course, it is up to the listener/reader who is unfamiliar with some or many of the artists and recordings in this guide, or perhaps even with progressive music as a genre, to experiment. If a recording sounds intriguing, seek it out, and others like it. The process of discovery is exciting and rewarding.

A

AGITATION FREE

MALESCH. Released December 1972. Spalax import.

Agitation Free was among the legendary German progressive rock groups that emerged circa 1970 along with Tangerine Dream, Guru Guru, and Ash Ra Tempel. The band, with Michael Hoenig on synths, recorded only two studio albums, of which *Malesch* was the first. A late arrival in comparison with the group's contemporaries, *Malesch* is the very definition of German prog rock. It's a classic all-instrumental album, with production values superior to most German releases from this period.

Agitation Free are masters of the buildup: music that begins slowly and lazily with stray guitar chords and drumbeats, but then builds in mood and groove to a frenzied, blazing, jamming climax. Mixing an Arabic feel evocative of whirling dervishes with very heavy Guru Guru–like psychedelic guitar rock, the band is incredible—a twin guitar attack, loud, deep bass notes, and an amazingly precise miking of stereo drum effects, with great stereo drum rolls across your speakers. Whether the music was improvised or composed is hard to tell. The musicians show enormous restraint in the beginnings of the songs, which adds to the effectiveness of the grooves when they start to cook. Hoenig provides the album's most experimental moments; there are many effective avant-garde transitions in the music that his synths provide. The tracks all flow together, giving the album a Pink Floyd–like conceptual feel.

The sound is excellent. This is the one of the best-sounding reissues from Spalax, who tend to flatten albums completely with their remastering process (the sad fate of the reissue of the Agitation Free live album, "Last"). *Malesch* has that infectious early 1970s stereo separation, which makes for truly fun head music. The only complaint is that there are vocals in Arabic on one track which are way, way too loud in the mix and quite irritating.

SECOND. Released December 1973. Spalax import.

This rewarding companion to *Malesch* never disappoints. The entire disc seems to go by quickly and smoothly, despite the fact that some of the sounds and transitions are quite unusual. *Second,* with its acoustic guitars and laid-back electronics, is less rocking than *Malesch.* Part of the rich German space music scene, it fits in quite well with other ethereal 1973 releases like Tangerine Dream's *Atem* and Popol Vuh's *Hosianna Mantra.*

The 8-minute "First Communication" opens with a rush of white noise that will make you jump. A low-key, embryonic jam slowly unfolds, leading to penetrating electric guitar solos and precise drumming by Burghard Rausch. The sound created is subtle but powerful, recalling the psychedelic excursions of American bands like Jefferson Airplane, Quicksilver Messenger Service, and the Grateful Dead. The 2-minute "Dialogue & Random" is a primitive and dissonant slice of musique concrète electronics by keyboardist Michael Hoenig. The piece fits in squarely with that of other German electronic music from this period, such as pieces by Kraftwerk and Conrad Schnitzler. The 1½-minute "Laila Part 1" is a mellow texture of guitars with rhythm section that quickly builds to a blazing rock jam. This leads into the 7-minute "Laila Part 2," with chunky pulses of bass, drums, and keys joined by spacey guitars that become ever more blistering. The psychedelic purism recalls the sound of *Obscured by Clouds*–era Pink Floyd.

The 6½-minute "In the Silence of the Morning Sunrise" features a masterful texture of electronic jungle sounds by Hoenig, which is combined with mellow keyboards, guitars, percussion, and bass. The piece is easy-flowing, fun, and attractive. The 9-minute "A Quiet Walk" resembles early Deuter and Popol Vuh. Soft electronics that resemble a stream of running water merges with ethereal percussion, growing in volume. Then a multiguitar jig ensues, again recalling Deuter, and also Steve Howe, creating a very spacey and introspective mood. The 7-minute "Haunted Island," where drummer Bausch recites an Edgar Allan Poe poem, is the album's only vocal piece. Bausch's vocal is altered, multitracked, and heavily echoed for effect, and backed by shrill electronics. The piece then explores Gothic, guitar-led jams with mellotron and concludes with an explosion of white noise.

The band produced this album themselves and the sound is good, with some hiss, and is quite similar to *Malesch,* with the odd but wonderful drum miking and extreme stereo separation. The cover art (also by the band), however, is unspectacular, indicating nothing about the music.

The two live Agitation Free discs—*Last* and *Fragments*—are really only afterthoughts, very seldom offering the creative excitement of *Malesch* and *Second.*

ALGARNAS TRADGARD

THE GARDEN OF THE ELKS. Released January 1972. Silence import.

A true landmark in the history of progressive music, *The Garden of the Elks* (the Swedish title is "Framtiden ar ett Svavande skepe, forankrat i forntiden") is a kind of Swedish *Ummagumma/Atom Heart Mother*—an embryonic step by young counterculture musicians toward an original music without boundaries, without precedents, blazing trails and creating radically new sounds. This 58-minute disc is one of the wildest, most experimental and deliberately psychedelic albums of its era.

A masterpiece of collage that features the extreme stereo separation so beloved during the early 1970s, *Garden* is concerned with the elements of sound and feel rather than the straightforward band approach of prog rock. The first track, "Two Hours over Two Blue Mountains with a Cuckoo on Each Side, of the Hours . . . That Is," is a 13-minute swirl of organ, violins, cello, electronics, and rhythm guitar that evolves into a classic structure, adding drums and chants, building up to a frenzy of space rock, then exploding in a burst of loud musique concrète electronics. This leads directly into the 6-minute second track, "There Is a Time for Everything, There Is a Time When Even Time Will Meet," which has a lighter feel of flute and percussion, into which are mixed the sounds of bells, clocks, and a dog barking, giving way to an Eastern psychedelia of sitar and tablas and ending with a duet of zither and acoustic guitar.

Next is the 3-minute "Children of Possibilities" (an apt title from this group), which features a female vocal, in Swedish. "La Rotta" is a 1½-minute folksy piece of violin, handclaps, and footstomps. "Viriditas" is a psychedelic 3-minute piece with a faraway, filtered male vocal. "Rings of Saturn," a powerful, spacey 7-minute piece of heavy guitar rock that is one of the disc's highlights, is evidence of the band's versatility. The 5-minute final track, "The Future Is a Hovering Ship, Anchored in the Past," is the disc's most introspective—a light bass drum beating ominously behind a wash of synth and violin.

Two bonus live tracks from later in 1972—*5/4* and *The Mirrors of Gabriel*—were added to the reissue. While these are in mono, they are definitely incredible and not the usual minor afterthoughts that so many "bonus" tracks are. The approach live is different from the studio sound. The group is more of a rock band here, but the psychedelic/space music element is totally at work, especially the electric guitar. A real spell is woven in the playing, leaving the listener entranced and drifting in space.

This disc has good sound, with some hiss and a few clicks. The cover art, however, is terrible and should have been redone for the reissue. The enclosed booklet contains great photos of the group.

JON ANDERSON

OLIAS OF SUNHILLOW. Released July 1976. Atlantic import.

This brilliant first solo album by the leader of Yes, an experimental work in every sense and a key work in progressive music, is totally outside the conventional popular and rock and roll idioms. It is certainly the finest solo album from any of the Yes group members, and proves that Anderson is the creative force driving that group.

It might be said that the term "concept album" was invented for a project such as this, which is an imaginative and complex conceptual work with fantasy overtones. The music is performed in its entirety by Anderson himself on synths, acoustic guitars, harps, and a wide variety of exotic percussion (bells, gongs, etc.), and the instrumental textures he achieves are stunning and extraordinary. Although known primarily as a vocalist, Anderson's instrumental soundscapes are more ethereally effective than many of the experimental sounds generated by Yes mates Wakeman and Moraz.

The album's construction, comprising space music, acoustic balladry, and world music–like percussives achieves its otherworldly goal, which seems a logical end-game extension of Anderson-led Yes works such as *Tales from Topographic Oceans* and *Relayer.*

Olias is alternately serene and frenetic, reaching almost messianic heights at times in the very spiritual and transformative style that is Anderson's forte. There are, for instance, some incredibly infectious vocal patterns ("Naon"), building in intensity to a kind of religious/ ceremonial climax. This is definitely a work of visionary genius—deeply felt and delivered with great passion and sincerity.

The album opens with "Ocean Song," a 3-minute instrumental in which the loud rumble and crash of cymbals lead into ominous keyboards and multiple acoustic guitars, creating a big sound with sweeping, swaying themes of almost cinematic grandeur. The 3½-minute "Meeting (Garden of Geda)"/"Sound Out the Galleon" features Anderson's layered tapestries of vocals, going into a playful jig of percussion, guitars, and keyboards. The rousing delivery of both the music and the vocals is impressive. The 4½-minute "Dance of Ranyart"/"Olias (to Build the Moorglade)" is a highlight, with its angelic harp effects and magical acoustic guitars having as much popular appeal as any Yes piece. The 7-minute "Qoquaq En Transic"/"Naon"/"Transic To" is another highlight, with a very picturesque and flavorful mix. Dewy washes of spacey synth lead to a deeply spiritual and heavy vocal chant by Anderson; then the music switches to a large, shamanistic, tribal percussion section with sitar, bells, and vocal, recalling the sound of Deuter's *D* and Dzyan's *Electric Silence.* The 3½-minute "Flight of the Moorglade," with its ballad form of multiple acoustic guitars, trippy sprinkles of synths, and vocal, resembles Yes's *Tales from Topographic Oceans* era.

The 5½-minute "Solid Space" is another high point, with ethereal, otherworldly textures of percussion, keyboards, and vocals, plus stereo phasing and tape effects, creating a sound mix that is unconventional and unique. The piece's transcendent theme is once again accomplished with epic-scale grandeur. The 13-minute "Moon Ra"/"Chords"/"Song of Search" has a crash of thunder that leads into a primal and relentless chant section, sung to a percussive beat, along with huge washes of orchestrating synth, leading to a lengthy instrumental section of dreamy, Kitaro-like synths and airy guitars. The 4-minute ballad "To the Runner" recalls both Yes's "Close to the Edge and "And You and I." The piece concludes with a serene bed of church music keyboards.

In collaboration with sleeve designer Roger Dean, the disc contains a narrative story booklet with illustrations which are rendered somewhat ineffective by having been shrunk in size for the CD format. Its look is reminiscent of filmmaker/ humorist/illustrator Terry Gilliam's work. If he were to do an album, it might resemble *Olias.*

Olias, which of course isn't a rock album, was greeted with contempt by the rock press at the time of its release. Lacking the critical initiative to be able to see the work on its own unique terms, reviewers simply dismissed it as just another of Anderson's incoherent indulgences, only worse because it didn't "rock." In other words, it went right over their heads, and their hearts. And those views have had unfortunate consequences. *Olias* is available only as an import, despite the fact that it sells very well. In the view of Yes fans and Anderson himself, *Olias* is his crowning achievement, yet audiences have to search harder for it than any of the Yes releases, including Anderson's other routine, sub-par pop albums.

ANDERSON BRUFORD WAKEMAN HOWE

AN EVENING OF YES MUSIC PLUS (video).

Recorded 1989, released 1993. Image laser disc/Griffin VHS.

This is indeed a very decent document, despite the fact that the self-titled ABWH disc released in 1989 was somewhat mediocre and not particularly progressive. Live, however, they are a formidable proposition. This concert delivers almost everything a fan could want, actually managing exciting (if slightly neo-prog) takes of "Close to the Edge," "Heart of the Sunrise," and "Long Distance Runaround." The Yes material sticks primarily to the 1972 era during which Anderson, Bruford, Wakeman, and Howe were members. This, plus brief solo sections for the four to showcase the elements that each brings to the Yes band, and a handful of the better songs from the ABWH disc, are put across reasonably well. For this reason, the video is strongly recommended over the CD release. One needs to see these legends in action, at the top of their form, rather than through less inspired studio recordings.

Anderson, Howe, and Bruford impress the most. Wakeman's late 1980s keyboard sounds are cheesy and flash (hence the "neo-prog" label used above), but his presence is welcome nonetheless. Although he is almost never the focus of the camera coverage, the excellent Jeff Berlin (of the Bruford band and Watanabe *Spice of Life* fame) is on bass, which ups the ante in musical excitement. The stage design is impressive, the audience ecstatic, and the picture and sound are excellent.

There is an unintentionally hilarious moment at the beginning of the program, where Anderson introduces the festivities from backstage before the concert. He waves enthusiastically to the camera about how wonderful the show is going to be, when—bam! he walks into a metal barricade. He deserves a lot of credit for leaving this sequence in the video release.

ANEKDOTEN

VEMOD. Released September 1993. Virtalevy import.

Vemod is one of the key releases from the current Scandinavian (Anekdoten are from Sweden) progressive rock scene. Rarely does any current vocal prog impress—too often they are corny prog clichés—which in comparison makes *Vemod* all the more impressive and potent because its vocals and lyrics (in English—very important!) really work. The seven tracks on this album are all strong and of a high standard. It is a true group effort by a young band and everything a prog rock outfit in this vein should be.

The key to the well-produced *Vemod*'s success is variety. Of the seven tracks, two are instrumentals. Anekdoten's sound is thunderous, crunching heavy rock (piercing electric guitar, propulsive bass and drums) combined with tasteful, serene moments of classical chamber music (cello, acoustic guitar,

Anekdoten. From left to right, Nicklas Berg, Jan Erik Liljestrom, Anna Sofi Dahlberg, Peter Nordins.

mellotron), much like Anglagard, Focus, King Crimson, and Rush. The performances of the four band members are exemplary. Comparisons to other bands are not the issue, for what comes shining through is the musical genre itself that *Vemod* is a part of. With this release Anekdoten surpasses many other vocal prog groups, both old and new.

Also worth mentioning is the visually interesting presentation of atmospheric cover art and booklet, another goal so often attempted, but rarely achieved, by other prog rock rock bands.

ANGLAGARD

EPILOG. Released November 1994. Hybris import.

Epilog, a major classic, is a prime example of where many new prog rock bands are currently at. Anglagard was (they have since broken up) the leader of the current Scandinavian rock movement. Their first album, *Hybris* (1993), featured Swedish vocals that were a bit alienating, whereas *Epilog* is an all-instrumental recording which quite rightly showcases their enormous talent for complex compositions. Their material is strong, mature, tight, tasteful, varied, and refined. There are textures to burn on this disc, which take you through a broad range of emotions, from the contemplative, light, and pretty to the heavy, frenetic, and jarring. Anglagard are masters of the transition, layering loud and quiet parts in an almost effortless way. This is not build-up music, but rather a system of tension and release set up by the many unexpected twists and turns. Yet somehow it works, and all is brought to a satisfactory closure. This is one hell of a band.

Epilog is framed by two short classically influenced pieces. It opens with the Gothic, dramatic "Prolog," with a string section, classical guitar, and mellotron, and closes with "Saknadens Fullhet," a brief, reflective piano solo similar in feel to Popol Vuh's "Spirit of Peace." But it is the three lengthy epics "Hostsejd," "Skogsranden," and "Sista Somrar" that are *Epilog*'s ambitious centerpieces.

The general sound of the band is similar to Jethro Tull à la *Thick As a Brick* and Focus à la *Moving Waves,* mixed with avant-garde twists à la Henry Cow's *Western Culture* and Scandinavian prog bands like Atlas. The music shifts from loud, hard-hitting drums and infectious, quirky bass riffs propelled by ominous organ and mellotron to tranquil acoustic guitars, flutes, piano, exotic percussion, and some very subtle wordless vocalizations. The performances are first-rate, the production and (especially) the mix are top-notch, and the sound is very good.

The cover art and disc booklet are among the best. There are dreamy, sepia-tinged photos of statues superimposed over outdoor scenes, giving the whole package a very strong hint of mystery, right down to the abstract design on the disc itself.

BURIED ALIVE. Released July 1996. Musea import.

As an comprehensive document of an Anglagard concert this is everything you could want. Unfortunately, this was their farewell appearance, recorded before an extremely enthusiastic audience at L.A.'s ProgFest in November of 1994 on the eve of the release of *Epilog.* Anglagard dissolved at a time when their impact was only beginning to be felt, and their too-brief career and early break-up are signals that Anglagard—and releases like this one—may attain legendary status.

The six-piece band performs material from their two releases *Hybris* and *Epilog,* with the ambitious selections averaging around 10 minutes each. The performances are excellent all round, except for the occasional vocal, here handled by guitarist Tord Lindman (somewhat surprising because on *Hybris* they were sung by flautist Anna Holmgren). The excitement of the music completely overshadows the vocals. In fact, the success of Anglagard's all-instrumental studio masterpiece *Epilog* over the now out-of-print *Hybris* reflects the realization that the vocals just aren't needed (especially so since the lyrics are in Swedish). By creating such complex classical prog rock compositions Anglagard has pointed out the conflict over vocals in modern progressive music, and with this live disc they prove that they are superfluous.

The strongest piece here is *Epilog*'s "Hostsejd." A true epic of the prog rock form, it is 13½ minutes of complex changes and unexpected textures, the right mix of chops and atmospherics. Quiet sections of flute and mellotron/organ are hammered hard by a crack rhythm section, with dual electric guitars in the angular Fripp/Anekdoten–like style overlaid on top. The bass riffing on this track is amazing, by the way.

The sound on this 72-minute disc is great, though there is minor hiss as well as a few stage buzzes. The track listing on the back cover neglects to mention "Hostsejd" and gets everything mixed up, including the running times. The cover art is unexceptional, though the booklet has some nice photos and notes.

The break-up of Anglagard is depressing enough, but it is infuriating that an acclaimed group can make their final recording before a rapt American audience, in a major U.S. city, yet not be able to have that product made available domestically in America.

LUIGI ARCHETTI

DAS OHR. Released April 1993. Admission To Music import.

Das Ohr (translated, "the ear") is a 61-minute collection of 35 amazing short pieces dedicated to the human ear, all performed on the electric guitar. Luigi Archetti, a Swiss composer, guitarist, painter, and member of the prog rock band Tiere der Nacht, wrote, performed, and produced this genuinely progressive work in September 1992. An artist concerned with different structures, new sound colors, and the appreciation of the act of listening, Archetti is a guitarist with all the range of David Torn and the poignancy of Terje Rypdal, which he combines with the sensibility of avant-garde sound constructionists like O + A and Syllyk. His guitar compositions are inventive stereo "sound environments," based mainly on concrète and collage forms, yet still including stylish, conventional soloing.

The keys to *Das Ohr* are conciseness, variety, and conceptual unity. The pieces range from a half a minute to 4 minutes in length, each concentrated in its focus, with none of them hanging around long enough to lose their direction or become unwelcome. Archetti creates unexpected sounds with his guitar, from drum-like percussion, to the sound of scissors cutting, to dripping water. But this is not just a hodgepodge of unrelated bits and pieces. The work is conceptually unified, with all of the different titles related to the parts and functions of the ear. The disc is also varied enough in the moods it chooses to evoke to have wide appeal and hold up to repeated listenings.

There is some truly beautiful music here, especially Archetti's searing, emotional guitar solos on less experimental tracks like "Round Windows," "Malleus and Incus," and "Cochlea," so do not be fooled into thinking this is too out there. There are a lot of musicians trying to find the right balance of the conventional and the experimental, but few succeed as well as Archetti does here.

The sound quality is excellent. Archetti also designed the cover art, which asks us to listen more closely to the environment around us.

ADRENALIN. Released February 1995. Rec Rec import.

Adrenalin, Luigi Archetti's second album, is a surprise after the low-key impressionism of his brilliant debut disc, *Das Ohr* (see above). Recorded in 1993, this 70-minute instrumental tour-de-force establishes Archetti as one of the most significant progressive composers of the current era. The amount of variety and challenge here is staggering. Each of the album's 28 pieces (most co-written with his bandmates) manages to break new ground. Far, far louder and more flat-out rock than *Das Ohr, Adrenalin*'s industrial collage compositions incorporate noise and dissonance as part of their structure, shredding like Torn/Karn/Bozzio's *Polytown* or bands like Happy Family, and the music stands you on your head. While this is still a collection of smaller vignettes (as on *Das Ohr* and the Tiere Der Nacht projects with Mani Neumeier), with each of the pieces in the range of 1 to 4 minutes, there are enough ideas here for three albums. What's immediately striking on this recording are its volume and playful stereo effects, and the album produces a strong, inescapable wall of sound that justifies its title.

Archetti, playing guitars, tapes, keyboards, mandolin, and melodica, is joined by Martin Gantenbein (drums, piccolo, keyboards), Urs Blochlinger (saxophones, flute) and Hubi Greiner (sampling). Song titles like "Spatial Illusions of the Insects," "Collections of Lines," "Drip Dry Drill," and "Tit?" are evocative of surrealism/Dada, and are entirely apppropriate for Archetti's rapidly paced but tightly constructed impressions.

There are a number of highlights. The 3-minute "Secrets of the Royal Psychic" is a titanic rock jam with a plethora of guitar effects that stomp everything in their path. The 2½-minute "The God, The Bad & The Ugly," and the 3½-minute "Inflammable & Electric" are both Ennio Morricone pastiches, with stereo keyboard effects, samples, percussion, and guitar, which recall *The Big Gundown,* a Morricone tribute album from 1986 by John Zorn. The 2½-minute "Seductive Edge" and the 1-minute "Chlorophyl" both feature very loud, over-the-top drum crashes and guitar atmospherics that feel like bomb attacks. The 4-minute "Half Way to Intelligence" is softer, with acoustic guitar, keyboard orchestrations, and strange percussion. The 3-minute "First & Last" combines laid-back and distorted electric guitar noodling, silly voices that sound like they are from radio broadcasts, and heavy breathing. In the 1½-minute "Urban Guerilla" an incoherent, babbling voice is heard as a fork runs over Archetti's guitar strings.

The sheer inventiveness of "Adrenalin" recalls the work of some of the progressive genre's most noted proponents—Pink Floyd (à la *Ummagumma),* King Crimson (the 1980s/1990s incarnations), Fred Frith (in the Massacre group), and David Torn (à la *Polytown, Tripping over God).* The disc's strange cover painting by Archetti is an unsettling picture of an eyeball stretching itself—an apt image to introduce the dislocating and frenetic experimental rock jams of *Adrenalin.*

ASH RA TEMPEL

INVENTIONS FOR ELECTRIC GUITAR. Released September 1974. Spalax import.

This is, rightfully, the most acclaimed Ash Ra Tempel release. Basically a solo release from guitarist Manuel Gottsching, it is a deceptively simple collection of layered guitar patterns, with stereo echo effects and soloing on top, recorded on a Teac 4-track. To present-day guitar aficionados and tech-heads this may not be very impressive, and may even be shrugged off as quaint run-of-the-mill noodling. But the sound is infectious, and the album goes by quickly and effortlessly despite its 46-minute running length.

There are three tracks on the recording: the 17½-minute "Echo Waves," the most aggressive and rhythmic piece; the 6½-minute "Quasarsphere, a softer, pure space music of drifting, floating sounds; and the 21½-minute "Pluralis," a minimalist rhythm pattern of shimmering tones, constantly added to and changed. All of the sounds are created with electric guitar, with lots of stereo panning, expanding the range of the musical palette. In keeping with other Ash Ra Tempel recordings, their music here has a heavy psychedelic feel, particularly the piercing solos. In the liner notes Gottsching refers to this guitar work as "electronic music." One can certainly hear similarities to the sequencers of mid-1970s Tangerine Dream and Klaus Schulze in the intricate tapestry of the rhythm guitar patterns. He probably had been listening to TD's "Phaedra!"

On the whole, the sound is quite good (with a little hiss), unlike some of the other Ash Ra Tempel discs available which may have been LP transcriptions.

ATLAS

BLA VARDAG. Released March 1979. A.P.M. import.

Bla Vardag (a.k.a. *Blue Tuesday)* is a shining example of breezy, sunny-textured prog rock/fusion, with memorable melodies and a slightly jazzy feel. A fine young Swedish band with a freshness and energy, Atlas has strong compositions and playing, but the sound isn't particularly busy. The group resembles Passport (though without saxophones) and Trilogy (there are two keyboardists), and has some of the classic prog band elements: instrumental compositions featuring a multitude of synths, organ, piano, and mellotron, with electric and acoustic guitar shadings, punctuated by a snappy rhythm section. Their sound is also a precursor to later similar Scandinavian prog developments like Anglagard. Despite some of the dated organ sounds, this is classic stuff.

The 7-minute "The Elizabetune" is an atypical slice of European symphonic prog rock, with melodic and friendly textures of sunny keyboards, spacey electric and acoustic guitars, and a tight rhythm section. The keyboards (electric piano, mellotron, synths, organ) dominate, and the band's sound recalls Terpandre, Bonfire, Trilogy, and early Genesis. The 14-minute "In the Street" is a highlight, with rousing themes and strong performances. A low-key but sprawling epic, the piece's lively jamming leads to a spacey center section of Steve Hackett–like guitars and piano breaks, but also, unfortunately, to a moldy organ solo.

The 7-minute title track is an unusually sweet and glowing piece of jazz/rock fusion; with its syrupy, snake-charming keyboards, it resembles film soundtrack music, . The 3-minute "Walking Tune" is very much in the vein of the U.K. Canterbury sound, with jazzy noodling that recalls Hatfield and the North. The 7-minute "The Path of the White Crane" is a storytelling form reminiscent of Camel's "The Snow Goose," with its bright and tuneful melodies. The sound is dated, but still enjoyable.

There are three bonus tracks. The first, "Bjørn's Craft," was recorded in 1980–81 when the band was down to a four-piece group and had a slightly chunkier rhythm attack. The just-under 8-minute "From Home," a 1995 reunion track, is an excellent and respectable effort, not at all below the heights achieved in the rest of the material. The final bonus track is a short 1978 recording for radio with terrible sound. The overall sound quality for this disc is very good, although there is a small amount of hiss.

If Atlas had to struggle to make it after *Bla Vardag* was released, it may be in part due to the terrible cover art—an ugly grey pencil drawing of a bulldozer demolishing a building. The cover should have at least been redone for the CD reissue, because the substandard artwork hides some great music.

LUCIANO BASSO

VOCI. Released January 1976. Vinyl Magic import.

There are very few gems in what is touted as the "Italian progressive scene" (which consists mostly of vocal-heavy operatic twaddle—dated, clichéd, badly produced organ-dominated prog rock), but Luciano Basso's *Voci* is a masterpiece of classically influenced rock, different from and preferable to groups like Emerson, Lake & Palmer, and Trace. Imagine a more classical Focus or Curved Air. The all-instrumental *Voci* is a real stunner: five grand, lyrical compositions by keyboardist Basso, a marvellous production and mix, and an excellent band (especially drummer Riccardo Da Par).

The 7½-minute "Preludio" is a compelling piece, with an opening of piano and violin that is at once romantic and very earnest. This is joined by searing but clean electric guitar notes, which are emotionally gripping. Adding synth and a tight rhythm section, the piece is an excellent example of driving classical rock, recalling Curved Air. The 4½-minute "Promenade 1" has a quaint organ-led prog rock intro section, similar to early Egg. A playful center section of multitracked clavinets is then joined by the superior backing band. The 6-minute "Promenade II," a breezy, symphonic prog rock jam with cascades of dreamy piano, bass, and tight drumming, along with equally dreamy strings and synth, recalls Clearlight.

The 11-minute title track is a serene and grand form of European prog rock, intricate and tasteful, and stands alongside other European artists like Focus, Finnforest, and Schicke, Führs & Fröhling. The themes are memorable and the performances ace. The 9-minute "Echo" opens with an emotional church music organ and choir of ethereal voices, then an ultra-spacey David Gilmour–like slide guitar joins the organ and choir, recalling Pink Floyd's *Atom Heart Mother.* The piece then explores some light, jazzy rock workouts with a Canterbury sound, concluding with a grand finale of strings and piano.

The excellent sound on this disc has a live feel to it—deep, rich, resonant, and punchy. The cover drawing, though, is fairly unspectacular.

ADRIAN BELEW

DESIRE CAUGHT BY THE TAIL. Released October 1986. Island.

This is a mature, extremely avant-garde impressionist work from one of the members of the 1980s/1990s King Crimson. Recorded in its entirety and produced by Belew, it is astonishingly experimental music. Stockhausen-like juxtapositions, tape collage, and bizarre percussion form the backdrops for Belew's inventive orchestra of dissonant guitar sounds. Take the more off-the-wall Crimson material, only much more stripped down and far more avant, and you've got music that is often more challenging than King Crimson releases like *Beat* or *THRAK,* or Summers and Fripp instrumental collaborations.

This is really too dissonant to be classified as mainstream impressionism (perhaps a better label would be *abstract* expressionism). However, "Laughing Man," "Portrait of Margaret," "Beach Creatures Dancing Like Cranes," "Guernica," and "At the Seaside Cafe" are all effective impressionistic evocations of what those titles might suggest to the imagination. "Tango Zebra" has a Jade Warrior–like Oriental feel, and many of the pieces use sound sculpture to tell a story, evidence of the influence of Laurie Anderson (note his contributions to her 1986 concert film *Home of the Brave)* prior to recording *Desire.* The whole presentation is more avant-garde than anything done at labels like ECM or CMP, and is certainly more bizarre than most instrumental albums released at the time. This is definitely not a new age recording!

Too many of Belew's imaginative guitar sound experiments are on the shrill, shrieking, and abrasive side, which can be off-putting at times and keeps the relatively short (at 33 minutes) album from the highest rating. The sound is good and clear, and there is a nicely appropriate cover painting by Margaret Belew. Unfortunately Mr. Belew has backed away considerably from projects like this in his solo career, releasing far too many sub-par pop recordings aimed (low) at the alternative rock market, where he appears to be more comfortable as the belter/balladeer rather than as the innovative composer/instrumentalist. Nevertheless, *Desire* is an important example of American progressive music.

KETIL BJØRNSTAD

WATER STORIES. Released November 1993. ECM.

This is an essential prelude to *The Sea* (see below). A conceptual work in the same vein, it is dark, ominous, moody music that is atmospheric and foreboding. Washes of introspective piano (by composer Bjørnstad) and cascades of percussion (Jon Christensen/Per Hillestad) are colored by the wailing, sometimes blazing guitar of Terje Rypdal, plus the bass of Bjørn Kiellemyr.

This 58-minute full digital recording is divided into two sections, "Blue Ice (The Glacier)" and "Approaching the Sea." While the music doesn't always rise to the promise of the imagery in the song titles (e.g., "Glacial Reconstruction,"

Ketil Bjørnstad. (Photo by Dag E. Thorenfeldt)

"Flotation and Surroundings"), it does so often enough to create some outstanding, evocative textures. Periods of serene tranquility and grandeur alternate with sudden outbursts of chaotic sound. Highly impressionistic in the usual ECM mold, this is intelligent, sophisticated music—a tasteful high-quality effort from these Norwegian masters.

Bjørnstad wrote the project to showcase Rypdal's playing, and this disc is essential for Rypdal fans. His guitar is at the center of most of these pieces, providing the music's most exciting moments with loud and piercing solos. With *Water Stories, The Sea,* and *The River,* Bjørnstad, along with Rypdal, reinvigorates the ECM label as a hotbed of major new progressive music.

KETIL BJØRNSTAD/DAVID DARLING

THE RIVER. Released March 1997. ECM.

The River, a 12-part, 55-minute work by composer/pianist Bjørnstad, is the essential companion to 1995's *The Sea* and in fact began as an outgrowth of textures from that disc). *The River* gives a larger voice to the dreamiest aspects of Bjørnstad's compositions, via the reductionist delivery of the duo, away from the expanded band efforts of *Water Stories* and *The Sea.* In some ways, *The River* is more of a showcase for Bjørnstad's solo talents than *Water Stories;* it contains his best work as a pianist (in that every note of his playing can be heard throughout). *The River* would have made an equally great solo piano album. Darling's contribution, some of his finest work, is huge. His cello sounds like a small orchestra or flute creeping in and out, behind and around Bjørnstad's piano, adding a brooding element to Bjørnstad's darker, sparser notes.

The 12 pieces range between 1½ and 7½ minutes, and the mood is very dreamy and serene, occasionally melancholic. Nothing is made obvious in the pieces; they are so understated as to be practically ambient (though not in the sense of being static). Like its title, the music flows by, relatively smoothly, at times active, at times barely there, never announcing itself or jarring with unexpected changes. The full digital recording gives it a very quiet and flat mix that is never loud, underlining the music's serenity.

According to Bjørnstad's liner notes, some of the pieces were influenced by the music of the late Renaissance. *The River* is precisely the kind of pure impressionism that the ECM label does so well, where a new classical music emerges, but influenced by jazz, ambient, new age, and space music. In this reductionist sense, *The River* may even be preferable to *The Sea* and is certainly preferable to a project like 1984's *Eos* by Terje Rypdal/David Darling.

The effective minimalist cover art by Mayo Bucher is just a pencil-thin line dividing up a blue background, which emphasizes the spaces found within *The River.*

KETIL BJØRNSTAD/DAVID DARLING/ TERJE RYPDAL/JON CHRISTENSEN

THE SEA. Released October 1995. ECM.

The Sea is a total success—a conceptual masterpiece, a major work of impressionism, and a hauntingly delicate full digital recording. It is a definitive album for active listening and just the kind of peak these ECM artists had been working toward.

The Sea is a 75-minute composition in 12 parts, written by Bjørnstad, basically a quartet of piano, cello, guitar, and drums in the true ECM style (a fusion of jazz, classical, and rock elements). Each of these master musicians has a staked-out sound territory for his instrument, and their timing and delicacy of touch are masterful—appropriate, tight, and with close attention to detail.

And it is detail that makes this album such a milestone. There is always someplace new to go inside this music. Fresh impressions and spaces can be discovered with each listen. The music has a gothic stateliness, a haunting, dreamy spaciness of truly remarkable subtlety. The digital mix—the powerful delineations of the instruments as they meet and coalesce, then disperse into deep, serene solos, and then back again, all executed with a resonant (if understated) flair and style—is also incredible.

The fabulously dreamy and appropriate cover art is also in inimitable ECM style. Although minimalist in the sense that it offers only one image to consider (a sea), the design sets the impressionistic tone perfectly.

BLUE MOTION

BLUE MOTION. Released December 1980. Laser's Edge.

Featuring former members of the Swiss group Circus, Blue Motion is a trio of two keyboardists and a percussionist. Stephan Ammann and Stephan Grieder utilize ARP synths, grand piano, Hammond organ, electric piano, and clavinet while Fritz Laujer plays drums, xylophone, and percussion. With all three members writing, the group digitally recorded 12 instrumentals live in the studio in two days during October of 1980, making this recording an early example of a full digital nonclassical release.

Blue Motion is notable for isolating and emphasizing the vital keyboard and drum interplay of symphonic prog and fusion, excluding guitars, bass, or vocals. The sound recalls the dynamics of other progressive keyboard/drum duos, such as Emerson/Palmer, Banks/Collins, Lumley/Collins, and Corea/White. Blue Motion's storytelling, actively paced compositions, which are classical in tone, are accomplished with flair and aplomb and create a variety of moods.

The two longest pieces are the best. The 14½-minute "Stromboli," with its plentiful organ and piano soloing, and the 12-minute "Stonehenge," with its rollicking keyboards, crashing drums, and cascades of xylophone, should both appeal strongly to fans of progressive music. The other ten pieces on this recording range from half a minute to 4½ minutes. "Fingers I" and "Fingers II" are brief solo piano interludes. "Moontales IV" and "Moontales I" are like early 1970s prog rock intros à la Genesis, with spacey organ and electric piano. The 1½-minute "Motions" is a restrained and tasteful drum solo, while the 2-minute pieces "3 and One Eighth" and "Parking" are classical/new age piano vignettes. The 3-minute title track and the 4½-minute "Slow Motion" are introspective pieces similar to certain ECM offerings, with stark, somber keyboard notes and superb accompaniment from Laujer.

Digital recording gives this an airy and fresh sound, and a very quiet soundstage. The cover has a colorful deep blue paint streak across a white background that suggests the light touch of the music. While Blue Motion is not well known, their deft distillations of the keyboard and drum foundations of progressive rock are very effective.

BONFIRE

BONFIRE GOES BANANAS. Released February 1975. Belle Antique import.

Upon hearing this recording—most of which is a top-notch production and a really fine job soundwise for a 1975 release—one wonders why Bonfire is not more popular. A Dutch group in the instrumental rock genre of their peers Finch and Focus, with a sprinkle here and there of Gentle Giant and Rush, Bonfire plays truly rocking progressive music that is rhythmic, tight and grooving, and loud. Pieces like "Circle" feature relentless band interplay. Everything works and each player is 100% on. The riff of the up-front guitars sometimes has has a bluesy feel. Drummer Gees Meerman is always on or ahead of the beat and has a huge drum sound, comparable to Phil Collins's. While Bonfire's music is more in the rave-up style than anything particularly experimental, their compositions are not without complexity. More importantly, though, their music is fun, and progressive should be fun.

So why isn't this recording more well known? There are several reasons. First, the silly title (they should have done better). Second, the cover art (a wretchedly unattractive parody of the *Meet The Beatles* cover). Ouch! Third, there is another band called Bonfire, a terrible heavy metal outfit. And fourth, this disc contains atrocious, irrelevant bonus tracks cut by a later lineup of the band many years after *Bananas*. This dreadful material sours an otherwise excellent example of a reissue done right and is probably the main reason for the group's obscurity.

BOUD DEUN

ASTRONOMY MADE EASY. Released January 1997. Cuneiform.

A new American band from Virginia, the groove-oriented Boud Deun is not earth-shatteringly progressive, but they do confidently reassert the forms of instrumental rock. More entertaining than groundbreaking, their emphasis is on energy and chops. *Astronomy Made Easy* features twelve solidly executed, high-octane workouts, ranging from 1½ to 9½ minutes. The quartet are amazing players, with a dynamic interaction that's rock-solid tight.

Boud Deun exemplifies a populist and uniquely American aesthetic. Their kind of prog rock is meant to be performed in club settings, and it would do nicely in those commercial forums if the current mainstream media accepted instrumental music as club-worthy, which it often doesn't. As a result, young rock bands like Boud Deun are categorized as progressive. Boud Deun adds a violin to the power trio slamming of the guitar, bass, and drums, which gives their music not the sonorous classical dimension you might expect, but rather a bluegrass feel—a new kind of fusion for a prog rock project. The fact that the other three instruments make like Fugazi-meets-Djam Karet is what keeps that fusion in the progressive realm. While the band's aggressive playing is devoid of pretensions, it's also devoid of ambition and context. The music doesn't tell stories; the only message is "Boogie!" Given that the group's appeal is their spirited live sound, the production values of *Astronomy Made Easy* are what make the album, capturing the sound of the band the way it should be heard with monster volume and clarity.

LIONA BOYD

PERSONA. Released January 1986. CBS.

Liona Boyd is a long-celebrated classical guitar virtuoso. *Persona,* her foray into the context of progressive rock–style instrumentation, is so

Boud Deun. From left to right, Matt Eiland, Shawn Persinger, Greg Hiser, Rock Cancelose. (Photo by Rob Gassie.)

impressive that after hearing it, you are likely to find her straight classical releases—just the classical guitar and never anything else—too thin and sparse. *Persona* puts Boyd's considerable talent into a more imaginative, varied setting, with other musicians and even environmental sounds to add dimension.

Persona is different from most of the other releases discussed in this book in that it lacks a true rock, jazz, or new age approach. Boyd's approach is purely classical. She has made no effort to shape her music into another, more popular, mold, which is good as such a move might have turned the recording into just an embarrassing imitation. And despite the presence of many guest stars, such as David Gilmour, Eric Clapton, and Michael Kamen, *Persona* is actually rather low-key.

The 5½-minute "L'Enfant" is a cover of a Vangelis tune, with icy piano and pedestrian electronic percussion and Boyd's dramatic classical guitar soloing over it, plus other guitar orchestrations. The piece is memorable despite the thin production and unfortunate percussion. The 3-minute "Sun Child" is the first of the album's three pieces written by Boyd, which are among the disc's highlights. Field recordings of children playing lead into a beautiful and infectious guitar tapestry, recalling Mike Oldfield. The gorgeous 3½-minute "Memories of a Thousand Moons," with wind sounds leading into introspective and moody chords by Boyd, accompanied by Kamen on strings and choir, is another highlight, despite its reverent sound. The 4½-minute "Sorceress" has some interesting sections, but is deeply marred by the unfortunate electronic percussion. The 5-minute "Mother and Sister" is a lush, sweetish piece of chamber music, with large, cinematic sways of multiple guitars and guest Yo-Yo Ma's cello. Subtle it's not.

The 4-minute "Labryinth" features bluesy licks by guest Eric Clapton, trading riffs with Boyd. The poor backing and percussion bog it down, however. The 4-minute "Phoenix Reborn" has environmental sounds accompanying a delicate, affecting storytelling solo guitar by Boyd. The 4-minute "Sea of Tranquility," a cover of piece by Brahms is serene, but mushy backing from the studio musicians make it unspectacular. The 3-minute "Destiny" is a nice, moody, Spanish-flavored piece. The 3-minute "Flight of the Phoenix" is another high point, with the sounds of wind, birdsong, bells, and strings accompanying Boyd's guitars. The piece is textural and low-key, creating spacey, drifting moods. The 4-minute title track is similar to "L'Enfant," but more understated, with acoustic tapestries, congas, and chimes. Midway through, guest David Gilmour unleashes a roaring Pink Floyd–like electric guitar solo. This contribution, like those of some of the other guest artists, is typical of *Persona* in that it somewhat overshadows the best tracks, which are those by Boyd with minimal accompaniment.

GLENN BRANCA

THE ASCENSION. Released January 1981. New Tone import.

The first in a spectacular series of releases by Branca, *The Ascension* is a combination of punk rock instrumentation with strict classical structures and forms. This fusing of low-brow and high-brow is inspired and successfully executed. The music is storytelling, with a gritty, dark mood that creates an underground, murky feel. The classical structure gives it a hypnotically repetitive form that drips with a sinister tension. Branca's consciously modern classical/rock fusion is a uniquely American alternative to the melodicism and refinement of European styles of classical/rock, although it is equally precise and symphonic.

The 5-minute "Lesson No. 2" opens with a grungy bass guitar intro, with the drums and four oddly tuned electric guitars marching in for a series of orchestral crashes. The 12½-minute "The Spectacular Commodity" has a King Crimson–like feel of menace, with its shrill, tense jams climbing edgy tonal scales, carried along by the drums and picking up to a racing pace. The 3-minute "Structure" has a punk rock–like form, recalling Siouxsie and the Banshees (à la "Sin in My Heart"). The 8-minute "Light Field (In Consonance)" has careening, minimalist guitar riffs which set the piece's course. The 13-minute title track begins with stray guitar and bass chords, which are punctuated by brief but large drum fills. The piece then becomes a dreamy, Ash Ra Tempel–like blizzard of drones.

Branca's aggressive sound influenced the earlier, artier phase of Sonic Youth, which is no surprise as one of this album's guitarists is Lee Ranaldo from that band. The sound is only fairly good, so it must be turned up. The cover is a black-and-white drawing of two men by artist Robert Longo.

BRAND X

UNORTHODOX BEHAVIOUR. Released July 1976. Caroline.

Brand X is a pivotal group in British progressive music. British fusion in the early 1970s was mainly represented by the Canterbury sax/keyboards of Soft Machine and the avant excursions of the violin/mellotron-heavy King Crimson. Breaking away from those approaches, Brand X was influenced more by the American fusion of Return to Forever and Mahavishnu Orchestra. By incorporating a more flat-out funkiness, turning up the rock-oriented side of the fusion equation, and applying a more composed, less improvised studio efficiency, Brand X paved the way for newer, rawer powerhouse fusion, which groups like Gong, Bruford, National Health, and others would later expand on.

Unorthodox Behaviour was cutting-edge progressive in 1976. Recorded in the fall of 1975, when Phil Collins had not yet become full-time vocalist in Genesis, *Unorthodox* reveals a Collins totally committed to adventurous instrumentation. That he has backed away so totally in his career from this original solo direction is something that many progressive music fans have never forgiven him for. To them he is a percussionist, not a pop singer. In fact, *Unorthodox* may be his finest hour as a percussionist, even when the clearly shining moments he has in Genesis and on his solo albums are considered. Collins and Genesis fans unaware of Brand X should check this band out. Collins's performances are historic, and his drumming some of the most colorful ever recorded. That so many people are unaware, or worse, dismissive of Brand X is unfortunate, and does progressive music as a whole a disservice. It is also a mistake to view Brand X solely as a Collins project. This was a fairly democratic band; he was only part of the equation.

"Nuclear Burn," the album's 6½-minute opener, is a definitive example of the music of Brand X. Percy Jones, as influential on bass guitar as Collins is on drums, virtually defines the increased role of modern bass playing, especially on fretless. Reminiscent of Jaco Pastorius, his monster bass sound just walks and struts through the track. Collins's drums here have his trademark sound—anyone familiar with *A Trick of the Tail* or *Face Value* will recognize it—but on this recording Collins is quintessentially *on,* from Godzilla-sized drum rolls to an arsenal of percussive colorations (vibes, tamborines, gongs, etc.). Jones's and Collins's tight playing benefits from precise engineering and mixing, which for 1975–1976 was state-of-the-art. *Unorthodox* advances the rhythm section much more to the forefront of the music, an approach which has been extraordinarily influential.

Guitarist John Goodsall and keyboardist Robin Lumley are at this juncture more textural, which is not always their usual role. Goodsall would go on to develop an aggressive axe-wielding persona in both Brand X and especially in his later band Fire Merchants (see review). On *Unorthodox* the guitars and keyboards (both electric and acoustic) are tasteful shadings. Though at times they are in front, mostly they are understated in an ECM-like style.

Brand X's sense of humor is evident (though unfortunately the CD reissue doesn't reprint the original LP insert loaded with Pythonesque jokes), both in the music and in their song titles. (This can be a bit off-putting sometimes. Titles like "Born Ugly" (8 minutes) and "Smacks of Euphoric Hysteria" (4½ minutes) may be fun, but they are perhaps a bit too flippant.)

While the sound on this disc is sharp and crisp, there are some distortions due to the close miking of Collins's drums, which is unfortunate (though almost charming). Another drawback is the poor cover art—a photo of someone looking through the blinds of a window. These are very minor criticisms—this is absolutely classic stuff.

MOROCCAN ROLL. Released April 1977. Caroline.

Moroccan Roll is Brand X at their most experimental, and, being a strong group effort, is also perhaps the definitive Brand X album. With this release they developed an even clearer identity, and each of its tracks reveals mature facets and styles. The lineup is now expanded to a quintet, adding percussionist Morris Pert.

And, amazingly, Phil Collins is still strongly committed to this group, despite the enormous pressure of having assumed the lead vocal role in Genesis, recorded two pivotal Genesis albums in 1976, and undertaken two lengthy career-making world tours with them, either prior to or during the recording of *Moroccan Roll.*

The opening piece, the 4½-minute"Sun in the Night" by John Goodsall, is an unexpected tour de force of Arabic-style swirls and exotica, complete with ethereal chants by Collins in his first vocals for the band. This track is a departure for the group in that it isn't their usual style of fusion, and as such is a real triumph.

"Sun in the Night" is followed by two tracks by Collins that are easily among his most avant-garde compositions. The first, "Why Should I Lend You Mine . . . ," is an 11-minute slice of very spacey twists and turns, with an extreme stereo separation sound palette. This is followed by the 2-minute ". . . Maybe I'll Lend You Mine After All," a quiet wordless vocal with piano accompaniment that is just as spacey as the companion piece.

Keyboardist Robin Lumley also contributes two key tracks. The first, "Collapsar," is a much-too-brief burst of pure space music similar to his compositions for his *Marscape* album (see review) with Jack Lancaster and the rest of Brand X. The second, "Disco Suicide," is classic Brand X. A cascading piano motif builds to grand heights, later joined by a vocal chorus, with the band adding thunderous fusion parts in between. The next piece, "Orbits," is the first of many Percy Jones experimental solo bass compositions. Like the above-mentioned cuts, the 1½-minute "Orbits" has a space music feel to it.

The rest of the tracks are in the style of the first album, a hard-hitting, funky fusion, albeit with a more eclectic and over-the-top style (the final piece, the 7½-minute "Macrocosm," concludes with the sound of a plane crashing!).

The sound quality is excellent—again a very crisp mix—although there is some hiss. The cover art by Hipgnosis is pretty goofy, as are the photos of the band, especially the one of a longhaired bushy-bearded Collins.

PRODUCT. Released August 1979. Caroline.

After *Moroccan Roll,* Phil Collins's main attention turned back toward Genesis. Robin Lumley, tired of performing, preferred writing and producing. Thus began a series of line-up shuffles that changed the nature of the band slightly. Brand X became more of a journeyman-type session group. Perhaps this fragmentation was responsible for the relative mediocrity of their next two albums, *Livestock* (1977) and *Masques* (1978). *Livestock* is a worthwhile but surprisingly timid live recording. *Masques* doesn't have Collins on it at all and moves Lumley into the producer's chair, adding Mike Clarke (drums) and Peter Robinson (keyboards). Although *Masques* still has some value, it's easily the flimsiest of the band's studio releases.

Product, then, is something of a return to form. All five members from the *Moroccan* lineup appear, plus Robinson and Clarke, and new man John Giblin (on bass). With most of the members making writing contributions, *Product* has quite a lot of variety. It is a very solid album, with more of a polished studio gloss than before, which works well for them. The sound is excellent, typically crisp and crystal-clear. The spacey, jazzy, experimental edges are de-emphasized (with the exception of Giblin's all-too-brief "April," a 2-minute solo bass meditation with environmental sounds) in favor of an even more rock-oriented, tighter, punchy jamming, with Goodsall and Jones assuming larger roles. All members' playing is incredible. Robinson's keyboards are more rhythmic and less melodic than Lumley's, and it's difficult to even tell when it's Collins on drums and when it's Clarke!

The surprise on *Product* is two vocals by Collins, "Don't Make Waves" and "Soho," which could be mistaken for slick Genesis cuts (à la early 1980s material like "Paperlate"). They're not progressive, but rather conventional FM-ready rock, complete with choruses. Perhaps this explains the album title?

Product is also notable for being the last Brand X album to have Collins's full participation. He even undertook a tour of the U.S. with them in 1979. The album contains Collins's 6½-minute ". . . And So to F . . . ," the only Brand X material to ever resurface in his solo career.

DO THEY HURT? Released April 1980. Caroline.

Do They Hurt? is a very good, solid album. It's not a masterpiece, and has a detectable lack of focus, but it is certainly a respectable part of Brand X's impressive catalog. *Do They Hurt?* is even more of a punchy, busy, rocking fusion than *Product,* and this is mainly Goodsall and Jones's group by now. They both have writing credits on all the pieces, though each of the musicians from *Product* put in appearances. The sound is very good, with the rhythm section coming on especially strong. The bass guitar work by Jones and Giblin is particularly noteworthy; both make breathtaking lightning runs of notes throughout the album.

Goodsall's 4½-minute "Cambodia" is one of Brand X's most outstanding tracks and a step forward for the band in that it operates as an unfolding narrative-type composition, with a build-up and release of raw but controlled electric guitars. The 7½-minute "Triumphant Limp" and the 8½-minute "D.M.Z." exhibit some of the swing and swagger typical of the original Brand X of *Unorthodox Behaviour,* albeit with a more hard-edge rock punch. In contrast, Goodsall's totally out of place "Act of Will" is easily the worst cut ever made by Brand X. An atrocious filtered vocoder-like vocal from Goodsall with a tired, formulaic arrangement and backing, this surprisingly poor piece of junk should never have been included. Fortunately, it is the album's only major musical mistake; all the other material is quite strong.

Two minor complaints concern the cover art (an alligator on a sidewalk—ouch!), and the absence of the hilarious liner notes by Michael Palin, which were not reprinted for the CD reissue.

XCOMMUNICATION. Released June 1992. Ozone.

This comeback album is as fine a Brand X recording as you could hope for, a definitive album not only for the group but for the genre of fusion itself. The recording proves that Brand X are still leaders in progressive music, and *Xcommunication* just gets better with each listen.

Picking up right where albums like *Do They Hurt?* left off, *Xcommunication* actually improves on them. This is Brand X as a louder, hard-hitting power trio, which is a good thing. Mixing the approach of classic Brand X with Goodsall's band Fire Merchants (see reviews), this incarnation has guitars at the center of the action more than before, with the rhythm section still very much in focus. This eclectic album was written completely by Goodsall and Jones (now playing fretless bass exclusively), and their playing and material are unbelievably strong.

This is an Americanized Brand X; the members now are all American citizens, living and recording in the United States, for a U.S. label. One doesn't even miss Phil Collins or Robin Lumley. New drummer Frank Katz is excellent all the way, adding extensive colorful touches just the way Collins did in the past.

The music of *Xcommunication* has lost the English feel of past Brand X fusion, and emerges with a sound similar to that of groups like Dark, Kazumi Watanabe (in Watanabe's *Spice of Life)* (see reviews), and, of course, Fire Merchants. Goodsall makes extensive use of MIDI guitar (triggering keyboards and samples), and if that sounds suspicious to you, you needn't be—it all works and adds some very welcome Adrian Belew–like avant touches around the edges, a necessary texture amid all the scorching guitars.

The 7-minute "Kluzinski Period" and the 6½-minute "A Duck Exploding" have a storytelling, unfolding structure similar to previous X numbers like "Cambodia," only now more complex (and therein lies the progression). Goodsall's "Healing Dream" is an entirely new texture for Brand X: a multiple acoustic guitar composition that's very welcome for the variety it brings to such a crunching powerhouse of an album.

The sound quality is excellent throughout. The cover art (again) is only passable. Also, forget the horrible Percy Jones solo albums, as they are so disappointing. You would probably do wise to avoid the 1982 Brand X release *Is There Anything About?*—it's a disappointment. The follow-up to *Xcommunication,* 1997's *Manifest Destiny,* is a splendid sequel and a must for fans.

BRUFORD

FEELS GOOD TO ME. Released December 1977. Caroline/EG.

Featuring one of the all-time great band lineups (Bill Bruford, drums/percussion; Jeff Berlin, bass; Dave Stewart, keyboards; Allan Holdsworth, guitars; Annette Peacock, vocals), *Feels Good to Me* was an eagerly anticipated, state-of-the-art, seminal progressive release in 1977–1978. Its highly acclaimed classic status is well deserved.

This is a group effort (the band is called Bruford), not merely a Bill Bruford solo album, as it is often perceived.

Feels Good to Me succeeds due to a variety of settings in which Bruford's many fusions are set. Several comparisons come to mind. "Sample and Hold" is reminiscent of Passport. "Either End of August" could be a Weather Report track. "If You Can't Stand the Heat . . . ," with its use of vibes and xylophone, sounds like *Gazeuse!*-era Gong. In addition, the touches of flugelhorn foreshadow Bill Bruford's Earthworks band, especially on "Springtime in Siberia," an almost ECM/Windham Hill–style piece that wouldn't be at all out of place on an Earthworks disc.

It is Berlin's notable bass playing that provides some of the strongest parts in the music. Similar in sound and virtuosity to Jaco Pastorius, he certainly has not received the acclaim so due to him. On the opening cut "Beelzebub," a tight, funky, breezy number, Berlin's bass just bops and punctuates throughout.

Feels Good to Me was notable for the return of Peacock (see reviews), absent since her 1972 album *I'm the One*. It was on the basis of her fine moments here that she resumed her extraordinary career, beginning with 1978's *X-Dreams,* which featured Bill Bruford on drums. Apparently Bruford could coax her back into performing when others such as David Bowie and Brian Eno couldn't. There are three vocal cuts featuring Peacock on this recording. "Back to the Beginning" is an irresistible, infectious slice of friendly, slickly produced Brit-rock. "Seems Like a Lifetime Ago" is a two-part piece, the first part a straightforward jazz vocal, similar to some of Peacock's solo material, with Kenny Wheeler's flugelhorn accompanying.

Undoubtedly the centerpiece of the album is the powerful concluding piece "Goodbye to the Past (Adios a la Pasada)," which has some of Peacock's finest lyrics sung in her celebrated introspective style. The piece opens with a supremely spacey synth intro by Stewart, and builds with scathing lead guitar by Holdsworth. It is an absolutely amazing cut.

Throughout, of course, Bill Bruford's drumming is the epitome of taste and economy, helped by the very crisp sound, with lots of high-end reproduction adding laser-beam clarity to the cymbals. (There is a good deal of hiss at times, though.) The album was produced by Robin Lumley (of Brand X) and Bill Bruford, and has a guest appearance on guitar by John Goodsall (also of Brand X).

ONE OF A KIND. Released March 1979. Caroline/EG.

A logical follow-up to *Feels Good to Me,* this is an all-instrumental release featuring that album's lineup of Bruford, Berlin, Stewart, and Holdsworth. Annette Peacock does not appear this time (having successfully resumed her own career), which is unfortunate because her vocal contributions would have provided some much-needed variety. This album is clearly classic stuff, but it is not the masterpiece it should be.

Stewart takes a larger role in the composition, and his ultra-modern synth sounds (for early 1979) mark the genesis of neo-power-prog sound, particularly in "Hells Bells" and "The Sahara of Snow." This particular sound, incorporated as it is within a tight instrumental format, became a big influence on later groups, such as the French progressive bands Minimum Vital and Tiemko.

Obviously there are some thoroughly incredible, amazingly tight grooves here, and of course this album is a must for fans of Bill Bruford's crisp drumming style. The concentration is on the players and the grooves rather than the compositions and moods. Regrettably, this leaves it a bit on the cold side, in that it doesn't take you to too many places other than into the playing of the band. This is not helped by the thin and slightly flat mix, either. The sound quality is good and clear, but lacks richness and vibrancy.

The best pieces on the album are the most jazzy. "Forever until Sunday," "Travels with Myself and Someone Else," and "The Abingdon Chasp" are still fusion in the Brand X/Gong/National Health style. There's nothing as traditional as Earthworks here, but these cuts focus less on chops and more on feel, allowing the tasteful bits to emerge from the compositions themselves. Also, the music is at its most compelling when it's just Bruford, Berlin, and Stewart. Holdsworth's playing here can be a bit aimless and emotionless (although that is not true throughout).

Despite the minor complaints, this is a noteworthy release (though it is not as good as their live shows of the time). It is, by the way, a miracle that records like this have not been stocked in the jazz sections of stores, but rather in the rock/pop sections.

Avoid the other two releases by Bruford. *Gradually Going Tornado,* released later in 1979, loses Holdsworth for another guitarist, but the real problem is the move toward more vocals and lyrics (poor in this case), and the whole album is a disaster. *The Bruford Tapes,* from 1980, is a release of an FM radio broadcast of a so-so live show, and the sound is only marginal.

HAROLD BUDD/BRIAN ENO

AMBIENT 2 THE PLATEAUX OF MIRROR. Released January 1980. Caroline/EG.

The best of Eno's *Ambient* series, *The Plateaux of Mirror* virtually defined a genre of modern musical impressionism, which in turn spawned the new age music movement. This is the most fully realized of all of Eno's many collaborations of the time (the others being Laraaji, Jon Hassell, and David Byrne), and the sound Budd defined on this recording became the foundation on which Eno built his prolific career.

Minimal in the extreme (Budd on acoustic and electric piano, Eno on other unspecified instruments and "treatments"), these serene, pristine, and very quiet piano works are as evocative and introspective as can be. The music passes like a dream, drawing the listener into a private space of thought, meditation, and reflection. The mind drifts into its own spaces with this music. Budd's playing is necessarily low key and understated, quite a masterful accomplishment.

Eno's treatments are even more subtle, as evidenced by the extremely quiet nature sounds that accompany "Steal Away," or the light percussion on the title track. This is not music to be played loud. Everything about it demands the listener's quiet attention, and rewards with a relaxed calm. The utterly pure impressionism of cuts like "Wind in Lonely Fields" was a key development in active listening music, and influenced countless other musicians and ambient, new age, and space music genres. Its can'at be overstated how unique a recording like this was at the time of its release, when there were no new age sections on the shelves.

Unfortunately, the recording has a high degree of hiss, which is an almost unforgivable flaw that should have been corrected at the time of recording. Note that although both Budd and Eno have released vast amounts of product since *The Plateaux of Mirror,* none of them (with the major exception of Eno's *Thursday Afternoon;* see review) have been radically different, or better.

KATE BUSH

NEVER FOR EVER. Released September 1980. EMI.

Kate Bush, a well respected singer/songwriter in the pop realm, had a definite progressive phase in her career (1979–1986), which has been quite influential. A highly visual artist, she took the conceptualizations of her videos and her 1979 tour into the studio, returning to modern progressive music that breakthrough feeling that it can be music which is suited to a vision, rather than the other way round. In this sense she often created sophisticated high-concept vocal pop prog, much like the psychedelic era Beatles (à la "I Am the Walrus," "A Day in the Life," or "Strawberry Fields Forever"). A good example of this is the song "Breathing" from *Never For Ever.* Adjectives that are often applied to Bush's music—*emotional, ethereal, feminine, eclectic, obscure, poetic, welcoming*—are particularly apt for music from her progressive phase.

Unlike her first two albums (*The Kick Inside* and *Lionheart* in 1978) and her more recent releases, with their somewhat conventional arrangements, *Never For Ever* (which she co-produced), puts Bush's imagination to work on the unusual arrangements and mix. This album just does not have the usual calculating sound that most popular recordings have. The stereo separation is odd, there is a proliferation of sound effects, and the disc has an uncommon mixture of modern synths and samples with traditional folk instruments. It is these off-the-wall elements, in combination with her increasingly conceptual songs, that put Kate Bush at the center of 1980s progressive music.

"Babooshka" substitutes broken glass crashes for a few of its drumbeats. "Delius (Song of Summer)" features electronic percussion, sitar, and voices in a unique tribute to the classical composer Delius.

"All We Ever Look For" has lots of folk influences, with Kate's brother Paddy providing things like balalaika and mandolin, both here and on other tracks. "Night Scented Stock" is an unbelievably effective (but way too brief) vocal. Throughout these tracks and others are incorporated sound effects, as if Bush was performing a live storytelling presentation, and it is these little charming performance art/collage touches that delight. Other cuts, like the frenetic "Egypt," "Violin," and "The Wedding List," are equally classic, although "Blow Away" is a bit too quaint and cute in this company.

"Breathing," the album's closer, is a major stunner. The way it unfolds continually surprises, with touches such as the monologue about a nuclear blast in the middle of the song, or the light tinkle of piano and bass rumble that ends the track on an ominous note. This is conceptual pop that is truly challenging. It goes by quickly, but only those who are paying close attention to these unusual juxtapositions and arrangements will be rewarded fully.

Not only was Bush responsible for the songs and arrangements, but she also did the art direction, and the cover art perfectly conveys the imaginative power of this record. The sound quality is good, although the German disc is preferable to the U.S. disc; it is more vibrant and less flat, with heightened clarity on the high end.

LIVE AT HAMMERSMITH ODEON (video).
Recorded May 1979. Released 1981. EMI VHS.

Recorded at London's Hammersmith Odeon on May 13, 1979, this 52-minute, 12-song video is a historic moment of high drama for modern music, significant for its unusually intense presentation of Bush's material. Using choreography, costumes, props, mime, dancers, and a bit of acting, this video puts you directly into the songs. This approach had been utilized before and has been since by other artists, but never so comprehensively and so successfully. Using these elements to open the songs outwards toward such theatrical heights, Bush made some rather small-scale songs seem like Shakespearean drama. It is with this tour that she began the progressive phase of her musical career.

Bush was helped visually by director Keef Macmillan, who added a significant amount of imaginative edits, camera coverage, and video effects, upping the ante even further. The dreamy opening shots of whale song, with its deep blue water images, are intercut with "Moving," to which Bush dances supremely sensuously—a true evocation of an archetypal feminine appeal. Bush was the first to use the headset microphone, a key component in the success of this program. With it, she is free to dance. Without it, this would have been a completely different show.

The material on the video is mostly from her first two albums; the exception is "Violin" from *Never for Ever.* The video is infinitely preferable to the albums as a document of Bush's art. The dancing routine for "Hammer Horror" is incredibly effective. Simply listening to the track on *Lionheart,* you would never expect so much could be done with it. However, when you watch the video, it's as if you are in Bush's mind, seeing the images come to life as she imagined them. Even more stunning is the interpretation of "James and the Cold Gun," which on *The Kick Inside* album doesn't sound like much. But here it is expanded in length and beefed up musically to heavy guitar rock proportions (unusual for Bush), and a gunfight scenario is acted out between Kate and her dancers. The drama of the blazing guitars matched with these visual enhancements creates a piece that is much more powerful than anyone could have expected from the sound alone.

The band is very, very good, although they are only seen playing in the background, receiving no closeups whatsoever—uncommon for a concert video. The sound track is in stereo, which sounds quite good if turned up enough. The program is shot on video, thankfully not with the sort of grainy film that was so often used in the 1970s, and the resolution and color are excellent.

This live video masterpiece captures Bush in her youthful, playful mode, exhibiting a free-spiritedness that is not really part of her current music. Sadly, only 52 minutes of the show were captured. Fans who want to see more will have to track down additional footage, which exists and is available through various fan networks. For instance, there is an incredible German TV special similar to this program which includes a spectacular dance routine for "Room for the Life." *Hammersmith* has also been in and out of print on Japanese laser disc. Bush fans may want to search for it, as it would be preferable to VHS.

Kate Bush.

THE DREAMING. Released September 1982. EMI.

In the hyper-digital, sample-ridden world of current pop music, *The Dreaming* may not sound all that radically innovative anymore, but it is still (when taken as a whole) one of the finest examples of a meeting point between pop invention and progressive elements. At the time of its release Bush was a high-profile commercial draw in the U.K., and in the ultra-trendy world of U.K. pop in the early 1980s this album was positively risky. A visionary surreal recording that was at first either critically rejected or ignored, *The Dreaming* slowly built an enormous international reputation over the years. It was on the basis of *The Dreaming* that Bush's devoted, fervent fan movement began.

All the songs here are mini-operas. Each of Bush's cinematic visions creates a definite landscape and sound environment all its own. Neither the music nor the lyrics are in any way obvious, though that is usually the criterion for a pop release. The opening cut, "Sat in Your Lap," although frantically paced, is really a song about a philosophical quest, but listeners who don't pay really close attention will never figure that out.

Using layers of voices electronically treated with echoes, reverb, and compression (the psychedelic mania of "Leave It Open" is a good example), Bush puts the vocal soundscapes front and center, and they are what carry these songs. There's quite a lot of vocal counterpoint, which at times may be a bit shrill and histrionic for some tastes, but all of this is just part of Bush's usual palette. The wall of backing vocals is a kind of wacky word painting—one of her trademarks.

The odd production techniques and unique and tight arrangements set *The Dreaming* apart from the conventional in 1982. Of all her releases this has the most subtle touches and sound effects, which are important as a needed background to the very up-front foreground vocals. Many of the changes throughout these pieces also take place in the foreground, and the combination of foreground vocals and changes would seem garish without the background atmosphere of the effects. The technique is central to Bush's cinematic approach.

Musically, *The Dreaming* is a wonder. On the title track earthy tribal drums, sparse piano chords, a menacing didgeridoo, and animal sounds (by a man named Percy Edwards) combine with Bush's dense vocal webs and Fairlight sampler to create an authentic atmosphere of poetic rhythm. It's mysterious, spacey, bizarre—and quite incredible. This segues into "Night of the Swallow," with its elements of Irish music, such as Uillean pipes and fiddle; bouzouki; and then piano, synth, drums, and bass.

"All the Love" is an extremely emotional and powerful piece. It is impossible to be unmoved by the somber tones of Kate's vocal and that of choirboy Richard Thornton. To the sparse bass lines and piano are added the voices from an answering machine tape! (Apparently Kate's answering machine had malfunctioned in a bizarre way, only playing back the goodbyes of various callers while eliminating the rest of the message. Incorporating all of this into the song was a masterful touch.)

"Houdini" is also an emotional knockout, with bass by ECM artist Eberhard Weber. The lovely cover art, which has a surreal, dramatic effect, illustrates a scene from that song.

HOUNDS OF LOVE. Released September 1985. EMI import (remaster).

This legendary classic of progressive pop takes the experimental breakthroughs of *The Dreaming* in two separate but similar directions. Having settled comfortably into confessional compositions with voices, Fairlight samples, and piano at their base, Bush creates a stripped-down, softer pop on the first half of *Hounds,* and on the second a delicately constructed conceptual piece entitled *The Ninth Wave.* Both approaches are remarkably similar in sound, yet are different in crucial ways. The first song on *Hounds,* "Running Up That Hill," is outside the progressive strata, being basically a pop song (with its primarily timid and thin electronic percussion). The title track and "The Big Sky" are also basically pop. The wonderful "Mother Stands for Comfort" features loud glass crashes and drumbeats with a mournful fretless bass, piano, and vocal. On this material her odd, tight, and memorable arrangements are, as always, a strength, and make it all sound so effortless that the album was easily slotted into the mainstream.

It could be said that Kate Bush occupied the same sphere of 1980s serious rock/pop as Peter Gabriel, Laurie Anderson, Danielle Dax, Genesis, and David Bowie. However, later Bush releases like *The Sensual World* (1989) had none of the more progressive elements in her earlier music, leaving her as little more than a mainstream rock/pop chronicler. For the purposes of this guide, *The Ninth Wave,* perhaps her most acclaimed accomplishment, is our primary focus. Conceptual works open up songs and production to experimentation and further elaborations, and it is within such a framework that Bush can be her most creative.

A cathartic voyage of self-discovery, *The Ninth Wave* takes the listener from emotions of sheer fear and terror to profound joy and bliss. The brilliant lyrics tell of several life experiences of awakening wonder and empathy glimpsed through the prism of an ominous crisis (the character/narrator may drown in the water after a boat accident). This linear story line is quite cinematic.

A film of the piece was going to be made (and no doubt would have been fantastic), and the structure works so well that the listener can almost conjure up the images that might have been used in such a film. Musically, the influence of Pink Floyd (especially with regard to sound effects) and the Beatles (in their imaginative use of orchestral arrangements) is obvious. All that is done musically is done for the concept; the piece is not particularly abstract. There are no solos. "Waking the Witch" is the most bizarre track from *The Ninth Wave,* with its thumping electronic beats, loud demon-like voices, and the sound of a helicopter relating a tale of hidden fears.

The last three pieces ("Jig of Life," "Hello Earth," "The Morning Fog") are particularly effective. "Jig . . ." is an outstanding example of Bush's use of traditional instruments. There is a break in this piece that is sheer genius. The music stops abruptly, Bush whispers softly in a stereo pan, and we get a romantic male narration done with reverential enthusiasm to an aggressive display of fiddles, percussion, handclaps, and Bush's trademark word-painting voices. The metaphysical "Hello Earth" begins with a NASA announcement, followed by a tortured vocal by Bush. The inherent situational drama is added to by a supremely mournful vocal choir, the softest of acoustic guitar strums, and submarine bleeps, ending with a whisper in German. "The Morning Fog" then bounces in, with a bright classical guitar (by John Williams) and a band. The catharsis is now complete; happiness and peace have been found in the company of loved ones. It literally ends with a happy note—from Williams's guitar. Masterful.

THE SINGLES FILE (video). Released 1983. EMI VHS import. **THE WHOLE STORY (video).** Released 1986. Pioneer laser disc/Sony VHS.

These visual presentations of Bush's music, like *Live at Hammersmith Odeon,* are not only essential pieces of the overall puzzle, they may even be the best way to experience the songs. While both releases contain a core of the same material, each has several key videos the other doesn't, making both necessary.

Even Bush's early videos (1978–1979) show that she was intent on adding something extra, such as her highly expressive choreography, rather than rely straight performance lip sync, as other artists did. From these embryonic beginnings ("The Man with the Child in His Eyes," "Hammer Horror," etc.) Bush's work evolved to the point where she became *the* conceptual video artist of the early-to-mid 1980s. While conceptual music videos are nothing new today, at the time Bush used them to illustrate to her audiences her increasingly conceptual music, which for the insipid pop market was pretty challenging. In the process she demonstrated that music video need not be eye candy—that it can be art. This truth has still not been embraced by the pop music world.

The emphasis in most of these videos is on drama, abstraction, and theatricality, as opposed to empty, flashy, fast-paced edits. Yet they are remarkably simple and uncluttered, often shot quickly in a studio with relatively few props, extras, or costume changes. Of course this, in part, is due to their being produced during the golden era of music video (when videos were actually shot on video and not film).

"Breathing," "Sat in Your Lap," "The Dreaming," and "Suspended in Gaffa" are all avant-garde video masterpieces, where images are presented totally outside any recognizable context. One enters a strange realm à la *Alice in Wonderland* where Bush wanders, dances, mimes, and sings. The songs themselves are some of her most progressive, yet these visual interpretations catapult you to a still higher plane. Instead of trying to simplify the concepts of the songs, the videos provide even more abstraction. At the time, these videos represented the progressive intentions of Bush's music perfectly, making clear to the viewer that they were different from the rest of the crass pop pack, requiring thought when watched.

Bush's approach to video carries over to some of her other more conventional songs as well, such as "There Goes A Tenner" and "Running Up That Hill," although here the videos actually have more depth than do the songs themselves. Although most of the concepts are hers, a lot of credit goes to her many video directors.

Throughout, Bush is energetic, uninhibited, and sexy. There is an aura of friendliness about these programs that gives them a universal appeal despite some of the more abstract images. By 1986, Bush was directing the videos herself, with clips for "Hounds of Love," "The Big Sky," and "Experiment IV." The sound on both programs is excellent stereo, and the visual quality is equally outstanding. Like the *Hammersmith* video, *The Singles File* may be available on import Japanese laser disc.

THIS WOMAN'S WORK. Released September 1990. EMI import box set.

Although much of this is on the commercial pop side, there is a good amount of Bush's best progressive material here. Unfortunately, to get this package one must consent to being heavily extorted by EMI. The two discs that comprise *This Woman's Work* can only be bought along with six of Bush's previous releases, in a box set of eight discs, at an import price! That caveat aside, it must be said that this set contains some of the artist's finest work. Typically, the level of invention is extraordinarily varied and fascinating, ranging from intoxicating, rollicking youthful swagger to mature, introspective romantic poetry. As usual the vocals are a bit too high in the mix, but beyond that the sound is excellent and is a superb mastering job.

That the *Hounds of Love* recordings could have yielded a quality double album is evidenced by the large number of pieces from that session, including "My Lagan Love," "Under the Ivy," "Burning Bridge," "The Handsome Cabin Boy," "Not This Time," and an alternative, quite different version of "Hounds of Love," plus a superb extended remix of "The Big Sky." "My Lagan Love" and "Under The Ivy" are pristinely delicate, sensual, warm vocal pieces, extremely romantic and affecting, closely miked, quiet, and intimate. These two pieces should ensure Bush's reputation as one of the most celebrated vocalists in progressive music. "The Big Sky" remix contains an unexpected delightful twist of different voices offering humorous conversational asides in the middle of the piece—something other artists simply would not have done.

"Lord of The Reedy River," from 1981, is a cover of a Donovan song with a Fairlight-constructed environment of light, airy, flutelike tones; mournful voices, whispers, and cries; and drips of water. It is quite fantastic. The four-song 1979 EP, "On Stage," a vital live document similar to the *Hammersmith* performances, is also included here, plus a 1986 remake of "Wuthering Heights" (preferable to the original, released in 1978), and the unusual "Experiment IV"—a rather thin pop single from 1986 about a military scheme to utilize music as a weapon. (How often do the pop charts get something like that?) The extended remix of "Experiment IV" is also included here and is the preferred version, with more of Nigel Kennedy's sorrowful violin and extra sound effects heightening the doomy nature of the song. We also get a rare and way-too-brief Bush instrumental, the 1-minute "One Last Look Around the House Before We Go," a solo piano piece.

The rest of the material is purely of archival interest: early short pieces that are fairly quaint; two French-language versions; and some pretty insipid and weak pop ("Ken," "Be Kind to My Mistakes," etc.). But if you appreciate Bush's more progressive moments, this is a must. It really should be made available as a two-disc set on its own.

CAMEL

THE SNOW GOOSE. Released April 1975. Deram import.

Throughout the course of their career, which began in the early 1970s, Camel has been a mainstay on the British rock scene. More in the vein of rock/pop vocal groups such as Caravan,

Supertramp, and the Alan Parsons Project, Camel did make occasional forays into progressive realms, but never with as much panache as they did with *The Snow Goose.* All instrumental, and a concept album to boot, this release is as seminal a classic of British prog rock as you're likely to find. It is a work of genius that has become legendary, and Camel's other, more conventional releases never even come close to touching it.

This is a major example of classically influenced modern rock music as storytelling. Since it is done entirely without words, the concentration is on the musical themes and their execution, and the evocations they conjure up. This is also light, friendly prog rock, an ideal introduction to progressive music.

The key to the album's power is, of course, the writing. The music was written in its entirety by guitarist Andy Latimer and keyboardist Pete Bardens (adding bass, drums, and flute to the melodic exchanges between the guitars and keyboard textures). The music goes through a variety of moods, mostly on the mellow side (by today's standards). All the tracks flow together in a ultra-melodic suite. This is prog rock at its 1970s height, with orchestral backing and arrangements by David Bedford (a longtime collaborator with Mike Oldfield), and produced by David Hitchcock (soon to produce Renaissance's 1975 classical rock tour-de-force *Scheherazade and Other Stories).* There is a precision and tightness to the playing, arrangements, and mix which indicate that great care was taken. Highlights are the refreshing scat vocalizing by Latimer on "Migration" and the female choir (à la Pink Floyd's "Atom Heart Mother") alongside Barden's synth blips on "Preparation."

The included booklet has excellent liner notes, explaining the commercial pressures the group was under and finally succumbed to. The reader is outraged to find that their record company actually expressed displeasure with *The Snow Goose* and demanded vocals on all further releases. Camel's 1978 release *A Live Record* contains an ace live presentation of *The Snow Goose* in its entirety, and comes highly recommended. Recorded in the fall of 1975 by the same lineup, it is in part even preferable to the studio version.

CHRIS AND COSEY/CTI

COLLECTIV THREE—AN ELEMENTAL RENDEZVOUS. Two LPs on one CD. **ELEMENTAL 7** released February 1984. **EUROPEAN RENDEZVOUS—CTI LIVE 1983** released November 1984. World Serpent import.

Chris and Cosey have a prolific output featuring several styles of music, from vocal pop to industrial dance. The "better" half of Throbbing Gristle with regard to solo releases, they produced some very interesting progressive music. Despite an extraordinary contribution to postmodern space music, their progressive work has not received its due, in part because of their fierce independence and the diverse number of musical directions they took.

Having already produced three albums by time *Elemental 7* was released (their industrial pop masterpiece *Songs of Love & Lust* had come out just a month before), Chris and Cosey formed CTI. The name was originally meant to indicate collaborative projects with other artists, but ultimately became just the two of them. With *Elemental 7* and *European Rendezvous,* their collaborator was visual artist John Lacey, who also appears briefly on these albums and did the designs for their concert visuals.

Very much in the independent/underground scene at the time, Chris and Cosey were an island of U.K. experimentation unto themselves. Because of Gristle's outre image and the dark obsessions of the 1980s industrial scene (exemplified by their former Gristle counterparts now in Psychic TV and Coil), their audiences had certain set expectations. Chris and Cosey, however, emerged with a new approach, friendlier perhaps than what those audiences were looking for, although they still retained an aura of mystery.

Elemental 7 is a combination of extended Gristle-like textures and a huge Tangerine Dream/German electronic-cosmic influence—lengthy tracks of atmospheric, mysterious, menacing synths. The 12½-minute "Temple Bar" and the 9½-minute "Invisible Spectrum" are miles ahead of what the more typical electronic progressive music leaders were doing at the time. The 4-minute "Mr. Evans" is collage music, with voices coming in and out of the mix as if remembered from a dream. "Well

Spring of Life" is 6 1/2 minutes of pure space music bliss, with nature sounds and the sound of a waterfall combined with subtle shimmering synths. The stereo effects on all of these tracks are brilliant. The 9 1/2-minute "Dancing Ghosts," "Sidereal," and "The Final Calling" are more in the mondo industrial mode, with technodance beats and screeching electronics and guitars. Although these variations break the space mood set by the rest of the tracks, they do add variety.

European Rendezvous is, sadly, only partially included; the liner notes state that all the original master tapes were lost. *European* is live, though it's difficult to tell as the audience sounds are mixed out. This is quite industrial, with a heavy concentration on beats and rhythms that invokes a trancelike state.

Both *Elemental 7* and *European Rendezvous* came out as excellent full-length videos; they were out of print as of this writing, but are soon to be re-released by Chris and Cosey. They are perhaps the best way to experience this music. This 76-minute CD has excellent sound, with great care taken in the remastering by Chris Carter. The cover art is different from that on the original LPs.

ALLOTROPY. Released March 1990. Staalplat.

A postmodern conceptual masterpiece, this moving 43-minute composition unifies three separate moods and styles into a single song. For the first 13 minutes, there is a light, lengthy intro, with new-agey synth and cheery electronic percussion, at times reminiscent of Edgar Froese's *Pinnacles.* From the 13th minute to the 25th the listener is moved into a chaotic tangle of distorted electric guitar and loud wipes of industrial electronics, plus breathy vocals by Cosey. At the 25-minute mark through to the end, this is replaced by somber, foreboding, introspective icy electronics, similar to Klaus Schulze's *Mirage,* with lush, sensual, emotional whispers by Cosey over it.

Allotropy was written for a video performance art project and recorded in 1987, then released in a remixed form for CD in 1990. This work is influenced by and quite similar to Cosey's Time To Tell solo album. In a way, it also takes the atmospherics of Throbbing Gristle's "In the Shadow of the Sun" and turns them into a solid form. *Allotropy* is Chris and Cosey at their most progressive, due to the hypnotic vortex of Carter's electronics, sound effects, and harsh rhythms and the most outfront ever guitar by Cosey.

The concluding third of *Allotropy* is very affecting romantic space music. Listen to Cosey's voice; it is so evocative of all the feminine, nurturing qualities. Her voice has that sensuous English cool, so enticing and sexy, drawing the listener into the spell the music is casting. The romantic confessions she coos are quite moving. The music fades out to her whispers during the final minute. Nice!

The sound is spacious, wide open, and extremely clear. The cover drawing is unique, but it evokes an atmosphere of fright, and is wrong for the loving nature of the music.

Chris Carter and Cosey Fanni Tutti.

THE LIBRARY OF SOUND—EDITIONS 1–3.
1—**METAPHYSICAL.** Released May 1993.
2—**CHRONOMANIC.** Released September 1994.
3—**IN CONTINUUM.** Released November 1995.
CTI/World Serpent imports.

These three separately sold titles are excellent additions to the ambient genre and to electronic music in general. Ambient music is by its nature subtle, so one cannot really expect excitement in the usual sense. Within that context these are successful releases. This is very light stuff, with an overall mood that is gentle and atmospheric. All is soothing, like the calm of a cloudy day with a steady, light wind.

Enough changes take place in the compositions to make *The Library of Sound* more interesting than the average ambient disc. The airiest Lightwave, Emerald Web, or Klaus Schulze tracks come to mind when looking for comparisons. Prolific and proficient, Chris and Cosey employ so many electronic goodies (as is the case with all electronic music) that the hand of the artists is almost invisible.

Most of the tracks in this series are practically interchangeable from disc to disc in terms of the overall ambient feel. *Metaphysical* is the most low-key. The sound and mix are very quiet and flat. *Chronomanic* is a bit of a departure, with more rhythm and a colder electronic sound. It also has the longest running time, and would have benefited from a shorter and stronger number of pieces. The third volume, *In Continuum,* is the most vibrant, spatial, and flowing of the three. It is a warmer sounding disc than the other two, with more definition to the sounds. All three come recommended, but start with *In Continuum.*

The artwork on *Chronomanic* (by Cosey) and *In Continuum* (by Chris and Cosey) is gorgeously colorful: *Chronomanic* is a yellow-dominated rainbow (evocative of its rhythmic focus), and *In Continuum* is a deep blue (evocative of its lush space music). Expect further volumes to be released in this series.

HANS CHRISTIAN

PHANTOMS. Released August 1994. Paraiso import.

Recorded in San Francisco, California, between 1991 and 1993, "Phantoms" is a minor masterpiece that crystallizes so many progressive areas so effortlessly that it is surprising that composer/instrumentalist Hans Christian is not more well known. On this amazing 62-minute all-instrumental disc, he proficiently plays cello, bass, guitars, keyboards, percussion, and didgeridoo, plus adds some sound effects. He also produced and engineered the recording. Christian's compositions are amazingly mature for a first release. Comparisons abound, from the more eclectic ECM artists like Steve Tibbetts, Eberhard Weber, and David Darling to the spacey fusions of artists like Vicki Richards, Forrest Fang, or even Voice of Eye.

The 4-minute "Backwards (With My Eyes Closed . . .)" opens, and the piece typifies the disc's richly layered mix and detailed production. Delicate tapestries of tabla, bass, and percussion are woven together, led by a joyful but earnest cello. The 6-minute "Coyotes Dance" features dark ritual percussion and didgeridoo, with sunnier, dreamier moments provided by the melodic keyboards. The 4-minute "Lindenflowers & Coronations" is a flavorful combination of multiple guitars, percussion, and keyboards. The 3-minute title track puts a hypnotic drumbeat to playful cello notes, washes of synth, and sound effects. The 7½-minute "Atlantis" is a dense and mysterious storytelling piece with classical themes, featuring spacey tabla and frame drums, cello, acoustic guitar, and keyboards. The compelling 6-minute "Desperado" has soaring, bowed cello notes and a memorable, emotional motif conveyed by seductively soft percussion and keyboards.

The 6-minute "Arabesque" is more tightly arranged, with its storytelling form verging on the cinematic and picturesque. Multilayered, exotic flavors of guitars, orchestrations of keyboards and voices, and a relentless tempo from the percussion create an ethereal mood. The 6½-minute "Scattered" is a highlight. Led by dewy, Eberhard Weber–like bass notes and spacey solos of electric and acoustic guitars that wind and drift over cello, percussion, and keyboards, the piece is easy to like. The 4-minute ". . . In the Pews . . . ," another highlight, is also reminiscent of Weber. Ghostly loops of voices, bass, and guitar create opt-out drones. The 4½-minute "The Sacrifice" is dramatic and poignant, with soft textures of cello, guitars, and keyboards. The 9-minute "Aftermath" sums up the entire album well, with more cello solos, guitars, bass, keyboards, percussion, and a brief, sensual, female spoken vocal.

The accompanying booklet has poems by Chera Van Burg (who speaks a few very brief lines on "Aftermath"), which are the inspirations for some of the pieces on *Phantoms.* It is interesting to note that these are included as a sort of poetic guide to the music rather than as a mandatory exposition via vocals. Christian thankfully lets the music do all the talking.

This disc has top-notch sound, and is a very high-quality first effort. Christian also designed the disc's cover art. Hopefully there is more to come.

CLEARLIGHT

CLEARLIGHT SYMPHONY. Released December 1974. Virgin import.

Clearlight, a sort of supersession group led by composer/keyboardist/producer Cyrille Verdeaux, were one of the most popular and influential groups of the French progressive scene. What elevates their three 1970s discs to classic status is the supremely ethereal, celestial feel of their space rock. *Clearlight Symphony* is an all-instrumental two-part work (each part is 20½ minutes) of classically influenced psychedelic space music, an amazing sort of musical fusion that not many people do anymore. The reputation of this recording as authentic head-bending opt-out music is well deserved.

Central to the success of this recording is Verdeaux's lush keyboards, which are the centerpiece of these compositions. His romantic grand piano, mellotron, and organ work provide a warm, organic element, to which Tim Blake (of Gong) adds both wildly avant and spacey VCS3 synth. To this is added the heavy rock element of electric guitar, drums, bass, and sax. The lively, spacious sound design of the mix, with lots of stereo panning and extreme separation, is crucial to creating the elusive space rock magic.

Part 1 of *Clearlight Symphony* is Verdeaux coupled with half of Gong (guitarist Steve Hillage, keyboardist Tim Blake, and sax man Didier Malherbe). This is some of Hillage's and Blake's finest playing. Hillage's guitar here is solidly in his searing, heavy psych solo mode. The pairing of Verdeaux and Blake, both space music pioneers, is a good one. Part 2 is Verdeaux playing with the French prog group Lard Free (guitarist Christian Boule, drummer Gilbert Artman, and bassist Martin Isaacs). Especially exciting is the combination of Verdeaux's wall of keyboards with Artman's drums.

This album was released by Virgin during that label's heyday of reaching out to progressive sounds of all kinds. The music of Clearlight has been quite influential. The careers of the collaborators (Hillage, Blake, and Lard Free) have all incorporated elements of the Clearlight sound, and comparisons can be made to the music of composer/keyboardist Luciano Basso and to French prog groups like Pulsar.

The cover painting by Jean Claude Michet is outstanding. Deep hues of blue evoke a plugged-in spiritual awakening.

Unfortunately, *Clearlight Symphony* is currently available on CD only from Japan, but it is well worth the effort to find it. Do not confuse this with the *Symphony II* disc by Clearlight on the French label Mantra (see below). The sound on this disc is good, except for a high degree of hiss.

FOREVER BLOWING BUBBLES. Released October 1975. Mantra import.

This is the larger, expanded Clearlight band: three other keyboardists besides Verdeaux; a core band of bassist/composer Joel Dugrenot, guitarist/flautist Jean Claude d'Agostini, and drummer Christos Stapinopoulos; and guests David Cross (of King Crimson) on violins, Lard Free's Boule and Artman again, and Amanda Parsons and Ann Rosenthal (vocalists from the Hatfield/Egg sessions). *Forever Blowing Bubbles* retains the wide open sound, stereo panning, and richly textured, lush, romantic feel of *Symphony,* yet in slightly different settings. These compositions are mainly keyboard-dominated, layered instrumental space jams, more rock than classical this time.

The opening track, the 5-minute "Chanson," is one of two compositions by Dugrenot, and it has vocals in French. Here, however, they work as atmosphere and do not dominate. The music on this is heavy symphonic prog rock—the core band as much in the fore at times as the walls of keyboards. In between each of the songs, linking the tracks, is the sound of electronic bubbles. There are also a lot of tape effects with parts speeded up or slowed down (especially the ending of "Way"). The space rock instrumentals (ranging between 4–8 minutes in length) "Without Words," "Way," "Ergotrip, " and "Et Pendant Ce Temps La" constitute the bulk of the disc, and are a joy. Dramatic, soaring, friendly, and moving at an inventive pace, *Bubbles* is the loosest and most rock-oriented of the Clearlight discs, while retaining an elusive, magical aura.

A departure is the 2½-minute "Narcisse et Goidmund," a short folksy number with harpsichord, flute, acoustic guitar, violin, and piano that includes vocals (in French again) by Brigitte Roy. Somehow this combination manages to suggest "otherness," like something from the Third Ear Band's *Music From Macbeth*. The closing track, the 2½-minute "Jungle Bubbles" makes you feel like you're swimming in some exotic tropical waterfall from an exploding electronic selzer bottle.

Like *Symphony, Bubbles* is a fine example of the cosmopolitan flavor of the mid-1970s European progressive scene. *Bubbles* has another lovely cover painting by Jean Claude Michel, which appropriately gives off that bubbly, airy space vibe. The sound quality is good, but hissy like *Symphony,* and there are a few flaws in the master tape that are exposed.

VISIONS. Originally released January 1978. Expanded CD version released December 1992. Legend import.

The third major masterpiece from Clearlight, *Visions* is a key pre–new age recording. This disc contains the original 38-minute six-song release from 1978, and adds four new pieces from 1992 recorded especially for inclusion as part of *Visions,* bringing the running time up to over 77 minutes. It is also a superior remaster. The sound is excellent, with little hiss this time.

Virtually all instrumental, *Visions* is a more light and serene Clearlight, despite having another large cast of contributors. The music here is more delicate, more introspective. The space rock elements and active pace are still present, but stripped down a bit and more jazzy. The flow and sound are remarkably similar to the previous albums, but with a more relaxing and calmer mood. Each of the tracks is connected by and features environmental sounds (wind, water, birdsong, rain, etc.). This technique, a key component of new age music, adds atmosphere in spades. Co-written with various band members and guests, composer Cyrille Verdeaux's lush keyboards, combined with flutes, modern synths, and exotic percussion, creates a place where modern electric music attains a mystical, alchemical dimension. Despite the ambitiously large compositions, band, and studio wizardry, this is still effective opt-out music. *Visions* walks all the tightropes brilliantly. There are no loose ends; all is tied up and flows perfectly.

The opening 7½-minute track, "Spirale d'Amour," contains some true magic. A majestic piano motif, grand and romantic, emerges from environmental sounds. This is combined with flute, followed by playful, soaring violin and sax exchanges with the backing band. During a break halfway through, there is the sound of a female sighing in intense pleasure—an unexpected and inspired touch. The 5½-minute "Guitare Elevation" opens with rain sounds, then goes into a grand piano-led symphonic rock jam, culminating in a spacey electric guitar solo. The 5½-minute "Crystal City" has sweet and danceable but very trippy Gong-like synths and infectious percussion. The 7-minute "Messe Caline" begins with wind sounds and birdsong, then voyages into another gorgeous texture of piano, synths, and violin. The 8½-minute "Shanti Lotus" is another highlight. Starting with animal sounds, the piece explores swirling and seductive mixes of tablas, synths, guitars, and bass, building to a furious jam. This track foreshadows the sound of later prog rock groups like Melting Euphoria and Ozric Tentacles. The 5-minute "Hewmae" foreshadows another later group, Emerald Web, with its combination of lovely lyricon notes, sparkling synths, and environmental sounds.

The 4-minute "Vision Nocturne" has jungle sounds that lead into another prog rock jam led by Verdeaux's piano, and concludes with spooky wind effects. The 4-minute "Songes de Cristal" is a reflective but pompous piano excursion by Verdeaux. Although the 7-minute "0 Rage 0 Espoir" is a disappointment (it verges on being wallpaper music), its inclusion is a minor flaw. The 10½-minute "Full Moon Raga" is a highlight, where a meditational mix of sitar, synth, voices, and tabla leads into a band jam with crowd sounds. The 6-minute "Au Royaume des mutants" is a lame vocal track (sung in

French) that seems wildly out of place. Avoid that one. However, the final piece, the 2½-minute "Paix profonde," is a real treat. A simple combination of sitar and field recordings of nature sounds, the piece recalls Deuter, David Parsons, and Dzyan.

The juxtapositional flow and editing are so masterful that it's difficult to tell which are the newer pieces. There are some familiar names here—Zao's violinist Didier Lockwood and Gong saxophonist Didier Malherbe (they are the soloists on "Spirale d'Amour"). The cover art is suitably visionary. *Visions* foreshadows Verdeaux's 1984 solo album, *Messenger of the Son* (see review).

SYMPHONY II. Released 1989. Mantra import.

This is a sequel of sorts to the original *Clearlight Symphony* album, but it is more of a Cyrille Verdeaux solo disc than a proper Clearlight release. (Note that this uses the same cover art as the first *Symphony* album, so be sure not to confuse them.)

Symphony II has 46 minutes of original music but also includes a poor sounding hissy master of Part 1 of the original *Symphony,* which is a big mistake. *Symphony II* is presented in six movements (consisting of 8- to 10-minute pieces), of which the older *Symphony* Part 1 is the 5th movement, sandwiched in between the new material. This is a bad idea, and this disc would've been much more respectable had this older track not been included.

That said, *Symphony II* has a lot to offer. It just deserves a more suitable presentation. In many ways it is quite similar to Mike Oldfield's *Tubular Bells II.* Verdeaux takes the original work and redoes it with modern technology. Using samples of flute, bass, violins, horns, piano, choirs, harp, and percussion, he becomes a one-man Clearlight band. Despite the technical brilliance of this (similar to Constance Demby's sampling tour de force *Novus Magnificat)* a real band would have been preferable, especially for the drums.

With the exception of Richard Prezelin on electric guitar, Verdeaux's samplers and synths give *Symphony II* a totally different feel. While the themes and motifs are the same, the organic sound is lost in favor of a glossy rhythmic one. It's still in the grand Clearlight style (if not as spacey), but the listener is always aware that everything is done via sterile high-tech methods, by one person, and all that programmed percussion is just not as good as the real thing.

Despite these considerable drawbacks, the ideas work. This is a decent refinement of the first *Symphony*'s themes. The 3rd, 4th, and 6th movements are especially successful. On the whole, the album is an interesting if not a major work.

COLLEGIUM MUSICUM

LIVE. Released October 1973. Pavian import.

The exciting music of this beloved Czech classical rock group is the purest definition of symphonic rock. While similar to but fundamentally different from groups like the Nice, ELP, Egg, Focus, and Trace, Collegium Musicum took the classical and rock fusion to its logical conclusion—instrumental music devoid of pop influences (save for their electric instrumentation). The trio of Marian Varga on organ, Fedor Freso on bass guitar, and Dusan Hajek on drums make this fusion seem effortless, pumping out the fanfares at a rapid pace with a panache and joie de vivre that's extremely effective.

The icing on the cake is that this is a raw live recording (from July of 1973) performed in front of an enthusiastic audience at a period in the 1970s when classical rock was a new form that appealed to two separate audiences, the hippie counterculture rockers and the classical academics, giving *Live* an authentic period feel. The sound is reminiscent of Genesis's 1973 live album (though without guitars or modern keyboards), with Freso's bass sounding like Mike Rutherford's. Although Varga's organ sounds are at times primitive and dated, they are still charming, with the organ representing the "old" in this trio equation, exuding an over-the-top Gothic quality.

Four lengthy compositions showcase their excellent performances, from the opening 10½-minute "Burlesque" to the 9-minute "You Are Impossible Part 1," which features a lengthy virtuoso bass solo that's simply mind-boggling. The 8-minute "You Are Impossible Part 2" features an organ solo, and the 14½-

minute "Monument" treats us to mucho stereo drum rolls in a lengthy, very hip drum solo. The sound quality throughout is good, if hissy, with great separation. While Collegium Musicum have other studio releases, their live context remains the most compelling.

COSEY FANNI TUTTI

TIME TO TELL. Released January 1994. CTI/World Serpent import.

The extraordinary *Time To Tell* provides a close-up look at Cosey and her many interests courtesy of the gorgeous plush packaging and accompanying extensive informative booklet which documents her explorations of performance art, modeling, and erotica. With *Time to Tell* one can gauge how much influence she has had as part of Chris and Cosey and Throbbing Gristle, and this release is just as notable as any of the important titles from those configurations.

Recorded mainly in 1982 and remixed in 1993, there are three superb lengthy tracks—"The Secret Touch," "Time to Tell," and "Ritual Awakening." The 9½-minute "The Secret Touch" is pure instrumental space music, with a light, airy, floating feel, a precursor of the CTI *Library of Sound* releases. It's calming and soothing, yet has an elusive element of menace and mystery. The instrumentation is the atypical Cosey textures of electronics, guitar, and cornet.

The 23-minute title track is an evolving electronic tapestry done for Cosey's 1980s solo multimedia performances about erotica (which, from the photos and descriptions, sound very interesting!). Swooshes and tinkles of synths, sound effects, percussion, and voices blend into a rich brew of sound, throughout which Cosey delivers a spoken monologue that becomes ever more hypnotic due to its being electronically altered and enhanced. It is seamlessly mixed near-psychedelia, putting the listener under its spell. It is not always easy to understand what she is saying, but that doesn't matter. This isn't a conventional monologue but rather a swirling vortex of sound. The words become a part of the music, which obscures them a bit but provides mystery and makes the listener pay that much closer attention. This is an excellent example of making the art form suit the vision.

The 16½-minute "Ritual Awakening" is similar to Chris and Cosey's *Allotropy.* Musically, it offers more of the spacey, minimal trance patterns of electronics, now joined by Cosey's up-front breathy poetic recitations and whispers, which are made compelling and very sexy by the powerful sensuality of her voice.

While in the notorious Throbbing Gristle, Cosey was also a nude model and stripper. *Time to Tell* is a partial record of this experience. The package is full of photos (yes, nude ones—perhaps Cosey is the first progressive composer/pinup girl?) and essays about this era, including an essential reprint of an interview from a late 1970s sex magazine about her work with Throbbing Gristle as a guitarist, performance artist, and model.

The sound quality is excellent. The music has the expansive stereo separation necessary to spin its mysterious webs of sound. With *Time To Tell,* Cosey Fanni Tutti proves herself to be an important artist in her own right.

CURVED AIR

CURVED AIR LIVE. Released February 1975. Deram (U.K.) import or Repertoire (Germany) import.

Recorded at two U.K. colleges in December 1974, this is a prog rock classic and the best way to experience the music of Curved Air. A straight-ahead British vocal prog rock band (with guitars, electric violin, bass, drums, and synths) comparable to Genesis, with the impassioned singing of the legendary Sonja Kristina, Curved Air has everything you would want from such a group—intelligence, passion, and extended pieces of instrumental virtuosity. Their previous studio releases had been rather stripped down, with horribly botched mixes and thin production. But live, the band plays up a firestorm, with more tight groove and chops. Kristina's vocals here have real fire in them, lacking on the earlier studio discs.

Curved Air Live has a huge, clear sound and is an awesome 49-minute audiophile gem. It's crisp, detailed, and loud. It's a state-of-the-art live rock recording that isn't the least bit dated. On this recording, the group performs the best material from their first three LPs: *Air Conditioning* (1970), *Second Album* (1971), and *Phantasmagoria* (1972). At the time this was the reunion tour of the lineup that recorded those releases, and it turned out to be a highlight of the group's career. If this live disc had been released four years earlier instead of the flatter studio ones, Curved Air would have been a front-rank rock act with more than a cult following.

The seven songs on this album are delivered at a lightning pace. The 7-minute "Marie Antoinette" (a song about political revolution) is properly angry; the guitars burn and Kristina screams bloody murder. "Vivaldi," perhaps the group's most famous piece, is here in all its glory, extended to 9 minutes and critically different from the abridged studio version which omitted Kristina's vocal. *Curved Air Live* is a definitive example of the celebrated 1970s British prog rock style. It captures all the excitement and aura of that famous genre.

The Deram and Repertoire releases are the same recording of the concerts, but are mixed differently. Each is outstanding.

LIVE AT THE BBC. Released December 1995. Band of Joy/BBC import.

Like *Curved Air Live, Live at the BBC* is absolutely essential, again demonstrating how much the band was undermined by its studio releases. Whereas the studio products had a dated prettiness, here the rawness of a bigger drum sound, the up-front guitars, and in general the more aggressive performances show Curved Air at their best.

The first part of this 66-minute disc is the original lineup, with three separate BBC recording sessions: November 1970, January 1971, and March 1971. The second part, equally exciting as the first, is the final lineup of Curved Air, retaining vocalist Sonja Kristina and violinist/keyboardist Daryl Way, but with a new guitarist, bassist, and drummer (Stewart Copeland). The later lineup is featured on a January 1976 BBC recording.

This release is a fascinating and valuable document of the beginnings of the British progressive rock movement. At the time of the first session in the fall of 1970, Curved Air was one of many English prog groups (post Floyd and Crimson) emerging at the same time. Others included Genesis, Egg, Yes, Gong, Gentle Giant, Van Der Graaf Generator, and ELP. The three tracks (in an excellent mono mix) from this 1970 session, especially "Vivaldi," must have been quite a breakthrough revelation for the radio listener at the time. This "Vivaldi" is different from the LP (*Air Conditioning,* also from November 1970) version. After blizzards of loud electric violin and feedback, 3 minutes into the piece Kristina comes screaming in, singing about music and madness, with a building crescendo that rises in intensity and emotion and then returns to the song's opening motif. The studio version mistakenly strips away all of this.

With the 1970 and 1971 sessions we get over half of *Air Conditioning*'s material, plus "Thinking on the Floor," a song from this era not available elsewhere. We also get "Young Mother in Style," which is a completely different version of "Young Mother," a track from 1971's *Second Album.* This is a shorter version with different lyrics and with both Way and Kristina singing. The January 1971 tracks are crude stereo, but after that the sound is excellent.

In the 1976 session the group, like their British prog rock peers during this time, was moving toward more conventional rock. Yet these tracks are the most comparable to the impassioned fire of the *Curved Air Live* disc. The sound and mix are equally sharp. The material is from the band's 1975 release, *Midnight Wire,* which is perhaps their most successful studio recording (though it is more rock than prog rock). Kristina's vocals are sexy here, with horny tracks like "Woman on a One Night Stand" and "Hot and Bothered." Kristina's image throughout Curved Air's history provided the group with a needed, focused persona, in her case a counterculture earth-mother vixen. So it is Kristina's face that adorns the cover of this CD. Her contribution in fronting this group is often overlooked by those rock historians who lament the lack of women in rock from this era.

This immensely enjoyable release isn't even all of Curved Air that is available from the BBC vaults. There is an entire 1975 session, plus more of the 1976 session. This material appears on the unofficial, hard-to-find CD *Stark Naked.*

D

DARK

DARK. Released 1986. CMP.

Dark, a not particularly well-known American band, was one of the best 1980s progressive groups. Their self-titled debut is a real stunner, breaking new ground with every track. It never lets up; the ideas and grooves just keep coming. The CMP label is known for its full digital recordings of sharp and realistic rhythm-instrument driven music, of which *Dark* is a prime example. This is hard-hitting audiophile fusion, with a wide-open stereo soundstage. Dark is a group with one HUGE sound.

Combining exotic percussion, drums, bass guitar, primitive synths, and wordless voice, Dark creates a world music–influenced guitarless fusion that exudes spiritual otherness, but also has a monster drum sound making this progressive music you can dance to. Comparisons can be made to the instrumentals of 1980s King Crimson or Gabrielle Roth and the Mirrors, as well as to the 1991 CMP band Let's Be Generous, of which the Dark musicians are a part. The only song with lyrics, the 3½-minute "The Spectator," sounds like Laurie Anderson. Catherine Guard is the vocalist. The other three members—Mark Nauseef, Leonice Shinneman, and Mark London Sims—each play percussion instruments and synth, with Nauseef handling most of the drum kit and Sims on bass guitar. The Casio synth work is especially interesting—shrilling and shrieking like horns or guitars or vocals. All compositions are credited to the band.

Dark (1988 lineup). From left to right, Mark Nauseef, Leonice Shinneman, Mark London Sims, Miroslav Tadic. (Photo by Fern Seiden. Used by permission.)

The 6-minute opener, the appropriately titled "Du Reptile," begins with environmental noises and frosty African drums, slowly building up with menacing bass guitar notes sent panning in the mix like a creeping lizard until a banshee scream startles and a full band sound is unleashed with bursts of sawlike percussion and a sinewy synth that is an absolute dead ringer for an electric guitar. This all fades out, but then suddenly comes back at full volume. This surprise ending is absolutely jolting.

The 7-minute "Republic of Darkness" is actually a sort of space music. Concrète-like slabs and bleeps and foghorn-like blasts from Nauseef on synth are selectively sprayed and washed by gongs and roto-toms, with Guard's light vocal texturing above them. This is evocative, storytelling music that is always building and and changing.

Dark is a great leap forward in 1980s progressive and is highly recommended. The cover art is suitably "dark."

TAMNA VODA. Released 1988. CMP.

Tamna Voda, the equally impressive follow-up to *Dark*, never disappoints. This is a different lineup, with vocalist Guard gone and guitarist Miroslav Tadic added, with guest appearances from violinist L. Shankar and guitarist David Torn. These changes move the music in the direction of a more conventional fusion, though overall it is still very much in the vein of the first disc. There is more rock groove here, with the band members having settled into their primary instruments, playing extremely tight, lightning-fast paces.

As before, there is lots of wonderful percussion and sinewy synth, now with the guitars (electric plus acoustic) adding a burn-'em-up excitement as well as similarly sinewy and restrained notes. "Trilok," the 5-minute opener, is an example of late Gong-like fusion, only much heavier. The lighter textures are presented with the acoustic guitar and violin, as on the 3-minute title track, the 6-minute "Merciful," and the cover of Jimi Hendrix's "Drifting."

Once again the smooth digital sound is a knockout. *Tamna Voda* punches very hard. Unlike *Dark,* the compositions are credited to particular members. The cover art is ugly and tells you nothing. For those looking for where to go after this, the *Let's Be Generous* disc is highly recommended.

DAVID DARLING

EIGHT STRING RELIGION. Released 1993. Hearts of Space.

Had *Eight String Religion* been released in the early 1970s it would be considered a classic of deeply felt fusion/space music with its atmospheric cellos, chanting, and environmental sounds. Without that chronological advantage, this recording comes across as merely a fine addition to the canon. Straddling the lines between classical, jazz, world music, and new age, this is similar to a release from the ECM or Celestial Harmonies labels, and apt comparisons abound—

David Darling. (Photo by R. J. Muna.)

from Popol Vuh and Eberhard Weber to Oregon and Hans Christian.

The eight pieces on this CD are marvels of low-key, modest simplicity. Darling never comes on in a big way; sparseness is what *Eight String Religion* is all about. Using cello, solid-body celli (sounding like a bass), piano, light wordless chants, and environmental sounds, the instrumentation remains varied, preventing this from being "just" a cello album. The environmental effects, while not employed often enough, are also a big help, directing the listener toward the desired mood. The chanting is also quite welcome, adding depth in a very simple way.

The showcase, though, is the cello. Alternately mournful or joyful, soaring or atmospheric, Darling explores these various potentials without ever showing off. For him the communication in the music seems to be his priority; he doesn't appear interested in impressing with technique.

Because *Eight String Religion* was recorded over a ten-year period, there's an inherent variety to the music. The disc features pieces recorded in both digital and analog formats. While this was probably not Darling's ideal plan for recording, it keeps this disc from being pigeonholed as a "cello album," providing it with an uncommon context that underlines its deeply felt musical expressions.

The sound is good. This is a very quiet album. The cover art, however, is lousy—blurry photos of Darling that tell you nothing about the personal nature of this music.

DANIELLE DAX

POP EYES. Released February 1983. Biter of Thorpe/World Serpent import.

Pop Eyes perfectly demonstrates the experimental underpinning of Dax's music, and is a good example of the totally new forms and sounds emerging during the early 1980s. This is Dax's first solo album; she was previously in the overrated underground band The Lemon Kittens. *Pop Eyes* is pure psychedelia, similar to early Pink Floyd and especially comparable to the prog pop of *The Dreaming*–era Kate Bush. Recorded on a four-track in 1982, it is a solo project. Dax plays all the instruments on the recording, including guitars, drums, bass, flute, keyboards, banjo, saxophones, trumpet, tapes, toys, and vocals.

As a result, *Pop Eyes* has a skeletal homemade feel, almost like a demo. All the rough edges are left intact; nothing is polished up (in strong contrast to 1980s music). Since Dax is such a private artist, this is the best way to hear her—with all her ideas as originally conceived and played by her, without being glossed over by band arrangements or a slick production. This is not to say that Dax is all that proficient instrumentally, but here the focus is on her totally off-the-wall compositions anyway. For example, the aggressive opening track, "Bed Caves," begins with a firestorm of percussion, to which a psychedelic banjo line is added, joined by rhythm guitar and Dax's sweet but menacing vocals. This is similar in feel to Kate Bush's "Sat in Your Lap." Like Bush, Dax is a great vocalist—her genius lies there as much as in the songs themselves. Each track in the disc is in a different style, and it is Dax's voice that puts the bizarre material across, with at times the most minimal of musical backings. Her excellent lyrics are very heavy. It is not in the least bit obvious upon first listen what these songs are about. If anything, the lyrics make the music even more obscure (it usually works the other way around).

In the late 1980s and early 1990s Dax was a very sexy (she is a beautiful blonde) commercial pop diva, retaining some of her unique psychedelic songwriting traits, though in the main her music was straightforward guitar-driven rock or sample-heavy dance house music. *Pop Eyes,* by contrast, is defiantly uncommercial, from an artier period when she utilized costumes and makeup. *Pop Eyes* even has a few instrumentals, something Dax never does anymore.

The tastefully grotesque and wonderful cover art (by Dax herself) perfectly evokes the weirdness of the recording. The sound is great, if charmingly primitive. Continuing in this vein, but more band-oriented, is 1984's *Jesus Egg That Wept* and her 1985 *BBC Session* (released in 1988). Both are impressive.

CONSTANCE DEMBY

SACRED SPACE MUSIC. Released 1982. Hearts of Space.

One of the notable releases to first draw attention to the growing new age realm of progressive music,

Sacred Space Music lives up to its reputation as a seminal new age recording. On this disc, composer/instrumentalist Demby features the sounds of the hammered dulcimer—a string instrument struck with small hammers that sounds like a cross between a piano and a harpsichord. This is an ideal instrument for producing space music tapestries, providing a warm acoustic alternative to the often thin synth-dominated new age genre. What is notable is that due to the use of this instrument, the recording operates in an entirely different realm (and with a different audience) than would a similar sounding electronic release (Klaus Schulze's *Mirage* comes to mind). What brings the recording into the progressive realm is that Demby does not rely solely on the hammered dulcimer. Her classically influenced, all-instrumental compositions work; the music successfully achieves its lofty spiritual (and spacey) goals.

The first piece, "The Longing," joins the dulcimer with piano (by Demby) and viola (by Toni Marcus). Worthy of its title (as is everything here), it achieves a mournful, sorrowful mood in a meditative vibe similar to perhaps Popol Vuh (especially the piano). It is the combination of instruments (Demby is not just getting by on the shimmering cascades of the dulcimer alone) that makes this recording so effective, even at 20 minutes. In fact, at a shorter length, this would not achieve the "otherness" that it does. The other piece, "Radiance" (also 20 minutes long), is equally deep, combining the dulcimer with synth, a vocal chorus, and bells. The vocal coloring is a splendid touch, adding to the spiritual feel.

The sound is very good; all is sparkle. The semireligious cover art is entirely appropriate. It looks the way the music feels.

NOVUS MAGNIFICAT. Released 1986. Hearts of Space.

Subtitled *Through the Stargate: Sacred Space Vol. II,* this is a worthy follow-up to *Sacred Space Music.* A lengthier two-part symphonic work, it is more ambitious in scope and more classical and romantic in tone. *Novus Magnificat* is one of the most popular and influential recordings of its kind, so much so that many new age releases

Constance Demby. (Photo by Irene Young.)

are merely different takes on what Demby is doing here. With nothing written in advance, she created a classically structured orchestra of sampled instruments (violas, violins, celli, bassoon, harp, organ, bells, tympani, and chorus) combined with synths and piano, to create a grand, lush, melodic music that is large in vision and nearly religious in its striving, reverent, and joyful reaching.

If there is a complaint it would be that all of this lush richness causes the piece to be too sweet. With any rock influences completely absent (as they wouldn't be with composers who have done similar work, like Cyrille Verdeaux or Mike Oldfield), any rough edges are gone (especially when so much of it is sampling). Despite the reverence the music aims for, it's all a little too painless; one feels that no real catharsis has been gone through to justify the continued building of the revelatory mood. The sound is polished to a high shine, and the clarity is great, but that reinforces the slickness of the production.

DEUTER

D. Released August 1971. Kuckuck.

D. and *Aum* (see below), Deuter's first two releases, are critical to appreciating the genesis of progressive music in Germany's "cosmic" music of the 1970s, and how this was crucial for the development of space music, and later new age. Both releases are firmly in the exploratory mode of Deuter's peers Tangerine Dream, Popol Vuh, Eberhard Schoener, Klaus Schulze, Agitation Free, and others, all of whom seemed to be unified in vision at the time. *D* is definitely opt-out stuff, a true head-bender. It's genuinely psychedelic collage experimentalism with a surreal and spooky mystery to it, and has a fantastic, infectious, multilayered psych-out headphone mix, with lots of stereo panning and effects.

The 15-minute opener, "Babylon," is tense buildup music, featuring lots of tape effects (slowed down, speeded up), beginning with combinations of guitar loops and the sounds of a baby crying. From this the recording segues to a bass guitar and acoustic guitar, with a savage, loud, and cutting electric guitar soloing over it. This is a serious psychedelic skronk-out, similar to that found on Tangerine Dream's *Electronic Meditation.* The track then moves into a Pink Floyd–like organ with surreal tape and sound effects, which dissolves into a mellow, drifting raga with distorted electric guitar, bass, and percussion taking the listener into a collage of different sounds—voices, ringing phones, footsteps, etc.

The 4½-minute "Der Turm/Fluchtpunkt" features chunky percussion and walls and waves of stereo minefield guitar noise (well before Robert Fripp's voyages into these areas). The piece even stays in a minimalist pattern for its final half—quite industrial! The 10-minute "Krishna Eating Fish and Chips" begins with a psychedelic organ intro that drifts off into multitracked sitar drones, which then build in intensity to such a rapid pace that listening to it is a genuinely ego-losing experience. The concluding piece, the 6-minute "Atlantis," is pure collage. Tape effects, the organic gurgling of tablas, synth, and water sounds are as ethereal as can be—everything seems to be just floating in the mix, taking the listener far away on a deep voyage.

D was a breakthrough release in modern music, where experimentalism (by a first-time recording artist) and collage techniques met with psychedelic rock and roll, producing an attractive, evocative, and mind-expanding new form of music.

AUM. Released 1972. Kuckuck.

Aum, another breakthrough psychedelic/collage classic from Deuter, is notable for its extensive use of environmental sounds. *Aum* forms a perfect trilogy with two other similar releases from 1972: Wendy Carlos's *Sonic Seasonings* and Popol Vuh's *In the Gardens of Pharao.* These three key releases integrated environmental sounds (sometimes electronically simulated) into the emerging genre of electronic space music.

Like his contemporaries in the 1970s German cosmic music genre, Deuter had a Midas touch. *Aum* is very likeable ego-dissipating music that takes the listener off into the void. The journey flows so smoothly, so naturally, that it is a special experience. All is mixed together, as if one was stirring a bowl of sounds.

Aum contains three lengthy tracks. The first, the 9½-minute "Phoenix/Aum/Soham," begins with a thunderstorm intro, which becomes a folky jig of guitars and percussion with birdsong; then comes a jump into a pool of water, with ethereal bass rumbles and insistent tablas. This leads to more sounds of nature and a sitar/tabla raga with meditative chants. The 12-minute "Offener Himmel 1/Gleichzeitig/Offener Himmel 2/Sattwa/Morning Glory" is an early example of the tribal/ambient/ritual sound, the organic nature of which is more interesting than what samplers could do. Here (as in all of *Aum)* everything is "hands on," with sounds personally collected on tape by the composer, and recording conditions manipulated for effect, divorced from the high-tech gloss of a studio. The piece begins with sounds of nature, followed by aggressive tribal drums, the sounds of motorcycles and cars and more percussive goodies, then drifts off, fading away, then returns to sections of acoustic guitar, sitar, and chants. The influence on other later organic collage music artists like Voice of Eye and Life Garden would be enormous.

The 21½-minute "Soma/Surat Shabda/Abraxas/Susani/The Key" again features such lush sounds as crashing ocean waves (in excellent stereo, too) accompanied by acoustic guitar. This moves to a Caribbean-style percussion dance, then a menacing and ghostly web of hovering electric guitar chords, with the voices of children floating in the mix. Next is a frosty spray of cymbals and bells with a light flute joined by a sitar, which leads to the final fade-out.

The collage nature of these works is well served by the environmental sounds, which Deuter uses to make smooth transitions between the varying instrumental parts. The sound is very good. The use of stereo is clever and well thought out—a serious artistic collage—and at the same time creates irresistible headphone candy. As usual, Deuter pays very close attention to the mix and production.

Aum is a personal form of music that became the blueprint for Deuter's subsequent releases. The cover photo of a blue sea, like a watercolor painting in its tranquility, perfectly imparts the earthy, inner voyages of this special music.

CELEBRATION. Released 1976. Kuckuck.

Bridging the styles of his early releases with those that would come later, *Celebration* is an important link in Deuter's development. This disc is still as much a collage as his early recordings, and quite experimental. What strikes one almost immediately is that this music practically announces its spirituality. It is as introspective as music can get, in that inner journeys continually unfold in these compositions.

The hallmarks of the Deuter sound—light, friendly, and very spacey textures of acoustic guitars (also some electric here), flutes, bells, synth, organ, and the extensive use of nature sounds—begin here with the music of *Celebration.* These elements are magic in Deuter's hands. "Von Hohen Himmel Ein Leuchtender Schweigen" is an important 11½-minute track in the classic German cosmic style. Eastern ragas, drones, and chants give way to dual acoustic guitars. The similarity to Popol Vuh is at its strongest on *Celebration.* This is very much like that band's mid-1970s group of releases, especially in the dreamy acoustic guitar textures of *Celebration*'s 7-minute "Grass Grows by Itself."

This release continues the environmental sound collages of his previous works, now produced more seamlessly than ever. The musical instruments are almost engaged in duets with the nature sounds. The 5-minute "Solitary Bird" is a mix of water sounds with acoustic guitars and mellow electric guitars. The 6½-minute "Easy Is Right" does the same with bird sounds. The exaggerated stereo sound gives everything atmosphere in spades. The production is a bit shaky and flat at the beginning, with a good amount of hiss and a few clicks, but it improves greatly after a few tracks and becomes fairly crisp.

The cover is a photo of a landscape (in miniature), which suggests the discovery of a special place or small miracle that brings personal joy and treasure—an excellent evocation of the music on *Celebration.*

SILENCE IS THE ANSWER. Released 1981. Kuckuck.

With *Silence Is the Answer* Deuter reaches the summit of what he seemed to be aiming for, and it sums up his musical career quite well. The first disc (of two) is a 43-minute six-part (title) track—a serious work of intense concentration. The second disc is perhaps the atypical Deuter release, showcasing the prettier, lighter style that his later 1980s releases would exhibit.

The title and title work of this release suggest a unifying theme that encapsulates his ambitions as well as those of the German cosmic music movement. This is one of the last works of its kind, achieving a magic, classic status—floating, ethereal, and very, very spiritual. As usual the mood is set as soon as the music begins. There is little doubt that Deuter is on a creative roll here. When most of his contemporaries were moving in an opposite direction, toward high-tech, shorter lengths, and more rhythm, Deuter moved toward silence (although it should be noted that silence isn't used here as it might be in an avant-garde piece à la John Cage). It is perhaps a project which stands as a plea for more active listening, and in this sense the first disc is a major progressive release. Throughout, Deuter represents himself as a composer interested in sound itself. He knows his limitations (and thus sticks to his primary instruments) but exploits the maximum possible potential of the sounds he is using. His oft-employed combination of nature sounds is not just a gimmick or coloration.

The conceptual title work features acoustic guitar textures, synth, flute, light chants, wind and water sounds, and lots of bells. The use of bells is in the vein of that of his label mates Henry Wolff, Nancy Hennings, and Frank Perry. The 12-minute second part of "Silence Is the Answer" requires silence to appreciate the lingering resonance of the bells. The third part sounds like Steve Hillage's *Rainbow Dome Musick,* with its cascading stereo synth space effects. The 1-minute fifth part is just the sound of a human whisper, extraordinarily delicate and poignant. It is a major work by any measure.

The second disc is a prelude to later releases, where synths become more integrated into Deuter's compositions. This works quite well for him—the electronic percolations and textures are seamlessly incorporated. The accent here is on joy. It is as if a catharsis has been experienced on the first disc, and now a fresh, exuberant radiance has emerged from that time of trial. Happy moods are evoked again using flutes, guitars, synths, tabla, and sounds of nature. It flows quite effortlessly, though it's a bit too sweet at times. On his later works, except for the shining *Cicada* (see below), Deuter is mainly repeating the style he perfects here.

The music on this CD was recorded in India under less than ideal recording conditions. Nonetheless, the sound is very good. There is some hiss, but what is sacrificed in audiophile considerations is made up for in authenticity. The cover photo of a barren desert complements the introspective silences of the title work.

CICADA. Released 1982. Kuckuck.

Variety, grand, memorable melodies, and a lush, attention-getting production make *Cicada* a sparkling classic that Deuter has understandably found hard to top. This is one of the recordings that began the new age category in earnest, and on a high note, in the early 1980s.

Synths take an a larger role here than before, but they are sunny and sprinkling in Deuter's hands, infectious and celestial. Sequenced rhythm patterns and electronic blips wash by, interwoven effortlessly with the acoustic instruments. *Cicada* is Deuter's best-produced album, with a lively expansive stereo mix that is not at all flat or thin like some of his later material. This is an important point. Deuter is a composer concerned with sound collage, and on *Cicada* all of his ideas are so successfully integrated they are, in effect, a genre of their own, a blueprint the musicians of the emerging new age music movement were to use, giving Deuter more recognition and fans than ever, but without many new musical challenges. After *Cicada,* Deuter became an artist on autopilot.

The shimmering acoustic guitars, bells, harp, sitar, synths, and sounds of nature are all here again, achieving a perfect synthesis. The 6½-minute title track features electronic blips combined with water sounds, not just as a short intro but as an integral part of the piece in its foreground. The piece recalls similar constructions by early Agitation Free and Popol Vuh, and on this album Deuter should still be seen in this context, not as part of the routine new age wallpaper. The 7½-minute "Alchemy" has a tapestry of bells and synths that are truly magical, while the final track, the 3½-minute "Between Two Breaths," ends the disc on a darker mood, with sinewy multitracked flutes.

The cover is superb, with a lovely, dreamy photo of a misty, meditative forest, perfect for this disc and for the imagery of the new age music genre in general, of which *Cicada* is an authentic progressive landmark.

DJAM KARET

REFLECTIONS FROM THE FIREPOOL. Released June 1989. HC Productions.

One of the most promising of the recent American progressive groups, Djam Karet is a fiercely independent outfit with a bizarre band name that proves that commerce is not their priority. *Reflections* is 65+ minutes of guitar-led instrumental rock, tightly played and arranged in pieces with atmospheric divergences mixed in. In many ways they are like a modern-day Finch, with a similarly big sound of guitars/bass/drums dominating the overall structure and mood. Other comparisons would be *Tamna Voda*–era Dark (e.g., the world music percussion in the 9-minute "Fall of the Monkeywalk" from *Reflections)* or *Wish/Animals*–era Pink Floyd (the heavy space rock of the 7-minute "Animal Origins"). It was an incredibly ambitious move for a California band to release a lengthy instrumental prog rock disc in the 1980s, and this recording really stands out.

The blazing guitar-led jams are the precursor to the band's 1991 masterpiece *Burning the Hard City* (see below). While *Reflections* delivers all the right elements for a prog rock release, not all of the sounds and structures work as well as they could (e.g., the cheesy keyboards on the opening of the 7-minute "Scenes from the Electric Circus") and there could be a bit more development within some of the pieces. Nevertheless, these are minor complaints and *Reflections* delivers the goods. This music tells stories—an important progressive

Djam Karet (1989–1991 lineup). From left to right, Mike Henderson, Henry J. Osborne, Chuck Oken, Jr., Gayle Ellett.

ingredient. The closing title track ends with classical and acoustic guitars and loud train sounds, creating a cinematic feel that is usually at work in this group's music. The production is very good, as is the artwork.

BURNING THE HARD CITY. Released September 1991. HC productions.

With *Burning the Hard City* and *Suspension & Displacement* (see below), two separate and ambitious 70-minute discs released in the fall of 1991, Djam Karet became a major influence on progressive musical directions. They are certainly regarded as one of the leading progressive groups in the United States (along with Voice of Eye), and on the strength of these two releases, they live up to that billing. *Burning the Hard City* and *Suspension & Displacement* demonstrate two different prog styles—instrumental rock and space music, respectively. That the group can achieve this compositional balance successfully is in itself no mean feat, but they also sustain the quality up to the length of 140 minutes of original material, recorded and released at the same time—Wow!

Burning the Hard City is electric guitar–led blistering high-volume band-oriented rock with a live sound. Exuding a white-hot, adrenalin-driven but controlled frenzy, this aptly titled disc is unrelenting and entertainingly so. While it is heavy, it is not heavy metal (though heavy metal fans would like it). This is storytelling music, not just grooves and chops or improvs and experiments. It is this mixture of storytelling and chops that makes it so successful. Influences or reference points would include Finch, Fire Merchants, and Frank Zappa's instrumental *Guitar* opuses, yet Djam Karet's compositions are more ambitious. It's still rip-'em-up-and-spit-'em-out prog rock, but done for the effect of dramatic exposition, not merely to show off instrumental prowess. And this is prog you can air-guitar to.

The first piece, the 9-minute "At the Mountains of Madness," opens with an emotional, heavy blues guitar, then races down several rhythmic workouts and hard-hitting solo bits. "Province 19: The Visage of War," the famous 8-minute second cut, begins with a swoosh of synth followed by rumbles, shrieks, and cries from electric guitars, during which is heard the distorted voice of a military commander. There is then a tension-and-release buildup, with tormented guitar scales and an icy, creeping bass guitar riff tugging us through the agonized pace of the notes. The piece ends with two guitars blazing in grinding, noisy feedback. An antiwar message in the track is attained via it's sound alone, without lyrics or vocals. This is a demonstration of the dramatic storytelling potential of instrumental rock, the communications without words that still eludes many popular music forms.

The music in the rest of the pieces on *Burning* also lives up to their titles (e.g., the fast fretboard runs on the 12-minute "Grooming the Psychosis," the irresistibly funky groove of the 6-minute "Topanga Safari"). Each member also contributes keyboards and other sounds in addition to their primary instruments. All in all, it is a more mature work than *Reflections from the Firepool.*

The production is excellent, although not quite as punchy as it could have been (the drums could be a bit bigger). The primary colors (yellow, red, orange) of the cover art indicate the music's mood. Djam Karet's keen, insightful postmodern take on instrumental rock is intelligent, tasteful, and emotionally raw.

SUSPENSION & DISPLACEMENT. Released September 1991. HC Productions.

An important and significant release, *Suspension & Displacement* both recalls earlier progressive styles and looks ahead by recombining those elements in new and successful ways. This is the space music companion to *Burning the Hard City,* and it is both somewhat unexpected (considering the band's hard rock reputation) and part of what makes the music work so well (space music as approached by rockers).

Suspension is difficult to describe, as each track is different. The electro-acoustic compositions all have a drifting feel to them. The disc is never startling; all is on an even keel. There is a lot of acoustic guitar here which provides many of the spaciest moments (similar to the opening acoustic guitar and synth of Klaus Schulze's "Ways of Changes" from *Blackdance).* The mixtures of guitars, bass, a wide variety of synths, and sparing use of percussion are augmented by tape effects and loops and samples, often utilizing minimalist drones and patterns, fusing classic space music textures, collage, ambient, industrial, ritual, and new age styles into a seamless whole.

The slowly unfolding 11-minute "Dark Clouds, No Rain" is alternately light and menacing, as the title implies, weaving a moody, cloudy day atmosphere. Beginning with an eerie, choirlike resonance and guitar effects, Fripp and Eno-like loops are added, along with trance percussion and sunny synths. The 4½-minute "8:15—No Safe Place" has a spacey texture of skidding, trippy stereo phased guitar notes, with sections of dreamy keyboards, guitar, and bass. The 5-minute "Angels Without Wings" opens with a drone, which is joined by exotic percussion, synth, and extremely light guitar textures, recalling the more subdued moments of the 1980's King Crimson. The excellent 7½-minute "Consider Figure Three" begins with a Steve Reich–like narrative tape loop of a pathologist's observed recitation about the internal organs. This voice slowly becomes obscured by guitar hums and synth atmospheres, with the piece dissolving into a dreamlike, formless cloud of sound. Unexpectedly, a sunny and fluid acoustic guitar section comes in, nicely sewing up the piece. The 13-minute "Erosion" has minimalist guitar loops, with low-key Robert Fripp–like soloing over it, along with percussion effects, lulling the listener into a sleepy state. Later, the piece adds colorful, inviting percussion and acoustic guitar, creating superb stereo headphone candy.

The 6½-minute "Severed Moon" is a highlight, with its tape effects, guitar, and percussion strongly recalling Steve Tibbetts. A section of bongos and shrill synths builds to a conclusion of multiple acoustic guitars. The 5½-minute "The Naked and the Dead" has more drifting atmospherics, with grumbling voice samples providing a primitive vibe. A gorgeous, storytelling acoustic guitar is added, along with light synth and a concluding segment of tribal percussion. The 3½-minute "Gordon's Basement" combines a radio voice and backward tape effects with musique concrète electronics, then becomes a garbled mass, adding percussion and guitar. The poorly titled 13½-minute "A City with Two Tales: Part One Revisited 1990" starts with a gooey, oozing, organic mass of electronics and percussion, dissolving into a chaotic morass of effects, culminating in an explosion noise. This leads into a playful section of more synths and percussion, with a Fripp-like guitar soloing over it. The piece ends with some unfortunately cheesy and screeching keyboards.

Djam Karet clearly knew what was required for this project to succeed. The compositions (as always) are the group's strongest asset, helped by the fantastic sound and rich stereo separation. One can detect a wealth of influences, from Brian Eno to Throbbing Gristle, from Tangerine Dream to Heldon. *Suspension & Displacement* is challenging, experimental music that is professionally produced, without any loose threads showing in its ingeniously woven musical tapestry. The group's follow-up to this, 1994's *Collaborator,* is in a similar vein but not as successful.

DAVID DUNN

ANGELS & INSECTS. Released 1992. Nonsequitur.

David Dunn is a composer interested in the "otherness" of sound. *Angels & Insects,* recorded in 1990–1991, features two lengthy experimental pieces. The first, the 28½-minute "Tabula Angelorum Bonorum 49," is an almost impossible-to-describe construction of computer-processed voices, evidently meant to give form to the sounds of the supernatural. It is divided into seven segments, each roughly four minutes in length. Consisting of strange groaning and gurgling sounds, complete with spatial stereo effects and a realistic volume that will shake your room, this is a very creepy and menacing voyage into the unknown, like a journey through Hades. The piece recalls Lightwave (à la *Mundus Subterraneous)* at their most unsettling. Other segments feature metallic, snapping sounds that recall the industrial music of artists like SPK, the Anti-Group, and *Nature Unveiled*–era Current 93. The subterranean, teeth-grinding unease becomes a bit repetitious by the final few segments, but nevertheless this is a fascinating creation.

The second piece, "Chaos & the Emergent Mind of the Pond," is a 24-minute collage of field recordings of microscopic insects and freshwater ponds, exploring the sounds of other life forms and the environment. It recalls the acoustic explorations of composers Annea Lockwood and Michael Prime. Slowly, light water/pond sounds fade in, which are then manipulated with spatial effects and other processing. A drop of water is amplified in one channel, creating a sound resembling a loud snap. Insect buzzes, high-frequency tones, and percolating liquid sounds are juxtaposed and heavily layered on top of each other. As subtle changes are made, a journey of sorts unfolds. The mood created is perfect for a humid, sunny day.

This full digital recording, a difficult and radically experimental disc, is a mature work. Composed, produced, and performed by Dunn, it comes with a very lengthy booklet in which Dunn provides detailed explanations of the methods used in creating the pieces.

DZYAN

TIME MACHINE. Released November 1973. Bellaphon import.

Stir up a mixture of Brand X, Jade Warrior, Oregon, Pink Floyd, Popol Vuh, Steve Tibbetts, and Third Ear Band, and you have the music of Dzyan. (If only the group's name was more pronounceable!) The music of Dzyan is at the very front rank of progressive artists. This utterly unique group not only lives up to its underground reputation, but goes well beyond, exceeding expectations.

Time Machine is an absolutely classic example of German instrumental fusion, a recording rich in detail and texture, with a spiritual, deep, otherworldliness. Combining Eastern influences and psychedelia with lively jazz/rock, *Time Machine*'s subtleties can be listened to repeatedly due to the meticulous attention to detail. The entire recording exudes an exotic opt-out "otherness" that so many of the psychedelic groups aim for but that few manage to achieve.

The four pieces on *Time Machine* consist of intricate tapestries, both electric and acoustic. The performances are outstanding and creative, bursting with ideas at every turn. They rock, yet can also be spacey. The sound is big and open, with incredible stereo separation. Eddy Marron's army of guitars provides an edgy element and bassist Reinhard Karwatky provides a chunky bottom, while drummer Peter Giger is the group's secret weapon. He's all over these pieces, coloring every section with masterful touches of amazing percussion, adding further depth to the already detailed textures.

The 8-minute "Kabisrain" introduces the group's detailed, crisply recorded sound. Icy, frosty percussion, bowed double bass, and guitars with an Eastern flavor create a spacey, complex, and playful form that strikes a brilliant balance between chaos and control. The 8½-minute "Magika" emphasizes the group's gritty, underground feel and heavy rock power-trio side. A tightly arranged groove of Giger's huge drum fills, Marron's rhythm guitar races, and Karwatky's thunderous bass combines jazzy playing with rock energy. A spacey center section grows into a monster rock workout, with an edgy electric guitar solo by Marron. The 3-minute "Light Shining Out of Darkness" recalls the sound of the artists on the ECM label, but with a much bigger production. The details in the sound mix are impressive. The piece foreshadows the material on Dyzan's next release, *Electric Silence* (see below).

The 17½-minute title track has an irresistible drum solo intro, which is joined by a racing guitar and bass. After falling back into a section of haunting, spacey guitar textures, the piece then slices through a lengthy, hot fusion section of tasty, infectious playing. The piece's concluding segment is a bit plodding, but the whole is so attractive that it doesn't matter.

The sound quality is excellent, and the cover photo (by Helmut Wenske), with its altered, twisted perspective, is an apt introduction to Dzyan's deep, otherworldly sounds.

ELECTRIC SILENCE. Released December 1974. Bellaphon import.

The stunning follow-up to *Time Machine, Electric Silence* is, like the earlier release, a masterpiece. Retaining the Eastern and psychedelic flavors of the first and adding a few new instruments to the already heady mix (mellotron, sitar, and tambura are all incorporated), this album builds on the group's sound without changing it. With the additional instruments, *Electric Silence* becomes more celestial, spacey, and less rock-oriented than *Time Machine*. The sense of spirituality and "otherness" is increased, especially on such cuts as "The Road Not Taken" and "For Earthly Thinking."

The disarmingly elusive 9-minute "Back to Where We Came From" goes by rather quickly, painting colorful pictures with its dreamy, unconventional sound mix. A trickle of soft vibes and echoed screeches from the string instruments lead to aggressive slices of jazzy guitar, funky bass riffs, and a punchy drum kit. The 4-minute "A Day in the Life" is an authentic piece of Indian music with psychedelic touches, featuring a driving and intense sitar, bass, and percussion, recalling *D*-era Deuter and George Harrison and Ravi Shankar. The 5-minute "The Road Not Taken" is an example of irresistible German 1970s period prog, very much in the same arena as Agitation Free and Ash Ra Tempel, with its eccentric, sparse fusion buildup structure.

The 5-minute "Khali," which has a more Eastern flavor, is a unique and delicately executed mix of celestial mellotron and electric guitar, creating a strongly spiritual and transcendent form of music. The 9½-minute "For Earthly Thinking" recalls early King Crimson and Jade Warrior, with its cinematic mellotron, throbbing bass notes, playful stereo effects, tumbling drums, and breezy guitar noodling. The 4½-minute title track is an interesting, low-key rock jam, with a moody, gangly, grungy feel. The combination of the rough rock edges with the band's otherworldly and cosmic approach creates a very palatable and easy-to-like sound.

The playing is as inventive as before, if a bit more jazzy. The stereo separation here is even more extreme than on *Time Machine,* increasing the introspective depth of the music. The sound quality is very good, with a little hiss. The cover painting (again by Helmut Wenske) is a completely zonked out, druggy sci-fi fantasy. It doesn't represent the music in terms of content, but does convey in its disorienting feel. *Electric Silence* is highly recommended to those looking for that elusive, spiritual, step-over-the-threshold kind of music.

EGG

THE POLITE FORCE. Released December 1970. Deram import.

The Polite Force is an enjoyable, rare slice of early British prog, notable for its radical experimentation and for predating Emerson, Lake and Palmer as a keyboard-led, classically influenced big-sounding trio. This is much more mature than the baby steps of their first self-titled album (from earlier in 1970), and is an amazingly uncommercial release from a major label.

The first two songs on the recording are dated but charmingly heavy Canterbury-style vocal pieces. They are nothing exceptional, but the pieces are beloved by fans. The sound on these cuts is abysmal, however, and the production is a horrible, swampy muddle. Adopting a jazzy, pub-band sound, keyboardist Dave Stewart (later of Hatfield and the North, National Health, and Bruford) covers for the lack of guitars by getting every conceivable sound out of his primitive keyboards, most notably the organ. Using an onslaught of layering, these organs do create a big sound, but it's now pretty dated, especially considering the poor stereo mix.

The third piece, "Boilk," is a different story altogether. The sound improves mysteriously and the stereo is excellent. "Boilk" is an incredible 9½-minute example of pure collage music, à la the Beatles' "Revolution #9," only much, much more bizarre. It starts off with what sounds like a toilet flushing, then it's off on a real head trip of sound and tape effects, going from spacey to chaotic and jarring—though mostly chaotic! This is as industrial as Throbbing Gristle (even more so in some ways), but more musical. In the context of 1970 (still very early for the progressive genre) this is quite an accomplishment.

Finally, the essential 20½-minute "Long Piece No. 3" may be the definitive Egg track, summing up their sound so well. An instrumental of heavy classical jamming in several sections, it goes through many changes. The piece is overall very enjoyable, if somewhat intellectual and heavily structured. The sound and production on this track are also successful.

Anyone interested in the early U.K. prog scene should check out *The Polite Force,* as should those who are fans of the Canterbury subgenre (in which Egg is one of the definitive bands). The cover art is, unfortunately, horrible.

THE CIVIL SURFACE. Released September 1974. Virgin import.

The final and much-beloved Egg release, *The Civil Surface* is perhaps their best album—a low-key classic of eccentric, charming, friendly, and varied instrumental music from the early Virgin era. The production (by the band) is much better than their previous two releases.

The $8^{1}/_{2}$-minute "Germ Patrol" opens with a clock-like ticking and toy box voices, joined by Dave Stewart's quaint organ, in a happy-pace workout with bass and drums. This is not the fast and flashy polished style of an ELP, but rather a jazzy classical fusion with a kind of feel-good vibe to it. Stewart plays piano and organ only—there are no synths. Also, Clive Brooks's drums have that full, open 1970s sound that is a key element here. Similarly, the 9-minute "Enneagram" is a prime slab of Canterbury prog—dense, unpredictable, infectious.

Kat Epple of Emerald Web. (Photo by Burnell Caldwell.)

Two tracks, the $2^{1}/_{2}$-minute "Wind Quartet 1" and the 5-minute "Wind Quartet 2," are lovely, short, airy pieces, featuring wind instruments (clarinet, flute, bassoon, and French horn). These are very nice and represent quite a change of pace from the trio jamming. Also in a light, floating vein is the 4-minute "Prelude," which has a vocal choir (Amanda Parsons, Barbara Gaskin, Ann Rosenthal) à la the kind used on the Hatfield and the North albums, here combined with organ and bass guitar.

There are some avant-garde touches on *The Civil Surface,* such as the brief and barely audible voices (from a phone) buried in the background, and the starts, stops, and delayed ending of the $3^{1}/_{2}$-minute "Nearch," a Henry Cow–like improvisation.

Keeping the disc from true classic status is "Wring Out the Ground Loosely Now," dreadful, dated tosh featuring the poor vocals of bassist Mont Campbell. At an overly long 8 minutes, this lumbering, plodding monstrosity of a rock number sounds like something from the late 1960s. Guest star Steve Hillage is on guitar, though he's hardly recognizable.

That flaw aside, *The Civil Surface* is a unique gem of eclectic prog. The cover art is nice—English humor at its driest. The sound is fairly good, but has a lot of hiss and is a bit thin.

EMERALD WEB

NOCTURNE/LIGHTS OF THE IVORY PLAINS. NOCTURNE released 1983. Lights of the Ivory Plains released 1984. Fortuna.

This release of two key masterworks of new age/space music is absolutely essential. In the 1980s Emerald Web set the standard for American progressive new age music. The combination of flutes and synths was magical in the hands of members Kat Epple and Bob Stohl. The group's music, unlike that of many artists in this genre, lives up to their evocative song titles.

Nocturne is a delicate, dreamlike album, elusive yet rich with memorable images. Listening to the music is like encountering a misty fog from afar that dissipates when you approach, though not without putting you under its spell. The music tells open-ended stories that suggest meanings and moods but leave enough room for expansion by the listener. *Nocturne* is a rare and special achievement, a major masterpiece of space music.

The first piece, the 4½-minute "Sunset," begins with soft sounds of nature and the light Celtic harp of guest Patrick Ball, joined by flute and bells. The 3-minute "Silver Tears" is similar, with both typical of the classic Emerald Web sound. It quickly creates an introspective mood, and its evocative textures are relaxing. It's like quietly staring at the intricacy of a soothing visual pattern; the experience is meditative and therapeutic.

The 2½-minute "Unfolding," a smooth wash of ethereal voices, lyricon synth, and Japanese shakuhachi flute, sends shivers up the spine. The 4½-minute "The Sandpainter," a high point among the band's compositions, has a mournful lead synth line with a memorable melancholic feel that is incredibly haunting. It's like a cloudy day spent recalling vivid memories and strong emotions.

Lights of the Ivory Plains is a more active album than *Nocturne.* The best track from *Lights* is the opening "Obelisk," far too brief at a mere 2 minutes. A faraway flute beckons, and suddenly some attention-getting thunderous chords and percussion wash across the wide-open stereo mix. This highly dramatic, storytelling track gives the listener the feeling of encountering an ancient totem or alien artifact in a secluded forest.

Most of *Lights* consists of three 8- to 9-minute pieces ("Diamond Passage," "Dew Point," and "Nether Flow"), which are synth-dominated. They are a bit more techno-sounding than the cuts on *Nocturne,* in a sunny and light mood, but retain memorable melodies and ingenious touches, rich with depth. The album's 4½-minute title track is comparable to the music of Tangerine Dream. The 5½-minute "Koto Blue" is similar to *Nocturne*'s "The Sandpainter," with its mournful synth line.

The stereo mix on these albums creates its own environment, providing crucial layers that other, similar projects lack. The sound quality is great, but there are a number of clicks, which is unfortunate in that they interrupt the deep moods set by the music. Sadly, there was one track omitted from *Lights* in order for the album to fit this CD. The cover art—a photo of sea waves on a beach at dusk—is wonderful, perfectly evoking the music's tranquillity. Since most of Emerald Web's releases remain unissued on CD, this disc is a great treasure.

TRACES OF TIME. Released 1987. Emerald Web/Stargate.

This 56-minute anthology of rare Emerald Web is essential progressive space music. Seven tracks varying in length from 3 to 12 minutes from the period 1979–1987 are previously unreleased and/or were cassette-only material. Rising far above the average new age offerings, these pieces have a depth of feeling; the pure melodic ecstasy of the flutes, synths, and lyricon is rich and harmonious. This music invites introspection, creating a warm, gentle, intimate glow that is relaxing and enticing. Emerald Web's flowing, cascading, caressing sounds have an organic feel, despite the synths, and any music which makes electronics sound organic must be regarded as a significant achievement.

The 11½-minute "Variations on Pachelbel's Canon," the disc's first track from 1987, showcases their friendly and joyous sound. The music is never flat, cold, busy, or flashy and achieves that (once again) elusive "otherness." While this is not as deep a space music as *Nocturne,* there is very spacious stereo, reinforcing the floating pace of their compositions. The 9-minute "Awakening," from 1986, unfolds as if something being recalled is slowly coming into clearer focus and understanding. The earliest piece here (from 1979) and unfortunately the briefest (at a mere 3 minutes) is "Whispered Vision," combining a light tinkling of bells with piano, synth, and flute. All the elements of Emerald Web's deep, emotionally rich sound are present at the start—the spirituality, the voyages into inner space, the gorgeous melodies. Also, the sound is very good, with little hiss. Tragically, Bob Stohl died in an accident in 1990, and Emerald Web's later releases, unfortunately, haven't been as successful. *Traces of Time* is now only available via mail from Kat Epple (see Appendix 6).

EMERSON, LAKE AND PALMER

EMERSON, LAKE AND PALMER. Released January 1971. Rhino.

Emerson, Lake and Palmer burst onto the early 1970s pop scene as the preeminent proponent of progressive rock music. A veritable supergroup with keyboardist Keith Emerson from the Nice, vocalist/bassist/guitarist Greg Lake from King Crimson, and drummer Carl Palmer from the Crazy World of Arthur Brown, ELP jettisoned the more fey, restrained elements of their former groups, concentrating on creating the biggest sound possible (oddly enough, without using much electric guitar) with an army of keyboards and the latest developments in synthesizers. Emerson created the persona of the modern keyboardist—an arsenal of equipment; a flashy, more centerstage presence; and the ability to carry the material in the absence of guitars and (occasionally) vocals. Given such a powerful and large sound, Palmer and Lake upped the ante to Emerson's level, so that each musician creates his own huge, macho wall of sound.

To some, the phrases *classical rock* and *symphonic rock* are synonymous with ELP. Their compositions from this self-titled debut are determinedly classical (e.g., there's no hint of rock and roll in the 7½-minute "The Three Fates"). ELP, by adeptly covering and incorporating so many classical styles, received a great deal of attention for its "serious rock music" from the (normally silent on these matters) classical circles.

While the band never totally lost its classical overtones, succeeding albums moved closer and closer to mainstream arena/FM rock (as on the 4½-minute radio hit "Lucky Man") and further and further away from truly progressive hybrids, such as the classical rock they pioneered. Listening to this debut, though, one can gauge their enormous impact on their British prog rock peers Genesis, Yes, Renaissance, et al. Lake's thundering bass, flowery lyrics, and authoritative vocals give this ELP album a sound similar to that of the first two King Crimson releases. The most compelling track is perhaps the 7-minute "Tank," which puts to maximum advantage the group's playing style.

The production and sound here are excellent—very live-sounding, with good separation and a open soundstage. The music is loud and aggressive and the playing virtuoso. This is a distinguished, landmark album, one which they regrettably never topped in terms of innovation. The group's other discs have much to recommend them to be sure, but ELP quickly succumbed to their own formulas and bombast, and the later recordings document their descent into less and less progressive realms. But in early 1971, at the time of this debut release, the autopilot had not yet been switched on and the trio were in peak form—vital, influential, and groundbreaking.

PICTURES AT AN EXHIBITION (video). Film released 1972. Laser disc import (Japan).
PICTURES AT AN EXHIBITION (CD). Released May 1972. Rhino.

The 1972 film entitled *Pictures at an Exhibition* is a 92-minute historic performance by ELP, who are at their peak, in a concert shot in 1971 after the release of their debut album. From that release they perform "The Barbarian," "Take a Pebble," and "The Knife Edge," plus the epic album-length "Pictures at an Exhibition," which is their famous take on the Mussorgsky composition. This video concert is one of the finest documents of the early 1970s U.K. progressive scene, and is the best way to experience the music of Emerson, Lake and Palmer—visually.

The laser disc is in stereo, with varied sound. Evidently, two separate recordings of the show took place. The debut LP material is shot on film, and has crude, hissy distorted sound, while the *Pictures* section is shot on video, with better, clearer sound. There are a lot of wonderful psychedelic visual effects throughout the program. Different exposures and intense colors are floated by and mixed in. The picture quality of both the film and video segments is excellent. The audience is an unusually attentive and curious young crowd.

ELP are at their classical rock best here. Each member of the trio—all amazing performers—demonstrates his oft-lauded virtuosity in spades. The band has a structured, carefully delineated sound, where each member has a large, staked-out territory that can be used either to solo, to augment another, or to go all out as one of a power trio. The instrumentation is organ, Moog synths, piano, clavinet, and acoustic guitar combined with the heavy rock rhythm section of bass guitar and drums. The four songs are lengthy classical rock workouts, mainly instrumental. *Pictures at an Exhibition* is a definitive example of symphonic rock. The music is grand and on a large scale, and is undeniably an important meeting place between the old music and the new music.

Lake's lyrics to "Pictures" are uncommonly perfect for the piece, adding emotion and poignancy to the occasionally bombastic structures. His commanding vocal style is very close to that of his performances in King Crimson, and his deep, authoritative voice suits ELP's grandeur brilliantly. Emerson is the funny, over-the-top showman, rubbing a long synth pad through his crotch, standing on top of his Hammond organ and playing it with his feet as if the keys were foot pedals, playing it upside down, playing it on his back, etc. Palmer is also a visual treat, often playing the drums when his entire head is obscured from view by long hair. There is an amazing sequence in "The Knife Edge" where Palmer solos using only foot pedals; reaching up to take his shirt off as he plays, he picks up two mallets and holds them in the air, eyes closed, bare-chested, his feet pounding out huge beats on his bass drums as he appears to be in a musical trance. The image and music are macho and spiritual at the same time.

These larger-than-life performances from 1971 were linked in the public eye to the progressive genre of classical rock, giving it a popular mystique for those who might otherwise have found such a hybrid unappealing. In making classical rock entertaining, ELP also deserve acclaim for repopularizing classical structures.

The CD of *Pictures at an Exhibition* was also recorded live in 1971, but was delayed for release until 1972 after ELP's second album, *Tarkus,* had been released. It has slightly better sound than the video, but this is music that really needs to be seen as well as heard. A VHS version of only the *Pictures at an Exhibition* piece from the full-length film is also available from Griffin video.

BRIAN ENO

DISCREET MUSIC. Released November 1975. Caroline.

Like *Zeit*–era Tangerine Dream, this is one of the early examples of ambient music, and was just as influential a release. Eno's liner notes make clear that his intention was to create music for a quiet, private, contemplative space, different from the active, flashy realms of popular music. Eno takes space music styles (from, for example, the early German cosmic music) and opens them up even further—to the space within that music, that is—so that it is softer and more introspective, and his work represents an important development in the origins of the ambient and new age genres.

The aptly named 30½-minute title track is the highlight of the recording, offering lots of depth, resonance, and texture. Layer upon layer of soft sounds (melodic synth lines with tape delay, reverb, and EQ altering the timbre) are unfolded

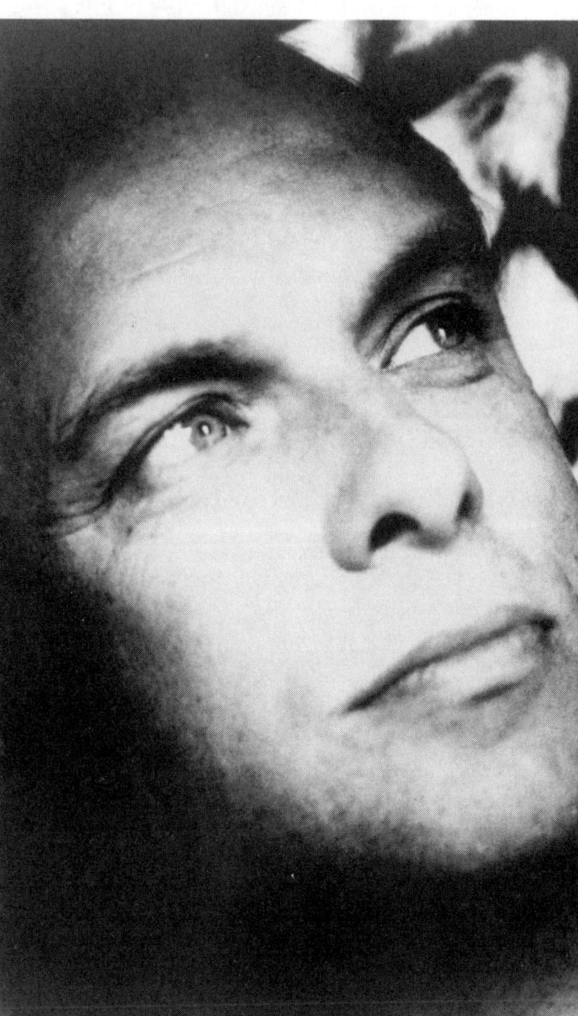

Brian Eno.

with extreme stereo separation, creating a warm, open, and inviting sound. Simplicity is the key here; there's nothing ultra-high-tech about it. The sound just flows over you and you disappear into it. This is what ambient music is all about. Although the hiss level is very high, try not to let that interfere with your listening enjoyment.

The second half of the disc is "Three Variations on the Canon in D by Johann Pachelbel." Unless you know this particular Eno track you'd think you were just hearing a straightforward classical recording. But Eno deconstructs the piece (in three sections) into fragments. The string section players were instructed to overlap and overlay each other's parts so that a new piece emerges. Again this is done with lots of stereo panning to gorgeous effect, and with better sound (less hiss) than the title track.

AMBIENT 1 MUSIC FOR AIRPORTS. Released December 1978. Caroline.

A logical step foward from *Discreet Music,* this is a landmark ambient/new age/space/quiet music release, continuing Eno's exploration of silence and resonance in sound and music. In active listening terms, this means that you have to listen to the notes in their entirety, concentrating on the sounds from first appearance to final fade-out. As in *Discreet Music,* there are sparse keyboard patterns, very low-key and simple, with lots of room for them to appear, resonate, fade, and disappear.

The first track, "1/1," was composed with Robert Wyatt of Soft Machine, who plays piano on it. "2/2" sounds like the German group Cluster—a quiet, meditative electronic voyage. Voices are used on "2/1" and "1/2"; this is a nice touch and these are the real highlights of the album, preferable to the keyboard parts. A light floating feel, very soothing, is conveyed by the cascading sways of the voices. Like the sparse piano notes, they resonate and fade, the effect of which is quite relaxing. All four tracks are different, providing welcome variety.

The instruments are closely miked and well recorded, but like *Discreet Music* there is an unfortunate amount of hiss for a recording such as this. Although this work has been surpassed by many of the ambient recordings that followed it, it is nonetheless a historic release. It is the best of Eno's *Ambient* series, and is the precursor to *Thursday Afternoon,* released a decade later.

THURSDAY AFTERNOON. Released November 1985. Caroline.

Thursday Afternoon is Eno's most mature ambient composition. A 61-minute piece recorded in 1984 (for the ambient video of the same name), this was one of the first works of its length for the compact disc era. In the liner notes Eno writes that the music is like a painting: it stays sitting while one moves in its presence. The recording achieves this goal, building on ideas and techniques developed since the *Discreet Music* and the *Ambient* series, creating a new music made for new listening spaces and new purposes.

Very, very low-key light piano and electronic treatments unfold slowly, with extremely subtle environmental sounds mixed in. There is little development, but that's the whole point. The piece holds up to repeated listenings and is indeed relaxing. The music shimmers with dewy radiance. It is an inviting, meditative work.

The music was co-created with Eno's regular collaborators, Daniel Lanois, Roger Eno, and Michael Brook, all of whom have released similar works. Again there is some hiss in the recording, but not as pervasive as on the previous discs. The ADD mix is also relatively low-volume. *Thursday Afternoon*'s lack of development is something of a problem, especially when one compares it to other ambient works that do incorporate more background development into their structure. A release like Bill Nelson's *Crimsworth* (see review), for example, tends to make *Thursday Afternoon* look a bit too thin in comparison. Perhaps the best way to view this work is as a blueprint for ambient music, the general outline which others can build on. In this sense, *Thursday Afternoon* is the core "original." And it is certainly Eno's ambient apex; later releases, like *The Shutov Assembly* and *Neroli,* essentially show no further progress.

EXTENSIONS

MOTIONS. Released 1994. EXT import.

Motions' unique, intricate, busy sort of fusion comes on like an early 1970s ECM disc, only with much more punch and panache. The combination of classical guitar with guitar/bass/drums is interesting, and seems to be more influenced by jazz than by classical (or rock). The classical guitar and the percussion dominate the mix, with crisp notes and extremely active drumming and avant-garde tasty colorations of all sorts. It is similar to Dzyan, though without the spacey and celestial overtones. The all instrumental pieces (mostly short, 2 to 3 minutes, but ranging from 43 seconds to $6\frac{1}{2}$ minutes) move at a brisk rhythmic pace, featuring chaotic bursts exploding in between the calmer moments.

Entirely written and produced by the band (here, a quartet), the disc has an excellent, very sharp live sound. In between the wild and woolly pieces such as "Chaos in Three Movements" and "Some Bizarre," there are some contemplative moods as well, such as "Gilisb," written by drummer Mark Van Overmeire for the solo classical guitar of leader Gilbert Isbin. The cover—nothing special—depicts an extended hand reaching out. The disc was recorded in 1993, and sports a successfully crisp ADD mix. For their next album *1, 54* (also released in 1994) the group shifted its compositional focus, changed the lineup, and added a vocalist, performing irritating avant pop. *Motions,* however, remains a recent gem of well-done fusion with new twists.

FERMATA

HUASCARAN. Released October 1977. Opus import.

Fermata were a Czechoslovakian symphonic rock group, and their second album *Huascaran* is a tasteful and fun all-instrumental gem. More modern than their Czech prog rock peers Collegium Musicum, Fermata incorporates their classical influences with funk and arena rock elements, recalling Finch, Return to Forever, Atlas, and Rush. Their material is written by keyboardist Tomas Berka and guitarist/keyboardist Frantisek Griglak,

Gilbert Isbin of Extensions.

and Berka and Griglak are joined by the crack rhythm section of bassist Ladislav Lucenic and drummer Karol Olah. Both the writing and the playing are first-rate, and the solidly rocking "Huascaran" exudes a gritty, live-sounding feel.

The album's first two pieces are the highlights. The 13½-minute "Huascaran I" opens with a lush intro of multilayered keyboards which then falls into a dewy piano, finally joined by the up-front and meaty bass guitar and drums. The band goes through a number of bombastic (but not too over-the-top) symphonic workouts before switching to a piano and violincello section that is reminiscent of Luciano Basso's *Voci*. A guest male wordless vocal is added, followed by a heavy rock jam that then recedes, only to return again along with a drum solo. The 7½-minute "80 000" has a plaintive electric piano intro that builds into a murky rock jam that picks up tempo, becoming thick and metal-like à la Rush, taking off into piercing guitar solos.

The 6½-minute "Solidarity" is an old-fashioned and loose jam, with infectious, jazzy band interplay that resembles the breeziness of Atlas. The 11-minute "Huascaran II" is a playful romp that strongly recals Return to Forever's "Romantic Warrior." Rapid-fire and tricky tradeoffs of keyboards, guitar, and bass are held together by some very hip drumbeats by Olah. The piece concludes with Pink Floyd/*Dark Side of the Moon*–like drum heartbeats and synth effects.

The disc also includes three excellent bonus tracks, recorded for Czech radio in 1976. The 4-minute "15" is a rollicking and tasty funk jam, with saucy guitars, a bass solo, and knob-twirling stereo effects. The 6-minute "Valparaiso" is another loose jam, with a wailing guitar solo. The 2-minute "Perpetuum 1" is jazzier, and includes a horn section.

The sound and production values of *Huascaran* are outstanding. The cover is a photo of the band onstage.

FIFTY FOOT HOSE

CAULDRON. Released December 1967. Weasel Disc.

Fifty Foot Hose was a very important American group, one of the most radical of the 1960s psychedelic era in the United States. Chronologically speaking this album is the earliest American recording included here, putting it on a par with the earliest British progressive recording, Pink Floyd's *The Piper at the Gates of Dawn.* The recording is remarkably similar to Jefferson Airplane's *After Bathing at Baxters* (particularly Grace Slick's songs) and the United States of America's early 1968 self-titled album (both of which also come highly recommended to progressive listeners). Despite these comparisons, *Cauldron* was evidently too weird for its time, and was denied the acclaim given to the aforementioned groups. As a result, the band quickly called it a day in 1968.

Cauldron is authentic psychedelia. The popular forms of 1960s rock have not yet been abandoned, though they are interrupted to a great extent by the weirdness of experimental guitar work, primitive electronics, bizarre vocals, and studio effects. The album's success is due primarily to the husband-and-wife team of David and Nancy Blossom, who front the band. David is the key songwriter and lead guitarist, while Nancy is the lead vocalist. The key tracks on this album are theirs ("If Not This Time," "Red the Sign Post," "Rose," "Fantasy," and the title track). Nancy Blossom's tripped-out, sexy vocalizing really makes the album, giving it both an otherworldly and a sensual appeal. Like Syd Barrett's vocals on *The Piper at the Gates of Dawn,* her vocals utilize echo, multiple tracking, and stereo panning. Cork Marcheschi is the wild-card element in Fifty Foot Hose, bringing the academic influence of composers like John Cage and electronics pioneers like Morton Subotnick. Electronic bleeps are floated throughout these songs, risking dissonance, though they are always colorful and welcome.

The 3½-minute "If Not This Time" is typical of the songs on *Cauldron.* The music is swirling and voluptuous, with that unmistakable late 1960s sound of vibrancy and confidence. David Blossom's lyrics here (and on the other tracks) are pure high-as-a-kite bliss. The 3-minute "Red the Sign Post" is tough and surprisingly modern political rock, led by guitar riffs, feedback, and effects. The lyrics invite listeners to take sides. "Fantasy" is a 10-minute opus (a length that was still quite rare in rock at that time) of several psychout grooves. The group also covers Billie Holliday's "God Bless the Child" in the same psychedelic manner.

The 5-minute title track, a work of ultra-surreal collage, is easily the most experimental. Manipulated vocals, shrieks and screams, tape effects, echoed percussion, and other wild sound effects conjure up a dark, doomy vision which none of the rest of the pieces on the album really prepares you for, given their relatively positive vibes.

The compositions by Marcheschi and rhythm guitarist Larry Evans are of considerably less interest. There are four thankfully very brief electronic works by Marcheschi which are totally out of place among the sunny psych-rock pieces. Basically these are just low-fi rumbles and hums, hissy and boring. Evans's "The Things That Concern You" is totally insipid, inept, repetitive, and trite pop psychedelia. The disc could use a nice scratch over this part.

The sound quality is surprisingly good, with a transfer that restores fullness and clarity to a thin source. Three early, low-fi demos are included here as bonus tracks, but they are of little interest.

FINCH

GLORY OF THE INNER FORCE. Released April 1975. Belle Antique import.

Loud, exciting, fast, driving, rollicking, propulsive—all of these adjectives can be applied to the music of the instrumental band Finch. They were perhaps one of the first groups of their kind in that they are full-on rock—there's little or nothing jazz or classical about them. The emphasis is on the *form* of instrumental rock, distilling the stylistic elements of progressive rock into its purest form—music only, no singing, lyrics, concepts, or radical experimentation. In this way they capture all the power and excitement of prog rock, but without imposing storytelling (beyond the song titles), concentrating solely on the grooves and the moods in a thoroughly entertaining and convincing way. And *Glory* is a monster in this genre.

In terms of comparisons, their sound (particularly here on *Glory*) is similar to an instrumental Yes. Imagine Yes songs like "Yours Is No Disgrace," "Perpetual Change," or "Siberian Khatru" without vocals or lyrics. Using the conventional rock instrumentation (guitars, bass, keyboards, and drums) Finch creates the ultimate huge band sound for the mid-1970s. They are a prog group with all the focus on the music, confidently blazing away without any need for further contextualization. This is a pure music, like jazz and fusion, but for rock it's quite rare, both now and then.

Glory features four lengthy pieces (ranging from 9½ to 13 minutes), plus two quality 3½-minute tracks left off the original LP due to time considerations. The leader of the group is guitarist Joop Van Nimwegen, who writes all of their material. There are excellent performances from all four members, especially by bassist Peter Vink, who here is as up-front in the mix as the guitar, getting in some truly amazing parts. Van Nimwegen's guitar is more rhythm-based on *Glory* (unlike the heavy blues soloing on later releases), and his solos are more angular. There is an unexpected dual acoustic guitar break in the middle of "A Bridge to Alice," unexpected because *Glory* is otherwise such a monster rave-up from start to finish.

The sound is excellent in every way. This is a Godzilla of an album. The cover design of a zodiac is nice if not particularly significant. Finch should be a much more popular band than they are.

BEYOND EXPRESSION. Released April 1976. Belle Antique import.

Beyond Expression is an attempt to take the Finch sound and open it up to lengthier and softer textures while retaining the fast-moving monster wall of sound groove they began with on *Glory of the Inner Force*. The band succeeds admirably; this is another irresistible classic.

The opening piece, the 20-minute "A Passion Condensed," begins loudly, with aggressive lightning runs for the first 8½ minutes. From there it moves into a wistful, quiet section of electric piano and subdued electric guitar, which lasts 3 minutes, shifts into a 2-minute heavy blues electric guitar blowout, then returns to the opening theme.

The 9-minute "Scars on the Ego" starts with a swaggering flash intro, gives way to a scathingly heavy power chording guitar rhythm, then moves into a chunky Rush (à la *2112)* meets Mahavishnu Orchestra sound. Another light break of piano and guitar continues the piece, followed by another of guitarist-composer Joop Van Nimwegen's stunning solos. The 14½-minute "Beyond the Bizarre" is in a similar vein to the others, with a number of dramatic themes and climaxes tastefully and sprightly executed.

The pyrotechnics of Van Nimwegen's Gibson Les Paul guitar is the cementing force in Finch's music—always at the center, with up-front solos that are extraordinarily powerful. On *Beyond Expression* the palette is expanded a bit further instrumentally, with acoustic guitars, Moog bass pedals, synths, and mellotron. Unfortunately, the organ in these tracks sounds very dated, a recurring problem for Finch. There is also a good amount of stereo panning on "Beyond," which expands their already huge sound even further.

Once again the sound quality is excellent—raw and punchy, hard-hitting, and close to being live. The cover depicts a human heart in space that's on fire, which is a good symbol for the explosive rock purity of the music on the album.

GALLEONS OF PASSION. Released 1977. Belle Antique import.

On *Galleons of Passion* composer-guitarist Joop Van Nimwegen moves the music of Finch in a clear spiritual direction, similar to that of John McLaughlin and Mahavishnu Orchestra. Titles like "Unspoken Is the Word" and "With Love as the Motive" signal that there is now a context to Finch's rock forms, and on *Galleons* the music lives up to the emotional pronouncements of those titles. This music is more refined and honed than the music on the previous two Finch discs—more symphonic, with flamboyant and grand gestures.

Again, Van Nimwegen's guitar is the centerpiece, but with a difference. Like McLaughlin, Van Nimwegen uses the heavy, dense, and complex blues of the blazing electric guitar as a transformative catharsis. But unlike the slick guitar sounds often found in fusion, Van Nimwegen's guitar is saucy, flashy, ballsy, frosty, and almost heavy metal, albeit now in a more serious and spiritual surrounding than on previous Finch releases.

Galleons is state-of-the-art instrumental rock. There is a lot of blowing and wailing here, but this time with more depth, intensity, and feeling. "With Love as the Motive" even has a very European shuffle to it, something not present in their previous music. The performances are powerful from all.

On this recording Van Nimwegen and bassist Peter Vink are joined by two new band members, keyboardist Ad Wammes and drummer Hans Bosboom. Two of the album's songs are co-written by Van Nimwegen with Vink and Wammes, respectively. The only complaint—and it is a minor one—is that many of the keyboard sounds are cringingly garish and dated in parts.

The sound once again is quite live and mondo gonzo—in other words, LOUD. The cover art is a garish, Roy Lichtenstein–style cartoon, not at all appropriate for this solid music.

FINNFOREST

FINNFOREST/LAHTO MATKALLE. FINNFOREST released 1975. **LAHTO MATKALLE** released 1976. Laser's Edge.

Another excellent band deserving of more acclaim, Finnforest (from Finland) produced these two gems of mid-1970s instrumental fusion. Led by brothers Pekka Tegelman (guitars) and Jussi Tegelman (drums), their music has an original sound, and the band's playing has a delicate, deft, playful touch that is never over the top.

Finnforest, their first album, has an understated dignity to it. It is serene, yet grooving—a difficult balance to achieve. The essence of the sound on these 3- to 5-minute pieces is the combination of tense but stately guitar soloing and a tightly controlled delivery of notes, with equally tight, crisp drumming, plus an ethereal backdrop of spacey keyboards (organ, grand piano, electric piano, synth) by Jukka Rissanen. As the titles of the pieces—"The Local Winds," "Oxygen," "I Felt Your Wings," etc.—suggest, the music falls in the realm of moody and atmospheric fusion. The album has no obvious comparisons, and it is quite impressive in that respect. The sound is good, but there are a few clicks and some hiss, and the volume of the mastering is a bit low. But it is a 100% improvement over the original vinyl version, and this reissue gives it a clarity it did not have previously.

Lahto Matkalle (a.k.a. "Starting a Voyage" in English) expands the lineup to a quartet, adding a bass player, and is quite different from the first. It is harder-hitting, with a more sophisticated and refined sound. There are more keyboards and less guitar, and the pieces are longer, in the 8½- to 11-minute range. Pieces like "Alpha," "Elvin," and "Don" are on the jazzier side, similar to the music of Return to Forever, with racing scales and the big-sounding interplay of synths and drums. The two-part title track fuses the funkiness of the band with a string section, which works quite successfully.

The sound on *Lahto Matkalle* is excellent. The artwork, new for this CD reissue, is outstanding. The photos of foggy marshes are particularly evocative of the group's music, especially the first album's low-key, dignified moodiness.

FIRE MERCHANTS

FIRE MERCHANTS. Released 1989. Medusa/Restless.

Fire Merchants are a hard-hitting instrumental rock power trio led by Brand X guitarist John Goodsall and bassist Doug Lunn. Their debut disc features Chester Thompson of Genesis on drums. The group's emphasis is on the economical, stripped-down forms of instrumental rock with the focus on chops. There's very little that is jazz here. This is certainly nothing like the original Brand X; it is a California-based group, strongly in the rock mold, featuring a whole new side to the playing of Goodsall (and Thompson). It is interesting to hear them in this muscular, macho context, with lots of power chording, riffing, and soloing, and insistent rhythmic chugging and crunch. The only reference point might be Mahavishnu Orchestra, because the guitar/drums interplay is similar to that of John McLaughlin and Billy Cobham.

Goodsall provides lots of high-quality guitar synth here as well. His MIDI guitar triggers synths and sampled horns, orchestrating the songs and adding colorations. The playing is excellent throughout. The group has a powerful sound! The disc consists of 4- to 6-minute pieces, typified by the piercing swagger of smokers like "Hamsterdam," "Divisions," and "Ignition." It almost makes the early Brand X seem laid back. Fire Merchants is pure rock; check out the guitar wailing on "Z104." Only the elegant, storytelling "Last Rhino" and "Black Forest" are more refined.

Fire Merchants' move away from jazz toward full-blown rock would have been a significant development for 1980s instrumental music—were it not for the fact that it arrived years too late. The economical tightening up (and turning up) of the instrumental rock form would have injected new life into the genre had this disc been released in the early 1980s, after the folding of the original Brand X. Then, the band might have fit in with the similar paring down of the new wave, and would thereby have provided a place at the table for instrumental music of like energy. But by 1989 the impact of a release like *Fire Merchants* was nil. Denied the status of a milestone release, the recording is still an enjoyable rave-up, with excellent punchy sound, though with a terrible, ugly, heavy metal–style cover design.

LANDLORDS OF ATLANTIS. Released May 1994. Renaissance.

Landlords of Atlantis is one of the heaviest progressive rock discs ever. This is gargantuan heavy metal–type instrumental rock, with very loud power chording and soloing pyrotechnics all the way. Heavier than its predecessor, or Djam Karet's *Burning the Hard City,* or Ozric Tentacles' *Live Underslunky,* this sets a standard of sorts as the most macho prog. As before, the emphasis is on form, groove, and chops.

The 61½-minute disc contains no filler. The pieces range from 3 to 9 minutes in length, and there is more bottom end than before in the absolutely crunching mix. Chester Thompson is gone; drumming is now by the equally impressive Toss Panos.

Guitarist John Goodsall again uses MIDI synths, which is the only element that is remotely jazzy in the instrumentation, keeping it from being pure heavy metal. In fact, rawer tracks like "Sybil," "Flamekeeper," and "Thing 15" are so balls-to-the-wall metal riffery and wailing that there is little progressive about them.

There is, however, "Worlds In Modulation" (by Goodsall), which uses its barrage of guitar styles to a Djam Karet–like storytelling effect, beyond mere chops. "The Last Future" (by bassist Doug Lunn, who writes 6 of the 10 songs on "Landlords") has more grand and precise notes, and is one of the best tracks on the CD. Goodsall's leads are his sauciest yet—witness the flailing on "9 28 91" and "Lifetimes." Also included is the

Fire Merchants' version of Brand X's acoustic "Healing Dream" (from *Xcommunication),* which works just as well in an electric setting, and even includes a flamenco-style solo.

Once again, *Landlords* arrived too late in the game for its own good: it would have been more of a revelation had it been done half a decade earlier. It also sports another hideous cover. But the sound is absolutely monster, one of the most crunching covered in this guide.

FOCUS

MOVING WAVES. Released January 1972. IRS.

Moving Waves is an easy-to-like, classic album from the golden age, and a perfect entry-level disc for anyone interested in progressive rock. It's very like an instrumental Pink Floyd, but with more of a classical influence. This is the band's best lineup: keyboardist Thijs Van Leer, guitarist-flautist Jan Akkerman, drummer Pierre Van Der Linden, and bassist Cyril Havermans.

The famous opening piece, the 6½-minute "Hocus Pocus," is the group's signature tune, and has been a radio favorite since its release. The simple power chords and riffing give plenty of breaks for the musicians to fill, and they play up a storm, milking the piece's structure for all its worth. Not to be outdone, Van Leer's unique yodeling and whistling provides the icing on the cake. "Hocus Pocus" demonstrated to early 1970s audiences that instrumental rock could entertain as well as explore and experiment.

After "Hocus" there are two short mellow instrumentals by Akkerman. The 2-minute "Le Clochard" features acoustic guitar, mellotron, and bass, while the 3-minute "Janis" has multitracked flutes with band backing, creating a nice spacey texture. The 2½-minute title track is a short vocal piece (with lyrics) by Van Leer, with classical piano.

The final two pieces, the 4-minute "Focus II" and the 23-minute opus "Eruption," are classic instrumental rock compositions (by Van Leer, with contributions from the others). "Eruption" consists of 16 smaller parts. The group's sound features strong, tight guitar/drum workouts, with solo bits for both, and breaks of Pink Floyd–like organ and Yes–like fanfares. Wonderful stuff.

Despite a number of clicks and some hiss, the sound is unusually good for a recording from this era. The miking and engineering of the drums are especially notable. This is an album with lots of stereo drum rolls! According to the liner notes, the band at the time were after a heavier, live sound, and they certainly achieved it here. Unfortunately Focus never surpassed *Moving Waves* in terms of successful compositions. *Focus 3,* from 1973, is probably the best of the rest if you want to hear more by this group.

EDGAR FROESE

AQUA. Released June 1974. Caroline.

Aqua is a major work, at the front rank of Tangerine Dream's releases (even though this is a solo album by Froese) and very much in the style of that group's *Atem* and *Phaedra. Aqua* continues the collage of environmental sounds with synthesizers begun by Wendy Carlos, Popol Vuh, and Deuter. The mix of water sounds with washes of dreamy, melodic synths is irresistible. The electronics used here are unique to their time and place. They have a warm, organic feel to them, unlike the coldness and rhythms of later Tangerine Dream. *Aqua* succeeds by combining these technologies with the linking thematic concept of water. This music is strongly mysterious, spiritual, and introspective.

The opening title track (17 minutes) begins with a burst of water sounds, followed by some relatively loud walls of gurgling synths, which collide with each other within the stereo spectrum. A swoosh of sound will emerge from one channel, then burst into the center, to finally fade out in the other. The 9½-minute "Panorphelia," which is at once soothing and enigmatic, opens with very soft bursts of noise, from which an electronic pulse emerges. The 3½-minute "ngc 891" mixes traffic noises with fluid synth patterns, which seems to emphasize the complexities of modern life, yet all is tied up into a harmonious whole. In the 6-minute "Upland," the final piece, an emerging, gurgling synth is joined by a churchlike organ soloing over it. It's a very deep journey, ending with a climactic storm of jarring tape effects. Each of these four lengthy pieces offers a wealth of ideas and developments.

The sound mix is sharp and loud. Unfortunately, there are several flaws in the master, such as distortion (especially in "Panorphelia" and "ngc 891") and clicks. The production creates its own stereo environment, making the room come alive. The cover artwork by Monique Froese is brilliant. A pure blue color nature photo, totally evocative of the music's organic warmth, perfectly sets the mood. *Aqua* is a masterpiece dripping with authentic atmosphere.

EPSILON IN MALAYSIAN PALE. Released September 1975. Caroline.

This is another major masterpiece from Froese, who certainly had the Midas touch in the mid-1970s. The year 1975 saw the release of two Tangerine Dream classics as well as this, Froese's second solo album. Like *Aqua* and T.D.'s *Rubycon, Epsilon in Malaysian Pale* is a thematically unified work, as important as any in the T.D. canon.

There are two lengthy pieces, each about 16½ to 17 minutes. The title track opens with what sounds like an environmental recording, but is actually an electronic simulation. This happens throughout. This is subtle, tranquil, serene, friendly, and relaxing space music. Above all, it is warm-sounding. The electronics are organic and flowing in a way that could never be duplicated today, which is why this disc is such an essential landmark in the space music genre. "Maroubra Bay" has a tenser opening, but develops toward the calmer feel of the first, where all floats so seamlessly that it's a wonder to listen to. The elusive, fragile stereo mix is very special, like a sort of daydream vision passing, perfect for headphones. The sound is very good, with no distortions this time, but there is a fair amount of hiss. Hopefully, Froese's catalog will receive the same revisiting as the new TD remasters.

Monique Froese's cover photo of warm, green plants does for *Epsilon* what she did for *Aqua*. It brilliantly evokes the organic solitude of this special music.

PINNACLES. Released August 1983. Caroline.

Pinnacles, Froese's final solo release, is another solid effort. This is a cheerful set of electronic music, with a juicy, sprightly feel to it, like a bright spring morning. It still sounds quite organic at times, despite the newer technology. Above all, the music isn't flat and avoids being wallpaper schlock. This has memorable melodies and appealing, layered sounds that fill the room. While not as challenging as Tangerine Dream's darker *Hyperborea* (released three months later), nor more space music like Froese's previous solo works, it's all-is-sunshine glow is easy to like.

The splashy 9½-minute "Specific Gravity of Smile" and the 4½-minute "The Light Cone" feature multiple layers of sunny synth percolations, which create a sound similar to that of *Lights of the Ivory Plains*–era Emerald Web. Despite these layers, most of the activity is in the foreground. The judicious use of sequencers and rhythm is deft and not overdone. The 7-minute "Walkabout" borders on space music, but not because of the use of sequencers. The 22-minute title track is the least successful, with some unfortunate discoid, garish sounds (à la Tangerine Dream's *White Eagle).* There is little development in the piece, so the length cannot be justified. This cut prevents *Pinnacles* from attaining a classic status.

The sound quality is good. Monique Froese's two breathtaking cover photos are exactly right for the music, but the reproductions on the CD booklet are too small to be fully appreciated.

FÜHRS AND FRÖHLING

AMMERLAND. Released March 1978. Brain import.

This is Heinz Fröhling and Gerd Führs of the German prog rock band Schicke, Führs and Fröhling. *Ammerland* is a completely melodic and delicate music of multiple acoustic guitars, mellotron, synths, and grand piano. These instrumental pieces, recorded between the SFF group's *Sunburst* (1977) and *Ticket to Everywhere* (1978), are very mellow and bright. This is a sort of pre–new age progressive music, reinforcing the cosmic underpinnings of German rock. It resembles (but is far preferable to) similar acoustic releases by Anthony Phillips, or the 1980s Windham Hill guitarists Will Ackerman and Michael Hedges. Another reference point would be the acoustic guitar/mellotron parts of the early King Crimson and Genesis.

Ammerland features seven short pieces (ranging between 2 and 5½ minutes in length) and one 13½-minute track. The music on this disc is lush, with memorable melodies that stick with you. The performances and compositions are top-notch, as is the first-rate production, with its full, richly layered hiss-free stereo separation. The music is bright, upbeat, and positive, moving at a sprightly pace. It is not high-tech or complex, but rather simple and organic, living up to the nature-based images of titles such as "Gentle Breeze," "Dance of the Leaves," and "Street Dance." It's a bit too pretty to be space music, and rather it occupies an impressionistic realm where the sounds convey a sense of quiet wonder at the beauty of nature.

The final piece, "Ammernoon," is the most avant-garde of the songs, with voices and laughs accompanied by a celestial mellotron, and orgasmic sighs from guitarist Fröhling, who composed all these pieces, except for the 13½-minute "Every Land Tells a Story," co-written with keyboardist Führs. The excellent cover photo of an expansive outdoor landscape as seen from a wooden bridge is totally appropriate for this superb recording.

RON GEESIN

FUNNY FROWN. Released 1991. Headscope import.

Ron Geesin is one of the pioneers in modern avant-garde music, with a history that reaches as far back as the pre–Pink Floyd era. His first album, *A Raise of Eyebrows* in 1967, was a collection of some of the most Dadaesque compositions in 20th-century music, as well as some fairly insipid monologues which were intended as humor. Most of Geesin's releases have this mix of music and monologue, and those that are music-only remain unissued on CD. So his best work, then, is actually represented by three recent compilations, of which *Funny Frown* is one.

The 57-minute-plus "Funny Frown" collects 17 extremely varied instrumental pieces recorded between 1980 and 1990, none of which was released until compiled for this disc. The pieces, which run from 1 to 10 minutes are a series of diverse vignettes, like a composer's notebook. The range in recording dates and contexts makes for a masterful, varied compilation; each piece is different. *Funny Frown* cements Geesin's position as a major modern composer.

Geesin's approach is so unique and eclectic that he is different from all other artists in this field. The music is mostly keyboard-dominated (synths, samples, and piano). The pieces range in mood from manic and bizarre to atmospheric and haunting to cute and humorous. Throughout, the music is energetic, lively, friendly, and very enjoyable. Due to the all-but-the-kitchen-sink diversity of sounds, Geesin creates unique mixes, usually in a collage structure. For example, the piece "Ample Sample" (from 1990) features milk churns, a model circular saw, wind sounds, car horns, door slams, and footsteps.

Geesin gives detailed descriptions of each piece in the disc's liner notes, but the titles themselves tell the story: "Hot Breath," "Piano Prance," "Mad Kite," "Slink," "Lonely Park," etc. The sense of playfulness in his music is an important facet for progressive music. The sound quality is fantastic, and the cover is a nice photo of the artist.

HYSTERY—THE RON GEESIN STORY. Released March 1994. Cherry Red import.

This is a classic compilation arranged chronologically starting with the newest material (from January 1994) and moving back to 1967. The CD is probably the most varied of his releases, as many different styles are showcased here. These short pieces are taken from Geesin's many releases (*A Raise of Eyebrows, Electrosound, As He Stands, Electrosound Volume 2, Right Through, Patruns,* and *Atmospheres)* and is a work of eccentric genius. You get the impression that the sounds you're hearing are very close to what Geesin hears in his head. The unadorned purity of his work is a major achievement.

"A Raise of Eyebrows" (1967) is an absolutely crazy stereo collage, with very LOUD smashing of plates and gurgling/burbling sounds from Geesin, ending with the sound of a television and a short, verbal incitement to violence. This is challenging Dada experimentation, going the extra mile for extreme effect. "Certainly Random," also from

1967, is Geesin playing banjo while scatting and randomly babbling. "With a Smile up His Nose, They Entered" (1970) has a light flute and church organ, composed for Nick Mason's (of Pink Floyd) wedding. "Affections For String Quartet" is snippets of orchestral music for Geesin's soundtrack to the excellent 1971 film *Sunday, Bloody Sunday.* "Vocal Chords," a 1972 radio track, is an experiment with voices and volume-dimensional sound, where Geesin approaches the microphone from different parts of the room while speaking, with added echo effects. 1973's ""Upon Composition" is a whimsical collage with a narration about his various compositions, reminiscent of something by the Bonzo Dog Band.

"Frenzy," from 1974, has scathing slabs of harsh synth coming on like a tornado. It's extreme and as industrial as any similar Throbbing Gristle piece. "Animal Autos," also from 1974, features flamenco guitars and sequencers. 1975's "Smoked Hips" is a solo piano piece, tense and dramatic. Geesin aggressively attacks the keys, but the superb sound is not Dadaesque, as in many of the others, but simply intense. There

Ron Geesin.

are several short 1980s tracks in the same realm as those found on *Funny Frown*—highly musical electronic vignettes.

The spoken parts are very English, as in pieces like "Where Daffadils Do Thrive." Geesin is not at his best with these. The latest piece, from 1994, is "Ron's Address," another brief spoken work. This material isn't funny, nor is it good poetry. The inclusion of these tracks prevents this compilation from being all that it could, interrupting and undermining the musical bits. The sound on the disc, however, is good. The cover sports a photo of Geesin in the studio during his early days.

LAND OF MIST. Released July 1995. Cleopatra.

Another fine Geesin compilation, his first in America, this selection emphasizes the industrial aspects of his electronic material—a good choice since he was years ahead of his time in this area. This 54-minute disc is a gold mine of musical oddities covering the period 1970–1988, with 19 largely unissued tracks and only a few overlapping with the selections on *Funny Frown* and *Hystery.* As in all of these compilations, Geesin gives detailed descriptions of each song in the disc's liner notes.

Six of the pieces are from 1972's *Electrosound* and two from 1975's *Electrosound Volume 2.* These are noisy, loud, attention-getting, "out there" experimental works, somewhere in between Karlheinz Stockhausen, Kraftwerk, Throbbing Gristle, Tangerine Dream, and Chris and Cosey. The same can be said of the two tracks from 1977's *Atmospheres,* "Morning Sundew" and "Solar Flares," which are brief, dreamy electronic music snippets. Equally unsettling is the dark 1980s material (1985's "Evil Engine" and 1987's "Heaven Split"). Even the more playful "Mominous" has an undercurrent of menace. 1988's "Throat Sweat" is an interesting collage of coughs, performed live. 1973's "To Roger Waters, Wherever You Are" (from *As He Stands)* is also a collage piece, with voice, wind, and fire sounds, as well as electronic bagpipes.

The sound is outstanding. The mastering is loud, further bringing out the industrial side of this music. The cover painting of an alien landscape from outer space is probably not the most appropriate for Geesin's music, but its dreamy quality does stress the mystery in it.

RON GEESIN AND ROGER WATERS

MUSIC FROM THE BODY. Released December 1970. Restless Retro.

Music from the Body is one of the ultimate "opt-out" albums of all time. A major work of authentic psychedelia and highly imaginative radical experimentation, it is groundbreaking nonelectronic collage music that is fun and easy on the ears. It is a milestone in both Geesin's and Waters's careers, and a landmark progressive release.

The disc, a soundtrack to a film about the human body, provides a context and overall concept for all of Geesin's off-the-wall vignettes. (The music undoubtedly also enlivened the mind-expanding possibilities for viewers of the film.) Waters adds lyrics recalling the magical optimism of childhood, enriching the context, giving the project a friendly, nurturing feel, and linking this radically new kind of music with themes of positive inquiry and questioning. The recording is in keeping with the other soundtrack work each artist was doing at the time—Geesin on the film *Sunday, Bloody Sunday* and Waters (with Pink Floyd) on *Zabriskie Point.* Both films link progressive music styles to images of social commentary and introspection. *Music from the Body* also verges on space music, with its radical stereo panning and separation, sound effects, and environmental sounds.

"Our Song," the first piece, opens with a lively collage of handclaps, whistles, hiccups, belches, farts, and breathing noises, accompanied by piano—a real attention-getter. Listeners in 1970 might have thought someone spiked their drink. "Sea Shell and Stone," "Chain of Life," and "Breathe" are Waters songs, with wistful folky vocals, environmentally conscious lyrics, and acoustic and bass guitar. "Sea Shell . . ." is later nicely reprised instrumentally as "Sea Shell and Soft Stone." "Breathe" is famous as forerunner of a piece with the same title on Pink Floyd's *Dark Side of the Moon.* "Body Transport" is thoroughly nuts, with Geesin and Waters whispering, laughing, and breathing heavily in a closely miked stereo collage.

Elsewhere, Geesin's eclectic multi-instrumental bits are all over the map. "Red Stuff Writhe" is violins and fiddles, "A Gentle Breeze Through Life" features ominous banjos, and "Lick Your

Partners" is an odd rhythm part. "More Than Seven Dwarfs in Penis Land," a collection of odd vocal bits, is unique, inspired, complex insanity. The final track, "Give Birth to a Smile," is classic, soulful hippie rock, with a vocal by Waters and featuring the rest of Pink Floyd as backing musicians.

That a major label like EMI released something this radical and off-the-wall was good news for the emerging progressive scene at the time. The diverse and bizarre sounds all flow together so fluidly and successfully that *Music from the Body* is essential for any progressive collection. The sound quality is very good, if mastered at a slightly low volume. But it is far superior to any vinyl version. The cover features a skeleton, which doesn't do justice to the playful and nurturing feel of the music.

GENESIS

NURSERY CRYME. Released November 1971. Atlantic.

Although Genesis is heralded as one of the legends of progressive rock, their progressive phase (from 1971 to 1977) really constitutes a rather short segment of their overall history. *Nursery Cryme,* however, is an essential slice of early U.K. prog rock, and its sound doesn't seem even remotely like the later directions of this group's lineup (Peter Gabriel, Phil Collins, Tony Banks, Mike Rutherford, Steve Hackett), especially when their current gigantic solo careers are considered.

At the time of its release, *Nursery Cryme* was representative of the new "serious rock." Influenced by early King Crimson, Yes, and ELP, the band's sound here is an attractive blend of 12-string guitars, flute, and mellotron with bass, drums, organ, piano, electric guitar, and vocals. It is storytelling music, alternating between vocal parts and instrumental sections.

Nursery Cryme is notable for three lengthy epics of power and grandeur: "The Musical Box," representative of the band's theatrical and visual style; "The Return of the Giant Hogweed," a bizarre chunky groove; and "The Fountain of Salmacis," a piece of spacey classicism with outstanding lyrics. These are eccentric, no matter how you look at them, and all three were long-time staples of Genesis' live shows. The connection with fantasy themes brings the music in a direction which allows for dramatic chord changes and extrapolations. An entire landscape is thus painted, and within it dialogues and conflicts are played out. With these three numbers, Genesis established a powerful prog rock persona, a style to be continued on their next few releases.

The rest of the album is more typical of the band's later and current approaches, such as the brief folksy "For Absent Friends" (sung by Collins) and ballad-style "Harlequin." These, plus "Seven Stones" and "Harold the Barrel," really aren't progressive, but rather straight-ahead rock, having more in common with other U.K. bands from the period such as The Who, Led Zeppelin, and Deep Purple.

The production is very good, capturing a live, raw feel, and introducing Collins's big drum sound, a key feature of the music of Genesis. The legendary cover art by Paul Whitehead portrays the fairy tales told in the music.

FOXTROT. Released October 1972. Atlantic.

This recording is another classic, so similar to *Nursery Cryme* it sounds as if they were recorded at the same time. Even from the perspective of 1972, Genesis was an odd band. The whole of *Foxtrot* is pretty bizarre, and an aura of mystery and subculture imagery permeates the music, the song titles, the lyrics, the cover art, and even the band's appearance. Again, the longer tracks work best for them, as they did live in concert.

"Watcher of the Skies" opens with a loud Gothic church organ intro, followed by a heavy rhythm section groove complete with lots of bass guitar riffs, anchoring the song's clearly defined structure and buildup drama (assisted by the piece's oblique lyrics). "Time Table" is another ballad more in the later Genesis style, with a prettiness that is more rock than prog. "Get 'Em Out by Friday," a lengthy tale of present-day class warfare, takes Genesis' concepts and jamming into the world of social commentary — something they would later expand upon. Unfortunately, the song is led by dated, moldy organ sounds and tamborine shaking. "Can-Utility and the Coastliners" is perhaps the pick for weirdest Genesis song; it is quite successful musically, but the lyrics are practically incomprehensible.

"Horizons" is an all-too-brief (at 1½ minutes) acoustic guitar instrumental by Steve Hackett. It's very nice. "Supper's Ready," the group's legendary dramatic epic, sums up the sound and approach of the band in this period, and served as a rallying point of sorts for the group's audiences. A 23-minute conceptual track with several sections, from soft acoustic to hard electric, its structure is (still) quite avant-garde. The lyrical content is actually the most avant-garde, with free-form poetic asides that culminate in an oddly metaphysical good-versus-evil imagery, providing the themes for the track's final minutes of catharsis. This new "serious" rock music was linked to a kind of transformative spiritual experience, supported by classically influenced structures and modern electric instrumentation, all of which are essential components of prog rock. The playing is top-notch all round, and the album is a superb, cohesive group effort.

The sound of the first half of the album is flawed; it has an erratic mix and a good amount of hiss, and the dynamics are not sharp or punchy enough. The sound quality thankfully improves for the second half. The cover art, again by Paul Whitehead, like the art for *Nursery Cryme,* illustrates the fairy tales found within the music.

LIVE. Released August 1973. Atlantic.

Recorded (at two locations) before appreciative audiences in February 1973, this first live album from Genesis is an effective representation of the band. Rawer than the studio versions of these songs, with ballsier instrumentation, higher volume, and energetic delivery, it presents Genesis as a heavy, loud prog rock group. This is a powerful, well-recorded set of five songs ("Watcher of the Skies," "Get 'Em Out by Friday," "The Return of the Giant Hogweed," "Musical Box," and "The Knife"). The major reason for Genesis' impact was not visual, as was so often claimed at the time, but

Genesis (1976 lineup with Bill Bruford). From left to right, Phil Collins, Mike Rutherford, Bill Bruford, Tony Banks, Steve Hackett.

musical. The tight and driving arrangements stand out, with the anchors of the group being Collins's crisp drums and Rutherford's muscular bass. The performances here are youthful and unpolished, representative of the group's music before they perfected their sound. It was shows such as that captured on *Live* that generated the acclaim Genesis began receiving.

Peter Gabriel was charming to hear in this era, presenting (although only briefly glimpsed on this release) a stage persona as a prog rock storyteller—a mysterious traveler illustrating and acting out the characters from the band's songs. This persona has been quite influential and oft-imitated, especially by many 1980s U.K. neo-prog bands. Hackett shows unbelievable restraint as a lead guitarist (too much so to some tastes). Only on "The Knife" does he really let it rip. Banks's keyboards are much further up-front, more at home with the rhythmic playing from Collins and Rutherford than with the guitar or vocals.

The classic sleeve photos of the band on a small stage, seen in dark blue lighting, and with Gabriel in a weird costume, exudes an undeniable aura mystery that makes anyone seeing this album for the first time want to know what it sounds like. *Live,* then, is a perfect introductory disc for the progressive rock initiate, with a potent Genesis proving themselves to be one of the genre's leading innovators.

SELLING ENGLAND BY THE POUND. Released September 1973. Atlantic.

Coming just a month after the release of *Live, Selling England by the Pound* is mainstream prog rock, another good entry-level disc for newcomers from a much beloved era of the Genesis band. The arrangements are more multitextured and opened up a bit. Acoustic colorations of 12-string and nylon guitars from Hackett (whose guitars are more in evidence here) are at the center of the sound, while Banks expands his sounds as well, with more synths in addition to the mellotron, organ, and piano. Collins's extra percussive touches are imaginative and lively. The sound is light, pretty, and easy to like. The lyrical focus is now totally on contemporary British themes in a distinctly narrative (and wordy) form. This was now the trademark Genesis approach, as exemplified by the first piece, "Dancing with the Moonlit Knight."

The 9½-minute "Firth of Fifth" is one of the band's finest songs. Supremely dramatic, with metaphysical lyrics, it's a perfect showcase for all of the members' talents: a rapid classical piano intro and outro from Banks; a flute solo from Gabriel; chunky bass lines from Rutherford; precise symphonic drumming from Collins; and a very emotional, spiritual, mournful spacey solo by Hackett's electric guitar. "The Battle of Epping Forest," an 11½-minute epic jam, is not a medieval tale but rather one about present-day street toughs. "After the Ordeal" is a low-key 4-minute instrumental—quite rare in their repertoire at the time—featuring acoustic and electric guitars, piano, flute, bass, and drums. It's nice but surprisingly fey, even for 1973, and the opposite of the loud approach on the *Live* disc. The interplay among drums, keys, and bass on the 11-minute "The Cinema Show," is a keynote of the Genesis sound. While the mix here is too thin, this is one of their best and most representative pieces.

"I Know What I Like" and "More Fool Me" aren't prog, but rather pop. "I Know . . ." was their first hit single, and "More Fool . . ." is notable as an early lead vocal by Collins.

The album's 54-minute running length was quite generous for a 1973 release. The sound quality is very good. The lovely cover painting reflects the album's lighter sound.

THE LAMB LIES DOWN ON BROADWAY. Released November 1974. Atlantic.

The Lamb . . . is Genesis at their most didactic and ambitious. The concept album to end all concept albums, this obscure, verbose, epic-scale work probably couldn't be done today. Genesis certainly deserves a lot of credit for the project. Just as they were breaking through in the charts, they performed this vast work in its entirety on tour in 1974 before it had even been released. What a crazy move!

The Lamb . . . , which is difficult and demands a lot from the listener, is not easily assimilated in a few listens. This complexity is what makes the album progressive, despite the fact that much of it is quite poppy, vocal, chorus-heavy rock (e.g., the title track, "Counting Out Time," "Carpet Crawl," "Lillywhite Lilith," etc.). It does go through a number of intriguing moods, though, and conveys classy sense of cerebral drama. A film of the piece was going to be made, but unfortunately it never happened. A problem with *The Lamb . . .* is that it really needs to be seen as well as heard. Genesis performed the work many times complete with an extensive slide show and costumes illustrating the story, but these performances were never filmed either.

The Lamb . . . contains this band's most experimental instrumental pieces, a side to the group that wasn't really developed to the extent that it could have been. "The Waiting Room," a 5½-minute track, begins with a number of odd percussions à la King Crimson, followed by a collage of tape effects, random synth sounds, and guitar noodling, eventually mutating into a full-band jam. This piece is a big favorite on bootlegs, as it was apparently played slightly differently each time. "Hairless Heart" and "Ravine" are two brief and similar pieces of soft guitar textures of poignant delicacy. "Silent Sorrow in Empty Boats" is a celestial low-key, keyboard-dominated instrumental, again too brief. One wishes Genesis had explored these instrumental areas further.

The group's forte is their vocal pieces. This was a showcase for Gabriel, whose lyrics here are truly fine poetry. Regrettably, the album is a bit *too* word-heavy, which at certain points obscures some fine musical colors that are part of the story line. (The subject matter—a street tough—was certainly an unexpected choice—an attempt on their part to avoid the flowery prettiness of their fantasy-heavy earlier material.)

"In the Cage" and "Riding the Scree" successfully capture the ominous new gritty feel, with rollercoaster keyboard/bass/drums workouts that demonstrate the by-now solidified core band interplay of Banks, Collins, and Rutherford. "Back in NYC," on the other hand, is somewhat plodding and murky in its attempt at a darker Genesis sound. Gabriel is most successful as a vocalist on this album, keeping the variety of moods (e.g., the cooing of "Cuckoo Cocoon" and the heavily filtered rants of "The Grand Parade of Lifeless Packaging") consistently intriguing. Hackett's playing is extraordinarily elusive throughout much of *The Lamb . . .*; it is difficult at times to pin down exactly what sounds are his, though by the second half his guitar is more at the forefront, taking center stage for numbers like the metaphysical wrap up masterpiece "It."

The sound mix of *The Lamb . . .* is interesting. The sound quality is good, particularly in the all-important remastered version (the others were murky), but the production itself is rather odd and too thin for the supposedly more muscular sound they were aiming for. The bizarre high-art photos by Hipgnosis that adorn *The Lamb . . .* brilliantly represent key abstract images from the story line.

A TRICK OF THE TAIL. Released February 1976. Atlantic.

This is one of the most successful and most popular of Genesis' prog-era releases. The Genesis sound is perfected here, with a truly first-rate production that rivals their later audiophile recordings like *Abacab*. The clarity and richness of the guitars and keyboards, and a drum sound that's way up in the front of the mix, produce a huge sound that's as rich as a high-calorie dessert.

Gabriel was gone by now, and Collins's vocal performance was a major landmark for him and for Genesis. His emergence as one of the music world's greatest vocalists is already well in evidence on *A Trick of the Tail*. The lyrics are also very strong, with a leftist sociopolitical perspective, as on "Dance on a Volcano" and "Squonk." Banks here has a writing credit on every track, and the successes of the 1976 era of Genesis is in large part due to his vision.

"Entangled" features an essential progressive rock texture—a gorgeous, silken web of multiple 12-string acoustic guitars combined with mellotron, organ, and grand piano. While they had used this sound for years, here it is true magic, with a recording standard they didn't have previously. All the subtleties in Hackett's and Rutherford's guitar playing are beautifully captured, with a fantastic stereo separation that puts you directly in the middle of those trademark textures.

A Trick of the Tail is a vocal-oriented prog album. There's a refreshing streak of romanticism in "Ripples" and "Mad Man Moon" that is perfectly suited to their sound. Collins's vocal delivery on these is exemplary. As usual, the lively interplay between Collins's drums and Banks's keyboards is the group's centerpiece, elevating basically pop numbers like "Robbery Assault and Battery" and giving them a prog rock excitement. There's not much in the way of electric guitar on *A Trick of the Tail*, but strangely enough it isn't missed given the melodic lushness of the 12 strings and keyboards.

"Los Endos" is one of Genesis' finest compositions. Compiling the musical themes of the various songs on the album, it's a compelling, driving, extremely entertaining instrumental, a great song in its own right and a perfect finale to the album. The sounds in the piece, all brilliantly recorded and mixed, represent all the facets of the Genesis prog era sound rolled into one.

The cover artwork emphasizes the playful fantasy elements that are found in the lyrics of the title track, giving the album a warm appeal.

WIND AND WUTHERING. Released December 1976. Atlantic.

The often-underrated follow-up to *A Trick of the Tail, Wind and Wuthering* is actually one of Genesis' best discs, and certainly one of their most progressive. This is Genesis at their most symphonic, with extended instrumental sections. An ambitious album similar in structure to *A Trick of the Tail,* the production is once again first-rate, lush and textured, with Banks's influence most prominent. The album is like a glossier, more polished *Foxtrot,* with keyboard-driven compositions of sophisticated, lengthy storytelling rock. The vocals are not too up front in the mix, putting the emphasis on the music. The mix of Hackett's acoustic, nylon, and classical guitars with Banks's ARP synth, grand piano, mellotron, organ, and electric piano, plus Collins's spot-on drumming, achieve a sound on that's as large and attractive as any in prog rock. Collins's vocals are keenly appropriate, especially considering he doesn't care for this material. Gabriel couldn't have done any better.

"One for the Vine" is one of the most notable Genesis compositions. Another lengthy (at 10 minutes) dramatic metaphysical tale that goes through a variety of moods and sounds, it's quite ambitious, and so successfully executed that it goes by almost a bit too smoothly considering its lyrical depth and musical grandeur. An amazing track. At the other end of the spectrum, however, is "Your Own Special Way," a blatant pop song sandwiched in between the progressive songs, which is more in the flavor of something from their 1986 *Invisible Touch* disc. "All in a Mouse's Night" sort of picks up where the fantasy themes in the song "A Trick of the Tail" ended, and is musically interesting, but too cutesy lyrically.

"Wot Gorilla?" is a 3-minute instrumental that comes on like a grander Brand X, once again focusing on the symphonic interplay between Banks's keyboards and Collins's percussion. "Blood on the Rooftops" is similar to the material from Hackett's *Voyage of the Acolyte,* with its classical guitar and spacey mellotron parts and a wistful vocal from Collins. "Afterglow" is more romanticism from Banks, and has excellent lyrics. Here Collins's vocal is too restrained, something he would improve upon on subsequent live performances.

The two-part instrumental "Unquiet Slumbers for the Sleepers . . . In That Quiet Earth" demonstrates what Genesis was capable of when they wrote nonvocal material. "Unquiet Slumbers . . ." features Hackett's sonorous guitar textures, combined with mellotron and bells. Spiritual, celestial, and spacey, it's a side of the group that's rarely heard.

The sound on this recording is very sharp, especially in the remastered version which is light years beyond the versions previously available, which were thin and muddled. The Hipgnosis cover is a dreamy painting of a gray landscape, perhaps inspired by the sonorities of "Unquiet Slumbers . . . ."

GENESIS IN CONCERT 1976 (video). Theatrical film released 1977. Laser disc import (Japan).

A 43-minute theatrical film of the Genesis summer tour in 1976 with Bill Bruford helping out on drums, this is perhaps the best way to experience the group's progressive era. It was the most successful filming of their performances up to that point. The footage of Genesis with Gabriel that had been filmed in past years for TV was darkly lit and suffered from technical difficulties. *Genesis in Concert 1976* is actually a wide-screen film, with a good stereo soundtrack, now available in this high-quality presentation on Japanese laser disc.

Not only are the performances outstanding, the visuals are truly remarkable. A slow tracking camera gives the concert footage a tense, unfolding feel. The visuals are well composed for the wide-screen format, and emphasize the dramatic aspects of the songs. The visual highlight is "Entangled," during which there is a fantasy sequence of a beautiful woman dancing on a beach as spacey effects wash through the picture.

Also visually notable is "Supper's Ready," which features imagery of the ruins of antiquity, a visual key to the song's message.

The film begins with "I Know What I Like," which is fun, particularly if you're a fan, though there's little that's really prog about it. "Fly on a Windshield" is next, an instrumental version of this cut from *The Lamb . . .* , and far superior to the vocal one. The band's dynamics here are much in evidence, as they go through a number of key prog rock moves despite the song's short running length. Hackett's soaring but modest electric guitar is the highlight. "The Carpet Crawlers" also features a superior guitar performance from Hackett (although the camera only shows us Collins singing). Hackett makes the piece his own with a silently suffering blues from the modest electric guitar, which quietly blazes away with tortured, low-key lament; it's the way the piece was meant to be heard, and is far superior to the thinner studio version on *The Lamb . . . .*

"The Cinema Show Pt. 2" is the instrumental section of that song, but with too much intercut footage of old silent movie comedies and not enough shots of the band. We do get to see a brief drum solo duet between Collins and Bruford, however. "Supper's Ready Pt. 2" is the more rocking half of the piece, and the performance is extraordinary. The bearded Collins looks like Jesus as he sings to the faithful crowd, which sways back and forth as he delivers the final lines, his image dissolving into a sea of red lighting, which then fades into the footage of the Greek ruins as Hackett solos on guitar. It's quite a transformative moment.

"Los Endos" concludes, and it's a ripping version, too, another real high point. The band plays up a storm, particularly Collins. The stereo sound is surprisingly good for a 1976 film recording, with wide separation, but not quite enough bass.

SECONDS OUT. Released October 1977. Atlantic.

The two-disc *Seconds Out* is a decent concert reprisal of selections from their entire progressive phase, from *Nursery Cryme* to *Wind and Wuthering*. While the group would continue to perform this material in the years to come, beginning with 1978's *And Then There Were Three*, the compositional focus of the group moves toward more conventional rock and pop. As a result, *Seconds Out* serves as a sort of farewell to the progressive Genesis.

Taken primarily from a 1977 show in Paris, this is Genesis at their arena-level dinosaur size, with a professional and calculated sound, quite removed from the small-sized rawness of earlier days such as that on 1973's *Live*. The expansive stereo mix is technically excellent, but at times the music sounds distant, lacking in color despite the clarity and volume. This was perhaps not the best time for Genesis to do a double live album. The 1976 tour was better, and there is one track ("Cinema Show") from that tour included here. The 1977 tour was a major trial by fire for new drummer Chester Thompson, who had to quickly learn some of the most complex drum parts in modern rock. He does quite well here, but would be even more in groove later on. With Collins away from the drum kit on half of this recording, the challenge for Collins as a vocalist is also formidable, and he's not as good as he could be. Songs like "Afterglow" would be delivered more passionately on 1982's *Three Sides Live*.

The first of the two discs is not as energetic as the second. The performances are a bit workmanlike, with a mix that emphasizes keyboards over guitars and bass. Although this was not necessarily a bad thing for Genesis, the sound occasionally lacks variety. Evidently Hackett's guitar was mixed down by the others after he left the band in 1977. The highlights of the first disc are "The Carpet Crawlers," a rendition where Collins's vocal eclipses Gabriel's, while Hackett's understated guitar tells the story; and "Firth of Fifth," another lucid moment of celestial sadness courtesy of Hackett's mournful soloing, made all the more effective by the dual drums of Thompson and Collins.

The second disc is excellent throughout. After a shaky start, "Supper's Ready" is pretty lively throughout and suitably dramatic, especially in the final wrap-up. Collins does quite well singing this, even though he has stated his dislike of the excessive verbiage of this era of Genesis.

The 1976 track "Cinema Show" with Bill Bruford has the best sound mix overall, with some lovely textures in the first half and a more up-front guitar. The extension of "I Know What I Like" is also groovy, and "Dance on a Volcano" and "Los Endos" display real instrumental fire, concluding *Seconds Out* on a high note.

THREE SIDES LIVE. Released May 1982. Atlantic.

Now reissued and superbly remastered in its original U.K. release format with all live material (the U.S. release replaced one-fourth of this with studio recordings), *Three Sides Live* contains tight and driving concert versions of some of their progressive era epics. This is a two-disc set taken mostly from their 1981 American tour for *Abacab,* and the first disc features selections from that album, *Duke,* and *And Then There Were Three.* This is well performed, albeit mainstream, rock. Beginning with the second track on disc two, the rest is solidly in the prog rock area.

"In the Cage," the "Cinema Show"/"Slippermen" medley, and "Afterglow" (all taken from the 1981 shows) move at an adrenalin-rousing pace and the transitions connecting the pieces are glorious. Collins's vocals (especially on "Afterglow") make these the preferable versions, his singing being more forceful, moody, and emotional than on previous releases. The rapid-fire drums of Chester Thompson and Collins are the prime movers of this recording, never missing a beat. The sound is good, even though the mix is at times a bit erratic.

A real treat are the 1980 concert versions of "One for the Vine" and "The Fountain of Salmacis" as 1980 was the last time they performed these pieces. The sound is great—crisp and lush. "One for the Vine" live is every inch the complex symphonic masterpiece it was on *Wind and Wuthering.* Thompson's drumming and Banks's keyboards are both exemplary here. "The Fountain of Salmacis" is fascinating; it's extremely interesting to hear Collins interpret this early material as a vocalist. And it's nice to hear the mellotron again, too.

From 1976 is "It/Watcher of the Skies," featuring Hackett and Bruford. "It" is performed in its entirety, while "Watcher . . ." is only a brief reprise. The two should have been separated in the disc's tracking, but they are decently done and the sound is good.

The track listing on this disc contains several errors. "One for the Vine" is divided over tracks 4 and 5. "The Fountain of Salmacis" and "It/Watcher of the Skies" are all part of track 6.

GOLEM

ORION AWAKES. Released 1973. Psi-Fi import.

Orion Awakes is a strange and entertaining form of instrumental psychedelic rock, from deep in the German underground scene of the early 1970s. This album is perhaps more potently psychedelic than any of the more famous German bands of that period, eschewing the sparseness of Agitation Free or the tightness of Guru Guru. Golem's focus is on the electric guitars (Willi Berghoff) and bass guitar (Mungo), with others on keyboards, drums, and additional guitar. Oddly enough, the sleepy guitar and bass drones are not that different from the instrumental moments of Sonic Youth. Murky, loud, and sloppy (they don't try to hide it), at first this doesn't appear to be all that extraordinary, but it unfolds as some of the dreamiest hard rock imaginable.

Berghoff and Mungo (who write all the material) deploy a variety of techniques to achieve their surreal atmospherics: feedback, wah-wah, processing, power chording, rumbles, and other textural combinations. Most notable about *Orion Awakes* is the way all the instruments seem to blend together, until none are really distinguishable. The keyboards and drums barely make their presence felt. Adding to the mood of opt-out trance is the unusually large amount of stoned knob twirling during the album's mixing—this is stereo panning galore—giving *Orion . . .* an unreal, thoroughly druggy sound.

The disc has five tracks, ranging in length from 6½ to 14½ minutes, with sci-fi titles like "Jupiter and Beyond" and "Stellar Launch." The sound quality is pretty good, with some hiss. Although *Orion Awakes* is now somewhat dated, that becomes an asset here, contributing to its otherworldly vibe. Evidently Genesis P. Orridge, later of Throbbing Gristle, was involved in this project as producer and co-writer (there can't be two people with a name like that!). The cover art is a Ron Cobb–like psychedelic drawing by Sandra Glenwright.

GONG

YOU. Released September 1974. Caroline.

You is a masterpiece of space rock, the best studio disc from the "classic" Gong lineup of Daevid Allen,

Tim Blake, Miquette Giraudy, Steve Hillage, Mike Howlett, Didier Malherbe, Pierre Moerlen, and Gilli Smyth. Previous Gong discs have a certain psychedelized folksy charm, to be sure, but the productions are weak and the material more vocal-oriented. This lineup is probably best represented by the many excellent live discs that are available (see below). However, *You* is the most successful studio recording from this era of Gong both because of crisper production values and because the various members are at their best in the lengthier numbers, of which there are many.

You is the third of the Radio Gnome trilogy, the first two being 1973's *Flying Teapot* and *Angel's Egg*. The lyrical and conceptual aspect of *You* is really more of a sound color for vocalists Allen, Smyth, and Giraudy, and provides a psychedelic fairy-tale context for the space rock jamming. It's easier to listen to than to follow as a story, so don't be overly concerned with knowing all the ins and outs of the complex fantasy concept.

You opens with three short (1 to 2 minutes each) pieces. "Thoughts for Naught" features brief drunken vocal exchanges, spacey flutes, vibes, and synth. "A P.H.P.'s Advice" is a sprightly ditty with vibes and sax. "Magick Mother Invocation" combines bassy ritual moans with Smyth's "space whisper" vocals and Blake's percolating synth. The 6-minute "Master Builder" begins with synth bleeps from Blake, accompanied by a creeping rhythm section, then grows more aggressive with the addition of Malherbe's sax. It then abruptly stops for some stereo nature sounds and Hillage's guitar licks, panning from one channel to the other, culminating in a driving, heavy space rock jam.

The 9-minute "A Sprinkling of Clouds" has a more celestial electronic opening, with an extended buildup from Blake's widely separated stereo synthesizer soundscapes, finally joined by Moerlen's jazzy drums and Howlett's bass. Hillage then unleashes a blazing acid rock solo, after which the piece returns to a jazzy swing with Malherbe's flute and sax. "A Perfect Mystery," a humorous folksy groove about police at your door is sung by Allen and Smyth.

The 10½-minute "Isle of Everywhere" is one of Gong's finest pieces—a beautiful example of instrumental space rock. It starts with a funky bass groove from Howlett and an aggressive percussion attack from Moerlen, with Smyth's space whisper and Blake's synth swooshes layered in, followed by raging solos from Malherbe's sax and Hillage's guitar, both in true spacey form. The final piece, the 11½-minute "You Never Blow Yr Trip Forever" is a return to Allen's early 1970s exploration of psychedelia, complete with unexpected twists and his bizarre scatting and vocalizing. There are some great grooves on this piece by the band.

You is a solid group effort, with all members giving impressive performances. The space rock sound of *You* is a direct influence on later prog rock groups like Ozric Tentacles and Melting Euphoria. The cover art, with its pyramids, stars, planets, and mandalas, emphasizes the strong cosmic context of the album.

SHAMAL. Released December 1975. Caroline.

Quite different from the Daevid Allen–led Gong, *Shamal* retains Howlett, Moerlen, and Malherbe from the *You* lineup, adding percussionist Mirielle Bauer (playing marimba, glockenspiel, xylophone, and gongs) and keyboardist Patrice Lemoine. The music is not free-form space rock, but rather composed and structured fusion with a virtuoso band interplay. With Nick Mason of Pink Floyd as producer, the group has a polished, smooth, clear sound and very few rough edges. All five members have writing credits. Howlett assumes lead vocal duties on this recording, his final appearance on a Gong disc. Guest Jorge Pinchevsky provides violin on several tracks, and is his playing a welcome element in the mix.

The 6½-minute "Wingful of Eyes" opens with a chunky bass groove, flute, vibes, vocals, and acoustic guitar. The lyrics are a clever, fantasy oriented type of social commentary. Steve Hillage and Miquette Giraudy guest on this track (and on "Bambooji"). Hillage contributes a saucy electric guitar solo on "Wingful . . . ," which then leads into the second track, the 7-minute "Chandra." The first half of this piece is funky jazz, similar to Weather Report and Zao, with sax and synth solos. The second part is a vocal section, which follows the funkiness of the piece with Howlett's rhythmic delivery of hippie-style pitter-patter lyrics. It's all quite a lot of fun.

The amazing 5-minute instrumental "Bambooji" is next, opening with wind sounds, Malherbe's bamboo flutes, xylophone, and a light vocal texture from Giraudy. It almost sounds like something by Deuter. The piece then goes into a classic groove, with bass, drums, and Hillage's electric, suddenly stops for a Jade Warrior–like Oriental break with bells, flute, acoustic guitar, and percussion, and finally ends with more wind sounds.

Two more instrumentals follow. The 7½-minute "Cat in Clark's Shoes" is a tasty fusion, with a great groove from the rhythm section and some infectious violin, sax, and synth parts. The 5-minute "Mandrake" is a kind of blueprint for the Gong sound that characterizes their next few releases, especially the sound found on 1978's *Expresso II* (see below). A percussion-dominated piece featuring vibraphones and xylophone, this is a showcase for Moerlen and Bauer. The concluding 9-minute title track has a heavy groove with bass, drums, sax, and violin, which mutates into a funky soul, almost commercial sound à la Steely Dan, with a guest vocal by Sandy Colley.

Shamal is an excellent album. Howlett's bass playing especially is notable throughout, and his vocals are competent. The cover photo of sand dunes reflects the flavor of "Bambooji," one of the recording's outstanding tracks.

GAZEUSE! Released December 1976. Caroline.

Quite different from earlier recordings, even from *Shamal, Gazeuse!* is a classic Gong disc, a strong ensemble all-instrumental effort. Moerlen, Malherbe, and Bauer are joined by Allan Holdsworth on guitars and violin, Francis Moze (from a 1973 lineup of Gong) on bass and piano, and two additional percussionists—Mino Cinelou and Moerlen's brother, Benoit. The music is very much percussion-driven, with a muscular, crispy production by Dennis Mackay (who produced Brand X at this time). Mackay does a fantastic job of layering the sounds of the four different percussionists. Pierre Moerlen's drumming is of the same calibre as Bill Bruford's and Phil Collins's. The album, with compositions by Pierre Moerlen, Holdsworth, and Moze, is in keeping with similar pioneer fusion groups of the era, such as Brand X, Bruford, Passport, and Return to Forever.

Gazeuse! begins with the 6-minute "Expresso," a swinging big-band fusion, with all the members playing up a storm. "Night Illusion" is next—3½ minutes of chunky, heavy rock fusion with Holdsworth's trademark tortured rhythm and lead guitar sounds, Moze's up-front bass, and aggressive drums by Moerlen.

"Percolations Parts 1 and 2" is a 10-minute showcase for bandleader Moerlen and the other percussionists, beginning with a light, gorgeous tapestry of sound and a nice violin texture from Holdsworth. Then the rock heavy drum solo by Moerlen kicks in, tasteful and not over the top. This track is essential for percussion fans.

The 7½-minute "Shadows Of" is similar to "Night Illusion"; it has a slower tempo and is more wistful, though it does include some heavy jamming, and a nice flute solo from Malherbe. The 8-minute "Esnuria" is another funky percussion showcase, with a beefy rhythm guitar, fretless bass, and sax. The final piece, the 4-minute "Mirielle," written by Moze for Bauer, is a welcome change of pace. A soft electric piano and acoustic guitar create a somber jazz texture, which then concludes with an acoustic piano.

The attractive cover art of a kaleidoscope of colors and shapes is simple, but effectively conveys the variety of colors in the album's excellent music.

LIVE ETC. Released October 1977. Caroline.

Recorded during 1973–1975, this 78½-minute disc is perhaps the best album from the group's "classic" lineup (see the review of 1974's *You,* above). And, despite the fact that Gong has always been better live than in the studio (due to the importance of the visual aspects of their shows), *Live Etc.* is a raucous and fascinating listen. The material is taken from *Camembert Electrique* (1971), *Flying Teapot* and *Angel's Egg* (both 1973), and *You,* making this a good introduction to all facets of this Gong lineup. This album is clearly tighter and more energetic than the studio releases, with excellent, crisp recording values and a drum sound that really cuts, all of which were lacking on most of the above discs. The album, co-produced by Howlett, has an attractive widely separated stereo sound that was characteristic of live recordings from this era (e.g., the lead vocals are set in one channel and then echoed in the other, and the stereo reproduction of Blake's synth effects is accurate).

Gong (1976–1977 lineup). From left to right, top: Allan Holdsworth, Pierre Moerlen, Didier Malherbe; from left to right, bottom: Francis Moze, Benoit Moerlen, Mirielle Bauer.

"You Can't Kill Me" and "Zero the Hero & the Witch's Spell" are from a May 1973 Paris show (the same concert found in its entirety on the Gong disc *Live In Paris—Bataclan 1973;* see review below). "You Can't Kill Me" is the ultimate Daevid Allen Gong song, perhaps the most well known and accessible, with his tripped out vocals, arena-sized riffs from Hillage, and lots of bashing and crashing drumming from Moerlen. "Zero . . ." is an 11-minute epic with Allen's trademark scats and echoed vocals, some very tight and active drumming by Moerlen, Smyth's "space whispers" and shrieks in French (also heavily echoed, which may be irritating to some and confusing to others, but that's the point), and space rock textures from sax and synth.

"Flying Teapot," from a September 1973 Edinburgh gig, is a key track of the Radio Gnome concept. It is one of their staple live numbers, livelier here than on the album of the same name. A rather chorus-heavy song, it nonetheless allows for some trademark space guitar and synth, as well as a drum solo.

"Dynamite/I Am Your Animal," "6/8 Tune," and "Est-Ce Que Je Suis" are from a Roanne concert August of 1973. "Dynamite/I Am . . ." opens with a playful sax and a heavy space guitar workout, going into creeping, teasing, mysterioso vocals and screams by Smyth, with Hawkwind-like swooshes of cheesy synth backing. This follows with "6/8 Tune," a jazzy fusion/space instrumental that sounds like a bizarre combination of Dzyan, Tangerine Dream, and Passport. The tune takes us directly into "Est-Ce . . . ," an irresistably grooving and fun number sung in French, with tour-de-force screwball vocal antics by Allen.

An absolutely masterful BBC radio appearance from January of 1974 is next, with Rob Tate sitting in on drums for Moerlen. "Radio Gnome Invisible" begins with a brief gurgling narration by Allen about the Radio Gnome story. Allen is truly in a psychedelic pied piper mode—his forte—on pieces like this. The song is an amalgram of styles, similar to the Bonzo Dog Band, with entertaining off-the-wall humor and time shifts. There is an incredible goofball vocal by Malherbe in the middle of the piece, and a loud, up-front ballsy guitar solo by Hillage, all accompanied by a space-cadet backing vocal from guest Di Stewart. The studio version sounds almost straight in comparison. This is truly a progressive music, pulling the listener into another perception of performance, groove, and song structure. "Oily Way" is a hilarious vocal number with flute and guitar tradeoffs. It's one of their most famous songs, and also very Bonzo-like. The brief "Outer Temple" is a short chorus about drinking tea, while the 5-minute instrumental "Inner Temple" features Smyth's space whispers and a classic rhythm section groove over which the guitar, sax, and synth solo in a drifting, supremely spacey fashion.

Interrupting the flow of the disc somewhat is the inclusion of "Where Have All the Flowers Gone," a studio cut from the *You* sessions. This uncharacteristic 3-minute folk number, with its harmonica solos, country western vocals, and hand percussion is strange and out of place here. It should have been a bonus track on the *You* CD instead.

Perhaps the highlight of *Live Etc.* is the all-instrumental set from London in September 1975, featuring the *Shamal* lineup with Steve Hillage and Miquette Giraudy still in the group (although credited here, Giraudy doesn't really have a presence on this disc). Here Hillage's guitar and Howlett's bass are much farther up front in the music than at any other point, and the four core members (Moerlen and Malherbe are the other two) deliver very, very tight virtuoso performances of the material from the *You* album. The recording quality of this show is immaculate.

"Isle of Everywhere" is 10½ minutes of space rock nirvana, thoroughly eclipsing even the superb version on *You.* Howlett and Moerlen begin an addictive groove, assisted by the keyboards of Lemoine and percussion from Bauer, followed by some truly memorable solos from Malherbe and Hillage. The beginning of Hillage's intense solo is the deft touch of a master guitar wizard. "Isle . . ." leads into the 2½-minute angular "Get It Inner," an improvisational piece with a fantastic anchoring bass by Howlett. This album's version of "Master Builder" is another superior live rendition. The disc concludes with a 2-minute reprise of "Flying Teapot."

EXPRESSO II. Released April 1978. Caroline.

Quite different from the previous releases *Shamal* and *Gazeuse! Expresso II* is another classic fusion album. The group is now totally percussion-led, retaining the Moerlen brothers, Bauer, and Hansford Rowe on bass. The writing is by all four members. There are no keyboards or sax, making the sound considerably different from before. Guesting on guitar is Mick Taylor (of the Rolling Stones), Allan Holdsworth (no longer a full-time member of Gong by this point), and Bon Lozaga (who was later to lead a group called Gongzilla with Benoit Moerlen in the 1990s). In addition to the drums, vibraphones, marimbas, bells, and xylophones of the three core percussionists, there is yet another percussionist, guest Francois Causse on congas. Daryl Way of Curved Air plays violin on some tracks, which is welcome and well suited to the lighter sounds of the various percussive instruments.

The 6½-minute "Heavy Tune" is an irresistable live-sounding rocking fusion number with audiophile-quality sonics. A monster groove is laid down by Moerlen's drums and the guitars of Taylor and Holdsworth, with up-front punctuating bass lines by Rowe. Despite the middle section of the piece being lightened by the vibes, the song lives up to its title. It's a good cut to test stereo systems with.

The 5-minute "Golden Dilemma" is a driving firestorm of percussion, both light and heavy, with simple rhythm guitar patterns giving the core band a groove to play off of. Fun stuff. The 7-minute "Sleepy" is vibe-dominated tasty fusion that goes through many changes and features solos from Holdsworth and Way. The plentiful bass riffery and atypical Holdsworth guitar sounds on the 7½-minute "Soli" give room for Benoit Moerlen's vibe solos, but the music begins to ramble a bit, as on the aptly titled 6½-minute "Boring."

The vibes are a major element of the compositions on *Expresso II,* and while the music is very good, the overall effect lightens the sound too much and too often for the tight, complex fusion context. Despite the sections of "vibes overkill," the sound is fantastic, and although the mix is a bit erratic at moments, the level of variety is wonderful when the vibes aren't dominating. The cover of *Expresso II* is the first Gong album to actually feature a gong on the front.

Pierre and Benoit Moerlen, Rowe, and Lozaga went on to form the group Pierre Moerlen's Gong, which released several albums beginning in 1979 and on through the 1980s. The compositions of that group, however, suffer in comparison to the previous albums made by Gong, and merely retool the sounds of "Expresso II." The best release by them is 1980's *Pierre Moerlen's Gong Live,* which contains several Gong-era numbers as well as new material, but has yet to be issued on CD.

LIVE IN PARIS—BATACLAN 1973. Released October 1989. Mantra import.

This is the entire 76½-minute May 1973 Paris concert, two tracks from which were featured on the earlier *Live Etc.* disc. It's a legendary performance, demonstrating that Gong was one of the oddest and most eclectic progressive bands of the 1970s. This concert recording captures a lot of musical moves not found on the studio discs. The 17-minute "Dynamite"/"I Am Your Animal" is Gong at their spaciest, with a lengthy intro by Blake's synth and Smyth's space whispers. It's a great buildup improv, gradually moving from the ethereal to the louder, harder, and sharper until a raging Smyth vocal with very successful echo delay effects kicks in, more aggressive and varied than usual, concluding with a psych-out solo by Hillage's guitar. "Tic Toc" and "Taliesin" are new titles for "Zero the Hero & The Witch's Spell" from *Live Etc.,* but the sound quality is not as good.

Smyth is at her best on *Live in Paris,* with works like "Inside Your Head" and "Pussy." "Inside . . ." has some effective constructions by the band, who use their respective sounds as a storytelling background to the bizarre occult lyrics. Smyth's vocals are alternately hypnotic and jarring, and authentically psychedelic. "Pussy" is an excellent 6-minute bizarre rock track, a vehicle for chanteuse Smyth's over-the-top mania.

The 4½-minute "Flute Salad" is a showcase for Malherbe's flute, an impassioned performance with a delicate vocal in French. "Flying Teapot" has a great drum solo by Moerlen, complete with huge echo effects. "Wet Drum Sandwich" is an energetic encore improv.

Unfortunately, the sound on this release isn't as sharp as on *Live Etc.,* having quite a lot of stage buzzes, clicks, and hiss, but the stereo is good. In the accompanying booklet, there is a lengthy text about the band, in French. There's also a great color centerfold photo of the band sitting meditating (albeit humorously) around a mandala.

LIVE AT SHEFFIELD 1974. Released 1990. Mantra import.

This album has the same lineup as *Live in Paris* but without Smyth (although she is credited in the booklet). The 58-minute *Live at Sheffield 1974* has much better sound than the Paris show, with a clearer and cleaner mix and less hiss and interference. All members are in peak form, especially Malherbe, whose playing is at the center of the music on this disc.

The 11-minute "Crystal Gnome" opens with some characteristic space synth from Blake, followed by a nice improv buildup by the band, with Allen's vocal scatting and Malherbe's sax blowing. This is prime Gong. The versions of "Radio Gnome I and II" and "Flying Teapot" are more subdued, with a jazzier tempo and more blowing than usual from Malherbe. All the instrumental transitions work smoothly for the band, and the vocal tradeoffs between Allen and Malherbe are classic.

"Mister Pyxie" and "Deep in the Sky" are "Zero the Hero & The Witch's Spell" retitled again, dominated this time by Malherbe with a jazzy flute solo that lightens the piece at first, but concludes with a blazing sax solo. "Wet Drum Sandwich" is another Moerlen drum solo, while the 3½-minute oddity "Mange Ton Calepin" is a piece of jazz rock by Malherbe, led by his sax and Allen's storytelling antics.

This essential Gong disc ends with a bonus track, a song recorded live from a 1989 Gong reunion lineup featuring Allen and Malherbe with

Gong (1996 reunion tour lineup). From left to right, Mike Howlett, Steffi Sharpstrings, Gilli Smyth, Daevid Allen, Didier Malherbe, Pip Pyle.

an unidentified female lead vocalist and band. The 10½-minute "Titicaca" is a folksy ditty, with Allen's acoustic guitar and Malherbe's flute accompanied by fiddles and percussion.

GOTIC

ESCENES. Released March 1978. Fonomusic import.

The most acclaimed progressive disc from Portugal, Gotic's *Escenes* is a true classic—one of the finest instrumental prog rock recordings ever. Delicate textures of flute, keyboards, and acoustic guitar combine with crisp drumming, virtuoso up-front bass guitar, and tasteful, sparing electric guitar solos. Nothing in the ingenious and very tight arrangements is out of place, and every ounce of melodic juice is coaxed out of each track. In terms of comparisons, this is similar to Camel's *The Snow Goose.*

Gotic is a four-piece group (Rafael Escote, bass; Jordi Marti, drums; Jep Nuix, flute; and Jordi Vilaprinyo, keyboards and violin) with several guests on guitars, percussion, and keyboards. The music on this album is easy to like—friendly, sunny, and bright. The performances are all incredible, though at 37 minutes *Escenes* goes by all too quickly. The production by the group is first-rate (except for some obtrusive hiss), with a widely separated and open soundstage. The compositions are by Escote, Nuix, and Vilaprinyo.

Escenes features six short pieces, ranging from 3½ to 6 minutes, and concludes with one long piece, the 10-minute "Historia D'Una Gota D'Aigua." The ultra-melodicism of Nuix's flutes and Vilaprinyo's keyboards, reinforced by Marti's percussion and anchored by Escote's bass, defines the sound of this band. "Jocs D'Ocells," with its breezy, memorable melodies led by the flute, deft cymbal brushes, and simple piano is typical of the music of *Escenes.* This is also storytelling music, as evidenced in the different movements of "La Revolucio." The lengthy final piece is a grand, symphonic buildup, opening with soft acoustic guitars and flute and ending with a restrained electric guitar, sparingly used to dramatic effect.

The lovely cover art paintings are similar to that of Roger Dean's inviting fantasy landscapes for Yes.

GRYPHON

RED QUEEN TO GRYPHON THREE. Released December 1974. Progressive.

Gryphon originally appeared on the U.K. music scene in 1973 as a somewhat old-fashioned folk band. In late 1974, they released this, their ambitious third album, which is a classic of instrumental symphonic prog rock. Amazingly adept at this change, the band constructed a huge, aggressive electric sound. The sound recalls Yes, though at times the music sounds like instrumental Jethro Tull à la their 1977 album *Songs from the Wood.* The music of *Red Queen . . .* is complex and lively, with lots of contrapuntal shifts, integrating such unlikely instruments as crumhorns, bassoons, and recorders with the guitars, bass, drums, and keyboards, giving this album a unique sound.

The performances of all players in this five-piece group (Richard Harvey, keyboards, recorders, crumhorn; Graeme Taylor, guitars; Brian Gulland, bassoon, crumhorn; David Oberle, drums; and Philip Nestor, bass) are brilliant. The mix is masterful and the sound is audiophile quality. The production is by the band, which certainly knew how to work in a studio. The music is multilayered and sophisticated, moving at a rapid pace.

There are four lengthy pieces, between 8 and 11 minutes ("Opening Move," "Second Spasm," "Lament," and "Checkmate") all written by the band. There are several attractive breaks for the crumhorns, bassoons, and recorder in each, all refreshingly welcome. Taylor's guitar work is notable, as on "Lament"'s gorgeous, lush, multiple acoustic guitar sections. Harvey's synths are also smoothly utilized, and are reminiscent of Rick Wakeman.

Throughout *Red Queen . . .* there are several moments where Gryphon reaches the heights of their U.K. prog rock peers, and if they had released more albums like this one, they might have achieved supergroup status. Evidently *Red Queen . . .* alienated their original audience, and on later releases they attempted a more commercial sound (similar to later Gentle Giant) with vocals and shorter songs. This approach didn't work for them either. *Red Queen to Gryphon Three* deserves the status of a 1970s prog rock classic, especially for its deft distillation of the most compelling and attractive elements of instrumental symphonic prog.

The cover is a great fantasy painting of a medieval philosopher contemplating his next chess move.

TOM GURALNICK

BROKEN DANCES FOR MUTED PIECES. Released November 1995. Nonsequitur.

Broken Dances for Muted Pieces is an incredibly inventive collection of 14 improvisational pieces, recorded live direct to digital (and sounding fantastic), using tenor and soprano saxophones that have been modified with homemade mutes and augmented by electronic processing and other reed-based instruments. To produce these compositions, composer-instrumentalist Tom Guralnick surrounded himself with instruments and technical gear, and it took some lively physical movement by him in order to pull it off. The construction of the pieces is sculptural, with musique concrète touches. It offers radical juxtapositions and extreme spatial stereo effects, reflecting a definite influence from avant-garde composers like John Cage and Karlheinz Stockhausen.

The result is a form of unique collage music which often sounds nothing like conventional saxophone playing. The mood is jittery and edgy, and at times unusually severe. The opening piece, the 4-minute "Broken Dance," which has skittish skronks careening through the mix and sounds like a tape machine playing at various speeds, is representative. In other pieces, such as the 5-minute "Whirled Weary," Guralnick unleashes cacophonous bursts that are woven into dense textures. Guralnick keeps the level of surprises very high, making this 56-minute disc one of the best of its kind. *Broken Dances . . .* certainly provides a strong avant alternative to the mellow ECM label saxophone excursions of artists like John Surman and Jan Garbarek. While at times the music is just as spacey as anything from that realm, at others it creates a good amount of John Zorn–like insanity. *Broken Dances . . .* is a very progressive album that's deserving of the highest recommendation.

GURU GURU

HINTEN. Released July 1971. Spalax import.

Guru Guru was a sensational and entertaining power trio from the German progressive scene of the 1970s. A loud, guitar-led psychedelic rock group, they took the innovations of earlier rock power trios (The Jimi Hendrix Experience, Cream, The Who) and distilled the most progressive elements of those bands, focusing on a free-form structure without the studio polish, playing lengthy, very live-sounding rock with plentiful psychedelic effects and little in the way of vocals. They recorded in the studio the way most groups played live in concert, delivering the goods in a cutting, driving manner, yet they were never sloppy.

Hinten, their second album, debuts the Guru Guru formula. There are four long tracks, all in the 10- to 12-minute range. Guitarist Ax Genrich is the star, performing along with throbbing bass by Uli Trepte and drums by Mani Neumier. The band dives headlong into high-energy adrenalin grooves, as heavy as any in rock at the time, giving lots of space for each member to play up a storm. Genrich unleashes hurricanes of feedback, noise, and all-out psychedelic soloing, with blazes of percussion from Neumier accompanying and at times leading. These pieces are virtually all instrumental; what vocals there are consist mainly of a few off-handedly delivered lines in each song. After several minutes, each track goes into a strange section of guitar-effects collage, veritable blueprints for psychedelic rave-ups. After a few minutes of this, the songs return to their original grooves for some final blowout pyrotechnics.

The production on this recording is excellent, and quite advanced for a German release from this era. The stereo separation is very wide, and there is a lot of characteristic stereo panning, especially from the multiguitar overdubs, which gives Guru Guru their monster sound. The cover is a hilarious underground-style photo of a nude man with the name of the band painted on his butt.

KANGURU. Released May 1972. Brain import.

Kanguru is widely acknowledged to be Guru Guru's best album. The lineup, structure, and sound are the same as on the album's predecessor, *Hinten,* with four lengthy tracks of brilliant, guitar-driven prog jamming with a minimum of vocals. The production is even better this time, with high-quality mixing, a very crisp, live feel, and one of the biggest drum sounds of that era. Given its unusually high production values, *Kanguru* doesn't sound at all dated.

Here Guru Guru is even more cutting, saucy, loose, and irresistable than ever before. Their music was never as formal as other prog rock. Eschewing the jazz, electronic, and "cosmic" influences that were being explored by others at the time, they instead favored a full-on rock approach to progressive music—maximum R&B rather than classical and jazz, the contemporary sounds of rhythms and noise over orchestral colorations. Vocals and concepts don't intrude; the band's focus is always on the directions the compositions take, with extended soloing that's more potently psychedelic than anything that was coming from the so-called American psychedelic music scene of the era.

The 10½-minute "Oxymoron" opens, a song about buying and smoking marijuana complete with the sounds of a water pipe. The 15½-minute "Immer Lustig" is a hard-rocking instrumental, beginning with a whistle blow and going through many changes and workouts, giving the members several opportunities to display their significant instrumental prowess. The middle section is another tornado of stereo guitar noise collage, pulling out all the stops, ending with nature sounds, echoed percussion, and other effects, before returning to its central groove. "Baby Cake Walk" and "Ooga Booga" (both 11 minutes in length) are very enjoyable, funky rave-ups.

The playing of Genrich, Neumier, and Trepte is more than exceptional, it is positively historic. The cover is a humorous painting of a kangaroo.

Guru Guru removes all pretension and stiffness from prog rock, emphasizing feel and a definite informality rarely found in the genre at the time. For their aesthetic advances and approach, Guru Guru ought to be hailed as a progenitor of sorts of the punk/alternative/grunge movements, but they aren't. Unfortunately, later Guru Guru releases went for a more commercial sound, adding more vocals (in German) and jazzier arrangements with an expanded lineup, all of which diluted the potency of the power trio format from which discs like *Kanguru* drew their strength.

STEVE HACKETT

VOYAGE OF THE ACOLYTE. Released October 1975. Caroline.

A key recording from the mid-1970s—a high point for major-label U.K. progressive rock—this ambitious first album from Hackett is a mature, polished work, extraordinarily progressive and exuding a mystery even beyond that of early Genesis (of which Hackett was still a member when this was released). *Voyage . . .* is notable for its formal structures and precise arrangements. This is heavily layered music à la early King Crimson (which this resembles) and Genesis—lush and melodic, with mellotron, acoustic guitar, flute, ARP synth, harmonium, bells, piano, and autoharp constructing a smooth and rich classical rock sound. Hackett's role in Genesis was always less clearly defined than that of the other members, and the mostly instrumental *Voyage . . .* makes explicit his considerable compositional talents. And with Phil Collins on drums and Mike Rutherford on bass, this album becomes an essential part of the progressive-era Genesis canon.

"Ace of Wands," the 5½-minute opener, is a lively, smoothly executed, multisectioned complex rock instrumental. "Hands of the Priestess," an astonishingly effective two-part instrumental, follows with acoustic guitar, mellotron, tape effects, bells, an ethereal oboe solo (from guest Robin Miller), and sparing, mournful electric guitar. The piece creates a cinematic atmosphere of authentic mystery, as if one was in ancient Egypt participating in a sacred ritual. "A Tower Struck Down" is a strange, heavy rock instrumental (with extra bass by Percy Jones, later of Brand X) with an unexpected collage section of coughs, voices, and crowds followed by a torrent of noise, then a few stereo pans of ominous mellotron notes, and finally a bass solo fade-out. "The Lovers" is a short, tasteful acoustic piece with some backward tape effects. It's very nice, though unfortunately there's a good amount of hiss on the track.

Steve Hackett. (Photo by Paul Cox.)

The vocal pieces are equally successful. "The Hermit" is a folksy ballad with a melancholy, far-away-sounding vocal from Hackett. The 7-minute "Star of Sirius" is formal classical rock, with vocals by Phil Collins and featuring poetic lyrics that evoke otherwordly, baroque images. The structure of "Shadow of the Hierophant" is even more formalistic, with airy vocals from Sally Oldfield. This incredible track is as well done as anything in this style can be, with properly symphonic accompaniment from the band, sweeping mellotron washes, delicate autoharps and oboe, and, of course, Hackett's guitars.

The sound quality (remixed for CD) is generally outstanding. The final few tracks do become rather hissy, however. The lovely, dreamy, fantasy-oriented cover paintings by Hackett's wife Kim Poor are perfect images for the music. Regrettably, Hackett's subsequent solo albums moved away from the direction of this classic disc, and none match overall its quality.

CLAIRE HAMILL

VOICES. Released April 1986. Art of Landscape import.

Claire Hamill is a very talented U.K. singer/songwriter, similar to Joni Mitchell, who released her first album, *One House Left Standing,* in late 1971. The very different *Voices* is a unique 43-minute conceptual experimental vocal work (without lyrics), with all sounds originating from Hamill's vocals. *Voices,* which was written, produced, and performed by Hamill, was released during the launch of the new age category in the mid-1980s and was strangely and unjustly ignored at the time. *Voices* reaches heights of sound construction seldom achieved by other vocalists or synthesists. Combining the organic realm of the human voice with the technological miracles available in modern recording studios, this release for the most part manages to avoid sounding overly technical. It is, rather, genuinely spiritual and celestial, uplifting, and even danceable at times.

The disc is divided into four sections—spring, summer, autumn, and winter. Evocative titles such as "Afternoon in a Wheatfield," "Icicle Rain," and "Mist on the Ridge" create highly visual images for the listener which Hamill's vocal constructions live up to. High points are the swaying layers of "ooh-hoo's" and central scatting vocal on "Leaf Fall" and the central emotional cries in "Tides." This is nurturing, loving music, and perhaps representative of one area where female artists are preeminent. *Voices* might not be the revelation it is if the voice were male.

The sound quality of the recording throughout is great, with an expansive soundscape that fills the room. Keeping *Voices* from masterpiece status, however, is the overuse of rhythmic beats, which sound too much like techno and undermine some pieces which would otherwise be unique.

The cover art is a photo of the sun peaking through the clouds in a blue sky, apt for the shining music found on *Voices*.

BO HANSSON

LORD OF THE RINGS. Released December 1970. One Way.

An early classic of space music from Sweden by acclaimed composer and instrumentalist Bo Hansson, *Lord of the Rings* exudes a hypnotic and mysterious atmosphere. It's not really jazz, rock, or classical, nor is it soundtrack music. At the time of its appearance there really were no precedents for an album like this. An all-instrumental conceptual work inspired by the writings of J.R.R. Tolkien, the music paints so many different pictures one need not be familiar with Tolkien or even know the song titles to be drawn into its aura. *Lord of the Rings* resembles the 1968–1970 era of Pink Floyd à la songs like "Set the Controls for the Heart of the Sun," only without vocals. The recording takes the most moody and spacey elements of that style and expands it to album length, quite an innovative move for 1970. The Tolkien concept reinforces the *Alice in Wonderland*–like otherworldliness of the music.

Lord . . . consists of 12 tracks, ranging in length from 1 to 5 minutes. It features Hansson himself playing most of the instruments, making this a more intimate form of music than his subsequent albums. Playing organ, guitar, Moog synth, and bass, Hansson creates an intoxicatingly Gothic and psychedelic atmosphere that is drifting, pulsing, organic, spiritual, melodic, and friendly. The organ is used to concoct thick webs of snake-charming spells, accompanied by echoed fuzz guitar riffs and murky Moog synth backgrounds. This mood is maintained consistently throughout all 12 pieces.

A core group of collaborators contributed to this album, including include Rune Carlsson on drums and congas, Gunnar Bergsten on sax, and Sten Bergman on flute. Each of these musicians would appear on later Hansson releases as well. In addition, Hansson utilizes some brief environmental sounds, such as the ocean waves on "The Grey Havens," which ends the album.

Lord . . . is one of the earliest space music recordings, and also one of the most popular. The album went gold in the U.K., and was undoubtedly influential on the emerging wave of progressive musicians there. The sound quality is excellent, and all of the frequencies (especially the lower ones) are restored on this One Way remaster.

The trippy fantasy cover paintings by Jane Furst are suitable for the authentically enigmatic music on this recording.

MAGICIAN'S HAT. Released 1972. One Way.

The incredible follow-up to *Lord of the Rings, Magician's Hat* retains the feel of its predecessor, but with an expanded group lineup and a bigger production. The sound is more layered, and still very melodic if not quite as mysterious. Another all-instrumental set, *Magician's Hat* proved Hansson's success was no fluke. His deft compositional skills deliver a music that recreates the charm of *Lord* . . . while still venturing into some very different areas.

The 11½-minute "Big City" is certainly different. A light jazz rock fusion with up-front sax and guitar solos, and even vocal chants, it's reminiscent of Weather Report, a group Hansson probably hadn't even heard when this was recorded. The 7-minute "The Sun (Parallel or 90)" is also quite fusion-oriented, dominated by bass, drums, and electric piano solos. "Excursion with Complications" is closer to rock, with fuzz guitar and lightning bass guitar runs. Joining Hansson, Carlsson, Bergsten, and Bergman on this outing are Kenny Hakansson on electric guitars, Rolf Scherrer on acoustic guitar, Bill Ohrstrom on congas, and Goran Freese on sax. This larger band opens up Hansson's compositions, taking them out of the space-music-only universe and breaking them down into separate styles, adding groove and some folksy elements without losing any of their magic. Eight of the titles on "Magician's Hat" are short pieces (1 to 3 minutes) that primarily feature Hansson and are similar to the heavy space music of *Lord of the Rings*.

Like all of Hansson's albums, *Magician's Hat* is an easy-to-like effortless listen. The sound is excellent, larger and crisper than *Lord . . . ,* with a first-rate remastering job. The cover is another incredible fantasy painting, this time by Jan Ternald, which takes the title of the album literally and also places this special music in the land of the imagination.

ATTIC THOUGHTS. Released April 1975. One Way.

Attic Thoughts is a true masterpiece of progressive instrumental music, very European in the style of Clearlight, Schicke, Fuhrs & Frohling, Luciano Basso, Mike Oldfield, and Focus. Infectious, flowing, and smoother than earlier recordings, Hansson's third album is immaculately recorded and mixed, with ultra-crisp highs, booming bass, and very little hiss—all rolled into a gorgeous symphonic rock whole. Hansson's arsenal of multilayered keyboards (organ, synth, mellotron) are at the center of these grand, ambitious compositions, but combined with the keyboards are rich, melodic textures of multiple acoustic guitars and restrained electric guitar. The bass and drums are rock-solid tight. Many of these pieces go through several varying moods, and some feature waltzlike sections, such as the irresistable track "Waltz for Interbeings."

The sounds and approaches vary throughout the nine pieces, most of which are in the 4- to 8-minute range. The band is more up-front here than in past recordings, adeptly moving from the spacey to the rocking. Here Hansson, Carlsson, Hakansson, and Bergsten are joined by Joran Lagerberg on bass and acoustic guitar, Roif Scherrer on acoustic guitar, Mats Glenngard on violin, and Thomas Netzler on bass. Some of the high points are the overlay of central keyboard notes that are as lush as dewdrops on "Waiting . . . ," the typically Euro prog keyboard and drum interplay in the opening of "The Hybrills," and the more formal structures of "Time for Great Achievements." This is still storytelling music, less otherworldly than *Lord of the Rings,* but more varied and sophisticated. Hansson was on a good path with a release like *Attic Thoughts.* It remains one of the most successful examples of the symphonic rock style of prog music, demonstrating all of that genre's attractive possibilities. The cover is a hilarious psychedelic painting by Jan Ternald.

HAPPY FAMILY

HAPPY FAMILY. Released May 1995. Cuneiform.

Happy Family are among the finest artists of the emerging Japanese progressive music scene. An instrumental quartet playing loud Fire Merchants–like fusion (à la *Landlords of Atlantis),* this is on the heavy metal side of prog rock, balls-to-the-wall and hard-hitting. Their debut album is a rather mature release from such young musicians (each in their mid-20s), putting their lightning-fast playing in a formally structured, almost symphonic context, with a dense variety of complex shifts, counterpoints, and poly-rhythms. While their music can be wearing and dark at times, needing more swing and fun, it always remains musical, never degenerating into posturing sludge.

Keyboardist Kenichi Morimoto (who wrote five of the seven tracks here) is the foundation of these compositions. Strangely enough, it's his synths and other keys that generally puts this music in the progressive realm. While some of his sounds can be garishly out of place, without him the band would simply be a full-on rock power trio. Bassist Tatsuya Miyano has a thunderous, chopping, up-front sound that slices up everything in its path. Guitarist Shigeru Makino at times resembles a less effortless Kazumi Watanabe, with more metal shredding, wailing, and flailing. Drummer Keiichi Nagase is always a treat, constantly contributing a number of fantastic percussive colorations. Nagase also designed and photographed the cover art, a collage of junkyard appliances. The sound on *Happy Family* captures a live feel and is well executed, although a full digital recording would have been more effective in presenting their crunching prog rock.

TOSCCO. Released May 1997. Cuneiform.

Toscco, the structured follow-up to Happy Family's self-titled 1995 debut, is just as macho, but more compositionally mature. The production is better (with a completely gargantuan sound), and the new guitarist Takahiro Izutani has a more natural flair for the band's material. The disc's nine pieces are written by keyboardist Kenichi Morimoto, bassist Tatsuya Miyano, and guitarist Izutani. Morimoto's keyboards here are less awkward than on the first disc, and the performances by all four players is truly exceptional, making this one of the most intelligent and genuinely exciting instrumental prog rock releases of the 1990s.

The 3-minute opener, "The Great Man," is a piece of heavy symphonic rock that incorporates sounds from field recordings. The 6½-minute "Overdrive Locomotive" and the 12-minute "The Three Leaves Insect" are both loud, dense, and relentless rhythmic heavy metal shredding epics, with a lot of clever counterpoint. The 5-minute "Nord Company Vs. Lead Company" begins with some very active percussion, its complex rhythms mushrooming into a fast-paced macho jam. The 4-minute "Filial Piety at the Dawn" and the 6½-minute "The Picture Book—X-Rated" both have Godzilla-sized, saucy, and playful grooves. The 11-minute "The Sushi Bar" opens with a simple piano intro. The first 2½ minutes have a somewhat laid-back pace, with textural tradeoffs between piano and guitar that establish a more storytelling form. From there the piece moves into immensely enjoyable jamming, with Gong/Melting Euphoria–like synths. The 4-minute "He Is Coming at Tokyo Station" is an ominous piece of symphonic bombast led by trumpet-like keyboards. The 1½-minute concluding piece, "The Great Man (Revisited)," is an unexpectedly mellow wrap-up, with acoustic guitar and harmonica-like keyboards.

Drummer Keiichi Negase once again designed the album cover art.

Happy Family. Clockwise, starting top left, Shigeru Makino, Tatsuya Miyano, Keiichi Nagase, Kenichi Morimoto.

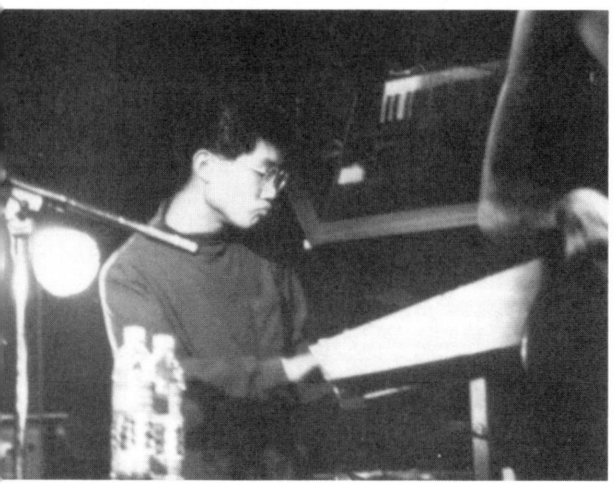

MICHAEL HARRISON

IN FLIGHT: PIANO SOLOS. Released 1987. Fortuna.

In Flight is a decent collection of eight solo piano pieces, typical of the high quality of a group of disparate recordings brought out in the mid-1980s under the new age umbrella. Classification is difficult with discs like this. It isn't classical; it isn't overtly jazzy; and it isn't the usual new age commercial schmaltz. So what is it? From a progressive perspective, this release resembles the skeletal piano sections that are at the heart of so many of the legendary symphonic rock bands' compositions. The gap between the two actually isn't that wide. For example, parts of the music on "In Flight" sound like the playing of Tony Banks (à la Genesis' "Firth of Fifth") or Rick Wakeman, and Harrison's writing and playing are impressive enough to stand up under such a comparison. Yet this is a solo piano album, so the impact is, of course, more delicate and less forcefully delivered than the piano sections found on prog rock songs.

This is not background music. It's neither spacey or meditative, but instead rather confident, with an active pace that makes the disc fly by. There's clearly a depth to this beyond the norm, with some appealing dewy notes that are sometimes sparkling, other times grand. Six of the pieces are played on a Yamaha piano with standard tuning, and two on a Steinway that is tuned with the natural acoustic intervals of just intonation. While Harrison's work is not quite as deep or as effortless as the solo piano compositions of Liz Story, this is a well-recorded, finely executed set of solid, original works.

The opening 6-minute title track introduces Harrison's delicate, introspective style. There are moments of color and grandeur, as well as some more rigid sections, and the piece concludes with some unexpectedly dewy notes. The 7-minute "The Swan Has Flown to the Mountain Lake" has a storytelling flow, and showcases Harrison's distinctive playing technique well, with a number of attractive timbres. The 4-minute "Because of You" has both a melancholy flavor and a rich poignancy. It goes by all too quickly. The 4-minute "Echo of Time" has an announcing fanfare intro, establishing a majestic motif, with an undercurrent of lush but highly disciplined notes.

Michael Harrison.

The strong delivery of the 3½-minute "The Joy of Life" recalls the piano parts of many prog rock groups. The 4½-minute "Ocean Dance" is a reflective, impressionistic piece that exudes a positive glow. The 5½-minute "Winter's Dream" has a schmaltzy Christmasy intro, but then goes in some interesting directions, offering sections of dramatic introspection. The disc concludes with the 5-minute "Mira," a piece of solemn romanticism. Harrison's 1992 album *From Ancient Worlds* continues in the same vein, and is recommended.

HATFIELD AND THE NORTH

HATFIELD AND THE NORTH. Released October 1973. Caroline.

The most successful band from the Canterbury-style 1970s U.K. prog world, Hatfield and the North are a progressive rock supergroup of sorts, with keyboardist Dave Stewart from Egg, drummer Pip Pyle from Gong, bassist-vocalist Richard Sinclair from Caravan, and guitarist Phil Miller from Matching Mole. Experimental, surrealistic, and astonishingly eclectic, their music is notable for self-referential lyrics, eccentric arrangements, and jazzy, free-feeling tempos. All four members share writing credits.

With all tracks separate but running together, "The Stubbs Effect," a very brief stereo keyboard pattern, opens. Next comes "Big Jobs (Poo Poo Extract)," a very short low-key number in which Sinclair sings in his trademark wistful, off-handed style about how the band hopes you will like their record. "Going Up to People and Tinkling" is representative of the Hatfield sound—light, airy jazz and ultra-Canterbury. "Calyx" has a multitracked scat vocal by guest Robert Wyatt of Soft Machine and Matching Mole. Clearly Wyatt had a big influence on these musicians. The 10-minute "Son of 'There's No Place Like Homerton'" has an instrumental first half, led by organ and the saxes and flutes of guest Geoff Leigh of Henry Cow, a band whose music this section resembles. The second half introduces the Northettes, a female vocal trio of Amanda Parsons, Barbara Gaskin, and Ann Rosenthal. Their choirlike vocals are similarly airy and light, and the ideal texture for this band. "Aigrette" is a breezy jazz scat by Sinclair. With "Rifferama," an instrumental, the band tightens up a bit; Miller steps forward for some sparing solos, and lots of odd sound effects are mixed in.

"Fol De Rol" begins the second half of the disc with a lazy tempo and nonsense vocals by Sinclair, plus bass solos, ending with the sound of a phone ringing and being answered, which then plays back Sinclair's vocal. This goes into the disc's high point, the 8½-minute instrumental "Shaving Is Boring," where the band really demonstrates their peculiar chemistry. A fuzz bass solo by Sinclair, with lots of sound effects verging on space rock and collage music, comes to a halt with some stereo footsteps; this is followed by a series of doors opening, and each time a door is opened, the sound of a particular place on the album is heard. This is playful, surreal stuff, with lots of stereo panning.

"Licks for the Ladies" and "Bossa Nochance" are two very English ditties by Sinclair, with downbeat vocals and hilarious lyrics about a plea for some more sensible music after all you've been hearing, something your girlfriend will understand. "Lobster in Cleavage Probe" and "Gigantic Land Crabs in Earth Takeover Bid" are more atypical Canterbury jams, with vocals again from the Northettes. The album ends with "The Other Stubbs Effect," another brief keyboard effect.

The disc also has two bonus tracks, the A and B sides of their first single. "Let's Eat (Real Soon)" is a lot like the other Sinclair material, if somewhat more old-hat. Pyle's "Fitter Stoke Has a Bath" is a rougher, sparser arrangement of one of their best songs, found later in a better version on *The Rotters Club*. The sound is decent, but could definitely use a remastering. It's thin and lacks both punch and definition, giving the music a fragility which it doesn't need.

THE ROTTERS CLUB. Released May 1975. Caroline.

A prime example of the Canterbury subgenre of U.K. prog, *The Rotters Club* is a much-beloved eccentric masterpiece. The music is very free, with a lightness and friendliness that give off a sunny, positive vibe. The lyrics are self-referential humor about the travails of the progressive musician. Guests Mont Campbell, Lindsay Cooper, Amanda Parsons, Jimmy Hastings, and Tim Hodgkinson—links with other Canterbury groups like Egg, National Health, Caravan, and Henry Cow—make a 1975 release like *The Rotters Club* representative of an entire segment of English progressive music of that era. Also included on this disc are several bonus tracks from *Afters,* a collection of rarities released after Hatfield's breakup, bringing the running time up to 63½ minutes.

Opening is "Share It,"a somewhat poppy song by Richard Sinclair about being stoned. "Lounging There Trying" is a nifty 3-minute Phil Miller–led jazzy instrumental. The dense, heavy Canterbury sludgefest of "(Big) John Wayne Socks Psychology on the Jaw" and the chunky bass solo of "Chaos at the Greasy Spoon" are brief links, bringing us to the 7-minute "The Yes No Interlude," a fusion jam that's a bit heavier than earlier pieces. This is a classic Hatfield instrumental; Miller is more up-front, and there are some savage solos and throbbing bass lines by Sinclair. The playing of Pip Pyle and Dave Stewart, however, is lighter and more old-fashioned. "Fitter Stoke Has a Bath" is a 7½-minute version of an earlier single, here smoother and better thought out. The lyrics by Pyle, which are more of the wry, self-referential type, are followed by a really free and liberating scat vocal by Sinclair. This takes us into a heavy guitar jam before the tempo slows, with a section of tape effects and vibes, leading us into "Didn't Matter Anyway," a tragic, understated, moving ballad featuring a flute solo.

"Underdub" kicks off what was side 2 in the vinyl era, a 4-minute fusion instrumental that's almost too light and sweet. The four part 20½-minute "Mumps" is a treat, featuring the return of the notorious Northettes (Amanda Parsons, Barbara Gaskin, and Ann Rosenthal). With their airy la-la's and choirs, their style is as much a signature of the Hatfield/Canterbury sound as anyone's. The first part of "Mumps" is the Monty Python–inspired "Your Majesty Is Like a Cream Donut," which has an Egg-like jam—one of their best and harder-rocking than usual. Sinclair's playing here is especially notable, anchoring all the twee noodling down into place with some heavy bottom from his bass guitar. This goes into the second part "Lumps," a short characteristic low-key vocal by Sinclair. The third part of the piece is "Prenut," with slicing licks by Miller and some very hip tradeoffs between him and the sax of Hastings. Part four is a return to "Your Majesty . . ." with some regrettably dated organ sounds from Stewart.

Kicking off the *Afters* tracks are alternate versions of "(Big) John . . ." and "Chaos . . . ," here more harder-edged. This leads into the single "Halfway Between Heaven and Earth." Their most popular tune, it's a lovely, breezy rock love song with a crooning-at-the-stars vocal from Sinclair. The 2-minute "Oh, Len's Nature!" and the 4-minute "Lying and Gracing" are live, with a huge, heavy metal–like Hatfield sound—very surprising and fun. This section is far too brief, though, and one wishes there was more of this kind of material. The sound quality throughout the disc is good, but could use a remastering.

HELDON

UN RÊVE SANS CONSÉQUENCE SPECIALE.

Released December 1976. Cuneiform.

Inspired by the music of Brian Eno, Philip Glass, King Crimson, and Tangerine Dream, former philosophy instructor Richard Pinhas began his own musical projects using the name Heldon, releasing his first album in 1974. The first four Heldon albums are basically Pinhas solo works, and are almost exclusively all-electronic synthesizer affairs. With *Un Rêve . . .* Pinhas convened a real band, featuring his most successful collaborator, drummer/percussionist Francois Auger, and another synth player, Patrick Gauthier. While Pinhas remained the leader, major composer, and producer, the Heldon group efforts are easily the most successful. This is primarily because of Auger's contributions, which put the later Heldon titles into the realm of electro-acoustic rock music, as opposed to the earlier (and more primitive) recordings, which were pure electronics.

While *Un Rêve . . .* is not a classic, the album is interesting for being absolutely nothing like any other kind of progressive music of the mid-1970s; it is awfully severe and bruising, especially for a 1976 release. While the album is not entirely successful, its underground feel and unusually active sound mix make it notably ahead of its time. The music of Heldon is like a combination of Klaus Schulze and Throbbing Gristle. The relationship of Auger's drums to the synths (particularly the Moog) of Pinhas and Gauthier is a dynamic similar to that found on Klaus Schulze's 1970s albums, with drummer Harold Grosskopf contributing solid human-performed drum kit rhythms to Schulze's spacey electronic voyages. A big complaint about Heldon is their garish synth tones, which always seem to be in the foreground and give the music an unfortunately stereotypical synth feel.

The 11½-minute opener, "Marie Virginie C," features haunting guitar tones, cymbal crashes, and synth bleeps which create an uneasy psychedelic tapestry. A drumbeat from Auger then picks up, along with plenty of Moog solos, and the piece becomes a blizzard of sound. The 8½-minute "Elephanta" is a showcase for Auger's exotic percussion. Chaotic and infectiously mixed, it's a wealth of different sounds that are loud and not one bit subtle, to which Pinhas adds industrial-like Moog blasts. The piece outstays its welcome, though, and ultimately becomes grating. The 6-minute "MVC II" is an early foray into industrial rhythms (hence the Throbbing Gristle comparison), with clanging metallic percussion, minimalist synth patterns, and punctuations from Auger's thumping bass drum. The disappointing 15-minute "Towards the Red Line" has swirls of synth, drums, and wailing guitar, but meanders for far too long.

An excellent bonus track recorded live by the group in 1978 is also included here: "Marie et Virginie Comp" is what the power of Heldon is all about—scathing, scabrous guitar soloing, huge drums, and chugging synths.

Richard Pinhas of Heldon.

INTERFACE. Released January 1978. Cuneiform.

With its fresh and immediate sound, *Interface* is a minor gem of all-instrumental rock. The production values here are better than most European projects from this period, giving the album a loud and attention-getting monster of a mix. Recorded in 1977, the album features the trio of Richard Pinhas (synths, guitars), Francois Auger (drums, percussion, synth), and Patrick Gauthier (synths, bass). This expanded group lineup (more than just Pinhas alone, as was the case for most of Heldon's early releases), particularly Auger's drumming, is what makes the later Heldon albums the most interesting. Alternating between short, active tracks and long, unfolding, blistering ones, the music on this album was far ahead of its time and rather different from the rest of space rock in the 1970s, which tended to be celestial and serene. *Interface*, on the other hand, is positively industrial—a kind of punk space rock.

The opening track, "Les Soucoupes Volantes Vertes," by Auger, is a $2\frac{1}{2}$-minute burst of driving synths and drums. The music stays locked in a pattern and thankfully concludes when there is no place further to go. Pinhas's 10-minute, two-part "Jet Girl" features his cutting, precise, and haunting guitar (backed by real drums). There's an admitted Robert Fripp influence, which is almost too obvious in Pinhas's playing. Long, dense blazes of drones weave dreamy but intense webs. Gauthier's hard-hitting $2\frac{1}{2}$-minute "Le Retour des Soucoupes Volantes," with its plateauing melody and electronics soloing by Gauthier and Pinhas, is a standout track, and is similar to late Schicke, Führs and Fröhling. Auger's $7\frac{1}{2}$-minute "Bal-à-Fou" also has a more positive glow compared to Pinhas's compositions, with its soft space music introduction. The track builds up with exotic percussion, like *Igaucu*-era Passport or late Gong.

Pinhas's $1\frac{1}{2}$-minute "Le Fils des Soucoupes Volantes (Vertes)" is another standout, the most rocking track on the album. Big stereo drum rolls, guitar solos, and percolating electronic percussion make this infectious and easy to like. Pinhas's 19-minute title track is also a high point. Beginning with sweeping stereo effects and snapping rhythmic buildups, the piece becomes a Lard Free–like vortex à la that group's *III*. A massive mix of drums and electronic percussion by Auger combines with Gauthier's electronics; the feel is very industrial. At $8^1/_2$ minutes into the piece, Pinhas's guitar begins slicing and shredding through the percussion, becoming a very loud rock excursion that moves at an adrenalin-driven pace.

Two great-sounding bonus tracks recorded live in Paris in 1978 are also included here. Both are interesting, shortened bits from the title track, done slightly differently. The 6-minute "Interface Live Part 1" adds some funk Moog bass lines. The 2-minute "Interface Live Part 2" is a slamming guitar/drums jam à la instrumental Frank Zappa.

The eerie cover art, a sci-fi photo of an alien in a space suit, is exactly right for the music on *Interface.*

STAND BY. Released January 1979. Cuneiform.

Recorded in 1978 by members Francois Auger, Patrick Gauthier, and Richard Pinhas, along with bassist Didier Batard, *Stand By* was the final Heldon album. Like *Interface,* it unleashes a hard-hitting, gritty sound that is not at all dated, and is unusually macho for this sort of electronics-dominated instrumental space rock. Batard's bass certainly gives the music needed bottom end, and as a result this album is the one of theirs that most closely resembles flat-out rock.

Pinhas's 14-minute title track is undoubtedly the band's finest ever. The extremely loud, disorienting opening of harsh electronics and percussion takes you directly into an absolutely shredding guitar/bass/drums groove that is a powerfully intense form of rock—insistent, driving, and relentless. Throughout, Auger's drum rolls are potent, punching very hard indeed, and Pinhas unleashes his most Fripp-like fiery solo. The track is such an over-the-top slaughterhouse that it gives you a body high.

Gauthier's 4-minute "Une Dr[cf]ole de Journée," by contrast, is a friendlier and lighter texture, reminiscent of 1980s Weather Report, but with more savage rhythms. Sequencers, synth, and drums are joined by the wordless voices of guest Klaus Blasquiz.

The $21^1/_2$-minute epic "Bolero" by Pinhas and Auger is similar to Tangerine Dream's "Force Majeure," only much darker and with heavier drums. The piece is an unfolding electronics-filled rock suite, dominated by synths and muscular drums, and the Tangerine Dream–like sequencer of guest Didier Badez. They could have done without the sequencer and also the silly vocoder injections from Pinhas. The piece concludes with icy, foreground synth landscapes, around which Pinhas wraps sinewy guitar solos.

Patrick Jelin's sci-fi cover of a person in a silver body suit, like some kind of shock trooper on a nuclear-meltdown, chemical-weapons-spill, or alien-encounter team, reinforces the tense immediacy of this adrenalin-jolting music.

HENRY COW

LEGEND. Released August 1973. ESD.

Henry Cow is a very important band in the history of progressive music. While their music is on the lighter and jazzier side of fusion (i.e., less rock), they are determinedly avant-garde, consciously avoiding the hooks and repetitions of the popular music forms. The group's compositions are hard to pin down and difficult to describe, going through so many unexpected changes that they never stay in any one place for more than a minute or two. After you've listened to them, you try to recall what the hell it was you just heard. This free-form, nonlinear, anarchic improvisational approach cuts through the artifices and formulas of the dominant popular styles like a knife. Such an approach forces one to listen closely, resulting in a greater appreciation of the diversity of sounds and the infinite number of ways those sounds can be arranged. Henry Cow actively cultivated these purely progressive explorations. They are also notable for explicitly linking their free form of music to leftist political expressions. While for some listeners Henry Cow is definitely an acquired taste, their groundbreaking experimentalism and no-compromise stance make them one of the greatest progressive bands.

On *Legend,* their debut, the lineup is Geoff Leigh (saxes, flute, clarinet, recorder), Tim Hodgkinson (organ, piano, sax, clarinet), Fred Frith (guitars, violin, viola, piano), John Greaves (bass, piano, whistle), and Chris Cutler (drums, toys, piano, whistle). It's notable that the members do not confine themselves to one instrument, and that all the members contribute to the writing. There are 10 pieces on the album, from 1 to 7 minutes in length. There's a lot of central blowing from the wind instruments, more so than from the other instruments (e.g., guitar), and the sound mix is as diverse and complex as you can imagine; Hodgkinson's remix for this CD imparts an open, airy feel. Henry Cow's form of fusion is an interesting alternative to others from this era. There's no gigantic arena-level riffing or soloing. Comparisons for this period of Henry Cow might be the 1973–1974 era of King Crimson at their most experimental; the Canterbury axis of Soft Machine, Egg, and Hatfield and the North; and the Mothers of Invention or Weather Report at their most jazzy and idiosyncratic.

Highlights of *Legend* are the ominous drums and vocal choir (by the band) on the opening of "Teenbeat," which goes into a flat-out jam with saxes and quirky rhythms with complex tempos, then suddenly falls into an acoustic guitar and clarinet section; "Teenbeat Reprise," with a raging Frith guitar solo and tight backing from bass, drums, and piano; and "Nine Funerals of the Citizen King," with deadpan vocals by the band delivering impossibly off-the-wall didactic lyrics.

The cover art is the first of three sleeves, each of which features a different kind of sock, designed by Ray Smith.

UNREST. Released June 1974. ESD.

The moody *Unrest* is Henry Cow's darkest and most experimental studio release. Replacing Geoff Leigh from the *Legend* lineup is Lindsay Cooper, playing bassoon, oboe, and recorder. This new element, particularly the bassoon, moves the band into the realm of modern chamber music. *Unrest* is representative of the height of eclecticism at the Virgin label (the album's original label) and in the progressive scene in general at that time. A glance at the liner notes (by the band) reveals a diverse list of artists who were influences: Mike Oldfield, Faust, Robert Wyatt, and Guru Guru. With the first four tracks composed beforehand and the rest of the album entirely improvised in the studio, *Unrest* solidified the group's avant-garde reputation. And indeed, much of that improvised material does take several listens to appreciate. But *Unrest*'s defiant noncommercialism produces some compelling experimental music. Unfortunately, the volume of the CD transfer is very low, creating a good amount of hiss. However, there are two bonus tracks included from the original recording sessions not available on the vinyl release ("The Glove" and "Torchfire").

The four composed pieces are some of Henry Cow's best. "Bittern Storm over Ulm," the 2½-minute opener, is a tight, enjoyable band-oriented fusion, with up-front bass lines, harder-than-usual drums, and a saucy Robert Fripp–like guitar from Fred Frith. The 7½-minute "Half Asleep; Half Awake" is another high point, having a Soft Machine–like sound, with organ, throbbing bass guitar, sax, and piano. The 12-minute "Ruins" was actually engineered in the Virgin studios by Mike Oldfield. Dark piano notes, dissonant wind instruments, low-key screeching guitar noise, and bells lead into a formal chamber music section with violin and bassoon, and toy percussions by Cutler. The 6-minute "Linguaphone" begins with random noodling and pulses from guitar and bass, joined by indescribable vocal shouts. This track also features bassoon, sax, percussion, and vocal parts that were recorded at half or double speed.

The production values decline somewhat on the improvisational pieces, but the 3-minute "Upon Entering the Hotel Aldon" improv is an excellent, free jazz romp 'n' stomp. The cover art is a gray sock this time.

IN PRAISE OF LEARNING. Released May 1975. ESD.

Radically different from their previous releases, *In Praise of Learning* is a conceptual vocal work of political rock. While parts of this recording are more symphonically structured, with orchestrated guitar, bass, and percussion sections, the band are as determined as ever to avoid clichés and pop hooks. The usual plentiful amount of changes in direction and sound effects are all still here, only this time there's more rock-oriented material, with Frith's tortured guitar sounds up at the front.

For this album, Henry Cow combined with another group, Slapp Happy. This added Dagmar Krause on vocals, Anthony Moore on piano, electronics, and tapes, and Peter Blegvad on guitar and clavinet. If Krause's vocals are not to everyone's liking, it may be in part due to the difficult lyrics (which she actually delivers quite well). It does take several listens for newcomers to get into Krause's style, though. The lyrics might be better as written poetry than as vocals in musical arrangements, and they have been variously called "difficult," "didactic," and "overly serious."

Henry Cow make their left-wing idealism explicit in ways other musicians seldom do. The CD booklet photo pictures the band at a 1976 Communist Party Festival in Italy. *In Praise of Learning* is radical not only because of the band's use of nonlinear structures and sound collages as a means of artistic expression but also because it exemplifies a dissenting political sensibility. The recording has a very European flavor to it, both in its sound and in its political poetry. A good example of this is the 15½-minute "Living in the Heart of the Heart of the Beast." An epic-scale work about the destructiveness of capitalism on the human spirit, this is music that takes sides.

The 6½-minute instrumental "Beginning: The Long March" features dissonant guitars and rhythms that are a prelude of sorts to the later Massacre band with Fred Frith (see review). The random noises and Stockhausen-like arrangement of these various sounds work quite well here. The group is so cohesive within these nonstructured pieces that it all somehow works. "Morning Star," another 6-minute collage instrumental, is more of the same. "Lovers of Gold" is frankly indescribable. Except for the lyrics, the 7-minute "Beautiful As the Moan—Terrible as an Army with Banners" isn't that far away from a Curved Air track (à la their 1971 epic "Piece of Mind" from *Second Album)*. This is a more recognizable ballad-like structure, led by piano and light cymbal work. All in all, *In Praise of Learning* proves that Henry Cow was the most radically progressive U.K. band at that time.

The remixed sound is excellent, and the production values are better here than before. The cover art is a red sock, appropriate for the disc's political sensibilities.

CONCERTS. Released 1976. ESD.

The two-disc set of Henry Cow's *Concerts* is a pinnacle of adventurous, improvisational complexity; it's a trip into the realms of musical density. Rambling, lengthy, and noisy, it may seem formless to the uninitiated, but for fans of experimentalism taken to extremes it's an exciting journey. The group's lineup for most of the material on *Concerts* is that of *In Praise of Learning*, minus Anthony Moore and Peter Blegvad.

The first piece is the 22½-minute "Beautiful As the Moon; Terrible As an Army with Banners"/"Nirvana for Mice"/"Ottawa Song"/"Gloria Gloom"/"Moon Reprise." This is Henry Cow's BBC Peel session from August of 1975. The sound is very good, with widely separated stereo. The track is a perfect example of the essence of Henry Cow's music. With *Concerts* one can see why this group is so obscure. This music is extremely challenging to the attention span of most listeners, and it's not at all easy to divine what it's about, either lyrically or musically. The piece opens with Dagmar Krause's vocals in one channel, counterpointed by Fred Frith's piano in the other. Frith covers a lot of territory on this track, switching from piano to a stinging electric guitar to shadings from the acoustic guitar. John Greaves's bass guitar is heavier here than on previous discs. The whole work is delivered with such grandeur that it assumes a unique place of its own in the prog rock music pantheon.

"Bad Alchemy"/"Little Red Riding Hood Hits the Road," recorded in London in May 1975, is, on the other hand, a low point, with very hissy, poor sound quality and Krause and Greaves singing some old-hat, dated, Canterbury-flavored material. A 16-minute version of "Ruins" from October 1975 in Italy follows. This is more frenzied than the studio take, with some great soloing from Frith. The sound isn't bad, but the recording standards aren't what they should be. "Groningen" and "Groningen Again," recorded in Holland in September 1974, are murky and hissy, and *Concerts* would be better off without them. It's more Canterbury sludge, with music that's thin and dated. These tracks conclude the first disc, which is 64 minutes in length.

The 60½-minute disc 2 opens with another major epic-length highlight, the 29-minute "Oslo," recorded in Norway in 1975. The sound is very good on this one, and it's an excellent track. With Frith on violin and xylophone, Lindsay Cooper on recorder, and Chris Cutler on piano, "Oslo" is a lot of improvisational noodling and lively percussion. Intersecting patterns of random sounds create a spacey, sparse, drifting music. The actual sound is like children fooling around with instruments they just discovered. This gives it a certain authentic naivete that's nonlinear in every way, with all the density and pretension that the group is famous for. The middle section has a torturous scatting and screaming vocal from Krause that is quite jarring for a performance from 1975.

Three tracks from the 1973 lineup of Henry Cow with Geoff Leigh are included as well. These are studio recordings transcribed from an LP source, and the sound is fairly crackly and poor. This is unfortunate, as the material is quite promising, exploring musique concrète sounds and the plucking of piano strings. Concluding is the 9½-minute "Udine," recorded in Italy, from the same source as "Ruins." It's fairly insubstantial, with cheesy organ by Tim Hodgkinson, and ultimately goes nowhere.

Concerts, then, is a mixed bag, containing both well-recorded, outstanding performances, and poorly recorded, mediocre performances. The cover art is an off-putting, ugly black-and-white drawing.

WESTERN CULTURE. Released March 1978. ESD.

An all-instrumental conceptual work, *Western Culture* is the most popular and accessible Henry Cow disc. It's still discordant and avant-garde (i.e., completely nuts), retaining the flow of the earlier releases, but the palette is larger and the album is more tightly constructed. It is a storytelling political work (without lyrics) where the music evokes a chaotic, crumbling, and difficult free market world. The complexity of the music continually reinforces the concept. The recording is not an easy listen, as the mood is dark and doomy and permeated by a sense of foreboding, but it's highly accomplished. The compositions create impressions with several meanings and possibilities. The remastered sound is truly excellent, with an attention-getting spacious stereo mix, and the percussion sounds come across particularly well. *Western Culture* is also notable as one of the most successful examples of a chamber music/rock fusion.

The lineup here is Fred Frith (guitars, bass, sax), Tim Hodgkinson (organ, sax, clarinet, guitar, oboe), Lindsay Cooper (bassoon, oboe, sax, recorder) and Chris Cutler (drums, percussion, piano, trumpet, "noises"), with guest Anne Marie Roelofs (trombone, violin), who plays a big role in these compositions. Cutler is more up-front than before; the music is colored throughout by his deft touches. (He also designed the cover art.) The album is divided into two 18-minute sections, the first written by Hodgkinson, the second by Cooper.

The first section begins with the 7-minute "Industry." The track opens with a dissonant, LOUD, thunderous cacophony of wind instruments and bashing percussion. This is a larger sound than usual for Henry Cow, with a bigger and crisper rhythmic attack. "The Decay of Cities," also at 7 minutes in length, begins with Frith's acoustic guitar, organ, and ominous trombone notes, then goes into a bizarre fusion that is indescribably complex, with slabs of electric guitar noise. It then returns to the stateliness of the opening, with violin and recorder exchanges accompanied by bass guitar. The 4-minute "On the Raft" is a drifting and unfolding fusion with a live feel, and lots of kit bashing from Cutler.

"Falling Away," which opens the second half of the album, is a 7½-minute piece with a dirgelike opening, followed by a very nimble bass and drums fusion section and violin solo, joined by Frith's electric guitar and every kind of cymbal sound from Cutler. "Gretel's Tale" has screwball piano notes backed by bass and drums. Little sections like this go off like sparks, and the band never milks any one idea for too long, quickly moving on to other sounds.

Western Culture was the final Henry Cow album. Each of the various members have prolific solo careers, although the whole is greater than the individual parts.

STEVE HILLAGE

RAINBOW DOME MUSICK. Released May 1979. Caroline.

A landmark in space music (and pre–new age), *Rainbow Dome Musick* is a clear, rich, and lush pure form of music (like the crystal pictured on the cover) from the unlikely source of Steve Hillage. *Rainbow Dome Musick* is nothing like the rest of his solo albums, which are mainstream guitar rock. This recording is an all-instrumental work of ethereal, cosmic mystery, continuing along lines traveled by early Popol Vuh, Wendy Carlos, and Deuter. Recorded in January 1979 for the Rainbow Dome Mind-Body-Spirit Festival in London, it has none of Hillage's trademark psychedelia hard rock soloing. Instead it contains tranquil, relaxing, flowing soundscapes, and was as influential on the emerging 1980s new age music movement as Brian Eno's *Ambient* series. It is also Hillage's most progressive release.

The first of two pieces is the 23-minute "Garden of Paradise" written by Hillage and longtime collaborator Miquette Giraudy. Hillage plays electric guitar, electric piano, and ARP synth, while Giraudy plays sequencer, electric piano, ARP synth, and Tibetan bells. The track opens with a gorgeous stereo recording of running water, which remains an integral part of the piece for the first 7 minutes. This environmental element is crucial, giving it an otherworldly mystery into which is floated the gentle, melodic synth, electric piano and guitar textures. Drifting, caressing cascades of dewy notes sprinkle past the listener like grains of magical fairy dust. The entire track is soothing and soft, featuring lots of hypnotic stereo panning.

The 20½-minute "Four Ever Rainbow" again features Giraudy on ARP synth and Tibetan bells, plus sleeve cover artist Rupert Atwill on the Eventide Harmoniser, and Hillage himself on electric guitar and Moog synth. The piece begins with Tibetan bells and some supremely spacey hums, echoed and looped guitar patterns, and subtle, haunting synth lines. The icy, chilling mood evokes the timeless expanse of the universe, making this space music as much about outer space as it is about inner. Hillage's guitars here are celestial and mournful, far more restrained than on any of his other projects.

By 1979 Steve Hillage had become something of a product machine. A pioneering force in early 1970s U.K. progressive rock with his band Khan and as a member of Gong, his many solo albums (beginning in 1975 with *Fish Rising,* his best vocal album) projected an arena rock guitar hero image, with vocal songs in the 3- to 10-minute range. In early 1979 he released his requisite double live album, *Live Herald,* and at the end of that year came the studio album of quirky new wave rock entitled *Open.* In between these releases came the enigmatic *Rainbow Dome Musick.* Despite being copied for later new age music releases as if it were a veritable blueprint, the album holds up as an important, timeless creation.

The sound quality is first-rate, with virtually no hiss. The colorful cover by Rupert Atwill consists of photos of a polarized silica-quartz crystal—the perfect image for this music.

Steve Hillage.

MICHAEL HOENIG

DEPARTURE FROM THE NORTHERN WASTELAND. Released January 1978. Kuckuck.

Since its original release on Warner Bros. Records in early 1978, *Departure from the Northern Wasteland* has been and remains a very important and beloved icon of electronic space music. Michael Hoenig, the keyboardist from the group Agitation Free, also had brief stints in the mid-1970s as a touring collaborator with Tangerine Dream, Klaus Schulze, and Manuel Gottsching. As one of the pioneers of the German cosmic music of the 1970s, Hoenig displays the touch of a master here on his first solo album, having total control over the project as composer, arranger, performer, engineer, mixer, and producer.

Departure . . . is a triumphantly deep and enigmatic keyboard extravaganza, similar to Tangerine Dream's *Phaedra* and *Rubycon.* Hoenig constructs a multilayered, multitextured, highly composed form of electronic music. The production is of a very high standard, and the mix is quiet and flat, emphasizing subtlety and avoiding garishness. This is important to the success of *Departure . . . .* The music is soft; its patterns, themes, transitions, and melodies flow together perfectly. This electronic music is not in any way dated, clichéd, or run of the mill. The 21-minute title track has the length necessary to display the many attractive facets of Hoenig's brilliant style of composition. Every idea is followed up and fleshed out. As soon as you hear the tranquil opening sounds, you know he's

Michael Hoenig.

aiming for an ethereal quality. Shifting, wide rhythmic spans, light and melodic, create detailed foregrounds and backgrounds to spectacular effect. The piece is storytelling, moody, introspective, soothing, and easy to enjoy. It evokes a memorable, significant journey, where a series of impressions from a particular time and space—perhaps from the present, perhaps being recalled—are unfolding. The piece ends with soft, electronically simulated gurgling water sounds, over which calming, celestial notes are layered, achieving a nirvana of sorts as it fades out.

The 11-minute "Hanging Garden Transfer" features soft rhythmic stereo sequencers which gradually pick up the pace over time. The notes really dance in these sounds! The piece eventually assumes a kind of grandeur, once again leaving the listener in an uplifted mood. The 6-minute "Voices of Where" is an important track. A somber, minimal, ambient work, poignant in its quiet dignity, the piece just glows. It's an extraordinarily comforting, radiating form of sound that surrounds the listener with a meditative aura. The piece ends with an eruption from a collage of voices, quickly and abruptly bringing you to another place entirely. Finally, the 4-minute "Sun and Moon" concludes the disc with more serene, rhythmic flows of sequencers and synth.

The cover photo by Dennis G. Hendricks of a cold blue landscape, one of the most striking covers of any mentioned in this guide, is the ideal image for this music, evoking the mysterious journeys the mind takes when listening to the music of *Departure from the Northern Wasteland.*

HUGH HOPPER

1984. Released March 1973. Mantra import.

This first solo album from the Soft Machine bassist underscores the experimental nature of the U.K. music scene of the time. While Soft Machine can no longer be considered experimental, *1984* is an unusually mind-expanding release, more concerned with sound collages than with conventional fusion jamming or songs. It has more in common with other U.K. avant-garde composers like Ron Geesin and the band Henry Cow than with anything from the Soft Machine canon. Rarely has an album from the roster of the 1970s Canterbury musicians emerged that was as radical as *1984.* It tests the limits of fusion both then and now, risks dissonance, and uses strange, unrecognizable sounds.

From the first few moments of listening to *1984,* it's apparent that great care was taken during the recording and production. The sound is extremely sharp. The instruments were closely miked, and the horn instruments positively sting. The drum sound is very hip, and Hopper provides innovative sounds from the bass guitar here not heard anywhere else. The stereo separation is very wide, and on some tracks there are completely different sounds in each channel. Such music is ideal for headphones. The production values clearly are a big step up from Soft Machine's releases, which tended to be thin, murky, and hissy. *1984* indisputably sparkles.

The 14½-minute "Miniluv" opens, with Hopper playing bass guitars, percussion, and mellophone. The sound immediately fills the room, and is quite attention-getting and atmospheric. Hopper plays multiple bass parts, using the inventive idea of trading off bass notes from one channel to the other and back. Over the background of the track's incredibly spacious percussion are psychedelic notes gurgling from the mellophone. The piece ends with a collage section of these various textures.

The crisp 3-minute "Minipax 1" is next, the disc's most conventional track. This is a swinging jazzy fusion number, with a much harder edge than Soft Machine, featuring some mean blowing from two saxes and a trombone, plus guitar by Caravan's Pye Hastings and drums by Soft Machine's John Marshall. "Minipax 2," also 3 minutes, is more of Hopper with the mellophone, sounding like Ron Geesin with a band. Snarling horns buzz in and out of the mix while showers of percussion sparkle in the background. The brief (at 1½ minutes) "Minitrue" is some more saucy jazz, with Hopper on piano and Marshall's big drum sound accompanied by saxes and trombones.

The second epic-length track, the 12½-minute "Miniplenty," is a major highlight. Accompanied by Marshall's percussion, Hopper plays his bass guitar through something called a "tootlebug"; also heard are hand bells and voice. This is a very experimental piece, with odd percussions dominating and huge industrial slabs of bass notes, over which are laid soloing notes. The cut becomes an ethereal, evocative vortex of sound that takes the listener's imagination to many places. The track ends with dissipating and dissolving saxes and percussion. This leads into the final piece, the 2½-minute "Minitrue Reprise" with Hopper on bass and sax and Marshall on drums.

1984 was released just one month after Soft Machine's double album *Six* (their most progressive and well-produced album), and Hopper continued to release several further solo titles, the best of which is the 1977 followup to *1984, Hoppertunity Box.*

I

IN BE TWEEN NOISE

SO DELICATE AND STRANGELY MADE. Released 1993. New Plastic Music.

So Delicate and Strangely Made is an apt title for this musical concoction, an eccentric American oddity of drone music accomplished via collage construction and the improvisational uses of unlikely instruments. A truly strange and diverse grab-bag of unusual sounds, this debut disc by In Be Tween Noise's composer/instrumentalist Steve Roden is not as successful as the later *Humming Endlessly in the Hush* (see review below), but is every bit as fascinating. Unfortunately, the disc has a high degree of hiss. The fidelity is otherwise good, but even minor defects detract from music of this subtlety. Nevertheless, this is an essential example of amateur eclecticism at its most inspired, seemingly oblivious to or unaware of any conventional musical forms.

The goal (and theme) of the album appears to be the creation of new types of drones, which is established with the minimalist accordion notes of the 2-minute opening track "So." The 8-minute "Straight Arrow (Navajo Prayer)" combines synth drum, bowed psaltry, bass recorder, harmonica, tapes, and percussion, producing loud, grating, primitive, and simple rhythms, and then becomes a trippy raga with a bass recorder solo. The 2-minute "Delicate" is ethereal, snake-charming music, with Thai guard pipes, samples, and Japanese prayer bell. The lengthy 11-minute "St. Francis' Vision of the Musical Angel" is intense plucked and bowed violin, with sharp and crisp resonances. This is unconventional and primitive music with a purpose, trance-inducing and hypnotic. The 2-minute "And" continues the exploration of drones, with a lap steel guitar and sampled Chinese flute producing airy, drifting, space-out tones.

The 11-minute "Phonography" combines Roden's meditative, high-pitched, soft singing, reverent and shivery, with murky accordion and recorder drones and interruptions from stray voice samples. The 2-minute "Strangely" is a totally abstract, concrète/industrial series of drones from a music box and sampled voices. The 11-minute "Cycle (re-)," which is reminiscent of the experiments of Annea Lockwood's *The Glass World,* produces a spacey landscape. Roden takes 53 glass, plastic, and aluminum cans, and subtlely blows into them, creating a sound like a distant foghorn; this is augmented by other sounds made by tapping and rubbing the containers. The disc ends with the 2-minute "Made," a high-pitched singing produced by microphone feedback, combined with hand drums and voice samples.

HUMMING ENDLESSLY IN THE HUSH. Released 1996. New Plastic Music.

In Be Tween Noise is the musical project of American visual artist Steve Roden, and *Humming Endlessly in the Hush* is perfectly representative of the elusive and thoroughly abstract independent releases that seem to comprise much of the current progressive music scene. This 66½-minute disc explores totally new areas of sound collage and space music. It doesn't even try to be musically conventional; it carries on as if the concept of music were being invented right there, with no preconceived ideas or influences. Primitive and improvisational, the album has a very intimate, homemade feel, taking music making away from slick professionalism and returning it to inspired amateurism. Roden brings sensibilities from other artistic disciplines to the music (these pieces are often used as sound installations as part of other projects), giving these uniquely strange sounds a rich, hypnotic quality.

The 5½-minute "The Wishing Bells (Part 2)" opens. A series of odd drones and subtle percussion, produced with an accordion, a toy lute, and a coffee can and string, is simple yet effective. The 7-minute "The Apostle" features voice (by Roden), bagpipes, and field recordings of street musicians. Gentle, meditative, multitracked vocal chants give way to a pipes solo. It's not really weird, except for the occasionally shrill background sounds. The 5½-minute "Dry Mouthed Insects on the Gates of Heaven" combines spooky, stereo-panned Micromoog frequencies with a glass bead being rolled in a Japanese prayer bowl, plus kalimba notes, and ghostly dreamlike radio waves are floated in. The effect is like Fiorella Terenzi meets Popol Vuh via O + A. The 7-minute "Meditation on the Memory of a Theme by Purcell" is soothing and dreamy collage music, with a melancholy lap steel guitar in the midst of stereo effects and the sounds of voices from a television.

The 6½-minute "Any Illimitable Star" employs saxlike bagpipes, bouzouki, and the shaking of an object inside a juice can, creating a mellow mood. The 6-minute "We Moved in a Varicolored Universe of Stories" has a totally unconventional vocal with words by Roden that is so sleepy and delicate that it becomes another elusive (and slightly incoherent) element in a collage along with recordings of a radiator and train sounds, plus lap steel guitar. It is very well done. The 5-minute "The Wishing Bells (Part 1)" is mysterious, evocative space music, with environmental sounds (of a lake) and church bells combined with pump organ and the plucked strings of a toy lute. The effect is reassuring and relaxing. The 5½-minute "Untitled" is an intense, heavy raga, with radical stereo separation, and superb textures of bowed banjo, African drums, and cymbal.

The epic 15-minute "Communicating Vessels" takes a bicycle wheel (in the spirit of Dadaist Marcel Duchamp's "ready-mades") and "prepares" it with paper clips and screws on its various parts, making percussive noises. To this are added environmental sounds (a recording of a bamboo fountain) and odd interruptions of voice, guitar, whistle, and choir loops. The effect is hypnotic. The concluding track is the 2½-minute "Etaropave," which is so low-key it's barely there, with the tiny, quiet sounds of a music box in one channel and field recordings of a Japanese fish seller in the other.

Every piece on *Humming* breaks new ground, and is unquestionably progressive. Most importantly, it takes avant-garde forms and concepts out of the high tech-professional realm and returns them to a do-it-yourself aesthetic. Listening to *Humming* . . . is very much like glimpsing up close the private dream world of a person creating a private entertainment by making strange sounds with commonplace objects that can be found in anyone's home. For this it receives the highest possible recommendation.

The sound quality is excellent, and the cover art is a Rorschach-like inkblot.

GILBERT ISBIN/RUDY DE SUTTER

ACOUSTIC DIALOGUES. Released 1995. Tern import.

Digitally recorded in one day on January 18, 1995 at the concert studio Conservatory in Kortrijk, Belgium, *Acoustic Dialogues* is an excellent collection of adventurous acoustic guitar/acoustic piano duets, done without calculation in a sophisticated way. Isbin, the classical guitarist from the group Extensions (see review), and de Sutter are both surprisingly good for being relative unknowns on a small obscure label. Not many people record like this anymore, even in jazz. It's the sort of recording with a sense of spontaneous immediacy that larger labels once prided themselves on.

The two musicians make a good team, pulling out cascades of scales and notes for this one session, achieving some poignant moments. The playing style of both here is low-key and gentle, even though Isbin goes all out for certain effects, utilizing experimental sounds by scratching and snapping the strings of his guitar or tapping out small rhythms on the body of the instrument.

"Dialogue 3" features romantic notes from de Sutter's piano, with tasteful additions from Isbin. The 1-minute "Dialogue 4" is quite avant-garde, with scatting vocalizing and random bursts of playing. "Blue Dusk" (by Isbin) reveals the delicacy of Isbin's approach, while "Colours" (by de Sutter) aims for an introspective form via de Sutter's piano. Each of these individually penned tracks showcases the performer in peak form. There is a lot of space in this music (especially in "Dialogue 7"), with the instruments resonating

Gilbert Isbin.

superbly, unencumbered by any surface noise courtesy of the full digital production. The cover is a black-and-white photo of the two gentlemen in shadow.

J

JETHRO TULL

THICK AS A BRICK. Released February 1972. EMI import (remaster).

An easy-to-like popular classic of British progressive rock in the style of other seminal works from 1972 like Yes's *Fragile,* Focus's *Moving Waves,* and Khan's *Space Shanty, Thick As a Brick* is the most progressive Jethro Tull album. While the band have several releases in a similar vein (1973's *A Passion Play* comes the closest), none has the conceptual unity that this has. In actuality, most of the band's recorded output generally falls well within the popular forms of FM/arena rock and folk music. *Thick As a Brick* is all one piece, running 43:15, divided into two parts. This kind of extended running length was an innovation, the first of its kind in rock circles.

Written by leader/vocalist/guitarist/flautist Ian Anderson, *Thick As a Brick* is quite formally constructed, using several motifs, all executed with precision. The recording is also one of the most successful fusions of classical forms and modern rock techniques. Yet it sounds raw and live, proving that the band certainly knew how to use the studio to enlarge their sound. The vocals, guitars, and flute are all multitracked, creating airy, wide-open spaces. The production values are state of the art for the period—a detailed mix with great separation and stereo effects that makes ideal headphone candy.

Thick As a Brick is also a conceptual masterpiece. The lyrics are a clever, Pythonesque, very English counterculture put-down of greedy, mean squares and other contemptible bourgeois types. For this, *Thick As a Brick* was warmly received in hippie quarters in the 1970s. While irony and humor are employed, for the most part the lyrics are quite serious and savage. The words are intense, and have teeth. They also work well as poetry and can stand on their own. The original LP sleeve employed a newspaper format, and looked something like an underground magazine. The EMI remaster reprints this in its entirety.

The lush and attractive opening immediately grabs the listener, with its dual acoustic guitars, flute, piano, bass, cymbals, and Anderson's impassioned vocals, which range from confident to vulnerable. The piece then moves into powerful heavy rock workouts with electric guitars, organ, bass, drums, flute, and tamborine. One of the most compelling elements of Jethro Tull has always been their formidable rock and roll chops. *Thick As a Brick* allows them the length necessary to let loose, one of the reasons why this album is among their most beloved. Martin Barre's guitars define the Tull sound as much as Anderson does, a sound constructed from duelling electrics and acoustics. The rest of the band is also exemplary and aggressive, particularly drummer Clive Bunker.

In the center of the piece are some atmospheric moments of wind sounds, which serve both as a transition and as a break from all the heavy rock. The album's high point is perhaps the visionary second half. The music is spiritual and cathartic, and Anderson sings here as if a revelation has been experienced and is now being earnestly communicated; he seems to be making a utopian appeal. The music is relentless and intense, racing around its main themes. The album ends abruptly, with a reprise of the main lyric by Anderson, minus the rest of the band. As fresh today as it was in 1972, *Thick As a Brick* stands as a demonstration of the wonderful possibilities inherent in the fusion of classical and rock forms. The remaster also contains a live version of the first half of the piece, recorded in 1978, and an interview with three of the band members.

KHAN

SPACE SHANTY. Released June 1972. Deram.

Space Shanty is a very exciting vocal prog rock album, deserving of more attention than it has received. The band Khan, led by composer/guitarist/vocalist Steve Hillage, performs a savagely hard rock form of progressive music, which evidently was too far ahead of its time in mid-1972, since the group quickly disbanded and Hillage joined Gong the following year. Hillage must have felt stifled in Gong compared with Khan. Even though Khan was a band and not a solo project, Hillage is at the center of things on *Space Shanty,* which is far and away more progressive and entertaining than his later solo releases, with the exception of 1979's *Rainbow Dome Musick* (see review).

Helping make *Space Shanty* the delight it is were its high production values. The performances have a strong live and in-your-face feel, which is captured with top-notch sound that never dilutes its muscularity. There's lots of stereo panning and stereo drum rolls, with only keyboardist Dave Stewart's (of Egg) organ sounds coming across as dated. Eric Peachey's drum sound is massive and hip, contributing active beats and fills that practically steal the show from Hillage.

The opening 9-minute title track startles with a loud introduction of provocative chords and drums. The lyrics, here and on the rest of *Space Shanty,* are authentic, tripped-out counterculture raps, giving the album a unique context for its heavy prog rock. The title track, with its long instrumental workouts, sets the tone for this album. Hillage's aggressive guitar orchestrations and powerful psychedelic soloing dominate here as nowhere else (certainly not in Gong), backed by what must be his tightest ever band (Peachey, Stewart, and bassist Nick Greenwood).

The 6½-minute ballad "Stranded Effervescent Psychonovelty No. 5" opens with a gorgeous acoustic guitar, accompanied by Stewart's sunny and jazzy Canterbury keyboards, but later moves into screaming guitar territory. The 7-minute "Mixed Up Man of the Mountains" is an inspiring cut, with an impassioned vocal delivery by Hillage about the joys of feeling free. The song, co-written with Greenwood, is bursting with ideas, going through several dramatic rocking and jazzy sections, with filtered vocal section, snake-charming organ, and bass notes also thrown in. The 9½-minute "Driving to Amsterdam" begins as the disc's most jazzy and ballady track, but then goes into some heavy metal guitar. The 5½-minute "Stargazers" also has same ripping guitar work but overall it is the disc's weakest cut, being the most vocal-heavy, with a chorus that becomes rather tedious.

"Hollow Stone"/"Escape of the Space Pirates," the concluding 8-minute track, is the most determinedly progressive track, with fantasy lyrics describing some sort of vision or personal epiphany. The opening, with lush dual acoustic guitars, is superb.

The cover art by David Anstey is similar to Ron Cobb's cover for Jefferson Airplane's 1967 *After Bathing at Baxters,* and is suitably psychedelic for this recording.

KING CRIMSON

IN THE COURT OF THE CRIMSON KING.

Released October 1969. Caroline.

A surreal modernist classic, *In the Court of the Crimson King* broke all kinds of new musical ground at the time of its release and is one of the recordings that formed the foundations of modern progressive music. The lineup here consisted of Robert Fripp (guitars), Pete Sinfield (lyrics), Greg Lake (vocals, bass guitar), Ian McDonald (keyboards, mellotron, reeds, woodwinds, vibes, vocals), and Michael Giles (drums, percussion).

"21st Century Schizoid Man," the demented 7½-minute opening track, was hard-hitting stuff in 1969, in some ways analogous to the music made by today's industrial noise or death metal rock bands. Actually, it's more of a jazz/rock fusion, but with its big, aggressive rhythm section, Lake's muted vocals, and screeching guitar and reeds it was one of the most outre rock songs of its era. "I Talk to the Wind," sung by McDonald, is a very English, folksy ballad—6 minutes of tastefully done wistfulness, with lyrics that are a philosophical statement reflecting the introspection of one's formative years. The woodwinds solos and artful drumming are lovely highlights of this song.

The 8½-minute "Epitaph" is a landmark track, introducing the genre of symphonic rock. Ominous, mature, and formal storytelling, the piece is delivered with somber, dramatic grandeur and is entirely convincing and moving. Huge dollops of mellotron orchestration, Fripp's acoustic guitar, and Lake's deep vocals relate Sinfield's pessimistic lyrics about the tragedy of failed leadership in human affairs. The 12-minute "Moonchild" is another crucial piece, the most modernist and ethereal track. It opens with a brief section of radically separated stereo, with Lake's filtered, faraway vocals in one channel and Fripp's sirenlike guitar textures beckoning in the other and various percussions dancing over and beneath them. A lengthy, quiet Stockhausen-like soundscape then develops, with short bursts of sounds of light guitar colorings, vibes, and percussion squeaking away on their own, occasionally all coming together in cascades of dreamy, otherworldly patterns.

The 9½-minute title track is more glorious symphonic pomp similar to "Epitaph," though with fantasy lyrics similar to "Moonchild." It's all put across with a kind of Gothic, self-involved majesty that is attractive even to those who claim to dislike this kind of formally structured art song.

Sinfield's words are actually formidable as poetry, and his combination of wry social commentary on the present and fantastic tales of bygone eras became the blueprint for the lyrical content of progressive rock. His contributions to the genre are as significant as those of the other members of the band.

In the Court of the Crimson King put King Crimson at the forefront of the musical counterculture. It's a solid group effort, unlike later releases led by Fripp. The band certainly had the artistic freedom to create such radically different directions, as their album is self-produced, rare for a debut major label release. The production is effective if thin and hissy.

The attention-getting historic cover art by Barry Godber is as notable as the music. The front cover painting is a screaming face, something like the one in Edvard Munch's "The Scream," in extreme closeup. The booklet painting is a surreal, twisting, grinning face. Both works are done in deep red colors, and were spectacular choices for presenting King Crimson's breakthrough music.

The two-disc set *Epitaph,* released in 1997, chronicles several live shows by the band in late 1969, and is a fascinating document demonstrating the innovations of this early era of King Crimson.

The mystical symphonic rock introduced on King Crimson's first three albums (*In the Court of the Crimson King, In the Wake of Poseidon,* and *Lizard)* influenced a large number of the early wave of U.K. prog rockers, including Emerson, Lake & Palmer, Genesis, Steve Hackett, Henry Cow, Van Der Graaf Generator, and Yes, and is still influential, as evidenced by the symphonic prog of 1990s Scandinavian groups Anekdoten, Anglagard, and White Willow.

IN THE WAKE OF POSEIDON. Released May 1970. Caroline.

The second King Crimson masterpiece retains the same structure as *In the Court of the Crimson King,* closely rewriting it (but with better production values), and giving it a more advanced and muscular sound. With the lineup coming apart in early 1970 and Ian McDonald gone, *In the Wake of Poseidon* begins the period of King Crimson that was "produced and directed" by Robert Fripp and Pete Sinfield. *In the Wake . . .* is written entirely by the two, except for two songs co-written by Fripp with McDonald. While Greg Lake and Michael Giles are on this album, they left the group during the recording. Expanding the lineup are Peter Giles, Michael's brother, on bass guitar, Keith Tippett on piano, Mel Collins on saxes and flute, and vocalist Gordon Haskell. Given all of these changes, it is amazing that *In the Wake . . .* was released only seven months after the appearance of the first album. And like *In the Court . . . , In the Wake . . .* is a veritable blueprint for the genre of serious, classically structured symphonic progressive rock.

Fripp plays a larger than usual amount of acoustic guitar on *In the Wake . . . ,* and it's nice to hear as he's quite good on the instrument. He also plays mellotron and "devices." Sinfield, assuming a more expanded role in the band, again shapes the presentation of King Crimson via his clever and cosmic lyrics, giving the project a philosophical depth, intelligence, and abundant sense of mystery. For this Sinfield deserves a great deal of credit, as he manages to maintain the high art principles which in the hands of so many imitators became hollow pretension.

In the Wake . . . opens with the brief (at 0:49) "Peace—A Beginning," which is a soft, echoed, and filtered solo vocal by Lake that introduces the bookending theme of peace. After a few gentle chords, the listener is launched into the 8-minute frenzy of "Pictures of a City." Like "21st Century Schizoid Man," this is a loud, hard-edged jazz/rock blowout, with snarling slabs of heavy guitars that are positively industrial and some very hip playing from the Giles brothers rhythm section. The 4½-minute "Cadence and Cascade," sung by Haskell, is another very English ballad à la "I Talk to the Wind," with lovely, light acoustic guitar and piano tradeoffs. The 8-minute title track, like *In the Court*'s "Epitaph," is ominous symphonic rock featuring mellotron, acoustic guitar, bass, and drums. Classical in approach and grand in execution, it all amounts to a very large sound, and a powerful form of poetic and philosophical storytelling.

"Peace—A Theme" is a 1-minute reprise of the opening theme on acoustic guitar. "Cat Food," their single at the time, is a driving, macho oddity, with an aggressive vocal from Lake, rollicking piano runs by Tippett, and for-laughs (though dark) lyrics by Sinfield. The 11½-minute "The Devil's Triangle" is an album highlight. A storytelling instrumental featuring mainly mellotron and percussion, it sounds almost like the soundtrack to a film. A lengthy, moody, murky buildup sets the scene for some imaginative images. A loud foghorn is then heard, and noises like an ocean tempest swirl loudly, until only a quiet clicking sound is heard, like an abandoned ship found floating on the sea. The final piece is the 2-minute "Peace—an End," with another emotional vocal by Lake and Sinfield's proto-hippie pacifist lyrics.

The imposing cover painting, *12 Archetypes* by Tammode Jongh, emphasizes the magnificent and mysterious qualities in this music.

LIZARD. Released December 1970. Caroline.

A revolutionary innovation in modern music, *Lizard* incorporates chamber music, jazz, and psychedelia into King Crimson's symphonic rock, creating a unique world in which to tell its musical stories. In many ways this recording is the most sophisticated King Crimson incarnation, way ahead of its time, and it confused as many people as it won over. The album is as much of a breakthrough in the realm of fusion as any from 1970, and it is as significant in its own way as John McLaughlin's *Devotion* or Miles Davis's *Bitches' Brew.*

Lizard is fresh and not at all dated, with advanced production values and a crisp mix that bring out the details of the layered arrangements. This advantage in sound quality was unusual in 1970, making *Lizard* seem more thought-out and complete by comparison with others from that era. The music goes down many different avenues, with each idea followed up. Despite the many changes taking place in the band's lineup, *Lizard* was released only seven months

King Crimson (1994–present lineup). From left to right, Robert Fripp, Pat Mastelotto, Bill Bruford, Trey Gunn, Adrian Belew, Tony Levin. (Photo by Kevin Westenberg.)

after the release of *In the Wake of Poseidon.* The lineup for *Lizard* is Robert Fripp (guitars, mellotron, electric piano, "devices"), Pete Sinfield (lyrics, sleeve, co-producer), Mel Collins (flute, saxes), Gordon Haskell (bass guitar, vocals), Andy McCulloch (drums), Keith Tippett (piano), Robin Miller (oboe), plus others on cornet and trombone.

The surreal aspect of *Lizard* is perhaps the icing on the cake. Studio effects, outstandingly wide stereo separation, mad carnival barker–like vocals from Gordon Haskell, and dense, oblique, poetic lyrics make this a King Crimson unlike all others. With wind instruments, piano, and an abundance of acoustic guitars, *Lizard*'s sound is more elaborate and ornate (in keeping with Sinfield's conceptual direction) than on their other releases.

The 6½-minute "Cirkus" retains the gargantuan mellotron and evocative lead acoustic guitar of the earlier albums, but takes the symphonic formulas into more obscure and eclectic directions. This is less straightforward, more abstract. The music is layered with smaller touches, less garish than the first two albums. Andy McCulloch does an amazing job throughout, providing huge drum fills; Michael Giles isn't missed. The 5½-minute "Indoor Games" has a saucy jam with electric guitars, bass, drums, and sax that's pretty savory. The 4-minute "Happy Family" features mangled, filtered vocals, tight drumming, and punctuating piano notes, with touches of coloring from Fripp's guitars. The middle section is dissonant, free, and glorious. Following all of this surreal madness comes the truly beautiful 2½-minute ballad "Lady of the Dancing Water." Romantic and formal, with lovely flute, electric piano, acoustic guitar, and gentle vocal by Haskell, it shows the heights that the poetic art song can reach.

The 23½-minute title track is one of the finest examples of progressive music. Conceptual, dramatic, and multistylistic, it's at once formal and modern, fusing classical, jazz, and rock elements. There's depth in spades throughout, both musically and lyrically. There are deft touches from all the players, though particularly from Fripp, Tippett, and McCulloch. The track is divided into four sections—"Prince Rupert Awakes," "Bolero—The Peacock's Tale," "The Battle of Glass Tears," and "Big Top."

"Prince Rupert Awakes" features vocals by Jon Anderson of Yes. Sinfield's lyrics relate an obscure tale, and since Yes was only beginning their progressive phase at this point, it is logical to assume that Anderson was greatly influenced by Sinfield's writing style. "Bolero—The Peacock's Tale" is tasteful, flowing chamber music, with piano, oboe, and bass, and a trombone solo. This embracing of overtly orchestral forms within the context of what was then a popular rock release was a big influence on later groups. "The Battle of Glass Tears," with its gigantic drum fills and walls of mellotron, contains some foreboding cinematic images. The section concludes with slabs of bass guitar and a menacing, screeching electric guitar. In this spacey yet scary section can be heard snippets of ideas that were to influence groups from Genesis to Heldon to Shylock. "Big Top" is a surreal stereo pan of circus-style organ, piano, and percussion, reprising images from the first song.

The flamboyant cover by Gini Barris is a portmanteau of fascinatingly detailed, dark scenes from the "circus of life"—both medieval and modern— on a gold-embossed art deco sleeve. It's very appropriate for the music.

1971's *Islands* continued the directions of *Lizard,* but far less successfully, having an inappropriately sparse and improvised sound which attempts to put across too many uncomfortable transitions and juxtapositions. It's one of their least-successful releases. After *Islands* Sinfield departed, leaving Fripp to remake King Crimson solely according to his vision.

STARLESS AND BIBLE BLACK. Released February 1974. Caroline.

The 1973–1974 era of King Crimson is another popular high point for the band, featuring aggressive, cutting, and harder-edged rock, in contrast to the jazzy, symphonic hippie floweriness of the Pete Sinfield era. Joining leader Robert Fripp in this new incarnation is Bill Bruford on percussion, fresh from Yes; violinist/keyboardist David Cross; and bassist/vocalist John Wetton. Also featured are lyrics by Richard Palmer-James. The music of this lineup combined loud, funky fusion with spacey improvisational textures, sort of like a strange hybrid of Mahavishnu Orchestra and Henry Cow. Palmer-James's lyrics deal with more contemporary themes, retaining Sinfield's detached poetics but exuding an even darker cynicism.

This band's forte was live concert performances, and the 1992 release of the four-disc box set *The Great Deceiver* (see review) makes the 1973 King Crimson studio album *Larks Tongues in Aspic* somewhat redundant, with the live presentations eclipsing the studio versions. *Starless and Bible Black,* with the exception of the first two tracks, is also a collection of live recordings. Because the audience is mixed out, most people didn't know the music was live until this was stated in the booklet of *The Great Deceiver.* All the material from *Larks Tongues in Aspic* is represented on *The Great Deceiver,* but the two 1974 King Crimson releases, *Starless* and *Red,* both contain several tracks not found on that set and so are reviewed separately.

Starless . . . opens with "The Great Deceiver," a rather clever, if somewhat mainstream, rock and roll number. The song is too chorus-heavy, which ultimately becomes grating. *Lament* is next, a self-referential take on the life of rock stars. Wetton's vocals are similar to Greg Lake's in that his deep voice and delivery are powerful, authoritative, and muscular. The tenacity and edginess he brings to songs like "Lament" are a rousing feature of the album.

The live material begins with the instrumental "We'll Let You Know," a concise representation of the music of this band. An embryonic improv, it begins slowly with textures from Cross, then follows with sharp slabs of punctuating bass guitar notes to begin a groove, joined by Bruford's monster drums and Fripp's characteristic angular and tight guitar playing. The funkiness of the piece, and of this band in general, was a real change from the then-current directions of U.K. prog rock.

"The Night Watch," on the other hand, successfully revisits a Sinfield-era style. A delicate ballad with lyrics referencing Rembrandt's famous painting of the same name, the piece features bells, violin, and Fripp's celestial guitar orchestrations and solos. This is some of Fripp's finest guitar work, and a standout track on the album.

"Trio," a 5½-minute instrumental, further elaborates on the band's chamber music directions, merely hinted at on previous releases. Using no percussion, the track is dominated by Cross's string instruments and the mellotron. It's spacey, gentle, and lyrical. "The Mincer" is a very odd track, with haunting guitar and some vocal parts that seem awkward and don't work very well. The 9-minute title track is more representative of this band. It's buildup music, starting with light percussion and random notes before finally coalescing into an all-out jam. Fripp's guitar sounds are savage waves of deadly serious, resonating screeches punctuated by Wetton's thick bass and Bruford's colorful playing.

The 11-minute "Fracture" is also an atypical example of the Crimson sound, both at the time and in later incarnations. A tricky and unique form of fusion, it chases down a groove, then retreats to something else, follows those new directions, then returns back to the earlier groove. It's more buildup jamming, led by Fripp's gaunt guitar style, which is somewhat cold but tight and energetic.

The sound is excellent throughout, and the live material is especially well recorded and mixed. The styles characteristic of this era of King Crimson have directly influenced a number of progressive bands, from Heldon and Univers Zero to Anekdoten and Happy Family.

RED. Released October 1974. Caroline.

Released only eight months after *Starless and Bible Black, Red* was the swan song of the 1970s King Crimson, after which Robert Fripp unwisely and somewhat hastily declared the band over and done with. Here on *Red* the band is down to the trio of Fripp, Bruford, and Wetton; Cross was no longer a full-time member. Several former members from the previous lineups make guest appearances on the album, including Cross, Ian McDonald, Mel Collins, and Robin Miller. Richard Palmer-James's dark lyrics are more down and dirty than ever before (similar to the approach taken by Peter Gabriel on Genesis' *The Lamb Lies Down on Broadway),* a move designed to escape the flowery fantasy that had become a staple of U.K. prog rock. This works well for the music of *Red,* which is the toughest and most straightforward rock and roll King Crimson release of the 1970s.

The 6-minute instrumental title track by Fripp opens with attention-getting heavy metal power chording and riffing. Powerful and relentless, it was the band's most aggressive track to date. "Fallen Angel" also has a gritty edge, with lots of saxophone blowing from McDonald. Unfortunately, the horns and Wetton's vocals here become too grating, as they also are on the 7-minute "One More Red Nightmare." The shrieking noisiness is an acquired taste.

The 8-minute instrumental "Providence" is more atypical Crimson buildup music, featuring Cross's violin. The final half of the piece has lots of whiny guitars and an especially hard-hitting rhythm section. The 12-minute "Starless," a favorite, opens with a melancholy mellotron dirge and a lengthy buildup led by Fripp's insistent guitar scales, and finally explodes in a powerful series of notes and another sax solo from McDonald.

The overall sound is appropriately muscular, and the playing, particularly by Wetton, constantly impresses. While *Red* is certainly a solid album, it has tended to be somewhat overrated by fans. The cover is a stark black-and-white photo of the trio on a black background.

THREE OF A PERFECT PAIR LIVE IN JAPAN (video). Released 1984. Laser disc import (Japan).

Like the 1973–1974 lineup, the 1981–1984 King Crimson is better in a concert setting than in the studio. While the three 1980s Crimson releases—*Discipline* (1981), *Beat* (1982), and *Three of a Perfect Pair* (1984) are not classics, they do have their moments. Since the 90-minute *Live in Japan* features most of the tracks from these albums, it stands as the ideal document of this era. With full digital stereo sound and high-resolution color video, this Japanese laser disc set a standard for audiophile-level video recordings of live events.

The 1980s King Crimson was yet another radical reinvention of the band by Robert Fripp. Instead of symphonic art song or jazz/rock fusion, this Crimson embraced head-on the conciseness and polished danceability of new wave rock, with a definite 1980s aesthetic sensibility similar to that of Peter Gabriel, Talking Heads, and Laurie Anderson, all of whom were collaborators at some point with Fripp and new vocalist/guitarist/lyricist/percussionist Adrian Belew. Drummer Bill Bruford returns, with session man extraordinaire Tony Levin on bass and keyboards rounding out the lineup. It is not an exaggeration to say that each of the four has become something of a living legend. This version of King Crimson also introduces the era where a mountain of high-tech gadgetry is trotted out, most notably the wealth of processing toys employed by the two guitarists, Bruford's electronic percussion, and Levin's Chapman stick (a basslike instrument).

The band retains the usual clever and tricky compositions, with a particular emphasis on rhythm that's dense in the extreme, leaving a lot of space in the music. Thick webs of guitars and bass carve out edgy, jagged, screechy, and rumbly grooves, which in a sense is what they've always done, only here it's polished to a tee. The sound is still big and muscular, and as tight as is humanly possible. The mix is precise and flat, emphasizing even more the well-rehearsed and beautifully executed arrangements.

"Larks Tongues in Aspic Part 3" sets the tone for the material and features a ripping solo from Fripp. The guitar tradeoffs between Fripp and Belew on "Frame by Frame" and "Discipline" are extraordinarily complex and difficult. These pieces really need to be seen as well as heard. "Industry" and "Dig Me" are positively industrial, with a machinelike precision from Levin and Bruford, over which Belew (in particular) and Fripp tease every kind of ominous squeak and whine out of their guitars. "Sartori in Tangier" is the most similar to the 1973–1974 Crimson, as is, of course, the chunky version of "Larks Tongues In Aspic Part 2." "Indiscipline" and "Elephant Talk" offer some of Belew's finest moments; as the group's front man in these pieces, with their many unexpected twists and turns, he manages to project an authentic "otherness." Belew is the first lyricist for King Crimson to come from the playing lineup of the band (the others were poets), and he does a spectacular job, for which he deserves more credit. Belew's element has usually been more pop-oriented styles, and his keen grasp of what was required lyrically for a serious group like King Crimson is one of his finest accomplishments.

On the other hand, tracks like "Man with an Open Heart" and "Three of a Perfect Pair" veer heavily into Talking Heads–like quirky pop, for which Belew's smooth-guy vocals and writing bear the lion's share of the blame. These tracks, along with other pop-single-style material like the love song "Heartbeat" and the danceable "Sleepless," caused many observers to compare the 1980s King Crimson to the 1980s Genesis—labeling both as 1970s dinosaurs that had capitulated to current marketplace demands in order to maintain their major label status. But given that half of the material here is instrumental, that comparison is not justified. *Live in Japan* is engrossingly compelling for those who have never seen a King Crimson performance, and is manna from heaven for the rabid Crimson fan. The camera coverage of the show is straightforward, the Japanese audience is responsive if overly respectful, and Bruford was virtually the only drummer in the 1980s to utilize electronic percussion with any ingenuity or attractiveness. For these reasons, for the instrumentals, and for their updating of the Crimson approach, *Three of a Perfect Pair Live in Japan* is essential progressive rock.

THE GREAT DECEIVER (box set). Released November 1992. Caroline/Discipline.

A four-disc set of concert material from 1973 and 1974, *The Great Deceiver* is a tasty, first-rate treat for fans of this era of King Crimson. All the discs are in the 70-minute range, and all have high-quality, monster sound. Not only are there a large number of instrumental improvisations and never-before-released tracks here, but the rawness of the live presentation makes *The Great Deceiver* preferable to studio albums like *Larks Tongues in Aspic* and *Red.* While fans will appreciate this box set, newcomers would probably be best served by *Starless and Bible Black,* which provides a more concise overview.

The first disc is the final performance of the quartet of Robert Fripp, Bill Bruford, John Wetton, and David Cross, recorded in Providence, Rhode Island, in June of 1974. Often Cross (on violin, viola and mellotron) is just stomped on in the live mixes by the hard rock blowing of the other three, and his departure is, in a way, a testament to the power of this band. "Larks Tongues In Aspic Part 2" is a somewhat academic form of instrumental heavy metal, with slashing guitar chords and monstrous slabs of bass guitar. "Lament" is more subdued at first here, but its loud parts are much more frenetic in concert. "Exiles" is a poignant and serene ballad, and one of lyricist Richard Palmer-James's finest works. The volume fortunately doesn't swamp this piece's lovely melody. "A Voyage to the Center of the Cosmos" is an 11½-minute improv, and the best of the improvs on the set. The first half features huge drumbeats and bass riffing, over which Fripp's squeaking guitar lines relay Eastern-style drones, only with massive amplification. The second half is a moody section, with violin, mellotron, bass, and light cymbals, returning at the end to the song's opening groove, accompanied by Bruford's powerful rim shot snare hits. "Easy Money" is tough muscular rock, with impudent, snotty guitar chords and bravado soloing. "Providence," here an improv, was later developed in the studio for *Red.*

Disc 2 finishes the Rhode Island concert with a decent version of "2lst Century Schizoid Man." Bruford gloriously bashes his way through this. From there the disc moves to an October 1973 show in Glasgow, Scotland. "Sharks' Lungs in Lemsip" is a low-key improv intro that segues into "Larks Tongues in Aspic Part 1." An excellent and energetic instrumental, the piece goes through several tricky shifts in pace with all four members cooking in an extremely tight and exciting arrangement. "Book of Saturday" provides a respite of soaring beauty from the heavy rock, with a vocal by Wetton, Cross's nice violin solo, and Bruford's exotic percussion. This is followed by the abrasive "Easy Money" and "We'll Let You Know," almost note for note the same as on *Starless and Bible Black,* as is "The Night Watch." An 8½-minute improv, "Tight Scrummy," follows, with salty percussion from Bruford. The piece becomes almost Mahavishnu-like, with sonorous passages from Cross and Fripp. Surprisingly, the Glasgow material concludes with two tracks from *In the Wake of Poseidon:* the soft 1-minute "Peace—A Theme," here performed on electric guitar, and "Cat Food," which has Bruford's playing all over it, with the rhythms from the piano (on the studio version) replicated here on drums. Two tracks from a June 1974 show at Penn State wrap up this disc—2 minutes of "Easy Money" and another buildup improv, the 7½-minute ". . . It Is for You, But Not for Us."

Disc 3 is a subdued, restrained performance from April, 1974, in Pittsburgh, Pennsylvania, before an enthusiastic crowd. "The Great Deceiver" retains the same form as the studio version, but with a slightly different guitar sound. The short, spacey improv "Bartley Butsford" features light bells, soft violin, and mellotron and flows into "Exiles." The 4½-minute improv "Daniel Dust" is a celestial guitar/violin duet, and a perfect intro into "The Night Watch."

The 5-minute "Doctor Diamond" is a vocal track that never made it on to any of the albums, with lyrics once again from Palmer-James. It's a fascinating if lumbering rave-up, a conventional rocker à la "Easy Money," with piercing solos from Fripp and Cross. "Starless" here is preferable to the one on *Red,* without the shrill saxophone and with more active percussion. There's an especially fantastic part where Fripp's guitar reprises the vocal section at the conclusion. The 6-minute improv "Wilton Carpet" is another atypical, edgy, embryonic buildup number, moving into the 5½-minute instrumental "The Talking Drum." The show concludes with 2½ minutes of "Larks Tongues In Aspic Part 2." The disc then returns to the June 1974 Penn State show for a loud rock improv entitled "Is There Life Out There?"

The fourth disc begins with a June 1974 show in Toronto, Canada, before a rowdy, enthusiastic crowd. The 11-minute improv "The Golden Walnut" is one of the disc's better instrumentals, an exciting hard rock number. Next come "The Night Watch" and "Fracture," which are similar to the versions on *Starless and Bible Black.* The 8½-minute improv "Clueless and Slightly Slack" is an opportunity for Cross to step forward. Cross lets the notes he plays hang by themselves for a while, while the other three prefer to romp 'n' stomp. Finally, there's material from a November, 1973 show from Zurich, Switzerland. A short improv, "Some Pussyfooting," begins, serving as a nice intro to "Larks Tongues In Aspic Part 1"; this piece is in top form here, alternately ripsnorting and low-key and tasteful. This is followed by the 9-minute improv "The Law of Maximum Distress Parts 1 and 2," and "Easy Money." The 6-minute improv "Some More Pussyfooting" features spacey mellotrons with occasional accompaniment from the rhythm section, leading into another version of "The Talking Drum." Whew!

Overall, *The Great Deceiver* is best experienced in small doses, one disc at a time. A definite sameness creeps up, especially in the improvisations. Yet it all remains interesting, and will please King Crimson fans.

THRAKATTAK. Released June 1996. Discipline.

The 1990's King Crimson retains the 1980's lineup, adding guitarist/bassist Trey Gunn and percussionist Pat Mastelotto. Crimson had quickly released three albums in succession in 1994–1995 (*Vrooom, THRAK,* and *B'Boom Live in Argentina)* that broke no new ground, merely regurgitating the forms of the 1980's Crimson, and so the appearance of a visionary achievement like *THRaKaTTaK* was quite unexpected. The recording is easily the band's most consciously radical and experimental work ever, one that will truly surprise those familiar only with their older material.

THRaKaTTaK assembles a number of disparate improvisations from Crimson's 1995 tour soundboard mix (as on *Starless and Bible Black,* the audiences are mixed out) and juxtaposes them next to one another without pauses. The album is a nonlinear, formless, and difficult creation, light years beyond the other 1990s material. Not by any standard an average rock recording, *THRaKaTTaK* comes across like a futuristic Karlheinz Stockhausen, or Henry Cow à la *Concerts.* It's postmodern and avant-garde to the core, and certainly reestablishes King Crimson's progressive credentials.

The song titles given to the works don't mean much, as they all run together, creating a single 57-minute work rather than a collection of separate pieces. *THRaKaTTaK* represents a pinnacle of high-tech music making, so much so that no layperson would be familiar with all the gear that's employed. Delays, filters, stereo panning, and an array of processors shape the normal rock band sounds in new ways, as if they were mere clay. A plethora of these soundscapes creates a dense and often confusing mix (e.g., keyboard sounds are triggered by the guitars and percussion); the level of technological manipulation here is astonishing.

The mood created by this production is dark and unsettling. Embryonic jams begin in the usual Crimson manner, but before they even take hold the band veers off into new territories. Random, dissonant, and bizarre sounds hang in the air, occasionally coming together to form patterns. There are still some thick, syrupy grooves from the rhythm section(s) and the occasional recognizable guitar solo, but not even Bruford's dependably solid drumming holds anything together here. Just as you're beginning to get the hang of the music, it seems to dissolve in front of you. This is a militantly psychedelic form of sound making, existing in an unreal world where a million things seem to be going on at once but the listener can't with certainty pin down any of it.

Being all textures and rhythms and lacking in melody, *THRaKaTTaK* is not at all an easy listen. It is not even close to having universal appeal, which is a definite drawback. Perhaps a more composed work would have been better, to give the production more focus and direction. Nonetheless, it's one of the most radical releases ever from a front-rank group. The full impact of the album cannot be evaluated yet, as *THRaKaTTaK* is certainly ahead of its time.

The full digital recording is loud, delivering great sound (if slightly shrill). The cover is a concert photo of the band, on which a sticker has been placed warning of "explicit improvisation." An understatement!

LIVE IN JAPAN 1995 (video). Released November 1996. Pony Canyon laser disc import (Japan)/Discipline VHS (domestic).

This 100+-minute concert recorded in October of 1995 in Tokyo, Japan, is the most successful King Crimson project since the 1970s, surpassing all of the band's 1980s and 1990s releases. With new members Pat Mastelotto (percussion) and Trey Gunn (guitars) joining Adrian Belew, Bill Bruford, Robert Fripp, and Tony Levin, the music is less sparse than that of the 1980s four-man lineup, giving the band a more layered sound. As always, King Crimson in concert is much more energetic than King Crimson in the studio; their playing here is at its all-time tastiest, giving this video document much more appeal than any of their recent recordings. The show is executed with verve and panache, mixing a strong sense of macho rock and roll with their trademark experimentalism.

The material is half instrumental, which is appropriate, as the virtuoso performances by the six members are absolutely jaw-dropping. Belew has several new sounds here, adding inventive guitar orchestrations such as a guitar-triggered keyboard and a drill-on-guitar sound on "Thrak," and his additional notes on "Red" are pure genius. Bruford has an enhanced intro of new fills on a marvelous version of "Indiscipline." Other highlights include the driving, heavy rock instrumentals "Vrooom," "B'Boom," and "Vrooom Vrooom;" "Sex, Eat, Sleep, Drink, Dream," and "People" (the two strongest vocal tracks of their 1990s compositions); an update of "The Talking Drum"; and Levin and Gunn performing a "Stick Duet" that is a textbook example of first-rate musicianship. The versions of 1980's tracks such as "Frame by Frame," "Matte Kudasai," "Three of a Perfect Pair," and "Elephant Talk" are the most impressive renderings to date.

The sound quality is perfect (co-mixed by Belew), bringing out the details in each member's playing. The camera coverage is excellent, providing up-close views one could never get when attending a concert. The darkly lit stage and the use of multicolored lights interfere with the resolution at times, but provides the program with a certain warm glow. *Live in Japan* certainly reaffirms King Crimson's status as one of the greatest progressive rock groups.

JACK LANCASTER AND ROBIN LUMLEY

MARSCAPE. Released November 1976. Ozone.

Marscape represents a time in the music industry of the 1970s when major-label session musicians from such U.K. groups as Brand X, Blodwyn Pig, and Penguin Cafe Orchestra could come together for a project with high conceptual and artistic aspirations. An all-instrumental work which evokes what its title suggests—a future journey to Mars—*Marscape* is an irresistable and essential progressive release.

Written and produced by Jack Lancaster (here playing lyricon wind synths, flutes, violin, water gong, and pan pipes) and Robin Lumley (on acoustic and electric piano, harmonium, Moog synth, autoharp, ARP synth, and Hammond organ), *Marscape* features the entire Brand X lineup from 1977's *Moroccan Roll,* including Lumley, drummer Phil Collins, guitarist John Goodsall, bassist Percy Jones, and percussionist Morris Pert. Penguin Cafe Orchestra's leader Simon Jeffes plays the koto and arranges the string quartet. With the abundant instrumental palette brought by these seasoned professionals, *Marscape* effortlessly achieves its imaginative musical goals. The various pieces range from 2 to 7 minutes in length, and on the sleeve each has a subtitle which further guides the listener's visualization.

The album begins with "Take Off," a gurgling and cold chill of synth, percussion, violin, acoustic bass, and electric piano. "Sail On Solar Winds" then introduces the main motif on Lumley's keyboard and Goodsall's rhythm guitar. Here and throughout, Lumley's lush keyboard textures are rich with spacey, dewy notes. The piece crashes into Brand X–like fusion, complete with Collins's drum rolls. "Arrival" is a far-away sounding piano piece, drifting in and out, much like Lumley's "Collapsar" from Brand X's *Moroccan Roll*. "Phobos and Deimos" is suitably celestial, with keyboards, harmonium, violin, percussion, and Collins's huge, echoed drums. "With a Great Feeling of Love," with keyboards, violin, sax, light acoustic guitar, and acoustic bass, has a relaxed spaciness. "Olympus Mons" starts with a Pink Floyd–like heartbeat synth sound, thumping quietly away as distant and sparse piano and sound effects scatter around it. Suddenly the listener is launched into more Brand X–style fusion, with a jazzy sax solo from Lancaster; this too then changes, moving into an unexpected synth section of gurgling, splooshing water sounds, before a return to the ripping jamming of Goodsall, Jones, and Collins.

"Homelight" continues with a bright, sunny, breezy fusion, with dual acoustic guitars reprising the main theme from "Sail On Solar Winds." "Hopper" is Jones' sequenced bass, which the band then joins, accompanied by some spacey keyboard solos. The remaining tracks are the recording's highlights. The two most experimental and imaginative tracks are "Dust Storm" and "Blowholes (The Pipes of Mars)." Pan pipes, bamboo and glass flutes, and wind sounds combine with an exotic "storm" of Jade Warrior–like percussion from Collins and Pert and Jeffes's koto to create truly outer space sci-fi soundscapes. "Realisations" is a grand finale wrap up of the theme, led by piano and a Pink Floyd–like choir. "Release" concludes on a moody note, with flute and koto (a precursor of the sound of the 1980s group Emerald Web).

Fusion sax jams are hardly the stuff of Mars journeys, and this could have easily degenerated into a low-rate soundtrack to an episode of *Space: 1999*. That it doesn't is a testament to the care taken in the writing and recording, which give a clear purpose and context to the fusion music of Brand X and offer an altogether different take on the genres of space rock and space music. This is the sort of project that Phil Collins once embraced, even while fronting Genesis, and he deserves a ton of angry mail for abandoning things like this.

The only drawback here is that the CD is an LP transcription—hardly ideal—with a good amount of surface noise during critical passages. The crisp treble of the guitars and drums comes across best. The cover photo of the darkness of space as seen from a Martian landscape evokes the mood of the album.

LARD FREE

III. Released August 1977. Spalax import.

Lard Free's *III* is an original, odd, and notable fusion of Terry Riley–like minimalism, psychedelia, electronic music, and space music. *III* is the brainchild of Gilbert Artman, the composer and leader of the group, an unusual French progressive band from the mid-1970s. This was the group's final album, and it's far and away their best. Artman handles most of the instruments himself, playing organ, piano, ARP synth, vibraphone, and drums. Also contributing are Xavier Baulleret (guitar), Yves Lanes (synth), and Jean-Pierre Thiraut (clarinet).

From the first few moments of the 17-minute opener, "Spirale Malax," the listener understands that this is some very otherworldly stuff. Pulses of space music organ and synth, Gothic and not at all high-tech begin, then rapidly pick up the pace. Listening to the way the sound unfolds and builds is similar to the experience of hearing an outdoor arena concert from the very back, as waves of echoed (but loud) sound wash through the speakers. Like some kind of huge engine churning away, the piece becomes a swirling and engulfing tempest. To this are added soaring and snarling electric guitar notes by Baulleret—loud and chaotic, yet still entrancing. It is as though one is nearing some vast, otherworldly time tunnel, ominous and unsettling, but beckoning at the same time.

The four sections of "Synthetic Seasons," with all tracks running together, follow a similar unfolding structure, though it is more varied. "Part 1.1" is a 3½-minute display of spacey keyboards, with approaching, echoed drumbeats encircling the mix. "Part 1.2" is more of the same, with stereo panning and effects joined by edgy guitars. Throughout, it is all very minimalist, with primitive, repetitive rhythmic structures from Artman's drums that are subtly shifted in hypnotic ways, an effect underlined by the stereo vibraphone notes that dance from channel to channel. The 3½-minute "Part 2" features a quietly dissonant, industrial guitar texture into which a piano and clarinet float, and eventually replace. The 5½-minute "Part 3" turns up the volume on the drums (still in a repetitive pattern), concluding with a piercing psychedelic guitar solo and loud gusts of synth that come on like a tropical storm.

Like the music of two other 1970s French space music/space rock groups, Clearlight and Heldon, with whom Artman often collaborated, Lard Free's *III* is compelling progressive music. The sound is good, if somewhat flattened by Spalax's ADD remaster. The cover art, though, is ugly—a drawing of empty bottles that conveys nothing about this evocative music.

LET'S BE GENEROUS

LET'S BE GENEROUS. Released 1991. CMP.

With its unconventional approaches to keyboards and guitar, *Let's Be Generous* is one of the most significant progressive jazz rock fusion discs of the 1990s, an example of progressive music at its best. The sounds this band plays are very new, and are captured in a totally live-sounding, full digital production. The quality is high at every level.

The band features two members of the 1980s fusion group Dark, percussionist Mark Nauseef and guitarist Miroslav Tadic. Those who know Dark's two superb releases will be delighted with this recording. The disc has the biggest rhythm section in recent memory, driven by bassist Tony Newton and Nauseef's collection of drums, gongs, cymbals, bells, and metal plates. The main feature of "Let's Be Generous, however, is keyboardist Joachim Kuhn, who constructs layers of electronic horn–like sounds that zig-zag to very effective and impressive heights. Taken together, Kuhn's squonking keyboards and Tadic's jagged guitar release growling polyphonic solos of angular, jazzy counterpoints. These wonderful harmonic progressions have an almost psychedelic effect.

The opening track on the album, a 12-minute cover of Eric Dolphy's "The Prophet," and the following 5½-minute "Always Yours" are perfect introductions to the band's sound. One comparison for newcomers might be the 1970s Miles Davis, only more hard-hitting. This band's four players wage what might be called the war of the gargantuans, where each player has a sound the size of a major metropolitan area. *Let's Be Generous,* then, is some major skronk, the kind of progressive music you can air-guitar or air-drum to.

The 4-minute "Senegal" has an echoed, guitarlike keyboard that, when coupled with Tadic's electric guitar, creates powerful, wrenching sounds which are then joined by bass and percussion. The 2½-minute "Avant Garage" features gongs and other percussion smashes along with staccato guitar patterns joined by bass. Another Eric Dolphy cover, the 3-minute "Something Sweet, Something Tender" is a heavy rock fusion run-through. The 4½-minute "Heavy Hanging" is some bottom-heavy funk, with explosions of percussion from Nauseef and a section of tricky stereo pans. Parts of it recall Return to Forever. "Don't Disturb My Groove" also has a Return to Forever–like funkiness, but with a Fred Frith à la Massacre guitar. The brief "Snake Oil" has keyboards and guitars that go off together like a loud saw blade. The 8½-minute final track, "Kissing the Feet," is a rave-up improv, a chance for all four members to demonstrate their chops, including more shrieks from Kuhn's keyboards.

The unremarkable cover painting by Ulf von Kanitz conveys little about the sensational music found here.

LIGHTWAVE

NACHTMUSIK. Released December 1990. Erdenklang import.

Lightwave is one of the most important progressive groups of the 1990s. They are the current leaders in the genres of electronic music and space music and heirs to the ambitious aesthetic of artists like Tangerine Dream at their creative zenith. Taking current technology into the realms of that kind of high-concept epic storytelling structure (à la TD's *Zeit* and *Atem),* their music makes the most of the possibilities available. Lightwave is the duo of Frenchmen Christoph Harbonnier and Christian Wittman. They are undisputed masters of sonic sculpturing, utilizing all manner of electronic instruments both old and new to create lengthy, climactic works, usually without rhythm, but incorporating shifting resonances that are distinctly unlike the conventional forms of electronic music. *Nachtmusik,* their debut, recorded in 1989 for the German label Erdenklang, was a breakthrough release.

The 23½-minute title track feels like an approaching storm. It is icy, eerie, Gothic, and haunting. Moody and atmospheric creaking noises, subtle human voices, and floating sounds hover (via a lot of stereo phasing) in and out of the foreground, while in the background, sounds like the ominous, occasional ringing of what resembles a cathedral bell leave the listener fascinated but chilled. Nothing about this music is stereotypical.

The 32½-minute "Just Another Dream" opens with a spray of rhythmic patterns, followed by a series of hums and growls that lead the listener into long and drifting notes which shimmer, resonate, sprinkle, and fade, with an intensity level that recedes, becomes chaotic, and then fades away into next to nothing.

The full digital sound is state of the art, lush but never garish in any way. The suitably

Lightwave. Left, Christoph Harbonnier; right, Christian Wittman. (Photos by J-M Pharisien.)

mysterious cover design by Harbonnier of a sky above houses on a darkened night perfectly suits the music. The liner notes feature lengthy and colorful descriptions by the group of the two compositions on the album. *Nachtmusik,* oddly enough, is the most relaxing Lightwave release, subtly taking the listener's imagination into many fascinating areas. It is a brilliant work.

TYCHO BRAHE. Released September 1994. Fathom/Hearts of Space.

A 58½-minute conceptual work inspired by the 16th-century Danish astronomer Tycho Brahe, this is a distinctive and enduring recording. *Tycho Brahe* combines elements of ambient, classical, new age, and musique concrète to create a sophisticated form of electronic music. The conceptual link between astronomy and electronic music is a good one, and is also the basis for Lightwave's live disc *Uranography* (see review below). Joining Christian Wittman and Christoph Harbonnier is former Tangerine Dream member (of that band's 1980s configuration) Paul Haslinger. Also contributing are guests Jacques Deregnaucourt on violin, Renaud Pion on Turkish clarinet, and Hector Zazou on synths.

The 17-minute "Uraniborg" is quite similar to the style of the *Nachtmusik* tracks, but adds Deregnaucourt's violin textures. The rest of the 10 pieces are in the 3½- to 6-minute range, projecting a wide variety of moods. "Mapping the Sky" features dewy, new age–like piano notes with an ambient electronic glow in the background. The haunting "Cathedral" recalls Klaus Schuize's classical/electronic fusions (à la *Cyborg* and *X),* only less rhythmic. The quiet, somber electronics of "Fuga Stellarum" recall "Sequent C" from Tangerine Dream's *Phaedra.* "Virtual Mechanics" is dense space music, proving that Lightwave is as adept with shorter tracks as they are with lengthier ones. The 6-minute "Tycho on the Moon" surprises with jagged concrète sounds, high-pitched piercing tones, and juxtapositions reminiscent of Throbbing Gristle.

When specific notes from the piano sounds and the violin continue for several minutes, as they do in tracks like "Apogee," it's clear that the compositional artistry is there, and that Lightwave is not only assembling moody atmospheres but can also wring them out of more conventional instrumentation as well. *Tycho Brahe* achieves that unique synthesis, which is the stated goal of electro-acoustic music, exceptionally well. The concluding track is another good example of this, with Renaud Pion's Turkish clarinet hovering within Lightwave's electronic mist throughout "Hymn for the Guild of Astronomers." The piece makes listeners feel as though they've stepped back in time to Tycho Brahe's 16th century.

The sound is excellent throughout. The cover art and booklet feature Brahe's astronomy charts.

MUNDUS SUBTERRANEOUS. Released December 1995. Fathom/Hearts of Space.

Mundus Subterraneous, Lightwave's third release, is one of the most important titles in all of progressive music. By incorporating and combining many avant-garde forms, it seems to sum up 20th-century music in general. Classical, musique concrète, new age, ambient, space music, and industrial styles are all assimilated and represented here. In *Mundus Subterraneous,* one can hear the influences of such electronic music pioneers as Karlheinz Stockhausen, Morton Subotnick, Tangerine Dream, Klaus Schulze, Throbbing Gristle, Chris & Cosey, Lustmord, Djam Karet, and Robert Rich.

Inspired by the strange illustrations in the book *Mundus Subterraneous* by 17th-century scientist Athanasius Kircher, once again Lightwave have taken on an ambitious, conceptually directed project of enormous artistic challenge, giving the music a strong direction beyond that of a collection of moods. The illustrations in Kircher's book were a mix of scientific and mythical images from a strange, fantastic underworld, filled with primary forces and shadows; they were detailed visions of an abyss, a bottomless pit in the universe. The cover art depicts such a scene, in striking red and black. Lightwave's *Mundus Subterraneous* successfully gives aural form to these chilling and haunting images, with music that scales the heights of abstraction while retaining a visceral, universal appeal.

Here the electronics/"sound design" lineup of Wittman, Harbonnier, and Haslinger is once again joined by Jacques Deregnaucourt on violin, electronics, alto sax, and voice and Charlie Campagne on guitars and loops. The contributions of these guest musicians are important, providing even further spacey elements. *Mundus Subterraneous.* is a 65½-minute work, with 10 pieces ranging in length from 4 to 9½-minutes. The sound design is indeed impressive, with an unusually complex, active, and layered mix, giving the listener an audiophile's tour of this other dimension.

"De Motu Pendulorum," the opening piece, interrupts cascades of warm, organic sways with loud, obtrusive crackles and creaking sounds, creating an uneasy combination of jittery abrasiveness and glowing, friendly harmony. "Cabinet de Curiosities 1" features some *Nachtmusik*-like atmospherics along with more concrète sounds. Distorted voices float throughout the mix. "Cabinet de Curiosities 2" opens with what sounds like a metal cylinder rolling across a floor; this is followed by loud, disturbing rumbles and crescendos of stereo effects rushing outward from the center, then scattering in both channels. "Nekyomanteia" evokes a vast, cold chasm, with outer space-like bleeps.

The next three tracks are all in the 9-minute range. "Sonnensturme" offers space music textures, with Deregnaucourt's icy violin runs sending chills down your spine. The piece keeps building to an unsettling volume. "Towards the Abyss" combines electronics, violin, and voice, creating evasive sounds that chase each other around in the mix before exploding into the sound of water. "Glissement d'Ame," which features Campagne's guitar loops, loud low-frequency space electronics, and violin, is the most *Tycho Brahe*–like.

"Roma Barocca" opens with atmospheric loops and electronic sizzling sounds like something cooking on a grill. The piece swirls through more washes of loops and bassy notes. "Ascension" is a CTI *Library of Sound*–like ambient work, with light piano and percussion sounds amid a smooth electronic foreground. This mutates into low-frequency rumbles with concrète sounds, then returns to its earlier glow. "Mapping the Earth" is also rather ambient, with distant, floating sounds in the background within a vortex of voices and atmospheres.

Mundus Subterraneous inhabits a multidimensional plane that transcends time and place.

URANOGRAPHY—LIVE AT THE NICE OBSERVATORY. Released July 1996. MSI import.

Recorded at the Nice, France, astronomy observatory in November of 1993, this is the Lightwave duo of Harbonnier and Wittman, a full three years after the release of *Nachtmusik* (which had developed a strong following), but well before the successes of *Tycho Brahe* and *Mundus Subterraneous. Uranography* is perhaps closest to *Nachtmusik* in the sense that it's difficult to describe and passes like a dream.

The group has wrapped this live concert in a conceptual framework, dedicating it to the Nice observatory and giving the 11 pieces on the album titles named after the planets described by a 19th-century astronomer from Nice, Auguste Charlois. The astronomy tie-in, and the location of the observatory for the concert, is an ideal project for Lightwave, linking the vast spaces of the universe with the spaces created by the group's music.

Uranography completely ignores the usual cliches of high-tech keyboard wankery. It's all pure abstraction and mystery, conveying an authentic sense of wonder and awe. This disc is perhaps the closest Lightwave comes to creating a more traditional space music, with a deep, celestial, outer-spacey feel. Nonetheless, it is neither relaxing nor calming, being too active to be purely new age or ambient, and it is not influenced by rock or jazz. There's no rhythm, and no popular music forms of any kind are utilized. The tracks all run together in this continuous 52-minute work. There are no audience sounds until the final applause. The full digital sound is excellent, with an extreme stereo mix for a live recording. The music explored ranges from jarring concrète sounds, to ambient piano chords, to extremely loud low frequencies (guard your speakers with this disc!), to miscellaneous collages of machinelike sounds. The cover art by Harbonnier of a swirling, deep blue vortex descending upon the observatory is an apt visual for what really happened during this concert.

Lightwave's 1996 CD single *In der Unterwelt* is in a similar vein to *Uranography,* being a 19-minute installation piece. It's well worth seeking out, as Lightwave is one of the major leaders in progressive music today.

ANNEA LOCKWOOD

THE GLASS WORLD. Released 1970. Nonsequitur.

The Glass World is an important early progressive music classic that explores the various sounds of common and industrial glass objects of varying sizes and shapes. All organic, with no high-tech embellishments, this is a fascinating and consciousness-expanding album that investigates a natural acoustic sound in all of its possible forms. Each single sound that's created is in itself a piece of music. *The Glass World* was performed live by composer Annea Lockwood around the world between 1966 and 1973, and this 1970 recording ideally captures the work. The almost hissless sound of this Nonsequitur remaster is a shining triumph, and the best this album has ever sounded. The vinyl versions were swamped with surface noise, encroaching on the extremely subtle and delicate resonances.

The 23 short pieces, ranging between a half a minute to 6 minutes, represent an astonishingly diverse collection of unusual and attractive sounds. Recorded with a precise stereo field, *The Glass World* creates its own environment of sound, one which is ideal for headphone listening. The effect of these various pieces is relaxing and ethereal, while at the same time creating for the listener a deeper appreciation for sounds and for the act of listening. Despite Lockwood's avant-garde, John Cage–like experimental purism, the album has a warm universal appeal.

There are a number of notable highlights. The 2-minute "Mini Mobile," where glass objects become stereo sprinkles of bell-like sounds, is irresistible. The 2-minute "Two Ribbed Discs" resembles an electronic synth gurgle, albeit concrète, before becoming a grating scratch sound. The 1½-minute "Spinning Discs" sounds like a bunch of coins rolling on a floor. The fantastic 1½-minute "Dialogue: Bottles and Jars" features incredibly delicate collisions of the title objects as they're rolled on a flat surface in a stereo field. The 1½-minute "Bubbling" presents various resonances made by the sound of water inside a glass jug. The 2½-minute "Breathing Machine" presents in one channel a rubbing of various glass surfaces that resembles the sounds of inhalation and exhalation and in the other channel a sound of percussive clashes. The 2½-minute "Medium Mobile" is like a symphony of chimes. The amazing 1½-minute "Micro Glass a Long Pane" has a series of scraping sounds that conveys an amazing range of frequencies, becoming its own form of a musical scale.

A SOUNDMAP OF THE HUDSON RIVER.
Released 1989. Lovely.

A Soundmap of the Hudson River is a fascinating and irresistable construction of sounds from natural environments by new music/collage composer Lockwood. The premise is a breakthrough idea—a 71½-minute continuous piece recorded at 15 different locations along New York's Hudson River, each site having its own aural texture. With transitions and edits that sound perfectly smooth, changes are made every 3 to 10 minutes so that the work quite literally takes the listener on a sonic journey along the length of the river. Purists should not dismiss this as being too nonmusical; it is an exploration of natural, acoustic sound. The album is a classic progressive release due to the way the piece makes us concentrate on sound—in this case, the sound of things we think we're familiar with—assembling and reconfiguring those sounds in forms that draw our attention to them in new ways.

This is not a typical environmental recording. The microphone placements are not static for the duration, merely capturing a block of time at a particular backdrop. Nor is this a combination of musical instruments with nature sounds à la new age/space music. Lockwood doesn't use these sounds as just one element in a larger compositional goal; she dispenses with everything else and utilizes *only* the environmental sounds to create the desired mood. In this sense, *A Soundmap of the Hudson River* picks up where pioneer recordings by Deuter, Wendy Carlos, and Popol Vuh left off, creating a sound canvas of a similar kind but using only the nature sounds to achieve it. The recording is in the spirit of the *Environments* series from Atlantic Records in the 1970s, which focused on the perception of unusual sounds, such as a human heartbeat or a hippie be-in. But while that series only observed and recorded events as they happened, Lockwood's construction has a more ambitious goal—to use the environmental recordings as the raw material.

Recorded between April and December of 1982, the sound is unusually rich and vibrant, with a glorious extreme stereo separation that fills any room and is ideal for headphones. Given the time gap between the 1982 recording dates and the disc's 1989 release, it's clear that painstaking care was put into this project.

Annea Lockwood. (Photo by Manny Albam.)

The piece begins with light white noise–like sounds at Mount Marcy's Lake Tear of the Clouds, at the highest elevation in the Adirondacks. Suddenly the sound of running water emerges in one channel. These dimensional transitions are crucial to how the work unfolds. The running water grows louder, and is joined by a similar but separate sound of running water in the other channel. The two sounds become fuller, picking up speed, before a central pouring sound takes over, followed by two separate pouring sounds. This slows and percolates. From there we hear the juicy sounds of wading and swimming. As we move into the calmer middle section, we hear splashing sounds, birdsong, crickets, and a horn blowing from a distant ship. This takes us to the up-close sounds of a frolicking seal. From this we go into the sounds of deep, echoed running water, as if in a great cavern. Following this are some frosty, foamy, spraying sounds that lead into windy gusts, which continue until finally fading out.

The disc's booklet unfolds into a map of the journey taken, with specific descriptions of the locations and the corresponding times each appears in the piece. *A Soundmap of the Hudson River* is highly recommended for its sophisticated collage techniques and for its ability to take the listener on such an evocative sound trek, one that's introspective, calming, and celebratory of our natural environment.

Lockwood's 1993 experiment with resonances of acoustic instruments on her *Thousand Year Dreaming* release is also of interest, if somewhat less compelling.

DIDIER LOCKWOOD/JANNICK TOP/CHRISTIAN VANDER/BENOIT WIDEMANN

FUSION. Released December 1981. JMS import.

Fusion is a potent 1980s example of the jazz/rock union by four members of the French progressive group Magma. However, unlike the music of that band (with its strange made-up languages and vocals that are an acquired taste, to say the least), this project is all instrumental. Given that each of the players is a celebrated virtuoso on his respective instrument, a release like this is actually of more interest than those by the Magma band. This is reinforced by the 1980s production values, which are a big improvement over the low-fi murkiness of the 1970s Magma recordings.

The music of *Fusion* was entirely improvised live in the studio. Lockwood's violin, Top's bass guitar, Vander's drums, and Widemann's keyboards (synths, electric piano) are all consistently impressive. The rhythm section of Vander and Top is rock-solid, Lockwood puts other violinists to shame (Jean-Luc Ponty, anyone?), and Widemann solos brilliantly with such unlikely improvisational instruments as a Minimoog. *Fusion* does not disappoint; it's precisely the kind of exciting recording you'd expect from musicians of this caliber.

The 24-minute opener "GHK Go to Miles" is representative of the band's approach. Tricky bass riffing, funky, crashing drums, spacey keyboard excursions, and soaring, white-hot violin solos make for relentless band interplay. Particularly exciting are the aggressive keyboard/drum passages. The 5-minute "Overdrive" is the tastiest of the tracks, with a plucking bass style and a wealth of violin/keyboard tradeoffs. The 6½-minute "767 ZX" has a breezier, jazzy feel, while the 8-minute "Reliefs" is a drifting buildup, with wandering keyboard lines, which then shifts into a very loud, heavier shuffle.

The volume of the mastering is a bit low, but otherwise the sound quality of the ADD mix is excellent—especially if turned up. The cover is a photo of a flashy red sports car on a yellow background. The hot colors are certainly appropriate for this equally hot fusion.

THE LUNCH FACTOR

THE LUNCH FACTOR. Released 1991. Lunch Factor.

Irreverent and anarchic "downtown" New York skronk, the music of the Lunch Factor is both refreshing and cacophonous, cutting through the dead-end 1990s music scene like a knife. Coming on like the Lounge Lizards and John Zorn meet an updated *Tadpoles*-era Bonzo Dog Band, this is music that's challenging and completely nuts. What makes it progressive is the radical juxtapositions of structure, combining such ultra-American forms as surf rock, big band, and cartoon music with hard-hitting jazz/rock fusion chops. The seven-piece band (with all members writing) features alto sax, trombone, guitar, keyboards, bass, drums, and percussion. The performances are excellent throughout.

There are thirteen tracks on *The Lunch Factor.* All have attention-getting mixes, and each is different from all the others. The 1-minute opener "Surf Tuna" is surf rock, which takes us into the 6½-minute fusion funk of the Monty Python–inspired

"Just a Bit Fucking Runny." (The title refers to a Python sketch where two characters exchange witty barbs with each other.) Appropriately, the track features whiny, conversational horns, backed by an irresistable rhythm section. The song suddenly switches its groove to a softer, moodier, slower tempo before going into a heavy free jazz jam with spacey wah-wah guitar.

"Calypso" and "Children's Tune" explore calypso and cartoon music, respectively. The 5½-minute "Shuffle for the Domestic Animals" has a space music intro with percussion effects and a lonely sax sound. This gives way to a heavy jam with bass, drums, keyboards, and trombone, the song going back and forth from that to the spacey parts it began with, as if it can't decide which direction to follow.

The 4-minute "Some Lunch Rap" has thick rhythm section grooves, over which the horns and guitar race, slicing them up like bread. "Ash Wednesday" is old-fashioned ragtime with some clever twists. A highlight is the 5½-minute "Dirge Movement," a buildup piece with a bass solo intro, and the cathartic blowing and bashing tension and release of the horns, drums, guitar, and babbling scat vocal. "Error Spasm" is complex Zorn-like fusion with savage sax attacks. It is impressive how effectively this band just tears through such rapid 2-minute numbers as "My Baby Digs Struedel" and "Or Not."

This privately released disc has excellent sound, very live and very punchy. The deliberately whiny tones from the horns grate at times, but overall this is an entertaining album of many bizarre fusions.

MAHAVISHNU ORCHESTRA

THE INNER MOUNTING FLAME. Released September 1971. Columbia.

Weak production values keep *The Inner Mounting Flame* from being the masterpiece it should have been, but this debut album from the legendary Mahavishnu Orchestra is still an important and historic release. Undisputedly the vision of leader/composer/guitarist John McLaughlin, Mahavishnu Orchestra was one of the finest groups the music world has ever seen: drummer Billy Cobham (whose keen interaction with McLaughlin was the magic fusion dynamic that launched countless similar progressive groups), violinist Jerry Goodman (who became the most visible performer on that instrument in the potent progressive scene of the early 1970s), keyboardist Jan Hammer, and bassist Rick Laird. All five players are masters.

Essentially a development forward from where McLaughlin's *Devotion* (see review) left off, *The Inner Mounting Flame* captured the public's attention far more than McLaughlin's solo album, and in the process introduced the genre of jazz/rock fusion to the world. All of the trademarks of that fusion style are here: volume, virtuosity, grandeur, ambition, length, mystery, instrumental compositions, and a mix of electric and acoustic pieces. McLaughlin and the band deserve enormous credit for moving in the direction of such serious artistry, which was a new approach, though a growing one, within the music industry at the time. The song titles give clues as to the goals set for the compositions—the 7-minute "Meeting of the Spirits," the 6-minute "Vital Transformation," the 7-minute "The Dance of Maya," the 5½-minute "A Lotus on Irish Streams," etc. Effectively grafted onto modern jazz and instrumental/conceptual rock were the notions of an intense spiritual release/catharsis, as well as a respect for nature and the diversity found in the world.

The Inner Mounting Flame was very loud music for 1971, and surprised both the traditional jazz constituency and the pop/rock mainstream. This is certainly not conventional jazz, not even by today's standards. It does, however, retain the improvisational methods of jazz combined with the volume and electric power of rock. It's also neither overly formal nor composed, which keeps the music intense and energetic (unlike the strained formalism McLaughlin would later impose on the 1974 Mahavishnu Orchestra release *Apocalypse).* Lightning runs from the guitar, violin, and keyboards race each other down, as Cobham bashes away like a flailing superman. It's a lot of blowing, and in a sense might benefit from more context and focus, but the band is so good that such considerations that don't seem to matter; the listener appreciates the instantaneous bursts of energy, which are like glimpses of a pure spiritual essence.

What's disappointing is that the sound isn't particularly good. The mastering is a bit thin, some hiss and clicks can be heard, the stereo balance is awkward, and the bass guitar is barely audible. These production drawbacks hurt, even given the relatively low expectations for a 1971 recording. A remastering is called for. Despite the sound, *The Inner Mounting Flame* is one of the few recorded legacies of this preferred Mahavishnu lineup. It is a crucial document of the beginning of fusion, and a testament to the artistic integrity of the early 1970s progressive music revolution, particularly in America.

BIRDS OF FIRE. Released January 1973. Columbia.

Birds of Fire is the poetic apex of American jazz/rock fusion. More composed and less frenetic on this album than on *The Inner Mounting Flame,* the band manages to communicate stoic and grand emotions while maintaining a generally unpolished feel. This makes the album both very accessible and a classic of its genre.

The band's sound is huge, with the rock influences coming on loud and clear. John McLaughlin's wailing, snarling guitar solos unfold in pure virtuoso fashion, and tradeoffs by all the players build in intensity, yet none of the musicians tries to take over. A standout example of this is the 5-minute piece "Sanctuary." Its emotional buildup and release convey a moving empathy in the face of tragedy.

The playing by all is once again fantastic, particularly by drummer Billy Cobham, McLaughlin, and violinist Jerry Goodman. Cobham gets to demonstrate the power of the modern drummer à la 1973 via the grooves and solo bit on the 10-minute "One Word." There is only one acoustic moment on *Birds of Fire,* and that's the lovely 3-minute "Thousand Island Park." The band also covers a Miles Davis tune in pure Mahavishnu fusion fashion with the 4½-minute "Miles Beyond."

McLaughlin's Eastern philosophical themes are once again prominent. The song titles, cover art, reprinted Sri Chinmoy poems, and even the sleeve photos of the band suggest an intense meditative absorption, underscoring the spiritual dimensions of modern instrumental music.

Unfortunately, *Birds of Fire* is a short disc, and is over far too quickly. The sound quality is merely adequate, and a high-definition remaster is urgently called for to preserve the majestic qualities which *Birds of Fire* possesses.

The impact of *Birds of Fire* and the Mahavishnu Orchestra in the early and mid-1970s was enormous in progressive music circles. The band Return To Forever began in 1973, led by Chick Corea, as a direct response to the fusion introduced by McLaughlin and Mahavishnu. Other fusion giants like Weather Report became increasingly more electrified, again partly as a result of the influence of Mahavishnu. In Britain, groups like King Crimson and Genesis incorporated into their symphonic prog rock the funkiness of the Orchestra's fusion jams. Brand X, Gong, and Bruford departed from the laid-back jazz precedents of Soft Machine and toughened up British fusion due in part to the inspiration of Mahavishnu. And in Germany, Klaus Doldinger remade Passport in the fusion image of Mahavishnu, and in the process provided that band with its best musical direction.

Foolishly, McLaughlin jettisoned the entire band (Cobham, Hammer, Goodman, and Laird) after this album and configured ridiculously similar lineups, complete with another violinist (Jean-Luc Ponty) and hard-hitting black drummer (Narada Michael Walden). While 1974's *Apocalypse,* 1975's *Visions of the Emerald Beyond,* and 1976's *Inner Worlds* certainly have their fine moments, momentum and fire are lost, and McLaughlin shamelessly goes over and makes formulaic the same ground that is covered on *Birds of Fire.* He also experimented with ideas that didn't work for Mahavishnu, such as lengthy orchestral passages and vocalists, and the production values took a downward turn.

A live album from the first Mahavishnu lineup was released in November 1973 entitled *Between Nothingness and Eternity.* It's a great performance and comes highly recommended.

MASSACRE

KILLING TIME. Released January 1983. Rec Rec import.

Massacre was a short-lived collaboration between Henry Cow guitarist Fred Frith and bassist Bill Laswell and drummer Fred Maher from the group Material. Thirteen tracks, both composed and improvised, were recorded live in Paris in April, 1981 and in a Brooklyn, New York studio in June, 1981. This is totally different music from Henry Cow, to say the least, being a very hip combination of instrumental punk rock and dissonant noise structures. The tracks embrace the concise nature of punk, most tracks being in the 1- to 3-minute range, and have an edgy, tense, and jagged feel. It all moves like some kind of amphetamine rush, verging on hard-core punk. Very loud, rhythmic and angular, the arrangements put Frith's guitar way out in front, employing a piercing, screeching wall of sound and noise behind which Laswell and Maher are a Godzilla-sized rhythm section—tight, aggressive, and extremely fast, and punctuated with colors throughout.

"Gate" is reminiscent of a Lydia Lunch/Teenage Jesus and the Jerks instrumental, which at the time was a radically new approach in progressive music. Frith adds inspired junglelike grunts to the primitive rhythms of "Aging with Dignity" and the extremely loud, blaring guitar shrieks he uses for "Corridor" would make any listener stand up and pay attention. It's obnoxious, in-your-face stuff, yet very entertaining.

The sound on *Killing Time* is completely raw, gritty, and hard-hitting. *Killing Time* is also one of the best-sounding albums of the 1980s, with a clear and full production that puts you in the moment.

It is unfortunate that the album's release was delayed for so long. If this had come out in late 1981 it might have been bigger news than Genesis' *Abacab* and King Crimson's *Discipline,* and would have given progressive rock a credibility it lacked at the time with many younger punk/new wave audiences. *Killing Time* could possibly have been marketed to the punk crowd, but it wasn't, and was appealing only to the New York scene and to Frith fans (who must have been really surprised by the album; anyone expecting something like Henry Cow's *Legend* was in for a major shock).

Killing Time is a crucial 1980s progressive title; it shattered all preconceptions, going in completely different directions from symphonic prog, electronic/new age, or jazz/rock fusion. Unfortunately, the group fell apart far too quickly, never recording a second album.

LOREN MAZZACANE AND SUZANNE LANGILLE

COME NIGHT. Released 1991. Nonsequitur.

Come Night is an example of one of those strange and unexpected American progressive hybrids that arrives out of nowhere. Electric guitarist Loren Mazzacane and vocalist Suzanne Langille, here joined by Brian Johnson (drums, percussion, vibes) and George Cartwright (tenor sax), combine jazz and blues influences with a progressive slant. Despite its rather conventional stylistic elements, the music on this recording makes no attempt to achieve the palatability of a more commercial sound. Instead, it follows its own idiosyncratic paths.

This half-vocal, half-instrumental disc contains 16 moody, sparse sound poems delivered in a low-key, downbeat, and breathy manner. These brooding, unpolished (they sound improvised) pieces range in length from 1 to 9 minutes. Langille's vocal style recalls the intense introspection of Annette Peacock, although their voices are not similar. The jagged, fragmentary instrumentals are equally delicate. The mood throughout is mysterious, and its plentiful nuances and intimacy grow and impress anew with each listen. The elusive qualities of the music make it worth chasing.

The sound is excellent, and the marvelous, meshlike fold-out cover symbolizes the music's elusive yet pleasing structures.

JOHN MCLAUGHLIN

DEVOTION. Released May 1970. Restless.

Devotion has a surreal, dreamy quality that exudes pure period 1960s opt-out. It's revolutionary, breakthrough music for its time, like a meeting point between Pink Floyd's *Ummagumma* and Guru Guru's *Hinten.* This is McLaughlin at his most attractive, and a major departure from his previous work. *Devotion,* his second solo album, is nothing like the traditional jazz of his first release, *Extrapolation* (1969), or his playing on Miles Davis's *Bitches Brew* (1970). One of the first all-instrumental non-straight jazz releases, it's also different from the poetic sonorities of the later Mahavishnu Orchestra. One of the first fusions of rock and jazz, it is perhaps more accurately described as a blueprint for space rock, with a psychedelic heaviness that is more potently druggy than most 1960s rock. The production and mix, with their extreme separation and imaginative construction, provide an authentic underground feel.

McLaughlin is joined on the recording by Buddy Miles on drums and percussion, Billy Rich on bass guitar, and Larry Young on organ and electric piano. McLaughlin's multitracked electric guitar parts were an innovation at the time, borrowing an expanded palette of orchestration and studio recording techniques from rockers like Jimi Hendrix. Strangely, the rest of the band comes across like Pink Floyd rather than anything overtly fusionesque, especially Young's Rick Wright–like keyboards.

The 10-minute "Marbles" opens with spacey guitar and keyboard, into which Miles's big, echoed drums enters. (*Devotion* was one of the first albums to center the drums in the mix, giving them a bigger, rawer sound.) The piece features solos by McLaughlin which fade; the band then moves into something else entirely, and then into further changes. These surreal transitions, complete with studio trickery, dominate throughout *Devotion.*

The piercing 4½-minute "Don't Let the Dragon Eat Your Mother" has screechingly loud soloing from McLaughlin. Some of the heaviest blowing heard on record at the time, it makes a powerful statement. Unfortunately, the drum sound on this track is unusually weak. The 4-minute "Purpose of When" has a more Gothic feel, with dark guitar tones and a carnival-like organ. The 11½-minute "Dragon Song" is the best-engineered track on the album. Its lengthy rock workouts led by McLaughlin's torturous guitars climb ever-increasing harmonic scales, providing the basis for the approach taken later in Mahavishnu Orchestra.

The sound quality of this essential disc is thin but enjoyable. The cover is a stark black-and-white photo closeup of McLaughlin. Regrettably, McLaughlin has never recorded another album like *Devotion,* preferring to retreat to more traditional jazz forms.

MELTING EUPHORIA

UPON THE SOLAR WINDS. Released October 1995. Cleopatra.

A modern, psychedelic all-instrumental space rock band, Melting Euphoria hail from San Francisco, and it's certainly refreshing to see such bohemian/hippie rock as this emerge from the staid, ultra-responsible, politically correct environment of 1990s America. Melting Euphoria features an extraordinary female vocalist, Beci. However, there are no lyrics, and her voice is used selectively. This keeps the concentration on the structure and overall feel of the compositions, restoring to the basic rock band form the ability to weave dreams via the music alone, unguided by words.

Melting Euphoria consists of Zero Devilin on Moog synth, DeFM on guitars, Anthony Who? on bass guitar and synth (he also produces), Michael Merrill on drums and percussion, and Beci's "space voices." While the band's music strongly evokes the space rock of the pioneers from the 1960s (Pink Floyd), the 1970s (Gong, Hawkwind, Steve Hillage), and the current era (Ozric Tentacles), what's most notable about them is that they represent the reemergence of a space rock constituency in America. Say what you will about the legacy of previous San Francisco giants like the Grateful Dead and Jefferson Airplane, none of those groups played music quite like this. Melting Euphoria's music is far more psychedelic than actual hippie-era music, and in large doses it becomes almost hypnotic. While the group doesn't break new ground, and they are stylistically similar to their space rock predecessors, they have much better production values, giving them a crucial edge. The sound of *Upon the Solar Winds* is huge, though not flattened under its own weight. There's a lot of stereo panning, and the mix doesn't often center instruments like the drums or bass guitar, a technique that recalls albums of the late 1960s and early 1970s.

This 52-minute disc features nine tracks, most of which are in the 4- to 7-minute range. The opener, "Leylines from Azimuth," introduces the basic sound of the group. Gong/Tim Blake–like synths, propulsive bass guitar à la Hawkwind, soulful Pink Floyd/Clare Torry/*Dark Side of the Moon* female vocals, and loud, crashing rock drumming. This isn't relaxing space music, but nuclear fusion space rock, soaring through the cosmos.

"Scarab Sands" is less rock-oriented, giving variety to the disc with its more atmospheric synth and percussion. "Harbour of Infinity" and "Crystalline Wind" are driving pieces of power rock with reach-for-the-stars guitar soloing. These pieces dissolve into flurries of synth effects, returning with attractively confident and powerful vocals and drums, then fading out with wind sounds (as on "Harbour . . ."). "Of Misting Eyes and Lavender" begins with some brief nature sounds, then launches into big Heldon-like synth and drum patterns with rhythmic charges from the bass and guitar.

"Venusian Skyline" has some awfully clichéd synth whooshes, but is redeemed by the powerful grooving from the guitarist, bassist, and drummer. "Astral Nemesis" is one of the longer tracks, a buildup with a drifting space rock structure.

Upon the Solar Winds is a superb reaffirmation of the space rock form. The cover art deliberately invokes 1960s poster art psychedelia.

BEYOND THE MAYBE MACHINE. Released August 1996. Cleopatra.

Beyond the Maybe Machine picks up right where *Upon the Solar Winds* left off, though with a few minor and subtle distinctions. No new ground is broken here, and some may consider the music of a group like this to be its own kind of formula. However, it's a strong and enduring formula, and the group certainly

Melting Euphoria.

sets a state-of-the-art standard by its purist execution and delivery of that form. In other words, *Beyond the Maybe Machine* is solid and well done from beginning to end. While hopefully Melting Euphoria will not end up where Ozric Tentacles found themselves a half dozen albums into their career, overly relying on the formula that brought them popularity, it's too early to demand such changes from this group.

The basic four-piece lineup of *Upon the Solar Winds* returns here, but Beci has been replaced by a different female voice, Jennifer Ruby. Stylistically these incarnations are similar, and equally impressive. The nine tracks on *Beyond . . .* all run together. The propulsive bass guitar, big drums, and ethereal, wordless vocals are all here and in top form. The guitar is more restrained this time, and the synths are a bit more subtle than before, occupying backgrounds as well as foregrounds. This gives *Beyond . . .* a more spacey, drifting aura, somewhat less groove-oriented and more plugged into cosmic vibes. All in all, the album is more sophisticated than *Upon the Solar Winds,* if slightly less of a revelation (which doesn't matter much if the first one you hear is *Beyond the Maybe Machine).*

The sound quality here is fantastic, with plentiful stereo effects and a fresh live sound. The cover art by bassist Anthony Who? is right out of a Grateful Dead collection.

NATIONAL HEALTH

COMPLETE. Three LPs on two CDs. **NATIONAL HEALTH** released January 1978. **OF QUEUES AND CURES** released January 1979. **D.S. AL CODA** released May 1982. **COMPLETE** released September 1990. ESD.

Complete is indeed a thorough set, collecting all three of the group's studio releases in their entirety, plus two bonus tracks. National Health was an all-star ultra-Canterbury fest, with a core band consisting of Dave Stewart, Phil Miller, and Pip Pyle from Hatfield and the North. Their music takes the Canterbury style (formal/classical keyboard-driven rock/jazz fusion) into more modern and loud electric realms, while retaining the genre's old-fashioned flavor. Naturally, the sound is very English.

The first disc begins with a 1½-minute excerpt of the instrumental "Paracelsus," by an earlier incarnation of the band, recorded for radio in February 1976. Here Stewart and Miller were joined by Bill Bruford, Steve Hillage, Mont Campbell, and Alan Gowen. It's a nice if insubstantial taste from this embryonic era, which is represented at length on the rather underwhelming National Health disc *Missing Pieces,* a compilation of rarities released in 1996.

National Health's self-titled debut was recorded in 1977, and is easily the best of their three releases. The lineup for this album was Stewart (organ, electric and acoustic piano, clavinet), Miller (guitar), Pyle (drums and percussion), Amanda Parsons (vocals), Neil Murray (bass), plus guests Alan Gowen (Moog synth, electric and acoustic piano), and Jimmy Hastings (flute, clarinets). By the time the album was released, Parsons had left the group, which is a real pity as her angelic vocals were perfect for the band's material. What Robert Wyatt of Soft Machine did for male Canterbury-style vocals, Parsons did for female vocals. And on this first National Health album the listener gets to hear the full range of her talents (unlike the brief appearances she makes on the Hatfield discs).

"Tenemos Roads," a 14½-minute epic, opens with a lengthy intro of multilayered keyboards, light and classical in tone, introducing the album's main musical themes, which recur throughout. From there a strong rock attack is led by Pyle and Miller, far heavier than Hatfield. A spacey center section of Hastings' flute and clarinet goes by all too quickly, and Parsons delivers Stewart's wistful lyrics brilliantly.

The 10-minute "Brujo" is light and friendly prog rock. A lilting vocal from Parsons, backed by playful keyboard and guitar parts, takes the listener into another spacey flute solo, which builds to a melodic jam. The 4-minute "Borogoves Part 2 (excerpt)" is a jazzy bass/electric piano/drums jam which tears into a ripping guitar solo. The 6-minute "Borogoves Part 1" is a

Bo Hansson–like polka, strongly recalling Egg and Hatfield with its organ-led fanfares, accompanied by another nice but brief wordless vocal from Parsons.

The 14$\frac{1}{2}$-minute "Elephants" opens with elephantine keyboard screeches and playful Moog soloing from Gowen. The track reprises "Tenemos Roads," with more vocals from Parsons. It fades out with flute and electric piano.

While Stewart's moldy organ solos are a problem, the production values here are better than most 1970s Canterbury, with a crisp, live sound.

Of Queues and Cures is a solid, all-instrumental affair, similar to work by groups like Trilogy, Terpandre, and Collegium Musicum. While Amanda Parsons is sorely missed, Neil Murray is replaced by the far better John Greaves (from Henry Cow). Again there are a number of guests: Jimmy Hastings on flute and clarinets and Georgie Born on cellos, plus several others on trumpet, trombone, oboe, steel drums, and voice. Although this should have given the album badly needed variety, these other players aren't used often enough or given much space, and the majority of the tracks are dominated by the loud jamming from the four core members.

Although the playing, arrangements, and production are excellent, a strong similarity in the material is evident. Despite the occasional Minimoog, Stewart plays no synths, which means there are more organ solos, and his organ solos already sounded dated in 1975, let alone 1979. The group's penchant for long compositions (the album is a whopping 55 minutes) and terribly precise and academic executions doesn't help, and *Of Queues and Cures* is not what it could have been.

D.S. Al Coda is also a disappointment. Recorded in 1981 as a tribute to Alan Gowen after his death, this was the last of the great

National Health (1977–1978 lineup). From left to right, Dave Stewart, Neil Murray, Phil Miller, Pip Pyle.

Canterbury roundups for some time. Half the people in that scene make an appearance here, including Richard Sinclair, Elton Dean, Amanda Parsons, Jimmy Hastings, and Barbara Gaskin. The material recorded by the core band of Stewart, Miller, Pyle, and Greaves is all written by Gowen, and in many ways he's a better writer than they are.

However, the domination of Stewart's garish synths and Pyle's thin electronic drums gives the group a slick fusion sound, coming across like a poor man's Chick Corea's Elektric Band or mid-1980s Weather Report. "Black Hat" and "Tales of a Damson Knight" revisit the airy Hatfield sound, with wordless vocals from Sinclair, Parsons, and Gaskin. While the effect is nice, it's nothing new. Giving much-needed variety are the multiple acoustic guitars of "Arriving Twice." In fact, Miller and Greaves come across the best on *D.S. Al Coda,* particularly on the pure fusion grandeur of "T.N.T.F.X." Overall, though, the album is pretty mediocre, and the sound quality is only fair.

The 1990 "reunion" track "The Apocalypso" is thoroughly bogus, just a retread of previous National Health bits, and only Stewart and Miller appear, with a drum "score" by Pyle. Stewart's tinny synths are hardly an improvement over those dated organs. The cover art of *Complete* isn't much either, replacing the original covers (which are not even reproduced in the package) with a silly photo of a monkey.

Bill Nelson. (Photo by Nigel Huntersdon.)

BILL NELSON

CRIMSWORTH. Released April 1995. Resurgence import.

Crimsworth, subtitled *Flowers, Stones, Fountains and Flames,* is a masterpiece of ambient music, one of the leading titles in that genre. It creates a true stereo environment in which to disappear, and it takes over whatever space you play it in. This is the best of Bill Nelson's instrumental albums, the sort of otherworldly, ethereal work he'd always been aiming for. Earlier Nelson releases such as 1988's *Chance Encounters in the Garden of Lights* (a double disc set now out of print) were also ambient projects, but *Crimsworth* eclipses them all.

The 62-minute disc is divided into two 31-minute pieces, both of which are variations of the same sounds. Brian Eno/*Thursday Afternoon*–like piano notes, bell sounds, gurgling and swooshing water sounds, Moog/synth blips that drip like raindrops, faint, low groanlike sounds, and light rhythmic sounds like the shaking of metal chains combine and veer from soft to loud and back again. The whole work is more like a mysterious, hovering living cloud than a composition, a strange phenomena that was always there and is merely being recorded.

Crimsworth is very relaxing—the perfect disc in which to immerse yourself. But make no mistake: this serious seduction of your imagination required true artistry to achieve. Crucial to the success of *Crimsworth* is the wide variety of sounds that constantly shift in the mix. The music is neither static nor totally minimal, as in so many other ambient projects. This provides a critical level of change that gives the listener something to look for in the work and provides a reason to listen closely.

The sound quality of *Crimsworth* is first-rate, with a very wide spatial scope. The cover art isn't particularly apt for these kind of opt-out sounds, however, being just a red background with streaks of black.

NETWORK

CORRODED PATH. Released 1993. Progressive.

Corroded Path is a minor treasure of U.K. fusion, directly picking up where groups like Brand X and Bruford left off. Eight tracks (each between 2½ and 7½ minutes), written by guitarist Tim Crowther and drummer Steve Clarke (who also produced the album), follow the friendlier and melodic paths of fusion, with a swinging smoothness that isn't earth-shattering but is easy to like. The five-piece band (which features Ted Emmett on trumpet and flugelhorn) is quite good. Most of these gentlemen are also members of other fusion bands on the Progressive label, such as Groon and Conglomerate. The accent here is on concise, jazzy arrangements, with Crowther's restrained guitar soloing recalling some of the best moments of Allan Holdsworth and Al DiMeola. Imagine Bill Bruford's Earthworks band electrified and you get the sound of Network.

While keyboardist Pete Jacobsen's sounds are sometimes a little cheesy, Emmett's Miles Davis–like solos are superb, particularly when he is more up-front as on "Obsessive Behaviour." Occasionally, the funky bass lines and piano breaks resemble Return to Forever, and Clarke's big drum sound vividly recalls Bill Bruford and the Phil Collins–era Brand X.

The sound quality is very good throughout, with production values ideal for an analog recording like this. Like Chad Wackerman's *The View* in the United States, Network's *Corroded Path* successfully continues the most attractive band dynamics of the jazz/rock fusion form.

MANI NEUMEIER

PRIVAT. Released 1993. Admission to Music import.

Recorded in 1992, *Privat* is one of the best progressive drum albums of all time, a tour de force showcase for every kind of percussion style. Although Mani Neumeier is the former leader and drummer of the German prog rock band Guru Guru, *Privat* sounds nothing like the psychedelic guitar rock of that band. Combining a powerful Sonor drum kit and tom-toms with cymbals, gongs, tavil gamelans, sampling electronics, environmental sounds, and brief voices, Neumeier, with the assistance of three other musicians, creates an inventive, lively, and punchy instrumental music that's all rhythm.

The disc's 18 pieces range in length from 15 seconds to 8 minutes, covering every conceivable ethnic/tribal/world music influence, from Indian to African to Oriental. The music's both danceable and fun, projecting a happy vibe. Given its melting-pot variety and compositional quirkiness, the recording sounds quite progressive. It neither falls back into anything resembling popular music forms nor resembles a purist version of world music. It inhabits its own universe.

The sound is of audiophile quality, with a realistic volume and a clean, detailed, totally infectious mix. The only drawback is the howlingly bad artwork—a poorly designed digipack with a truly wretched cover painting that presents images totally unsuitable for the exciting music of *Privat.*

O + A

RESONANCE. Released January 1995. O + A import.

Composed, produced, and privately released by Bruce Odland and Sam Auinger, the aptly titled *Resonance* is a remarkable expedition into the world of sound, an entire disc of fascinating collages made from natural environmental sources. The music is enormously inventive, intelligent, adventurous, and challenging, and it is not easy to figure out what sound-processing techniques the duo used to achieve their effects. However they did it, the result is thoroughly mind-altering, focusing our attention on environmental sound with a laserlike accuracy.

The 4-minute "Weather," culled from a rain source, sounds a little like someone is snapping pieces of metal with their fingers, although here it's a flurry of these sounds, which, when jumbled together, sounds like falling rain. The 6-minute "Yampa" originates from the sounds of oar strokes and wind. Like a huge turbine cylinder of liquid spinning around in a repetative gurgle, it mutates into big industrial rumbles that rattle your room.

The next four tracks are subtitled "R4 Cities" and feature sounds recorded in four different cities of the world. The 5-minute "Rome: Traffic Mantra" uses as its source the resonance of passing motor vehicles. The sounds all flow together, becoming pulses of rumbles, wind, and spacey frequencies. The 2½-minute "Salzburg" also originates from traffic sounds, recorded in a tunnel this time, but the original sounds are then eliminated and only the "resonances" of them are used, revealing cascades of (stereo-panned) low frequencies. The 2-minute "Berlin" collects sounds from a bus stop, resulting in loud, low-frequency rumbles, with a cloaked, misty background. The 4½-minute "New York: Hostage Variations" is more straightforward and recognizable at first, with apocalyptic sounds of traffic sirens, police, and gunshots, but these mutate into more musical sounds, like the warm up from a far-away orchestra pit.

The 5-minute "The Letter F" is a meditative, lingering glow of bowing harp sounds and water—truly resonant. The 7-minute "Stories," collected from the sounds of boulders, is edgy and tense, with high-pitched buzzing and rolling sounds that are like fingernails on a blackboard, and is somewhat hard to take given its length. The 4-minute "Water Raga," taken from a river flood, sounds nothing like that, with waves of whiny sounds that have a bubbling undercurrent. The hypnotic 6½-minute "Infrastructure Harmonics—Grand Central" is taken from sources such as ventilation fans, air conditioners, lighting systems, traffic, and passing crowds. A gigantic whirring dominates the foreground, while the sounds of the various sources can be made out in the background.

No explanations are given for the 20-minute epic "Coremeltz," which is perhaps the recording's highlight. The duo goes all out with the stereo effects for this piece. Beginning with what you might hear if someone ran a hand through a deep pit of plastic objects, the sound becomes water-like, then mutates into a buzzing sound with an angelic, choirlike background before all the sounds are sent into a giant swirl. The dynamics of it are almost like the roaring feedback of an electric guitar solo. The piece has become completely psychedelic by this point. Hypnotic, trance-inducing, and indescribable, it's an authentic step into another dimension.

This 67½-minute disc (an ambitious length for a debut) has a quiet soundstage and subtle mix, not in-your-face, though occasionally jarring. The brilliant, highly spatial stereo effects give these experiments their magic, making this ideal for headphones. The band must have had an enormous amount of fun collecting, processing, and presenting these sounds—a fact that should become obvious to listeners brave enough to share their journey into the nature of sound itself. The duo's excellent photography for the booklet represents gallery-quality photojournalism. *Resonance* is a truly ground-breaking work that celebrates the protean, ever-evolving nature of matter and sound.

MIKE OLDFIELD

TUBULAR BELLS. Released May 1973. Virgin.

An important milestone in progressive music, the lengthy instrumental work *Tubular Bells* is one of the first of its kind, and the most popular. Developing and unfolding like a symphonic classical suite, its structure joins the old with the new, and it is this fusion of styles that gives the album such a universal appeal.

Recorded in 1972 and early 1973 by the young, then-unknown session musician Mike Oldfield, the work is a series of small, very catchy musical vignettes grafted together so seamlessly that each section flows naturally into the next. Oldfield's compositions have a real warmth to them.

Oldfield is the ultimate multi-instrumentalist, playing acoustic, electric and Spanish guitars, bass guitar, mandolin, grand piano, organ, and several kinds of percussion, including glockenspiel and, of course, tubular bells. As a guitarist, Oldfield is similar in style to Steve Howe, constructing vast, layered soundscapes, while avoiding bluesy clichés and the darker, harder-edged attacks of rock (a fact which has always put him at odds within rock circles).

Joining Oldfield for *Tubular Bells* are a number of progressive music luminaries, including Jon Field of Jade Warrior on flute, Lindsay Cooper of Henry Cow on string basses, Vivian Stanshall of the Bonzo Dog Band doing a brief narration, Oldfield's sister Sally adding voices, and producer Tom Newman on acoustic guitar.

"Tubular Bells Part 1" opens with the famous cascading piano chords which establish the piece's themes and which have become Oldfield's most popular calling card. From there the theme is repeated on guitar and flute, until suddenly a section of gnarly electric guitars and thick slabs of bass guitar notes create a heavier rock feel. This disappears into some sunny acoustic guitars and bells, with a rephrasing of the theme on Spanish guitar and piano. After this, more tricky guitar sections, both loud and quiet, move into some space music organ, bells, and acoustic guitars. The chunky electric guitars and bass riffs return, until the famous closing section of Part 1 begins with Stanshall's narration. Each musical instrument is given an introduction in a grand fashion by Stanshall, and then in turn each plays a little riff to demonstrate its place in the composition, ending, of course, with the tubular bells. This section is a celebration of the joys of music in general, and makes it easy to see why this album was such a hit.

"Tubular Bells Part 2" begins with a lengthy pastoral section of space music textures from guitar, bass, organ, and Sally Oldfield's voice. This leads into attractive sections of calming and sweet multiple acoustic guitars, which grows into a stately orchestra of guitars that has the sound of a Middle Eastern group of pipe players. The rousing "Piltdown Man" section is next. This famous section, which features loud primeval grunts from Oldfield as the piece tears into its most rocking grooves, with chunky bass, drums, and piano over which tasty electric guitar licks are added, is especially popular with younger listeners, who appreciate its primal feel. The piece then returns to the spacey, pastoral textures of earlier sections. The conclusion is a tear through the traditional "The Sailor's Hornpipe," which connects Oldfield's music to the timeless music of the British Isles.

The sound of *Tubular Bells* is intimate and private, the cut-and-paste assembly painstakingly done by Oldfield himself without today's high-tech methods and without the help of a large group of backing musicians. This reinforces the ambition of the work, in that Oldfield's music has always had a huge "cinemascope" breadth to it. Here, however, those lofty goals are accomplished note by note, devotedly and methodically, on the small scale of a studio project done by a then-unknown musician who had no idea that his music would become such a runaway success.

Tubular Bells was also the album that launched countless other ambitious instrumental projects. The success of the album virtually created Virgin Records, enabling that label to release some extremely avant-garde and eclectic works throughout the 1970s. With *Tubular Bells,* the genre of progressive music took a giant leap forward.

HERGEST RIDGE. Released August 1974. Virgin import.

A refined, pastoral classical work not at all a part of the rock/pop idioms, *Hergest Ridge* is not an obvious follow-up to *Tubular Bells.* While like *Tubular Bells, Hergest Ridge* is to an extent a collection of several smaller tracks making up a cohesive whole, it largely concentrates on only a few main themes, with a more natural flow and a low-key eclecticism that has a sense of the baroque and Gothic to it.

A veritable warehouse of instrumentation is again employed by Oldfield more or less single-handedly, with some assistance from June Whiting and Lindsay Cooper on oboes, Ted Hobart on trumpet, Mike's brother Terry on flute, the voices of Clodagh Simmonds and Mike's sister Sally, and string and choir sections conducted by David Bedford.

Mike Oldfield. (Photo by Jill Fumanovsky.)

"Hergest Ridge Part 1" begins with organ, flute, and bells, followed by soft pulses from the string section and bass, giving way to sunny organ patterns, rhythm guitars, and soft electric guitar solo notes. A more aggressive orchestration ensues, with multiple guitars joined by a faraway sounding trumpet fanfare. There follows a lovely section of delicate acoustic guitar parts, along with oboe, trumpet, and select electric guitar notes. After a buildup with timpani and bells, the piece crashes into a thick bass guitar solo. This then moves into a rather jolly section, with sleigh bells and organ, an emphatic electric guitar solo, and a churchlike choir, which makes the piece revelatory, inspirational, and reassuring.

The album's softest pastoral section opens "Hergest Ridge Part 2," with light acoustic guitars, organ, oboes, and strings, and breezy electric guitar notes floated in. This goes into a gorgeous multiple acoustic guitar, bass, and Spanish guitar section, with a female choir and crescendos of cymbals and quietly understated electric guitar notes. A solemn church organ and bass return, with an electric guitar reprising the main theme. This crashes into piano notes and the famous "thunderstorm" section, where for several minutes all the instruments create a loud and very intense swirling effect, topped off by soaring electric guitar solos. The piece concludes by returning to soft church organ and understated acoustic guitars, which reprise the main theme, along with the vocal choir and string section.

Hergest Ridge is a favorite of Oldfield fans, once again showcasing his strong compositional talents and demonstrating that *Tubular Bells* was only the beginning. Despite being so conspicuously outside any conventional pop forms, this album was a very big seller and instantly went to No. 1 at the time of its release. The sound quality is good, although the stereo separation during the first few minutes is hardly ideal (this is soon remedied). The inviting cover art is a trick photograph of an arc of earth (on which a dog sits) that seems to be surrounded on all sides by a circle of blue sky and clouds. The effect is evocative of the all-encompassing tranquillity of the music of *Hergest Ridge.*

OMMADAWN. Released October 1975. Caroline.

Ommadawn is another two-part epic, juxtaposing Oldfield's usual spirited arrangements with darker, Gothic elements. *Ommadawn,* Oldfield 's first self-produced album, has a gorgeous, lush sound that's fuller than his previous releases. For the record, Oldfield plays electric, acoustic, classical, and 12-string guitars, acoustic and electric bass, harp, mandolin, banjo, bodhran, bazouki, grand piano, synths, organ, glockenspiel, and percussion. He's joined by Paddy Maloney's Uillean pipes, Herbie's Northumbrian pipes, Leslie Penning's recorder, brother Terry Oldfield's pan pipes, Pierre Moerlen on timpani, plus others on cello, trumpet, and percussion, a section of African drum players, and a vocal choir that includes Sally Oldfield, Bridget St. John, Clodagh Simmonds, and a children's choir.

The 19-minute "Ommadawn Part 1" opens with voices and multi-guitar textures, ominous keyboards, and bass, plus a classical guitar solo (stereo-panned) that states the main motif. From there enter some spacey electric guitars and dense textures. At the seventh minute, a jolly if fairly loud section of recorder, bazouki, banjo, and acoustic guitar dissolves into a light sprinkle of guitars, voice, and cello. This follows with one of Oldfield's most famous sections, with African drums, Celtic vocals, timpani, and pan pipes. Hypnotic and swirling, the section continues for several minutes, building up as precise electric guitar notes lead. Part 1 concludes with a dissolve back to the African drums until the final fade-out.

"Ommadawn Part 2" begins with another very famous section constructed of 62 guitar overdubs, which creates a loud, extremely dense syrup of sound that's both ominous and menacing. This 5½-minute section is Oldfield at his darkest and most murky, with the guitars taking on an almost orchestral form. At points the section resembles early Philip Glass, à la his 1974 Virgin release *Music in 12 Parts.* After this comes a pastoral section that features bagpipes, guitars, and recorders with added synths and bass; it jumps to a spirited jig, which is then neatly all sewn up by Oldfield's guitar soloing.

Ommadawn concludes with a 3½-minute vocal track, "On Horseback," a very English ballad with a wintry feel. It's like a sing-song for the lads down at the pub, and why this trite nonsense even appears here is a mystery.

The misty, reverent cover photo close-up of Oldfield (with a beard) makes him look like

Christ, reinforcing both the comforting nature and the seriousness of the music of *Ommadawn*.

BOXED. Released October 1976. Virgin import.

Although *Boxed* is a three-disc set containing *Tubular Bells, Hergest Ridge,* and *Ommadawn,* the package is made essential by the inclusion of a fourth album, *Collaborations,* which is not available elsewhere and ranks among Oldfield's finest releases. In its original vinyl form *Boxed* was four LPs. The CD version divides up the *Collaborations* material, adding its tracks to the ends of each CD. The version of *Tubular Bells* included here is extended by a few minutes, and *Hergest Ridge* is a remix, but neither are fundamentally different. The mix of *Ommadawn* is inferior to the point of being a complete botch, with the sound mostly grounded in one channel! Because of this drawback, *Boxed* cannot serve as a way to get all of Oldfield's first three albums in one go. And while some of the *Collaborations* material made its way onto the later Oldfield *Elements* retrospective box set, not all of it did, making *Boxed* the only release that has all of these spectacular early tracks.

Collaborations is notable as a collection of oddities that spotlight Oldfield at his most baroque, classical, Gothic, and folksy. Half of the tracks are excerpts from albums by David Bedford, a classical composer who was perhaps the Virgin label's most eclectic artist in the 1970s. Bedford appears on most of Oldfield's works from this era, conducting the string and vocal choirs. In turn, Oldfield provided Bedford's albums with their best moments, guesting on electric guitar. The other half of *Collaborations* is Oldfield's very popular mid-1970s explorations of traditional songs with recorder player Leslie Penning.

The 6½-minute "The Rio Grande," from Bedford's 1975 album *The Rime of the Ancient Mariner,* is extremely old-fashioned, the kind of thing you'd hear in a church. A children's vocal choir from London's Queen's College sings a hymn, followed by an orchestral section with a light, restrained, serene electric guitar solo from Oldfield. A 7½-minute extract from Bedford's 1974 album *Stars End* is next, and is the highlight portion of that album, recorded with the Royal Philharmonic Orchestra and Henry Cow's Chris Cutler on percussion. A menacing orchestral buildup leads into a ripping electric guitar solo that is very intense, psychedelic, and Steve Hillage–like, conjuring images of outer space/cosmic phenomena. The 4-minute "The Phaecian Games" from Bedford's 1976 album *The Odyssey* is a standout track. With Bedford on ARP synth, string synth, grand piano, and electric piano and Oldfield on electric guitar, the piece is a dense, fiery, symphonic, celestial fest recalling Yes, with Oldfield's guitar soaring skyward. Another major highlight is the 6-minute "First Excursion," by Oldfield and Bedford, recorded for *Collaborations.* With Bedford providing a background of grand piano and string synth, Oldfield steps away from his usual sunny moods for moodier, powerful guitar notes, letting them resonate here longer than usual.

The three traditional songs with Leslie Penning are each irresistible highlights. The 4-minute "Argiers" is a favorite, with Oldfield's lovely multiple acoustic guitar strums accompanying Penning's gentle recorder. The short (at around 2 minutes each) hit singles "In Dulci Jubilo" and "Portsmouth" demonstrate a reinvigorated purist aesthetic. These tracks make clear how much influence traditional music has had on Oldfield's own compositions. "Portsmouth" is active, fun, and jolly, with Oldfield playing accordion, mandolin, kettledrum, and string synth, and he and Penning stomping along with their feet to the music. "In Dulci Jubilo"'s multiple guitars, with the addition of a snare drum over which an electric guitar wails, becomes a rousing, inviting march—a tendency present in many of Oldfield's works.

The sound quality on this recording is fairly sharp, though some of the Bedford tracks are marred by hiss.

INCANTATIONS. Released November 1978. Caroline.

An extremely ambitious 74-minute four-part work, *Incantations* is the composition Mike Oldfield should be remembered for, rather than *Tubular Bells.* With adventurous fusions of classical, rock, Celtic, and even world music forms, *Incantations* is sophisticated, but sounds natural and fresh. Its large scope seems to encapsulate all of Oldfield's previous releases. Above all, its uplifting nature makes it music of great joy.

As always, Oldfield plays a huge number of musical instruments, which by now had become too numerous to list. Assisting are Mike Laird on trumpet, Gong's Pierre Moerlen on drums and vibes, Maddy Prior of Steeleye Span on lead vocals, Sally Oldfield also on vocals, Terry Oldfield and Sebastian Bell on flutes, plus the Queen's College Girls Choir, the African drums of Jabula, and a string section conducted by David Bedford.

The 19-minute "Incantations Part 1" opens with a female vocal choir and a cymbal crash, which moves into a very attractive, rousing string section, like a flurry of spring clouds. This is joined by sprinkles of vibes, exotic percussions, and a whirling dervish–like Middle East–flavored electric guitar playing the main theme. This gives way to a different variation with flutes and African drums, with a series of fantastic trumpet-led sections which provide a sharp delivery of the theme. A bass/keyboard/percussion section then leads into the truly inspiring Celtic vocals of the girls choir. This is supported by flute riffs, handclaps, and percussion, giving the piece an outdoor celebratory feel. The piece concludes with a reprisal of the theme with strings and flute.

The 19½-minute "Incantations Part 2" begins with gorgeous flute-led textures, with strings and keyboards. A symphonic burst from the strings, a soft, deliberate pulse from a drum, and celestial guitar notes then create a sonorous, near-religious variation of the theme, with a return of the choir that lends a chantlike earnestness. Loud voices and percussion intensify the mood. This gives way to the most beautiful moment of *Incantations.* Stereo African drums, joined by vibes and synth, establish a hypnotic texture. The angelic vocals of Maddy Prior then takes us by surprise into a flowing, unfolding delivery of Henry Wordsworth Longfellow's famous poem, "Song of Hiawatha." This section is among the all-time high points in progressive music, providing *Incantations* with a transformative, deeply spiritual, and poetic moment. By choosing this poem, which extols the wonders of nature, Oldfield reinforces the elemental nature of the music of *Incantations.*

The 17-minute "Incantations Part 3" begins with washes of vibes, percussion, synth, and bass, and Oldfield unleashes some of his most soaring, stinging guitar soloing. Charging into a whirling-dervish rock jam, like some kind of massive cavalry attack across an Arabian desert, the synth, drums, and bass are encircled by flutes, embarking on a smooth rhythmic course for some loud, powerful rock guitar solos by Oldfield. The 17-minute "Incantations Part 4" rambles a bit, with the first half of the piece dominated by very Gong-like vibes, which are too loud and trebly in the mix and go on for far too long. This is the album's only really inferior piece. At the halfway point the piece shifts to some chunky rhythms and more blazing guitar. Unfortunately, the finale isn't nearly triumphant enough, despite the return of Prior's vocals, relying again on the rambling vibes. The live concert version of *Incantations* on *Exposed* corrects these errors to an extent.

The soundstage of *Incantations* is a wide, spacious stereo, with very crisp highs. The cover is a photo of Oldfield standing on a seashore among crashing waves and rocks, with a blue-sky background; like the Longfellow poem, it serves to underscore the elemental forces that *Incantations* evokes.

EXPOSED. Released July 1979. Caroline.

Exposed is a live two-CD set that ranks as one of Mike Oldfield's very best releases, and also as one of the finest concert recordings in progressive music. The translation of his music to a live context is very interesting, as up until this time Oldfield's live performances were fairly rare, with studio recording taking priority. What's notable is that Oldfield was popular enough to play at the arena level, and the large scale actually complements his rather personal and intimate compositions from the early and mid-1970s, rather than crudely simplifying them. Oldfield is a performer who faces audiences fully equipped with compositional brilliance; he doesn't rely on his instrumental prowess or any kind of dressed-up media image. The input of a larger than usual backing band (as opposed to the studio versions, where it's mainly just Oldfield himself) also adds a lot, giving the music cohesion, muscle, and extra confidence.

Exposed features two of Oldfield's most successful works, "Incantations" and "Tubular Bells." The arrangements and instrumentation are quite different from the studio ones. These versions being preferable, focusing on the strongest parts of each, eliminating entire sections but achieving a more effective synthesis that's both rousing and exciting. *Exposed* is taken from recordings made in Spain, Germany, Belgium, Holland, Denmark, and England during March and April of 1979. The tour ensemble included a number of very talented artists, including Steeleye Span vocalist Maddy Prior, Gong percussionists Pierre and Benoit Moerlen, Swedish composer Pekka Pohjola (here on bass guitar), and conductor David Bedford. The rest of the extended band contains two other guitarists (besides Oldfield himself), two percussionists, three trumpets, two flutes, six violas, six violins, four cellos, two basses, and an 11-member female choir.

The 26-minute "Incantations Parts 1 and 2" and the 21-minute "Incantations Parts 3 and 4" both emphasize the classical elements within the work, making *Exposed*'s "Incantations" Oldfield's most traditionally symphonic recording. The piece has some of the most attractive and uplifting strings and choir arrangements in recent 20th-century composition (although the choir should be louder in the mix). The guitar-led section of precise soloing notes is bewitching here, and Maddy Prior's vocal, eagerly anticipated (the crowd applauds before she even starts), is a strong highlight of the piece. The band-oriented jams are as intense as the studio version, but not as loud. The vibes section is thankfully shortened, and the finale is improved.

The 28½-minute "Tubular Bells Part 1" and the 11-minute "Tubular Bells Part 2" have a core rock band dynamic that gives the piece a real groove and swagger—quite different from the studio version—with a more conventional prog rock interaction of guitars, bass, keyboards, and drums. But Oldfield also adds new sections with strings, vibes, horns, and flute, thereby emphasizing the classical dimensions of this piece, while at the same time balancing it with the heated-up rock sections. A high point of Part 1 is the wonderfully different section starting at around the seventeenth minute, with chunky guitars, massive drums, keyboard runs, and a flute solo, which then becomes a raging charge from the rhythm section led by guitar solos. Part 2 opens with an attractive section of strings, horns, and flute before returning to a rock band jam, the flute moving into some rather intense blowing.

Following "Tubular Bells" is the 6-minute song "Guilty," Oldfield's first real foray into commercial songwriting. A sequenced disco beat, plucking bass guitar, synth solos, and a repetitious vocal chorus bounce along nicely. The piece is fun, with a sharp sound mix, and actually reprises bits from "Incantations" and "Tubular Bells."

The production values of *Exposed* are strong, although the mix is flat and could be a lot meatier. The cover has a number of photos from the tour, but they are too compressed in size to be effective.

PLATINUM. Released November 1979. Caroline.

Platinum is one of Mike Oldfield's most attractive albums, and also one of his most varied. A stronger rock and even a jazz feel is explored, helped by Pierre Moerlen, Morris Pert, and Allan Schwartzberg on drums, and others on bass, keyboards, and bells. Oldfield confines himself to electric and acoustic guitars, synth, piano, vibes, and marimba. An American influence is brought to Oldfield's music with a horn section arranged by New Yorkers Peter Gordon and Michael Riesman, along with engineer Kurt Munkasci. These names are known in the New York avant-garde scene for their work with composers like Philip Glass. *Platinum* was something of a departure for Oldfield, with a sparser sound that's in contrast to the dense intricacy of earlier works. The production and mix are quite precise, giving *Platinum* a crisp, sharply defined execution that is a contrast to the layered tapestries of *Hergest Ridge* or *Ommadawn*. And *Platinum,* with its snazzy horns, is actually a danceable prog rock.

The first four instrumental pieces run together as the centerpiece "Platinum Parts 1–4," even though they are all actually very different from each other. The 5-minute "Airborn" opens with extremely crisp synth rhythms, bass guitar, a large drum sound, and a vibraphone, all led by Oldfield's electric guitar. This is not the usual sort of fusion, despite the drums/vibes influence of Gong's Pierre Moerlen, but rather a more ragtime–like jazz. The flavorful 6-minute "Platinum" is one of Oldfield's best-ever tracks, and one of his most rocking compositions. A smooth but flat-out rhythm section marches along with Oldfield's clean, soaring electric lead lines. The piece is catchy, easy to like, and exciting. It's an air guitar favorite. "Charleston," a 3-minute jazzy piece with a slicing, attention-getting horn arrangement, a bouncy rhythm section, and a shivery wordless vocal by Wendy Roberts, is equally enjoyable. Despite its tight execution, the piece has a loose feel. The 4-minute "North Star"/"Platinum Finale" is a cover of Philip Glass's "North Star," with a rousing guitar solo and chorus of voices leading vibraphone, synth, piano, bass, drums, and acoustic guitars. The piece is as nimble and as fluid as the rest of the recording, quite unlike the somewhat stiff feel of Glass's compositions.

The second half of *Platinum* is a mixed bag. A definite highlight is the 4-minute instrumental "Woodhenge," perhaps Oldfield's most space music–like track. A flurry of vibraphone, marimba, and woodblocks is joined by light guitar and synth textures. The piece has an approachable, natural glow, and one wishes he would do more in this vein.

The 5-minute "Sally" is utterly dispensable trite tosh, an old-hat jazzy pop song with a wretched disco beat. The lead vocal by Wendy Roberts, however, is superb. The 5-minute instrumental "Punkadiddle" is equally dreadful, with garish synths and more disco beats. Everything about the piece is unattractive: the title is a mistake and the track has uncalled-for audience applause, managing to make what Oldfield does look formulaic.

Platinum concludes with a 4½-minute version of George Gershwin's "I Got Rhythm." It's a ripping cover with a passionate vocal from Roberts, who was Oldfield's best vocalist. For more of their work together, try to find the now-rare 1980 concert video release entitled *The Complete Mike Oldfield,* produced shortly after the release of *Platinum.* It features Roberts's fantastic and sexy vocal textures on both "Tubular Bells" and "Ommadawn."

The cover art is a photo of a butterfly in the glow of a spotlight on a blue background, a nice visual image for the enjoyable music of *Platinum.*

QE2. Released October 1980. Caroline.

QE2 is another interesting Oldfield album, a bridge between his sprawling 1970s works and his later 1980s pop releases. Still primarily instrumental and featuring the same extended grab bag of instruments that he used throughout his previous opuses, *QE2* is nevertheless an attempt to forge a contemporary updating of his trademark sound and to break some new ground in the process. The most major musical change is the extensive use of synths, vocoder, and exotica such as Aboriginal drumsticks. *QE2* was co-produced by David Hentschel (Genesis, Renaissance). Although the album is still primarily an Oldfield solo affair, it also sees the initial convening of his 1980s core band (vocalist Maggie Reilly, drummer Morris Pert, and keyboardist Tim Cross), plus an expanded guest lineup that includes Phil Collins on drums.

The 10-minute "Taurus 1" is a poor choice for an opener, being the album's weakest track. Oldfield's mandolin and Reilly's Celtic vocals are led by tinny electronic percussion. Thankfully a bigger groove ensues, with some saucy electric guitar licks and Collins's drums, but this switches into a cheesy vocoder part with African drums. The 3½-minute "Sheba" is similar but better, with Reilly's world music–like vocals (a very welcome new element, actually), vocoder, and synth patterns. Things really pick up in the track when Collins's huge drum rolls kick in. The 3-minute "Conflict" is a highlight, with aggressive African drums, cascades of synth, and soaring electric guitar soloing, with sprinkles of acoustic guitars. The 2½-minute "Arrival" is a cover of an ABBA song, and Oldfield certainly makes it his own. With a richly detailed sound palette, including a vocal choir, it's not bad, though a bit too Muzaky and inconsequential in the final analysis.

The second half of *QE2* is the best. "Wonderful Land," a popular single at the time, is a 3½-minute cover of a traditional song, very much in Oldfield's classic style à la the *Collaborations* tracks from *Boxed,* with celestial electric guitars and David Bedford's string section. The 4-minute "Mirage" and the 7½-minute "QE2/QE2 Finale" are both very similar to the material on *Platinum,* which is a good thing. Exciting, smooth horn arrangements (with two trumpets, a trombone, and a sax), a more interesting use of synths, and sophisticated mixes create active, atypical Oldfield buildup marches, led by brisk electric guitar solos. The 3-minute "Celt" is another highlight, similar to "Sheba" but better. Hard-hitting African drums and Reilly's vocals are more infectious here, and Oldfield's guitar solo on this track is really great. *QE2* concludes with "Molly," an all-too-brief (at a scant 1 minute) textural toss-off of mellow electric guitars with soft bass and vocoder added. It's nice, but just too minor.

QE2 exudes a summery, outdoor vibe, but unfortunately half of it has a tendency to be too light-sounding, and the up-front synths are not up to the standard of the rest. Too many of the tracks are like expensive musical wallpaper, elaborate but conveying little. While *QE2* is redeemed to a great extent by its excellent second half, the music press of the era (in both the U.K. and the U.S.) pounced on it with a vengeance at the time, condemning Oldfield's progressive forms as one of the true stylistic enemies of the emerging young rock bands. This was of course a bogus charge (did they really prefer it when he switched to shorter, tougher vocal rock songs, as in 1983's "Shadow on the Wall"?). Perhaps they were jealous of *QE2*'s advanced production values, which are some of his best. (By this point Oldfield had become a master of ear-candy mixes.) Or perhaps it was the terrible cover art of *QE2* that got the critics down, with its lines of primary colors that convey nothing about the music.

AMAROK. Released August 1990. Virgin import.

Amarok is Mike Oldfield's most radically experimental disc, and a popular one with his fans. A 60-minute piece without pause or interruption, the work is certainly an unexpected move, coming as it did in between two of his most pop releases, 1989's *Earthmoving* and 1991's *Heaven's Open.* With its jaw-dropping total of 65 different instruments (all listed in the disc's booklet), *Amarok* is a Ron Geesin–like loony musical collage, employing such sounds like toys, whistles, spoons, water, glass breaks, door slams, and tools. While previous Oldfield collaborators like Tom Newman, Paddy Maloney, Clodagh Simmonds, and Bridget St. John make contributions to this disc, the recording is not a homage to Oldfield's 1970s works, nor is it even an updating of them, but rather something totally new.

Amarok presents Oldfield's penchant for collections of smaller musical vignettes without any unifying concept or theme. Without any symphonic or rock band arrangements, his music is completely avant-garde—absurdist, nonlinear, chaotic, disorienting, and dissonant. This difficult-to-describe piece moves at such a jarring pace that something different happens every 10 seconds.

While the number of inventive and attractive textures here is plentiful, the surprises wrought by the crashing, screeching notes littered throughout the piece are just too shocking. The juxtaposition of these with the softer textures is extremely jarring and uncomfortable, and this is *Amarok*'s main flaw. Also, at a full hour without a break music this complex is a rough ride. That said, *Amarok* is the pinnacle of spacious Oldfield ear candy—incredibly detailed, with a full digital mix. Even though there isn't much synth here, this is still the epitome of high-tech recording, with digital editing creating a sound that's nothing like the painstakingly constructed older releases. It's louder, cleaner, and more precise, but has lost some warmth and charm.

The cover photo is like a slick, updated *Ommadawn*—very 1990s, and tastelessly so. At the time of *Amarok*'s release, Virgin ignored the album, giving it no promotion and no U.S. release. It was a very strange way to treat the man whose album sales more or less made the label what it is.

TUBULAR BELLS 2. Released October 1992. Reprise.

A sequel of sorts to 1973's *Tubular Bells,* this work is similar to the earlier album, but though they share many themes, they are fundamentally different. All 14 tracks of the 58½-minute *Tubular Bells 2* run together, and these separately titled divisions give clues as to how Oldfield constructs a larger whole out of the various smaller bits. The main difference between the first album and this one is the updated technology, providing the recording with a larger scope and giving it a clean, precise execution. Despite all the high-tech gloss, the overall structure of *Tubular Bells 2* is actually quite classical and less contemporary than albums like *QE2* or the radical *Amarok*.

Tubular Bells 2 is a good introduction to Oldfield's music, and certainly ranks among his best; it is also one of the major progressive releases of the 1990s. The only significant complaint about it is that some parts of it are too sweet and mushy (often due to atypical synth sounds). These sections make it sound like new age music, which is unfortunate because the label "new age" implies limitations, and keeps the album from being regarded as something larger. However, the disc does flow very smoothly, and could use more rough edges.

For the record, Oldfield plays electric, acoustic, flamenco, and 12-string guitars, banjo, mandolin, grand piano, synths, digital programming, Hammond organ, timpani, glockenspiel, triangle, tambourine, cymbals, toys, handclaps, and, of course, tubular bells! Additional musicians contribute drums, vocals, Scottish and Celtic bagpipes, and digital programming.

"Sentinel" opens with a more reflective piano variation on the *Tubular Bells* theme, joined by attractive, breathy female vocals, which provide the work with its most soulful element. An infectious, danceable buildup groove begins, with guitars, keyboards, voices, bass, and percussion. "Dark Star" is more of a guitar rave-up, but still quite friendly in its sound. "Clearlight" is indeed light, with soft textures of guitars, keyboards, and voice. "Blue Saloon" lays down catchy pulses of bass, keyboards, and guitar, switching to a shrill guitar and then a flurry of banjos and saloon-style piano. "Sunjammer" has driving, edgy rhythm guitars joined by multiple acoustic guitars, but is sweetened by light percussion. "Red Dawn" is a highlight, an all-too-brief acoustic guitar and angelic female vocal; it is beautiful and poignant. "The Bell" is the introduction section of the various instruments (as on the first album), concluding with an acoustic jam and handclaps.

"Weightless" is a mellow stroll through the clouds, with airy patterns of floating vocals and guitars joined by light piano and percussion. "The Great Plains" begins as another of Oldfield's pastorals with acoustic guitars and banjos, but then becomes quite bouncy with stereo keyboard effects. "Sunset Door" continues this light texture, punctuated by bass guitar licks. "Tattoo" is a quintessential Oldfield march of bagpipes and keyboards, injected with guitar rave-ups. "Altered State" is another high point. A very loose, rollicking piano and drums groove plunks merrily along, with a brief lead nonsense vocal and grunt, and female voices repeatedly questioning what the hell is going on. All of this is topped off by ripping guitar solos. All told, "Altered State" is enjoyable, off-the-wall, drunken-frenzy-type music. "Maya Gold" is a calm respite after "Altered State," with bass, keyboards, mellow electric guitars, and sprinkles of percussion and acoustic guitars, plus deep, electronically processed "ooohs" by Oldfield. The romping "Moonshine" concludes, with a down-home, country banjo finale.

The sound mix is the usual Oldfield ear candy, being lustrous, spacious, vibrant, and detailed. The cover is similar to that of the original *Tubular Bells,* only with a solid blue background.

TUBULAR BELLS II—THE PERFORMANCE LIVE AT EDINBURGH CASTLE (video). U.K. TV broadcast from October 1992. Laser disc import released 1992.

In the same way that the *Exposed* disc presented a preferable live version of the original *Tubular Bells,* this video concert is also the best way to experience *Tubular Bells 2.* While this doesn't make changes to the piece the way *Exposed* did for the first one, it does flow more naturally than the too-clean studio version. Plus, the huge band lineup gives the work a certain collective cohesion, solidity, and dynamism. Overall, it's simply a treat to be able to see the work performed. The complexity of such a creation as this is here given an up-close look in all its splendor.

Besides Oldfield himself, the band consists of three guitarists, three keyboardists, one pianist, a bassist, a drummer, two percussionists, a banjo/mandolin player, a fiddler, a bluegrass banjo player, and the Royal Scots Dragoon Guards on bagpipes and drums. Four female vocalists (Edie Lehmann, Suzanna Melvoin, Jackie Quinn, and Linda Taylor) are here involved, providing some of the concert's best moments, especially during "Sentinel," "Red Dawn," and "Altered State."

The size of the gig is massive (it even includes a fireworks show at the end), with the castle setting reinforcing the essentially British nature of Oldfield's music. The audience is attentive and responsive. The concert is executed with such flair and precision that it must have been a phenomenal undertaking to organize. The whole affair is on such a grand scale, and succeeds so well, that this live presentation of *Tubular Bells 2* assumes a timeless quality.

All of this is captured with state-of-the-art visuals and sound. The sound mix is by Oldfield himself, and is just incredible. The video image has crisp resolution, particularly for an evening outdoor show, and the camera coverage is ideal. A highly recommended viewing.

SALLY OLDFIELD

WATER BEARER. Released October 1978. Castle import.

Sally Oldfield's *Water Bearer* is one of the major classics of the vocal progressive rock genre;

Sally Oldfield.

everything about the album is extremely well done. The older sister of Mike Oldfield, she's a virtuoso acoustic guitarist, and as talented a multi-instrumentalist as her brother. *Water Bearer* is her first solo album, and her only progressive one. After this she moved strongly in the direction of commercial pop.

Water Bearer is notable for a number of reasons. First, it's such a solo tour de force, with Oldfield writing, arranging, performing, and producing. On the recording, she plays acoustic, electric, and Spanish guitars, piano, Moog bass, synths, marimba, glockenspiel, harpsichord, tubaphone, mandolin, and vibes. Her talents are very similar to brother Mike's in these respects, and she is deserving of more attention. Secondly, the album has an unusually advanced, attention-getting, state-of-the-art production—crisp, heavily layered, and detailed; it even eclipses Mike's great-sounding late 1970s releases. Thirdly, the album's lyrical themes are earthy, optimistic ultra-hippie paeans to universal love and romantic passion, giving the album a sensual, deeply felt emotional intensity—a goal matched by the music. *Water Bearer* invites the listener along on a profound spiritual (but also fun and sexy) experience.

The 6½-minute title track opens with the sounds of a river leading into a gorgeous tapestry of multiple guitars, angelic lead and background vocals, and percussion. The next section is a transformative conceptual piece comprised of four separate tracks, entitled "Songs of the Quendi." This is the highlight of the album. Ostensibly influenced by the writings of J. R. R. Tolkien, the piece also touches on New Testament and hippie/counterculture themes. It is almost impossible not to be moved by these four tracks; the fragile vulnerability of Oldfield's voice on these tracks has been known to bring people to tears.

The 3-minute "Night Theme" sets the scene, with suitably soft vibes and Moog bass. The 3-minute "Wampum Song" is a ballad about how societies could be organized around love. The 5-minute "Nenya" has majestic, sweeping orchestrated movements (constructed mainly with a multitude of guitars), adding guests on male tenor voice and bongos. The 2-minute "Land of the Sun" is the most affective, with Oldfield on acoustic guitar and vocals that anyone would find moving.

The rest of *Water Bearer*'s seven songs are each in the 2½- to 3½-minute range. "Mirrors" is like a 1967 "All You Need Is Love" plea, inspiring if sweet. "Weaver" is irresistibly tuneful, similar to early Kate Bush, with catchy keyboard/bass/guitar interaction. "Night of the Hunter's Moon" is a highlight, perhaps the album's most famous track and certainly the one with the strongest rock credentials. A huge, thumping Moog bass line is joined by multiple acoustic guitars, with lyrics about a lustful female on the prowl. "Song of the Bow" and "Fire and Honey" are in a similar vein. "Child of Allah" veers toward sickly-sweet pop, but the production is so lavish it doesn't matter—the thick tapestries of guitars are pure ear candy. "Song of the Healer" is one of Oldfield's best songs, with more sparkling guitar work.

The cover photo of a robed Oldfield standing over a magical waterfall is the perfect image for the disc, underscoring the harmony-with-nature aspect of her music as well as its sensual side. The previous CD issue of *Water Bearer* on the Bronze label has even better sound than the current Castle version, and also has a more complete booklet, with the lyrics.

Despite the hostility in late 1978 toward progressive rock (and hippies), particularly in the U.K. press, *Water Bearer* actually made it through that climate because it's so easy to like, establishing Sally Oldfield with a career that lasted into the 1980s. While the rest of her releases don't come close to the sophistication of *Water Bearer, Celebration* (from 1980) retains some of the same flavor, and is a solid album.

HANS OTTE

THE BOOK OF SOUNDS. Released April 1984. Kuckuck.

Hans Otte is a German composer, pianist, and artist who is concerned with active listening—the possibilities of immersing oneself in sound and transforming one's awareness in the process. *The Book of Sounds* is a 71-minute 12-part work performed on a Steinway piano and was recorded in November 1983 at the Academy of Music in Munchen, Germany. Basically a minimalist form, the piece uses small harmonic changes, alternating between colorful cascades of notes and sections of sparser dispersions that have space to resonate. The pieces range from 3 to $8^1/_2$ minutes, and each explore the dynamics of the piano and its timbres.

By concentrating on the organizations of the notes, Otte never draws attention to himself with any overt technique. Key to the success of this work is the extremely quiet, full digital soundstage; it is very flat, and not at all spatial. Otte is all subtlety, and has a light touch, always understated. To the literal-minded *The Book of Sounds* may sound simple and unvaried, but the active listener will perceive enormous depth. A classic minimalist landscape is painted, where foreground and background are merged. The pieces become like a faint, radiant glow that hovers and dances around the room, like the sunlight at dusk. It's a reassuring sound that seduces the senses, but is approachable, friendly, and very relaxing.

While Otte is somewhere in the area of a Harold Budd or a Terry Riley, *The Book of Sounds* is outside any strict classical, jazz, or contemporary

Hans Otte.

style, including that of ambient or new age. It has its own style, and is thus very progressive.

OZRIC TENTACLES

STRANGEITUDE. Released September 1991. IRS.

Ozric Tentacles were a breath of fresh air for the progressive rock genre (particularly for U.K. prog rock) when they first appeared in the mid-to late 1980s. While sharing an underground, hippie, bohemian aura with previous generations of prog rockers, their music is undeniably different from most of the forms preferred by earlier groups. Combining psychedelia, gritty guitar-led space rock, and space music with unexpected elements like reggae and acid-house/techno-rave music, they created a bizarre new fusion hybrid of danceable, boom-box space rock with an exotic flavor. Their music is like an intricately designed tapestry of loud colors.

A five-piece group led by guitarist/keyboardist/composer/producer Ed Wynne, along with his brother, bassist Roly Wynne, and others on synths, drums, and flute, Ozric Tentacles are an all-instrumental band, in contrast to the neoprog rock U.K. bands of the 1980s, with their penchant for conceptual verbiage. The Ozrics have an extensive number of releases. However, the standard complaint about them is that their material has few surprises or developments after a certain point, and that they concoct more and more bombastic ways of exploring their own formula. While this is a valid criticism, two of their releases stand out from the others—their 1991 third studio album *Strangeitude* and the concert recording *Live Underslunky,* released in 1992 (see review below). Although their other releases are worthwhile, they cannot sustain their often uncalled-for length, eventually succumbing to unvaried, obviously derivative patterns. *Strangeitude,* then, is a representative sample of all Ozric's studio releases, and a good introduction.

The 6-minute "White Rhino Tea" opens the disc with active synth percolations leading into the gargantuan band interplay and volume, with wailing guitars and synths backed by a massive rhythm section. The piece has some Middle Eastern–flavored notes, typical of Ozric exotica. The 6½-minute "Sploosh!" begins with a splash of water and a simple synth rhythm, followed by a powerful drumbeat. It's quite danceable, and includes teeth-grinding synth solos. The 7½-minute "Saucers" has an active acoustic guitar leading the band through hard-rocking psychedelic sways, along with flute, bubbling synths, and a heavy beat. The piece drifts into a blaring guitar solo which despite its loudness can produce a trancelike state in the listener.

The 7½-minute title track has a middle section of Eastern-flavor synth and light percussion, which then chugs away like an engine, becoming dissonant, and instead of fading or taking a turn into something else adds a monster-sized drumbeat and continues. The enjoyable 4-minute "Bizarre Bazaar" is led by Wynne's electric guitar riffs and solos, laying down a bouncy groove and joined by an effects-enhanced flute. Slippery and panoramic at the same time, it comes at the listener like a hurricane. Both the 7½-minute "Space Between Your Ears" and the 7-minute live track "Live Throbbe" are dominated by heavy reggae/dub beats, with saucy electric guitar solos from Wynne.

The production values here are incredible, and set a standard of sorts for the time. The appropriately psychedelic cover art, which features rings of earthlike pods drifting in space, is reminiscent of *Silent Running,* a 1972 sci-fi film.

LIVE UNDERSLUNKY. Released April 1992. Dovetail import.

Moving at an even faster pace than their already adrenalin-charged studio albums, *Live Underslunky* is clearly the best Ozric Tentacles release. Energetic, driving, fast-paced, and very loud, it's a hard rock instrumental affair, with the sharp focus on leader Ed Wynne's electric guitar. This 73-minute, 11-song disc, recorded at two U.K. gigs in November 1991, is a concise representation of the band in their ideal setting—in concert. The sound quality is first-rate, as it should be, with up-front guitars/bass/drums, de-emphasizing to an extent the synths and flute. Hard rock/heavy metal fans would love *Live Underslunky.* Each of the five band members here is excellent, though it's mainly Wynne's show. The only complaint is that some of the synth sounds are too obvious, too familiar. For those unfamiliar with the sound of *Live Underslunky,* picture Jethro Tull combined with Fire Merchants, via Gong and Steve Hillage.

Ozric Tentacles. (Photo by Martin Goodachre.)

The first two minutes of the 8-minute opener, "Dots Thots," is space music synths and percussion which shifts into an insistent rhythm guitar, bass, and drums groove that's jagged and irresistible, accompanied by gripping guitar solos by Wynne. The 9½-minute "Og-Ha-Be" features funky flute and keyboard interplay with bass and drums, adding power-drive rhythm and lead guitars. The 5½-minute "Erpland" is heavy psychedelic guitar blowing à la Jimi Hendrix, followed by a somewhat drowned-out flute solo. The 5½-minute "White Rhino Tea" has a fast, goofy opening with synth and vocals recalling Gong, before a dissolving synths and percussion section with a Middle Eastern flavor takes over. The 4-minute "Bizarre Bazaar" is a fantastically nimble flute and drums groove, giving way to concise, soaring electric guitar solos. The 8-minute "Sunscape" also contains more guitar-dominated workouts, but eases up the tempo slightly for some breezy synth flights.

A lighter texture is established with the 3½-minute "Erpsongs," being an all electronic space music voyage that's really pretty good. A chunky bass-led groove launches the 3½-minute "Snake Pit," a workout with synth, samples, and drums. The 5-minute "Kuck Muck" is a dizzying, intoxicating, potently psychedelic track led by Wynne's whirling dervish guitar. It's lightning-fast and tight. The 5-minute "0–1" opens with a flute solo before returning to more blazing guitar rock. The sound falters a bit on the 14½-minute "Ayurvedic," where a dreamy opening leads into a buildup with an extended reggae beat.

The cute cover drawing depicts a hippie tour follower, plus some good tour photos and a mandala.

PANGEE

HYMNEMONDE. Released December 1995. Pangee import.

Pangee are a French Canadian quintet from Quebec, whose sound is similar to the classically influenced rock of Gryphon, early Genesis, Shylock, Egg, and Univers Zero, but without the rough edges. The self-released *Hymnemonde* is a refined, all-instrumental oddity, using 6- and 12- string guitars, violin, bass guitar, clarinet, keyboards, bass pedals, and percussion. Pangee's music is complex but not overly so, avoiding flat-out rock by including very spacey, long passages that have a likeable, warm quality. The sound of the group is unconventional, with a high-quality ADD mix which is not the power crunch of a typical fusion project, but that of a subtle form of chamber rock.

The 19½-minute "Quartus Frenesis" begins with drifting guitar and violin textures, establishing a lazy tempo with keyboards, drums, and clarinet. The overall convergence of these instruments makes a strange sound, like a giant harmonium. The piece builds up with more drumming and precise guitar notes, pausing for some solo drones from the violin, then picks up with melodic textures from the 12-string guitar and bass pedals. This goes into a tight rhythm section with some nimble bass playing, along with spacey and occasionally shrill soloing from the keyboards, guitar, and violin. The piece keeps the listener guessing as to where it's going; while experimental, however, it's not difficult to follow.

The 11-minute "Cataracte" is led by an angular electric guitar à la King Crimson or Shylock, only more laid-back and not so severe. There are many tricky, rhythmic chord changes from the guitar and violin, but there's no conventional rock style soloing from these instruments. The piece then changes to sunny Genesis/"Supper's Ready"–like chords, adding light vibes, bells, assorted percussion, chunky bass lines, and up-front synth.

The 16-minute "Le Sanctuaire d'Euterpe" is a symphonic but understated drum march, with guitars, bass, organ, and gentle, supportive texturing from synths. The piece has a reverent, celestial feel, yet it bounces along at an lively pace. Although it does become more aggressive, this doesn't threaten the established mood.

The strange cover art by drummer Jean-Vincent Roy is a painting of a bearded man in close up with no eyes, only hollow black sockets, done in burning colors. An odd cover, appropriate for the uncommon musical directions of *Hymnemonde*.

DAVID PARSONS

TIBETAN PLATEAU/SOUNDS OF THE MOTHERSHIP. TIBETAN PLATEAU released 1982. **SOUNDS OF THE MOTHERSHIP** released 1980. Fortunna.

David Parsons is a composer from New Zealand who combines synthesizers with Indian music, creating dreamy, highly meditative new age/electronic compositions that are serious and not schlocky, serene and not corny. Indian instruments (harp, sitar, sarod, etc.) and environmental sounds (bird song, water streams, crickets) mesh with subtle electronics, and this level of variety (beyond just keyboards) gives Parsons' releases extra doses of authenticity and mystery. No popular forms are even acknowledged in his music, which goes in a completely opposite direction to that of other electronic/new age musicians in the 1980s. Parsons' music seems to be concerned with carefully unifying all of the elements (synths, Indian music, environmental sounds) within his compositions, so that one larger resonance is created that makes the pieces speak with one voice. His albums reveal a painstaking care that is all his own: he writes, performs, engineers, and produces all of his releases.

This 74$\frac{1}{2}$-minute disc collects Parsons' first two albums on one CD, starting with his second one, *Tibetan Plateau* (1982), first. The album's 13$\frac{1}{2}$-minute title track opens with all-electronic, drifting synth tones and unfolding movements. It's an extremely quiet, ambient piece. The 11$\frac{1}{2}$-minute "Gangotri" is also rather ambient, beginning with Indian sitar drones which are then taken over by more swaying synth washes. The 4-minute "Meditation on a Lonely Pool" is briefer (and better for it) and has a more spacious mix. The piece is a gentle glow of Indian harp and synth. The 10$\frac{1}{2}$-minute "Devaloka" is the recording's highlight, with a gorgeous stereo field recording of running water streams, to which harp and synths are added. It's a meditative, trance-inducing music at one with nature (like that of Deuter, whose music Parsons' work often resembles).

Sounds of the Mothership is the best of the two albums due to a sparser, less polished approach. The 5$\frac{1}{2}$-minute "Separation" has Terry Riley–like synth delays with a more up-front Indian instrumentation. The 11-minute "Tree Spirits" combines water streams and birds with the Indian instruments, plus some soft (if somewhat dated) electronic percussion. The 6-minute "Durga" and the 11$\frac{1}{2}$-minute "Spheres" are two of Parsons' most hypnotic music-only pieces. Similar again to Terry Riley, there is a lot of space in the music, with reverent synth hymns, swirls of Indian sounds, and a few more playful stereo effects.

The sound on both albums is excellent. Each has plenty of definition; every small detail in the mix is revealed. The original cover of *Tibetan Plateau,* a gorgeous color photo of the Himalayan mountains, is used for this package.

HIMALAYA. Released 1989. Fortuna.

With *Himalaya,* composer David Parsons demonstrates that he is one of the great new age/electronic music texturalists. Inspired by trips to India and the Himalaya mountains, Parsons combines synths and samples with field recordings of environmental sounds, creating impressions of the scenery of sacred sites. The music is primarily Indian melodies and sustained synth chords, creating relaxing moods. While not every one of Parsons' synth sounds is otherworldly, most of them are, and certainly more so than others in this genre. The 72$\frac{1}{2}$-minute *Himalaya* paints vivid, picturesque landscapes on a panoramic scale.

The 19$\frac{1}{2}$-minute title track sets a serene tone, with a lead synth line that sounds alternately like a flute, pipe, or voice, along with a soft, quiet, hovering background. The piece is more a "presence" than anything else, like the timeless Himalayas themselves. The 13-minute "Kailasa" unfolds with a barely audible sparkling, to which are washes of windlike rumbles. The track begins to sound like emanations from some vast mountain cavern—the listener can almost feel the cold mist. The 6-minute "Akbar" is a haunting work, creating a feeling that one might have upon stepping into a darkened woods. A more spacious synth scape, light drum sounds, and a voice recorded in a tomb make this track a highlight.

The 10$\frac{1}{2}$-minute "Varanasi Dawn" is another key track, with a gorgeous stereo recording of the Ganges River at dawn mixed with sitar-like drones and majestic, sweeping synth lines. The piece is one of Parsons' most representative and successful tracks. The remaining works are of an equal standard. The 14-minute "Rishikesh" blends chanting and claps of thunder recorded at a festival in the town of the same name, with more sitar drones and subtle, selectively placed synth glows. The 10-minute "Varuna Deva" has a tabla-like percussion which, while appearing to be played live by a human, is a sample. It is very delicately done.

The sound is clean, layered, and of a high quality. The cover photo of the Himalaya mountains sums up the focus of this music.

YATRA. Released 1990. Fortuna.

A sprawling two-disc set of 124 minutes of music, *Yatra* follows directly in the vein of David Parsons' previous releases. A musical sound voyage through the Indian countryside that moves on to the landscape of Tibet, *Yatra* is more of the artist's combinations of electronics, samples of Indian instruments, and field recordings, once again all performed and produced by Parsons himself.

The first five tracks (ranging in length from 3½ to 8 minutes) are the most untypical, with garish synth work and up-front electronic percussion. While these tracks are still dreamy when combined with location recordings and environmental sounds, they resemble more conventional electronic/new age forms, like early 1980s Tangerine Dream.

Two other shorter tracks are much better. The 5-minute "Ram Bhakta" is a highlight, with the very faint chanting of an Indian guru and the sound of crickets taken over by subtle synth colorings that create a floating feel. The 8-minute "Earth Mother" opens with the sounds of frogs and a night-time, outdoor vibe that disappears into calm and soft ambient electronic glows.

Making up the bulk of *Yatra* are three lengthy tracks, the disc's centerpieces. The 29½-minute "Abode of Shiva" begins with the sounds of frogs on a quiet river and synth, with a ceremonial bell heard faintly in the background. There is no percussion here, just a pure dream world. The 21½-minute "Maha Puja" is an ambient piece, with sleepy, caressing tones, drowsy chanting voices, faint bell sounds, and a more judicious use of percussion. The track is reassuring and comforting, with a grandeur like that of lonely, wintry mountain peaks. The 28-minute "Manasarover" is more of the same, though somewhat sunnier.

David Parsons.

Yatra is preferable to similar new age journeys made by artists such as Steve Roach or Michael Stearns, and Parsons' ego-dissolving space music is ideal for mental picture painting. The production values of *Yatra* are Parsons' best. The cover includes color photos of the mountains, from India and other parts of the world. The CD version has a considerable amount of music not included on the cassette version, which eliminates many of *Yatra*'s key tracks.

PASSPORT

LOOKING THRU. Released January 1974. Atlantic import.

The German jazz/rock band Passport released four easy-to-like albums during the period 1974–1977 which rank as classics of the fusion genre. With a more ethereal progressive sound than most American and British fusion groups, Passport had an ability to be genuinely spacey and dreamy within this form while still being both rocking and funky.

The lineup during this classic era of Passport was Klaus Doldinger (saxes, Moog synth, mellotron, electric piano), Curt Cress (drums, percussion, electronic percussion), Wolfgang Schmid (bass guitar, guitars), and Kristian Schultze (electric piano, organ). All four are great players. Doldinger, the leader of the group, composed all of the material and produced the recordings. Influenced by 1970s-era Miles Davis and the Mahavishnu Orchestra, this mid-1970s lineup was a break from the more traditional jazz forms of the early Passport, and light years more accomplished than the band's 1980s fusion-lite wallpaper. The rhythm section is hot but restrained, and the melodic keyboards of the period gives them a sound akin to much of 1970s prog, recalling everything from Schicke, Fuhrs and Frohling to Klaus Schulze, Embyro to Agitation Free, Return to Forever to Weather Report.

The eight tracks on *Looking Thru* range from 1½ to 8 minutes in length. "Eternal Spiral" opens with infectious mellotron and synth textures which are attacked aggressively by drum fills, bass, and acoustic guitar, leading into some bright electric piano solos. The 8-minute title track is a sax excursion with artful drumming, mellotron, and electric piano, exuding an otherworldliness rather than a strict live feel. The brief "Zwischenspiel" is a classic texture of piano and acoustic guitar. "Rockport" is an enjoyable, sparse, and simple number, beginning with an electric piano groove and big drumbeat that is joined by breezy sax blowing. The music is danceable and not too complex.

"Tarantula" menaces with creepy, reverbed sax wails, adding murky electric piano, bass, and drums. It then launches into a funky groove led by sharp, mean sax lines. "Ready for Take Off" has a chunky bass groove, joined by Cress's full-sounding drums, organ, and electric piano, with mellow sax layered over it. The approach is refined and exciting, but not flashy. "Eloquence" begins with Agitation Free–like concrete electronic percussions, along with huge drum fills. It then goes into a mellow sax solo and jam. "Things to Come" has dreamy outer space Moog and mellotron, plus psychedelic stereo pans joined by the rhythm section.

The production values are excellent for the era, and Cress has a drum sound that's very big and brilliantly engineered. The volume of the disc's mastering is a bit low, however. The cover art by Wandrey's studio is a series of eye-catching deep blue colored paintings done specifically for the band; they adorn *Looking Thru* as well as the next two Passport releases.

CROSS COLLATERAL. Released February 1975. Atlantic import.

Thoroughly enjoyable from start to finish, *Cross Collateral* is one of the greatest 1970s jazz/rock fusion releases, having an unusually broad progressive scope, sounding like a cross between Soft Machine, Miles Davis, Genesis, Klaus Schulze, and Weather Report. *Cross Collateral* has a European flavor (with a tiny pinch of Gothic to it) that makes it unlike most other fusion projects, including Passport's other albums. Leader Klaus Doldinger plays as many keyboards here as he does sax, so his sax work doesn't dominate. Most of the solo space is given to the other excellent players in the band, especially Curt Cress's phenomenal John Bonham–sized drum sound (one of the biggest of the 1970s music scene). The production is first-rate (their best), and captures a lot of the ambience that takes *Cross Collateral* in the direction of prog rock.

The 6-minute opening track, "Homonculus," is representative of this approach. Layers of attractive and spacey electric piano, mellotron, organ, and Moog synth by Doldinger and Kristian Schultze interact playfully with Cress's thunderous drums. The 13½-minute title track is a real tour de force, with a monster groove led by heavy sax blowing with a fast drumbeat behind it. A hip drum solo then leads into chunky keyboard patterns, followed by a Brand X–like section with bass riffs from Wolfgang Schmid and electric piano solos from Schultze.

The 3-minute "Jadoo" is a fast number, with a funky electric piano riff, a thumping rhythm section, and some heavy sax soloing. The 6-minute "Will-o' the-Wisp" has an infectious drumbeat and monster bass guitar notes that move into a playful but spacey sax. The hooks here are memorable, being more prog than jazz. The 5-minute "Albatross Song" begins with a soft electric piano and bass with washes of mellotron. This is joined by drumbeat and percussion led by bass riffs, as the dreamy keyboards continue and a mellow sax solo is added. The lovely 4½-minute "Damals" is a basic introspective texture, with a mournful sax, Schmid's acoustic guitar, sparse electric piano, cymbals, and bass.

Klaus Doldinger of Passport.

INFINITY MACHINE. Released April 1976. Atlantic import.

Infinity Machine is in the main a thrilling *Cross Collateral* part 2, with the same lineup, instrumentation, and vibe as that disc, making it essential Passport.

The first track, the 10-minute "Ju-Ju-Man," is a slight departure from the rest, with a more American feel. A gargantuan funk beat is laid down by the drums, joined by thick bass and keyboard lines, and a sax solo, plus an extended percussion solo. This danceable piece is similar to *Jack Johnson/On the Corner*–era Miles Davis, with Klaus Doldinger's echoed and delayed sax blowing. The 5½-minute "Morning Sun" is a playful number, with a catchy lead sax line exuding a positive vibe, along with acoustic piano, cymbal brushes, electric piano, and bass, eventually growing and adding drums and guitar. The 3-minute "Blue Aura" is a contemplative track, with a dignified, low-key voice by Doldinger accompanying his bluesy sax and keyboards. The piece is in a sense similar to something by the mid-1970s Popol Vuh.

The second half of *Infinity Machine* is the most like *Cross Collateral*. The 5-minute title track is a keyboard buildup attacked by the rhythm section, going into a breezy sax solo with a solid rock backing. The 7½-minute "Ostinato" has an airy feel, with infectious, dreamy synths and gurgling electric piano leading a smooth bass and drums pattern. The piece even throws in a celestial mellotron at the end, accompanied by exotic drum fills. The 6½-minute "Contemplation" is pure space music, combining a smooth ECM-like sound with new age textures. Fragile tinklings of glasslike percussions, light synth, and dewy electric piano notes are joined by soft dual acoustic guitars for a dignified jazz sax solo, building up with drums. Superb.

The production is again excellent, but the CD transfer is strangely bassy, muting the crisp highs a bit. It sounds fine, though a remastering may be in order.

IGUACU. Released April 1977. Atlantic import.

A big departure from their previous style, *Iguacu* is not dreamy prog but instead an unexpected plunge into the danceable rhythms of world music. *Iguacu* was one of the first explorations into those new directions by a major-label Western band, and a very musically credible one it is, too. This was not just a trendy expression of current influences or a timid experiment, though it was somewhat surprising coming from a group like Passport.

Retaining the same four players (Doldinger, Cress, Schmid, and Schultze) and instrumentation as before, *Iguacu* adds brothers Roy and Elmer Louis to the lineup, on guitar and percussion, respectively, plus seven other guests on percussion, guitar, and ethnic instruments. Leader/composer/saxophonist/keyboardist Klaus Doldinger begins to dominate here, with his sax playing more up front and his keyboard playing de-emphasized. This gives *Iguacu* a tastier, more driving jazz form. Guitarist Roy Louis is unremarkable, though, falling into a more laid-back fusion style that is sometimes funky but really adds very little.

Iguacu is a potent combination of Brazilian rhythms with the Passport four-piece band interplay of the previous three albums. The playing and arrangements are tight, and it all works very well, recalling in part similar world music/jazz/rock fusions by the German band Embryo, but far more polished and rocking. The sound quality of *Iguacu* is excellent, with a detailed, live-sounding, smooth, and infectious mix.

The 6-minute "Bahia Do Sol" begins with brief field recordings of a Brazilian street dance, going into a confident jam led by a very strong sax arrangement of memorable, clearly defined notes by Doldinger. The piece then falls back into sections of exotic percussion, along with bass, keyboards, and sleepy guitars. The 4-minute "Aguamarinha" features a funky rhythm guitar and an up-front sax solo with the rhythm section, followed by a laid-back guitar solo. The 5½-minute "Bird of Paradise" has toy whistle–like sounds and percussion, with the sax dominating the band jam. This still has the basic Passport elements, including the killer interplay between Cress's drums and Schmid's bass guitar, although here it's jazzier and lighter. "Sambukada" is 4½ minutes of wild jungle dance music that really swings. Doldinger wraps saucy sax lines around tribal rhythms and the plentiful percussion.

The 8½-minute title track starts with the same sounds that "Sambukada" ended with, then goes into a more typical Passport prog groove, which then retreats to a "Bird of Paradise" feel with punctuating bass riffs, barking sax lines, rhythm guitar, bass, and drums. The final three tracks, "Praia Leme" (3 minutes), and "Heavy Weight" and "Guna Guna" (each 4½ minutes), are all upbeat, saucy funk grooves. Cress and Schmid are precise but muscular. Very danceable and lots of fun.

After *Iguacu* the whole lineup fell apart, with Doldinger re-creating a series of completely different Passport bands whose music had none of the invention of the mid-1970s titles. The wretched late-1970s Passport even added a ridiculous vocalist, with duff, trite pop lyrics by the former King Crimson lyricist Richard Palmer-James!

ANNETTE PEACOCK

SKY-SKATING. Released March 1982. Ironic import.

Annette Peacock is one of the true geniuses of modern music, and her albums all have an extraordinarily high level of intelligence, poetry, and artistic credibility. Peacock has released a fair number of criminally ignored titles, and deserves much more attention than she has received. Beginning as part of the American avant-garde free jazz and counterculture scene of the 1960s, she composed for and played with Paul Bley, Albert Ayler, and Gary Peacock. She also pioneered some of the first explorations of the early Moog synthesizer, and briefly hung with the likes of Timothy Leary, Salvador Dali, Charles Mingus, and Allen Ginsberg. Moving to Britain in the 1970s, Peacock was sought after by both David Bowie and Brian Eno for various projects, but turned them down. She is perhaps best known for her brief stint as the vocalist in the Bruford band on their 1977 album *Feels Good to Me* (see review).

Sky-skating marked Peacock's fifth solo album as well as the launch of her own independent label, Ironic, in 1982. Having total artistic control, Peacock writes, performs, arranges, produces, and even paints the cover art. *Sky-skating,* which was recorded on location at Wellington College, is not at all the conventional singer/songwriter approach. There's no band, no acoustic guitars, no chorus-heavy songs, no hard-traveled media image. Instead Peacock uses her voice expressively as the main storytelling instrument (she says she tries to sing the way Miles Davis played the trumpet; she was perhaps also influenced by jazz singers like Nina Simone), along with playing acoustic and electric pianos, synths, and a tiny amount of drum machines and percussion.

The sound of *Sky-skating* is incredibly sparse and quiet, creating one of the most intimate albums ever made. *Sky-skating* is progressive in its creation of an emotionally complex, introspective, low-key music. The sound environment is soft and sensual, like the whispers from a lover across the bed, hardly the kind of material suited to the commercial markets of radio, video, or the concert hall. Peacock combines a delicate, inventive tapestry of lead and background vocals with her always-brilliant lyrics and minimal but equally expressive keyboards. *Sky-skating*'s 12 songs range from 1 to 5 minutes in length. The album's progressive nature is underscored by the fact that it really requires repeated listenings, as Peacock's minute vignettes each contain such enormous depth and sophistication that not every nuance can be grasped in one listen.

"Take Your Shoes Off" begins the album, opening with the sounds of public hallway traffic; this changes into Peacock's piano, combined with a vocal that invites the listener into her private thoughts. "Taking It As It Comes" is representative of her caressing, up-close, multitracked vocals. The title track, "Sky-skating," has a drum machine, dreamy carnival-like keyboards, and a guest vocal bit by Peacock's daughter that's out of sync with the rest of the album. "Rap with the Trees" is a sexual song about all the earth being a wonderland of passion. "Until Untrust Unties" has minimal electric and acoustic piano, with a cute, short vocal and some humming.

"Trust" is a conversational vocal, with a sexual honesty rare for the period and a single keyboard playing very subtle melodies. "The Outness Queen's Travelling Theme" is a clever observation with several vocal effects. "Nothing Outside Us" begins with a fragile, quiet, and emotional wordless vocal, then goes into a spoken, conversational vocal with carefully chosen piano notes. "Warmer Than Gold" has a mysterious, deep vocal with poignant lyrics and romantic piano. The album concludes with "Pride," a keen self- examination with romantic overtones. The piece's sensual whisper at the end is an amazing finale.

The sound quality is great throughout, and Peacock's cover painting of a nude woman as seen from behind underscores the emotional rawness and honesty of the priceless *Sky-skating.*

I HAVE NO FEELINGS. Released January 1986. Ironic import.

I Have No Feelings is the strong follow-up to Peacock's masterful *Sky-skating,* and is equal to the quality of that album, being in almost exactly the same style. Here, though, the mood is darker and more emotionally wrenching, far less romantic than *Sky-skating.* The recording is also different in that percussionist Roger Turner accompanies Peacock on half of the disc's 12 tracks, adding tiny avant-garde colorations in support of the album's pessimistic moods.

The construction of Peacock's small (the pieces are between 1 and 4½-minutes), confessional vignettes is fascinatingly sparse—all the sounds that are used are there solely to support the intended mood. In this sense *I Have No Feelings* is a decisive departure from band-oriented forms, and a strong (and progressive) dissent from the larger lineups preferred by the commercial, popular forms since the 1980s. Also notable is Peacock's free-form compositional style, which is close to that of the way a person's thoughts unfold—sometimes going off in wild, energetic, verbal directions, at other times deep and completely introspective. The way her vocal and piano arrangements convey this, each following the other so closely, is a marvel. It's all very tightly controlled, yet outside all conventions and totally unique.

On *I Have No Feelings,* Peacock's vocals have a purer tone and are more tightly arranged than those on *Sky-skating,* creating much of the album's tension. As usual she has total artistic control, writing, producing, and playing keyboards, bass, and toys. Turner's percussion has a lot of echo and resonance, and is not at all like that found within the popular musical genres.

Opening is "Nothing Ever Was, Anyway," a song that has appeared on several Paul Bley albums in many versions. Here (for the first time) it has downbeat lyrics, delivered with an orchestra of vocals by Peacock and low-key crashing percussion by Turner, underlining the things-fall-apart theme of the lyrics. "Butterflies" features Peacock's high-pitched vocal dynamics, with some suitably fluttering percussion. "I'm Not Perfect" has some truly dark chords, with electric piano, bass, and percussion, and ends with a muted vocal. The title track moves at an appropriately melancholy pace, interjecting occasional horn samples. The equally pessimistic lyrics of "The Cynic" are accompanied by more of Turner's exploding percussion. This leads into "The Carousel," a ballad with sampled sax notes and Turner's cymbals.

"You've Left Me," a song of emotional disappointment, has a vocal that sounds like it's being sung through a hollow tube, along with Gothic organ-like notes and chaotic percussion. This leads into "Sincereless," a piece with similar vocal effects and percussion. "Freefall" and "This Almost Spring" run together. They are more romantic than the rest of the recording, and are similar to the material on *Sky-skating*—lovely, impressionistic pieces. "The Feeling's Free" is a jazzy ballad with piano, cymbal brushes, and brief, awkward sax samples. "A Personal Revolution" is a radical feminist pastiche. The disc concludes on a downbeat mood with "Not Enough," a spiritual song with a political rap in the middle and more sax samples.

I Have No Feelings, like all of Peacock's releases, is a perfect example of the progressive vocal form. The sound is great, and the cover is a superb portrait of Peacock by Alfreda Benje.

ABSTRACT-CONTACT. Released July 1988. Ironic import.

On *Abstract-Contact,* Annette Peacock embraces the popular forms of rock, jazz, and funk, while retaining her intensely personal style and insightful, ingenious lyrics. The disc is similar to her 1979 tour de force *The Perfect Release* (now tragically out of print), only with a more immediate and ultramodern sound. Peacock's vocals and keyboards here are joined by the drums of Simon Price and the bass guitar of Ed Poole. Price and Poole provide strong counterpoints to Peacock's playing style, and together the three create heavy, hip rhythms.

Peacock peppers the more conventional forms of *Abstract-Contact* with lyrics that are a veritable philosophical feast, combining detailed political diatribes and intense, self-searching confessionals. Although this in some ways makes the music more accessible, the poetics are intellectually rigorous enough to completely sidestep and undercut the trivial frivolities usually associated with such forms. The lyrical themes of *Abstract-Contact* establish Peacock as one of the most articulate voices of the left in the progressive music scene.

The 13½-minute "Elect Yourself" is the epic-sized centerpiece of the disc. In this insistent, funky rap track (progressive rap? Yes, it is possible!), Peacock speaks a political tract over a hard-hitting, relentless, strident piano/huge drums/plucky bass jam, laying out an empowering manifesto on the self-deception of individuals in the face of corrosive capitalist greed, hollow consumerism, religious hypocrisy, conformity, and sexual repression.

The 5½-minute "Lost in Your Speed" has a snazzy and tight jazz beat, with Peacock singing a low, smooth vocal, accompanied by sampled sax. The 5-minute "Disparate X's" and the 4½-minute "Happy with My Hand" (a paean to masturbation) similarly exude a classy jazz cool.

The 1-minute "Memory Is" and the 30-second "Living Is A" are very brief interludes of piano/bass/drums/vocal grooves. The 7½-minute "We Are Adnate" is another spoken rap, with slabs of guitarlike synth lines and a funky rhythm section in a locked groove. The lyrical focus here is not overtly political, but rather existential.

The closing 3-minute "Down in Blue" is so well done it should be considered practically a standard of the jazz torch song ballad. But Rickie Lee Jones was never like this. This is some of Peacock's best singing.

Also among Peacock's finest vocal performances is the 4-minute bonus track "No Winning, No Losing." Recorded in the 1970s and released on the hopelessly rare (sadly, not yet issued on CD) 1983 LP *Been on the Streets Too Long,* the track is perhaps her best song. Peacock's voice and lyrics combine with the music and guitar of David Terry, who creates spacey atmospherics with his playing.

"No Winning, No Losing" captures an otherworldly, elusive ambience, using a lot of echo on the guitar. It is the height of Peacock's romanticism. Her conversational delivery and lyrics articulate what it means to love and be loved, conveying a hopeful thread of optimism for the future that's tempered with a definite realism and vulnerability. This inspiring and moving piece is concerned with conveying a deeply felt conviction, but uses only the most minimal musical sounds to achieve its goals; it is completely oblivious to any trend-driven forms, remaining as close to the vision as possible.

The production of *Abstract-Contact* is crisp, live-sounding, and first-rate. The CD cover replaces the original (and better) LP cover with another photo—a close-up of Peacock.

ANNETTE PEACOCK/PAUL BLEY

DUAL UNITY. Released December 1988. Freedom import.

Recorded live in Paris in 1970, *Dual Unity* is a crucial early example of American progressive music. Paul Bley, the noted traditional jazz pianist, had a long-standing partnership with Annette Peacock in the late 1960s and early 1970s, and together they acquired (at Peacock's insistence) a Moog synthesizer to incorporate into their compositions. They were among the first musicians to use the instrument in the 1960s, and the effect of doing so was alienating to Bley's core audience, who found it too avant-garde.

Dual Unity is a rare and priceless document of an early moment in the battle between revolutionary progressive forms and entrenched, traditional precedents. By integrating the chaotic and unruly bleeps of the early, primitive synths with the already exploratory form of free jazz, Peacock and Bley created an avant-garde sound that was psychedelic to the power of ten. *Dual Unity* just drips atmosphere, and is a more evocative recording from this heady era than most. The recording (very good, if hissy) leaves all the rough edges intact, and has the extreme stereo separation characteristic of the period.

The 17-minute "M.J." (a.k.a. "Mister Joy") by Peacock is a piece that appears in several different (and shorter) forms on many of Bley's albums. On this version Bley plays synth and electric piano and Peacock plays bass guitar and sings; Han Bennink is on drums. Bley's slow, dreamy keyboards are joined by Peacock's unique slides of bass guitar and Bennink's crashing drumming. Bley and Peacock exchange a series of wonderful notes, followed by a nice solo by Bley. This version has lyrics and vocals (earlier versions were instrumentals). Peacock's vocal here is perhaps the emotional highlight of the album. Though her vocal stylings at the time were occasionally reckless, they are soulful. The lyrics are fairly simple as compared with those on later Peacock releases, but the subject matter is one of intense self-realization and catharsis. This is very important, not only for being the genesis of Peacock's style, but because it ties what was an extremely radical new form of music to a theme of deeply felt personal resolve.

The 4½-minute "Gargantuan Encounter" (co-written by Peacock and Bley, as are the remaining pieces) is practically formless, and certainly among the most successfully dissonant pieces of American music circa 1970. Bley unleashes high, fast, shrill synth blowing, along with Peacock's low and growling treated electric piano and Bennink's drums. The group interplay is excellent, particularly the clever rapport between Bley and Peacock.

The 8-minute "Richter Scale" is an ideal example of intense avant-garde free jazz featuring Bley's squeaking synth. This track replaces Bennink with drummer Laurence Cook and bassist Mario Pavone. The larger rhythm section leads to a good deal of loud bashing from Cook, with juxtapositions that are jagged and disturbing. Bley (also on electric piano) and Peacock (acoustic piano) exchange many colorful moments.

The 3-minute title track, also with Cook and Pavone, is a lighter approach. Mild piano doodling, cymbals, acoustic bass, and a few synth blips follow notes similar to those in "M.J.," but in a more drifting mood. Peacock scats along with synth notes, which is fun to hear.

The small but superb cover photo of Peacock and Bley is very amusing. Peacock is all smiles in a revealing dress, while Bley is a mass of beard and long hair, in sunglasses. *Dual Unity* is a hard-to-find Japanese import, but it's a key title in progressive music history.

SHAWN PINCHBECK AND MARION GARVER

RESONANCE. Released November 1995. Pinchbeck & Garver import.

Resonance is pure space music with a huge sense of mystery (a crucial ingredient for the genre, but one rarely seen these days). Shawn Pinchbeck is a Canadian composer interested in creating abstract environments of sound utilizing synthesizers, tapes, electronic treatments, and field recordings. Garver is an American flautist with a background in 20th-century classical and jazz music. Recorded between 1991 and 1995, the 66-minute disc was produced and engineered by Pinchbeck, with 9 of the 10 tracks written separately either by Pinchbeck or Garver, and 1 track that's co-written by the two of them. While *Resonance* seems to be mainly Pinchbeck's baby, Garver adds a crucial nonelectronic human element, lightening some of the disc's darker moments. Pinchbeck and Garver's music is strongly reminiscent of Emerald Web, though it is not quite as light in tone.

The 5½-minute "Spirit and Flesh" is a Gothic opening, with ominous, dense, church organ keyboards (sounding like a mellotron) that are joined by a faraway drumbeat. The 8½-minute "Temporal Reality" combines windlike swooshes of synth and flute with an up-front electronic drumbeat (not the best choice, but still effective) and interruptions of loud, industrial collage noises. The 1½-minute "For Swrm" is a nice interlude solo flute by Garver followed by the 5½-minute Emerald Web–like "Open Heart," with celestial new age synths and a light flow, as well as a lot of low-frequency rumbles. The 3½-minute "The Sand, the Sea, the Stars" is a combination of trance and active electronics, with haunting synth lines. The 2-minute "Dave, David, Davidson" showcases Garver's flutes, with a fluttery technique enhanced by reverb. The piece has a Renaissance-era feel to it. The 6½-minute "Transformation No. 1" is electronic mist with moody flute that evokes a macabre, ghostly realm. The piece becomes dissonant (taking the flute in these directions as well) and goes into a bizarre section of stereo concrète sounds, recalling artists like Lightwave, Klaus Schulze, and Lustmord. The 5-minute "Opal" is a simple electronic rhythm, with dreamy synth lines in the foreground and a faint glow in the background. Garver's 3-minute "Dziwna Mitosc," a reflective piano solo, is somewhat unexpected, and adds variety.

Shawn Pinchbeck and Marion Garver.

The standout track is the 23-minute concluding piece, "Endangered Spaces." It begins with up-front environmental sounds (wind, bird songs), then an ambient electronic low frequency sound emerges, slowly becoming brighter. The piece unfolds very delicately, adding soft flute, percussion, and guitar-like sounds. Similar to Bill Nelson's

Crimsworth, it's even more introspectively fragile than that work, quietly celebrating the private moods it creates.

The production values of this self-released disc are excellent, with a mix that brings out all the details in the music. The exceptionally gorgeous and lavish packaging—a multicolored foldout cover—is very appealing. However, the disc itself is wrapped only in a colored paper, held together with string, which is both inconvenient and an all-too-fragile way of storing the disc. It does, on the other hand, turn the disc into a kind of sacred object, to be handled with great care.

PINK FLOYD

THE PIPER AT THE GATES OF DAWN. Released August 1967. Capitol/EMI.

The Piper at the Gates of Dawn is the earliest album-length example of modern progressive music. The original Pink Floyd lineup at this time was Syd Barrett (composer, guitars, lead vocals), Roger Waters (bass guitar, vocals), Rick Wright (organ, piano, vocals), and Nick Mason (drums). Barrett was the leader of the group, and this first Pink Floyd album is mainly his vision.

The Piper . . . is significant in that it did not accept the pop forms of the era as it found them, choosing instead to create playful, surreal stereo soundscapes—mini storytelling vignettes of collage psychedelia. The album's 11 tracks (ranging in length from 2 to 9½-minutes) have a great deal of authentic psychedelic tension. Instruments veer off as if trying to escape the stereo field they're in, pushing outward and dissolving, but inevitably being reined back in. The pieces combine small bits of song forms and sounds into a tenuous whole that can and does change direction at any moment, always in flux. The lyrics contain sharp and vivid images in the vein of Lewis Carroll's *Alice in Wonderland,* and are quite fantasy-oriented, having a strong dose of clever absurdism and an eccentric, very English sensibility. The vocals are multitracked in order to create a range of ultra-surreal textures and moods, giving the songs an immediate sense of the otherworldly and mysterious. All of these innovations in *Piper*'s production, mix, composition, lyrics, and vocals can be attributed to Barrett's breakthrough style.

From the first few moments of the opening track, "Astronomy Domine," we know we're in for something very different. A strange, heavily filtered, distorted voice is talking . . . . Is this a transmission from another galaxy? What the hell *is* it? In addition to the pioneer space rock style heard in this piece and others, *The Piper . . .* explores a number of other avant-garde fusions. The vocal patterns of both "Pow R. Toc H." and "Take Up Thy Stethoscope and Walk" are pure Dada. "The Gnome" is old English balladry, with the production and vocal effects making it sound different from artists like Donovan, even though the material is intrinsically similar. "Scarecrow" fuses children's/carnival music with a psychedelic abandon. "Bike" is a Summer of Love slice of psych/pop, not too different from something by the Small Faces during this period, but again the avant production puts it at another level.

The 9½-minute instrumental (rare for a pop album in 1967) "Interstellar Overdrive" was *the* psychedelic freak-out jam of the era, with its guitar-led madness and driving rhythm section. The piece explores noise and dissonance; at times it just disappears into formless voids and drifts, and it ends with a series of spatial stereo pans and studio knob twirling.

Barrett's electric guitars on *The Piper . . .* are edgy and twitchy, very different from the smooth guitars of his successor David Gilmour. Wright successfully attempts to wring every kind of dreamy, spacey, outer-limits sounds he can out of the organ, virtually founding the genre of space music keyboards.

The remastered version of *The Piper at the Gates of Dawn* is excellent, restoring vibrancy, a more precise stereo separation, and a realistic sense of volume. The expanded booklet provides lyrics (for the first time) and extra photos. The cover art is a swirling photomontage of the four band members. The album is critical to understanding the radical breaks from the popular styles that progressive music introduced.

UMMAGUMMA. Released October 1969. Capitol/EMI.

Replacing Syd Barrett with guitarist David Gilmour, Pink Floyd in 1968 had the rare opportunity to completely reinvent themselves, with each of the four members now writing material in their own unique styles, taking as a starting point the heavy psychedelia of Barrett's original direction, but adding new twists. The members have since claimed that in the period after Barrett's departure they didn't really know what they were doing, and on the evidence of their next two releases—1968's *A Saucerful of Secrets* and 1969's *More*—one is inclined to agree, as both are fairly patchy.

Ummagumma, however, is as much of a revolutionary breakthrough for the four members as writers as their first album was for the Barrett-led Floyd. A two-disc set—one live, one studio—*Ummagumma* is essential Pink Floyd, and a crucially important title in progressive music history, one that influenced a number of (particularly European) progressive artists at the time and throughout the 1970s.

The live disc was recorded at two U.K. locations in June of 1969. The quality is good, although there is a large amount of hiss. The 8½-minute "Astronomy Domine" here becomes a kind of anthem, flowing more smoothly than before, soaring as opposed to edgy. The 8½-minute "Careful with That Axe, Eugene" is the track that launched a thousand freak-outs, with its bloodcurdling scream by bassist Roger Waters. The music is a buildup and release, with a tortured guitar sound, and combined somber jazz with a heavy blues. The 9½-minute "Set the Controls for the Heart of the Sun" and the 12½-minute "A Saucerful of Secrets" are both tracks from the album *A Saucerful of Secrets.* The original studio versions are shorter and seem more tenuous and undeveloped compared with these extended concert versions. "Set the Controls . . ." is an intense form of raga rock, employing drummer Nick Mason's mallet-driven percussion and creating a large tabla-like sound, only softer. Waters's whispering vocals and Rick Wright's snake-charming organ drones enhance this mood. The track is deeply introspective, yet somehow an escapist sci-fi flight of fantasy at the same time. "A Saucerful . . ." is a radical avant-garde instrumental. An embryonic bass/keyboards/drums buildup becomes stormy and tempestuous, with guitar effects, cymbals, synth bleeps, and percussive piano. A solo drum pattern then leads into a jam with maximum space guitar and a wordless vocal by David Gilmour which seems to call out to the cosmos in both agony and wonder.

Gilmour was a remarkable replacement for Barrett, knowing exactly what colors were needed to create a space rock guitar palette. His style is much more precise than Barrett's, however. Wright provides a wealth of gentle organ textures which are a soft cushion to sink into after the guitar rave-ups.

These concert tracks are extended by several minutes from their original studio versions, which gives the pieces both an unfolding quality and also some quieter moments of poignancy. Even before *Ummagumma* was made, the band had developed a fondness for sleepy pacing, which had manifested itself in longer instrumental passages, but here this form has a more symphonic structure, with a sense of high drama and grandeur.

The studio disc is the more significant half of *Ummagumma,* and is perhaps one of the most adventurous recordings ever released by a major-label group. The band divides the album into four sections, each composed and primarily performed by the featured band member. The group's members were developing a certain conceptual framework and aesthetic that were unique for a rock band in 1969, and this example of their new approach succeeds admirably.

Wright's 13-minute "Sysyphus" is a four-part work. Part 1 is an ultra-Gothic, menacing combination of murky mellotron, organ, and drums. Part 2 is a piano excursion of dark, active chords, adding light cymbals and sound effects. This is a side of Wright's playing that was barely glimpsed in the band's previously recorded output. Part 3 is an extremely avant-garde collage piece, with minimalist keyboard and drum patterns mixed with screaming, screeching sounds; it is jarringly psychedelic and shrill. The first section of Part 4 has the kind of ambient glow later explored by so many others in the 1970s. A mellotron combines with subtle environmental sounds, creating a peaceful, tranquil mood. This is violently interrupted halfway through by noisy, shocking organ chords and collage sounds, then returns to reprise the themes of Part 1.

The Waters section contains two pieces. The 7½-minute "Grantchester Meadows" has stereo swirls of environmental sounds combined with gentle, dual acoustic guitars, creating a very attractive spacey ballad sung by Waters in a deep, double-tracked voice. The lyrics celebrate both nature and memory, and the piece ends with the sound of a man chasing a fly. The 5-minute "Several Species of Small Furry Animals Gathered Together in a Cave and Grooving with a Pict" is a completely insane, brilliant Dadaesque work of ultra-collage. There's a strong Ron Geesin influence, and the piece presages the sounds and forms explored on Geesin and Waters's 1970s *Music from the Body* album (see review).

Gilmour's 12½-minute, three-part "The Narrow Way" juxtaposes the spacey directions of very attractive multiguitar textures with loud, dissonant noises during Part 1, while Part 2 has heavy, dark raga guitar drones, along with percussion and loud electronic effects. Part 3 opens with sustained drones and ominous chords, then goes into a vocal section with the rest of the band backing.

Mason's 9-minute, three-part "The Grand Vizier's Garden Party" is directly influenced by the composer Karlheinz Stockhausen, with parts of this piece resembling his famous work *Kontakte.* Parts 1 and 3 are brief, flute-like mellotron fanfares, with drum rolls; they are very classical and sweet. Part 2, however, is a collage of percussion and tape effects with an extreme stereo separation. The piece explores various percussive juxtapositions and a textbook of timbres, spiced with a number of rumbles and scratches. Incredible stuff.

Ummagumma, then, is Pink Floyd's most determinedly progressive album, going in directions that take them far, far away from all popular forms, and it stands as their most challenging release, even today. Many German artists at the time found it a liberating new lease on musical life, with bands such as Tangerine Dream and Cluster claiming it as a direct influence. This remastered version contains two generously thick booklets, with lyrics, extra photos, and a poster.

ATOM HEART MOTHER. Released October 1970. Capitol/ EMI.

Like *Ummagumma, Atom Heart Mother* is a solid group effort, and an important title in progressive music history. This self-produced album offers a lazily paced, yet more serious form of symphonic psychedelia. Clearly this is still "out there," but its execution is, surprisingly, rather old-fashioned. The mix of the album is awkward, with extreme separation that grounds the rhythm section in one channel, rendering it somewhat ineffective. The album's various tracks were so much more immediate in a live setting (locate if possible the 1971 BBC concert of "Atom Heart Mother") that the production here is, in the final analysis, a letdown. Nonetheless, the music paints interesting and unusual pictures with its various elements, and exudes a strange, murky atmosphere throughout.

The 23½-minute title track is the recording's highlight, co-written with composer Ron Geesin. A horn section, string section, and the John Aldiss Choir interact with the group, and in many ways end up dominating, with Geesin's strong and lovely arrangements for them eclipsing those of the Floyd band. A soft keyboard rumble opens, incorporating the sound of a motorcycle, with the band, horns, and strings establishing the main theme, along with David Gilmour's simple, spacey, mellow electric guitar notes. The odd vocal patterns of the choir section, accompanied by organ and bass, are unusual in every sense, establishing a deadly earnest and eerie mood. Rick Wright has a marvelous section of "Sysyphus"-like collage, with church organ, outer-space synth bleeps, and the sound of train wrecks. In fact, Wright and drummer Nick Mason are standouts on *Atom Heart Mother.* Ostensibly a classical suite, the piece nonetheless has an opt-out feel, like a journey to some bizarre wonderland.

The second half of the disc features four shorter tracks, each (like the studio *Ummagumma* disc) devoted mainly to one of the individual members, with backing by the other three. Roger Waters's "If" is a moody vocal ballad, with acoustic guitar, bass, piano, percussion, and a light blues by guitarist Gilmour. Wright's "Summer '68" is a garish pop song with a big production. Gilmour's sleepy "Fat Old Sun" is the most typically Floyd-like. With distant-sounding cathedral bells and Gilmour's delicate, solemn vocals, the piece evokes the kind of mood one might feel lying in a wooded field at sunset, calm yet filled with wonder. The band performed an extended version of it live, which was preferable to this studio version.

The 13½-minute "Alan's Psychedelic Breakfast" is a three-part collage, blending the repetition of various phrases by a spoken male voice with the sounds of a person in a kitchen cooking something to eat. The piece begins and concludes with the sound of water dripping from a faucet. Into this, three low-key musical interludes are inserted. "Rise and Shine" is a playful, melodic, surreal jam with piano, organ, guitar, and cymbals. "Sunny Side Up" has sleepy acoustic and slide guitars. "Morning Glory" is a nice buildup spotlighting Mason's drums.

The remastered CD by Capitol is the finest-sounding version of this album available, eclipsing that of all other versions, including Mobile Fidelity's gold disc. The cover art by Hipgnosis is a collection of photos of cows on a farm, a literal interpretation of the "mother earth" concept, but yet somehow wonderfully abstract for an album cover. The remastered disc's booklet contains a generous amount of new photos and artwork. Also notable is the disc's 53-minute running length, which was quite long for a record in 1970.

Atom Heart Mother was one of the very first forays by a contemporary major label pop group into lengthy, instrumental classical/rock fusion, and was also one of the most popular. It was a number one album in the U.K. charts at the time of its release (which is almost hard to believe given today's perspective), and represents the breakthrough of early progressive music into the mainstream media consciousness.

MEDDLE. Released November 1971. Capitol/EMI.

Meddle was another important step in Pink Floyd's evolution. The elements that were to make them the prototypical prog rock band—multilayered sound textures (instrumentation augmented by sound effects), loud and heavy rock alternating with laid-back folk and blues elements via psychedelia, and lyrical symbolism—had been in place, but by the time *Meddle* was released they had achieved a fine polish.

The 6-minute "One of These Days" begins with a slow fade-in of the sound of wind. Roger Waters runs his bass guitar through an echo unit that allows him to set a pulsating tempo (sounding like two bass guitars) that's kept throughout the piece. Wright's keyboards join in, accenting Waters's changing of the bass note. Nick Mason adds to the primal nature of the beat with thumping bass drum and reverse cymbals. Once this motif has been set up, David Gilmour's deceptively simple yet searing slide guitar enters the mix. Dark and bluesy, it builds for a short while before breaking down quickly into a more rhythmically free section. There's a completely acid moment in the piece, where everything seems like it's going to fall apart. Then an evil growl is heard, emitting the only vocal in the song ("One of these days, I'm going to cut you into little pieces"), after which the listener is taken back to the original groove, this time with even more power. After more soloing by Gilmour, the piece winds down to the airy sounds again. Quintessential and uniquely Pink Floyd, the elements utilized in "One of These Days" would help to create similar moods on subsequent releases.

The blowing wind sounds create a perfect segue into "A Pillow of Winds." This acoustic guitar-laden track continues the restful mood. Enhanced by a melancholy Dobro guitar, plaintive Hammond organ, and sliding bass lines, the listener is lulled into security. The acoustic setting of this track, as well as the following track, "Fearless," follow in the style found on the band's soundtrack albums (1969's *More,* 1970's *Zabriskie Point,* and 1972's *Obscured by Clouds).* These songs continue in a well-established tradition and are templates for acoustic compositions found on all subsequent Pink Floyd releases.

"San Tropez" and "Seamus" show the humorous side of the band, although this type of humor would soon be replaced by irony. "San Tropez," with its bouncy, jazzy beat, recalls quaint, World War Two–era popular songs. "Seamus" is a short and pithy blues tune augmented by the sound of a howling dog. Retro rather than progressive, these two tracks, along with the balladry of "A Pillow of Winds" and "Fearless," would give the band a wider acceptance by an audience not typically disposed to the progressive genre.

The 23½-minute "Echoes" is the album's centerpiece. Illustrating concepts of evolution, spiritualism, and theism, the piece begins with a single note (by Wright) that resembles a drawn-out radar blip. Shimmering keyboards set up a rippling wavelike mood, followed by Gilmour's single-note, clean guitar sound. Harmony lead vocals by Wright and Gilmour enter, evoking a suboceanic, prehistoric world. This gives way to some powerful jamming by the band. A surreal section of albatross-like cries startles, then fades into a hymnlike keyboard, and the band builds up dynamically so that Gilmour can take the listener still higher with his majestic guitar heraldry. Rising tonal effects close out the piece as the music fades, enhancing the feeling that a higher level has been attained.

The sound of the remastered CD version is exceptional, far preferable to previous versions. The cover features a photo of rippling water superimposed over an extreme close-up of the (human) inner ear. A perfect image for active listening music.

PINK FLOYD AT POMPEII (video). Theatrical film released November 1972. Polygram laser disc/VHS.

The 85-minute film *Pink Floyd at Pompeii* is as fine a document of the band's progressive era as could be hoped for. It's also a crucial, up-close look at the form of progressive/space rock during the genre's formative period by one of its most effective proponents, complete with excellent stereo sound.

Filming primarily in the ruins of the ancient city of Pompeii, director Adrian Maben constructed an innovative and powerful work, utilizing locations, scenery, murals, lights, stereo panning on the soundtrack, divided screen images, and slow, precise tracking camera compositions. Shots of misty terrains, bubbling volcanoes, and images of antiquity (statues, architecture, painted faces on ruins) combine with the dreamiest of Pink Floyd's material to conjure up visions of ancient truths and the primeval forces of nature. Far more than an expensive or vapid advertisement for the band, it stands as a fine example of cinema in its own right. What the 1970 film *Woodstock* was for hippie rock, *Pink Floyd at Pompeii* was for progressive rock.

The band's performance is energetic throughout, especially drummer Nick Mason, who comes across as the most visually dynamic of the four,

Pink Floyd (1968–1980 lineup, from *Live at Pompeii* film). From left to right, David Gilmour, Nick Mason, Rick Wright, Roger Waters.

and as a result is given more camera time by Maben. The film also includes interesting scenes in the recording studio, as the group assembles their masterpiece *Dark Side of the Moon.* The interview sections are disappointing and inconsequential, however, save for a brief, spirited exchange between Roger Waters and the unseen interviewer over the issue of commercial music versus "art" music.

"Echoes Part 1" begins the film, and it (as well as Part 2) is superior to the studio version. Shot in the bright, outdoor sunlight of an empty, ancient stadium, the presentation is the very definition of arena-sized space rock. The same is true of "A Saucerful of Secrets," which looks a lot bigger (and sounds a lot louder) than you might think it would in this setting. David Gilmour's guitar effects, Rick Wright's avant-garde piano technique, Mason's massive-sounding drums, and Waters's over the top gong bashes create a music that is a grandiose hymn to the cosmos. A milestone.

"Careful with That Axe, Eugene" makes full use of the location, intercutting the band with close-ups of faces painted on the ruins and ominous volcanoes, emphasizing even further the drama inherent in the song. "Set the Controls for the Heart of the Sun" is similar, with the band surrounded by a large number of various lights, appropriate for the warm glow this raga exudes. The effect is *extremely* spacey, making it by far the finest version of the song.

"One of These Days" concentrates solely on Mason's drum performance, which is incredible. The brief "Mademoiselle Nobs" is an oddity, being an instrumental variation on *Meddle*'s "Seamus," complete with whining dog. "Echoes Part 2" closes the film, ending on a sleepy, subtle note.

DARK SIDE OF THE MOON. Released March 1973. Capitol/ EMI.

The conceptual apex of progressive rock, *Dark Side of the Moon* is notable for an almost perfect synergy between refined experimentalism, musical technique, and lyrical subject matter. To build an album solely around one concept (which was a relatively new approach) cohesively and succinctly was a great achievement. The album was the band's last amicable group effort (almost democratically so in that each member writes), and marks an end of sorts to a certain era of Pink Floyd, before radio in the 1970s turned them into a dinosaur, taking the band in different directions. While bassist Roger Waters writes all the lyrics here, he's still only one-fourth of the equation, not dominating with intensely personal lyrics as he would on later Pink Floyd releases. In addition to their primary instruments, Gilmour, Waters, and Wright each play VCS3 synthesizer, and both Mason and Waters are credited with tape effects. The group cohesion, coupled with the fact that the album had been fleshed out during live performances throughout 1972 prior to its being recorded, makes the disc an astounding success.

The album begins with "Speak to Me" and "Breathe." "Speak to Me" is credited to Nick Mason, whose drumming is tasteful and unobtrusive throughout the album. The sound of a heartbeat fades in, followed by a short audio montage featuring sound effects and voices that resurface throughout the album. These chaotic elements build to a wailing voice that abruptly stops. Next comes the "Breathe" section, which is a variation on Waters's songs on *Music from the Body* (see review). "On the Run" follows, a collage of tape and sound effects, voices, and synth. This track sets the intended mood better than a traditional vocal song or purely musical instrumental, creating an environment and a development of the broad story being told in the album. Like a film, "On the Run" is a scene that carries and develops the plot. The transition to "Time" is a seamless cross-fade, like the previous two tracks. Ticking clocks and heartbeat-like percussion lead to a gaggle of clock alarms going off, setting the tempo and the tone for the piece, the lyrics of which lament the inevitable passage of time. Gilmour and Wright split the vocals here; Gilmour's are an angry resignation, Wright's a melancholy reflection. Wright's "The Great Gig in the Sky" is one of the most transcendent and cathartic moments in progressive music, and the definite highlight of the album. Wright's acoustic piano and big Hammond organ create a powerful background for the emotionally wrenching, gospel-tinged wordless vocals by guest Clare Torry, eventually joined by the rest of the band. Torry's vocal seems to encompass all human suffering, and the ability to overcome that suffering. Her vocals are delicate and rich in nuance, and even after countless listenings have power to move the listener.

"Money" is one of the most popular and accessible prog rock singles ever. The rhythmic collage construction of coins jingling, cash registers ringing, and receipts ripping sets the groove, with Roger Waters's bass pattern picking up and augmenting the funkiness of the tune. The round tone of the bass guitar accents the bouncy, yet quirky beat. Wright's electric piano dueling with Gilmour's guitar also works to great effect here. Guest saxophonist Dick Parry then solos with a distinctive, bluesy feel that shifts into a straight-ahead rock beat for a tasty guitar solo by Gilmour. This segues into the mini-epic "Us and Them," with themes of alienation, violence, and war. The verse section is laid-back and plaintive, building to a loud chorus. This is another song with a distinctive Wright influence in that it has a church organ sound. Parry returns for another saxophone solo, and a small contingent of backup singers adds to the choir sound of the chorus. The entertaining and quirky instrumental "Any Colour You Like" has a trippy synthesizer solo and a funky guitar solo, with a plentiful amount of stereo effects. "Brain Damage" and "Eclipse," written by Waters, illustrate vividly the album's all-encompassing conceptual theme, serving as both climax and epilogue for the work, with "Eclipse" fading out with mumbling voices and a heartbeat.

The production is crisp, seamless, and multilayered. It is an amazing achievement that utilizes musicianship, technology, and artistry with a sense of purpose.

WISH YOU WERE HERE. Released September 1975. Columbia Mastersound gold disc.

While their previous albums were organic in feel and celestial in their goals, in *Wish You Were Here* Pink Floyd creates a modern, futuristic sound, more heavily reliant upon synth structures while still being built around extended songs. Like *Dark Side of the Moon, Wish You Were Here* interweaves each of its tracks, creating a sort of audiocinema that achieves its visual qualities through the combined elements of music, voice, sound effects, and montage. The lyrics, all by Roger Waters, condemn the impersonality of modern life on all levels. Steeped in irony, with a sharp, anti-establishment tongue, the words reach out to many separate audiences, from adolescent rebels to counterculture subversives. Waters often uses the music business as a metaphorical framework for his statements about modern life, which also works as a way to express his ambiguous feelings about the band's newfound success.

The two-part "Shine on You Crazy Diamond" is the conceptual centerpiece of the album. Rick Wright's shimmering synths are prominently featured, with a sound similar to that of Klaus Schulze. The 13½-minute "Shine On . . . Part 1" begins the disc. Glittering beds of organ are coupled with string synths, slowly shifting under epic rock performances by David Gilmour, Nick Mason, and Waters. Gilmour's wailing, bluesy guitar is counterpointed by Wright's lead synth. Waters's poetic focus here is a loving tribute to the sad plight of their earlier leader, Syd Barrett, but the words have a universal appeal because they could represent anyone's feelings about a close friend, and are not necessarily specific to Barrett. "Welcome to the Machine" is next. Pulsating, spitting synths evoke steam turbines cranking out products—be they consumable goods or people themselves. Cold-blooded, machine-like vocals enhance this mood.

The chunky, guitar-driven "Have a Cigar" is an obvious criticism of the music business. The track features smart-assed lead vocals by guest Roy Harper, plus funky electric piano and saxophone. The segue into the following track, "Wish You Were Here," is pure audio theater. Gilmour's guitar solo on "Have a Cigar" becomes filtered, as if coming out of a radio speaker. A radio dial is turned, stopping on various stations, then finally remaining on a station that is playing the intro to "Wish You Were Here." Gilmour's acoustic guitar solo joins in, and the song builds into a slow, folksy ballad. Waters's lyrics here are among his best, being a strong caution to radicals not to sell out and settle for material comfort. The 12½-minute "Shine on You Crazy Diamond Part 2" is like a slowed-down "One of These Days," fading in with windlike effects and a searing slide guitar solo. The last verse acts as a final chapter to the story, and the song fades out with a funky jam and sirenlike lead synth.

The production values of *Wish You Were Here* remain at the high standards that were established on previous Pink Floyd releases, and are part of the reason that these works have held up to continued scrutiny and repeated listenings throughout the years. The only way to experience the full sonic glory of the recording, however, is via the Mastersound gold disc from Columbia, which is light years ahead of the regular CD version, which is not even a remaster. The cover art of the album has varied, depending on the format and country of release. The images convey themes of alienation and dislocation, reinforcing the lyrical concerns as well as reflecting the tension between the group's members during the recording of the album.

ANIMALS. Released January 1977. EMI import.

Animals is a classic of conceptual vocal prog rock that ranks among Pink Floyd's best work. Here composer/lyricist/bassist Roger Waters, who by this point was dominating the direction of the band, created an allegorical political work, a concept album seething with anger at the status quo. Now words more than instrumental freak-outs are used to convey a subversive, countercultural message, and Waters's lyrics focus on the personal as well as the political, with as much raw contempt for wrong-headed individuals as for systems.

Animals (which follows the structure of George Orwell's *Animal Farm)* is unrelentingly anticapitalist in its view of personal greed as the source of both a violent, competitive social Darwinian reality and a numbing, hollow, dehumanizing conformity. The music is far darker than the opt-out suites of "Atom Heart Mother," "Echoes," or "Shine on You Crazy Diamond." On a personal level Waters was known as being the most intense and outspoken member of Pink Floyd, and it could be said that these characteristics are what drive the fierce and vehement lyrics (amongst Waters's best) and the flat-out rock and roll style of the album. Waters also uses his bass guitar throughout as a running motif, an undercurrent of menace that's a reminder of the tension brewing inside this music. The album seems to go by very quickly and smoothly, no doubt aided by the fact that the group had been performing the material in concert for some time prior to recording it, so it was well fleshed out by the time they brought it to the studio.

The brief (at 1½ minutes each) "Pigs on the Wing (Part One)" and "Pigs on the Wing (Part Two)" bookend the album, and are much gentler and more hopeful than the rest of the tracks. Both are folksy ballads with dual acoustic guitars, sung by Waters, here sounding more low-key and even vulnerable. The theme of both is universal equality; the mood of the first is shattered by the events depicted in the songs that follow, but Part 2 reaffirms the moral lesson.

The 17-minute "Dogs" begins with attractively mixed but rather unsettling acoustic guitars aggressively playing tense chords. This is joined by Rick Wright's ominous synth lines, more minimal here and far less dreamy than before. David Gilmour, Wright, and (mainly) Waters take turns singing the vocals, relating a disturbing allegorical look at modern life, joined by Nick Mason's drums, playing in a more symphonic style. Gilmour unleashes very angry electric guitar solos, with a blues/hard rock influence, in the usual tortured, grandiose Pink Floyd style. Midway through, the piece settles into a nice section of textures by Wright, with Mason's thumping drumbeats and the incorporation of dog barks restating the group's penchant for collage elements. The final vocal section (sung by Waters) asks a series of painful and specific questions directly of the audience, making more explicit the link between the listener's own experience and the conditions laid out earlier in the piece. Images of isolation and the crushing of the spirit are put in question form, implicating corrosive and selfish individuals in our families, homes, workplaces, and political institutions.

The 11½-minute "Pigs (Three Different Ones)" directs its attacks at three specific types of people who all in their own way enforce conformity—bosses (in the workplace), nosy old ladies (who interfere in relationships), and censors (who operate in many areas)—until there is no freedom left. The piece begins with pig noises, which continue throughout. A simple keyboard pattern by Wright is joined by Waters's bass, and is sliced up by Gilmour's impudent guitar slashes, going into a basic riffing groove and Mason's cowbell-led beat. The vocal sections are delivered by Waters with utter contempt. Underlining this mood is Gilmour's savage guitar soloing, which concludes the piece.

The 10-minute "Sheep" is a tale of sudden revolution taking place in the midst of a complacent majority who aren't even aware of what's going on. Waters seems to be repeating the view that while those who have power will be replaced, the nature of power remains unchanged, so perhaps an entirely new model is called for. The piece begins with the sound of sheep, soft electric piano notes, and bass, adding more aggressive guitars and drums. There's a strange center section of a "Lord's Prayer"–like recitation (here turned into an angry hymn against oppressors) with churchlike organ and Waters's subtle, ever-present bass lines.

The remastered version (not available in the United States in any form) sounds incredible, restoring power and volume to this raging diatribe. As usual, this is one of Pink Floyd's big productions, polished to a diamond brilliance. The legendary cover art of a huge, inflatable pig flying over industrial factories underscores the album's political message.

This era of Pink Floyd was ridiculed at the time by the emerging punk movement, which was a self-defeating move as *Animals* is one of the most overtly anti-establishment musical albums ever made, and perhaps the most popular. Politically, if not musically, Pink Floyd and punk should have been allies, not foes.

PEKKA POHJOLA

KEESOJEN LEHTO. Released April 1977. Love import.

This first album by Finnish composer/bassist/keyboardist Pekka Pohjola was originally released by Virgin Records as *The Mathematician's Air*

Pekka Pohjola. From left to right, Markku Kanerva, Seppo Kantonen, Anssi Nykänen, Pekka Pohjola. (Photo by Samoil/Arffman.)

Display. Virgin was not interested in reissuing it, so *Keesojen Lehto* is the Finnish version, with the title credits printed in the Finnish language. Recorded in 1976, this is Pohjola's best album and the most popular; his compositions here have a more natural flow than those on his other releases, which gives them wider appeal. Pohjola and his band (guitarist George Wadenius, drummer Vesa Aaltonen, keyboardist Wiodek Gulgowski) are here joined by Mike Oldfield on guitars, harpsichord, mandolin, and whistle, Sally Oldfield on vocals, and Gong's Pierre Moerlen on drums and percussion. While *Keesojen Lehto* is a great album in its own right, these three guests add an undeniable appeal.

"The Sighted Light" is the 5-minute opener, featuring Pohjola and his band playing a unique, very European-flavored instrumental rock, similar to a less hard-edged Schicke, Führs and Fröhling. Driven primarily by keyboards, warm-sounding guitar solos, and spacey whooshes of synth, this is music that's easy to like. The 4½-minute "Hands Calming the Water" features Pohjola with the two Oldfields. A baroque piece of music combining harpsichord with Sally Oldfield's lilting, lovely wordless vocals and Mike Oldfield's typically celestial guitars (à la *Ommadawn),* this is an irresistible combination. The 7-minute title track is another fascinating lineup of Pohjola, Mike Oldfield, and Moerlen. A light jam of melodic, symphonic rock, this is also very European, with a sense of storytelling grandeur; though it is led by Pohjola's bass and keyboards, Oldfield's mild guitar soloing does make an appearance. The mix here is much too thin, however, especially for Moerlen's drums.

Next is "The Consequences of Indecisions," the album's two-part high point. Part 1 is the 4½-minute, classically structured piece "Time Heals All Wounds." The first 3½ minutes feature Pohjola on piano and bass, playing distinctive, poignantly expressive notes. This is one of Pohjola's most dramatic moments both as a composer and an instrumentalist. For the concluding minute Pohjola is joined by Oldfield's guitar and Moerlen's cymbals, presaging the piece's symphonic conclusion. This goes into the exciting 11-minute edgy fusion of "Comfort with a Stranger," another ingenuous piece combining both Pohjola's band and Oldfield and Moerlen. Beginning with a piano intro, drums, and guitars, the track goes into a very tight marching groove, with Pohjola's bass guitar as the lead instrument playing a series of clearly defined notes which are counterpointed by jazzy synth bleeps and angular guitar licks. The 2-minute "False Start" concludes the album with the two Oldfields and Pohjola. A wildly mad, racing folk tune with whistles, this is dominated by the Oldfields and closes the album on a nimble, active vibe.

The sound quality is very good throughout. Later Pohjola releases are in a more conventional fusion style, and as a result lack the charm of *Keesojen Lehto.* The best of his other albums is 1986's *Flight of the Angel,* although all have their fine moments.

POPOL VUH

AFFENSTUNDE. Released April 1971. Spalax import.

Formed in 1969, Popol Vuh is a very important group in the history of progressive music. Taking their name from a sacred book of the Mayan Indians, their music has always striven to be enigmatic, mixing a huge sense of brooding mystery with a more private, intimate feeling.

Affenstunde (translated from the German, this means "The Time of the Monkey King") is their first album, and it's a solid group effort, with Florian Fricke on the Moog synth, Holger Trulzsch on percussion, and Frank Fiedler on synth and mix-down; Bettina Fricke co-produced and photographed the cover art. Combining primitive synths with percussion in an all-instrumental setting, the music evokes primeval, primordial forces, making *Affenstunde* an early classic of electronic and space music. During this period Popol Vuh were as popular as Tangerine Dream, with both groups exploring similar themes. The synth/percussion palette of the later 1990s ritual music genre owes a great deal to recordings like *Affenstunde.*

The 3½-minute "Ich Mache Einen Spiegel" opens the disc, with environmental sounds and a splash into water leading into spooky and murky synth tones, like entering some kind of underwater cavern. Loud stereo pans of lead synth lines drift from channel to channel while a hovering, misty electronics haunts the background. The effect isn't subtle enough by today's standards, unfortunately, due to the volume of the phased synth lines. The 5-minute "Dream Part 4" is more of the same, adding the light percussion of hand drums. This crashes head on into the 4½-minute "Dream Part 5." A jarringly loud exotic percussion segment by Trulzsch, the feel is very tribal, and fascinating when placed in the context of all the rest. It also has a more spatial stereo mix. This disappears into the 7½-minute "Dream Part 49," one of the album's highlights. A thoroughly abstract electronic mist, the piece is elusive, spacey, and dreamy, adding the faintest of percussion taps. The music is very conducive to mental picture painting.

The standout 18½-minute title track opens with the sound of a crackling fire, and exudes a wealth of ambience. It then goes into a strange percussion pattern with a moderately loud beat, along with synth, achieving an organic feel. The piece is Gothic to the core, sounding like the soundtrack to an early 1970s vampire film. This is the era when synths were generally used to create outer-space moods, but here Fricke and Fiedler take them into the realm of inner space.

The sound is good throughout, but is flattened somewhat by Spalax's ADD mix. The disc is best experienced on headphones, where its spatial effects are more discernible. The low frequencies cause too much rumble when played at a loud volume. The cover and booklet photography by Bettina Fricke are appropriately Gothic and mysterious.

IN DEN GARTEN PHARAOS. Released June 1972. Spalax import. **IN THE GARDENS OF PHARAO/AGUIRRE.** Releaseed 1983. Celestial Harmonies.

In the Gardens of Pharao, Popol Vuh's second release, is their most well known, and is an extremely important album in progressive music. The recording has aged better than their debut album, constructing a timeless realm with its soothing, opened-out sound. This is another solid group effort by the same lineup as on *Affenstunde* (Florian Fricke, Holger Trulzsch, Frank Fiedler, and Bettina Fricke), using Moog synth, conga, Turkish percussion, and cymbals, and adding electric piano and organ.

The 17½-minute title track is irresistible to anyone's ears, combining attractive stereo sounds of water with mysterious Moog synth and congas. The sound here is sharper than on *Affenstunde,* replacing the dark mood of that disc with a much friendlier one. The piece unfolds so naturally that it becomes a journey of sorts, like following the path of a river on a cloudy day. The music is genuinely ethereal, introspective, and relaxing. This track is very similar to the music on two other 1972 releases, Deuter's *Aum* and Wendy Carlos's Sonic Seasonings, each being a delicate soundscape where the acoustics of the natural world merges with that of musical performance, producing a spiritual, inner harmony.

The unique 20-minute "Vuh" aims for the transformative from the very start. Recorded in Bavaria's Baumberg Cathedral, the piece has an intensity of devotional fervor. Sustained, ceremonial organ notes and loud, heavily echoed Turkish cymbals are joined by choral voices from the Moog synth, becoming a gigantic whirlwind of evocative sound. Despite the volume the music is quite trance-inducing.

The Spalax import digipack retains the original cover art, a radiating orange background with a bird, egg, and flower in its center, haloed by a yellow glow—thoroughly appropriate for this album's harmonious, peaceful vibe. The digipack also retains Bettina Fricke's photos of the band.

The Celestial Harmonies version doesn't include any of the artwork, but it does have a cleaner, more vibrant mix, making it the preferable version. Also included on this release are two other important Popol Vuh tracks, bringing the total running time up to 65 minutes.

The 6-minute "Aguirre," also recorded in 1972, is very much in the vein of "Vuh," with its haunting, hovering synth lines and chorus of voices, like a near-religious chant. The piece was used as part of the soundtrack for the 1972 Werner Herzog film *Aguirre, The Wrath of God.* A separate 1976 album (on Spalax) entitled *Aguirre* contains alternate versions of this track. The three-part 20½-minute "Spirit of Peace" is a quiet, personal solo piano work by Florian Fricke, digitally recorded for this Celestial Harmonies disc in 1980. It's one of the finest (and spaciest) solo piano pieces in progressive music, capturing something undefinable that allows the consciousness to drift in uncharted regions. The piece seems to be searching for something. It's introspective, meditative, reflective, and calming, stripping Fricke's music down to its barest elements, with a lot of space between the notes, giving the listener time to reflect on what has already passed, to savor the resonances.

HOSIANNA MANTRA. Released April 1973. Spalax import. **DIE NACHT DER SEELE** (subtitled **TANTRIC SONGS).** Released November 1979. Spalax import. **TANTRIC SONGS/HOSIANNA MANTRA.** Released 1981. Celestial Harmonies.

With 1973's *Hosianna Mantra,* Florian Fricke assumed the center role in Popol Vuh, and has remained so ever since. An entirely different lineup is convened here, with Fricke on piano, Conny Veidt (of the German prog rock band Amon Duul II) on electric guitar and 12-string guitar, Djong Yun on vocals, Robert Eliscu (of the German prog/space music band Between) on oboe, Klaus Wiese on tambaura, and Fritz Sonnleitner on violin. Fricke felt it was important to switch to mainly acoustic instruments to achieve the ethereal Popol Vuh sound, no longer relying on the Moog synth. He was dismayed that groups performing space music (like Pink Floyd or Tangerine Dream) couldn't even play music until truckloads of equipment had been set up. Given that *Hosianna Mantra* succeeds so well in producing an acoustic space music, this unconventional (and uncommercial) move on Fricke's part gives him a lot of credibility as a composer and anchors Popol Vuh's progressive forms in an earthier, chamber music format.

Fricke also dispenses with rhythm on this album, concentrating on the cascades of sparkling notes from his piano and Veidt's fluid electric guitar. Yun's far-away, space-child vocals have a minimum of words and add a welcome feminine texture. The oboe and violin provide a baroque flavor, and the tamboura gives a hint of the East. The sound is all gorgeous melody—a quiet, delicate, and fragile form of music that creates a floating feeling and radiates an inner-directed beauty. The album's eight spacious tracks, ranging in length from 45 seconds to 10 minutes, all follow this pattern. The album is not too light; this is timeless music of great depth and reverence.

The Spalax reissue of *Hosianna Mantra* contains the original artwork and a number of band photos.

1979's *Die Nacht Der Seele* ("The Night of the Spirit") is all acoustic, but much, much darker in feel. An exploration of Tantric themes, the 11 tracks (ranging between 1-and-one-half to 5 minutes) feature Fricke on piano and vocals, Yun on vocals, Daniel Fichelscher on guitars and percussion, Renate Knaup (of Amon Duul II) on vocals, Susan Goetting on oboe, and Al Gromer an sitar.

Titles such as "In the Realm of Shadow," "Wanderer Through the Night," "Angel of the Air," and "Mantra of the Touching of the Heart" each explore moody, inner caverns by combining deep vocal groans with ominous ritualistic percussion. Depending on the listener's personal predelictions, this music can be conducive to meditation and spiritual exploration music or to unsettling horror-show spookiness. Other tracks explore combinations of acoustic guitar, sitar, cymbals, piano, and tabla, similar to the style of mid-1970s Popol Vuh albums like *Coeur de Verre* (see review below), only sparser and less densely layered.

Die Nacht Der Seele ignores popular forms, going in a completely opposite direction to that of the music industry at that time.

The 76½-minute *Tantric Songs/Hosianna Mantra* disc from Celestial Harmonies includes *Hosianna Mantra* in its entirety, the more purely Tantric and bizarre half of *Die Nacht der Seele*'s material, and most of another 1979 Popol Vuh release entitled *Bruder des Schattens—Sohne des Lichts* ("Brothers of Darkness—Sons of Light"). The two tracks from that album included here are the 6-minute "Listen He Who Ventures" and the 16½-minute "Brothers of Darkness—Sons of Light." Both feature Fricke, Fichelscher, Gromer, Goetting, Eliscu, and Ted de Jang on tamboura, and are in the same haunting style as the material selected from *Die Nacht der Seele,* but are longer, more unfolding works. Coupling the *Die Nacht . . .* and *Bruder . . .* material is an excellent idea (Fricke's), and is probably the preferable way to hear these pieces. The sound of this disc is cleaner and sharper than the Spalax discs, although the tracks not included here from *Die Nacht . . .* make that album worth owning as well. The rest of the tracks from *Bruder* that are not included here are unremarkable.

COEUR DE VERRE ("Heart of Glass"). Released January 1977. Spalax import. **SING, FOR SONG DRIVES AWAY THE WOLVES.** Released October 1993. Milan/RCA.

Coeur de Verre is one of Popol Vuh's best albums, representative of the prolific mid-1970s period of the band and in keeping with the sounds established on previous releases like 1974's *Einsjager and Siebenjager* and 1976's *Aguirre* and *Letzte Tage—Letzte Nachte.* This era of Popol Vuh is all- instrumental, full-blown raga rock. Pianist Florian Fricke is still the leader and composer, and despite the critical addition of Al Gromer's sitar, these releases are dominated by Daniel Fichelscher, who plays a multitude of guitars, drums, and percussion, and also composes. The seven tracks (ranging from 3½ to 8 minutes) have a somewhat unconventional and elusive production which gives the album its otherworldly, meditational sound, something like Third Ear Band meets Ravi Shankar via Algarnas Tradgard and Ragnarok. The album is ostensibly a soundtrack to the 1976 Werner Herzog film *Heart of Glass.* Returning from the first Popol Vuh lineup is engineer Frank Fiedler, plus another long-time Popol Vuh member, vocalist Renate Knaup. Knaup didn't perform here, but co-produced the album.

Highlights are "Keepers of the Threshold," an intoxicating, heavy, whirling-dervish form of swirling trance rock; "Der Ruf," a more straightforward rock track with a soaring electric guitar solo; and "Sing, For Song Drives Away the Wolves," featuring Fichelscher's sweet multi–electric guitar textures.

The disc *Sing, For song Drives Away the Wolves* is yet another in a series of confusing compilations for the American market assembled by Fricke. The album is a remix of eight tracks from *Coeur de Verre* and *Einsjager and Siebenjager,* adding a few new instruments. This worthwhile venture is not significantly different from the original mixes, except for the improved sound quality, which is a big plus.

Included is *Einsjager*'s 19½-minute "You Shouldn't Awake Your Beloved Before It Pleases Her." This track, one of Popol Vuh's best, features only Fichelscher, Fricke, and vocalist Djong Yun. Their interaction here is splendid. Fichelscher's contribution is particularly striking, as he constructs intricately detailed, attractively mixed multiguitar and percussion parts that keep moving the piece to new, higher plateaus. It's a joyful and inspiring song.

MICHAEL PRIME

AQUIFERS. Released 1993. RRR.

Fun and cryptic at the same time, *Aquifers* is an excellent example of collage music. The approach sound constructionist Michael Prime takes is aggressive, creating works that are not meant to be conventionally ambient, new age, or space music. If anything the aesthetic is rather industrial. It is in some ways similar to the music of the Hafler Trio or Lustmord, but this comparison can't be taken too far, as Prime's audio manipulations are all taken from natural sound sources, using no musical instruments. The intent is to present a series of impressions of our natural audio environment, with the various sounds actively juxtaposed and somewhat randomly mixed together, which is quite different from the seamless, purist concentration on single acoustic sounds by artists like Annea Lockwood. The overall effect can be somewhat chaotic (hence the use of the label "industrial"), but Prime's sound mixes are playful, his compositions putting the listener directly "inside" the sounds of the particular audio sources.

The 7-minute "Racked" was partly recorded at the British Music Information Center in November of 1991. The sound source is a metal storage rack, and Prime wrenches from it a number of doomy, echoed thumps and vibrations. Screeching scratches combine with more spacey drifts. This piece could easily be mistaken as musique concrète or industrial electronics, but it is just a manipulation of various metallic sounds.

The 13½-minute "Aquatic Synapse" was recorded live at the Rising Sun Institute in Reading, England, in April of 1992. Here Prime combines field recordings of street sounds and traffic sounds with a live link to the outside toilet of the venue. Playful stereo effects of loud running water merge with a heavy blanket of crowd sounds. Later a series of footsteps, car engines, crowds, voices, thumps, rumbles, and loud clangs coalesces into a wild and jarring aural landscape. The effect of the performance is to sensitize listeners to the diversity of the urban sound environment.

The 15½-minute "Rotifers" is an exploration of Prime's homemade instrument, the water machine. (For a description of the water machine, see the review of *Cellular Radar,* below.) A thoroughly abstract piece, it begins with cricketlike water sounds and percussive thumps, creating a relaxing mood. Then the pace and volume increase, making a sound like a combination of loud rain and engines churning away.

The highlight of the disc is the 19½-minute "Timeslips," consisting of various environmental sounds recorded by Prime in the U.K. The piece has a truly amazing stereo mix, ideal for headphones, taking the listener on a mini-tour of our modern world. Beginning with attractive water splashes, the track visits the sounds of barking dogs, distant foghorns, traffic, street vendors, voices, thunder, crowd applause, and seagulls, to name a few. Less chaotic than the previous three pieces, "Timeslips" is an irresistible, brilliantly edited compilation of so many of the sounds that we hear—but routinely ignore—in our daily lives, awakening both our awareness and appreciation of them.

The sound quality of this 57-minute disc is sharp and clear. The cover and booklet photography, by Prime and A. Warley, ranks among the finest of any cover art discussed in this volume. The striking blue cover is an oozing organic structure. Elsewhere a series of outdoor photos depicts odd, spindly, unsettling images.

CELLULAR RADAR. Released 1996. Mycophile import.

Cellular Radar is an incredible tour of sound itself. Radical, challenging, and noisy, the self-released 73-minute album is a completely dislocating experience.

Michael Prime, an ecologist who became interested in creating collage soundscapes from natural sources, invented what he calls a "bio-activity translator," which translates the voltage potential of living creatures into sound, and a "water machine," a system of pumps and valves in a chamber, which is amplified and processed. By combining these strange instruments with field recordings, tape manipulations, and electronic processing, Prime creates sound environments similar to those created by artists like O + A and Syllyk, with a stereo soundstage that is as spatial as can be imagined given modern recording techniques.

The 23-minute "Finis Terra" opens with the environmental sounds of an outdoor setting. Engine hums, human breaths, wind sounds, grinding sounds, and thunder each make appearances, getting very loud and becoming hurricanes of white noise. This dissolves into human whispers and stereo pans of noise, switching to crowd sounds, like those at a restaurant, before segueing into water splashes and finally falling back to silence. The piece fades back in with a totally cacophonous sine wave–like buzz, morphing into the up-close sound of a blaring airplane engine.

The 21½-minute "Climb Down the Ladder of Carbon" has radical stereo pans of water sounds, with percussive shakes like objects rattling. More spatial effects of voices and machinelike rumbles continue until they become disorienting, eventually evolving into a swirling tunnel of sound. The piece falls into silence, which is jarringly interrupted by more of the same kind of sounds, then switches to the sound of someone shoveling, followed by more silence and ending with voices, machines, and a helicopter.

The 13½-minute "Instar" features loud, assembly-line metallic grinding, like a warehouse of forklifts and welders, adding insectlike buzzing and more harsh, machinelike sounds. This goes into the sounds of animal grunts, an automobile engine, and loud churning noises, and these sounds then disappear as if going down some kind of metallic chute.

The 14-minute "Nocturnal Resort" takes the chirping of crickets and speeds them up and then slows them down, creating a shrill singing in the foreground and low grumbles in the background, later adding train engine rev-ups.

The excellent cover and booklet photos by Emma O'bong recall the best of Monique Froese's photography for Tangerine Dream's sleeves. Her mysterious landscapes of an organic world that is constantly in flux are perfect for the sounds of *Cellular Radar.*

PROPELLER ISLAND

HERMENEUTIC MUSIC. Released 1988. Erdenklang import.

Propeller Island is mainly the brainchild of Lars Stroschen, with the assistance of Torsten Hentschel. An all-instrumental work of primarily postmodern electronics, with touches of grand piano and gongs thrown in, this music is high-concept expressionism inspired by various themes from philosophy, science, and literature.

The disc begins with the 41-second "Hanne's Jingle," wherein an electronic goblin bids listeners to throw their telephones out the window. "The Jungle of Sizzling Stones" is a trance-inducing, atmospheric piece that immediately puts the listener at ease. Breaking the mood is the humorous 1-minute "Mystic Cocktail," with creaking doors and a mocking Germanic voice. The calming mood is resumed though, with the 5½-minute new age piano composition "Thundernight." "A Short Trip to Some Eastern Country, But Coming Back Soon" is an 8-minute organic development, with indigenous instruments entering the mix to illustrate the setting. This piece has moments reminiscent of Wendy Carlos's abstract sonic impressions, especially her forays into synthesized gamelan music. The 6-minute "Hope" is more celestial in direction, with shimmering sounds that fly through the stereo mix over slowly shifting audio landscapes, continuing the German space music tradition of Tangerine Dream.

The 25½-minute, 10-part, expansive epic of "The 5th Generation—Trial and Error of a System" was inspired by the development of the largest computer system ever built. The sonic exploration of this technology's possible effect on humankind results in an extensive range of musical styles and experimentation. Stroschen and Hentschel have created some challenging all-electronic compositions through techniques using computers and modern synthesizers. There are frequent moments here that recall the works of electronic classical composers like Morton Subotnick and Tod Machover. The subject serves as a base from which to create and explore the musical questions posed without forcing the listener to overintellectualize.

Although the sound production techniques have a 1980s glossy sheen, the disc does sound spacious beyond the boundaries of most electronic releases, and is great for headphone listening.

RAGNAROK

RAGNAROK. Released February 1976. Silence import.

This charming, all-instrumental debut by the six-piece Swedish group Ragnarok is representative of the European flavor brought to progressive music in the mid-1970s, when countries such as France, Spain, Italy, and Sweden began developing fertile progressive music scenes, joining what up until then had been an American, British, and German-dominated field. The six members of Ragnarok play electric and acoustic guitars, bass guitar, flutes, and drums, with half of the group members playing more than just one instrument and all of the members contributing to the writing. The album's ten tracks, ranging in length from half a minute to 8 minutes, are generally in a mellow mood, delicate and flavorful, augmented by occasional keyboards and saxophone. The vibrant production, with its wide stereo separation, low-key mix, and close miking, gives the album an intimate and warm feeling, like the band is playing in one's living room.

The opening piece, "Goodbye Copenhagen," features gorgeous multiple acoustic guitars, reminiscent of the sound of Fuhrs and Frohling's 1978 *Ammerland.* "Walks" and "Factory Funk" are spacey, melodic rock, with laid-back electric guitars, thick bass guitar, and drums recalling *Meddle*-era Pink Floyd, but without the vocals. "Fresh Baked Bread" and "Calm—Breaking Up" are irresistible, ultra-melodic folksy tunes led by lively acoustic guitars and flutes. The 8-minute "Foam of the Days" opens with very subtle multi–electric guitar textures, later joined by flute, bass, piano, and drums, with a jazz-flavored electric guitar solo. "Tatanga Mani" is a solo acoustic guitar pastoral, similar to the work of Anthony Phillips, later adding flute and bass. The brief "Fiottot" resembles a Bo Hansson *Attic Thoughts*–era polka. "Pools of Water" even brings the *Looking Thru*–era Passport to mind, with its electric piano, saxophone, bass, and drums.

RAPOON

DARKER BY LIGHT. Released June 1996. Soleilmoon.

Robin Storey, a.k.a. Rapoon, is a talented texturalist in the currently flooded market of ambient and industrial electronics. Storey is a member of the group Zoviet France, but his Rapoon projects are really nothing like the work of that band. *Darker by Light* is the third (and the most progressive) in a series of Rapoon projects; the first two discs were released a month before this one.

The 72-minute disc features nine long tracks, with most of the pieces in the 8½- to 10-minute range. Sounding deceptively simple at first, these works are highly seductive, with rhythmic pulses that lull your senses into a trance state. The structures are elusive, but very effective. The listener is slowly pulled into a hypnotic and dreamy void, making *Darker by Light* a classic of recently produced space music. But this is a space music influenced by the electronics of industrial artists (such as Lustmord), as opposed to the cosmic music of the melodic 1970s or the new age excursions of the 1980s. Rapoon mixes strong opt-out flavor and typical industrial darkness with a more playful bounce, as on "Lies and Propaganda," which uses rhythm as a seductive tool.

Most of *Darker by Light,* though, explores regions of deep space, without overt rhythmic elements. "Flight" and "Winter's Edge" are fleeting electronic presences, barely even there. "Prayer" and "Tidal Transmissions" both gurgle a relatively organic ooze, while "Sunday's Shadows" includes light environmental sounds (or are they?). The rest of this enigmatic disc follows similar paths, with dreamworld titles like "Night That Thunders" and "From Sleep Awake."

The sound is fantastic, with a smooth and subtle mix. The cover art is appropriately abstract, but the booklet provides no information whatsoever, typical of releases from this genre. *Darker by Light* stands out as a masterful, genuine, ultra-modern form of space music.

RENAISSANCE

ASHES ARE BURNING. Released August 1973. One Way.

A very important and much-loved British group of the 1970s, Renaissance was as fundamental to the U.K. progressive rock scene of that era as groups like Pink Floyd, Yes, King Crimson, and Genesis, and had a long, uninterrupted run of excellent releases. They never achieved the status of those other groups, however, because in the late 1970s and early 1980s they made an unwise move toward more popular forms, demonstrating just how disastrous commercial directions can be for a progressive band. Renaissance is *the* classical rock group, exploring lighter acoustic textures (as opposed to darker, hard rock ones) and stirring symphonic structures, with brilliant arrangements, poetic lyrics, and a penchant for high drama.

Their first album, 1972's *Prologue,* introduced the lineup of Annie Haslam (vocals), Jon Camp (bass guitar, bass pedals, backing vocals), Mike Tout (piano, organ, harpsichord), and Terry Sullivan (drums), and the songwriting team of guitarist Michael Dunford and poet/lyricist Betty Thatcher, who were not part of the performing group. Pieces like "Sounds of the Sea," "Rajah Khan," and the title track on *Prologue* feature what was to become the classical/rock fusion format they later followed, but this debut album is generally spotty, and the rest of the material is less successful.

On 1973's *Ashes Are Burning,* the conceptual direction of the band is solidly in place, with Dunford assuming the role of acoustic guitarist for the band in the studio, and soon joining as a full-time member. Dunford and Tout's concentration on acoustic instruments, along with Haslam's multioctave vocal range, allowed the group to operate within the bounds of classical formalism, which is more difficult in many respects than to explore entirely new experimental forms. The success of this era of Renaissance is due mainly to the conceptual framework provided to the band by Dunford and Thatcher. It was common in the U.K. rock scene at the time to have a poet provide lyrics for the songs of rock bands (as was the case with King Crimson and Procol Harum), and Thatcher provided Renaissance with romantic and dramatic themes (often with a very hippie-world flavor, like Sally Oldfield's lyrics or Kate Bush). Thatcher's lyrics, specifically written for Haslam's beautiful and emotional voice, create a gentle, feminine aura. (Haslam's voice fronts the sound of the band, but she herself never wrote for the band.) By combining the old (classical structures, poetry) with the new (modern studio techniques, rock, folk, and pop influences) Renaissance carved out a unique niche in progressive music.

The 10-minute opener "Can You Understand?" introduces this style. The piece is led by Tout's piano, adding Dunford's gorgeous multi–acoustic

Renaissance (1972–1979 lineup). From left to right, Jon Camp, John Tout, Annie Haslam, Mickey Dunford, Terence Sullivan.

guitars, Camp's up-front bass guitar, and Sullivan's restrained, nonflashy drumming style. (Sullivan's drumming represented a brave departure from 1970s rock's fascination with huge, flamboyant drums.) The sound is rather baroque, adding bells and a string section. Haslam's enthralling vocals and the crisp, full production values put the icing on the cake.

The 4-minute "Let It Grow" and the 5-minute "On the Frontier" are more popular ballad forms, and not really progressive. The group made a lot of these songs, but they're particularly fresh here, resembling tracks like "I Know What I Like" or "More Fool Me" on Genesis's *Selling England by the Pound.*

The 3½-minute "Carpet of the Sun" is perhaps their signature song, and one of their best. Bouncy multi–acoustic guitars, sunny piano notes, an irresistible string arrangement, Haslam's tour-de-force vocal, and the all-is-harmony vibe of the lyrics encapsulate, in this one short and lovely tune, all the Renaissance elements. The 3-minute "At the Harbour" is formal storytelling at its finest, with just a low-key acoustic guitar part accompanying Haslam's delicate vocal. The 11-minute title track is among the group's most well known, and was long a concert favorite. An epic poem about the passing of time, there's a soaring moment of pure drama when Haslam's wordless vocal chant joins with Camp's thick bass notes, producing an operatic, attention-getting sound. The track ends with an electric guitar solo (the only one on the album), provided by Andy Powell of Wishbone Ash.

TURN OF THE CARDS. Released August 1974. Repertoire import.

Turn of the Cards is a quality release on which the group's best elements are emphasized. The same instrumentation and lineup of *Ashes Are Burning* are featured here, with vocalist Annie Haslam, keyboardist John Tout, bassist Jon Camp, drummer Terry Sullivan, and composer/guitarist Michael Dunford (who by this point was playing in concert with the band as well as in the studio). Five of this album's six songs are written by Dunford and Betty Thatcher, with arrangements by the band, who also co-produce.

The two 9-minute epics, "Running Hard" and "Mother Russia," among the band's most popular songs, are epic-scale, driving pieces of classical rock, each with a center section of jaw-dropping vocal antics by Haslam. The concert versions of these songs on the later *Live At Carnegie Hall* disc are perhaps preferable, as the vocals are too up-front in the mix on the studio recordings, but this was an understandable move as Haslam is such an amazing front person.

The 3-minute "I Think of You" and the 6½-minute "Black Flame" are also album highlights, with an absolutely gorgeous mix of multiple acoustic guitars, lush vocals, and dramatic lyrical themes, adding bass, piano, and drums. Also notable is the 3-minute "Cold Is Being," a song about loneliness with only church organ and a stately vocal by Haslam. This baroque track is positively old-fashioned, yet so effectively delivered that the extreme formalism of it doesn't detract. On the other hand, the 9½-minute "Things I Don't Understand," written by Thatcher and Jim McCarty, which has the atypical Renaissance textures but is also definitely a pop form, is not one of their better tracks, and does come across as dated.

The performances are polished throughout, helped by the excellent sound and ideal production values. This disc also stands as the best Renaissance studio CD transfer, along with the next two releases; the Repertoire reissues all have flawlessly clean and sharp sound.

SCHEHERAZADE AND OTHER STORIES. Released August 1975. Repertoire import.

Renaissance's fourth album, *Scheherazade and Other Stories,* is a high point for the band, and for the genres of vocal and conceptual progressive rock. This is grand storytelling music in the traditional classical form, combining the orchestral scope of an album like King Crimson's *Lizard* (though this is warm, rather than sinister and surreal like that album) with the smooth professionalism of other U.K. prog rock groups of the mid-1970s like Camel, Curved Air, and Genesis. *Scheherazade* is co-produced (along with the band) by David Hitchcock, who at the time also produced albums by most of the aforementioned bands. The album also benefits from the accompaniment of a full orchestra, arranged by Tony Cox.

The 11-minute "A Trip to the Fair" has a playful stereo mix, with laughing voices, conjuring images of a carnival. A piano-led intro builds up with bass guitar and percussion, with Annie Haslam's vocal and the orchestra leading. The 3-minute "The Vultures Fly High" is one of the band's liveliest numbers, led by Michael Dunford's acoustic guitar. The moving 7-minute "Ocean Gypsy" is a definite highlight. Emotional and poetic prog balladry, it is among lyricist Betty Thatcher's best writing for the band—a tragic tale about the gift of love a woman brings, but then loses. An evocative synth background (new for the group) and piano solo by Tout, Terry Sullivan's delicate drumming, and especially Haslam's spellbinding vocal make this piece one of Renaissance's finest songs (although the version on *Live at Carnegie Hall* is preferable) .

The 24½-minute "Song of Scheherazade," in nine subtitled sections, is the band's conceptual interpretation of Rimsky-Korsakov's *Scheherazade.* Written by Dunford and Thatcher with Tout and bassist Jon Camp, the piece is a strong group effort and their most explicitly classical composition. Although the piece is somewhat old-fashioned, it's so attractively paced and engaging that such a criticism seems superfluous. Horn fanfares and a vocal choir open, and the nimble interaction of the band with the orchestra makes for compelling listening. Pianist Tout has the finest moments overall. The lead vocals are by both Haslam and Camp, which is not a good idea (a male vocal seems out of place). The highlight is the beautiful section entitled "The Young Prince and the Young Princess As Told by Scheherazade." Accompanied only by Dunford's delicate acoustic guitar (later slowly joined by the orchestra), Haslam's vocal is very moving, with sensitive, touching lyrics (once again about the gift of love) by Thatcher.

The high-quality production is lush and gorgeous, with an attention to detail that makes *Scheherazade and Other Stories* ideal for headphone listening. The clean CD transfer is far better than any vinyl release of this album, giving it an entirely new lease on life, its fragile orchestral passages no longer sabotaged by surface noise.

LIVE AT CARNEGIE HALL. Released June 1976. Repertoire import.

Live at Carnegie Hall is Renaissance's most representative album, and one of the finest concert releases of the progressive rock genre. The recording and production values are ideal; it's hard to imagine this sounding any better than it does. Recorded with the New York Philharmonic Orchestra before appreciative audiences at three shows in June of 1975, this is epic-scale music—lengthy songs performed on a huge stage, all delivered with grandeur and authority. The group's best and most classically oriented material (of the period 1972–1975) is emphasized, demonstrating that the band knew what the strongest pieces in their repertoire were. The quality of the writing stands out, along with Annie Haslam's fantastic singing.

The lively 7½-minute "Prologue," from their debut album of the same name, is one of the most entertaining examples of Renaissance's classical/rock fusion. A rollicking piano, thick bass, and drums are led throughout by Haslam's airy vocals. This disc's version of "Ocean Gypsy" is the best one, with more up-front drumming by Terry Sullivan. You can tell Haslam has the audience completely under her spell. This song, and the rest of the material from the *Scheherazade . . .* album that appears here, had not yet been released at the time of this performance, yet the audience responds enthusiastically, despite the fact that it's rather a lot to take in—especially the lengthy "Song of Scheherazade."

"Can You Understand" is lightened a tiny bit due to the setting and the live orchestra, although the same factors strengthen the versions of "Carpet of the Sun," "Running Hard," and "Mother Russia."

The 28½-minute "Song of Scheherazade" remains very close to the studio version, and all goes smoothly during the performance of this ambitious piece. The highlight, as on the studio version, is "The Young Prince and the Young Princess As Told by Scheherazade," which receives loud applause from the audience. The 23-minute "Ashes Are Burning" is here as well, extended for a band jam and topped off by a lengthy bass guitar solo by Jon Camp, who engages the crowd in an arena rock fashion with an aggressive lead instrument bass reminiscent of Yes's Chris Squire.

Throughout *Live at Carnegie Hall* pianist John Tout gets a lot of soloing space, and Sullivan's drumming is clearer in the mix than before. These two members are perhaps the most responsible for the band's classical sound. The overall sound quality is a vast improvement over the vinyl version, making the album quite an audiophile's treat.

The CD reproduces all the album's original gatefold color photos (some by Haslam) of the performances and the backstage antics, albeit in a compressed format. These photos would have made a better cover than the drab drawing that was used for the front.

NOVELLA. Released March 1977. Sire/Warner Bros. import.

Novella is one of Renaissance's best studio albums, and was a strong group effort. Still all acoustic and consisting of mainly soft passages, this is an incredibly baroque album for 1977, totally outside the hard rock trends of the era. Recorded in late 1976, the arrangements and the production are all by the band, with the emergence of bassist Jon Camp as a composer, co-writing with guitarist Michael Dunford.

The 13½-minute "Can You Hear Me?" by Camp, Dunford, and Betty Thatcher is a song about modern-day loneliness, ideal for Annie Haslam's authoritative vocal style. A surprise buildup opening sees the group charging into one of their more raucous arrangements, with the rhythm section more muscular in the mix than usual. The piece has a stirring main theme, joined by a string orchestra and Dunford's characteristic multiple acoustic guitars.

A major highlight is the 7-minute "The Sisters," by Dunford, Thatcher, and keyboardist John Tout. A song about the holiness of charity and the search for meaning in the midst of suffering, this is one of the group's finest achievements. An orchestral piece with chimes, piano, horn fanfares, and a reverent vocal choir (by the band), later joined by bass and drums, it has a near-religious piety that is miles away from commercial styles. Haslam's vocals here are also among her finest, evoking a precarious balance between doubt and confidence. The piece ends with stereo pans of voices and intense, Spanish-flavored guitar by Dunford. It is an extraordinarily delicate track.

The 5½-minute "Midas Man" by Dunford and Thatcher is a folksy, Incredible String Band–like ballad about greed and how it steals time and happiness from us all. Dunford weaves a thick tapestry of several acoustic guitars, with Camp contributing a unique bass pedal solo.

The 4-minute "The Captive Heart" by Camp and Dunford is the least of the album's tracks; it comes across as a syrupy pop ballad, and is not progressive. However, the 9½-minute "Touching Once (Is So Hard to Keep)," also by Camp and Dunford, is a real surprise highlight, with excellent poetic lyrics (written without Thatcher) about romantic longing. A playful piano intro with a Tin Pan Alley shuffle (very odd for Renaissance) leads into the atypical group arrangements with bass, drums, acoustic guitar, and strings. There's also a pastoral center section with a variety of keyboard textures by Tout, and the piece concludes in a sweeping finale of high drama.

The sound is very good, with an incredibly fragile mix, but it's not as crisp as the Renaissance CD transfers from the Repertoire label. The cover painting by Pamela Brown of a woman reading from a storybook to children, creating images of peace and imagination, is the perfect imagery for *Novella.*

A SONG FOR ALL SEASONS. Released May 1978. Sire/Warner Bros. import.

A Song for All Seasons makes radical changes in Renaissance's instrumentation and sound. With production and engineering by David Hentschel, the focus was on bringing the band into line with more popular (commercial) forms. Hentschel gives Renaissance a huge 1970s dinosaur production, and electrifies the band. Keyboardist John Tout switches to synths, Michael Dunford and Jon Camp both play electric guitar (while still retaining their acoustic guitars), and Terry Sullivan's drumming style becomes more rock-oriented. This bigger, electric sound is a mixed bag for the band. The approach works well for them on their more sophisticated compositions (such as the title track), but it just makes their shorter songs (which were far less progressive already), sound rather ordinary. While the overall failure of *A Song for All Seasons* is due to the weakness of the material, this change in instrumentation also completely changed the overall concept of the band itself. The album is basically half progressive, half pure pop—a bad move for the group, stripping away most of the elements that made them successful.

The first three tracks are written by Camp and Dunford. The 4-minute "Opening Out" is a highlight, and should have been developed further. The atypical Renaissance textures here, and brief additions of things like bass pedals and horns, make it similar to something from the *Novella* album, with its poetic earnestness.

The 9½-minute "Day of the Dreamer" is another highlight, giving Renaissance a more rock-oriented feel. A muscular symphonic bass, drums, and guitar combine with the Royal Philharmonic Orchestra, and the interaction between Camp's aggressive bass guitar and the orchestra is the kind of classical/rock fusion path the rest of the album should have followed. The track also has some nifty drum grooves, which are new for drummer Terry Sullivan. Unfortunately there's a dreadfully poppy chorus in the song, which should have been toned down; however, the rest is excellent. The middle section of the track featuring Haslam's vocal is the high point—one of those emotional moments that she's so good at. The lyrics here are about remaining true to one's dreams, and empathizing with those brave enough to stick to their chosen paths.

The 3-minute "Closer Than Yesterday" is a ballad not unlike "Let It Grow" from *Ashes Are Burning,* though far less successful. This is definitely in mainstream territory, not even remotely progressive. The next three songs, "Kindness (At the End)," "Back Home Once Again," and "She Is Love," are wretched low points for the band, and should not have been included. "Back Home . . ." is a plodding theme for a TV series, and the other two are syrupy schmaltz embarrassments sung by Camp. Try and pretend these three songs do not exist. The 4-minute "Northern Lights" is also chorus-heavy pop, and was actually a hit single at the time. However, it does serve as a good showcase for each of the member's styles.

The 11-minute title track is the album's centerpiece, written by the entire band (sans Haslam), along with Betty Thatcher. The first 4 minutes are an aggressive instrumental symphonic jam, and the group's most thunderous foray into rock forms. This majestic song about the changing of the seasons features a loud, rousing arrangement with the Royal Philharmonic, and the combination of the orchestra with the newly electrified Renaissance creates a formidable sound.

The band continued to shed its unique characteristics on the overtly commercial, Hentschel-produced *Azure d'Or* album in 1979. While a few of its tunes stand out, it's mostly drivel. Continuing their artistic suicide, the band proceeded to fire Sullivan and Tout, rejected their major label offers, and then switched entirely to a quirky, rhythmic new wave pop rock sound for two reprehensible albums in the 1980s. In the 1990s both Haslam and Dunford front two different Renaissance groups, regrettably continuing their middle-of-the-road tendencies, coming across like late 1980s Sally Oldfield retro schlock. Despite these mistakes, the progressive era of Renaissance in the 1970s remains a superior musical achievement.

KING BISCUIT FLOWER HOUR PART 1.

Released February 1997. King Biscuit.

Recorded live for radio at London's Royal Albert Hall on October 14, 1977 with the Royal Philharmonic Orchestra, this somewhat unexpected two-volume CD set (separately released) is quite a treat. *Part 1* is the first 63½ minutes of the show, which is then continued on *Part 2.* Because the show was never aired in its entirety, these albums are of particular interest.

The band's performance is flawless, captured on a detailed 24-track master, bringing out all the nuances in their playing. Although this master was remixed in 1997 by composer/guitarist Michael Dunford (with Gary Lyons), it isn't as immaculate as it should be, and includes an unfortunate series of stage buzzes obtrusively intruding on what were ideal recording conditions.

Nevertheless, musically everything goes right. Although this set is virtually the same material as on *Live at Carnegie Hall,* it is about equal, if not preferable to, that recording. Making *King Biscuit* of further interest is that it is from the *Novella* era, which was a strong period for the band. *Part 1* features a 14-minute version of *Novella*'s "Can You Hear Me?" which lacks the teeth of the studio cut, being lightened considerably by the orchestra. Overall the execution on this track is somewhat awkward.

Another curiosity on *Part 1* is an 8-minute orchestral arrangement of "Prologue" performed without Renaissance by the Royal Philharmonic. This track is not marred by the stage buzzing, and its crisp dynamics are impressive. The piece demonstrates the quality of Dunford's writing, being as exciting in a strict classical setting as it is when done by the band.

The rest of *Part 1* has excellent versions of "Can You Understand," "Carpet of the Sun," and "Song of Scheherazade." The cover photo is fantastic: Annie Haslam singing her heart out.

KING BISCUIT FLOWER HOUR PART 2.
Released March 1997. King Biscuit.

Picking up where *Part 1* left off, *Part 2* continues the 1977 Royal Albert Hall show, and also includes one song recorded live in 1979 in addition to an 8½-minute unreleased studio track from 1984 entitled "You," the disc is just a few seconds shy of 80 minutes.

Part 2's Royal Albert Hall material has interesting versions of two tracks from the *Novella* album. The 4½-minute "Midas Man" is effective enough, with the awkward sound of the maximum amplification of Michael Dunford's acoustic guitar and some additional lilting vocal hi-jinx by Annie Haslam. The lively 10-minute "Touching Once (Is So Hard to Keep)" is excellent here, moving at a more natural and exuberant pace, throwing in some horn solos.

Also making *Part 2* different from *Live at Carnegie Hall* (in ways that *Part 1* is not) is the 28-minute version of "Ashes Are Burning." Even more extended than it was at the Carnegie show, this has an enjoyable band jam totally different from the 1975 performance of it. A rhythm section part leads into a brief solo by drummer Terry Sullivan (a real surprise—not a drummer you'd associate with solos!). This switches to the full band, with each of the members making clever additions, along with mournful operatic cries from Haslam. After this comes Camp's bass solo, and this too is different from the one on the *Carnegie* disc. The versions of "Running Hard" and "Mother Russia" have a more orchestral presence than on the *Carnegie Hall* show, though not for the better. And like *Part 1, Part 2* contains the unfortunate stage buzzes.

From a July 1979 show in Asbury Park, New Jersey, comes a fascinating 8-minute live version of "A Song for All Seasons," here mistakenly credited as "Prologue." Presented in the band's later rock arrangement phase, with synths, bass, and drums comprising the bulk of the sound, and without a backing orchestra, it's unusual to hear this song in such a thin arrangement. In many ways this approach robs the piece of its grandeur, causing Haslam to strain her voice to cover the empty spaces in the arrangement. This is a song that really requires an orchestra.

"You" is certainly a departure from their classical fusion sound, dominated again by synths, drums, and bass and resembling something like Kate Bush circa 1980. The lyrics are trite, though, which is a disappointment.

Fans of Renaissance's concert recordings would do well to seek out the rare *Live in London 1975* disc released in 1992, dating from around January of that year, which has the band's BBC sessions for the John Peel show, as the sound quality is outstanding. The material is more or less the same as that covered on *Live at Carnegie Hall.*

RETURN TO FOREVER

HYMN OF THE SEVENTH GALAXY. Released October 1973. Polygram.

Return to Forever were an important and well-liked American jazz/rock fusion band of the mid-1970s. *Hymn of the Seventh Galaxy* is their best album, and their most rock-oriented. Like most fusion pioneers, the four members all came to this project as noted jazz virtuosos (the two previous Return to Forever albums were done in traditional jazz styles). Leader and producer Chick Corea plays electric and acoustic piano, organ, harpsichord, and gongs, joined by Stanley Clarke (bass guitar), Bill Connors (electric and acoustic guitars), and Lenny White (drums and percussion). While comparisons with other fusion groups of this era like Mahavishnu Orchestra and Passport are obvious, the all-instrumental music of Return to Forever also fits comfortably alongside such 1970s British prog bands as ELP, Egg, Genesis, and Khan, and was a clear influence on later U.K. fusion groups like Brand X and Bruford.

The band seems very eager to impress with their newfound rock dynamics, particularly Connors, with his wailing electric guitar solos, and White, whose impressively large drum sound has more in common with John Bonham or Bill Bruford than with anyone from the traditional jazz spheres. The song titles, with their outer-space themes, convey an interesting choice of imagery, underlining the album's larger-than-life fusion sound. Corea, the acknowledged leader, wrote five of the album's six tracks.

The 3½-minute title piece introduces the band's style. Loud stereo panned keyboards take us into a rhythmic rock workout, with the clear spotlight on White and Connors. The 8½-minute "After the Cosmic Rain," by Clarke, is an exciting highlight. A fantastic jam, it's fast-paced, but with a very tight structure. Savage, penetrating electric guitar notes trade off with bass and keyboard solos while White just bashes the hell out of all of it. The 9-minute "Captain Senor Mouse" begins in a jazzier vein, led by Corea's breezy organ solos, adding bell tree by Clarke. Later it grows into a more rock-oriented sound, with solos by Connors and White tearing it all up with his drumming.

The 8½-minute "Theme to the Mothership" is a loud, guitar-led fusion with teeth. It then switches to a huge rhythm section groove led by Corea's Canterbury-sounding organ. The 5½-minute "Space Circus" begins with the warm, glowing tones of Corea's electric and acoustic pianos, then the rest of the band kicks in, led by White's drums, for a funky rock workout with bass riffs from Clarke. The 6½-minute "The Game Maker" is a lot like Passport (à la *Cross Collateral),* opening with acoustic guitar and electric piano, then shuffling into a raucous electric guitar–led jam.

The sound quality is good, if a bit dated, but that's actually an asset here. Connors left the band after this album, to be replaced by Al DiMeola. Connors's approach was more flat-out rock, which brought out the rock tendencies in White's drumming, whereas DiMeola's playing owes more to jazz styles. The cover art is a painting of a bird flying high in the clouds, an appropriate image for this free-feeling fusion music.

The cover clearly states the album to be by Return to Forever, yet the CD spine and disc now credit the album solely to Corea, which is somewhat strange.

WHERE HAVE I KNOWN YOU BEFORE.
Released October 1974. Polydor.

Where Have I Known You Before presents some very spacey themes, showing the band's willingness to take the fusion genre out to its furthest limits. With original guitarist Bill Connors replaced by the young Al DiMeola, the group settled into its most famous lineup, with all of the members, not just leader Chick Corea, composing.

The 8-minute opening track, "Vulcan Worlds" (by bassist Stanley Clarke), sets the mood with its outer space/*Star Trek* title and percolating funk rhythms that highlight all the players' soloing abilities. The 7½-minute "The Shadow of Lo" (by drummer Lenny White) begins with an ethereal electric piano and a medium tempo. DiMeola is given the opportunity to emote with the very lyrical melody before Corea takes over the lead line with a sweet-sounding synth. At around the halfway point the band kicks into double time, as Clarke's bass sets up a cyclical groove locked in with White's tight drumming. DiMeola has a short moment of burning, and he and Corea lock into sync playing a melody with angular lines, reminiscent of Egg, yet not as classically structured. The crunchy funk that ensues is downright liberating.

The thumping 3-minute "Beyond the Seventh Galaxy" (by Corea) has very tight unison lines by Clarke, Corea, and DiMeola, with White thrashing away in the background. The big sound has its counterpoint in appropriately expansive moments where the individuals separate and just create moments of atmosphere. The 3½-minute "Earth Jam" (by the band) is a heavy rock jam that sounds almost improvisational, as if it popped out during rehearsals. The motif is repetitive, with lots of guitar wailing and DiMeola showing off his ax abilities. Thankfully the band knows when not to drag an idea out, and the piece ends just at the right time.

Three short (1 to 2 minutes) Corea tracks, which are basically tone poems—"Where Have I Loved You Before," "Where Have I Danced with You Before," and the title track—are interspersed throughout the rest of the material on the album, presumably to give it a loose sense of unity. Performed as solo acoustic piano pieces, they're really nothing special.

The final track is the 14½-minute epic "Song to the Pharaoh Kings." Beginning in a hymnlike fashion, with organ backing a solo synth, it then moves into a full band section with an Egyptian snakecharmer double-reed sound for the melody. A tribal percussion jam follows, and Clarke takes a tasty solo. The use of repetitive motifs makes a hypnotic basis for further spacey jamming. Building to a climax with solos from DiMeola, the band quickly breaks it down into an early 1970s Miles Davis–like electric piano solo. Very impressive.

The sound is good throughout, but the production is marred by a thin mix exposed by the CD transfer. The cover photo features an amber, glowing sunlike object hovering over what looks like rippling water, suggesting a cosmic mood. The band's next release, 1975's *No Mystery,* continues the sound of this album, but combines it with a rather large amount of funk.

ROMANTIC WARRIOR. Released June 1976. Columbia.

Romantic Warrior demonstrates an evolution and a breakthrough in Return To Forever's sound. The album is structured around the unlikely concept of Arthurian and medieval legends. Chick Corea's synth arrangements are here more baroque, with more counterpoint and varied textures. The band had not totally dismissed the funk elements that are present on albums like *No Mystery,* but has rather elevated and refined them, adding a more symphonic sound without sacrificing the rock qualities.

The opening track, "Medieval Overture," jumps right into the high-energy fusion the band is known for, though guitarist Al DiMeola's influence is stronger here than on previous albums. This concise 5-minute piece features many short sections, with textures which range from funky to ethereal and which create cinematic moods. "Sorceress" (by drummer Lenny White) has the rhythm section laying down a smooth funk groove, giving plenty of room to Corea and DiMeola to solo. The lyrical 11-minute title track (by Corea) puts the band in an all-acoustic setting, with grand piano, acoustic guitar, and a bowed acoustic bass.

The precise 5-minute "Majestic Dance" (by DiMeola) has burning, fuzz-tone electric guitars over Corea's clavinet. The 5½-minute "The Magician" (by Stanley Clarke) is an appropriate follow-up, with the piece transforming itself into a celestial soup, and then into a quaint, carnival-like melody. The 11½-minute concluding track "Duel of the Jester and the Tyrant" (by Corea), takes advantage of both the individual and collective talents within the band. With grand orchestral movements and strong playing throughout, there are contrasting elements of humor (the jester) and power (the tyrant).

The sound quality is badly flattened by the murky remastering job, dampening the highs somewhat. But if the volume is turned up loud, it sounds all right. The cover art depicts a knight in battle armor astride an armored horse with a beautiful green pastoral setting in the background.

After this album White and DiMeola left the band, and Corea and Clarke carried on, releasing one more studio album and a sprawling, lengthy triple live album. This later incarnation adds Gayle Moran (Mrs. Corea) on vocals, with a sound similar to that of her contributions to the mid-1970s Mahavishnu Orchestra. The lyrics are trite, creating a sort of fusion-lite that seems to be aiming for commercial (radio) success. This is interspersed with a return to the band's original explorations of traditional jazz. While the playing and production values improved, this version of Return To Forever is a far cry from the genuine fusion breakthroughs of the earlier albums.

ROBERT RICH/BRIAN LUSTMORD

STALKER. Released 1995. Hearts of Space.

Inspired by the moods and concept of Andrei Tarkovsky's 1979 film *Stalker,* electronic composers Robert Rich and Brian Lustmord (a.k.a. Brian Williams) create dark ambient soundscapes, setting the stage for a deep exploration of the psyche. All seven tracks of this 68½-minute work flow into one another, like a trip through an uncharted, haunted territory. Rich and Lustmord's titles—for example, "Undulating Terrain," "Delusion Fields," "Omnipresent Boundary," and "Elemental Trigger"—create a psychological metaphor, suggesting landscapes both of the earth and of the mind. Slowly shifting, dark, and dissonant sounds set up an eerie mood which is sustained throughout. Found sounds and gloomy low-frequency rumbles (more characteristic of Lustmord's hand than Rich's) sans melody create atmospheric and introspective sound paintings for the listener to explore. Sounds creep in and out like the stalker of the title, like different aspects of the self.

The sound is rather transparent, intensifying the intended moods. The cover art, depicting grey scenes of shorelines, suggests that one is at the edges of what is known, about to cross over into the unknown. *Stalker* is a standout release of ambient/industrial/electronic space music.

VICKI RICHARDS

PARTING THE WATERS. Released December 1989. Third Stream (via Projekt).

Parting the Waters is worthy of the highest possible recommendation. It's an album that possesses genuine beauty, poignancy, and depth of feeling. It has all the sensitive moments of Third Ear Band, Popol Vuh, and the acoustic side of Mahavishnu Orchestra, and also recalls a number of ECM label artists (such as Steve Tibbetts), while maintaining a totally fresh American sensibility. Composer/instrumentalist/producer Vicki Richards emerged at the height of the new age music media blitz of the late 1980s, but was not signed by a major label, which is tragic, as she is clearly a leader in the field.

Recorded in Miami, Florida, this 55-minute disc is described as a voyage into the third ear, the third world, the stream of consciousness, and the energy of the female warrior within. The musical influences are many and diverse, ranging from European classical to North Indian classical. Richards plays violin, electric violin, kalimba, bass kalimba, and koto. By using sound-processing devices, she achieves a purity of tone with her violins, giving her an overwhelmingly attractive and warm sound. Richards is joined on this album by her husband Tim Richards (tabla drums, log drum, frame drum, bells), Amit Chatterjee (electric and acoustic guitars, koto with sticks), and former Weather Report member Robert Thomas Jr. (congas, bongos, tambourine, Peruvian flute, ocarina, percussion). All four musicians contributed to the writing. The production is a work of subtlety, with a quiet mix and a wide stereo separation, giving the music a very intimate feel.

Vicki Richards. (Photo by Pli Brylok.)

The 6-minute title track introduces the album's reassuring and friendly style. A soothing, soft mix of Peruvian flute, ocarina, acoustic guitar, and kalimba sets the stage for Richards's gorgeous violin soloing, which then builds with drums. The 4½-minute "Rising Sun" is instantly seductive, with koto and acoustic guitar establishing a positive vibe, like the beckoning of a sunny day. The 5½-minute "Endless Radiance" is a major highlight; its extremely affecting and poignant violin notes really send shivers down the spine. This exquisite track is basically a raga with tabla, acoustic guitar, and cymbals. The 6-minute "Logarhythm" and the 5½-minute "Windhorse" each establish a violin loop pattern, adding percussion over which Richards solos on violin. The sounds created are sensual and sweet, never aggressive, and have not a hint of flashiness.

The 4-minute "Dance for Jaco" irresistably combines Richards's violin with a lively koto, frame drum, bongos, and percussion. The 5½-minute "Prayer of the Heart" features entrancing, soft patterns of electric guitar, electric violin, and tabla. The 4½-minute "Skater's Dream" is Richards' solo violin, with a definite classical influence (perhaps Vivaldi). However, her processing effects give the instrument a different resonance, making it more dreamy. The 5-minute "Kalahari" has cascading, floating patterns of melodic violin and acoustic guitar. The concluding 7½-minute "Monsoon" is another highlight. A solo piece by Richards, it features soft violin drones and light sprinkles of bass kalimba and bells. The effect is haunting, creating a deeply introspective mood in the listener.

Parting the Waters is an authentic example of raga/classical fusion and space music, with so many extraordinary qualities that it achieves a rare universal appeal. Richards's hard-to-find 1987 cassette *Quiet Touch* is equally stunning.

TERRY RILEY

A RAINBOW IN CURVED AIR. Released October 1969. CBS.

A Rainbow in Curved Air is an important, very early American progressive album, as influential in its era as Pink Floyd and King Crimson were in the U.K. Going beyond the scope of the minimalist label that's synonymous with composer Terry Riley, *A Rainbow in Curved Air* (his second album) is not as intellectually rigid as the rest of his works, and exudes an inspired sense of otherworldly, opt-out playfulness.

The extremely wide separation of the ear-candy stereo mix is the key, with spatially separated delay imaging provided by Glen Kolotkin. The sound of the CD is excellent, having been digitally remixed.

The 18½-minute title track is jubilant and uninhibited music, with Riley playing electric organ, electric harpsichord, dumbec, and tambourine. Opening with lush organ pulses, the piece unleashes rapid-fire cascades of electric harpsichord, with bursts of notes similar to the work of Philip Glass. At around 6½-minutes the piece combines loud, up-close tambourine shakes with organ pulses, creating an ethereal, chilly feeling. Riley's loud organ soloing is like some kind of mad church music. Later, adding dumbec percussion, the piece assumes a lively raga bounce until the final fade-out. It's an attractive and enjoyable piece of music.

The 21½-minute "Poppy Nogood and the Phantom Band" is a more somber side of Riley, similar to the paths followed on later releases. Playing electric organ and soprano saxophone, the piece consists of slowly building and dense organ patterns, with subtle drones from the saxophone, creating a sleepy, hypnotic trance music. Interrupting the mood are psychedelic jolts of tense notes, which then become a part of the piece's minimalist structure, repeating like the rest of the sounds until fully absorbed, and until the track ends suddenly.

Riley's liner notes basically define the philosophical optimism of the late 1960s, and the music conveys this optimism. Here music is both art and change agent, transforming awareness and mirroring social change. The impact of *A Rainbow in Curved Air* was immediate, and had an obvious influence on the direction of minimalist composers like Philip Glass and that of the album's producer, David Behrman. The early career of Klaus Schulze was a more psychedelicized extension of the sound Riley introduced here. The prog rock band Curved Air takes its name directly from this album, and the French group Lard Free and guitarist David Torn have both cited this as a major influence.

TERJE RYPDAL

TERJE RYPDAL. Released December 1971. ECM import.

The debut release by Norwegian composer/instrumentalist Terje Rypdal (pronounced Tear-yay Rip-doll) is an early jazz/rock/chamber music fusion classic that's bursting with ideas. The sound of this album combines a distinct John McLaughlin/*Devotion*–Miles Davis/*At the Fillmore–Jack Johnson* flavor with the more mellow instrumental moments of rock bands such as Pink Floyd (à la *Atom Heart Mother)* or Country Joe and the Fish (à la instrumental songs such as "Eastern Jam" and "Colors For Susan" from the 1967 album *I Feel Like I'm Fixin' to Die).* Rypdal concentrates on the most otherworldly aspects of these influences, deemphasizing the funk, blues, and pop elements and creating a serious, impressionistic space music with its feet sometimes in jazz, sometimes in rock, but mostly following its own unique sound, which the artist has continued to modify and refine on a number of extraordinary albums up to the present day.

Underlining the atmospheric goals of this album is the exaggerated stereo separation of the period, which gives the recording a strange, unconventional mix that sounds fantastic and has now been remastered for CD with a more realistic volume. Here Rypdal (playing electric guitar and flute) is joined by longtime collaborator Jon Christensen (drums), Jan Garbarek (saxes, clarinet, flute), Inger Lyse Rypdal (wordless vocals), and Eckehard Fintl (oboe, English horn), plus four others on electric piano and electric bass. The choice of instruments, such as flute, oboe, and English horn, introduces a classical/chamber music element to the album, making Rypdal's style of fusion more eclectic and adventurous than that found anywhere else at the time (for example, in the fusion of bands such as Mahavishnu Orchestra in the United States or in bands such as Soft Machine in the U.K.).

The sparse 12-minute "Keep It Like That—Tight" establishes an embryonic and slowly built-up groove, with thick bass guitar riffs and bass drum thumps added to by Rypdal's spacey guitar. Garbarek injects a loud sax solo, followed by a snarling guitar solo. This piece is more streetwise than usual for Rypdal. The 7-minute "Rainbow" explores the more classical and experimental sides of Rypdal's composition, and virtually defines the ECM label sound. An ethereal and moody chamber music sound poem, the piece features the spacey combination of guitar, flute, double bass, English horn, clarinet, bells, cymbals, and shakers.

The 15½-minute "Electric Fantasy" is a completely authentic fusion of space, psychedelic, jazz, and classical musics, with a strange, enigmatic sound mix that strives for the otherworldly right from the start. An electric piano provides a soft underbelly for textures of flute, bass, and drums, with an excellent wordless vocal by Inger Lyse Rypdal adding even more mystery. The piece concludes with a heavy jam (at a psychedelic pace) led by intense soloing from Rypdal on guitar. The 3-minute "Lontano II" is even more spacey, with dark, menacing rumbles and stray notes. The piece is formless and (quietly) chaotic, resembling early Tangerine Dream or Ash Ra Tempel. The 4½-minute "Tough Enough" is a simple guitar riff with echo, going into a piercing rock solo à la Jimi Hendrix that's somewhat atypical of Rypdal's usual sound.

1974's *What Comes After,* Rypdal's second album, is in a similar mood, if a bit more conventionally jazzy, and is also recommended.

WHENEVER I SEEM TO BE FAR AWAY. Released December 1974. ECM import.

Terje Rypdal's third album, *Whenever I Seem To Be Far Away,* is one of his best. Divided into two parts, the first half is a tasteful jazz/rock fusion with the emphasis on rock, similar to the 1973–1974 era of King Crimson and *Devotion*-era John McLaughlin. The second half is a classical composition for electric guitar, strings, oboe, and clarinet, similar to Mike Oldfield's recordings with David Bedford, such as "Star's End" from the *Collaborations* album on Oldfield's *Boxed.* The writing throughout is excellent, and both approaches suit Rypdal's compositional style and guitar playing very well.

The first two pieces feature Rypdal (on electric guitar), Jon Christensen (drums, percussion), Pete Knutson (mellotron, electric piano), Sveinung Hovensjo (bass guitar), and Odd Ulleberg (French horn). The 14-minute "Silver Bird Is Heading for the Sun" opens with a loud French horn, which leads into ominous and murky mellotron, establishing a dark and Gothic mood.

This is underlined by some very up-front bass guitar by Hovensjo. Rypdal's guitars here are slices of jagged and dangling riffs that skate around spatially in the mix, giving the piece an edgy, psychedelic tone uncharacteristic of his later style. This, in combination with the mellotron, bass guitar, electric piano, and French horn, creates a surreal and druggy fusion that's dripping with mystery and atmosphere. The same is true for the 5-minute "The Hunt," although it's less intense and more jazzy.

The 17½-minute title track, with the Sudfunk Symphony Orchestra of Norway, is attractively recorded (up close) on a small soundstage, capturing a good amount of ambience. The piece opens with solo viola, and then solo violin, going through some moody and delicate passages. The entrance of Rypdal's guitar is powerful at first, but then suddenly falls back for a series of mournful notes. Rypdal is formidable in this context, having a genuine flair for serious classical composition.

The sound is excellent and full, with a strange mix of exaggerated, spacious separation that reinforces its occasionally psychedelic tendencies. The cover photo by Tadayuki Naito—a darkened seashore colored a deep blue—is also outstanding and provides an ideal image for the dreamy but ominous music of *Whenever I Seem to Be Far Away.*

ODYSSEY. Released December 1975. ECM.

Odyssey is perhaps Terje Rypdal's most representative album of the first half of his career. It's the point where his compositional talents had matured to such a degree that each of the pieces on the album features his distinct signature. Here all the facets of the Rypdal sound that were explored on his previous release, *Whenever I Seem to Be Far Away,* are refined and expanded upon. The music of *Odyssey* is a tasteful and precisely executed fusion of classical, jazz, and rock forms where the compositions take precedence over musicianship and soloing. What emerges is a rather moody and studious impressionism, with touches of romanticism and Gothic atmosphere creating an intensely introspective style of music.

Throughout, the instrumental palette remains diverse (if sparsely used). Rypdal himself plays an ensemble of string instruments in addition to his virtuoso electric guitar, and contributes a tiny amount of soprano sax as well. Bassist Sveinung Hovensjo is retained from the *Whenever . . .* lineup, adding Torbjorn Sunde (trombone), Brynjulf Blix (organ), and Svein Christensen (drums). The strings and the trombone are given as much prominence here as the other instruments. The sound mix is flat and very quiet, reinforcing the precision of the music and enhancing its subtlety.

The 3½-minute "Darkness Falls" opens with a piercing electric guitar, which is joined by bass and fluttery cymbals before dissolving into a spacey trombone solo with organ. The 16½-minute "Midnite" establishes a lonely mood with simple, low-key bass notes; later, organ, drums, and a slightly bluesy trombone creep in, adding to the mood. The music is icy and hypnotic, full of storytelling imagery. Rypdal ends the track with an intense, Pink Floyd–like (à la "Mudmen" from *Obscured by Clouds)* bluesy space guitar solo.

The 13-minute "Adagio" begins with a soft organ pulse that leads into gentle strings; a melancholy trombone is added, and finally a mournful, soaring guitar solo comes in with loud, sharp, screaming tones, piercing the dreamy mood established by the earlier sections. The 7½-minute "Better Off Without You" combines elusive guitar textures, delicate cymbals, and organ, with Hovensjo's up-front bass guitar solo unfolding slowly with loud, powerful notes. Rypdal concludes the piece with another David Gilmour–like guitar solo.

The 4½-minute "Over Birkerot" is the most rock-like track on the disc. Similar to the material on the first half of *Whenever I Seem to Be Far Away,* it's a dense and atmospheric mix of edgy guitars, thick bass, and drums. The sleepy 11½-minute "Fare Well" is similar to "Adagio," with strings, melancholy trombone, and stinging guitar solos. The 6-minute "Ballade" is a brooding, tortured, and memorable guitar solo by Rypdal.

Odyssey was originally a double album on vinyl, with another excellent 20-minute piece entitled "Rolling Stone" which was sadly eliminated here in order to fit the recording onto one CD. A double disc set would have been preferable in order to preserve the track, as its absence is a glaring omission. The sound quality is excellent throughout. Strangely, ECM avoids the opportunity to use an abstract interpretation on the cover (rare for the ECM label); instead, there is a straightforward photo of Rypdal with his guitar.

Terje Rypdal. (Photo by Steinar Buholm.)

AFTER THE RAIN. Released December 1976. ECM import.

After the Rain was a rare departure for Terje Rypdal, a true solo album where all the instruments are played by the artist himself, with the only other contributor being Inger Lyse Rypdal, whose voice is occasionally heard. Rypdal concentrates on the most impressionistic, romantic, and classical elements in his music, and the recording is Rypdal at his most melodic and textured. Soaring and glorious, these compositions are friendly yet quietly intense, recalling the mid-1970s music of Mike Oldfield. Rypdal becomes his own mini-orchestra (like Oldfield), playing electric and acoustic guitars, string ensemble, electric and acoustic piano, flute, bells, and soprano sax.

The 4½-minute "Autumn Breeze" attractively combines piano, strings, and electric guitar with slightly darker shadings provided by Inger Lyse Rypdal's voice. The piece certainly evokes its title, creating a feeling akin to stepping out into the fresh fall air. The 4½-minute "Air" continues these impressionistic moods, with a typically fluid electric guitar solo and with electric piano. The 3-minute "Now and Then" is a solo acoustic guitar piece, quite rare for Rypdal. The all-too-brief 1½-minute "Wind" is a space/ambient music flute solo. The hymnlike 6-minute title track is spiritual and serene, with sustained electric guitar notes that are sweetened by strings, all awash with sprinkles of bells. The piece recalls the reverence of Popol Vuh's *Hosianna Mantra.*

The 4-minute "Kjare Maren" is a solemn classical piece, with soft electric guitar and romantic piano and strings. The command Rypdal has over the tiniest of tones and resonances is masterful. The poignancy of his arrangements and his delicate touch as an instrumentalist can clearly be heard on this track. The mellow 1½-minute "Little Bell," a simple duo of flute and electric piano, is really just a fragment. The 3½-minute "Vintage Year" is representative of the album's strong impressionism. An introspective duo of piano and piercing electric guitar soloing evokes a moment of remembering or searching. The 3-minute "Multer" is a moody but not very interesting acoustic guitar solo, the least engaging of the album's tracks. The concluding 6-minute "Like a Child, Like a Song" is a highlight. A soaring wrap-up with piano, electric guitar, and Inger Lyse Rypdal's voice, the album ends with this brightly reassuring glow.

The sound is good, though unfortunately there's a large amount of hiss on some of the tracks. The cover photo by Giuseppe Pino is an appropriately impressionistic landscape of a barren field against a blue sky.

DESCENDRE. Released January 1980. ECM.

Recorded in March of 1979, *Descendre* is one of Terje Rypdal's finest releases, and his most atmospheric. The album is serene and sleepy, conveying an enormous sense of self-absorption and introspection, but with an underlying darkness and touch of the Gothic. These elements have always been present in Rypdal's music, though on *Descendre* they are more dominant. Intimacy is established (as it was on 1975's *Odyssey)* by the very quiet mix, which is detailed and crisp, putting the listener inside the music. For this album, Rypdal (playing electric guitar, keyboards, and flute) employs a trio format, joined by Palle Nikkelborg on trumpet, flugelhorn, and keyboards, and Jon Christensen on drums and percussion. The performances by all three musicians are among their best.

The reverent and spacey 5½-minute "Avskjed" opens with a somber church organ, which stays with the piece throughout. To this is added a morose and serious guitar and drums, with short bursts of flugelhorn, soft trumpet, and bells. The standout 11-minute "Circles" features a stellar recording of Christensen's drum kit, with restrained, playful stereo drum rolls, that makes for glorious headphone candy, giving the feeling one is inside his drum set. Added to this are slow, jazzy snorts of flugelhorn and trumpet, with Rypdal sailing guitar atmospheres and solos throughout the mix. The 3-minute title track has the beautiful sound of bells, piano, cymbals, and fleeting guitar notes, all of which pass like a sweet daydream. The remaining three tracks ("Innseiling," "Men of Mystery," and "Speil"), each 8 to 8½-minutes in length, are more of the same amazing textures as the rest.

The sound quality is very good, and the cover art and design by Dieter Rehm, depicting three landscapes seen through the blinds of a window representing *Descendre*'s trio of musicians, all in deep blue colors, are wonderfully abstract.

CHASER. Released December 1985. ECM.

Terje Rypdal consistently released quality instrumental music throughout the 1980s, and *Chaser* is the first album to feature his semipermanent collaborators Audun Kleive (drums and percussion) and Bjorn Kjellemyr (electric and acoustic bass). Rypdal's style on this and several ensuing releases is more streamlined and gritty than before. It focuses on more conventional rock and jazz structures, which distinguishes these releases from the classical, romantic, and impressionistic compositions that were to be explored at length on later straightforward classical releases like 1990's *Undisonus Ineo* and 1993's *Q.E.D.* This concentration on contemporary forms robs Rypdal's music of much of the eclecticism of his previous works, but nevertheless albums like *Chaser* are immensely enjoyable and solid, and to some may be more accessible.

The 8½-minute "Ambiguity" and the 6-minute title track surprised many at the time for being a foray into rock trio jamming, with Rypdal launching into simple riffing and power chording in a style that was a departure from his previous guitar playing. Kleive's and Kjellemyr's backing keeps these in jazzier structures, so from a rock perspective these tracks are actually quite mild, never over the top, and even perhaps a bit too refined, though Rypdal's guitar provides a rare clarity to the power trio format.

The 6-minute "Once Upon a Time," the 5-minute "A Closer Look," and the 6-minute "Ornen" veer into other new areas for Rypdal, exploring country western and blues styles, similar to the work of Ry Cooder. Featuring Kjellemyr's acoustic bass and Kleive's brushes, these pieces have slow, unfolding tempos with a lot of ambience. Rypdal's soloing contains a lot of echo and establishes a style and mood that show the stylistic influences described above but at the same time are very much his own.

The 6-minute "Geysir" (written by the band) is a jazzy trio sound, but with enough tasty soloing to be entertaining and enough complexity to dazzle. The 1½-minute "Transition" is a very brief keyboard texture, while the concluding Eastern-flavored "Imagi (Theme)" is a dreamy piece with soft percussion.

The sound quality on this recording is pretty good, if a bit too flat and quiet for the styles explored. The humorous cover photo by Dieter Rehm is a literal depiction of London Bridge falling down, no doubt meant to suggest a reaction to the unexpected rock structure of the album's title track.

BLUE. Released July 1987. ECM.

Recorded in 1986 with the same lineup and instrumentation as *Chaser* (see above), this is a sequel of sorts to that album. A crucial difference between the two is that this is a full digital recording, giving it a cleaner, slicker, and punchier sound (too flat, however; it has to be turned up). *Blue* is also louder (appropriately) and even more contemporary, attempting to wring sophisticated new grooves out of the trio format while still remaining strongly within the framework of Rypdal's previous oeuvre.

The 1½-minute opener, "The Curse," is a brief rock instrumental, setting the stage for the rest of the material with its painstaking precision. The 6½-minute "Kompet Gar" is led by the rhythmic groove of bass riffing and drums, adding low-key synths until Rypdal's edgy guitar soloing takes over. This is more cutting and rocking than the *Chaser* material. The 5-minute "I Disremember Quite Well" recalls the moody spaciness of Rypdal's 1970s music, but with a different sound due to the slick production. The 5½-minute "Og Hva Synes Vi Om Det" is pure space music atmospherics, and more effective than "I Disremember . . . ," with synth, bass, and percussion augmented by plenty of echo and effects.

The 3½-minute "Last Nite" puts Rypdal's David Gilmour–like bluesy soloing to loud percussion beats and crashes. The 5-minute title track is similar, if more low-key, with Rypdal's bluesy twang guitar solo over big drumbeats. The 4-minute "Tanga" is a tricky fusion, with a bass drum beat and bass guitar setting the scene for a series of guitar squeaks, culminating in a wailing solo. The 3-minute "Om Bare" is an awkward conclusion, with Rypdal's solo guitar interrupted by symphonic synth bursts. Dieter Rehm's cover art is appropriately blue.

IF MOUNTAINS COULD SING. Released April 1995. ECM.

In the same way that 1975's *Odyssey* (see above) was representative of Terje Rypdal's first 10 years as a recording artist, *If Mountains Could Sing,* recorded in 1994, encapsulates his 1980s/1990s period. What makes this disc so successful is its variety of styles, which fuse Rypdal's classical forms, such as that found on his superb 1993 classical recording *Q.E.D.*, with the slick jazz/rock of releases like *Blue*. This album also features Rypdal's best production values, with a crisp full digital recording that's state of the art. There's a strong attention to detail, and the compositions are so tightly arranged that they are almost *too* precise. The same lineup from the *Blue* disc returns here, alternating with a string ensemble of violin, viola, and violoncello, with Christian Eggen conducting.

The 5-minute opener, "The Return of Per Ulv," is similar to the material on *Blue*, only far more inviting and friendly. This rock piece is positively catchy, with sunny guitar textures by Rypdal. The 4-minute "It's in the Air" begins as a variation on the sound of the *Q.E.D.* disc, with guitar atmospherics, strings, and cymbals, but then switches to a tortured section of loud, whining guitar solos put to a bass drum beat. The 5-minute "But on the Other Hand" is the first of many shining examples of a current classical/rock fusion on *If Mountains Could Sing*. A crisply recorded, tight, and edgy violin and viola make conversational exchanges, and halfway through the piece they are replaced by the rock trio, with more anguished guitar from Rypdal. The juxtaposition of the two forms sounds utterly appropriate. The title track is a different though equally successful classical/rock fusion. This is another of Rypdal's typically moody combinations of attractive strings and spacey guitar effects, creating a powerful storytelling form of music. The 5-minute "Private Eye" continues these fusions, adding a *Chaser*-like power-chording rock jam to the string ensemble, finally fading with a melancholy section of guitar and strings.

The 4½-minute "Foran Peisen" is an extremely subtle form of ambient jazz. While the bass is up-front, the guitar and drums just hover, barely present, creating a drifting, wandering space music. The 3½-minute "Dancing Without Reindeers" combines nimble, screeching strings with a huge bass drum beat, which is then sewn up by an atypical Rypdal guitar solo. The 5-minute "One for the Roadrunner" is a rare excursion into free jazz, with Rypdal's dissonant guitar soloing cutting its way through the raunchy bashing of the rhythm section. The 3-minute "Blue Angel" is a trio ballad à la *Chaser*, but with a flutelike string section added. The 3½-minute "Genie" is another atypical Rypdal trio, with soaring guitar. The concluding 3-minute "Lonesome Guitar" sounds just like its title.

If Mountains Could Sing is one of the finest progressive discs of the 1990s, displaying Rypdal's compositions at their most mature and complex (not many artists are so accomplished in three separate genres—classical, rock, and jazz) while at the same time increasing the music's accessibility. It's an extraordinary accomplishment. The excellent black-and-white cover photo by Michael Trevillion of sunshine breaking through the clouds over a mountain and sea underscores the resounding musical triumphs of this disc.

RYPDAL DEJOHNETTE VITOUS

RYPDAL DEJOHNETTE VITOUS. Released January 1979. ECM.

Recorded in 1978, this album is absolutely atypical of what is known as the ECM sound. Here Terje Rypdal (playing electric guitar, guitar synth, and organ) is joined by two legendary jazz musicians, Jack DeJohnette (drums) and Miroslav Vitous (double bass and electric piano). The juxtaposition of styles works well, though it's not radically different from other Rypdal albums of this period, such as 1980's *Descendre*. What's notable about this particular trio release is that it contains a significant amount of depth, bearing up to repeated listenings, due to the plentiful nuances in the playing. This music has an intimate feel, with an up-close miking and mix that give it a lot of atmosphere.

The 8½-minute opener, "Sunrise," establishes the style and sound of the trio. DeJohnette's drumming has a light touch, concentrating on the cymbals, more in the traditional jazz style as opposed to the big beats and fills of many jazz/rock fusions. Vitous's murky bowed double bass, reminiscent of David Darling, is also a nonrock element. To this relatively jazzy scenario Rypdal adds a delicate background of guitar synth, then polishes off the track with another of his characteristic guitar solos. The 6½-minute "Den Forste Sne" is moody and melancholy, with stereo pans of Rypdal's guitar synth joined by Vitous's bass and incredibly delicate cymbal brushes by DeJohnette. The 8-minute "Will" creates a similar mood, with exciting interactions of electric piano, cymbals, and drums. The transitions within the piece are deftly handled.

The 6½-minute "Believer" is another atmospheric buildup, with guitar synth, bass, and drums. This piece has an inner tension that's finally released with Rypdal's guitar solo. The final two tracks, both written by the trio, are the album highlights. The 5½-minute "Flight" has skidding patterns of Vitous's bowed double bass backed by DeJohnette's lively drumming, which is more aggressive here than before. Over this Rypdal floats in some low-key guitar soloing. The 7½-minute "Seasons" announces itself with some chaotic, abstract patterns, then becomes a spacey jazz excursion, and is topped off by Rypdal's soloing.

Throughout, the music exudes a feeling of foreboding, like an overcast rainy day, and the stunning cover photo by Dieter Rehm of an approaching storm over the plains of a field is absolutely perfect imagery for this music. The sound quality is also excellent. A 1981 sequel by the trio entitled *To Be Continued* is more of the same, and is recommended.

PETER SCHAEFER

THE MYNAH. Released September 1996. FARN import.

Peter Schaefer's *The Mynah* is a privately released 66½-minute collection of high-quality, abstract, ambient space music collages (without rhythm) recorded between 1993 and 1995. Written, arranged, performed, and produced by Schaefer, this recording takes the styles of composers like David Parsons and Eberhard Schoener and combines them with the more avant-garde sensibility of artists such as Michael Prime. Schaefer utilizes Moog synth, samples, tapes and tape loops, cello, and other electronics, combining them with environmental field recordings made in Malaysia and Australia. The mood of this music is very

Peter Schaefer.

aptly indicated by the cover art and design (also by Schaefer), with mysterious location photography and abstract paintings that evoke images of antiquity and myth.

The 11-minute "Back on Track" opens with loud, murky subterranean electronics, but at the third minute switches suddenly to odd environmental sounds (what sounds like cows), then adds dark tape manipulations and mysterious crackling and groaning sounds before concluding with a strange, repetitive tape loop. The 10-minute "Gulf Savannah" features loud, treated environmental sounds, going into more murky electronics similar to that of the previous track, but then settling into mellow and dreamy space music atmospherics.

The 11-minute "Tropfentanz" is a highlight, combining night-time environmental sounds (e.g., crickets) with cello, talking trumpet, and electronics. The piece goes through a series of hypnotic, detailed, and moody cascades, adding percussion effects, oozing gurgles, and bleeps, producing a very heavy space music. The hissy 21-minute "Der Paradiesvogel und das Melancholisahe Cello" is also spacey, but has enough tension to prevent it from being relaxing. A high-pitched singing drone combines with floating textures and cello effects, with the occasional odd squeaks and spatial effects. Later, anguished cello and drifting background tones create a haunting mood. "Subway Rounddance," a live track recorded in 1996, concludes the album. The 12-minute piece is in the same murky, low-key, and dreamy style as the studio recordings. Throughout the disc the sound quality is very good, with occasional hiss.

SCHICKE, FÜHRS AND FRÖHLING

THE COLLECTED WORKS OF SCHICKE, FÜHRS AND FRÖHLING. Three LPs on two CDs. Symphonic Pictures released 1976. **SUNBURST** released 1977. **TICKET TO EVERYWHERE** released 1978. **THE COLLECTED WORKS** released July 1993. Laser's Edge.

The all-instrumental music of the German trio Schicke, Führs and Fröhling virtually defines the European prog rock sound of the mid- to late 1970s, fitting squarely alongside similar bands such as Bonfire, Clearlight, Finnforest, National Health, Shylock, and Terpandre. This supergroup produced some of the most lush, melodic symphonic rock of the era, with each of the musicians displaying formidable multi-instrumental talents. On these recordings Eduard Schicke plays drums, percussion, xylophone, metallophone, and Moog synth; Gerhard Führs plays acoustic and electric piano, mellotron, clavinet, and other electronic keyboards, especially the Moog synth; and Heinz Fröhling plays bass guitar, acoustic and electric guitars, mellotron, and Moog synth. These three albums are classics, each much beloved by progressive fans.

The group's debut, *Symphonic Pictures,* co-written by all three members, is the most orchestral in its compositional style and sound. Each of the five tracks is multifaceted, with varied and contrasting motifs and changing rhythms. The 9-minute "Too" opens the album with suitably symphonic textures, including thick, dual mellotrons and string ensemble keyboards played by Führs and Fröhling, which provide an expansive backdrop for Fröhling's melodic guitar line. Other sections are very baroque in nature, with Schicke's solid drumming providing a forward-driving force. The 3-minute "Solution" follows, a pastoral sound painting with the mellotrons, synths, and mallet percussion providing the melody. The clean arpeggiated electric guitar provides a nice folksy accompaniment. The 5½-minute "Dialog" contains dissonant keyboards, snare-heavy percussion, and a very Steve Howe–like guitar performance. The 2½-minute "Sundrops" is a dance that showcases the band's keyboard orchestration abilities. The album closes with their 16½-minute "Pictures," a mini rock symphony that many consider to be the band's high point. Dark, with moody sections that are perhaps reminiscent of Russian composers like Stravinsky and Prokoviev, this piece has wild synthesizer sounds and effects that make it very modern-sounding.

The equally excellent second album *Sunburst* is written primarily by Führs and Fröhling. The clever, flat-out 4½-minute fusion jam of "Wizzard" opens, with flying single and dual lead guitars setting the pace, daring the hip rhythms of the drums and keyboards to keep up. They rise to the challenge, pushing the guitars further ahead in a style very much reminiscent of Gong, Brand X, and Return to Forever. The 4½-minute "Autumn Sun in Cold Water" shows more of a Tangerine Dream influence (à la *Stratosfear),* with lots of echoing lead synth melody and synth bass. The music and title are a perfect match, painting an aural picture of a majestic natural vision. The 5½-minute "Artificial Energy" sees the trio moving into a more impressionistic phase, with the slow tempo of the bongos and arpeggiated guitar tied with the washes of synth, creating a celestial mood that's both strange and beautiful. The biting tone of Fröhling's electric guitar enters, occasionally doubled by a sawblade-like synth sweeping across the stereo field. The short 3½-minute "Driftin" is a slice of spacey jazz/rock similar to Passport.

The 7-minute "Troja" marks a return to the strong symphonics of the first album. This piece presents lead electric and classical guitars à la Genesis with an extensive use of effects. The 5-minute "1580" follows, with Fröhling's acoustic guitar playing the romantic ballad melody along with Führs' grand piano. The development of this track is more linear than previous SF&F. pieces. The final track is the 5-minute "Explorer." Heavy on synth textures with delay effects, the perky rhythm of the piece conveys the exploration of inner and outer realms. The buildup to the dual lead melody of synth and electric guitar sends the listener off into the great beyond.

The trio's third and final album, *Ticket to Everywhere,* is composed primarily by Fröhling. This release, marked by a move toward brighter textures, is really only half good, with much of the album not living up to the promise of the rest. An obvious commercial approach is taken on some of the tracks, such as the wretched disco of "Song from India."

The unquestioned highlight is the album's final track, the 4-minute "Folk 'n' Roll," a medieval-flavored folk jig that recalls the best moments of the two previous albums. Other strong tracks include the 5½-minute "Here and Now," an Oldfield-esque song replete with an unusually rousing vocal part; the 4-minute "Spain Span Spanish," a synth-tinged piece that recalls the Latin-flavored songs of Chick Corea; and the 8-minute "Slow Motion," which has shimmering keyboards and midtempo drumming that is reminiscent of late 1970s Tangerine Dream.

The production and sound quality of all three albums are staggeringly good, making this package an audiophile's dream. Completing *Ticket to Everywhere* are two bonus live tracks from 1978. The brief "Every Land Tells a Story" is a pastoral number from the Führs and Fröhling disc *Ammerland.* The 10-minute medley of "Explorer"/"Wizzard" is a fair document of the band's live abilities as well as their willingness to experiment with the arrangements of their pieces. Schicke bridges the two pieces with a nice drum solo, demonstrating imaginative and tasty chops. After the breakup of SF&F, Führs and Fröhling continued their projects, releasing two more albums following 1978's *Ammerland.*

EBERHARD SCHOENER

MEDITATION/SKY MUSIC—MOUNTAIN MUSIC. Two LPs on two CDs. **MEDITATION** released 1973. **SKY MUSIC—MOUNTAIN MUSIC** released August 1984. Celestial Harmonies.

Composer Eberhard Schoener is one of the most important German progressive artists, emerging from the same "cosmic music" scene that introduced Tangerine Dream, Popol Vuh, Klaus Schulze, and Michael Hoenig. While he's as prolific as his peers, most of his recordings have yet to be reissued on compact disc. Fortunately, this Celestial Harmonies double disc set contains two of his most important releases, both masterpieces of enigmatic, ethereal, and experimental space music.

Meditation, from 1973, achieves one of the most authentically opt-out and dreamy sounds in the history of the space music genre. Using the Moog synth, Schoener possesses an incredible talent for coaxing the most soothing, deep, and seductive sounds from that instrument. The best comparison would perhaps be the Wendy Carlos album *Sonic Seasonings.* Schoener's liner notes state his intention that this music be used as a tool for self-awareness, and also that it be seen as part of the Western, rather than the Eastern, tradition. Both of these goals are unquestionably progressive.

The 17-minute "Meditation Part 1" features washes of electronically simulated ocean waves, with a murky background of hums and an ever-present soft blip sound that recalls a submerged submarine. The piece conjures up images of a lone craft adrift on an expansive ocean, rocking to and fro, gently swaying as if in the grip of a spring breeze. These sounds are stereo-panned, and the effect is friendly and relaxing, but also undeniably mysterious.

The 18½-minute "Meditation Part 2" is a series of extremely subtle, soft resonances, at times voicelike, added to by bells. The piece is more a "presence" than a conventional musical composition; it's barely there at all, passing like a dream. Its drones are reassuring, pulling the listener in, and before one knows it, one is completely carried away. The most apt comparison would be the soft bell composition that appears on the *Environments #2* disc entitled "Tintinnabulation."

Meditation is indeed an extraordinary achievement, producing a music so elusive that it feels like stepping into a different dimension. The very flat and quiet sound mix underlines this elusive quality. The excellent cover art—an all-black square except for a small stained glass design in the center—seems to indicate that this album will be like a light at the end of a tunnel, a way out of the dark and into a more peaceful state of mind.

1984's *Sky Music—Mountain Music* is an equally important disc, and stands as one of the major progressive releases of the 1980s. Totally outside the corrosive trends of that decade, it fits very well alongside *Meditation;* it doesn't sound at all like there's a 10-year gap between them. As on *Meditation,* Schoener has full artistic control, composing, performing, producing, and even co-engineering the album. Here he plays the Fairlight synth, the Oberheim synth and sequencer, and the Roland synth. Despite the array of electronics, the music emerges sounding organic.

The 21½-minute "Sky Music" does, in fact, originate with the organic world. Schoener placed carrier pigeons in a wind tunnel, with tuned whistles and bells attached to their chests. The first minute of this piece is a recording of this. From there, sparse and dreamy synth notes take over with pure and bright tones. The mix is unusually spatial. The bird sounds return, altered and processed, combining with the synths. Schoener's intention was to create a "sky organ," a sort of "above" stereo imaging, and he accomplishes his goals, as the piece has an abundant ambience with a floating presence. The track exudes an open, joyful yet deep outdoor vibe.

The 23-minute "Mountain Music" takes the natural sounds of blackbirds and bullfinches and electronically processes them, adding sparse wood blocks as percussion. Indeterminate bleeps, taps, and bird tweets weave in and out of the piece's low-key mix, adding entrancing synth lines. There's a great deal of space in the sound, which is given an otherworldly, strange, and extreme (though subtly executed) spatial stereo separation. This effect creates interesting juxtapositions that are disarming but smoothly done. Very much like a work by John Cage, this track is completely avant-garde, but with clear compositional logic and goals.

Although *Sky Music—Mountain Music* is experimental, it has a universal appeal that's instantly attractive, making it a classic progressive release. Like the sound on *Meditation,* the sound here is excellent, with a flat and quiet mix underlining its enigmatic qualities. The amazing cover art by Nancy Hennings (of the *Tibetan Bells* series fame) is a David Hockney–like photocollage of various skies and mountains with several perspectives, echoing the spatial juxtapositions in the music.

TRANCE-FORMATION. Released November 1977. Innovative Communications.

Trance-Formation is another essential Eberhard Schoener release. Experimental and unique, it's a bizarre and twisted psychedelic/Dadaesque interpretation of Indian, Chinese, and Balinese trance musics. Composed, arranged, and produced by Schoener (here playing Moog synth, organ, piano, and mellotron), he's joined on the recording by Andy Summers (later of the Police) on electric guitar, the orchestra of the Munich Chamber-Opera, the monks of the monastery of SAMA, Mary Gregoriy on (wordless) vocals, and others on bass guitar, percussion, and keyboards. The sound mix is odd, but in a positive way, with the instruments seeming to dangle at the ends of the stereo spectrum.

The 5½-minute "Falling in Trance" establishes the album's unsettling mood, with strange rhythmic patterns of guitar, bass, and keyboards mixing with trippy vocal chanting. It has an edgy, uneasy quality, and nothing seems conventional.

Summers throws in some surprisingly loud power chords in the piece's center section. The 12½-minute "Shape of Things to Come" is a dreamy keyboard fest of space music, unfolding in a fashion similar to Tangerine Dream's *Stratosfear.* It's very much in the style of Schoener's albums on the Celestial Harmonies label (see reviews above), but more ordinary.

The 5-minute "Frame of Mind" is a more fluid mix of the vocal chants with bass, mellotron, and percussion, plus a tortured guitar solo by Summers, in a combination of the gritty (rock) with the gentle (chanting). The piece ends with a children's choir. The 3-minute "Signs of Emotion" is a reverent track of church organ and electric guitar, moving into some drifting Moog lines. None of the above tracks quite prepares one for the furious intensity of the 12-minute concluding title piece. Beginning with Klaus Schulze/*Cyborg*–like dissonant electronics (see below), Schoener creates a thunderstorm of crackles and swooshes, complete with a plethora of stereo effects. Into this sails Gregoriy's voice in a shrill choral manner. From there a mad church organ charges into some more nimble, spatial electronics, to which Summers adds a shredding guitar solo, followed by more cries and screams from Gregoriy. The piece is dislocating, jarring, and militantly psychedelic.

The cover art is an ominous photo of a spindly tree in a deep blue background, reinforcing the feeling of hallucinogenic unease this music creates.

KLAUS SCHULZE

CYBORG. Released October 1973. Spalax import.

Klaus Schulze was a pivotal figure in progressive music in the 1970s, consistently releasing revolutionary and experimental music. A founding member of two of Germany's earliest progressive bands, Tangerine Dream and Ash Ra Tempel, he embarked on a solo career in 1972. His first album, *Irrlicht,* resembles a deranged, Dadaesque Terry Riley, featuring extremely loud electric organ music rife with bizarre stereo delay effects, and is somewhat of an acquired taste. However, his second release, *Cyborg,* a double album from the fall of 1973, is a major classic of electro-acoustic music. Lengthy (with four compositions over 23 minutes), symphonic, and very psychedelic, *Cyborg* is an epic sci-fi musical environment. This is one of Schulze's most dense and challenging releases, and it established him in the area of cosmic music and avant-garde keyboards. (Other peers/influences in the same realm at that time were *Rainbow in Curved Air* Terry Riley; Tangerine Dream; Rick Wright of Pink Floyd, circa 1969–1975; and Agitation Free's Michael Hoenig.)

Like Tangerine Dream's *Zeit* (see review), *Cyborg* combines a classical string section with Schulze's Farfisa organ space music and VCS3 synth avant-garde electronics, but on a much larger scale. A "cosmic orchestra" of 12 violoncellists, 3 double bassists, 30 violinists, and 4 flautists is deployed, and in this kind of odd setting they become the most interesting aspect of *Cyborg,* often more so than Schulze's keyboards. This was still an early era in progressive music, and these kinds of experiments were totally new. Legend has it that the contributing classical players thought this project was lunacy. During this same time Schulze was also part of the Cosmic Jokers, an LSD-soaked German supersession group, and was composing music for a Berlin mental hospital for use in therapy. It was in this context that the thoroughly opt-out music of *Cyborg* was recorded.

The 23-minute "Synphara" begins with loud, murky rumbles and high-pitched electronic rustles, like a field of crickets in a swamp. This is joined by a melancholy section of cellists and bassists. The mood created is Gothic, creepy, and ultra-mysterious, underlined by head-bending stereo pans. Later, shrieking and primitive electronics and organ are added, a bit shrill at times, but becoming sleepy and trance-inducing. The piece concludes with an ocean of white noise that fries the synapses.

The 26-minute "Conphara" is a series of electronic loops and pulses, ominous and unsettling, adding a subtle undertow of whistling notes (like a very soft bagpipe) which become a buzzing pulse. The string section and Schulze's organ join in, sounding very Gothic. Finally this psychedelic piece oozes and pulsates, carrying the listener away until the fade-out.

The 24-minute "Chromengel" (translated, "chromium angel") opens with an organ pulse and streaks of colorful synth lines, recalling Terry

Riley's "Poppy Nogood and the Phantom Band, but even more somber. To this are added gooey, shimmering electronic percussive effects and outer-space synth shrieks and bleeps. Once again a tense, druggy mood is created. The 25-minute "Neuronengesang" combines high-frequency bristles with belching storms and walls of electronics; it all sounds like a giant laser battle on an inhospitable alien terrain.

Cyborg is a combination of *cyb*ernetic and *org*anic, as used in the Frank Herbert novel *Destination Void.* The album is best listened to at low volume (and is especially a treat on headphones) as its frequencies can be far too abrasive at louder levels. The disc's spatial effects take over any room it's played in. The Spalax remaster is fantastic, yielding incredible sound. The set comes in an attractive double-foldout full-color digipack. The cover has Schulze staring reverently at a light shining on his face, and in the background looms a large, round, glowing red object—some kind of alien sphere. All of this aptly communicates the otherworldly dimensions explored in the music of *Cyborg.*

BLACKDANCE. Released June 1974. Caroline.

Blackdance is easily one of Klaus Schulze's finest releases, and his most accessible. The album's flowing tranquility virtually defines the genre of space music, fitting in beautifully with the mid-1970s work of Tangerine Dream. All the elements are in place here, retaining strands of the psychedelic, the Gothic, and the cosmic. More importantly, this is still electro-acoustic music; the electronics are only a part of the overall whole, not dominating as they do so completely on later releases. *Blackdance* is written, arranged, performed, mixed, and produced by Schulze, and the instrumental palette is unusually large (for Schulze), including performances (albeit brief) of 12-string acoustic guitar, piano, phase trumpet, and percussion, in addition to the usual synths and organ.

The 18-minute "Ways of Changes" is one of Schulze's most successful compositions, taking the space music textures/fusions of earlier influences like Terry Riley and Pink Floyd to newer heights, along with a more polished and smoother execution. The piece opens with an enigmatic, murky organ, which is then joined by 12-string guitar for a series of disarmingly spacey stereo pans. The use of guitar is extremely rare for Schulze, and is a most welcome element here. To this tapestry is added the percussion of hand drums and cymbals (further welcome acoustic touches), and a final section is provided by some outer-space bleeps from the synth, which are a tad bit too loud in parts for the flow of the piece, but still very effective.

The 8½-minute "Some Velvet Phasing" is a high point of Schulze's electronic compositions. ARP and VCS3 synths establish seductive and dark unfolding tones (resembling a mellotron), dripping with atmosphere and lulling the listener into a serene state. The overall effect is like a combination of the minimalism of Riley and Philip Glass (à la 1974's *Music in Twelve Parts)* with the soundtrack of a Hammer horror film, emerging like one of the ephemeral pieces on Tangerine Dream's *Phaedra* (see review).

The 22½-minute "Voices of Syn" opens with the echoed, operatic bass voice of guest Ernst Walter Siemen, accompanied by an organ pulse. This is a marvelous combination, the effect of which is dramatic, Teutonic, and surreal. At the sixth minute the piece goes into a rhythmic phase loop percussion (like a loud clicking sound), continuing with more organ pulses. The effect is initially hypnotic, but the piece goes on for far too long without any development. Finally, sprinklings of stereo piano effects are added, but the track really should have ended about 8 minutes sooner.

The sound quality is very good, with an opt-out mix that's perfect for headphone listening. Note, however, that some pressings incorrectly identify the first track as "Waves of Changes." The truly outstanding cover and booklet paintings by Urs Amman depict surreal fantasy landscapes dripping with mystery, which are a perfect match for Schulze's music.

PICTURE MUSIC. Released October 1974. Spalax import.

Picture Music is one of Klaus Schulze's most innovative and beloved releases. Recorded after *Cyborg* in late 1973, but before *Blackdance,* this was released after *Blackdance* for contractual reasons. *Picture Music* is a blueprint for the forms and structures of many of Schulze's mid- to late 1970s releases, in particular the two soundtrack albums Schulze recorded in 1976 for a sex film entitled *Body Love.* Combining the dreamy fantasy of outer-space electronics (now ARP and VCS3 synth) with the organic rhythms of a drum kit, *Picture Music* bridges the gap between Schulze's early beginning as a drummer for Ash Ra Tempel and percussionist for Tangerine Dream and the synthesizer-wizard persona he had settled on by the mid-1970s. The album flows and unfolds seamlessly, setting a standard for the genre of space music. This is also Schulze's best-sounding production, being quite loud and extremely crisp (especially on the incredible Spalax remaster).

The $23\frac{1}{2}$-minute "Totem" opens with a 9-minute section of ultra-spacey synths and organ textures, less harsh than that of *Cyborg*, recalling the tranquility of Tangerine Dream. Schulze adds his active drumming and percussion to the rest of the piece, creating an infectious music that percolates and cooks. A large amount of stereo phasing emphasizes the music's spaciness, giving the danceable rhythms a strong sense of opt-out, dreamworld fantasy.

The 24-minute "Mental Door" puts the rubbery sound of fast rhythmic synth patterns in the foreground, with softer melodic lines in the background. The sound created is unique and inviting, the mood hypnotic and trance-producing. The piece concludes with a surreal Terry Riley–like church organ, recalling Schulze's first LP, *Irrlicht*.

The Spalax disc comes in a fabulous gatefold color digipack, with the remarkable surrealist paintings of Urs Amman creating an appropriately abstract tone for the music.

TIMEWIND. Released August 1975. Caroline.

Timewind is the most popular Klaus Schulze disc, and perhaps his most atypical. At an epic 59 minutes total running time, this was an extremely lengthy release for its era, with vinyl barely able to accomodate it. The themes of the album are the sound of wind and the passing of time, which Schulze evokes with a nearly all-electronic instrumentation of ARP and EMS synths. While organ and piano are credited, there's very little of them to be heard. *Timewind* is dedicated to the classical composer Richard Wagner, whose Teutonic scope Schulze admires.

The $30\frac{1}{2}$-minute "Bayreuth Return," named after Wagner's opera house, was recorded live to two-track. Opening with spacey electronic wind sounds, the piece launches into loud sequenced patterns similar to those found on Edgar Froese's *Aqua* (see review). Here Schulze displays his deft textural touch, maintaining extremely subtle changes throughout the unfolding of the piece and conveying the elusive passing of time. Light and warm notes, dreamy and entrancing, mix with some occasionally jolting ones. When the listener is thoroughly disarmed, Schulze ends the track suddenly with an excruciatingly loud noise that makes one think the home sound system has just exploded. Look out!

The $28\frac{1}{2}$-minute "Wahnfried 1883," named after Wagner's home and the year of his death, is more spacious. Again opening with evocative electronic windstorms, here the liquid, soft lead synth lines are more luscious. The form is like that of a suite or sonata. Despite its calming feel, the synths are rather foreground (too much so, actually), at times closer to the electronics of Heldon than to that of Eberhard Schoener or Michael Hoenig.

The sound quality is excellent, retaining a live feel. The darkly surreal fantasy paintings by Urs Amman lend an immediate otherworldly, sci-fi appeal to *Timewind*, offering an unusual set of images for listeners to ponder.

MOONDAWN. Released April 1976. Brain import.

Like *Picture Music* and *Timewind*, *Moondawn* is comprised of two extended tracks. Both pieces follow the established organic developmental style that is signature Schulze. While uniquely different compositions, they're complementary, and provide for an uninterrupted deep listening experience. Schulze's synths are augmented by the tasteful drumming of former Ash Ra Tempel associate Harold Grosskopf. Grosskopf's style is firmly rooted in the precedent laid down by Schulze's drumming on *Picture Music*'s "Totem." Grosskopf's drums would accompany Schulze on several ensuing releases, including the two *Body Love* albums, the epic *X*, and 1980's *Live*. Grosskopf's percussion keeps the listener centered as Schulze expands his electronic vocabulary by leaps and bounds and also grounds the music firmly in an electro-acoustic rock setting.

The 27-minute "Floating" is built in an arc, beginning slowly and quietly, and then building to a more intense level. Shimmering synth textures and wind chimes set the tone, until subtle key changes and a repeating sequence lead up to mild drumming that fades in at the middle section of the piece. Grosskopf delicately focuses on the cymbals, adding to the feeling of floating.

The adventurous 25-minute "Mindphaser" opens with sounds of ocean waves and thunder that fade in under a bed of string synthesizers. The environmental sounds are most welcome, and rare in Schulze's repertoire. The first half of the piece is glorious and hymnlike, with a high lead melody similar to an operatic arioso. This evokes a mood of searching and exploring. The halfway point is like a dawning revelation as the drums kick in heavily with a swoosh. Above that, a drone note is held for a long time while other instruments and timbres explore the space around it.

The sound is very good, if rather trebly. The drums, in particular, need far more bottom end. The appropriately dreamy cover art is a portrait of Schulze superimposed over a photo of clouds above a woody ground. The early 1980 Schulze release *Live* contains the 51-minute "Sense," recorded in October 1976 with Grosskopf. This piece revisits the forms of *Moondawn* in a punchier context (i.e., a better drum sound) and comes highly recommended, even though the rest of *Live* is a major disappointment.

MIRAGE. Released April 1977. Brain import.

Heralded as one of the earliest ambient (i.e., without rhythm or percussion) albums, *Mirage* continues the subtle stylistic variation changes within a composition introduced on *Timewind.* And like that album, this is a 58-minute epic with two lengthy tracks. By this point Schulze's synth equipment has become too numerous and complicated to list (like Tangerine Dream's), and *Mirage* is his first purely all-electronic release. A favorite with Schulze fans, this disc is a bit overrated, but remains an essential part of the Schulze canon.

The 28-minute "Velvet Voyage" begins with soft tones (reminiscent of Rick Wright's intro to Pink Floyd's "Echoes") that are cold and icy, slowly growing louder and increasing in pace. The music is haunting and chilling, and the occasional spatial effects of incoherent voices buried in the mix take the listener by surprise. In this unfolding minimalist structure one can hear elements of Terry Riley, Tangerine Dream, Richard Pinhas, and Philip Glass. Eventually the piece builds into a scary, ominous vortex of sound, with an unsettling undercurrent of bass notes. The track continues after this with few changes until its final fade-out.

The 29-minute "Crystal Lake" is lighter, but still has an uneasy undercurrent always threatening to bubble up to the surface. Sprinkles of shimmering, tinkling tones, once again rather minimalist, begin the piece, and these gradually increase in intensity. Buzzing, fluttering, and glowing lines are intermittently added. The middle section is the highlight, where the piece shifts to a dreamier level, evoking a winter blizzard (which could be the theme for the icy *Mirage),* until returning to the patterns of the track's opening.

Mirage is, sadly, difficult to find on CD, but well worth the search. The sound is good if hissy, and the stereo separation can be awkward in parts. The cover is a blue-and-white portrait of Schulze.

X. Released September 1978. Brain import.

The ambitious, epic double disc set *X* is Klaus Schulze's best album, the summit of all he had been aiming for. Combining a symphony orchestra with electronics, this is not the psychedelic severity of *Cyborg,* but rather a sweeping and majestic electro-acoustic classical music hybrid executed on a vast Wagnerian scale; it is lush, Teutonic and haunting. Subtitled "Six Musical Biographies," each of the six pieces is a separate audio portrait of an individual who influenced Schulze as a composer. Schulze is again joined on some of the tracks by drummer/percussionist Harold Grosskopf, who anchors the music in place.

The 24-minute "Friedrich Nietzsche" is a suitable homage to the great German philosopher. Basically a single-mood piece, with the activity and volume ebbing and flowing throughout, it begins with a slow wash of string synths, developing into Grosskopf's active drums, with a grounded bass and eerie choral leads shifting slowly above. The track, which is very spacey, with an almost Middle Eastern groove, stays in a single key, while the rhythms induce a trance-dance feeling, and the solos are very cyclical. The 5½-minute "Georg Trakl," dedicated to the 19th-century Austrian poet, is the shortest piece on the album. A repeating bass sequence sets up a restful mood, with a clarifying, plaintive lead synth line, and a percussive single note hammers out a rhythm. The Tangerine Dream–like shifting key changes make this relatively short piece surprisingly effective.

The 10½-minute "Frank Herbert" is dedicated to the noted author of speculative fiction. A very alluring track, it's driven by a straight-ahead rock beat from Grosskopf's drumming. The choral synth sounds are prominent throughout, and the shifting chord changes create tension and release. It has a faster tempo, which is appropriate to Herbert's writing style. The addition of electronic sound effects adds to the futuristic mood. The 18-minute "Friedemann Bach," named after composer Wilhelm Friedemann Bach, opens with a neo-baroque synth and orchestra section, but the percussion and sound effects make it more modern. The middle section turns into a sort of evil Russian jig, and overall the piece has a dark, self-absorbed tone, similar to Tangerine Dream's *Zeit.*

The 28½-minute "Ludwig II. von Bayern" is a musical collage of that composer's stylistic elements, with a modern twist to it. Strains of orchestral music reminiscent of Beethoven fade in and out, with familiar motifs juxtaposed onto modern synth timbres and compositional styles. In spite of its radical approach, it's still a direct linear descendant of Beethoven's music in its power to elicit moods and suggest landscapes. This impressive piece gets progressively more abstract toward the end.

The ominous 29½-minute "Heinrich von Kleist" is an homage to the late-18th-century poet. This excellent piece is by far the most abstract track on *X,* and has influenced later electronic composers. Slowly shifting tones and sound effects abound, while percussive rhythms are kept to a minimum and made hazy through processing.

The sound quality of this monumental work is excellent, capturing the right amount of large-scale grandeur needed for these compositions. The vinyl release originally came with an extensive booklet, which is only partly reproduced for the CD. After *X,* Schulze concentrated solely on all-electronic music, moving into the realms of full digital instrumentation and recording. An undeniable coldness is apparent in his releases after the triumph of *X.* A number of experiments with vocals and danceable beats elicited strongly negative reactions from most fans, while his spacey excursions were nothing more than inferior revisits of his 1970s material.

SHYLOCK

GIALORGUES. Released January 1977. Musea import.

Shylock was one of the finest French progressive rock bands, releasing two excellent instrumental albums for the CBS label in the late 1970s. *Gialorgues,* the first of the pair, has a remarkable compositional maturity given that the band members were all in their early twenties at the time. The lineup for this debut is the trio of Didier Lustig (mellotron, mini-Moog, clavinet, organ, electric piano), Frederic L'Épee (guitars, bass guitar), and Andre Fisichella (drums, percussion). The music of *Gialorgues* is a playful and accomplished exploration of the grand symphonic rock style with a strong sense of the baroque. The album fits comfortably alongside such seminal classical/rock projects as King Crimson's *In the Wake of Poseidon,* Focus's *Moving Waves,* Mike Oldfield's *Ommadawn,* and Steve Hackett's *Voyage of the Acolyte.*

The 13-minute "Le Quatrième" establishes the classical/baroque feel with Lustig's opening clavinet notes, which are then joined by lush orchestrations from the mini-Moog and mellotron. A rock section ensues, led by a Robert Fripp–like electric guitar from L'Épee that's precise, angular, and piercing, along with thick bass guitar notes and a full drum sound. A breezy mix of textures continues, adding acoustic guitar. The various sections are dreamy and storytelling, and it's all very well done. The 4-minute "Le Sixième" has a keyboard intro that sets a brisk, Oldfield-like marching pace, which is then taken up by a tight and loud rock workout, led by L'Épee's chunky bass guitar and edgy, tension-filled electric guitar lines.

The 19-minute "Le Cinquième" opens with an irresistible intro of goofy percussion effects from Fisichella, recalling McDonald and Giles or a livelier Pink Floyd. The sound of smashing glass ends the intro, and the piece switches into a funky rhythm section led by spacey electric guitar and mini-Moog. This is sophisticated and multilayered symphonic rock, with majestic, sweeping sections of power and grandeur conveying the sort of high drama the genre is famous for. A wonderfully twisted, chaotic section ends the piece.

Five excellent bonus tracks recorded in September of 1981 are also included on this recording, featuring Lustig (playing piano, organ, and synths) and L'Épee (electric guitar). The 3-minute "Pendule" is a low-key but lively piece of romanticism. The 6½-minute "Sons une Arche de Pierre" is a superb and adept classical piece, and is a highlight—particularly Lustig's piano. The 2-minute "Prelude a L'Éclipse" bears the closest resemblance to the textures of "Gialorgues." The 2-minute "La Robe et le Chat" is a rhythmic workout. The 1½-minute "Pour le Bal des Pauvres" features Lustig's surreal, carnival-like keyboards.

The production and sound quality of *Gialorgues* are very good (with some hiss) and are helped by a number of playful stereo effects. The cover is a stark black-and-white drawing of an old abbey.

Frederic L'Épee of Shylock.

ÎLE DE FIEVRE. Released June 1978. Musea import.

Île de Fievre (translated, "Island of Fever") retains the same lineup and instrumentation as Shylock's first album, *Gialorgues,* adding only Serge Summa on bass guitar, thus expanding the group from a trio to a quartet. Living up to its title, this album moves away from the baroque feel of the group's debut and turns up the volume and intensity, creating them a hard-hitting, live-sounding crunch without losing the quirky textures. The effect is to place *Île de Fievre* closer in feel to albums like King Crimson's *Red,* Rush's *A Farewell to Kings,* Heldon's *Interface,* and the first National Health album.

The 13-minute title track opens with a 1½-minute intro by keyboardist Didier Lustig that revisits the classical approach of *Gialorgues* with a dense fugue comprised of thick layers of clavinet and piano. This gives way to a very loud band jam which at first is also quite reminiscent of *Gialorgues,* but guitarist Frederic L'Épee's terse solos are more severe and Richard Pinhas–like, and the complex, extended jam by the group is far more driving. The 5½-minute "Le Sang des Capucines" begins as a fleeting improvisation of sorts, with stray, spacey notes, but then kicks in with Andre Fisichella's drums for a muscular and macho band workout that has won the listener over by its end.

The 2-minute "Choral" is a keyboard fest by Lustig. The 5-minute "Himigene" is a highlight, with a huge rhythm section that recalls King Crimson and McDonald and Giles. Penetrating guitar runs and keyboard riffs slice it up. The piece then switches to a percussion section with vibes that is pure ear candy. The 2-minute "Lierre d'Aujourd'hui" is another highlight. In a Genesis-like moment of high drama, ominous bass guitar notes lead a faraway sounding guitar, keyboards, and drums for a cutting rock jam. The 10½-minute "Laocksetal" focuses on the guitar/bass/drums for some intense power trio slice-ups that recall Heldon and Rush. A concluding section of Klaus Schulze–like Moog madness (with mellotron) by Lustig is extremely loud and jarring, and a somewhat off-putting way to end the album.

An unspectacular and low-fi 9-minute bonus track from 1979, "Le Dernier," is also included. The sound quality of *Île de Fievre* is outstanding throughout. The darkly surreal cover montage by Guy Bariol is a superbly "feverish" depiction of the album's title.

Regrettably, Shylock's record company pressured them to go in commercial directions (as detailed in the disc's liner notes), but they refused, and instead disbanded—a sad ending to one of France's most promising progressive bands. Guitarist L'Épee is currently a member of the group Philharmonie, who have had several releases on the Cuneiform label in the 1990s, but that band is nothing like the dynamic Shylock.

SOLSTICE

SILENT DANCE. Released November 1984. Progressive/Brainworks.

Silent Dance is a genuine treasure of 1980s vocal prog rock, reasserting the genre's hippie, folk, and arena rock elements. Solstice was a very promising British group from the early and mid-1980s who were more of a live act than a recording one. Its five members were Sandy Leigh (vocals), Andy Glass (guitars, backing vocals), Marc Elton (violin, keyboards, backing vocals), Mark Hawkins (bass guitar, bass pedals), and Martin wright (drums, percussion). Their songs recall the populist and counterculture moments of many classic U.K. prog rock artists, such as Yes, Sally Oldfield, Curved Air, Renaissance, Steve Hillage, and Jon Anderson, and are also comparable to the German group Werwolf, who also released their only album in 1984. The band's lyrics are strong, conveying dramatic storytelling imagery that has a philosophical depth to it. The production is a major disappointment, though, with a terribly thin mix that no doubt was a hindrance to their future recording prospects. The strength of Solstice is clearly Leigh's authoritative vocals and Glass's electric guitar, which put across the excellent material despite the production limitations and pedestrian playing from the other members.

The 6½-minute "Peace" is a rousing track, featuring Elton's dreamy violin and Glass's powerful Hillage-like rock guitar solo. The 6½-minute "Earthsong" opens with a Steve Howe–like acoustic guitar and Leigh's plaintive Annie Haslam–like vocal, then goes through bright exchanges of guitar, piano, violin, and cymbals. The 4-minute "Sunrise" has a grandeur that takes one by surprise with its powerful sound of Yes-like proportions. The 5-minute "Return of Spring" is an instrumental, led by Elton's violin solo (recalling Curved Air) and Glass's acoustic guitar. The melodies are very sweet, almost too much so.

The 6-minute "Cheyenne" is a highlight. An acoustic guitar-led ballad during its first half, the piece echoes every kind of 1970s arena rock act, from ABBA to Led Zeppelin, as well as many comparable prog rock artists. The piece is Leigh's finest moment. Midway through the track, she leads a Jon Anderson–like vocal chant (à la *Olias of Sunhillow*) which the group then joins with percussion and backing vocals. Another highlight is the 8½-minute epic "Brave New World," which is also very Yes-like. The rhythm section and synth lay down a groove, adding a rather dated organ, but the vocal and guitar interaction really soars. The piece is an emotional plea for a different world and better future, and Glass's cathartic guitar solo helps makes the case. The breezy 6-minute "Find Yourself," which closes the disc, is not really a progressive form, but rather a mainstream soft rock ballad, resembling 1980s Genesis.

While the album's mix is a botch, the sound quality is good if the volume is turned up. The lovely cover art by Martin Higgins is a colorful and inviting mandala. Solstice reappeared briefly in the 1990s with a completely different lineup that aimed for a more commercial sound than that of *Silent Dance,* but ended up sounding like a low-rent Jefferson Starship (the one without Grace Slick and Marty Balin)—hardly a progressive move.

LIZ STORY

SOLID COLORS. Released December 1982. Windham Hill.

Liz Story is one of the most significant composers of the current era, restoring intimacy to challenging instrumental music—always a progressive move. Her solo piano pieces are not overtly jazzy or classical in any strict sense, and neither are they stereotypically new age fluff; rather, she creates her own category. Her playing is absolutely rich with nuance, and her distinctive signature is writ large in each of the compositions. The reductionist move of confining compositions to a single instrument during an era of ever-larger arena-level armies of musicians and equipment is an important one. While the credit for this move does not belong solely to Story, she's the most effective proponent of this purist approach—more so than her solo piano peers George Winston, Tim Story (no relation), and Philip Aaberg. With this aesthetic, composition takes precedence over all other considerations (such as profit and fashion), and those who think that the world of progressive music consists solely of prog rock supergroups or electronics wizards often underestimate or ignore artists like Story, which is a crucial error.

While the Windham Hill label has yielded little of genuine significance in the progressive arena for some time, its original conception in the early 1980s was similar to that of other esoteric progressive labels like ECM and Celestial Harmonies. *Solid Colors,* which was among Windham Hill's first releases, has an intelligent and refreshing musical aura that's highly individualistic, and also impressionistic—perhaps to a fault. Story's solo storytelling Steinway piano compositions are genuinely memorable, yet accessible. The depth and shading are such that one can return to recordings like *Solid Colors* time and again and be consistently rewarded with new impressions.

There is perhaps no finer example of this than the opening 5½-minute piece "Wedding Rain." The shivery chords of the introductory motif draw the listener in, and this intro is as uniquely memorable as that of Mike Oldfield's *Tubular Bells.* The piece seems to mark time, and is both romantic and introspective. The 3-minute "Pacheco Pass" is rich with variety. Each minute change resonates with the listener, and everything about the piece seems just right somehow; nothing is out of place. The 4½-minute "Without You" is haunting and lyrical. The 4-minute "Hymn" features irresistable notes that are tuneful and inviting. The lively 3-minute "Things with Wings" is almost symphonic in nature.

The 4½-minute title track is another highlight, with its chords unfolding in cinematic sweeps. Its romanticism is gorgeous at times, but it is never sweet—a key feature of Story's writing. The 4½-minute "Bradley's Dream" is a lighter variant on some of the themes from the previous tracks. The 2-minute "White Heart" is spacey yet grand, and is quite substantial despite its short length. The 3-minute "Water Caves" continues the extraordinary level of invention, exuding a breezy, classical flow. The 5½-minute "Peace Piece" closes the album. A cover of pianist Bill Evans's song (Evans was Story's main influence), this is pure somber introspection.

Solid Colors, the first of five masterful releases by Story, goes by all too quickly. The sound is excellent, with no audible hiss. The fantastic impressionist cover painting by Michael S. Moore is absolutely perfect for the music.

UNACCOUNTABLE EFFECT. Released January 1985. Windham Hill.

Unaccountable Effect is the successful sequel to *Solid Colors.* Just as memorable, introspective, and storytelling as those on that album, Story's solo Steinway piano compositions here are an extraordinary treat, now bolstered by a full digital recording. The opening and concluding tracks expand the instrumentation beyond that of the piano, an excellent move that adds further colors to Story's music (and would be explored at greater length on her next release, *Part of Fortune).*

The 8-minute title track opens the disc, and is a collaboration with composer Mark Isham. A piece of spacey electro-acoustic music, Isham's haunting and low-key synth combines with Story's dewy cascades of piano. It's a very good blend, with a chamber music feel. The 3-minute "Devotion" is a subtle and poignant observation, refined and intelligent. The 4-minute "Mostly the Hours" is an album highlight—Story at her finest. A series of impressions unfolds, bringing with them a number of emotions. The piece is a recollection, a remembering, marking time in an expressive fashion that is Story's forte. The 4½-minute "Starfinder" is a more playful and nimble piece, yet retains a serious undercurrent.

The 6-minute "Rope Trick" is a challenging, uncategorizable piece that is uniquely Story. This is a deadly serious form of music, a good example of how substantial her writing is. This track stands as incontrovertible proof that those who consider Story's work as "background sounds" are making a serious error. Romantic and emotional, the 4-minute "My Heart, Your Heart," by Dick Grove (Story's mentor/collaborator) and Joy Bryan, is like tragic silent film music, but with Story's distinctive signature. The 4-minute "Leap

Liz Story. (Photo by Steve Hathaway.)

of Faith" is grand and dramatic, with a classical feel. The concluding 6-minute "Deeper Reasons" is another highlight. To her piano, Story adds the subtlest of drum textures (which she plays), along with percussion by Bob Conti, who adds shivery sprinkles of sounds like bells or tinkling glass. This is pure space music, understated and seductive, recalling early Emerald Web.

The sound of this recording is very good throughout, and although the quiet and flat mix deprives the piano of some vibrancy, that isn't a major drawback. The superb cover photo by David Lorenz Winston of an abstract sand pattern underscores the enigmatic qualities of this music.

PART OF FORTUNE. Released December 1986. BMG.

Part of Fortune is Liz Story's most diverse album, a juxtaposition of tracks half featuring solo piano and the other half piano with other instruments. What's notable about this disc is the contrast between the two approaches. It's fascinating to compare the compositions that concentrate on the piano with those that add layers of different instruments. Both approaches work well for Story, and for those interested in hearing something other than solo piano from her, *Part of Fortune* is a wonderful release.

The opening track, the 3½-minute "Toy Soldiers," is a splendid example of such a combination, placing the marching notes of Story's piano with drums and triangle percussion. The piece has a sprightly pace and a cinematic feel. (It's important to note that the piano could carry such a piece on its own.) The next five tracks are all solo piano compositions. The 5-minute "The Elephant Trainer" is sprawling, ambitious, and almost operatic. The piece is sophisticated and complex, and Story's playing is confident. The 2½-minute "Teased Hair" is a lively and tightly arranged observation. The 3-minute "Myth America" is a pastiche of patriotic songs, which are easily recognizable, but it does, thankfully, use some darker chords. The 3-minute title track moves at a rapid pace, showcasing Story's technique as a player with an aggression that foreshadows her later disc *Escape of the Circus Ponies*.

The 4½-minute "Reconciliation" is another album highlight. Dramatic and deadly serious, this is the style that would be explored on Story's next album, *Speechless*. The 6-minute "Duende" adds a sweeping orchestral section to Story's piano, creating a very full sound that's grandiose, rousing, and aggressive. The string arrangements are a bit too large and too much like soundtrack music, but it's nevertheless a fascinating experiment. In the 5-minute "Ana," a major highlight, strings and cello solos mix with Story's sad, downbeat notes for an authentic piece of classical chamber music. Here the other instruments underscore the piano rather than compete, and the piece is all the more effectively emotional as a result. The 3-minute Gregorian chant "Ubi Caritas," which has no piano at all, fits in with the moodiness of Story's music well.

The sound of this full digital recording is sunny and sharp, but not quite as full-bodied as it could be. The credits strangely fail to identify any of the other musicians that appear. The cover is a straightforward photo portrait of Story. For *Part of Fortune* Story was scooped up by a major label, and received a good amount of promotion as a result.

SPEECHLESS. Released August 1988. BMG.

Recorded in three days in April of 1988, *Speechless* is Liz Story's most serious work, with lengthy pieces that make the most of the solo piano format within the framework of the artist's style. The disc's flat, full digital recording emphasizes the darker qualities inherent in Story's music, but also conveys her aesthetic purism. Despite its ambition, this album is effortless and palatable, and doesn't rely on jazz or classical clichés to carry it. An album like *Speechless* is the polar opposite of the overblown, arena-sized, new age mega-fluff that's exemplified by superstars like Yanni, John Tesh, Kitaro, and Jean-Michel Jarre. It is completely a progressive form, returning instrumental music to the intensely private world of reflection and memory.

The 9-minute "Forgiveness" is a pleading appeal, with its insistent chords and repetition of sections. The first half of the piece has a slight error (either from the recording or mastering), causing a tiny but audible distortion in one channel. Thankfully it disappears after a few minutes and doesn't intrude too much on this memorable track. The 3-minute "Frog Park" is a real contrast to the mood set by "Forgiveness," being a freewheeling and fun romp that could almost be a Ron Geesin piano piece. The rest of the tracks are strong examples of everything Story is about as a composer and pianist. All are among her finest recordings. The 7-minute "Welcome Home" is in the style of her Windham Hill discs, with opening notes that then move into cinematic sweeps. Like many of her compositions, a landscape is painted and made to yield various impressions before an unexpected commentary on them is injected. The same is true for the 7-minute "Hermes Dance," which is a bit more baroque and utterly compelling. The 6½-minute title track is among her most poignant. It's cold and icy at times, but is also deep and full of nuance. Story's playing technique ensures that there's always something more for her to add to the piece, such as the little riff at the end of the theme and the final fade-out of notes. The 4-minute "Back Porch" is a classic impressionist track, romantic and rollicking, with an understated populism. The concluding 8½-minute "Vigil" is one of Story's best compositions, a mature and storytelling form. She establishes a soft undercurrent of notes, then intersperses a series of dramatic comments, conveying the passing of time and a sequence of events. The piece is ominous and austere, creating images of loneliness and hardship. A truly amazing work. The cover photo portrait of Story in shadow is a fine intimation of the earnestness of *Speechless.*

ESCAPE OF THE CIRCUS PONIES. Released November 1990. Windham Hill.

Escape of the Circus Ponies is Liz Story's most aggressively ambitious album, throwing out a large number of ideas at the listener, almost too rapidly to be digested in one sitting. It is a work of undeniable maturity, yielding a bountiful amount of virtuoso solo piano compositions. An impressionist classic that is an intrinsically American form of modern music, its various titles and structures elicit a number of picturesque landscapes and images. *Escape . . .* is also Story's most vibrant-sounding recording (she co-produced), giving her piano a more lustrous, loud, and lush resonance.

The 4½-minute "Broken Arrow Drive" is an exciting and rousing opening track with majestic and deftly executed themes that have a built-in universal appeal. The 3½-minute "Inside Out" is an introspective piece, done in larger than usual style, but with a resigned dignity. In the 6-minute title track, which does justice to the images conjured up by its title and is one of Story's most aggressive pieces, she uses some different scales than before, but retains her usual technique. The 6-minute "Church of Trees," a challenging and austere piece similar to the tracks on *Speechless,* exudes an outdoorsy, harmony-with-nature vibe. The 3½-minute "The Sounding Joy" is also evocative of its title, with bright cascades of melodies conveying a sense of urgency.

The 7½-minute "Another Shore" is dynamic and intense epic storytelling, with a wide, sweeping soundstage that's almost too relentless. The 7-minute "Incision" recalls "Vigil" from *Speechless,* with dense, strong notes and a rich sound. The 4-minute "Worth Winning" is like a track from *Solid Colors* or *Part of Fortune,* only more aggressive. The 7-minute "The Empty

Forest" is a loud and marvelously evocative album closer, with a center section of stunning notes.

Escape of the Circus Ponies represents the last (for now, anyway) Liz Story release of original compositions, which is odd in that her albums have all been so universally successful. Since then she has retreated toward more conventional and commercial forms by covering the material of others, such as jazz standards and Christmas songs. While her playing is always interesting, this is absolutely the wrong path for a composer of her stature to be following, as her own material is consistently innovative. Hopefully, in the future there will be more treasures to come.

SYLLYK

ASCENDRE, À L'OMBRE DU VENT. Released May 1996. La Legende Des Voix import.

Eric La Casa, a.k.a. Syllyk, is an experimental sound sculpturist similar to Michael Prime, O + A, and Annea Lockwood. Using studio manipulations of field recordings, *Ascendre, à l'ombre du vent* (translated, "Ascending, in the shadow of the wind") is a self-released 66-minute environmental/ambient/industrial journey into sound. Reminiscent of the works of the Hafler Trio (in that they both create lengthy sound manipulations employing dissonance), Syllyk's *Ascendre . . .* is more conceptually unified, and also far friendlier than the recordings by that group. The extensive use of water sounds certainly recalls the works of Lockwood and Prime, but is also from the same aesthetic school as Deuter's *Aum,* Bill Nelson's *Crimsworth,* and Kit Watkins's *Circle.* This makes for some supremely picturesque headphone candy (due to the plentiful spatial effects). However, *Ascendre . . .* is also jarring (and should be played at a relatively low volume), keeping it quite safe from being labeled as new age background music. Even when development within the work stalls for a bit, the piece retains its overall aura of mystery.

The recording begins with nearly a minute of silence before the very quiet opening of ocean waves and wind fades in. Whistles of wind from a calm seashore mix with soft scraping sounds, and they become much louder as the sea ebbs and flows, until they explode in a torrent of white noise. With the clang of a bell, the piece falls back to the environmental sounds heard earlier, now combined with bell resonances. Sudden clangs lead once again to more white noise assaults, before returning to faraway-sounding ritual bells, conveying a sense of the sacred. After this, a tempest of extremely loud and abrasive white noise assaults the listener (a mistake, being much too harsh) before evolving into churning ocean waves; the water sounds by degrees dwindle to a trickle, and are finally reduced to the tiniest of water drips. Syllyk focuses on the most minute and detailed resonances of those drips, adding rustling sounds of wind and birds, which create a sleepy, relaxing mood. A distant thumping sound then emerges in one channel, grows closer, and is then echoed in the other channel. Bells and scratching sounds return, until quiet dripping water is again heard. There's another moment of silence, then seashore splashes emerge, adding subtle electronic sounds and children's voices; the work concludes with another minute of silence.

The cover of the recording, an inset photo of a hill as seen from far below, is a depiction of a goal to be attained, the ascending journey of the disc's title.

SYLLYK/KOJI MARUTANI

OTHER-WISE. Released February 1996. Digital Narcis/Touch import.

Other-wise is a collection of five unusual pieces of experimental audio collage and field recordings, three by Eric La Casa (Syllyk), and two by Koji Marutani. Both artists share a fascination with the relationship between humans and their acoustic environment, desiring to liberate the diversity of sound from the imposed constraints of the music industry. These works paint highly visual sound environments, and the various juxtapositions ensure that the level of surprise remains very high. The artistry, then, lies in the plentiful transitions, taking the listener on a veritable grand tour of sound.

Syllyk's three pieces, recorded in 1994, resemble in part his *Ascendre . . .* disc (see review above), but they are perhaps preferable to that work. The 11½-minute "Ouroboros 3" is the most jarring of the three. Running water, sawing sounds, a background chant, and the minimal clanging of various objects are interrupted by loud clock chimes; then gusts of machinelike sounds are heard, and a crackling fire, with clocks, owls, and ocean waves added. The mood is silly and light-hearted, recalling the structure of Pink Floyd's "Alan's Psychedelic Breakfast," but far more varied and chaotic.

The 9-minute "Ouroboros 4" opens with a gorgeous stereo recording of running water, with a number of spatial variances. This switches to loud walking sounds (as if in a wet jungle terrain), very loud bell-like clanging, and footsteps on a stairway. From there the piece moves into more water sounds and the sound of children playing, before concluding with a trickle of water.

The 15½-minute "Ouroboros 5" opens with a minute of silence, then flows into a trickle of water and bells, which becomes louder. A series of chimes, clocks, and chants are added, and the piece then switches to the juxtaposition of bizarre percussion in one channel and walking sounds in the other. More water sounds and some singing in French ensue, until another minute of silence concludes the track.

Marutani's pieces, recorded in 1995, incorporate field recordings made in major cities (Tokyo, Paris, London, and Rome) and also a small amount of keyboards and samples. The 12½-minute "Scenes 1" has rain and street sounds savaged by a loud crumpling noise. Switching to bird sounds, a spacey high-pitched singing resonance is added, along with the sound of scraped metal fragments. The 23½-minute "Scenes 2" is great audio theater with a cosmopolitan flavor. A subtle and hypnotic singing pitch creates a caressing structure. Five minutes in, quiet environmental sounds are added. The running water and harmonious resonances exude a tranquil, peaceful vibe. A moment of silence around the 14th minute gives way to a series of city sounds. Crowds, subways, and announcements lead to church bells, and then to the wonderful ambience of bluesy music at a French cafe.

The sound quality of this recording is excellent throughout, with no hiss, and the mix is a hundred percent spatial effects, guaranteed to deliver a wealth of audio surprises. The cover is a photo of a building at the moment of a nuclear blast. The liner notes by the two artists encourages listeners to record their own audio creations.

T

TANGERINE DREAM

ELECTRONIC MEDITATION. Released March 1970. Sequel/castle.

Electronic Meditation is a genuinely revolutionary form of surreal, ultra-psychedelic instrumental rock, and is one of the truly authentic freak-out albums of the hippie era. A protégé of artist Salvador Dali, founding member Edgar Froese named the band after a lyric found in the Beatles song "Lucy in the Sky with Diamonds." The band's early aesthetics were to a large extent influenced by the unconventional musical structures preferred by young political radicals in the counterculture, who rejected song forms in favor of lengthy and noisy instrumental jams. The explorations of Pink Floyd (especially their *Ummagumma* album) were also a major influence.

Recorded in a rented factory in October of 1969 and released in early 1970, *Electronic Meditation* is Tangerine Dream at their most abrasive, with a primitive, low-tech, and completely underground sound rife with stereo effects. Froese, here playing a stinging lead electric guitar as well as organ and piano (and also producing), is joined by Klaus Schulze on drums and percussion, and Conrad Schnitzler on cello, violin, and flute. The band and its growing success paved the way for a German progressive music movement that was more experimental than any other scene at the time.

From the opening moments of the 6-minute "Genesis" it's apparent that this is definitely music from the other side. Strange guitar chords and cymbals merge with a murky and Gothic-sounding cello. The string instruments screech and howl like mad baboons or UFO blips on a radar warning system. Then a flute solo leads into primal drums and drones. The 12½-minute "Journey Through a Burning Brain" opens with jagged, sharp-edged electric guitar noise and riffing, recalling Amon Duul and Pink Floyd. A Rick Wright–like organ drifts in reverently, joining the primitive guitar noises and weaving a spacey tapestry. This builds into a groove with guitar soloing and radical stereo effects. The odd mix contributes heavily to the music's surreal twists. Froese's soloing is hard-edged, and the piece is an electric raga of sorts.

The 11-minute "Cold Sweat" marries an organ pulse with Schnitzler's strings, creating a spacey effect; loud jolts of percussion then interrupt, with the organ being sent off into some shrill notes. This is authentic psychedelia in an embryonic state. Midway through, Froese tears into a snarling electric guitar solo with drums, flute, and synapse-shredding stereo effects. The piece switches suddenly to the sound of someone breathing hard (a very LSD moment), then goes directly into the 4-minute "Ashes to Ashes." More jagged guitar soloing is joined by organ and thin-sounding drums. Though not as harsh as the preceding track, it's just as bizarre. The 3½-minute "Resurrection" opens with a very loud church organ, like something from a Hammer horror film. Into this is floated a stereo pan of a backward-playing voice (reciting the instructions for going through German customs). It's eerie, to say the least. The piece concludes with ghostly strings from Schnitzler, reprising the opening of "Genesis."

The sound quality of the Sequel remaster is extraordinary, restoring volume and clarity, and far surpassing all other previously available editions. The cover photo by Monique Froese of a baby doll wired onto an electronic pad is classic imagery for this album, for the genre of psychedelia, and for the emerging "serious" rock of the time. Schulze and Schnitzler left the band after this album, with Schulze joining Ash Ra Tempel and Schnitzler joining Kluster. Later both began prolific solo careers. *Electronic Meditation* is such a historic recording that it's displayed in the Museum of the History of the Republic of Germany in Bonn.

ALPHA CENTAURI. Released February 1971. Sequel/Castle.

Eagerly anticipated in the musical counterculture of the time, the second Tangerine Dream release eschews the blaring guitar rock of their debut album in favor of cosmic space excursions. While the space music genre would soon encompass the realms of inner-space self-discovery and introspection, in early 1971 lengthy instrumental excursions of the sort found here were generally intended as expressions of imaginative sci-fi/futuristic concepts, and were often inspired by the NASA missions of the era as well as the increasingly rich texts of speculative fiction writers. With *Alpha Centauri,* space music assumed its own language and form, going one step beyond Pink Floyd, where psychedelia and surreal rock joined to take the listener on journeys to unknown voids.

Recorded in January of 1971 and released a month later, *Alpha Centauri* retains the opt-out stereo fantasyland of Tangerine Dream's first album, but with improved production values, giving the band a fuller sound. Edgar Froese, here playing guitar, bass, and organ (and again producing), is joined by Christopher Franke (a jazz percussionist who played with Agitation Free at the time) on drums, percussion, flute, VCS3 synthesizer, piano harp, and zither, and Steve Schroeder on organ, plus two other guests on flute and synth. It's important to note that while this is the first TD album to use a synthesizer, it's mainly employed for sound effects and texturing support, with the rest of the instrumentation carrying the bulk of the sound.

The 4½-minute "Sunrise in the Third System" opens with appropriately spacey, delicate guitar chords, with echo, in combination with emerging organ pulses. A few outer-space synth blips are added, creating a drifting, mysterious sound. The 13½-minute "Fly and Collision of Comas Sola" begins with utter chaos and evolves into a trio jam. Very, very, very LOUD synth shrieks skate by, meant to convey the vastness of space and cosmic phenomena. These are replaced by plaintive electric guitar strums and reverent organ, building up with flute and synth textures and becoming a vast, whirring soup of sound. Into this Franke's drum kit enters, bringing some form to the chaos, along with a flute solo. Franke's drums add a strong rock element, giving the piece a psychedelic raga form.

The 22-minute title track is another floating, surreal brew of organ pulses, flute solos, and shrill synth textures, once again evoking the immense expanse of space. The piece drifts for quite a long time, exuding a haunting, dreamworld vibe. An electronic choral section emerges, predating the sound of Popol Vuh's *Affenstunde.* The finale has a spiritual recitation (in German) with stereo effects and choir.

Alpha Centauri is an essential title from the early era of progressive music. The Sequel remaster gives the album the best sound it has ever had. The abstract artwork by Edgar and Monique Froese effectively communicates the spacey themes of the music.

ZEIT. Released June 1972. Sequel/Castle.

Zeit (meaning "time") continues the outer space/sci-fi explorations of *Alpha Centauri,* and also marks the point where such explorations lead to the examination of inner space. A historic and groundbreaking release, *Zeit* is a double album (74½-minutes on one CD) of soft electro-acoustic music, featuring four lengthy tracks. A challenge for those expecting the rock textures of TD's first two albums, *Zeit* has no rhythm. *Zeit* is a product of the analog keyboard technology and production techniques of its time, and a recording like this probably could not be replicated today. Listening to it is like stepping into another dimension; its appeal is completely to the imagination. and you get out of it what you bring to it.

Recorded in May of 1972 and released the following month, *Zeit* features an unusually expanded lineup for TD. The idea of convening an orchestra of diverse musicians in order to produce the most totally "outside" music possible was a radical one. Edgar Froese (supplying delicate electric guitar textures), Christopher Franke (VCS3 synth, cymbals, keyboards) and new member Peter Baumann (VCS3 synth, organ, vibraphone) are joined by previous member Steve Schroeder (organ) and Florian Fricke of Popol Vuh (Moog synth), plus four members of the Cologne Cello Quartet.

The 20-minute "Birth of Liquid Plejades" opens with murky cello, establishing an ominous storytelling mood with their drones. Mysterious organ and synth are then added, creating a sound that's dark, menacing, and Gothic to the max, but is later lightened by warmer organ and Moog pulses.

The 18-minute "Nebulous Dawn" features ethereal, resonating hums and rumbles, with lighter tones in the background. This is a fuller exploration by the band of the softer possibilities for synthesizers. Later the piece veers into more avant-garde sections, recalling Pink Floyd's Rick Wright à la "Sysyphus," before concluding with bubbly and gurgling Moog sounds that exude an organic flow.

The soothing 19½-minute "Origin of Supernatural Probabilities" combines very soft electric guitar textures with quiet hushes of organ and synth. The effect is that of a sort of ghostly presence, the "supernatural probabilities" of the title. Later, some wobbly, rubbery synth lines, low-frequency rumbles, and whale song–like sounds are added, increasing the piece's ethereal qualities.

The 17-minute title track is similar to "Origin..." and is completely enigmatic. Despite its primitive construction, this is a timeless sort of music that one can disappear into, like some kind of sci-fi vortex.

Zeit is the first consciously ambient album, and had a direct influence on a number of space music composers, such as Brian Eno, Klaus Schulze, Eberhard Schoener, and Popol Vuh. The incredible, eye-catching, and utterly appropriate cover art by Monique and Edgar Froese of an eclipse-like phenomenon is almost more effective than the music itself.

While the Sequel remaster is an absolute revelation compared to the previously botched editions of *Zeit* (restoring a badly needed, much improved stereo imaging), the master tape had deteriorated, creating a number of bothersome clicks throughout the disc.

ATEM. Released May 1973. Sequel/castle.

Atem ("breath") is one of Tangerine Dream's finest releases, and solidified their reputation as leaders in the world of progressive music. With this album the band properly began its classic trio phase of Edgar Froese, Christopher Franke, and Peter Baumann, the lineup which recorded the majority of the group's most important compositions. With *Atem* their production values became more sophisticed, yet retained the early psychedelic authenticity of earlier albums. This is electro-acoustic music with a universal appeal, with synthesizers (here VCS3) combining with mellotron, drums, percussion, organ, piano, and guitar.

The 20½-minute title track exudes an aura of antiquity; it has a wide scope, like a sun-drenched ancient Egyptian panorama. A strange, oozing, wind tunnel–like sound opens, to which is added a grandiose but faraway sounding mellotron pattern, joined by Franke's drums and murky synths, creating a heavy, otherworldly raga, reminiscent of the most intense, center-section moments of Pink Floyd's "Set the Controls for the Heart of the

Sun." The sound mix is unconventional, giving the piece its appeal. An explosion is then heard, and the track falls into a morass of Gothic mellotron and warm, liquid-like synth percolations, creating a floating feeling, finally culminating in the return of the wind tunnel opening, becoming a vast whirlpool of mysterious sound.

The 11-minute "Fauni Gena" sounds so organic it positively drips like a dewy liquid. Very spacey organ, mellotron, and synth unveil a series of tranquil, soothing, and ultra-melodic notes, weaving a seductive tapestry. Combining various keyboards into an attractive whole is what the band does best. The piece unfolds with a lot of space between the notes, and listening to it is much like watching a painter methodically sprinkling colors on a canvas. The track is also reminiscent of a natural environment, with electronics simulating bird song.

The 6-minute "Circulation of Events" offers more of the same elusive and delicate harmonics. The piece just *glows*, painting its pictures with subtle changes of color and mood. It's storytelling music, but very sophisticated. The sound attained here was very influential on artists like Michael Hoenig, Cluster, Eberhard Schoener, and Chris Carter.

The 4½-minute "Wahn" is a major surprise, with jolting drums and percussion accompanied by supremely twisted, Dadaesque vocalizing. It's loud, with a lot of echo and stereo-effect madness, and is quite inventive, rivaling the wildest of Ron Geesin. Unfortunately, there's nothing else like it in the band's repertoire.

The sound of the recording is excellent, with some hiss. The Sequel remaster restores the music's dynamism and subtle stereo separation. The attention-getting cover, a Monique Froese painting of a baby's face in the center of an abstract universe, is one of their best, reinforcing the strong mystery of the music of *Atem*.

PHAEDRA. Released February 1974. Virgin import (remaster).

Recorded in December of 1973, *Phaedra* is a space music classic and one of the band's most important releases. Here the emphasis shifts away from the instrumentation of guitars and drums, and toward that of sculpting a keyboard-dominated vocabulary consisting of Moog and VCS3 synths, mellotron, organ, and electric piano. Each of the three group members now adopts keyboards as their primary instrument. Edgar Froese, who produced the album, adds brief electric guitar and bass guitar textures.

Phaedra is notable for several reasons. The sound of the group is a cutting-edge mix of styles, retaining surreal and psychedelic flavors, but also adding a variety of impressionistic moods and a classical storytelling structure. The mix of the various keyboards is seamless and elusive, creating a tranquil sound that occasionally evokes a transcendent spiritual mood, but also often makes it difficult to tell what specific instruments are being played. The fluency of the keyboard tapestries is not slick, however, but rather experimental, having been successfully mixed in the studio, with the band finding their way as they went along. *Phaedra*'s stereo mix (the band's most advanced production up to that point) provides the music with a high degree of theatricality and drama via a large amount of phasing and pans, giving the music an enigmatic quality.

The 17½-minute title track opens with rubbery chords from the Moog synth, to which is added electric piano. This shifts into a sequencer with mellotron, then into an equally rubbery basslike bottleneck guitar by Froese. The sequences resume, adding richly melodic synth tones and shivery bursts of flute by Peter Baumann. The piece becomes quite rhythmic, reaching a climax with a fluttery electronic cymbal-like sound by Christopher Franke. Some seagull-like sounds are then followed by an angelic Moog, mellotron strings, and phased electric piano. The piece concludes with a field recording of children playing in some kind of hallway, which is an excellent element to include in this kind of music. By this point Tangerine Dream had incorporated as many influences from pioneering German electronic composer Karlheinz Stockhausen as they had from Pink Floyd.

The 10-minute "Mysterious Semblance at the Strand of Nightmares" is a sweeping and thoroughly lush mellotron fest by Froese, with Baumann adding synth and electric piano. Alternately romantic and Gothic, this brilliant piece paints cinematic images of the ethereal and the ghostly; listening to it is like coming upon an apparition on a foggy night. The swooshing wind sounds produced by the keyboards are constantly in flux in the stereo mix, creating an unusually spacious and sweeping sound.

The 8-minute "Movements of a Visionary" is similarly inventive, and even more spatial. The piece begins with chaotic sounds, but finishes with an internal calm. Electronic voice echoes spit like garbled whispers, colliding and cascading in the left/right stereo field in a manner that's certainly attention getting. This moves into sprinkles of dewy, shimmering notes and a playful sequencer, along with a spacey organ. This music is very much in the style of Stockhausen (and many other "academic" electronic composers) and makes for striking headphone listening. The 2½-minute "Sequent C" is a Terry Riley–like fugue by Baumann. Minimalist flutelike keyboards are delayed until all lines disappear into one for a superbly low-key and lovely ending.

Phaedra was the first album by TD for the Virgin label, and on word of mouth alone it hit the U.K. Top 10. The high-definition super-bit-mapping remaster adds luster and detail. Strangely, Virgin has not licensed the most crucial mid-1970s TD remasters for release in the United States, despite their clear superiority to all previous editions. The sleeve design and cover by Edgar Froese features a misty cranial X-ray on a gray background, appropriate for the introspective direction the band had embarked upon with *Phaedra.*

RUBYCON. Released March 1975. Virgin import (remaster).

Rubycon is Tangerine Dream's most ambitious and artistically successful album-length thematic work. It's a quiet album of serene, soft, and caressing sounds—the epitome of lush, floating music. Consisting almost entirely of layered keyboards (mellotron, electric piano, Moog and VCS3 synths, prepared piano, organ, and ARP synth), the mix of instruments is difficult to pick apart, with all the sounds merged together in what may be the ultimate multiple keyboard composition.

The sophisticated music of the self-produced *Rubycon* takes the band's previous albums *Zeit* and *Phaedra* to the next logical step, but retains the warm, flowing, liquid feel of those discs. *Rubycon* is a work of pure abstraction, with a number of experimental sounds and avant-garde techniques, but these are all so accessible that even the most resistent listener can absorb them without conscious effort.

The 17-minute "Rubycon Part 1" and the 17½-minute "Rubycon Part 2" each feature airy, windlike drifts that are highly melodic, friendly, and soothing. The stereo mix is once again extremely enigmatic and elusive, making *Rubycon* pass like a sweet daydream. As usual, images of floating and of water predominate. The various techniques used to accomplish these sounds are complex, incorporating a number of tape effects. Edgar Froese adds a backwards tape of a guitar with echo, and both he and Christopher Franke contribute soft gong sounds. Franke and Peter Baumann scrape the strings of a grand piano with pieces of metal, place pieces of wood between the strings, and then play these sounds back at varying speeds to produce new pitches.

The sound of the Virgin high-definition remaster is a revelation for an album as subtle as *Rubycon,* restoring needed vibrancy. Monique Froese's cover photo of a deep blue pool of water is the perfect image for this harmonious music.

RICOCHET. Released November 1975. Virgin import (remaster).

Ricochet is a classic live document of Tangerine Dream at their peak, when their approach was fresh and new. Recorded in the autumn of 1975 in France and the U.K., the self-produced *Ricochet* is representative of the growing creative heights of the progressive music movement during the mid-1970s. In concert, Tangerine Dream seldom reprised their albums, choosing instead to focus on improvisations, creating keyboard-dominated electro-acoustic space music that emphasized the rock side of the band's sound. Using sequencers and electronic percussion, the group's live music was far more aggressive than that of their studio albums (like *Phaedra* and *Rubycon),* often bringing them closer to the realms of artists like Kraftwerk or Heldon.

At this point in their history Tangerine Dream were at the pinnacle of their experimentalism. They utilized not only a light show, but also (for a brief time) ballet dancers who, by improvising free-form movement, demonstrated the expressive possibilities inherent in the music. The band deployed a quadraphonic sound system, and were interested in the acoustics of venues like cathedrals for their concerts. Tangerine Dream became synonymous with state-of-the-art gear, especially in keyboard technology, often being among the first to use the very latest instruments. And, of course, in addition to modern synthesizers and sequencers, they continued to embroider their music with mellotrons, organs, electric pianos, and guitars.

The 17-minute "Ricochet Part 1" opens with a low-frequency electronic shuffling and windlike sound, from which a pulse emerges, accompanied by percussion and a repeating guitar riff. The drum sounds are very realistic and effective, almost identical to an acoustic kit. An interruption of spatial sounds of speeded-up babbling voices is an unexpected, welcome element. A whirlwind of percussion and a heavy sequencer kick in, with tasty guitar licks and a series of lead synth lines over them. Finally, loud and relentless drum patterns carry the piece to its conclusion.

The 21-minute "Ricochet Part 2" begins with 2½ outstanding minutes of piano and flute-like mellotron, creating a lovely and gentle serenity. Sunny rhythmic textures then take over, with a series of sparkling, liquid-like percolations and percussion. Haunting lead lines and tempo and volume changes maintain the variety. A marvelously chaotic section at the 13th minute is followed by sweet mellotrons and a spacey tapestry of synths and sequencers. As usual, the transitions between the various sections are tangible evidence of Tangerine Dream's genius.

The sound is excellent, with some hiss. The Virgin remaster restores a realistic volume and a wealth of definition, particularly to the keyboards. The cover photo by Monique Froese of dead trees standing like totems on a seashore, with the sun creeping out from behind one of them, is eerie and mysterious, and a suitable image for this music.

STRATOSFEAR. Released November 1976. Virgin import (remaster).

With *Stratosfear,* Tangerine Dream once again proved that at this point in their history they had the Midas touch, and could effortlessly produce timeless recordings such as this one. By now a very clear language for their compositional style had been developed, and *Stratosfear* is among the most popular and palatable albums in the band's catalog. There are an abundance of acoustic instruments here, so it's a mistake to view this era of Tangerine Dream as solely electronic. With the touch of conventional instrumentation, *Stratosfear* fits comfortably alongside other prog rock delights from 1976, such as Schicke, Führs and Fröhling's *Symphonic Pictures* and the two releases that year by Genesis, *A Trick of the Tail* and *Wind and Wuthering.*

Rich with melodicism and imagery, the music of *Stratosfear* is intelligently done, and has a spiritual side, defining both the band at this time and the period. In addition to the usual array of keyboards (mellotrons, Moog synths, electric piano, and organ), Christopher Franke contributes harpsichord and percussion; and Edgar Froese makes the largest acoustic contributions, with 12- and 6-string guitars, grand piano, mouth organ, and bass guitar.

The 10½-minute title track opens with Froese's lushly melodic 12-string guitar and mellotron, and is reminiscent of the textures of Genesis's "Entangled." This leads into rapid-fire sequencers and soaring lead Moog lines that continually move the melody to new plateaus. Percussion by Franke is added, followed by an electric piano solo of the theme by Peter Baumann and stray guitar chords from Froese. By current standards the percolating sequenced rhythms are simple, but these were a revelation at the time. The lead analog keyboard lines glow with a warm feeling and have a large harmonic range. A brief but startling and searing electric guitar chord winds the piece down for a reprisal of the opening, which concludes the track.

The 4½-minute "The Big Sleep in Search of Hades" is a highlight, and one of the band's most interesting tracks. Featuring harpsichord, bass guitar, and flute-like mellotrons, the piece creates a baroque/ Elizabethan/Renaissance-era ambience, rich with memorable melody and high drama. A center section of dreamy keyboards of all kinds is more modern, creating haunting and ghostly sounds before returning to the baroque flavors.

The 9-minute "3 AM at the Border of the Marsh from Okefenokee" opens with an ethereal mouth organ, with very sparse swooshes of Moog pulses and soft percussion. Building up with organ and mellotron, it becomes a dark, rhythmic bog of murky keyboards, with very spacey and lazy lead soloing lines. The piece has a hint of loneliness to it. A nice but brief touch of electronic animal-like sounds appears, then the piece returns to Froese's mouth organ and ethereal Moog synth for the final fade-out.

The 11½-minute "Invisible Limits" begins with stereo trade-offs of synth blips, with quiet atmospheres of Moog, mellotron, and electric piano. A brief drum buildup and attention-getting psychedelic chords lead into an active, nimble section of rhythms and solos, with very brief touches of Froese's acoustic guitar. In the closing section the piece falls into a formless and chaotic drift before switching to a sweet finale of grand piano and mellotron.

The sound of the Virgin remaster is smooth and vibrant. The colorful photomontage of sky and land by Cooke-Key Associates is the ideal cover imagery for this album. Unfortunately, the superb inner LP gatefold photography by Monique Froese was not reproduced for the CD booklet.

ENCORE. Released October 1977. Virgin.

A double live album recorded in North America during March and April of 1977, this 71-minute disc is a solid and well recorded release that's perhaps equal to Tangerine Dream's 1975 live album *Ricochet,* but does not surpass it. Very different indeed from the electro-acoustic heights of *Stratosfear, Encore* marks the era when the focus began shifting toward a greater reliance on electronics. Digital synths, Oberheim synth, and vocoder were added to the usual array of keyboards, and of the three band members, only Edgar Froese continued to play any instruments other than keyboards (in this case, electric guitar). The band's tendency toward sequenced rhythms was becoming a more and more prominent part of their instrumentation, and this would eventually lead their music down more pedestrian paths by the 1980s.

Encore was the final release by the trio of Froese, Christopher Franke, and Peter Baumann. Despite the band's internal friction and the embrace of colder rhythms, the trade-offs between the members in the live setting establish a compelling improvisational dialogue, which *Encore* captures quite well. While the melodic sections remain the best, the driving energy of the band in concert was such a contrast to the enigmatic meshes of their albums that it almost seemed as if there were two Tangerine Dreams for the fan to enjoy—a studio version and a concert version. *Encore* stands as an important document of the live TD, certainly more so than later live albums by the group.

The 16½-minute "Cherokee Lane" is the least of the album's four lengthy tracks. A loud and appreciative audience cheers as roaring electronic outer-space whooshes begin. By this point the band had developed a certain level of volume and bombast in concert to compensate for their necessarily static stage presence. An atypical TD sequencer kicks in, along with mellotron and a number of sunny lead synth lines. The piece is fun, but somewhat empty.

The 19½-minute "Monolight" begins with a rushed piano intro, accompanied by spacey electronics. After some Klaus Schulze–like chaotic sounds, an electronic drumbeat sets up a marching pace, with a memorably wistful double lead synth soloing over it. This disappears into a tempest of more chaotic electronics, out of which another rhythmic pulse emerges and dances. This leads into a brief version of "Stratosfear," which is promptly abandoned for other directions, until concluding with a reprisal of the opening.

The final two tracks are the highlights of *Encore,* and perhaps would have made a stronger single live album. The 17½-minute "Coldwater Canyon" sets up some announcing chords as a rhythm, into which Froese adds his famous ultra–space rock electric guitar solos and textures, with a penetrating space blues recalling David Gilmour or Steve Hackett. Froese's guitar performance was a staple of the band's live show, and is a major highlight, underscoring and updating the core rock and psychedelic origins of the band. The exchanges between the keys and the guitar are tense and immediate, but also supremely spacey, rewarding those listeners who may not be particularly enamored of electronics.

The 17½-minute "Desert Dream" is the most surreal and spacey track, with elusive mellotron and haunting, ghostly lead synth lines. The bell-like keyboards recall the abstract tapestries of *Rubycon,* and adds a few thumping bass notes. At around the 12th minute a lyrical lead line backed by mellotron and electric piano sews up the piece with a timeless, orchestral drama.

The sound is very loud and crisp, with the Virgin remaster adding further definition. The cover is a photo of the band onstage with their light show, inset over an American flag. To the band's detractors, the release of a double live album at this time made them just another prog rock dinosaur. In the same period of late 1977 and early 1978, double live albums were also released by Gong, Genesis, Camel, and Jethro Tull, plus a solo double studio album by Edgar Froese entitled *Ages*. This was viewed as excessive, and the band's reputation as an ultra-hip underground phenomenon was damaged. Athough at the time this criticism was unfair, later, in the 1980s, when the band had released scores of film soundtracks and four more live albums (including yet another double), that charge was right on target.

FORCE MAJEURE. Released June 1979. Griffin.

After 1978's lackluster but interesting *Cyclone,* Tangerine Dream released the last of their 1970s classics, *Force Majeure,* in 1979. Surprisingly, this is a return to the world of guitars and drums, giving the band their most polished and mainstream sound, similar to that of Pink Floyd's *Wish You Were Here*. Composed, produced, and mixed by Edgar Froese and Christopher Franke, the album was recorded in the fall of 1978 with drummer Klaus Krieger (who had joined the band with the *Cyclone* album). *Force Majeure* is full of good ideas, which all go by rather quickly. It's also perhaps the band's most popular album, as it was released when the group was at a peak of popularity with audiences, having produced a spectacularly prolific run of high-quality releases over the last decade.

The active 18½-minute title track has an attention-getting opening of liquid-like futuristic synths, mournful, soft pulses of voices, and bird call–like notes, all forming a classical suitelike structure. This moves into a bass pulse, followed by a breezy piano/guitar/drums workout that is reminiscent of Clearlight, Atlas, and Mike Oldfield circa *Platinum*. These polished textures are embellished by Froese's multiple acoustic guitars (a most welcome element). Krieger's simple yet crisp drumbeats set the stage for some mellow but up-front electric guitar soloing from Froese. The main theme, played by the keyboards, is memorable and quite enjoyable. The piece dissolves into a series of haunting synth effects and the sound of a train, leading to some rich and sunny synth textures, followed by perky rhythms.

The 7½-minute "Cloudburst Flight" opens with a very spacey and Pink Floyd–like acoustic guitar, with a soft keyboard background. This is replaced by bright, *Stratosfear*-like lead synth lines with Krieger's drums and percussion. After the soaring keyboard soloing plateaus, Froese's spacey electric guitar takes over, but in the final analysis his playing is too restrained. Some sweet synth solos that presage the later *Green Desert* conclude the track.

The 14½-minute "Thru Metamorphic Rocks" is led by a haunting, processed piano with synth, conjuring a watery scene. Krieger's drums kick in, and Froese solos some more on electric guitar, but again is too safe and mellow. The piece disappears into *Ricochet/Tangram*-like whooshes and pulses, joined by Krieger's percussion and strange voices. One can almost see the exploding colors of the light and laser show that would accompany a live performance of this section. The piece becomes a swirling void, throwing in a few wolf cries as it dances along. This track is a forerunner of the techno/ambient genre of the 1990s.

The sound quality is excellent throughout this recording, and the outstanding cover art by Monique Froese depicts the vanishing points of a vortex—ideal for the fantasy themes of the song titles. 1980's *Tangram* continues the sunny textures of *Force Majeure* and is a recommendably solid album, but adds nothing new of any significance, instead concentrating on synthesizers, eliminating the drums (Krieger had left the band, despite improving his performance considerably after *Cyclone),* and lightening even further Froese's already too mellow guitar playing.

HYPERBOREA. Released November 1983. Virgin.

After a number of distinctly mediocre albums in the early 1980s (*Exit, White Eagle, Logos Live at the Dominion),* Tangerine Dream released their final significantly progressive work, *Hyperborea,* at the end of 1983. By this point the band was virtually all electronic, and had been so for some time. Organs and mellotrons (and increasingly even Edgar Froese's guitar) were no longer utilized, and like post-1970s Klaus Schulze, the Tangerine Dream of the 1980s put a growing reliance on digital electronics, sacrificing much of the warmth and atmosphere that had for so long characterized their style of music.

While this same criticism could be applied to *Hyperborea,* here these digital changes make a far more convincing case for their new direction, notably bringing about a postmodern evolution and development—that is, a progression—of the Tangerine Dream sound and approach. This is very much a storytelling form of music, in the fashion of their 1970s classics. Similar to Edgar Froese's *Pinnacles* (which was released three months earlier), *Hyperborea*'s electronics flow quite well, move at a nonthreatening pace, and radiate a warm glow. Appropriately, the album's title is a term from Greek mythology about a land of sunshine known as Hyperborea. The lineup for this album consists of Froese, Christopher Franke, and Johannes Schmoelling, a member since 1980's *Tangram*.

The 9-minute "No Man's Land" opens with a Middle Eastern drone, adding active electronic tabla percussion that dances from one channel to the other. Over this, twitchy and jittery synth lines unfold like a nervous pulse. The effect of these elements is a rather musical form of high-tech raga, and the structure keeps it from sounding overly cold. The 8½-minute title track is a more slowly unfolding structure, with serene and mournful lead lines that sway to and fro, painting a vast, chilly landscape. The 4-minute "Cinnamon Road" is a loud and rhythmic piece with some good ideas, but the redundant themes and cold percussion are not very endearing. The track is useful, though, as an example of the direction the band would take for the next ten years.

The 20-minute "Sphinx Lightning" opens with jarring, trebly, announcing chords, leading into a lengthy section of choppy electronic percussion. Halfway through, this dissolves into a center section of serene notes that are disarmingly sweet and relaxing, recalling the title track. The piece returns to the sequencers and percussion sounds heard earlier, which carry on until the final fade-out. The track is padded, to be sure, but it's an epic updating of the early Tangerine Dream sound, albeit overly futuristic and less spacey.

The outstanding sound of the Virgin remaster is crystal-clear, with a richness of tone and realistic volume. Monique Froese's superb cover art is a circular inset photo of ice floes floating on blue water, with a sunlike orb composed of rippling, golden-hued liquid hovering above. Beneath the artwork sits a crass bar code, effectively ruining the effect of Froese's fantastic images.

GREEN DESERT. Released January 1986. Sequel/Castle.

Recorded in 1973 after the *Atem* album and before *Phaedra* by Edgar Froese and Christopher Franke (third member Peter Baumann was on a temporary leave from the group), *Green Desert* is an essential addition to the TD canon, and a real treat for fans of that era of the band. Remixed in 1984 by Froese (who added a small amount of unobtrusive synth embellishments), this is one of their more rock-driven albums, employing Froese's electric guitar and Franke's drum kit. As a result of this instrumentation, the recording is rather compelling. The album, in general, actually recalls the sound of *Force Majeure* (albeit far more subdued), and Franke's drum performance recalls his playing on *Alpha Centauri,* being in the same space rock style as Harold Grosskopf's drumming for Klaus Schulze.

It's curious that an album of the caliber of *Green Desert* was kept on the shelf for so long. The group ceased work on it when they began recording *Phaedra,* a project they preferred. At the time the band was unusually prolific, so that even strong efforts like *Green Desert* could be set aside. It's interesting to speculate as to whether the success of the band on Virgin Records in 1974 would have been greater had *Green Desert* been released along with *Phaedra* as a double album.

The smooth 19½-minute title track of the album opens with a Pink Floyd/*Atom Heart Mother*–like rumble, evolving into classic keyboard space music textures. At the fourth minute Franke's drums enter, with a slow, deliberate tempo and stereo miking that instantly recalls "Fly and Collision of Comas Sola" from *Alpha Centauri.* The pace and volume of the keyboards and drums increase, with Froese adding some minor and mellow electric guitar. It's a classic of electro-acoustic raga.

The 5-minute "White Clouds" is a combination of airy and breezy synths with drums, conveying a floating feeling as indicated by the piece's title. The 7-minute "Astral Voyager'" puts an active sequencer pulse to shooting and soaring lead synth lines. The piece bounces along attractively, with bird song–like notes that are colorful and luscious. The 7-minute "Indian Summer" is a warmer glow of sweet, recorder-like synth notes, evoking windy outdoor images.

The sound of this Sequel remaster is excellent. The new cover photo by Monique Froese of a colorful balloon is not preferable to her original cover art for the 1986 release on the Relativity label, which was a serene fantasyland set in the desert.

TEENAGE JESUS AND THE JERKS

EVERYTHING. Released 1995. Atavistic.

Recorded live in New York City in late 1977 and originally released as part of Lydia Lunch's *Hysterie* compilation in 1986, this is a 19-minute musical assault of primitive and radical power trio noise rock that was an attempt to forge a new rock language. The goal of vocalist/guitarist/composer Lunch was to offend and repel with a minimal, impudent, dark, and extremely loud presentation in an effort that was actually as much anti-punk as it was anti-mainstream rock. In fact, she so effectively achieved her goal that *Everything* has not yet taken its place among the pantheons of the new wave revolution in popular music during the late 1970s and early 1980s.

Lydia Lunch of Teenage Jesus and the Jerks. (Photo by David Arnoff.)

Like Throbbing Gristle in the U.K. during this new wave era, Teenage Jesus and the Jerks were far, far too extreme and abrasively revolutionary for most fans of 1970s style prog rock and jazz/rock fusion, who were more comfortable at the time listening to Caravan, Al DiMeola, and Alan Parsons Project albums, and extremely uncomfortable with music like this. While the band attracted the interest of people like Brian Eno (who wanted to produce them), their music was widely rejected as unlistenable noise, and their legacy is one of a brief attempt to storm the Bastille of the popular music world.

The 20-second instrumental "Red Alert" sets the tone for the rest, with simple chord progressions and minimal rhythms played loudly and at lightning-fast pace. The 2½-minute "Orphans" is a tale of frightened children running through landscapes of bloody snow, with a marching tempo and Lunch's screechingly loud electric guitar. The thunderous 4-minute "The Closet" is equally disturbing, inspired by Lunch's background as an abused child. Increasing scales of cacophonous guitar and tortured, screaming vocals lead to some genuinely cathartic bashing. The 1½-minute "Burning Rubber" is another dark screamer, with a plodding structure that stomps everything in its path. The 3-minute "I Woke Up Dreaming" is a form similar to that of "The Closet." Maximum guitar noise, slabs of rubbery bass, and cymbal crashes create an entertaining power trio workout. The 41-second "Freud in Flop" is a very fast instrumental that goes off like an alarm. The 1½-minute "Baby Doll" is even more severe than any of the above, being another personal catharsis for Lunch. The 1-minute "Race Mixing" is a chopping instrumental, like a piece of steel crashing on concrete. The 42-second "Crown of Thorns" is a rhythmic assault, with castigating vocal shouts. The concluding 20-second "Red Alert MKII" is a reprisal of the first track.

In the early 1980s, artists such as Glenn Branca, the early Sonic Youth, and Massacre would incorporate elements of Teenage Jesus's gritty and adrenalin-driven approach into their instrumental rock forms.

Lunch disbanded the band in 1979, embarking on an eclectic solo career that has encompassed more conventional punk/alternative rock forms. Unfortunately she seems to have given up her raucous guitar playing. More recently, she's been a spoken word performance artist, constantly taunting the establishment with her confrontational delivery and provocative sexuality.

Everything also contains two obscure bonus tracks, "My Eyes" and "Less of Me," neither of which sound anything like the blitzkrieg of the live material. The cover is a black-and-white photo of Lunch from 1977, and the disc's sound quality is excellent.

DR. FIORELLA TERENZI

MUSIC FROM THE GALAXIES. Released July 1991. Island.

Fiorella Terenzi is an astrophysicist and musician who had the novel idea of collecting radio waves emitted from celestial bodies, translating them into numbers via a computer program, and then converting them with a synthesizer into an audible collection of mysterious whooshes that are, literally, the sounds of the galaxies. This "acoustic astronomy" (as Terenzi refers to it) creates a huge sound of new timbres, running the gamut from the loud, shrill, and shrieking to the pulsing, oozing, and cascading. The result is a unique highlight of 1990s experimentalism.

While Terenzi's disc originates with her scientific research rather than from any influences in the musical world, the sound often recalls the early synthesizer experiments of Klaus Schulze (particularly *Cyborg)* and Tangerine Dream (*Alpha Centauri*'s "Fly and Collision of Comas Sola"), and can therefore take its place beside these and other space music and musique concrète projects. The disc's seven pieces, ranging in length from 2 to 11 minutes, all evoke vast expanses, due mainly to the imaginative stereo mix, a very wide and spatial soundstage across which the various sounds are phased and panned. This gives the album one of the strongest opt-out sounds extant—so much so that it's actually frightening at times. Produced by Terenzi, this full digital recording has an incredible dynamic range, requiring caution when played at a high volume.

The titles of the pieces indicate the various moods, such as "Stellar Wind," "Collision," and "Plasma Waves." The sound of these pieces generally consists of huge whirring and whooshing patterns. The 7-minute "Cosmic Time," co-created by Terenzi with engineer and mixer Gordon Bahary, is an attractive combination of music with the whooping, whirring sounds, and is a highlight. The cover art is a truly awful and garish illustration that ought to be replaced with something more suitable.

TERPANDRE

TERPANDRE. Released March 1981. Musea import.

Terpandre were a French prog rock band whose sole album is a gem of instrumental symphonic rock. The album was recorded in August of 1978, but the group didn't immediately get a record deal and had disbanded by the time of its eventual release in 1981. The instrumentation of this sextet is built from the foundation of two keyboardists (playing acoustic and electric piano, synths, mellotron, and clavinet) and a rhythm section, and is occasionally rounded out by an electric guitarist and electric violinist. The core of the band's interaction, though, is between the keyboards and the bass and drums, and their romantic and melodic music is strongly in the European prog rock tradition, recalling Schicke, Führs and Fröhling, Shylock, and the 1976–1977 era of Genesis.

The 7-minute "Le Temps" begins with an odd clicking effect that leads into an overture-like orchestral arrangement of its theme, then kicks into a tight and fast groove with lively percussion, rhythm guitar, and synth leads. This is followed by a violin solo, a romantic piano interlude, and finally a recapitulation of the theme. The 5-minute "Conte en Vert" is a lyrical highlight. Medium in tempo and rich with romanticism, the piece's memorable structure of dreamy keyboard melodies (played on the mellotron and electric piano) punctuated by the rhythm section is the very definition of the Euro-prog symphonic sound. The style of the lovely 5½-minute "Anne-Michaele" is so seamlessly matched with the preceding track that the two could be taken as movements in a mini-symphony of sorts, with gorgeous and baroque mellotrons and piano.

The 6-minute "Histoire d'un Pecher" has a playful ensemble pace, and its synth/bass/drums dynamics recall Clearlight and Genesis. The 13-minute "Carousel" opens with some snarling electric guitar, which gives way to handsome sections of mellotron, percussion, and especially solo piano. The transitions between sections are smooth, and the piece paints many scenic landscapes.

Two bonus live tracks from 1977 are included, but these are marred by appalling sound quality, unlike the rest of the disc, which sounds fantastic. The appealing cover photo by Pierre Chassain of a hazy lake scene evokes the pastoral, melodic qualities of Terpandre's music.

THIRD EAR BAND

ALCHEMY. Released June 1969. Demon import.

Along with Pink Floyd and King Crimson, Third Ear Band is a legendary group from the very early era of progressive music, one whose odyssey continues up to the present day. They began as a psychedelic rock outfit in 1967–1968, but after their equipment was stolen one night, they decided the best thing to do was go acoustic. The music that emerged was an instrumental fusion of Indian raga and classical chamber music, with a modern sensibility, that exuded dreamy opt-out qualities. Their debut album, *Alchemy,* from the summer of 1969, is a classic of authentic hippie space music that was and remains quite popular. The group was fashionable enough to open for John Lennon and Yoko Ono at the Royal Albert Hall in early 1969, and to play the free concerts in Hyde Park with the Rolling Stones and Blind Faith that summer. They then signed a three-record deal with EMI's Harvest label, which was also the home of Pink Floyd.

Glen Sweeney of Third Ear Band. (Photo by Lucia Baldini.)

The lineup on *Alchemy* is Glen Sweeney (tabla, hand drums, wind chimes), Paul Minns (oboe, recorder), and Richard Coff (violin, viola), with guest Mel Davis (cello, slide pipes). The performances are masterful, and the music achieves an intensity that makes it a potent, other-dimensional, and mysterious brew, conducive to introspection and meditation.

The 6½-minute "Mosaic" introduces the group's spacey sound. A tabla pulse, sitarlike viola plucks, and textural oboe and cello solos create a seductive, snake-charming aura. The 10½-minute "Ghetto Raga" begins with a wistful intro of pipes, strings, and oboe, then becomes a melancholy raga with hand drums and sinewy wind instruments. Listening is like taking a magic carpet ride over a barren desert. The piece builds to an edgy climax of tension and drama with an oboe solo. The 3½-minute "Druid One" follows; it's a friendly aria, with lovely, caressing notes from the strings and wind instruments. The 3½-minute "Stone Circle" features dense, unified group interaction, led by oboe and simple percussion.

The 9-minute "Egyptian Book of the Dead" begins with ethereal wind chimes, very subtle strings, and recorder, creating a floating feeling. This evolves into a sparse raga with hand drums and violin. The piece strongly recalls the sound achieved on parts of Vicki Richards's *Parting the Waters* (see review). The 8½-minute "Area Three" is a darker, moodier tone poem, with strings and wind instruments that switch to the usual raga form with tabla and a subdued oboe. The $5\frac{1}{2}$-minute "Dragon Lines" mixes a medieval, classical style with raga forms. Ending the album on a joyful note, the $2\frac{1}{2}$-minute "Lark Rise" is a playful, Celtic-style dance.

The sound is excellent, with a gritty, live-sounding feel and extreme stereo separation that underscores the music's spacey qualities. The cover is a drawing by Dave Loxley of a medieval alchemist.

THIRD EAR BAND. Released May 1970. BGO import.

The second Third Ear Band album is a crucial early progressive classic, evoking the elemental power of acoustic music. The group is in peak form, performing four lengthy tracks that are a part of a conceptual theme constructed around the four elements of earth, air, fire, and water. The chamber music side of the band is emphasized, along with a strong sense of the spiritual. The lineup of *Alchemy* returns, now joined by fourth member Ursula Smith on cello. *Third Ear Band* is the group's best-sounding album, with rich production values. Glen Sweeney's percussion has much more power than on *Alchemy,* and the mix of Paul Minns's oboe, Richard Coft's violin and viola, and Smith's cello creates complex and delicate floating music. Released originally by EMI around the same time as the Beatles' *Let It Be,* this was a high-profile title, an opt-out album that received a lot of play within countercultural circles.

The $10\frac{1}{2}$-minute "Air" opens with ethereal wind sounds, with Sweeney's bubbling stereo percussion beats gently coming in until becoming loud enough to be the center of the listener's focus. Minns's oboe and Coff's violin then trade off airy solos. The 10-minute "Earth" is a traditionally flavored, folksier piece, playful and friendly. The string instruments are plucked like guitars, picking up with light percussion and becoming a sprightly jig.

The 9-minute "Fire" is a dense and heavy raga, with each of the band members playing nonstop throughout. Its drones are relentless and detailed. The 7-minute "Water" opens with very soft ocean waves, subtly bringing in pulses from the strings. The percussion lays down a mild raga beat, joined by mournful strings and oboe, creating a somber but relaxing mood, then concludes with a fade-out of sea sounds.

The cover art by Hipgnosis is a photo of thick white clouds above a landscape, tinted with deep hues, underscoring the floating feel of the music.

MUSIC FROM MACBETH. Released January 1972. BGO import.

Recorded in 1971 for director Roman Polanski's superb film of the famed Shakespeare play, this was the final release by the original Third Ear Band. This much-beloved album functions as both a soundtrack and a regular group release. The lineup here retains original members Paul Minns (oboe, recorder) and Glen Sweeney (percussion), and expands with Paul Buckmaster (cello, bass guitar), Simon House (violin, VCS3 synth) and Denim Bridges (guitars). Despite the incorporation of electric instrumentation, *Music from Macbeth* actually emphasizes the classical side of the group, going in some different directions from the previous albums but without drastically changing the sound of the band.

The album consists of 16 shorter pieces, exploring baroque, medieval, and Renaissance-era styles, plus traditional music, orchestral passages, and some rather avant-garde moments as well. The disc's booklet provides lengthy descriptions of where each particular track fits into the play, and the various pieces do, in fact, conjure up the images suggested by their titles.

The 4-minute "Overture" takes the usual Third Ear Band sound of hand drums, oboe, and strings and very sparsely adds jagged bass guitar, electric guitar, and synth. The sound created is dark, tense, and menacing. The 2-minute "The Beach" is odd and ethereal, combining violin textures with environmental sounds. The 1-minute "Inverness: Macbeth's Return/The Preparation Fanfare/ Duncan's Arrival" features playful percussion, acoustic guitar, and oboe and violin workouts, with haunting call-and-response fanfares of multitracked oboe with gurgling synth. The $1\frac{1}{2}$-minute "The Banquet" adds a mellow electric guitar to the group's usual raga sound, until the piece collapses into the sound of thunder. The $2\frac{1}{2}$-minute "Dagger and Death" has stinging electric guitar notes, with grinding strings, dark synth, and nimble percussion.

The 3-minute "Court Dance" begins with some playful bird song effects on oboe before taking off into an authentically executed medieval jig. The 4-minute "Fleance" is a real treat, with acoustic guitar, recorder, and percussion accompanying an adolescent male voice (unidentified in the credits) singing a romantic Elizabethan song. An unexpected and brilliant touch, the piece makes you feel like you've just stepped into the 16th century. The 3-minute "The Cauldron" is unusual, with subtle synth percolations, guitar atmospheres, cymbals, and dark strings. The 1½-minute "Prophecies" is equally strange, with wind chimes, whistles, percussion, growling synth, and stray violin plucks, ending with the smashing of glass. The 1½-minute "Wicca Way" puts a simple, repeated guitar riff to strings and hand drums, building to a tense climax until it ends rather suddenly.

The sound quality is very good throughout, with some hiss. The cover art is by Roger Dean, who departs from the style of his famous colorful sleeves (for Yes) with an ultra-Gothic painting of three witches.

After a 16-year absence, Sweeney reconfigured a new Third Ear Band lineup in 1988. This group mainly revisits the raga tradition of the original band, while adding a few new elements (such as high-tech guitar atmospheres), and remains true to the purity of the genre of raga, even incorporating jazz and world music influences. The best release by this new lineup is their latest, a concert recording entitled *Live,* released in 1996 by Voiceprint.

THISTLE

THISTLE. Released 1996. Ventricle.

The debut release by the American duo Thistle is a surprising return to the ultra-surreal, being a contemporary form of psychedelic, flower-child mysticism. The group is fronted by the completely tripped-out voice and lyrics of a woman known only as Danielle, whose luminous feminine mystique recalls Gong's Gilli Smyth, and also Fifty Foot Hose's "Cauldron." Music, instruments, and production are by Kelly, the other single-name member of the duo, and the compositions use no rhythm, creating a totally abstract sound that alternates between the dark and the sweet. Consisting entirely of keyboards and Danielle's voice, the various sounds are processed, phased, and panned ad infinitum, producing a nonstop stereo fantasyland. While this over-reliance on effects betrays a conscious lack of variety, the duo does achieve a purely enigmatic and mysterious form of music.

The 5½-minute "Circle Star" sets the tone for the disc. Ethereal stereo-panned synths, church organ, and Gothic vocal whispers create a feeling of floating. The 3½-minute "Leaves Caught in My Hair" continues the mood, with church organ and heavily distorted vocals. All the sounds are swirled together until they become blurry and extremely strange. By the time the 5½-minute "The Department of Cloud Control Department" begins, one realizes that these bizarre effects have taken over the form of the album. The piece even employs moments of silence. The 3-minute "The Chambermaids" is an obscure spoken vocal with foghorn-like atmospheres. The 6-minute "And Then There Were Two" is more of a collage construction than a real song, consisting of windlike swooshes and various vocal effects.

The 5½-minute "These Things . . . (May Not Be the Usual Things)" begins with a fantastic stereo recording of a crackling fire, adding murky keyboard atmospheres and an obscured vocal, until disappearing into a thunderous cacophony of sheets of white noise. The 8-minute "A Glitch in Time" consists of industrial rumbles, far-off screams, and a Gothic organ that recalls something out of a Vincent Price/*Dr. Phibes* horror film. The remaining two pieces, "The Stars Pinned the Black Sheets to the Wall" and "Remember," continue in the vein of the previous tracks.

Thistle is similar to Mauve Sideshow and Torn Curtain, two other bands on the Ventricle label. Thistle is preferable to those artists, and more accessible by comparison. The sound quality is very good, and certainly makes for ideal headphone listening due to the variety of effects. The outstanding cover photos by Carmen Resendez of a young girl in the thistle of a forest of woods is the ideal romantic image for this surreal music.

THROBBING GRISTLE

THE SECOND ANNUAL REPORT OF THROBBING GRISTLE. Released December 1977. Mute/Elektra.

The legacy of the legendary group Throbbing Gristle is unique in the history of modern music. From the year of their initial formation in 1976 until well after their dissolution in 1981, the band seldom received acclaim or even acceptance, a state of affairs which continues to this day in many circles. What's most notable about Throbbing Gristle is that they took progressive music forms to their logical, end-game conclusion, to an aesthetic realm of pure improvisation, a musical world ruled by collage, nonlinear forms, parody, and noise. This was—and still is—a radical idea, as the music world wasn't—and isn't—ready for it.

Throbbing Gristle consisted of four unique individuals. Genesis P. Orridge, lead vocalist, bass guitarist, and violinist, was the quintessential agent provocateur, bringing an outspoken fanaticism to the group's approach and giving them an impudent, anti-establishment edge that threatened a dangerous extremism. For many, he was the persona of the band. Cosey Fanni Tutti was very much the naughty English pin-up girl, with a cleverness and charm that helped balance Orridge's more extreme moments. Her style of anti-technique electric guitar playing is exceptional, and one of the band's most interesting elements. Chris Carter was the electronics expert and musical backbone of the group, a behind-the-scenes figure. Were it not for TG's unconventional musical direction, Carter could have convincingly joined Tangerine Dream. Peter Christopherson designed trippy album covers for the Hipgnosis company, including many prog rock sleeves. He brought the group's collage experiments to the fore, with his tape techniques being a forerunner of modern sampling. The other three members adopted these techniques, incorporating them with their other instruments.

They worked entirely outside the music industry, and their first album, *The Second Annual Report,* was released on their own label, Industrial Records. While it isn't their best album, and probably would have meant very little if they had never released anything else, *The Second Annual Report* is easily one of the most out-in-left-field recordings in music history. The extremely primitive mix (with no overdubs) is totally outside that of any conventional forms. The band's intent at this early stage of their history was to create music devoid of entertainment value, and, looking back, it's hard to see how they established an audience base with this album.

The 1-minute "Industrial Introduction" is a machine-like hum (hence the term "industrial") that starts slowly and then builds, leading into the low-fi 4½-minute "Slug Bait," recorded in October of 1976. Rubbery grinding noises and rumbles churn along as Orridge relates a twisted tale. In its mix, all is obscured, as if intentionally, including any remnants of musicality. No listener at the time could have had any idea of what was going on. The second track, also titled "Slug Bait," is 2½ minutes recorded live in May of 1977. Bass guitar riffs play ominously in one channel, while in the other skids some shrieking race car–like electronics, with a collage of media voices. On the third track, again entitled "Slug Bait," 1 minute of dark and gloomy electronics accompanies slabs of low-frequency rumbles and more voices, including that of a serial killer.

Four tracks, each entitled "Maggot Death," are next. The first, 3 minutes recorded live in May of 1977, features formless patterns of squeaks, obscure voices, bass, and grinding noises. The effect is like turning a radio dial across several channels of the broadcast spectrum. The next 4½ minutes, recorded in the studio, consist of churning sounds and grisly grinding noises, with stereo pans of voices and chainsaw-like guitar shrieks. A 1½-minute piece of bassy rhythms and electronic pulses with more odd voices follows; this concludes with 1 minute recorded live at a Throbbing Gristle gig, where a crowd of unruly punters chastises the band by taking control of the microphone.

The highlight of the album is the 20-minute "After Cease to Exist," recorded in July of 1977. Totally different from the chaos of the first half of the disc, this is actually a piece of ambient space music, not unlike the more experimental sections of Pink Floyd's "A Saucerful of Secrets," but with a Henry Cow–like sensibility. Soft tones of synths and stray chords of guitar and bass, plus other effects, begin an embryonic buildup, adding light buzzing sounds and voices, just drifting until the final fadeout. Like other prog groups of the era,

Throbbing Gristle was manipulating a huge mass of modern equipment, but the difference with TG was their embrace of unpredictability, letting the equipment participate in the composition. This piece is the precursor to their later ambient album, *In the Shadow of the Sun* (see review below).

Two singles from this period are included as bonus tracks. "Zyclon B Zombie" is a dark, off-putting mix of grinding, machine-like electronics and a distorted lead vocal. On the other hand, "United" is a very important track, a forerunner of the techno-dance sounds of the 1980s and 1990s. An ultra-slick dance song, with a beat, chorus, high-tech glossy production, and a reasonably conventional lead vocal, this sounds like an entirely different group. The origin of both schools of the industrial genre (the experimental noise aesthetic and the techno-disco dance aesthetic) can be traced to these singles.

The remastered sound (mixed by Carter) works wonders for this album, restoring needed clarity. The cover is a minimal white sleeve with only the title and recording date printed in the center. It's a

Throbbing Gristle.

sign of some progress that this and other TG albums are now available in America through Mute/Elektra, a Time/Warner company.

D.O.A. Released December 1978. Mute/Elektra.

D.O.A. is the most varied and diverse Throbbing Gristle album, having a broad appeal and strong production values. Belying the threatening image the band was by then associated with (which they often cultivated), this unique disc virtually defined cutting-edge experimentalism for a long time, incorporating collage, live concert madness, and electronics, and did so in an amusing and approachable way. The group's playful sense of inspired amateurism created an atmosphere in which there was no preconceived notion of what an album should be. This sense of liberation is at the heart of progressive music, and TG was as formidable a creative force as Pink Floyd or Yes, assuming the underground mantle of progressive experimentation in the late 1970s and early 1980s that those supergroups had worn in the late 1960s and early 1970s. In fact, like Pink Floyd's *Ummagumma* and Yes's *Fragile, D.O.A.* displays four solo sections, one by each member.

The 2½-minute "I.B.M." features fragments of droning and bleeping machines, adding ominous keyboards, voices, and guitar screeches. The 2½-minute "Hit by a Rock" is a live track recorded in September of 1977, led by bass, synths, and Genesis P. Orridge's deadpan vocal. "United" is 16 seconds of a speeded-up tape effect. The 4-minute "Valley of the Shadow of Death" is Peter Christopherson's solo track. A work of pure collage, it incorporates voices, traffic sounds, dishes, the ticking of a clock, and other stray sounds. By current standards it's unremarkable, but at the time of its release it was a novelty. The 6-minute "Dead on Arrival" is another live cut, recorded in London in May of 1978. This piece establishes an atypical TG style; it features large, clunking, repetitive electronic rhythms by Chris Carter and savage guitar slashes by Cosey Fanni Tutti, creating a strange, teeth-grinding, cutting sound. The 5½-minute "Weeping" is Orridge's solo track, and one of his best. The piece uses four types of acoustic violins run through a space echo unit, exploring soft plucks and resonances, and adding a depressed, nasal vocal. The track recalls the eccentricity of Ron Geesin.

The 4-minute "Hamburger Lady" is an irritating, gangly jangle of electronics, bass, and guitar, with Orridge's odd vocal swamped with effects. The 3½-minute "Hometime" is Cosey's solo moment, and a definite highlight. Impressionistic and minimal guitar atmospheres combine with drifting collage sounds of a young girl's voice and laughter. The mood of this piece also recalls Ron Geesin (in this case, his soundtrack to the 1971 film *Sunday, Bloody Sunday).* The 4-minute "AB/7A" is Carter's solo track, consisting of very foreground harsh electronics and rhythms, recalling Heldon and Richard Pinhas. The piece, however, lacks development. The 4-minute "E. Coli" is a highlight; the voice of a clinician discussing bacteria, heavily altered with stereo effects, is accompanied by droning synth pulses and slide guitar. The piece recalls Djam Karet's "Consider Figure Three" from *Suspension and Displacement.* "Death Threats" is half a minute of slightly garbled vitriol taken off the band's answering machine. The 3-minute "Walls of Sound" lives up to its title, being a torrent of noise recorded live at various locations in the U.K. The concluding 1-minute "Blood on the Floor," also live, has a chugging pace and deadpan vocals by Orridge.

D.O.A. contains two singles from the period as bonus tracks. Both "Five Knuckle Shuffle" and "We Hate You (Little Girls)" are examples of Throbbing Gristle at their most off-putting, with noisy electronics and screaming vocals. The sound quality of *D.O.A.* is excellent, with very crisp separation. The cover is a photo of a young girl sitting by her home stereo, with an inset photo of the same girl with her skirt up.

20 JAZZ FUNK GREATS. Released December 1979. Mute/Elektra.

20 Jazz Funk Greats is Throbbing Gristle's most popular, polished, and accessible album, and also one of their most musical. Like *D.O.A.*, this is surprisingly diverse, and includes what seemed like unlikely directions for the group, such as space music and pop music parody. The instrumentation is also expanded, with the members playing vibes and cornet in addition to their primary instruments. The moods veer in several different directions, from Tangerine Dream–like space-outs, to Martin Denny–like exotica, to Bonzo Dog Band–via–Kraftwerk lunacy. A sense of humor prevails, and the disc is boosted considerably by the advanced production values (their best), giving it a crisp, realistic volume.

The attention-getting 2½-minute title track features thumping electronic percussion (now dated, but still enjoyable) and jazzy vocal whispers, with multiple cornets by Cosey Fanni Tutti and Peter Christopherson, while Chris Carter plays some searing lead synth lines. The 3½-minute "Beachy Head" is space music, with murky, foghorn-like atmospheres of sparse synth, and seagull sounds. The 5-minute "Still Walking" is a loud and danceable track of stereo-phased sequencers (a lot of knob twirling here), grinding guitar, and obscured, occasional vocals in the background. The 2-minute "Tanith" is more space music, and one of Genesis P. Orridge's finest musical moments, featuring rubbery bass guitar, a skidding violin, and light vibes. The amusing 5-minute "Convincing People" is a sparse pop parody led by Orridge's typical deadpan vocal delivery, Carter's simple sequencer and synth, and Cosey's fuzz-effects guitar. The 2½-minute "Exotica" is similar to "Beachy Head," with spacey synths and vibes providing an interlude of delicate, quiet music.

The 4½-minute "Hot on the Heels of Love" is the band's disco parody, with Carter's danceable electronics embellished by the sound of whip slashes. The synth notes are garish, and odd growling sounds and vibes only increase the sense of absurdity. Cosey briefly teases with a breathy, erotic whisper of the song's title, foreshadowing her later vocal style. The 6½-minute "Persuasion" is the band's most famous track, due to Orridge's hilarious lyrics and matter-of-fact vocal delivery. This song has been embraced by would-be ladies' men everywhere as an anthem, and its novelty cannot be denied. Huge slabs of meandering bass guitar—so ridiculously simple a child could play them—set the sparse, plodding tone. Occasionally jolting voice samples by Christopherson and screeching guitar notes by Cosey emphasize the song's ironic sense of erotic longing, but also suggest a hint of self-loathing.

The 3-minute "Walkabout" is another slice of Carter's much-too-foreground electronics, but with a sunny lead line recalling Tangerine Dream's *Tangram*. The 4½-minute "What a Day" is a much more polished foray into the abrasiveness of the band's earlier singles. Loud machine-like rhythms, superb guitar effects, and Orridge's screaming vocal all pass by unobtrusively. The 2-minute "Six Six Sixties" features metallic, cold electronics, with a spoken vocal by Orridge. The mood is edgy and tense, and the sound here is the precursor to the band's next studio album, *Heathen Earth*.

The two bonus tracks are both very loud live renditions of "Discipline," a concert favorite. The song was basically a chance for Orridge to provoke the audience, its impact regrettably being mainly visual. The song's noisy rhythms completely lack variation and quickly become rather irritating, but the piece does give a good indication of the bruising severity of the band's live shows.

The color cover photo of the band standing outdoors is used to humorous effect in two ways. First, anyone unfamiliar with TG might think this is an album by an actual jazz/pop combo. Secondly, the back cover has the same photo, but in black and white, and with a nude woman lying at their feet.

1980's *Heathen Earth* is another solid group effort, a conceptual/thematic work that comes recommended, though it relies too heavily on Carter's clunky, churning electronic rhythms for its sound, which becomes tedious given the lengthy running time of the tracks.

IN THE SHADOW OF THE SUN. Released February 1981. Mute import.

Recorded in 1980 as the soundtrack to a boring experimental film by Derek Jarman, this is one of Throbbing Gristle's finest releases. The album consists of an entirely improvised 57-minute track, and the band is in peak form, producing an early classic of ambient, nonlinear, instrumental space music. The group's outre image notwithstanding, the aesthetic here is the same as that found on other early ambient recordings, such as Tangerine Dream's *Zeit*. The listener is induced to float in a kind of other-dimensional dreamworld, and the level of nuance required to make music with these effect qualities is abundantly present here. The album is full of good ideas, and the transitions made throughout the piece as it unfolds are masterful.

A series of intermittent bass guitar notes and rumbles by Genesis P. Orridge joins with dewy, bell-like sounds, accompanied by stray notes and slides of spacey electric guitar by Cosey Fanni Tutti. Cosey's unconventional guitar work is notable, both moving the piece forward as well as commenting on it. Random snatches of Chris Carter's scratchy, rolling, tumbling keyboard patterns interrupt the otherwise spacey drift of the piece, but add a surreal, haunting feel. Continuing in this vein, a horror movie–like organ (recalling the 1962 film *Carnival of Souls)* enters, with scary, shivery, echoed voices by the band members coming in like screams, then resonating and fading in the distance. The piece ebbs and flows in this manner until its final fade-out.

The sound of this remaster is excellent, with a detailed mix and a wide stereo separation. The cover is a plain light grey with the title printed in the middle.

JOURNEY THROUGH A BODY. Released 1981. Mute import.

Recorded in five days in March of 1981 and composed directly onto tape in the studio, this was the final Throbbing Gristle album, and a truly experimental work that lives up to the band's reputation. Using a large amount of found sounds and a number of eclectic musical styles, this is TG at their most avant-garde. *Journey Through a Body* influenced the developing industrial genre in the U.K., with artists such as Nocturnal Emissions, Nurse with Wound, SPK, and Current 93 embracing the aesthetic approach of the album as a springboard for their experimental music.

The 15½-minute "Medicine" is a radical piece, and when played will clear the room of any nonbelievers. A very LOUD high-frequency tone opens the track, and remains for most of the piece's length, creating an on-the-edge tension. A playful but ultra-strange stereo mix of collage sounds unfolds, with crumpling paper, television and radio broadcasts, walking, rattles, and blowing sounds, all interrupted by indescribable clicks and echo chamber roars. The organization of the various sounds is chaotic but not overly cluttered. The 8-minute "Catholic Sex" has the typical TG sound of Chris Carter's chugging electronic rhythms, rubbery bass notes, cornet, voice samples, and a downbeat spoken vocal by Genesis P. Orridge, accompanied by church organ.

The 4-minute "Exotic Functions" is a bizarre but lighter-sounding Spanish-flavored type of lounge music incorporating piano, vibes, percussion, and the sound of running water (or maybe, given the title, it is a trickle of a different sort of liquid). The 8-minute "Violencia (The Bullet)" continues the Spanish flavor, with insistent piano notes, Cosey Fanni Tutti's gnarly guitar noise, and Peter Christopherson's scratchy scream effects. The 3½-minute "Oltre la Morte, Birth and Death" is a rather uncharacteristic TG track, with dual prepared pianos that create a moody and dark aura.

The sound of the disc is excellent, with some hiss. The cover is a drab and plain dark grey color, but the booklet contains a number of nice black-and-white band photos. The tracking of the disc is a botch, collecting the first two pieces onto one track, and the final three onto a second track, instead of properly dividing them.

CD1. Released September 1986. Mute import.

Recorded in March of 1979, *CD1* is one of Throbbing Gristle's most representative works. The piece consists entirely of an experimental 42-minute, untitled instrumental track, and its long form (as on their *In the Shadow of the Sun* album) allows each member to display their individual contributions to the TG sound. This is a revolutionary form of music, totally outside of all conventional structures. The only reference points for the listener in this thoroughly abstract piece are to the band's own style, and the music creates an enveloping aural environment that sounds like a transmission from outer space. The mood is neither overly dark nor harsh, but rather strange nonetheless. The group employs their usual instrumentation of electronics, electric guitar, tape effects, bass guitar, cornets, violin, and other special effects. The large foldout booklet for the disc contains essential statements by all four members regarding the aesthetic goals of this nonlinear music, as well as that of the industrial genre they founded.

The piece begins with an attention-getting blast of snarling guitar, bass, and unusual synths, creating a whirlwind/vortex/wall of sound. Cosey Fanni Tutti's unconventional, chunky guitar riffing is at the forefront on this disc, and is a highlight. Peter Christopherson adds a number of mysterious voice samples, giving the piece a dreamy, surreal quality. Chris Carter's chopping, clunky electronic rhythms somehow work better here than on albums like *Heathen Earth*, demonstrating a pure industrial aesthetic with machinelike patterns. At the halfway point the piece disappears into a spacey drift, not unlike Tangerine Dream or Pink Floyd, a precursor to *In the Shadow of the Sun*'s ambient sound. The track then returns to the dominance of Carter's rhythms, until the final fade-out.

The sound quality is excellent throughout, and the cover is the band's famous lightning bolt logo. *CD1* was the first available Throbbing Gristle compact disc (hence the title), and undoubtedly was in part responsible for the growing importance of the industrial scene in the late 1980s.

Another post-breakup TG release is the four-disc set *Throbbing Gristle Live Vols. 1–4,* released in 1993. This collection is an interesting contrast to King Crimson's four-disc live set *The Great Deceiver.* Whereas King Crimson's material was liberated somewhat in the live context, Throbbing Gristle's all-improvisational methods benefited more from the discipline of the studio environment. While this live set is a fine document of TG's concert mayhem, its extravagant length prevents it from having any chance for a wide appeal. While preferable to TG's other live album, *Mission of Dead Souls,* and a treat for fans, a one- or two-disc release would have been a wiser move.

After Throbbing Gristle disbanded, Carter and Cosey formed Chris and Cosey and Orridge and Christopherson formed Psychic TV, with Christopherson later forming the group Coil.

Steve Tibbetts. (Photo by Jonette Novak.)

STEVE TIBBETTS

STEVE TIBBETTS. Released January 1977. Cuneiform.

Written, performed, and recorded by a young Steve Tibbetts in the summer and fall of 1976 in St. Paul, Minnesota, this originally self-released recording is a classic of instrumental psychedelic progressive music from the unlikely region of grassroots middle America. (Progressive music out of St. Paul, Minnesota, seems perhaps even less likely than symphonic rock bands out of Iron Curtain–era Czechoslovakia [e.g., Collegium Musicum and Fermata].) Tibbetts, who describes his debut album as Tomita meets Leo Kottke, takes the acoustic Americana of artists like John Fahey and Kottke and places it in the druggy, psychedelic wonderland of Pink Floyd and Heldon—a thoroughly original development for the time. Because the album was recorded early in the progressive era, it's difficult to pinpoint any concrete influences (for example, in 1976 Minnesota, Tibbetts couldn't possibly have known about Heldon).

Playing electric and acoustic guitars, primitive synths, bass, and using a number of tape effects, Tibbetts makes music that is is warm, intimate, and inviting, with an up-close glow that's quite attractive and mellow, despite its experimentalism. The stereo mix is playful and delicious, an especially inspired achievement given the do-it-all-yourself amateur execution.

The 4-minute "Sunrise" opens with a strange rumble which moves into bright and vibrant multiple acoustic guitars, with the occasional addition of tape effects. Tibbetts's friendly guitars have a universal appeal. The 4½-minute "The Secret" adds wind sounds and simple electronics to the wistful acoustic guitars, creating a seductive yet opt-out sound. The 4½-minute "Desert" features stereo pans of liquid gloops of electronics and tape effects, then adds gorgeous acoustic guitar strums and playful chord progressions, followed by a synth solo. This leads into the 2½-minute "The Wonderful Day," with more multiple acoustic guitars. Although the piece is derivative of the preceding tracks, that's a positive in this case. Following is the ethereal 1½-minute "Gong," which alters percussion sounds with tape effects and adds brief environmental sounds.

The 5½-minute "Jungle Rhythm" features driving, primitive Richard Pinhas–like synths in the foreground, but is a tad smoother than Pinhas's style. The 2-minute "Interlude" has soft, quiet acoustic guitars with a wonderfully trippy electric guitar solo. The 4-minute "Alvin Goes to Tibet" contains more electronics, but this time they're icier and moodier, with lots of stereo effects and a very avant-garde and psychedelic voice tape effect. The 5-minute "How Do You Like My Buddha?" is a frenetic, odd, and savagely acid jam with bass, electronics, and a roaring electric guitar.

The cover is a brilliantly surreal black-and-white drawing that is absolutely perfect for this music.

YR. Released August 1980. ECM.

Yr, Steve Tibbetts's raucous second album was composed, engineered, produced, and self-released by him in 1980 (the ECM label picked it up in 1988). Recorded in Minneapolis, Minnesota, it's a classic of exotic instrumental prog, with high-energy, eclectic, inventive fusions. This album is the blueprint for Tibbetts's later releases, and is a favorite with his fans. It's attractively paced and lively, going by rather quickly, and features an expanded band lineup and instrumental palette. Tibbetts (here playing electric and acoustic guitars, kalimba, and synth) is joined by his regular group of collaborators, including Marc Anderson (congas, drums, percussion), Tim Weinhold (bongos, vase, bells), Bob Hughes (bass guitar), and Steve Cochrane and Marcus Wise (tablas).

The 4½-minute "Ur" opens with the attention-getting sound of handclap-like percussion from Weinhold's vase, playing along with Tibbetts's acoustic guitar. This leads into a series of bright and sunny multiple acoustic guitar textures, with mellotron-like synth topped off by a dirty-sounding electric guitar solo with drums, and concludes with a fade-out of bells. The 4-minute "Sphexes" combines congas, bells, and a sinewy electric guitar, then falls back into breezy, lighter sections of percussion with an island/tribal feel. This tapestry of percussion continues with the 7½-minute "Ten Years," with tablas, congas, bongos, low-key washes of synth, bass, and a Mike Oldfield–like web of acoustic and electric guitars by Tibbetts. The piece disappears into a mesh of electric guitar, then builds up again with the multilayered percussion. The 2½-minute "One Day" is a gorgeously executed, flowery acoustic guitar ballad, with more conventional chords, recalling the music of Ralph Towner, Leo Kottke, and Will Ackerman.

The 5-minute "Three Primates" is an intricate tapestry of guitars, percussion, and bass, going through a variety of moods, ranging from the unusually tasty (for Tibbetts) to the soft and pretty. A restrained electric guitar solo is stereo-panned, and the piece becomes quite lively toward the end with tabla percussion. The 7½-minute "You and It" is romantic and dramatic, with mellotron-like synth washes and acoustic guitars embellished by bells and percussion. A unique and elusive electric guitar solo then takes over for an aggressive rock section. The 3½-minute "The Alien Lounge" recalls *Electric Silence*–era Dzyan, with a gorgeously layered tapestry that assumes spiritual dimensions. This leads into the 3½-minute "Ten Yr Dance," which is like a track from *Led Zeppelin III* via an acoustic Al DiMeola. A playful multiguitar piece, the instruments are sent scurrying in psychedelic pans within the mix.

The production values on the recording are excellent, with a wide-open, airy stereo soundstage and a crisp, detailed mix. The cover photo of ancient ruins by Dieter Rehm emphasizes the timeless nature of this music.

SAFE JOURNEY. Released May 1984. ECM.

After his disappointing 1982 album *Northern Song,* Steve Tibbetts rebounded with the superb *Safe Journey,* his most refined and mature release. Recorded in 1983 in St. Paul, Minnesota, the album is rich with picturesque imagery, recalling the more flavorful instrumental moments of the mid-1970s recordings of King Crimson, Popol Vuh, and Jade Warrior. The recording is a synthesis of the inviting acoustic intimacy of his first self-titled album with that of the well-produced, exotic rock of his second album *Yr,* plus a huge dose of mystery and touches of impressionism. The influence of this particular fusion sound can be heard in the music of later 1980s artists like David Torn, Dark, and Vicki Richards. Tibbetts (here playing electric and acoustic guitars, kalimba, and tape effects) is joined by his usual collaborators Marc Anderson (congas, steel drum, percussion), Bob Hughes (bass guitar), Tim Weinhold (vase), and Steve Cochrane (tabla). With this album Anderson assumes a much larger role, co-writing four of the disc's ten tracks, and he remained Tibbetts's regular percussionist and collaborator on all subsequent albums.

The 6-minute "Test" starts very slowly with soft guitar atmospheres, bass, and frosty percussion, building up to a shamanistic frenzy of electric guitar and drums, but quickly falling back into dreamier textures, only to rise again with a tense rock jam until concluding with ethereal stereo percussion effects. The 4-minute "Climbing" combines kalimba with Anderson's low-key and infectious steel drum rhythms, creating a soft and sensual sound over which Tibbetts floats atmospheric electric guitar textures. The 3-minute "Running" has an echoed, clicking percussion effect that just drips ambience, with the piece drifting into sunny acoustic guitars. The 7-minute "Night Again" is space music, featuring wonderfully delicate, soft, and plaintive multiple acoustic guitars, with a floating guitar loop effect. The 4-minute "My Last Chance" is similar, but less spacey and more tuneful, adding percussion.

The 5½-minute "Vision" craftily sails breezy electric guitar notes into a drift of attractive percussion and kalimba. The 4-minute "Any Minute" is quite similar, exuding a summery vibe. The 4-minute "Mission" has some Eastern drones along with kalimba and Anderson's nimble congas. The 3-minute "Burning Up" is a hypnotic and seductive blend of ethereal percussion and guitar atmospheres. The epic 10½-minute "Going Somewhere" is a highlight, and quite an experimental space music construction. A tape loop creates a serene, voicelike singing, accompanied by a mild kalimba, followed by the sound of a young child and stereo pans of engine/traffic sounds. This mutates with more tape effects into an incredibly delicate section of floating guitar resonances and twinkles of wind chimes, until finally returning to the beautiful voice of the earlier loop effect. The piece is one of Tibbetts's finest compositions.

The sound quality is excellent throughout the recording (although there is some hiss), and the immensely detailed mix highlights the innovative percussion tapestries. Tibbetts repeated the formula of *Safe Journey* on all of his subsequent releases. These albums (1986's *Exploded View,* 1989's *Big Map Idea,* and 1994's *The Fall of Us All)* are all of high quality releases, but break no new ground. The best of the three is his latest, *The Fall of Us All.*

DAVID TORN

BEST LAID PLANS. Released January 1985. ECM.

Best Laid Plans, David Torn's debut release, is his finest recording, as well as being one of the most significant progressive titles of the 1980s. Recorded in July of 1984 in Oslo, Norway, the album introduces Torn's highly influential electric guitar style, which incorporates various washes of tonal colors, spacey atmospheres, and processing and tape loops.

Notable here is that this disc is a collaboration with the extraordinarily talented drummer/percussionist Geoffrey Gordon, whose role is so large that he really ought to have received co-billing with Torn. Together, Torn and Gordon create an unusually effective form of electric raga, achieving a rare purity and seriousness that give the album an almost meditative quality. While the style is improvisational and abstract, there's a clear linear flow to the compositions, making them easy to follow and enjoy, giving the project a wide appeal. There's a lot of space in this music, which is occasionally minimal and often quite impressionistic. The interaction between Torn and Gordon recalls that of other ECM-label guitar and drum teams such as Terje Rypdal and Jon Christensen, and Steve Tibbetts and Marc Anderson.

The 6½-minute "Before the Bitter Wind" begins with roaring but controlled guitar notes that blare and then solo, but then stop to resonate, while active drums and percussion dance around in the mix; the piece concludes with some primitive chording. The 7-minute title track introduces Torn's atmospheric guitar loops, with a lead line that then weaves a loose tapestry over it. Halfway through, Gordon adds drums, and cymbals with an exotic flavor, joined by Torn's lead line. The 3½-minute "The Hum of Its Parts" has a light and churning loop with a tortured lead line soloing over it, joined by tabla percussion and huge tom-tom rolls, becoming rather intense. The 2-minute "Removable Tongue" is Torn without Gordon, featuring more tortured soloing and atmospherics.

The 6-minute "In the Fifth Direction" has a laid back Rypdal-like intro by Torn, with Gordon adding nimble percussion. Torn then unleashes sparse, bluesy, whining solos, faraway sounding and spacey; the piece then builds in power before falling back into some dewy, David Gilmour–like notes. The 7-minute "Two Face Flash" is a dynamic interaction between the two musicians, with Torn playing lovely, singing, delicate notes and solos, and Gordon adding an insistent drum kit and tom-toms. The 8½-minute "Angle of Incidents" has misty, fleeting, atmospheric effects with a quietly hesitant, shrieking, and angular lead line, accompanied by Gordon's percussion.

The disc's sound is very good, especially the stereo mix of Gordon's percussion. The mastering could use more volume, though, and the album is best when played loud. The cover design and photo by Dieter Rehm of primitive, repeating symbols obscuring a photo of a government building comprise an interesting choice of imagery for this recording, suggesting perhaps the victory of the primal over the civilized.

CLOUD ABOUT MERCURY. Released March 1987. ECM.

Recorded in March of 1986 in Oslo, Norway, *Cloud About Mercury* was one of the genuinely high-profile progressive releases of the late 1980s, with a supergroup lineup that features David Torn (here playing guitars, koto, and tape effects) and the renowned composer Mark Isham (trumpet, piccolo trumpet, flugelhorn, synth), in addition to, fresh from the just-disbanded 1980s King Crimson, Bill Bruford (electronic drums, percussion), and Tony Levin (Chapman stick, synthesizer bass). This lineup is a good combination, resulting in a number of exotic instrumental textures. The music on this recording is a solid and disciplined fusion of high-tech rock and cinematic jazz, quite different from the sparse raga of Torn's *Best Laid Plans* debut.

The 1-minute "Suyafhu Skin" is a fleeting, dreamy prologue by Torn, with a Middle Eastern feel, awash in reverbs and guitar loops which then fade into silence. The Asian-flavored 7-minute "Snapping the Hollow Reed" then fades in, with a rich and distinctive stereo tapestry of multiple koto patterns which are counterpointed by Bruford's playful, repetitive synth tone pattern played on electronic drums, recalling parts of King Crimson's *Waiting Man* and also Bruford's playing on Kazumi Watanabe's *Spice of Life* video (see review). Isham's long trumpet tones, run-through reverbs, and harmonizers add to the atmosphere. The 6½-minute "The Mercury Grid" is led by Isham's trumpet and flugelhorn, accompanied by Bruford's flavorful percussion and guitar soloing from Torn. The 7-minute "3 minutes of Pure Entertainment" is a jam once again featuring Isham's memorably skidding trumpet lines over Levin's chunky synth bass. Torn's shrill guitar soloing recalls King Crimson's "The Sheltering Sky."

The 8-minute "Previous Man" is led by Torn's processed, staccato guitar riffing, going into shredding solos for a more aggressive workout, with quirky rhythms provided by Levin's Chapman stick. The 5-minute "The Delicate Code" is primarily a Torn tone poem, with a hypnotic cyclical pattern that breaks down after a couple of minutes, then develops into a droning, surreal section, hinting at a sort of transcendence. The 10½-minute "Egg Learns to Walk"/"Suyafhu Seal" begins with the ensemble locked in a tight and snappy groove, with Isham's brass instruments punctuating Torn's angular soloing, creating a dark mood. The final minute is a reprisal of the album's opening piece, giving the work a sense of thematic cohesion.

The sound of the disc is crystal-clear, allowing the nuances of the individual instruments to shine through. The sci-fi cover art by Dieter Rehm is a close-up of a television image, depicting a deep red orb in a blue field. While eye-catching, the cover signifies nothing about the music. Of Torn's several 1990s solo discs, 1995's *Tripping over God* is the most successful.

DAVID TORN/MICK KARN/TERRY BOZZIO

POLYTOWN. Released May 1994. CMP.

Completely improvised in the studio during the summer of 1993, *Polytown* is one of the most significant progressive recordings of the 1990s, composed and produced by the titanic supergroup of guitarist David Torn, bassist Mick Karn (of bands Japan and Rain Tree Crow), and drummer Terry Bozzio (Missing Persons, Frank Zappa, U.K.). An adventurous work of complex, narrative instrumental rock structures, the bruising music is a raw power trio workout that shreds all in its path. Incorporating shamanistic and tribal elements, this rock-and-roll gateway into dreamtime explores spiritualism and the deep recesses of the psyche.

Polytown's powerful full digital recording gives the disc a massive, and hard-hitting punch. The immaculate, dinosaur production values recall the sound of other CMP label artists, such as Dark, Let's Be Generous, and Chad Wackerman, with other possible reference points being Djam Karet, Happy Family, and King Crimson (both current

From left to right, Terry Bozzio, Mick Karn, David Torn.

and past). Torn (who at the time of this recording was recovering from a brain tumor that left him with hearing in only one ear) contributes guitars, Hammond organ, harmonica, and his trademark tape loop atmospherics. Karn, in addition to bass guitar, adds bass clarinet. Bozzio provides bodhran, dumbek, and piano, as well as his gargantuan drum kit and tom-tom polyrhythms.

The 5½-minute "Honey Sweating" is a passionate, state-of-the-art prog rock classic. The listener is assaulted by an attention-getting groove of live, very up-front-sounding drums, rubbery bass lines, and a stinging lead guitar tone. The piece then slips into a half-time mode, with Torn's signature guitar atmospheres. The 6½-minute "Palms for Lester" continues the intensity, driven forward by Bozzio's exotic, repeating rock beat and Karn's crunching bass, with Torn's fuzz-tone lead melody piercing through. The second half of the piece breaks down into a somber, ambient soundscape, accented by stabs of percussion, a harmonica loop, and a piano passage. The 4½-minute "Open Letter to the Heart of Diaphora" is a hard rock, snake-charming raga with a Middle Eastern flavor. Torn's twangy, slippery guitar dances through Bozzio's primal dumbek beats and Karn's snaky fretless bass, weaving an irresistibly seductive and hypnotic tapestry, with a short interlude of organ and guitar feedback. The 7-minute "Bandaged by Dreams" has a gigantic, slow groove from the rhythm section, with Torn adding his atypical guitar loop atmospherics. The structure of the piece allows for a number of spaces within the composition for the players to insert tricky additions, such as Karn's somnambulistic bass clarinet.

The 5-minute "Warrior Horsemen of the Spirit Thundering over the Hills of Doubt to a Place of Hope" is a mysterious showcase for Bozzio's percussion, Torn's ghostly swashes of tones, and Karn's bass clarinet. The ominous 9½-minute "Snail Hair Dune" encapsulates the sound and approaches of the previous tracks and turns them into an epic-length piece, taking the listener through a land of shadow and desolation and incorporating brief bits of piano and bass clarinet. The 3-minute "This Is the Abduction Scene" is one of the disc's loudest moments, with a chomping and grinding rhythm section and edge-of-the-seat tempo. Torn's tortured soloing over the main theme adds even more tension. The 4½-minute "Red Sleep" is hypnotic, with a Gothic church organ, mournful bass, and Bozzio's primal tom-tom beats. The 3½-minute "Res Majuko" is similar, with organ, rubbery bass lines, slamming snare hits, and unusual guitar work. The 3½-minute "City of the Dead" is a tour de force of exotic percussion by Bozzio. Created in the style of Tibetan ritual music, it's replete with loud, noisy, and jarring gongs, cymbals, bells, and a groaning French horn. The piece is like the soundtrack to a George Romero or Dario Argento horror film set in ancient Egypt.

TUU

MESH. Released April 1997. Fathom/Hearts of Space.

TUU are a very promising U.K. space music group, whose fourth album, *Mesh,* is a successful example of electro-acoustic, ambient/ritual space music with exotic flavors. The band, led by percussionist/producer Martin Franklin, with keyboardist Myki O'Dempsey and flautists Nick Parkin and Rebecca Lublinski, employs every kind of trance-producing instrumentation, including flutes, synths, shells, gongs, pots, bells, guitar loops, and samples. On all tracks both electronics and acoustic instruments are present, creating an elusive sound that often makes it difficult to distinguish one instrument from another. Although the execution is rather refined and a bit slick, and less electronics would have been preferable, the recording manages to do everything right in creating an effective space music sound. The group's style places them in the company of artists such as Voice of Eye, Lightwave, Forrest Fang, Emerald Web, Stephan Micus, and Robert Rich.

The 8-minute "Crack Between the Worlds" features Triton shell, shakers, ney flute, and synths, creating a loud, ghostly, and scary voice-like gale of airy, unsettling, Eastern-like sounds. The 7½-minute "Migration" consists of water drums, clay pot, vocoder, suling, flutes, synth, and samples, with the vocoder and percussion recalling some of the pieces on Mike Oldfield's *QE2,* albeit far more subdued and layered. The 5-minute "Kalpu Taru (Tree of Wishes)" has flute, shakers, bansuri, harmonium, synth, and kenong, creating Eastern drones that are both subtle and seductive, particularly the rain sounds made by the shakers.

The 12-minute title track is a disappointment. Despite the promising mix of water drums, clay pot, synth, flute, e-bow, and guitar loops, the piece's bouncy percussion beats are a bit pedestrian, and the guitar loop that runs throughout is quite tedious. The remaining three tracks are the album's highlights. The 5-minute "Stone To Sand" features Triton shell, bamboo, synth, and flute, creating a dissolving sound suggested by the piece's title. The 8-minute "Four Pillars" has Tibetan bells, gongs, synth, and chanting samples, and its spacey, spatial drifts make it go by rather quickly. The 6½-minute "Great Wheel" consists of singing bowls, bowed bells, synths, shortwave, and mantra samples, producing a subtle, reverent, glowing sound.

The recording's sound quality is excellent, creating a lush, enveloping aura.

CYRILLE VERDEAUX

MESSENGER OF THE SON. Released 1984. Musea import.

Messenger of the Son is the superb solo album from Cyrille Verdeaux, the leader of the French prog rock band Clearlight. With a sound similar to Clearlight's *Visions,* these unique and solid instrumental compositions are centered around his grand piano and synths, accompanied by several others on synth, bass guitar, drums, violin, and electric and acoustic guitars. The style is friendly and serene, yet grand, with an unmistakable element of romanticism, and the effect is a layered sound that is attractively ultra-melodic, like a rich dessert of sweet melody. The sound is neither overtly jazzy nor straightforward rock, and though it is not strictly classical either, it does occasionally embrace symphonic forms.

The 7-minute "Overture" is representative of Verdeaux's lush, cinematic style, featuring his piano and synths accompanied by drums and percussion. The 5-minute "Astral Journey" is an ethereal, electro-acoustic space music comprised of synths and grand piano solos. The 5-minute "Energy" is a surprise, opening with island-flavored rhythmic percussion, reminiscent of Passport's *Iguacu.* The piece then moves into breezy keyboard solos with bouncy drums and playful stereo pans. The 4-minute "Ballad in 7 Steps" recalls the group Blue Motion, with rollicking piano and rapid-fire drums, adding layers of dewy synths. The 6-minute "The Key of Enoch" has outer space–like synth whooshes, with an ominous, low-key bass guitar and light drums, going into a spacey drift.

The 8-minute "Vibrato" is an active symphonic prog rock workout, with a dynamic of cascading keyboards backed by a nimble rhythm section, recalling *Wind and Wuthering*–era Genesis, and occasionally falling back into piano sections and breezy synth leads. The 4½-minute "Magic Circus" opens with a gorgeous tapestry of multiple acoustic guitars (a very welcome texture), adding light keyboard sprinkles before moving into synth solos backed by the rhythm section. The 4-minute "Deep Death" is a multiple-keyboard construction with memorable chords, similar to *Clearlight Symphony.* The 6-minute "Full Sun Raga" is more of the same, but spacier. The 3-minute "Remember Jonathan" combines an introspective piano with awkward ocean sounds in the background.

The disc includes four bonus tracks from Verdeaux's 1988 album *Rhapsodies pour la Planète Bleue,* bringing the total running time up to 75½ minutes. The first three pieces fit in well with the *Messenger . . .* material, though there are a few annoying clicks in these transfers. The 6½-minute "Voyage à Atlantis" is a very strong track, opening with environmental sounds (wind, birds, sea), then going into a more serious and melancholy multi-keyboard structure, complete with a classical-sounding violin solo, until concluding with more nature sounds. The 6½-minute "Creation Synthétique" is similar, combining environmental sounds with spacey synths. Unfortunately, though, the mix is too overloaded, creating a muddy sound. The 4½-minute "Rêve avec Krishna," another fine track, recalls David Parsons, with serene electronics and environmental sounds. The 4½-minute "Set the Spirit Free" is to be avoided, being an abridged, re-recorded version of "Clearlight Symphony," but with vocals and trite lyrics.

Throughout *Messenger of the Son* the sound quality is very good, with some hiss. The cover is a lovely and sublime painting by Alain Robert, giving a hint of the album's diverse melodic colors.

VOICE OF EYE

MARINER SONIQUE. Released December 1992. Cyclotron.

Voice of Eye is the duo of Bonnie McNairn and Jim Wilson. Their approach to instrumental electro-acoustic music is a real breakthrough, making them America's most important progressive group of the 1990s. Using homemade instruments, flutes, voice, samples, percussion, sheet metal, and guitar, they produce thoroughly abstract and hypnotic tapestries of what has come to be known as *ritual sound,* a combination of various other genres and subgenres, such as ambient, industrial, trance, tribal, and raga. Basically this is sleepy space music created on an epic scale, but the sound achieved is surprisingly intimate. It is also somewhat elusive and obscure, as the sound is drawn primarily from homemade instruments and samples, making it difficult to describe in specific terms. *Mariner Sonique* is the duo's 63-minute debut.

Voice of Eye. Top, Jim Wilson; bottom, Bonnie McNairn. (Photo courtesy of John Lee.)

The 6-minute "Transmission," refusing to stay locked into only a few sounds, has a great deal of variety and establishes a haunting mood with swirling swooshes and drones, and lively but ominous percussion. The 4½-minute "Strange Attractor" is very dark, with primitive percussion, rumbles, and a dreamier drift led by flute. The 3-minute "The Shadow I Knew" is rather unusual, consisting of airy, windlike, floating sounds. The 9-minute "Deja Heir" features more windlike atmospheres, with cymbals, drones, voice, and flute. The 11-minute "Melange Nun" has ethereal, processed voice with echo, dewy tapping sounds, an airy flute, and bass, creating another windlike drift.

The 4½-minute "Descending a Stare" is a track that virtually defines the ritual sound, with percussion of all kinds, including sheet metal. The 4-minute "Eros and Innana" features very strange demonic groans. The 9-minute "Deep B E Vox" is a highlight, with its soft, stereo-panned sounds recalling Tangerine Dream and Lightwave, but without using synths or keyboards. The 11-minute "Epitaph for King Lear" is more of their windy drones and resonances, but is overlong and grows tedious.

The sound of the recording is excellent throughout, with a detailed mix. The cover art (by the group) is an odd, surreal collage of various images.

VESPERS. Released September 1994. Cyclotron.

Vespers is a totally enigmatic and visionary work, and one of the greatest opt-out masterpieces of progressive music. The album is thoroughly dislocating, hypnotic, spiritual, and shamanistic, plugging the listener more directly into dreamtime than perhaps any other space music recording.

The disc is all mystery, explaining nothing about itself, creating a trance-inducing journey at the end of which awaits transcendence. The introspective mood is intimate and private, giving the project a universal appeal.

Bonnie McNairn and Jim Wilson utilize voice, flute, homemade instruments, percussion, samples, shanai, sitar, slide whistle, guitar, and bass, with a good amount of digital effects processing. No synths are used, making this primarily an acoustic construction. While there is a distinct tantric raga feel, there are no discernible influences from the worlds of classical music or popular music (rock, jazz, etc.), putting the work completely outside all conventional forms. As is usual with Voice of Eye's odd palette of instrumentation, the music on *Vespers* is largely indescribable, but totally inviting.

The 66-minute disc is basically one lengthy thematic composition, with seven consecutively run subtitled segments offered as reference points—"Waking," "Breathing," "Blooming," "Waning," "Melting," "Drifting," and "Dreaming." Various seductive tapestries are produced by the band, with voices, whistling drones, flute, and infectious tribal percussion, all heavily processed with stereo effects. The moods range from the sleepy, to the floating, to the near-religious (hence the disc's appropriate title), all delivered in a very smooth and palatable fashion, neither abrasive nor startling. Two moments toward the end are worth noting. "Drifting" has an unexpected ghostly narration by McNairn, and "Dreaming," after fading into a minute of silence, goes into a trippy, tape-phased vocal section that concludes the disc with an affirming mantra.

The sound is excellent, and the disc is perfect for headphones, being the very definition of "head music." The strange cover and booklet photos reinforce the music's enigmatic qualities.

TRANSMIGRATION. Released December 1995. Cyclotron.

Transmigration is Voice of Eye's equally successful follow-up to their brilliant *Vespers* disc, and a superb companion piece to that work. Inspired by passages from the Tibetan Book of the Dead, the music is about the forced introspection that approaching death requires, making the recording a much darker creation, in stark contrast to the brighter first album. This occasionally frightening disc still brings the listener directly to an altered state, but here the mood is more primordial. All the sounds produced by Bonnie McNairn and Jim Wilson are acoustic (with processing), with no synths, samples, or sequencers used. The 67½-minute disc has all of its tracks running consecutively (as on the previous record), but here the various pieces are generally separate works and not just reference points, despite the overall thematic link and the flowing transitions.

The 19½-minute "Transmigration (Bardo I)" opens with a barely audible singing resonance, which grows louder with airy drones. The piece becomes another of the duo's beckoning vortexes of mystery, its drifts ebbing and flowing with a whirlwind of wind chimes and ominous bass drum, until disappearing into soft but unsettling vocal drones by McNairn and concluding with loud foghorn blasts. The 7½-minute "Transcendence" has a murky, Gothic opening that leads into drums and percussion with vocal textures, recalling the heavy, swaying space music of *Vespers*. The 6-minute "Sirens (Bardo II)" is a louder drone, with ghostly sounds, adding voice, sparse percussion, and hornlike textures.

The 5½-minute "Tempest" is a louder, windlike roar, with drums and percussion. The 4½-minute "Garden of Earthly Delights" has more atypical drones and voice, with industrial-style metallic percussion in the background. The 24-minute "Oblivion (Bardo III)" is a bit overlong, but that does not detract from its effectiveness. A thoroughly abstract mesh, the piece seems to conclude with a lengthy, serene, angelic drift, and then a moment of silence, but the sound abruptly returns with a strange collage of voices and effects.

The sound quality is excellent throughout. The cover art and booklet by the group are unique. Animal bones are placed inside a huge ring of fire, and are photographed both in a static position as well as in flight. The striking, primal image is perfect for this authentically enigmatic music.

VOICE OF EYE WITH LIFE GARDEN

THE HUNGRY VOID VOLUME TWO: AIR. Released 1995. Cyclotron/Agni.

Recorded live and in the studio during the summer of 1994, this is a collaboration between Voice of

Eye and Life Garden, a similar space music group from Arizona. The first volume of this two-disc collection (separately released), *The Hungry Void Volume One: Fire,* is less compelling than this second volume, and not as worthy of attention. The material is entirely improvised, utilizing voices, digital loops, multiple-effect processors, and a wide variety of eclectic instrumentation, including a number of tribalistic percussion instruments.

By this time a definite formula for these projects had emerged, and as a result this recording seems less essential than the other Voice of Eye releases, lacking a certain magic. But it's still an incredible album of extremely opt-out sounds, rich with mysterious, spacey drifts, hypnotic drones, ritual percussion, and ethereal male and female voices. As usual, it's difficult to identify what specifically is being played and by whom, but that's the idea. All the sounds are blended and stirred together, intentionally obscured, creating a dark, intoxicating, primordial soup. At 74 minutes, the disc, divided into 10 untitled sections, with all the tracks running consecutively, is slightly overlong.

The sound is excellent, with a detailed mix. The crystalline computer art by David Oliphant of Life Garden is unsettling, looking like a kind of spindly, frightening alien organism.

WALLENSTEIN

BLITZKRIEG. Released January 1972. Spalax import.

Wallenstein's debut album is an early German prog rock masterpiece, and the band's main claim to fame. Recorded between September and December of 1971, this is loud, driving, high-energy, primarily instrumental rock. While it has the energy of Guru Guru, there are no psychedelic or cosmic elements, and few symphonic or classical ones. Instead, this is flat-out, tight, power-chording, live-sounding rock and roll, anticipating the style of later bands such as Finch and Fermata by many years. Wallenstein may have been influenced by Guru Guru and Agitation Free, and Focus and Mahavishnu Orchestra are possible suspects.

While the group is led by composer/keyboardist/vocalist Jurgen Dollase, this album really belongs to electric guitarist Bill Barone, an American, who plays in an impudent, ballsy style that almost recalls the Stooges and the MC5. The band also features famed drummer Harold Grosskopf, later to play a prominent role as a percussionist on several key Klaus Schulze projects. His playing here is far more aggressive. Rounding out the lineup is Jerry Berkers on bass guitar. The playing is immaculate by all, with the group going through a number of rhythmic workouts, led by solos from Barone's guitar and Dollase's keyboards.

The 12-minute opener "Lunetic" is a fast and bombastic heavy metal instrumental, with a relentless pace. The style is strikingly sophisticated for its 1971 recording date. The 9½-minute "The Theme" has a laid-back intro, then launches into another heavy jam. Dollase's brief vocal (in English) passes unobtrusively, with the band arrangement dominating, especially Barone's screaming guitar. The 13½-minute "Manhattan Project" is another irresistible heavy rock instrumental jam, with a big, full drum sound, gritty guitar soloing, and mellotron and piano breaks. The 7½-minute "Audiences" is another vocal track, similar to the style the band would follow on their less interesting later releases. The conventional structures of the band's song forms are not particularly exceptional, despite their obvious talents.

The production of *Blitzkrieg* is remarkably advanced considering when it was recorded, and the sound is fantastic.

KAZUMI WATANABE

THE SPICE OF LIFE IN CONCERT (video). Released 1987. Pioneer laser disc import (Japan).

The Spice of Life in Concert is an impeccable 70-minute performance of state-of-the-art instrumental fusion by three master musicians: Kazumi Watanabe (guitars), Bill Bruford (electronic drums), and Jeff Berlin (bass guitar, synth). This is a live presentation, in its entirety, of the now-out-of-print 1987 album *The Spice of Life* by Watanabe, a famous Japanese instrumentalist and composer, and featuring Bruford and Berlin. These recordings are easily preferable to their somewhat restrained studio counterparts, with an energetic and tougher edge which adds considerably to the already tight arrangements.

Watanabe's playing has a purity of tone, producing airy and fluid solos and textures that are very attractive. He's also adept at loud power chording and fast, arena rock fingerwork. Bruford is a marvel to watch here, this show being one of his finest moments. It's also the best performance on electronic drums a listener is likely to encounter. Berlin constantly surprises with his playing as well, often taking the lead. While the sound of the trio certainly recalls elements of the both the Bruford band and 1980s King Crimson, these are only reference points. The group's style is far tastier and busier than those bands.

The opening "Melancho" has a spacey intro of solo guitar with synth effects by Watanabe, then moves into a sprightly and bouncy jam led by his power chording. "Hiper K" is a slice of breezy, rhythmic tastiness, with Watanabe's wailing notes leaving a lot of room for additions by the other two players. "City" is a highlight, being a furiously fast and macho rock jam with a blazing lead guitar. "Period" is similar to "City," only more textured. "Na Starovia" is a glossy, storytelling piece with a cutting and impressive arrangement. Parts of this are intercut with a lovely, romantic video of ballerinas, rain, and candles. Berlin's "Bass Solo" needs to be listened to rather than seen—it's too easy to concentrate visually on his performance and forget about the work as a piece of music. "Sayonara" is another highlight, a lyrical, jazzy ballad with a poignant melody. The piece is deftly executed, and the nuanced subtlety impresses after the flashiness of the rock material.

"Half Blood" is another breezy workout, similar to "Hiper K." Led by Watanabe's skittish guitar, "Lim-Poo" is high-tech funk with Eastern flavors. Bruford's "Drums Solo" is out of the ordinary and adventurous, utilizing the new electronic drum technology in ways most others of this era did not. Rather exotic and flavorful, the samples include things such as bell and frame drum sounds. "J.F.K." and "UNT" are both power-chording jams, with screaming guitar soloing by Watanabe.

The production values on this recording are immaculate. The sound mix is perfect, and the visuals were shot on crisp, color video, with multiple camera coverage, a light show, and special additional sequences.

KIT WATKINS

CIRCLE. Released January 1993. Linden.

Circle is one of the true innovative classics of environmental/ambient/collage space music, taking listeners on a seductive 59-minute journey through the sounds of water, wind, rain, musical instruments, animals, insects, objects, and machines. It's a soothing, drifting, and picturesque travelogue that honors our natural environment. Relaxing, positive, and never abrasive, *Circle* has a totally universal appeal—anyone, anywhere, of any age, would like this.

Kit Watkins, former keyboardist for the late 1970s American instrumental prog rock band Happy the Man, composed and painstakingly assembled *Circle* in 1992 in his hometown of Linden, Virginia. The disc recalls similar environmental recordings by Annea Lockwood, Bill Nelson, Syllyk, Michael Prime, Deuter, and Edgar Froese. Although there are a spate of releases on the market that combine music and nature sounds, they are mostly produced by hacks. *Circle,* however, is a standout, both because of its variety and because the masterful transitions between the various sounds (which never break the flow) draw the listener into an awarness of the construction of the pieces, as opposed to offering a static, unchanging canvas of relatively few sounds that functions merely as a background.

All of *Circle*'s tracks run together. The first four pieces are subdivided into a section entitled "Outer Boundaries." The 4-minute "All Things" is a slow and sensual intro, a gorgeous recording of crickets, owl, and deer. The 7-minute "The Harbinger" builds to a more ominous level, with a filtered keyboard, crickets, rattles, and geese. The 7-minute "Under Temporal Blankets" is comprised of jazzy space music textures, with Gary Burton–like vibes, English horn, and owl sounds. The 5-minute "Man/Machine" features the slightly startling sounds of a train.

The next three pieces are folded into a section entitled "Sanctuaries." The 2-minute "Song of Spring" is lush, sweet, and dewy, with the very friendly and inviting sound of bird song. The 4½-minute "Snake Dance" is a minor foray into the ritual/tribal sound, with tambourine bells, drums, voice, rainstick, shells, flute, and triangle. The use of an altered voice is not a great idea here, but neither is it obtrusive. The 3-minute "Awash" is a luscious recording of a stream.

The final five pieces are grouped into the section entitled "Gathering Surfaces." The 3-minute "Heated Sky" combines the resonances of cicadas with thunder and wind, giving these familiar sounds a new depth. The 6-minute "Around and Around" is reminiscent of the opening minutes of Tangerine Dream's *Rubycon,* with the soothing sounds of metal bowls, crickets, and train cars. The final three pieces are a continuous mixture of caressing water sounds. The 4½-minute "Circle of Rain" features the sounds of rain, a brook, hummingbirds, and vibes. The 3-minute "Tumble" adds to this the light percussion of drums and a wood block, as well as the sound of a hawk. The 9-minute "Dawn's Return" effortlessly winds the proceedings down to a minimal water drip, and along the way visits the sounds of wine glasses, a dove, an owl, a kitten, and grouse.

Perhaps the most striking feature of *Circle* is its crystal-clear, extremely spacious sound, which is virtually perfect, filling any space it's played in, and making for ideal headphone listening. Watkins's cover design, consisting of a lush blue circle, is also very attractive.

EBERHARD WEBER

THE COLOURS OF CHLOE. Released March 1974. ECM.

Eberhard Weber is a unique and gifted German composer and instrumentalist. His eclectic compositions showcase a refined side of German progressive music that's totally different from most prog artists from that region. Weber's music is an exotic but low-key and somewhat hard to classify fusion of traditional jazz, modern

Eberhard Weber. (Photo by Christina Naura.)

classical chamber music, minimalism, and various snippets of jazz/rock. His compositions unfold slowly in an open and airy fashion, and are highly impressionistic. The overall sound is always gentle and inviting, with mournful moments sometimes rising to the fore.

The Colours of Chloe, Weber's first album, is an early classic from the ECM label that established Weber and attracted what was to become a devoted cult following. Weber's spacey and introspective form of fusion does not depend on volume or instrumental chops, but instead concentrates on juxtapositions, successfully combining a diverse mix of elements, usually within a subdued and extremely delicate musical structure and a low-key production. Weber's music might be compared to the lighter side of the U.K. Canterbury sound, typified by artists such as Henry Cow and Egg, or to a less rocking Dzyan (from the German scene), or even to *Hosianna Mantra*–era Popol Vuh.

On *The Colours of Chloe,* Weber (playing bass, cello, and ocarina) is joined by his longtime collaborator Rainer Bruninghaus (electric and acoustic piano, synth), Dzyan's Peter Giger (drums, percussion), Ack van Rooyen (flugelhorn), the choir voice of Gisela Schauble, and the cello of the Stuttgart Sudfunk Orchestra.

The 6½-minute "More Colours" establishes a moody pulse of cello, occasionally going into dramatic and romantic directions. Over this, Weber solos on bass, creating a lonely sound, a feeling enhanced by sparse piano notes. The 7½-minute title track opens with tiny synth colorings, delicate cymbals, and the cello orchestra. A Renaissance-like section of lovely, lilting voice by Schauble and anchoring bass notes impresses, then switches into a moody center section of piano, bass, brushes, and strings, lightening considerably with its jazzy feel and solos. The 6-minute "An Evening with Vincent Van Ritz" opens with a 2-minute section of ethereal choral voices, ominous cellos, and bass. If the instrumention had instead been via mellotron, it would sound like King Crimson. The piece then jumps into a tasty, chunky jam of bass, piano, flugelhorn, and very light jazz drumming, until reprising the opening, adding more colorful percussion.

The highlight of the album is the 19½-minute "No Motion Picture," with its attention-getting motif, featuring an infectious, rollicking bass line, along with repeating, hypnotic, minimalist patterns of Terry Riley–like synth, subtle background percussion colorations by Giger, and accompanying cello. Alternating with this repeated theme are sections of Schauble's vocal, Weber's virtuoso bass solos, spacey, impressionistic piano solos, a nimble, tropical-flavored percussion solo, and a brief flugelhorn solo.

The sound quality is excellent, despite the flat, low-volume mastering. The cover art by Maja Weber is cutesy but pleasing.

THE FOLLOWING MORNING. Released April 1977. ECM import.

By the mid-1970s, Eberhard Weber was solidly a part of the ECM label's roster of eclectic, hard-to-classify composers/instrumentalists, including Terje Rypdal, Ralph Towner, Jan Garbarek, Pat Metheny, Carla Bley, and John Surman. While *The Following Morning* is not quite the breakthrough that some of Weber's other albums are, it's still an essential example of the type of musical impressionism that both his music and the ECM label are synonymous with. Fusing jazz and classical chamber music, this disc is low key in the extreme, with sparse instrumentation and a very quiet production. The minimalistic compositions are moody and reflective, and from this inwardly directed flow emerges a somber drama, creating a supremely private, contemplative form of music.

The album was recorded in August of 1976 in Oslo, Norway. Weber (here playing bass) was joined by collaborator Rainer Bruninghaus on electric and acoustic piano, along with members of the Oslo Philharmonic Orchestra on cello, French horns, and oboe. The instruments are very closely miked, giving the music an in-your-living-room feel. Each of *The Following Morning*'s four long tracks consists of spacey, overlaid textures, softly caressing the listener with its gentle sounds.

The 10-minute "T. On a White Horse" recalls the sound of Weber's first album, *The Colours of Chloe.* A lonely bass and dewy, minimal electric piano patterns are joined by cello and short, subtle bursts of French horn. The piece floats by so effortlessly that the transitions pass unnoticed. The 11-minute "Moana" establishes a very quiet pulse of cello and horns, adding shivery electric piano, oboe, and bass. This is followed by a section of impressionistic tones on acoustic piano, bass, and cello.

The 12-minute title track has a minute of the ambience of the recording stage incorporated into the piece as its opening, which immediately gives the listener a sense of the album's delicacy. A gentle and ethereal mix of moody cello, oboe, and electric piano leads into a very fluid, almost mournful, multitracked bass section by Weber (a highlight), followed by a jazzy section of lovely acoustic piano and bass. The spacey 8-minute "Moana II" has a sparse, barely-present intro of a screechy horn, cello, and bass, until Weber takes over with a furious bass solo, with Bruninghaus adding further colorations on acoustic piano.

The sound on this disc is very good, with some hiss. The cover is a tiny, inset pointillist drawing of a tree and animals by Maja Weber which evokes the sheer delicacy of this music.

FLUID RUSTLE. Released August 1979. ECM.

Fluid Rustle is Eberhard Weber's most popular release, and is among his finest recordings. This ultra-ethereal album has a number of memorably fresh, airy, floating textures, and stands refreshingly outside any conventional jazz or classical idioms. The most notable of these are the voices of Bonnie Herman and Norma Winstone, whose feminine textures are the album's most attractive feature. Once again, Weber's disciplined compositions are intimate and private zones of contemplation, and this disc is a masterpiece of introspection. Also notable is that there is a glowing, wide-eyed optimism to the proceedings (despite Weber's typically dour bass notes), making this a nurturing, reassuring form of space music.

Joining Weber (playing acoustic bass and tarang), Herman, and Winstone are two legendary players, Bill Frisell (guitar, balalaika) and Gary Burton (vibraharp, marimba). *Fluid Rustle* showcases Weber as an innovative, experimental composer rather than as an instrumentalist, and this is where his music is at its best. There are many points within these sparse compositions that are inhabited by spaces of silence, making this Weber's most delicate project. The production is so closely miked one can hear the inhales and exhales of the vocalists.

The 17½-minute "Quiet Departures" opens with extremely soft, gentle pulses of vibes, bass, and guitar and the caressing dual vocals of Herman and Winstone (consisting of soothing "aahs")—a gorgeous sound with universal appeal. The music builds in scope and variation, with a center section by Frisell of balalaikas and tiny electric guitar notes soloing over them, joined by Weber's bass and the voices of the women. This is followed by an exotic section of bass, marimba, guitar, and tarang percussion.

The 7½-minute title track begins with a very quiet mix of vibraharp and voices, building to a passionate level with loud "aahs" from the female voices. This is followed by an alternately lively and staid section of Burton's marimba and Frisell's soft, Terje Rypdal–like guitar, joined by Weber's bass, until the vocals return for a rousing reprisal. The 9-minute "A Pale Smile" is another irresistible combination of soothing vocals and Rypdal-like guitar, with a number of solos by Burton (whose playing never becomes boring in the context of this album). The 5-minute "Visible Thoughts" also has a very effective sound, with a quietly menacing bowed bass playing dark notes, accompanied by a series of echoed, stereo whispers by Herman and Winstone. The sound is quite haunting and attention-getting, but is lightened by the vibes and guitar.

The sound is great, but hissy. The cover is a series of miniature impressionist miniature paintings by Maja Weber that reflect the friendly serenity of the album.

LATER THAT EVENING. Released December 1982. ECM.

Later That Evening epitomizes the sound of both Eberhard Weber and the ECM label, and is a masterpiece of 1980s musical impressionism. Rich with nuance, this is a form of progressive music that creates atmospheres rather than relying on a series of attention-getting jazzy solos; as a result, the music passes like a daydream. Everything about the album is understated—the players assert themselves only in the most subtle of ways— and it all fits together perfectly. Here Weber (on bass) is joined by Paul McCandless (of Oregon) on soprano sax, oboe, English horn, and bass clarinet, Bill Frisell on guitar, Lyle Mays (of the Pat Metheny Group) on piano, and Michael DiPasqua on drums and percussion. The full digital recording gives Weber's distinctively delicate approach the quiet soundstage his music requires.

The 8-minute "Maurizius" opens with Mays's gentle, introspective, faraway-sounding piano, which then switches to dewier solo notes when joined by DiPasqua's jazzy cymbals and bells. A tapestry of McCandless's reassuring horn lines and Frisell's drifting, barely-present guitar chords is then added, creating an attractive sound with universal appeal. The 16½-minute "Death in the Carwash" opens with unexpected, nonsense sounds of backward voices and haunting tape effects with percussion. From there a mellow bed of McCandless's wind instruments shrouds the percussion with sleepy, narcotic-like resonances, a feeling reinforced by DiPasqua's cymbals and bells. The sound is relaxing, but mysterious. After this Weber takes a tiny bass solo, which is followed by an equally delicate guitar solo, and the tempo then increases for a piano solo.

The 11½-minute "Often in the Open" is improvisational, with Weber's bass and McCandless's bass clarinet providing a murky undercurrent to the light airiness of Mays's short piano bursts and DiPasqua's percussion. These drifting moods are continued with guitar and wind instruments. The moody 6½-minute title track recalls Weber's *The Following Morning* album, with upfront solo bass notes, accompanied by the spacey resonances of McCandless's wind instruments and Mays's piano.

The sound of the recording is excellent, but the volume of the mastering is low. The cover is a lovely, inset pointillist painting by Maja Weber, delicate and refined.

Weber's next three releases (1985's *Chorus,* 1988's *Orchestra,* and 1993's *Pendulum)* all come recommended, but lack the variety and charm of his most acclaimed titles due to their concentration on solo bass compositions, which tend to become dull and plodding at a full album length. The best of the three is perhaps *Chorus;* it's a trio lineup, and not a virtuoso solo bass affair like the other two.

WHITE WILLOW

IGNIS FATUUS. Released March 1995. Laser's Edge.

Ignis Fatuus ("will-o'-the-wisp"), the debut release by the Norwegian band White Willow, is a masterpiece of refined, pastoral, vocal prog, structured around folk and classical influences, and rich with mysticism and romanticism. Recorded between 1992 and 1994, the material on this 67-minute disc is both strong and varied, and equal to that of the masters of this genre. Fronted by gorgeous female vocals and poetic lyrics, the music exudes a friendly and gentle aura of mystery. These magical qualities are reinforced by the album's restrained mix, which has a stereo separation reminiscent of recordings circa 1968–1972.

The instrumental palette of White Willow is unusually vast. The band is led by primary composers/producers Jacob C. Hoim-Lupo (playing 6- and 12-string guitars, classical guitar, and bass guitar) and Jan Tariq Rahman (mellotrons, synths, clavinet, electric piano, recorders, crumhorns, sitar, bass pedals, bass guitar, and vocals), who are assisted in the writing and producing by Audun Kjus (flutes, whistles, pipes, bodhran, and vocals) and Tirill Mohn (violins and classical guitar). The group's lineup is completed by lead vocalists Eldrid Johansen and Sara Trondal, and bassist Alexander Engebretsen, with guests on drums, percussion, bass, cello, guitar, and vocals.

Many possible influences on White Willow can be named, including *U*-era Incredible String Band, *Midnight Mushrumps*–era Gryphon, Steve Hackett's *Voyage of the Acolyte,* early King Crimson (particularly *Lizard*'s "Lady of the Dancing Water" and *In the Court of the Crimson King*'s "I Talk To the Wind"), the more ballad-like material from Renaissance (such as *Ashes Are Burning*'s "At the Harbour"), and early Genesis.

The 6½-minute "Snowfall" opens with a tape effect intro that goes into melodic acoustic guitars and a reverent female/male dual vocal by Johansen and Rahman. The mood established is lush and instantly baroque. Adding drums, ethereal keyboards, and bass, the piece begins a jam, but then falls back to acoustic guitar, until picking up again with snappy snare hits and keyboard orchestrations, concluding with a section of recorder, crumhorns, cymbals, and acoustic guitar. The 7-minute "Lord of Night" is very Gothic, with Anne Rice–like fantasy lyrics. A mellotron and mild vocal by Johansen lead into a dark jam, led by exchanges of skronky keyboards, shivery flutes, and violin, plus rhythm section. The 2-minute "Song" is a real departure, with a guest vocal ensemble. The piece is a slice of Elizabethan-era English folk, with flutes, pipes, crumhorns, and bodhran. It sounds totally authentic.

The 3-minute "Ingenting" has lovely textures of violin, flute, and acoustic guitar, but is sung in Norwegian by Kjus and seems out of place. The 7-minute "The Withering of the Boughs" is an acoustic ballad with weak vocals by Kjus (in English). However, the instrumental textures are classic, consisting of mellotron, female backing vocals, nimble bass lines, percussion, and solos for flute and synth. The 5-minute "Lines on an Autumnal Evening" is a pastoral instrumental featuring chamber music textures from cello, flute, violin, clavinet, bass, and classical guitar, each of which has a small solo part, which are neatly sewn up by Johansen's lilting Annie Haslam–like vocal. The 5½-minute "Now in These Fairy Lands" is enchanting. A pastoral intro of acoustic guitar and flute leads into a rousing vocal by Johansen backed by the bouncy pace of Rahman's clavinet with the rhythm section. The 1½-minute "Piletreet" is a plaintive choral piece, with Johansen's emotional wordless vocal, an airy mellotron, acoustic guitar, and bass.

The 3½-minute "Till He Arrives" opens with environmental sounds, quickly moving into synth and acoustic guitar, and a soft, sensual, Kate Bush–like vocal by Johansen. The delicate execution recalls the Incredible String Band. The 11½-minute "Cryptomenysis" is the band's epic. A reverent church organ intro leads into a buildup ensemble section, with a soothing vocal by Trondal (Trondal sounds very much like Johansen, less powerful perhaps, but equally sensual). After breaks for piano and a tragic-feeling violin, the piece toughens up a bit with loud drums, then returns to Trondal's vocal, which concludes the piece. The 2-minute "Signs" has lyrics by the famed poet Samuel Coleridge. This haunting, delicate baroque piece features guitars, flute, bass, percussion, and Trondal's vocal, and one wishes it weren't so brief. The 11-minute "John Dee's Lament" puts a meatier drum sound at its center, along with keyboards and tiny electric guitars.

White Willow (in concert). From left to right, P. C. Svendsen, Jacob C. Holm-Lupo, Danny Young, Sara Trondal, Tirill Mohn, Jan Tariq Rahman.

Rahman's sensitive lead vocal recalls the style of the women's vocals. A jam ensues with violin solos and breaks for keyboards and guitar, accompanied by the rhythm section.

The sound quality is excellent, but the volume of the mastering is too low for the album's quiet, fragile mix. The brilliant cover art (with baroque blue, red, and black images) and booklet by Thom Ang convey perfectly the music's friendly mystery. The lineup of White Willow underwent a number of changes after the release of *Ignis Fatuus,* but future projects are forthcoming. On the strength of this disc, White Willow is one of the most significant progressive groups of the current era.

XAAL

EN CHEMIN. Released November 1991. MSI import.

Xaal were an exceptional instrumental prog rock power trio from France, and one of the most promising groups of the 1990s. Unfortunately, they called it quits after recording only two discs. *En Chemin* (translated, "On the Way") is a loosely defined thematic work of mature, flowing compositions and top-notch performances. Influenced by the esoteric French prog group Magma, the band plays cutting high-energy rock with sophisticated twists, recalling Fire Merchants, Quidam, Happy Family, Minimum Vital, and the re-formed Brand X, but within a more deliberate, conceptual context.

The trio's material is written by drummer Patrick Boileau and guitarist Jad Ayache, with Nicolas Neimer rounding out the lineup on bass guitar, and guests on trumpet, saxophone, and keyboards. Ayache's Hendrix-inspired electric guitar playing is extraordinary, but his injections of some very unfortunate guitar synth keeps *En Chemin* from achieving masterpiece status.

The 6-minute "L'Enfant (The Child)" opens with a brief intro of loud field recordings (footsteps, ticking clocks, noises), then establishes a precise, tight groove, led by smooth guitar soloing and orchestrations of guitar synth. The piece increases its pace by degrees, culminating in a series of fast, rocking sections. The 5½-minute "Ballade (The Walk)" is an album highlight. This infectious jazz/rock fusion is led by very hip and swinging horn arrangements, with lots of tasty blowing. The piece is dynamic, punchy, and memorable. Clock and nature sounds lead into the 4-minute "Le Jardin (The Garden)." A gurgling guitar riff is joined by bass, and the piece turns into a power-chording jam led by Ayache's soaring, clean-sounding guitar. The 6½-minute title track establishes an irresistibly funky groove with a nimble fretless bass and piano, joined by guitar riffing and drums. The piece falls into a hideous guitar synth, but then switches back to a different tempo for an all-out tension-and-release jam. The 5½-minute "Talisman" creates a lighter mood of breezy fusion, with another ripping guitar solo by Ayache.

The 7½-minute "Le Vieux Chasseur de Papillons (The Old Butterfly Hunter)" opens with spacey guitar synth atmospheres that lead to more airy fusion, then switches halfway through to a funky jam, and finally concludes in a chugging, thrashing heavy metal style. The 6½-minute "Ascension" is perhaps the album's most storytelling piece, beginning with lighter sections of subdued guitar and climaxing in a controlled but intense jam. The 11-minute "Byblos" is also a grand bit of storytelling music. A tortured symphonic workout with bubbling bass lines, soaring guitar solos, and bruising horns, the piece has many fine moments, but Ayache's lame guitar synth additions do not work. Look out for the concluding piece, the 1-minute "Final," a freak-out jam with a surprise bloodcurdling scream.

The sound on the French MSI label disc is excellent, with a loud, raw mix. The previously available U.S. version on the Progressive label was an inferior mix, so the import is well worth seeking out. The cover of *En Chemin,* a strange sci-fi painting, is not really an accurate image for this music.

SECONDE ÈRE. Released May 1995. Musea import.

Recorded in 1993, *Seconde Ère* is the final release by the beloved French instrumental rock band

Xaal. The trio of Jad Ayache (on electric guitar, guitar synth, synth, percussion), Patrick Boileau (drums, percussion, synth), and Nicolas Neimer (electric and acoustic bass) is dynamic, tight, hard-hitting, and entertaining. Xaal's music has great power and depth, producing an epic-sized grandeur. As on the earlier *En Chemin,* the compositions are by Ayache and Boileau, with the band producing.

The 9-minute "Rah (He Went)" balances lighter sections with scary jams, with guests on alto sax and trumpet. The piece opens with a loud rumble that shakes your room, incorporating stray bits of faraway-sounding guitar and drums. A descending scale of ominous, announcing chords sets a deadly serious mood, building slowly into a powerful rock march led by heavy hits from Boileau's drum kit. Falling back into a vocal choir, the piece then releases a power-chording guitar with horns. The 6-minute "Jamais Tranquille (Never At Rest)" begins with an active segment of bass drum and other percussion by Boileau, switching to a tapestry of rubbery fretless bass notes with guitar and cymbals. The piece then becomes a loud, precise, Rush-like jam.

The 10½-minute "Al Abad (Eternity)" is a change of pace, with guest Alex Ferrand on soprano sax. Ayache's Middle Eastern–flavored, bright guitar solos and Neimer's chugging acoustic bass create an airy feel, later joined by Ferrand's snake-charming, Coltrane-like sax solo for some fiery blowing by all. The piece recalls Gong's "Isle of Everywhere." The 6½-minute "Piège (Trap)" has an embryonic intro of percussion charges, with soft, floating guitar notes reminiscent of Steve Howe. The piece then switches to an entirely different shade, with piercing notes of guitar and synth leading a furious but tightly controlled jam. The 6½-minute "Force (Strength)" establishes a churning tempo of foreground synth, guitar, and drums, led by Neimer's chunky bass notes and finally topped off by Ayache's saucy guitar solos. The piece is catchy and layered, with an unmistakable European flavor reminiscent of Schicke, Führs and Fröhling.

The sound quality and production are very good, with some hiss. As with the art on *En Chemin,* the cartoonish cover art of *Seconde Ère* doesn't begin to hint at the strengths of this music.

YES

THE YES ALBUM. Released March 1971. Atlantic.

Yes's first two albums consisted of syrupy love ballads and covers of Stephen Stills and Richie Havens songs, but this, their third release, ushered in the genre of true symphonic prog rock. Friendlier than King Crimson, more disciplined than Pink Floyd, and less bombastic than ELP, Yes's sound was smooth, with a natural flow that was almost impossible to dislike, yet did not seem calculated. Recorded in the autumn of 1970, *The Yes Album* is a veritable blueprint for progressive rock forms, so much so that it's impossible to be familiar with the genre without being fully aware of Yes. During their progressive phase (1971–1976), the band had a Midas touch, and did as much or more than any other group or artist to advance the language of the new "serious" rock.

Although *The Yes Album* is led by the smooth, soaring vocals of Jon Anderson, and in fact the majority of the band's material was vocal-oriented, this release is the first evidence of the group's brilliant use of virtuoso instrumentalists. Their music and compositional style become more important then the vocals, despite the fact that the vocals are very much up-front in the mix, and the group's most polished aspect. The titanic musicianship of guitarist Steve Howe, drummer Bill Bruford, bassist Chris Squire, and keyboardist Tony Kaye was a force to be reckoned with, as were the album's attention-getting production values (by the band and Eddy Offord). *The Yes Album* is one of the finest audiophile rock albums ever made, with its unusually live-sounding, wide soundstage, sharp separation, loud volume, and playful stereo effects.

The 9½-minute "Yours Is No Disgrace" sets the stage for the trademark Yes sound. Squire's thunderous bass (as much a lead instrument in Yes as any other), Bruford's tumbling drums, Howe's chunky rhythm guitar, and Kaye's grinding organ charge into an infectious groove, which flows into a fluid, tasty jam with lightning-like guitar notes. A sunny vocal section is then sung by Anderson with Squire and Howe, followed by a barrage of head-spinning guitar by Howe, rife with stereo knob twirls. Howe continues to dazzle by weaving multiguitar tapestries, with acoustic guitar, a spacey Pink Floyd–like solo, and tasty jazz licks, until the vocal section resumes. The 3-minute "The Clap" is another showcase for Howe, being a solo instrumental piece for acoustic guitar. Recorded live in London, the track is a playful romp, sounding like a livelier Mike Oldfield. The 9½-minute "Starship Trooper" is a sci-fi tale, opening with a rushing burst of organ, bass, drums, guitar, and Anderson's clear, multitracked vocals. Once again Howe impresses, with a lightning-fast center section on acoustic guitar, and then a swirling, triumphant buildup of multiple electric guitar parts with savage exchanges of solos serving as the piece's climax. The mixture of fantasy subject matter with the rest of Anderson's contemporary spiritual themes is the basis of the band's modernist context, a realm where philosophical poetics joins forces with the potent immediacy of loud, driving, high-tech music making.

The 7-minute "I've Seen All Good People" is a Crosby, Stills, Nash and Young–like hippie folk rock anthem led by acoustic guitar. The detailed, advanced production and the concluding heavy rock jam give the piece its unmistakable Yes trademarks. The 3-minute "A Venture" begins with a dreamy, faraway-sounding piano intro with teasing guitar chords, then establishes a bouncy, romping tempo with a King Crimson/"Cat Food"–like jam of piano, bass, and drums, which like the rest is given a large production. The 9-minute "Perpetual Change" recalls "The Knife" by Genesis, with its chugging organ, adept bass, and savage guitar notes. A singsong but pretty vocal by Anderson lightens the piece; then comes an unusual, psychedelic touch—a totally different type of jam is phased into one channel while the previous section of the song reemerges in the other channel.

FRAGILE. Released January 1972. Atlantic.

Recorded in September of 1971, this popular classic of the progressive rock form is masterful in every respect and an inspired triumph. With Tony Kaye departed, new keyboardist Rick Wakeman brings a large palette of keys, including organ, mellotron, synths, harpsichord, grand piano, and electric piano. With *Fragile,* vocalist Jon Anderson introduces his new lyrical style, which is more sophisticated and intellectual, but still very much in the realm of wide-eyed, hippie dreamer poetics. Most notable here is that the recording is an uplifting and passionate form of music, with a breezy, positive vibe. The disc captures the band at their freshest, when their innovations were brand-new. The arrangements, particularly the vocals, are more disciplined and polished than any in prog rock in the early 1970s. This disc is another audiophile treasure, produced by the band and engineer Eddy Offord, yielding immaculate sound quality in its remastered form.

The 8½-minute "Roundabout" opens with Steve Howe's oddly inviting acoustic guitar tune-up intro, followed by Chris Squire's thick, pumping bass, creating a huge sound with its tricky, chunky rhythms, keyboard and guitar orchestrations, and rousing vocal structure. The piece is the ultimate in widely appealing, symphonic arrangements, a point of intersection between the new "serious rock" and the world of Top 40 pop singles. *Fragile* gives each member of the band a brief solo track, similar to Pink Floyd's democratic delegation on *Ummagumma.*

Rick Wakeman's 1½-minute "Cans and Brahms" is an adaptation of extracts from Brahms's *Fourth Symphony in E Minor,* Third Movement. Like Keith Emerson of ELP, Wakeman puts modern instruments (electric piano, synths) in the place of the traditional acoustic ones. It's nice, but not very important. Anderson's 1½-minute "We Have Heaven" is an imaginative stereo fantasyland of gorgeous guitars, percussion, and multiple vocal parts, the piece announcing itself like a spiritual anthem. The 8-minute "South Side of the Sky" is an album highlight. Wind sounds and the crack of thunder leap into Bill Bruford's huge drums and Howe's snarling lead electric guitar, with an aggressive vocal and abstract lyrics by Anderson and a nice, over-the-top piano solo by Wakeman.

Bruford's 30-second "Five Per Cent for Nothing" is a quirky, fragmentary, minimalist, Canterbury-like segment played by the band. (The piece's sarcastic title indicates that Bruford didn't much care for doing solo tracks at the time.) The 3½-minute "Long Distance Runaround" is a memorable, tightly executed ballad, with irresistible melodies,

Anderson's standout vocal and poetry, and Howe's fluid guitar. It has an elusive, dreamy quality, despite the piece's highly rhythmic structure. This leads into Squire's 2½-minute "The Fish (Shindleria Praematurus)," where all the riffs, rhythms, and melodies are produced by Squire's bass guitar. It's a priceless, appealing instrumental, with seamless performances by Squire and Bruford. Howe's 3-minute "Mood for a Day" is a classical-sounding piece consisting of multiple acoustic guitars. A sequel of sorts to *The Yes Album*'s "The Clap," it has more possibilities than the former piece; it also recalls Mike Oldfield. The 10½-minute "Heart of the Sunrise" is a Yes fan favorite, with a thunderous symphonic structure featuring some of Anderson's finest vocals, vulnerable yet resolute, with lyrics about feeling overwhelmed by the pace of modern-day life. Delivered with power, grandeur, authority, and high drama, the piece is an emotionally gripping track of classical, poetic storytelling.

The spindly cover painting by Roger Dean is his first cover for the band, and a prelude to his artwork for Anderson's solo album *Olias of Sunhillow.* The disc's booklet faithfully reproduces the band photos and Dean paintings originally included as a separate booklet in the early vinyl releases.

CLOSE TO THE EDGE. Released September 1972. Atlantic.

Recorded by the lineup of the previous Yes album, *Fragile* (see review above), *Close to the Edge* is a cornerstone of conceptual, symphonic progressive rock. While Yes were late arrivals on the scene in terms of extended, multimovement, conceptual compositions (preceeded by Egg, Soft Machine, Pink Floyd, Tangerine Dream, ELP, Popol Vuh, and Jethro Tull), they took the form to a new level. By putting the emphasis on emotional transcendence via loud, hard rock (instead of a drifting spaciness) and via Jon Anderson's philosophical lyrics, Yes created a challenging, spiritual form of modern rock.

Close to the Edge marks the mature period of Anderson's poetics, which are by now often abstract and obscure. This is an important development in the band's history because it's not at all obvious (to the uninitiated) what this music is about—it must be listened to closely. However, the use of music with liturgical antecedents helps anchor listeners, signaling specific emotional cues.

The title track on this disc is an 18½-minute, four part opus. The first section, titled "The Solid Time of Change," opens with very brief, rainforest-like environmental sounds, slowly fading in keyboardist Rick Wakeman's swirling notes, abruptly changing into a mini-overture. Chris Squire's climbing bass notes and Steve Howe's skidding, cutting, lead electric guitar lines release a powerfully hard-rocking groove, fluidly establishing the piece's motif. Segueing into the second section, entitled "Total Mass Retain," the band moves through an incredible rhythmic counterpointing as Anderson's vocal introduces the subject matter. The third section, entitled "I Get Up I Get Down," is dreamlike, with Squire and Howe's vocals creating a mysterious backdrop for Anderson's hymnlike lead vocal. An atmosphere of reverb-soaked guitar and keyboards underlines the religious mood of the piece. Wakeman's slow, staccato chording builds to a murky and loud swamp of pipe organ fanfare, at an over-the-top arena-level volume. A spiritual summit is attained with the fourth section of the piece, "Seasons of Man." Wakeman takes an extended organ solo, the main vocal melodies are recapitulated, and the piece fades out with environmental sounds.

The album's highlight is the 10-minute "And You and I." Howe's unmistakable acoustic guitar intro develops from relaxed noodling to become the track's motif, with a moody baroque feel underlined by Wakeman's misty backgrounds. The piece then launches into a gorgeous tapestry of multiple acoustic guitars in a folksy strumming rhythm to accompany Anderson's vocals. An expansive mellotron brings in the whole band, with Bruford's precise drums competing with Squire's huge bass, exploring themes of sweeping grandeur and atmosphere, topped off by Howe's celestial pedal steel guitar; the conclusion is a simple, folksy coda of the main theme. Although the piece utilizes distinctly Christian liturgical imagery, its impact is universal.

The 9-minute "Siberian Khatru" is an infectious, very English, bouncy groove. Howe's angular guitar leads the track, with Anderson's disciplined, intricate, choral vocal arrangements (including some rather aggressive vocal segments) providing more Christian references in their lyrical themes. Bruford's whip-crack drumming style is intellectual yet sensitive, with attractive snare hits and deft rhythms.

Close to the Edge is another audiophile classic, and has long been held as a state-of-the-art prog rock production. Although Roger Dean's minimalist cover art signals very little of the disc's content, the inner gatefold painting (not one of his best actually) suggests a visit to a place for solitude and meditation.

YESSONGS (CD). Released May 1973. Atlantic.
YESSONGS (video). Theatrical film released 1974. Image laser disc.

Originally a three-LP set (now on two CDs), the 130-minute *Yessongs* is perhaps the ultimate prog rock concert album. Recorded during the fall and winter of 1972, Yes virtually re-released *The Yes Album, Fragile,* and *Close to the Edge* for this live project. At the time, this move was seen as somewhat excessive, but is now—in the CD/box set age—considered standard procedure. The remastered version surpasses all other previously available editions, yielding excellent, well-recorded sound, despite occasionally awkward moments during the mix. The band generally sticks to faithful renditions of their songs, but executes them with a more raging, youthful rock power, and at higher volume. The performances are exemplary, and the group is in peak form throughout, with fiery and energetic playing and a friendly, easy-to-like presentation. This album was recorded during the era just prior to the advent of the giant, arena-sized dinosaur gig, and benefits from being removed from the impersonal nature of the stadiums Yes usually plays. Here the sound is captured more up-close, in front of a very receptive audience.

Although drummer Bill Bruford left the group in the fall of 1972, he is still featured on some of the *Yessongs* CD tracks, including "Perpetual Change" and "Long Distance Runaround"/"The Fish." His replacement, Alan White (previously John Lennon's drummer), is extremely impressive. Joining the band suddenly that fall, White had to learn the most complex drum parts in rock (at the time) for this tour. He adapted brilliantly.

The accompanying CD booklet reproduces all of the many Roger Dean paintings that appeared in the plush vinyl version. These are some of Dean's finest and most famous works, with vast,

Yes (live in 1973). From left to right, Jon Anderson, Alan White, Chris Squire.

colorful, sprawling sci-fi/fantasy dreamscapes which complement nicely the ambitious, large-scale music of Yes.

The *Yessongs* film, directed by Peter Neal, is a 72-minute theatrically released motion picture that documents a Yes show at London's Rainbow Theatre in late December of 1972. While the soundtrack is in stereo, it cannot compare with the fidelity of the *Yessongs* CD, and has a low-volume, murky, faltering separation. Though White's drums are often lost in this muddled mix, the material comes shining through. The performances are fresh and lively, and when taken as a companion piece to the CD, make for an entertaining viewing. Nonetheless, this package is not considered to be preferable to the video of the band's 1975 show at London's Queen's Park Rangers Stadium (see the review of *Live at Q.P.R. 1975,* below).

The combination of the deep colors used in the film and the darkness of the band onstage exudes a mysterious aura. The camera coverage is up-close and first-rate, and it's fun to observe how effective dry ice, colored lights, and a glitter ball could be in adding drama to the band's presentation. During "Close to the Edge," the film's highlight, Neal intercuts conceptual footage of microbial life and underwater seabeds with the group's performance. While hardly the cinematic tour de force that *Pink Floyd at Pompeii* (see review) is, the film still stands as an authentic artifact from an early era of prog rock.

The Image laser disc is a treat, with a gatefold sleeve containing multiple Roger Dean paintings, the bonus inclusion of a few theatrical trailers for the film, and an essay by members of a Yes fan club.

TALES FROM TOPOGRAPHIC OCEANS.

Released November 1973. Atlantic.

This brave, controversial recording has become the ultimate whipping boy for every kind of prog rock put-down imaginable, a fate that is totally undeserved. The overall structure of the album works, and is really not very different from what the band had done on albums like *Close to the Edge* and *Relayer. Tales . . .* is a serious attempt to create an intellectual rock music. It's a visionary, challenging work that has yet to be fully accepted and understood. Unified by an imaginative, all-encompassing thematic concept, the album's lyrics touch on spirituality, philosophy, history, art, genetic memory, and modern life.

Tales . . . has a number of superb motifs, melodies, and rhythms, as well as some of the band's most creative performances (particularly sections with Steve Howe's guitar and Alan White's drums and percussion). The esoteric nuances in the playing are a real treat for fans, and much of their renowned polish remains intact here. Vocalist/lyricist Jon Anderson's dominance is made more explicit here, and his leadership shapes the project. Once again Anderson's lyrical focus is on achieving transcendence, in several different senses. Like *Close to the Edge, Tales . . .* is not in any way obvious, rewarding only those who care to take the time to listen carefully and try to understand it. The recording for the most part jettisons the church music religiosity of *Close,* . . . a move which is definitely progressive. To those who question whether this is a work of conventional rock and roll, the answer is, it isn't. What it is is a new, progressive form of music that incorporates rock and classical structures, and as a result goes right over the heads of fans looking only for the latest dance groove.

The 20½-minute "The Revealing Science of God—Dance of the Dawn" begins a unique, multitracked vocal intro, then expands with symphonic workouts of building keyboards, percussion, and backing vocals. The density of the arrangement in parts seems unsure and lumbering, but the piece generally moves along at a sprightly pace, with spacey sections, atypical Yes vocal harmonies, instrumental flash, and full-blown jams.

The 20½-minute "The Remembering—High the Memory" has a group vocal with plaintive guitar that's frankly a bit ponderous, but a spacey multi-keyboard section by Rick Wakeman goes into a multiple acoustic guitar jig by Howe and leads to some more lively, haunting lead guitar and icy textures.

The 18½-minute "The Ancient—Giants Under the Sun" is an album highlight. Primarily instrumental, it's easily one of the band's most experimental tracks. Howe and White in particular shine here, with exotic, Middle Eastern–flavored, stereo-panned percussion and searing electric guitar, as well as Wakeman's soothing mellotron. The exploratory sections of guitar and drums are really wonderful, despite the occasionally awkward sound mix. While White's role in Yes is often overlooked, his unique percussion work—on what was his first studio recording with the band—is extraordinary. Another highlight is the 21½-minute "Ritual—Nous Somme du Soleil." Here Anderson's philosophical themes are mixed with a strong streak of romanticism, and the piece seems more naturally flowing than the previous tracks, bouncing along at the usual adept Yes style. Led by Squire's bass guitar, the track is a unique and unconventional symphonic rock jam, with a fiery, loud, and unexpected tour de force of complex drums and percussion by White—one of the high points of his tenure with Yes.

The sound of the remaster is excellent, though it does have some hiss. The production is once again by the band and Eddy Offord. Roger Dean's fabulous fantasy landscape cover painting is one of his best, and is ideal for this music. In concert, the album's compositions improved on the shakier transitions of the studio versions.

Tales from Topographic Oceans represents an optimistic period in progressive music history—a period when a recording like this could be made with full artistic freedom, the full support of a major label, and media attention.

RELAYER. Released November 1974. Atlantic.

Relayer is an essential Yes title, in the same experimental vein as *Close to the Edge* and *Tales from Topographic Oceans.* Both challenging and poetic, it forges a storytelling, epic-scale prog rock music form. This is a much harder-edged album than any of the band's other releases, and represents a period in their history where they had refined a theatrical approach to their presentation and were at their artistic zenith as leaders of the prog rock genre. Steve Howe's guitars are at the forefront of the album's sound, and he has the key musical moments. Rick Wakeman had left the band, and keyboardist Patrick Moraz here takes his place, playing more synths than any previous Yes keyboardist. Also contributing a number of tape effects is guest Genaro Rippo.

The 22-minute "The Gates of Delirium," one of Yes's finest tracks, is an example of the symphonic rock form at its peak. Without the religiosity of *Close to the Edge,* and far more modern than that release, it has moments that are dark and macho, with angry political lyrics that inject a touch of venom into the Yes style, a new element for the group. The piece is performed at an arena-level volume and the latest in keyboard and recording technology. It opens with a swirling effect of multiple keyboards, guitars, and cymbals, punctuated by Chris Squire's monster bass guitar, as leader/lyricist Jon Anderson's aggressive vocals relate a tale of titanic conflict. This leads into a lengthy center section that proves to be one of their loudest, biggest, most powerful jams, like a battle of the ancient gods. Relentless, continually building, violent jolts of guitar, keyboards, and bass finally culminate in chaotic percussion effects by drummer Alan White. Settling into a floating dust of space music for its concluding segment, Howe's slide guitar effects and Moraz's keyboards establish a gentle, tranquil, reflective mood, into which Anderson injects a quiet acoustic guitar and one of his finest vocals, with transcendent, spiritual lyrics about the hope of a new awakening. It's uplifting, emotional, and everything that Yes stands for. The execution of this ambitious, lengthy piece is more effective than that of most of the tracks on *Tales from Topographic Oceans.*

The 9½-minute "Sound Chaser" opens with a loud, rapid-fire, unusual rhythm section motif, leading into an adrenalin-driven heavy rock jam that's both noisy and live-sounding, with a screeching, deafening guitar solo by Howe. The equally loud vocal and keyboard sections seem awkward, however, and overall this is one of the group's most bizarre tracks. The 9-minute "To Be Over" has a hissy mix, with a vocal arrangement (as on "Sound Chaser") that's too loud and awkward. Nevertheless, the instrumental textures are appealing, with a drifting and spacey bed of acoustic guitars and keyboards that have an Eastern flavor, culminating in a Howe-led jam.

Produced by the band and Eddy Offord, the sound quality is excellent, with the exception of "To Be Over." Roger Dean's sumptuous, grey-colored fantasy painting is the ideal image for this album.

Later Yes studio albums, such as 1977's *Going for the One,* 1978's *Tormato,* and 1980's *Drama,* are only sporadically progressive, with the band returning to less ambitious, shorter tracks similar to those on their first two albums. While some of the material on those recordings is an embarrassment, each disc has its fine moments, and though they added nothing significant to the innovations of the group's previous releases, they come recommended. After *Drama,* the progressive elements in the band's music were effectively in the past.

LIVE AT Q.P.R. 1975. Volumes 1 and 2 (videos). Released 1992. Laser disc imports (Japan).

A complete Yes concert from the spring of 1975 at London's Queen's Park Rangers Stadium, this is the group's high point in terms of performing their most progressive material. These 150 minutes of professionally shot, clear color video on two Japanese laser discs (separately sold) are easily preferable to the *Yessongs* film, due primarily to the larger range of material included. While the soundtrack is in hi-fi mono, it's still an improvement over *Yessongs'* botched sound. The stadium where this was recorded is a huge, open-air sports auditorium, and the size of the show is gigantic. The stage design by Roger Dean is a real treat, surrounding the band with a sci-fi environment of strange, psychedelic objects.

Vocalist Jon Anderson is certainly in his element here, looking like a Biblical prophet with long hair and beard. This was an era when he was an instrumentalist in the band as well, playing a number of guitars and percussion instruments. Chris Squire also demonstrates a larger range, playing acoustic guitar, harmonica, and percussion, in addition to his role as bassist and backing vocalist. Patrick Moraz is the keyboardist for this show, and his playing is interesting for those who have seen only Rick Wakeman or Tony Kaye. Moraz expertly combines the fiery classical technique of Wakeman with the rock emotion of Kaye, yet his performance is never derivative. Moraz's unique ear for synth textures and deeper exploration into jazz-fusion territory marks an important yet all-too-brief period for Yes. The band bravely puts their lengthiest numbers at the beginning of the set. "Sound Chaser," "Close to the Edge," "To Be Over," and "The Gates of Delirium" are the first four numbers. The band's playing on "The Gates . . ." is a real highlight, revealing a super-aggressive delivery and real fury. "Long Distance Runaround" is another highlight, with a slightly different arrangement, and leads into a nice piano solo by Moraz.

"Ritual" is a major highlight, with the full mise-en-scène of the light show, Dean props, stage fog, and extra percussion effects creating a stunning form of operatic rock theatre. The execution of this track from *Tales from Topographic Oceans* is masterful, including exemplary performances by Anderson on vocals, percussion, and acoustic guitar, Squire's lengthy bass solo, Howe's emotional slide guitar, and White's aggressive, exotic percussion.

Elsewhere are ripping versions of "I've Seen All Good People," "The Clap," "And You and I," "Roundabout," "Sweet Dreams," and "Yours Is No Disgrace." Occasionally there are glaring sound-mix problems and stage buzzes (particularly on "Sound Chaser," "To Be Over," and "I've Seen All Good People"), but the show is so compelling that these technical glitches do not really distract for long.

Although this import set is hard to find, it stands as the essential visual document of Yes at their progressive pinnacle and is well worth the search. For an audio-only equivalent, the two-disc CD *Yesshows,* released in 1980, presents two tracks from a superior 1976 show, with ace versions of "The Gates of Delirium" and "Ritual." The rest of the album's material, however, consists of sub-par versions of tracks from their weaker late 1970s albums *Going for the One* and *Tormato*.

Another video release (on Atco laser disc and VHS) from 1992 is the documentary *Yes Years.* Recorded during rehearsals for Yes's 1991 *Union* tour, it features lengthy interviews with all Yes band members past and present and deals head-on with the many issues involved in the making of progressive music.

Z

ZAO

KAWANA. Released December 1976. Musea import.

Zao was a French progressive band that began as an offshoot of another French prog rock group, Magma. Zao uses no guitars, and their danceable (and at times even wild) tempos recall Weather Report, Passport, and *Visions*-era Clearlight, though with a more rocking, symphonic approach. *Kawana* (translated, "pure intention"), a minor gem of instrumental jazz/rock fusion, is the band's best production. Previous Zao albums were a total botch in terms of fidelity, making *Kawana* sound positively glossy by comparison. Led by composers Francois Cahen (playing acoustic and electric piano and synths) and Yochk'o Seffer (saxophones, piano), the quintet is rounded out by the talented rhythm section of bassist Gerard Provost and drummer Jean My Truong, and violinist Didier Lockwood, who provides a number of unique solos. *Kawana* was Zao's most well-received recording, and had a U.S. release at the time. Regrettably, the band fell apart in 1977 just as they were taking off.

The opening 7-minute "Natura" is quietly intense, featuring a bed of grand multiple keyboards, thick, rubbery bass lines, hip, Brand X–like drums, unusual violin, and mellow, Soft Machine/Karl Jenkins–like sax solos. The 9-minute "Tserouf" is quite an amazing workout, combining Return to Forever/Stanley Clarke–like funky bass lines, blaring sax orchestrations, and violin solos with Genesis-style rapid-fire keyboard and drum exchanges. The 2½-minute "F.F.F." is a lovely piece of classically flavored chamber music, featuring violin, piano, and bowed acoustic bass.

The 4-minute "Kabal" is a monster-sized fusion number, with its bass, aggressive sax soloing, and a huge drum sound recalling Passport and Brand X. The 3½-minute "Sadie" is more typically jazzy than the rest, with dual leads by violin and sax over low-key backing and atmospheric wind effects. The 10½-minute "Free Folk" is bookended by an unusual vocal choir. As on "Tserouf," the keyboard/rhythm section workouts impress, with furious blowing from all the members in this funky Return To Forever/Weather Report–like fusion jam.

A lively 13-minute bonus track from 1973 is also included. "Salut Robert!" has a different Zao lineup (apart from leaders Cahen and Seffer), and recalls the early Passport or Embryo, with the emphasis more on jazz than on rock. The sound is good, but not as sharp as on *Kawana*.

APPENDIX ONE

THE CANON: 100 CLASSIC PROGRESSIVE RECORDINGS

The main text of *The Billboard Guide to Progressive Music* reviews over 325 titles that are key to understanding the progressive music genre, its myriad forms, and its many subgenres. The following list pares down the original compilation to its essential bare bones: 100 important, influential, and beloved recordings which represent milestones in the history of progressive music. Let these represent the genre and all that it stands for—the best of the best, as it were.

This list is intended both for readers interested in building a collection and looking for a place to start, and for those with an interest in the works of a particular artist who want to know which titles are most notable. The list also includes video works, as there are some truly historic live performances that surpass the audio-only releases and need to be seen because they are crucial to a complete understanding of the genre. Whether audio or video, each of the 100 titles in this list represents a pinnacle of ambition, concept, composition, performance, and sound quality. They are the undeniable masterpieces.

The list includes as many progressive forms as possible. When more than one title from a single group/artist appears on the list, the listed releases represent a definite progression—a new stylistic development, a new aesthetic approach, or at least a more solid and successful recombination of earlier ideas. These are arranged in chronological order by release date.

A bit of confusion exists concerning the titles, as some CDs contain more than just a single album. However, CD releases consisting of more than one album are still counted as one title. For example, the Schicke, Führs and Fröhling release listed here contains three albums. The Eberhard Schoener title, the two Popol Vuh titles, and one of the Emerald Web titles also refer to two-album releases. Also, the two volumes of the Yes laser discs, *Live at Q.P.R.*, are counted as one selection, as they are both from the same show.

The canon, then, in alphabetical order, is as follows:

Algarnas Tradgard—*The Garden of the Elks*
Jon Anderson—*Olias of Sunhillow*
Bjørnstad/Darling/Rypdal/Christensen—*The Sea*
Camel—*The Snow Goose*
Chris and Cosey—*Allotropy*
Clearlight—*Clearlight Symphony*
Clearlight—*Visions*
Cosey Fanni Tutti—*Time to Tell*
Curved Air—*Curved Air Live*
Dark—*Dark*
Deuter—*D*
Deuter—*Aum*
Djam Karet—*Burning the Hard City*
Djam Karet—*Suspension and Displacement*
Dzyan—*Time Machine*
Emerald Web—*Nocturne/Lights of the Ivory Plains*
Emerald Web—*Traces of Time*
Focus—*Moving Waves*
Edgar Froese—*Aqua*
Edgar Froese—*Epsilon in Malaysian Pale*
Ron Geesin and Roger Waters—*Music from the Body*
Genesis—*Genesis in Concert 1976* (laser disc)
Gong—*Live Etc.*
Gotic—*Escenes*
Gryphon—*Red Queen to Gryphon Three*
Steve Hackett—*Voyage of the Acolyte*
Bo Hansson—*Lord of the Rings*
Bo Hansson—*Attic Thoughts*
Hatfield and the North—*Hatfield and the North*
Hatfield and the North—*The Rotters Club*
Henry Cow—*Western Culture*
Steve Hillage—*Rainbow Dome Musick*
Michael Hoenig—*Departure from The Northern Wasteland*
In Be Tween Noise—*Humming Endlessly in the Hush*
Jethro Tull—*Thick As a Brick*
King Crimson—*In the Court of the Crimson King*

King Crimson—*Lizard*
Lightwave—*Nachtmusik*
Lightwave—*Mundus Subterraneous*
Annea Lockwood—*The Glass World*
Annea Lockwood—*A Soundmap of the Hudson River*
Massacre—*Killing Time*
John McLaughlin—*Devotion*
Bill Nelson—*Crimsworth*
O + A—*Resonance*
Mike Oldfield—*Tubular Bells*
Mike Oldfield—*Incantations*
Mike Oldfield—*Exposed*
Mike Oldfield—*Tubular Bells II—The Performance Live at Edinburgh Castle* (laser disc)
Passport—*Cross Collateral*
Annette Peacock—*Sky-skating*
Annette Peacock/Paul Bley—*Dual Unity*
Pink Floyd—*The Piper at the Gates of Dawn*
Pink Floyd—*Ummagumma*
Pink Floyd—*Pink Floyd at Pompeii* (laser disc/VHS)
Pink Floyd—*Dark Side of the Moon*
Pink Floyd—*Animals*
Popol Vuh—*In the Gardens of Pharao/Aguirre*
Popol Vuh—*Tantric Songs/Hosianna Mantra*
Renaissance—*Live at Carnegie Hall*
Vicki Richards—*Parting the Waters*
Terry Riley—*A Rainbow in Curved Air*
Terje Rypdal—*Whenever I Seem to Be Far Away*
Terje Rypdal—*Odyssey*
Terje Rypdal—*If Mountains Could Sing*
Schicke, Führs and Fröhling—*The Collected Works of Schicke, Führs and Fröhling*
Eberhard Schoener—*Meditation/Sky Music—Mountain Music*
Klaus Schulze—*Cyborg*
Klaus Schulze—*Blackdance*
Klaus Schulze—*X*
Liz Story—*Solid Colors*
Liz Story—*Speechless*
Liz Story—*Escape of the Circus Ponies*
Tangerine Dream—*Electronic Meditation*
Tangerine Dream—*Atem*
Tangerine Dream—*Phaedra*
Tangerine Dream—*Rubycon*
Tangerine Dream—*Ricochet*
Third Ear Band—*Alchemy*
Third Ear Band—*Third Ear Band*
Throbbing Gristle—*D.O.A.*
Throbbing Gristle—*In the Shadow of the Sun*
Throbbing Gristle—*CD1*
Steve Tibbetts—*Steve Tibbetts*
Steve Tibbetts—*Safe Journey*
David Torn—*Best Laid Plans*
David Torn/Mick Karn/Terry Bozzio—*Polytown*
Voice of Eye—*Vespers*
Voice of Eye—*Transmigration*
Kazumi Watanabe—*The Spice of Life in Concert* (laser disc)
Kit Watkins—*Circle*
Eberhard Weber—*The Colours of Chloe*
Eberhard Weber—*Fluid Rustle*
Eberhard Weber—*Later That Evening*
White Willow—*Ignis Fatuus*
Yes—*The Yes Album*
Yes—*Fragile*
Yes—*Close to the Edge*
Yes—*Tales from Topographic Oceans*
Yes—*Live at Q.P.R.* Volumes One and Two (laser discs)

APPENDIX TWO

FIVE PROGRESSIVE MUSIC STYLES

Many artists and recordings in this book are directly or indirectly influenced and inspired by the forms, aesthetics, and styles of specific schools in the other arts. It is for this reason that such tags as "art rock" are often used when speaking of progressive music. Five distinct schools have been selected here—classical formalism, impressionism, surrealism, Dada/absurdism, and postmodernism—and for each is given a list of 10 recordings discussed in Part 2 of this book that most clearly reflect the influence of that school.

Classical Formalism

First, the school of classical formalism. Each of the following 10 recordings is an ambitious, grand, and complex conceptual "composition." Each is a linear, storytelling work. Some utilize motifs. Others utilize sectional pieces in several "movements," each part of a lengthy whole. This school ("classical rock," "symphonic rock," etc.) is the most widely pointed to when progressive music is chronicled.

Camel—*The Snow Goose*
Clearlight—*Clearlight Symphony*
Emerson, Lake and Palmer—*Pictures at an Exhibition*
Gryphon—*Red Queen To Gryphon Three*
Jethro Tull—*Thick As a Brick*
Mike Oldfield—*Hergest Ridge*
Mike Oldfield—*Incantations*
Mike Oldfield—*Ommadawn*
Mike Oldfield—*Tubular Bells II*
Yes—*Tales from Topographic Oceans*

Impressionism

Second, impressionism. Each of the recordings below tends to be quiet and gentle, with a clear emphasis on the melodic as opposed to the rhythmic, underscoring a lightly colored, textured sound, alternately serene and cascading, though sometimes forceful. Each is nonvocal, emphasizing the more personal, introspective nature of the mood the sounds are designed to create and de-emphasizing the hand of the artist. The musical touch characteristic of this school is delicate, eschewing anything too grand or too bizarre.

Bjørnstad/Darling/Rypdal/Christensen—*The Sea*
Harold Budd and Brian Eno—*Ambient 2 The Plateaux of Mirror*
Emerald Web—*Nocturne/Lights of the Ivory Plains*
Brian Eno—*Ambient 1 Music for Airports*
Brian Eno—*Thursday Afternoon*
Edgar Froese—*Epsilon in Malaysian Pale*
Terje Rypdal—*After the Rain*
Liz Story—*Solid Colors*
Liz Story—*Speechless*
Eberhard Weber—*Later That Evening*

Surrealism

Third, surrealism. Each of the 10 recordings listed here explores a world of dreamlike imagery, a world of grotesque and distorted realities, switching back and forth between the hysterically humorous, the dryly whimsical, and the darkly twisted, and doing so with a sense of gleeful intoxication and uninhibited abandon. Most have obscure, poetic lyrics, underpinned by a kaleidoscopic, near-schizophrenic stereo-effects-laden soundscape of instrumental freak-out. This is the multicolored world of psychedelia.

Kate Bush—*The Dreaming*
Danielle Dax—*Pop Eyes*
Fifty Foot Hose—*Cauldron*
Gong—*Live in Paris—Bataclan 1973*
Gong—*You*
Hatfield and the North—*Hatfield and the North*
King Crimson—*Lizard*

Pink Floyd—*The Piper at the Gates of Dawn*
Pink Floyd—*Ummagumma*
Thistle—*Thistle*

Dada/Abdurdism

Fourth, Dada/absurdism. Each of the following recordings constructs a cacophonous, dissonant nonlinear collage of (almost) thoroughly improvised and completely abstract sound which many might not consider to be music at all, but rather a form of performance art. Ranging from the nonsensical to the irritating to the incomprehensible, this school constantly defies popular description.

Ron Geesin—*Hystery—The Ron Geesin Story*
Ron Geesin and Roger Waters—*Music from the Body*
King Crimson—*THRaKaTTaK*
O + A—*Resonance*
Mike Oldfield—*Amarok*
Michael Prime—*Cellular Radar*
Syllyk/Koji Marutani—*Other-wise*
Throbbing Gristle—*CD1*
Throbbing Gristle—*Journey Through a Body*
Throbbing Gristle—*The Second Annual Report*

The Postmodern

Fifth and finally, the postmodern. Although the term *postmodern* means very different things to different people, each of the recordings included in this category is at once a deconstruction and economical reconstruction of musical forms, where the very process itself may be visible and part of the form of the work. Each is a musical collage—brilliantly eclectic, all-encompassing, multistylistic—forming the ultimate hybrid high-tech music for a global village. Although much of the progressive music produced since the early 1980s can be called postmodern, the following titles are particularly representative.

Luigi Archetti—*Das Ohr*
Chris and Cosey—*Allotropy*
Djam Karet—*Suspension and Displacement*
In Be Tween Noise—*Humming Endlessly in the Hush*
Lightwave—*Uranography—Live at the Nice Observatory*
Bill Nelson—*Crimsworth*
Fiorella Terenzi—*Music from the Galaxies*
Voice of Eye—*Transmigration*
Voice of Eye—*Vespers*
Kit Watkins—*Circle*

APPENDIX THREE

THE TOP 30 SPACE MUSIC RECORDINGS

The intent of space music is to induce a trancelike, altered state (similar to a drug-induced state)—to take the listener on an introspective journey, or to evoke otherworldly, mysterious landscapes. Although some of the elements often associated with the aesthetics of space music—stereo separation, longer than usual tracks, and the use of subtle, hard-to-identify environmental sounds—are indeed characteristic of that genre, it's a complex, hard-to-define form.

Space music is, undeniably, stereo personified. The separation between the two channels must leave plenty of "space" in the left/right sound field to create its own environment. This is essential, because space music is a contrivance made possible by modern audio technology. It often defies a "live" reproduction and the straightforward "live" sound of conventional musical instruments. The primary instrument, therefore, becomes the sound field itself, created both in the studio and on the tape. While this is not the case with all of the examples below, the goal is always a very complex layering of sounds within the mix which becomes the composition and the performance.

Recordings in the space music genre are usually lengthy pieces (10 to 25 minutes at least, over an hour at most) that are conducive to creative visualization because they give the listener's mind the time to relax and connect with the piece. In addition, environmental sounds are often employed, water and liquid elements in particular. Some of the sounds found on the more well-known space music recordings are so subtle and complex that the listener often cannot readily identify just what's making the sound, adding to the music's mystique. It is a mistake, however, to think that space music is always subtle (or that all quiet, subtle music is space music). Space music is not necessarily quiet or ambient, and can even be rather harsh. It's also incorrect to assume that all space music is new age music, or that it always involves a keyboard or synth excursion.

Although many space music classics are not well known, to fans of the genre, space music occupies a very special, and to some even spiritual, place, one in which music becomes a private, deeply introspective, uniquely personal experience, and listening to it requires an environment of solitude, without distractions. Headphones, while not essential, are highly recommended.

The following list contains the 30 finest opt-out recordings available. Regrettably, many of these recordings may not be well known or widely distributed, and are often relegated to mail order-only status because most stores don't carry them. They are all well worth tracking down.

Clearlight—*Visions*
Deuter—*Aum*
Emerald Web—*Nocturne/Lights of the Ivory Plains*
Emerald Web—*Traces of Time*
Edgar Froese—*Aqua*
Edgar Froese—*Epsilon in Malaysian Pale*
Steve Hillage—*Rainbow Dome Musick*
Michael Hoenig—*Departure from the Northern Wasteland*
In Be Tween Noise—*Humming Endlessly in the Hush*
Lightwave—*Mundus Subterraneous*
Lightwave—*Nachtmusik*
Lightwave—*Tycho Brahe*
Bill Nelson—*Crimsworth*
David Parsons—*Tibetan Plateau/Sounds of the Mothership*
Popol Vuh—*In the Gardens of Pharao/Aguirre*
Popol Vuh—*Tantric Songs/Hosianna Mantra*
Rapoon—*Darker By Light*
Eberhard Schoener—*Meditation/Sky Music—Mountain Music*
Klaus Schulze—*Blackdance*
Klaus Schulze—*Cyborg*
Klaus Schulze—*Timewind*
Tangerine Dream—*Atem*
Tangerine Dream—*Phaedra*
Tangerine Dream—*Rubycon*
Tangerine Dream—*Zeit*
Throbbing Gristle—*In the Shadow of the Sun*
Tuu—*Mesh*
Voice of Eye—*Transmigration*
Voice of Eye—*Vespers*
Kit Watkins—*Circle*

APPENDIX FOUR

THE TOP 30 BEST-SOUNDING RECORDINGS

What a superb sensual treat it is to listen to a high-quality audiophile recording on a good sound system, or on headphones, and be dazzled by the detailed layers of sound. While the majority of music titles in this book have outstanding sound quality, these 30 have that extra punch throughout, that extra "oomph," that makes them among the finest to be heard anywhere.

There are definite aesthetic criteria involved in these choices. This list is very different from the list of space music discs. Here, the emphasis is on the actual sound of the instruments themselves during performance and recording. The music comes not from a contrivance of studio and tape effects designed to create an otherworldly sound environment, but from the dynamics of a straightforward and realistic "live" delivery, sounding as if the performance were taking place in front of the listener. Central to this are a full and rich sound, with a sharp clarity of different instruments within the mix, and perfectly centered, balanced stereo, with low or no hiss.

A well-engineered, loud, and powerful drum sound (centered in the mix) is key to a live sound, as is a realistic sounding bass guitar—loud, smooth, with no unwanted rumble. All other instruments must convey a crisp richness and depth, and not be drowned out by the drums, or otherwise distorted, or mixed too high and trebly so as to become shrill. It's amazing how many recordings out there, even from the current high-tech era, get these things wrong.

Although the 30 recordings in this list are weighted toward a very tight, loud electric band sound, there are several superb acoustic moments as well. Only a few of these recordings are full digital, or even ADD mixes, which says a lot for the continuing versatility of analog (and for the importance of getting everything right the first time when recording and mixing). In addition, most live recordings suffer from assorted technical nightmares, making the few actual in-concert recordings listed here all that much more remarkable.

Bonfire—*Bonfire Goes Bananas*
Boud Deun—*Astronomy Made Easy*
Curved Air—*Curved Air Live*
Dark—*Dark*
Dark—*Tamna Voda*
Finch—*Glory of the Inner Force*
Fire Merchants—*Landlords of Atlantis*
Genesis—*Wind and Wuthering*
Gryphon—*Red Queen to Gryphon Three*
Guru Guru—*Kanguru*
Happy Family—*Toscco*
Jethro Tull—*Thick As a Brick*
Khan—*Space Shanty*
Let's Be Generous—*Let's Be Generous*
Massacre—*Killing Time*
Mani Neumeier—*Privat*
Mike Oldfield—*Tubular Bells II*
Sally Oldfield—*Water Bearer*
Ozric Tentacles—*Live Underslunky*
Ozric Tentacles—*Strangeitude*
Passport—*Cross Collateral*
Annette Peacock—*Abstract-Contact*
Renaissance—*Live at Carnegie Hall*
Renaissance—*Turn of the Cards*
Terje Rypdal—*If Mountains Could Sing*
Schicke, Führs and Fröhling—*The Collected Works of Schicke, Führs and Fröhling*
David Torn/Mick Karn/Terry Bozzio—*Polytown*
Xaal—*En Chemin*
Yes—*Fragile*
Yes—*The Yes Album*

APPENDIX FIVE

ADDITIONAL RECOMMENDED TITLES

The world of progressive music is so vast that to cover absolutely everything connected with it would require at least three volumes this size. This appendix lists recordings that are on the periphery of progressive music. While these titles are not as significant as those selected for in-depth review, they are certainly worthwhile, and do help to fill in the gaps and complete the picture for fans and collectors.

For the purposes of this book, the following titles do not represent a complete discography for all artists, nor do they include any pop crossovers or "best-of's." Artists who are not dealt with in the reviews of Part 2 are also represented here, though space allows for only a brief elaboration on their work.

Rare or out-of-print CDs and cassettes are listed as well for the most rabid of collectors. An asterisk (*) denotes a recording that is particularly recommended. Release dates and labels are also provided, if known.

Affront Purdu. *Fin de Siècle.** (Released March 1997. Mass and Fieber import.) A series of formless, lengthy, and loud improvisations from a trio led by Luigi Archetti, this combines his Frith/Belew/Torn guitar atmospherics with cello, piano, and drums. Interesting and well recorded, with great performances, but its wanderings are a bit hard to digest.

Agitation Free. *Last.* (Released January 1976. Spalax import.)

Laurie Anderson. *Home of the Brave* (video).* (Released 1986. Lumivision laser disc.) This theatrically released film of Anderson's 1984 tour showcases extraordinary stage design visuals and monologues, as well as extremely impressive ultra-modern high-tech music. The band features both Adrian Belew on guitar and percussionist David Van Tieghem.

Anglagard. *Hybris.* (Released 1993. Out of print import.)

Ash Ra Tempel. *Join Inn.* (Released February 1973. Spalax import.)

Ash Ra Tempel/Timothy Leary. *Seven Up.* (Released March 1973. Spalax import.) This is a far more minor affair than the reputations of its principals might suggest.

Robert Ashley. *Private Parts.* (Released December 1977. Lovely.) Very low-key space music over which Ashley relates lengthy, softly spoken tales. The first of his many releases in this style.

Bon. *Bon to the Bone.* (Released 1996. Lolo.) A fusion power trio led by composer-guitarist Bon Lozaga and bassist Hansford Rowe (two musicians from Gong's 1978 album *Expresso II),* this instrumental rock disc features guest David Torn and his trademark guitar atmospherics. Of the many releases by the bands led by Lozaga (Gongzilla, Project Lo, and Sonic Abandon) this is the most successful.

Tim Boone. *Swimming in the Clouds of the Summit.** (Released 1994. Boone Tunes.) A collection of effectively dreamy and spacious electronic music, reminiscent of mid-1970s Klaus Schulze. While this is not a masterpiece, it is a very strong recent contribution to the genre, possessing a wide scope, and avoiding any new age cliches.

Glenn Branca. *Symphony #5.* (Released 1984. New Tone import.)

Brand X. *Livestock.* (Released November 1977. Caroline.)
—*Masques.* (Released July 1978. Caroline.)
—*Is There Anything About?* (Released October 1982. CBS import.)
—*Manifest Destiny.** (Released February 1997. Pangea.)

Bruford. *The Bruford Tapes.* (Released 1980. Caroline.)

Kate Bush. *The Kick Inside.* (Released February 1978. EMI.)
—*Lionheart.* (Released November 1978. EMI.)

Camel. *Mirage.* (Released 1974. Deram import.)
—*A Live Record.** (Released April 1978. Deram import.)

Chris Carter. *The Space Between.* (Released 1980. Mute.) Recorded while Carter was still a member of Throbbing Gristle, this recording features several styles of synth rock, from the danceable to the spacey.

Chris and Cosey. *Heartbeat.* (Released September 1981. World Serpent/Play It Again Sam import.)
—*Trance.* (Released May 1982. World Serpent import.)
—*Songs of Love and Lust.* (Released January 1984. World Serpent/Play It Again Sam import.)
—*Exotika.* (Released June 1987. Out of print.)
—*Trust.* (Released Nay 1989. Out of print.)
—*Collectiv 4. Archive Recordings.* (Released 1990. World Serpent/Play It Again Sam import.)

Barry Cleveland. *Mythos.* (Released 1986. Out of print.) Guitarist Cleveland with guests Emerald Web creates some fairly effective space music textures.

Curved Air. *Air Conditioning.* (Released November 1970. Warner Bros. import.)
—*Second Album.* (Released August 1971. Warner Bros. import.)
—*Phantasmagoria.* (Released May 1972. Warner Bros. import.)
—*Midnight Wire.** (Released October 1975. Repertoire import.)
—*Airborne.* (Released May 1976. Repertoire import.)
—*Lovechild.** (Released August 1990. Castle import.)
—*Stark Naked.** (Released 1993. Import.)

Danielle Dax. *Jesus Egg That Wept.* (Released 1984. Biter of Thorpe/World Serpent import.)
—*The BBC Sessions.** (Released 1988. Strange Fruit.)

Daniel Denis. *Les Eaux Troubles.** (Released 1993. Cuneiform.) This second solo album from the leader of Univers Zero is the most accessible release from the artist or his band. It contains a wide variety of styles and more importantly, a larger rock influence and big drum sound from Denis.

Deuter. *Haleakala.* (Released 1978. Kuckuck.)
—*Ecstasy.* (Released 1979. Kuckuck.)
—*Land of Enchantment.* (Released 1984. Kuckuck.)
—*Wind & Mountain.** (Released January 1996. Relaxation Company.)

Djam Karet. *Collaborator.* (Released September 1994. HC Productions.)

Egg. *Egg.* (Released 1970. Deram import.)

Emerald Web. *Whispered Visions.* (Released 1980. Emerald Web cassette.)
—*Sound Trek.* (Released 1980. Emerald Web cassette.)
—*Valley of the Birds.* (Released 1981. Emerald Web cassette.)
—*Aqua Regia.* (Released 1981. Emerald Web cassette.)
—*Catspaw.** (Released 1986. Emerald Web cassette.)

Emerson, Lake and Palmer. *Trilogy.* (Released 1972. Rhino.)
—*Welcome Back My Friends to the Show That Never Ends.* (Released 1974. Rhino.)

Brian Eno. *Ambient 4 On Land.* (Released 1982. Caroline.)
—*Apollo: Atmospheres + Soundtracks.* (Released 1983. Caroline.)
—*The Shutov Assembly.* (Released 1992. Opal/WB.)

Extensions. *1,54.* (Released 1994. EXT import.)

Forrest Fang. *The Wolf at the Ruins.** (Released May 1989. Out of print.) Fang has several discs available in the world music style, featuring Chinese influences and instruments. This recording, however, applies his compositional stylings to the genre of space music, with exceptional results.

Focus. *Focus 3.* (Released February 1973. IRS.)
—*Live at the Rainbow.* (Released November 1973. EMI import.)

Bill Frisell. *Rambler.* (Released February 1985. ECM.) Frisell has several titles to his name, each a minor gem of Henry Cow-like quirky instrumental rock. This is his best — a combination of Fred Frith-like guitars, Miles Davis-like compositions, and that unique ECM production, which gives the recording an ethereal flow.

Edgar Froese. *Stuntman.* (Released 1979. Caroline.)
—*Kamikaze 1989.* (Released 1982. Out of print.)

Kay Gardner. *A Rainbow Path.** (Released 1984. Ladyslipper.)
—*Garden of Ecstasy.** (Released December 1989. Ladyslipper.) Composer/flautist Gardner operates in feminist circles, with ambitious compositions drawing on classical structures combined with low-key new age and space music textures, all of which make for an appealing form of fusion deserving of a wider audience.

Ron Geesin. *A Raise of Eyebrows/As He Stands.* (Released 1967; 1973. See For Miles import.)
—*Magnificent Machines.* (Released 1988. Themes International import.)

Genesis. *Trespass.* (Released October 1970. MCA.)
—*Abacab.* (Released September 1981. Atlantic.)
—*Three Sides Live* (video).* (Released 1982. Laser disc/VHS.)

Philip Glass. *Music in Twelve Parts.** (Released 1974. Virgin.)
—*North Star.** (Released 1977. Virgin.)
—*Dance Nos. 1-5** (Released 1988. CBS.) More at home in the classical realm than anywhere else, minimalist composer Glass nevertheless has been quite influential on progressive music. The three titles listed here are those closest to contemporary and progressive forms, and all come highly recommended.

Gong. *Magick Brother.* (Released 1970. Spalax import.)
—*Camembert Electrique.** (Released June 1971. Spalax import.)
—*Flying Teapot.** (Released March 1973. Spalax import.)
—*Angel's Egg.** (Released October 1973. Caroline.)
—*Live On TV 1990.* (Released March 1993. Code 90 import.)
—*Camembert Eclectrique.* (Released 1995. GAS import.)
—*The Birthday Party—25th Anniversary.* (Released 1995. GAS import.)

Gryphon. *Midnight Mushrumps.* (Released 1974. Progressive.)
—*Raindance.* (Released 1975. Progressive.)

Guru Guru. *UFO.* (Released September 1970. Spalax import.)

George Harrison. *Wonderwall Music.** (Released November 1968. Apple/Capitol.) A charming slice of instrumental psychedelia and Indian space ragas, this was an influential release at the time, but today looks less progressive, especially in light of the fact that Harrison never recorded anything like it again.

Michael Harrison. *From Ancient Worlds.* (Released April 1992. New Albion.)

Hatfield and the North. *Live 1990.* (Released May 1993. Code 90 import.)

Barbara Held. *Upper Air Observation.* (Released 1991. Lovely.) A new music/classical composer, flautist Held has some surprisingly avant-garde moments on this album, including collage music sections.

Heldon. *Agneta Nilsson.* (Released 1976. Cuneiform.)

Steve Hillage. *Fish Rising.* (Released May 1975. Caroline.)
—*L.* (Released 1976. Caroline.)
—*Green.* (Released March 1978. Caroline.)

Allan Holdsworth. *Velvet Darkness.** (Released 1976. CBS import.) Holdsworth was one of the top progressive guitarists in the 1970s, with tenures in Soft Machine, Gong, Bruford, and U.K. This is his first and best solo album, alternating between band-oriented fusion jams à la Mahavishnu Orchestra and solo acoustic guitar compositions.

Hugh Hopper. *Hoppertunity Box.* (Released 1977. Import.)

Isildurs Bane. *Mind Volume 1.** (Released April 1997. Isildurs Bane import.) An obscure Swedish band who play more instruments than Mike Oldfield, this eclectic, all-instrumental, conceptual symphonic rock disc easily eclipses their mediocre spate of releases from the 1980s and early 1990s. With an immaculate full digital production and lavish packaging, this is a slick and ambitious foray into an intricate classical/rock fusion.

Teiji Ito. *Mesh.** (Released April 1997. Nonsequitur.) Ito is a legendary composer/instrumentalist whose mystical, visionary compositions precede what is commonly known as the progressive genre. His training and travels embraced every conceivable influence, and his work was a significant contribution to the beginning of modernism in 20th-century music. This disc features three lengthy pieces, two being soundtracks for films by Maya Deren from the 1950s, and one for a theatre production in 1982. The sound is good, and this is definitely music for entering the dreamtime.

Jade Warrior. *Elements: The Island Anthology.* Contains four albums: *Floating World* (1974), *Waves* (1975), *Kites* (1976), and *Way of the Sun* (1978). These four all-instrumental releases by this eclectic British band incorporate Oriental musical forms with long, orchestrated, conceptual, picturesque pieces. The juxtapositions between the pastoral sections and the heavy rock jams are far too jarring to be successful overall, however. *Floating World* and *Way of the Sun* are the best of the four.

Jefferson Airplane. *After Bathing at Baxters.** (Released November 1967. RCA.) One of the few authentic examples of 1960s psychedelia, this is easily the Airplane's most experimental album, with exceptional compositions by Grace Slick and Spencer Dryden. The whole album is wrapped in a conceptual framework that exudes counterculture imagery, this time with music that really is revolutionary.

Jethro Tull. *Aqualung.** (Released March 1971. Chrysalis.)
—*Living in the Past.* (Released November 1972. Chrysalis.)
—*A Passion Play.** (Released May 1973. Chrysalis.)
—*Songs from the Wood.** (Released March 1977. Chrysalis.)
—*Bursting Out.* (Released 1978. Chrysalis.)

King Crimson. *Islands.* (Released December 1971. Caroline.)
—*Larks Tongues in Aspic.** (Released March 1973. Caroline.)
—*Discipline.* (Released September 1981. Warner Bros.)
—*Beat.* (Released June 1982. Warner Bros.)
—*Three of a Perfect Pair.* (Released March 1984. Warner Bros.)
—*Vrooom.* (Released October 1994. Discipline.)
—*Epitaph.* (Released April 1997. Discipline.)

Lightwave. *In der Unterwelt.** (Released 1996. Lightwave CD single import.)

Annea Lockwood. *Thousand Year Dreaming.** (Released April 1993. Nonsequiter.)

Lustmord. *Paradise Disowned.* (Released September 1986. Side Effects import.) A pioneer of the dark industrial music movement of the late 1980s (along with Nocturnal Emissions, SPK, Current 93, and Master/Slave Relationship), this disc is actually rather appealing once the listener accepts the horror-soundtrack-like premise, and it yields some effectively experimental and compelling soundscapes.

Maat. *Sie.** (Released 1994. Dragnet import.) Maat is a German female artist about whom little is known. This great release features some extremely abstract electronics—swirling spurts of sound that tumble out at the listener, over which her icy wordless vocals are layered, sending chills down the spine. A combination of Terry Riley (minimalist patterns of various tones) and Lightwave (spatial, atmospheric space music), Maat's recording is difficult to find but well worth seeking out.

Mahavishnu Orchestra. *Between Nothingness and Eternity.** (Released November 1973.)
—*Apocalypse.* (Released September 1974. Columbia.)
—*Visions of the Emerald Beyond.* (Released 1975. Columbia.)
—*Inner Worlds.* (Released 1976. Columbia.)

Maneige. *Libre Service.** (Released 1978. Out of print import.) The level of compositional intricacy is high on this recording by the Canadian fusion group with a light percussion-dominated sound à la early Spyro Gyra. It's certainly an interesting alternative to Rush.

Marillion. *Script for a Jester's Tear.* (Released May 1983. Capitol/EMI.) The epitome of the 1980s neo–prog rock U.K. bands, Marillion never lived up to their promising debut, which took progressive rock closer to a hard rock/heavy metal form, but never really worked. Here, however, on their first album, it is fairly successful.

Nick Mason and Rick Fenn. *Profiles.* (Released May 1985. Sony.) Along with Fenn, a guitarist from the early 1980s Mike Oldfield band, Mason created what's really the only progressive Pink Floyd solo album. Mostly instrumental, it's a sprightly collection of upbeat tunes, bogged down only by two atrociously poor vocal tracks and that dreaded 1980s electronic percussion.

McDonald and Giles. *McDonald and Giles.** (Released January 1971. Atlantic import.) The only release from these original members of King Crimson, this is solidly in the area of that group's first album, only with a poppier and lighter flavor. Throughout it's inventive and very entertaining, and has remarkably advanced production values for its era.

John McLaughlin. *My Goals Beyond.* (Released January 1971. Rykodisc.)
—*Shakti.* (Released 1976. Columbia.)
—*Live at the Royal Albert Hall.* (Released 1990. Polygram.)

Michael McNabb. *Computer Music.** (Released 1983. Out of print.) An early classic of advanced electronic music, McNabb's album is warm, very musical, and creates vivid pictures for the imagination.

Patrice Moullet/Alpes. *Rock Sous la Dalle.* (Released 1993. Spalax import.) Moullet and Alpes were the backing band for 1970s French chanteuse Catherine Ribeiro. This disc is an unusually fluid example of electronics and sampling, with a sound like Art of Noise and early 1990s Klaus Schulze meets the Lounge Lizards. Ultimately it's all too tech-sounding, but the music is very free and imaginatively constructed, with extreme stereo separation.

National Health. *Missing Pieces.* (Released November 1996. ESD.)

Bill Nelson. *Chance Encounters in the Garden of Lights.* (Released 1988. Out of print.)

O Yuki Conjugate. *Equator.* (Released November 1994. Staalplat.) A decent example of the sinister and dark industrial/ambient/tribal genre. This is abstract, all-instrumental music for the dreamtime, better than most releases in this vein, finding the right balance with a variety of stylistic fusions.

Mike Oldfield. *Five Miles Out.* (Released March 1982. Caroline.)
—*Crises.* (Released May 1983. Caroline.)
—*Voyager.* (Released September 1996. Reprise.)

Mike Oldfield and David Bedford. *The Orchestral Tubular Bells.* (Released February 1975. Virgin import.)

Sally Oldfield. *Easy.* (Released 1979. Castle import.)
—*Celebration.* (Released 1980. Castle import.)

Oregon. *Music of Another Present Era.* (Released 1973. Vanguard.)
—*Distant Hills.* (Released 1973. Vanguard.)
—*Winter Light.* (Released 1974. Vanguard.)
—*Out of the Trees.* (Released 1977. Vanguard.)
—*Oregon.* (Released 1983. ECM.)
—*The Crossing.* (Released February 1985. ECM.)
—*Ecotopia.* (Released 1987. ECM.)
—*49th Parallel.* (Released 1989.) Long a favorite of progressive audiences (as are the releases of Oregon guitarist Ralph Towner), Oregon is on the lighter side of fusion to be sure, and their albums are somewhat interchangeable, but the level of musicianship and group interaction is phenomenal, and their jazz is some of the spaciest ever recorded.

Ozric Tentacles. *Pungent Effulgent.* (Released 1989. Dovetail import.)
—*Erpland.* (Released July 1990. Dovetail import.)
—*Afterswish.* (Released January 1992. Dovetail import.
—*Jurassic Shift.* (Released July 1993. IRS.)
—*Vitamin Enhanced* (box set). (Released 1993. Dovetail import.)
—*Arborescence.* (Released July 1994. IRS.)
—*Become the Other.* (Released 1995. Dovetail import.)

The Alan Parsons Project. *I Robot.** (Released June 1977. Arista.) Easily their most successful release, the group could be considered prog rock lite, given the pop simplicity their albums proffer. This recording has the most and the best instrumentals, and the concept (albeit very light when it's even discernible) is pure Pink Floyd "us vs. them" drama with a touch of mystery.

David Parsons. *Dorje Ling.* (Released 1992. Fortuna.)

Passport. *Hand Made.** (Released 1973. Atlantic import.)

Annette Peacock. *X-Dreams.* (Released April 1978. Great Expectations import.)
—*The Perfect Release.** (Released November 1979. Out of print.)

Penguin Cafe Orchestra. *Penguin Cafe Orchestra.* (Released January 1981. Caroline.)

—*Signs of Life.* (Released 1987. Caroline.) This loosely knit ensemble led by Simon Jeffes is as bizarre as Henry Cow, but in a more palatable way, with classical influences so much in play that it brings them to the edge of 20th-century classical music. Elements of avant-garde collage and eclectic instrumentation make the group rather compelling, but nevertheless an acquired taste due to the almost too low-key approach.

Anthony Phillips. *The Geese and the Ghost.* (Released 1977. Voiceprint import.)
—*Private Parts and Pieces.* (Released March 1979. Voiceprint import.) Phillips was the original guitarist in Genesis, and his albums have that trademark 12-string sound, and *Geese . . .* has Phil Collins and Mike Rutherford playing on it. The *Private Parts . . .* series is a multivolume ongoing collection of various instrumental works (there's been about one every year since the first). They feature gentle acoustic passages, and are not overly significant.

Richard Pinhas. *Chronolyse.** (Released December 1976. Cuneiform.) Pinhas was the leader of Heldon, and this, his first solo album, is in a similar vein, only without the group's rock band dynamics. Here it's just electronics and guitar, but his synth work is totally head-bending and attention-getting.

Pink Floyd. *A Saucerful of Secrets.* (Released July 1968. Capitol.)
—*More.* (Released June 1969. Capitol.)
—*Relics.* (Released May 1971. Capitol.)
—*Obscured by Clouds.* (Released June 1972. Capitol.)
—*The Final Cut.* (Released March 1983. Columbia.)
—*Pulse* (video).* (Released 1994. Columbia laser disc/VHS.)

Pekka Pohjola. *The Visitation.* (Released 1979. Fazer import.)
—*Katkavaaran Lohikaarme.* (Released 1980. Fazer import.)
—*Space Waltz.* (Released 1984. Pohjola import.)
—*Flight of the Angel.** (Released 1986. Pohjola import.)
—*New Impressionist.* (Released 1987. Out of print.)
—*Changing Waters.* (Released 1992. Pohjola import.)

Popol Vuh. *Aguirre.* (Released January 1976. Spalax import.)
—*Letze Tage.* Letzte Nacht. (Released 1976. Spalax import.)
—*Sie Still, Wisse ICH BIN.* (Released January 1981. Spalax import.)
—*Agape Agape, Love Love.* (Released 1983. Spalax import.)

Present. *Triskaidekaphobie/Le Poison Oui Rend Fou.** (Released 1980; 1985. Cuneiform.)
—*Live!** (Released 1996. Cuneiform.) Present is led by former Univers Zero member Roger Trigaux. The first disc is a dense and dark instrumental prog rock, similar to mid-1970s King Crimson—instrumental, tricky, lengthy, and more rock and rollish than Univers Zero. The live disc adds vocals, but turns up the volume and goes for an all-out rock and roll approach, with blazing and wailing guitars. How progressive it all is is another matter, but it's certainly refreshing and entertaining.

Quidam. *Reflets Rock.* (Released 1991. Musea import.) A four-piece French prog rock instrumental band similar to Fire Merchants, this is one of the more promising 1990s French groups. Adding dreamy keyboards to the guitar-led power jamming, their material is fun and exciting. A guest female vocalist (words in French) on one long track is a bad idea, though.

Layne Redmond and the Mob of Angels. *Since the Beginning.* (Released 1992. Redmond.) A unique group of percussionists led by Redmond, they represent a meeting place between composers like Kay Gardner and groups like Voice of Eye. They use percussion as a form of spiritual ritual, accompanied by suitably sacred recitation, but although the music is interesting and exudes an otherworldliness, it has an overly literal approach and mediocre production values.

Steve Reich. *Drumming/Six Pianos, etc.* (Released 1974. Deutsche Grammophon.)
—*Octet/Music for a Large Ensemble/Violin Phase.* (Released 1980. ECM.)
—*Tehillim.** (Released 1982. ECM.)
—*Early Works: Come Out/Piano Phase/Clapping Music/It's Gonna Rain.** (Released September 1987. Elektra Nonesuch.)
—*Drumming.* (Released September 1987. Elektra Nonesuch.) Reich's many distinguished compositions

have been a peripheral influence on progressive music, especially his tape and collage works, and all are recommended.

Renaissance. *Prologue.* (Released October 1972. One way.)
—*Azure d'Or.* (Released June 1979. Sire/WB import.)
—*Live In London 1975.** (Released August 1992. Genschman import.)

Return to Forever. *No Mystery.* (Released July 1975. Polygram.)
—*Music Magic.* (Released 1977. Columbia.)
—*Live.* (Released 1978. Columbia.)

Robert Rich. *Numena/Geometry.** (*Numena* released 1986. *Geometry* released 1987. Fathom/Hearts of Space.) Rich is an American electro-acoustic composer, and these are his two finest solo albums. Featuring synths, lap steel guitar, flutes, kalimba, percussion, and environmental sounds, both are first-rate examples of serene space music. Rich's music often recalls that of Edgar Froese, and *Numena* could be considered his *Epsilon in Malaysian Pale,* and *Geometry* his *Pinnacles.* Both have been remastered, and the cover art is excellent.

Robert Rich/Alio Die. *Fissures.** (Released May 1997. Fathom/Hearts of Space.) Similar to Rich's and B. Lustmord's *Stalker, Fissures* is in some ways preferable. This is conceptual and very effective space music disc featuring synths, samples, flutes, and a lot of exotic, evocative percussion. Rich releases titles like this nearly every six months and spreads himself too thin, but *Fissures* is certainly one of his more successful projects. The colorful cover art is exceptional.

Vicki Richards. *Quiet Touch.** (Released 1987. Out of print cassette.)
—*Live in India.* (Released 1988. Out of print cassette.)

Richter Band. *Richter Band.** (Released 1992. Import.) A Czech trio utilizing guitars, bass, and many forms of percussive instruments, the band creates an unfolding series of rhythmic structures, usually soothing and relaxing, that are often quite minimalist. Not an earthshattering form of prog fusion, but certainly a unique one. Hard to find, but worth tracking down.

Terry Riley. *In C.* (Released November 1968. CBS.)
—*Shri Camel.* (Released January 1980. CBS.)
—*No Man's Land.* (Released 1985. Out of print import.)

Jeffrey Roden. *Mary Ann's Dream.** (Released 1993. Big Tree/New Plastic Music.) This charming, low-key disc of nine sparse instrumentals featuring Roden's bass guitar augmented by soft guitars and percussion is a minor gem of inspired and friendly impressionism.

Rush. *2112.* (Released June 1976. Mercury.)
—*A Farewell to Kings.** (Released October 1977. Mercury.)
—*Hemispheres.** (Released November 1978. Mercury.)
—*Moving Pictures.** (Released March 1981. Mercury.)
—*Exit . . . Stage Left* (video).* (Released 1981. Laser disc import.) Rush had the potential to be a major prog rock band, but went in other, more radio/video-friendly directions. The majority of their output both before and after these recordings makes their progressive phase look awfully brief. Combining classic prog rock forms with the power of heavy metal, they played with panache and finesse, their lyrics were true poetry, and their production values were state of the art. But among all the glorious hard rock prog were some grossly juvenile rock clichés to which the band eventually succumbed. The entire Rush catalog is now remastered.

Terje Rypdal. *What Comes After.** (Released January 1974. ECM import.)
—*Waves.* (Released January 1978. ECM.)
—*Undisonus Ineo.* (January 1990. ECM.)
—*Q.E.D.** (January 1993. ECM.)

Terje Rypdal/David Darling. *Eos.* (Released April 1984. ECM.)

Rypdal DeJohnette Vitous. *To Be Continued.** (Released 1981. ECM import.)

Sonic Youth. *Sonic Youth.** (Released 1982. Out of print.)
—*Confusion Is Sex.** (Released 1983. DGC.)
—*Sonic Death—Live Early Sonic 1981–1983.* (Released 1984. Out of print.) The early releases by this famed punk rock band actually fit quite comfortably in progressive circles, with lengthy instrumentals and noisy experimentation, and come recommended to fans of Glenn Branca, Massacre, and Teenage Jesus and the Jerks.

Suso Saiz. *Mirrors of Pollution.* (Released March 1994. No CD import.) Spanish guitarist Saiz is a great texturalist, creating ambient soundscapes similar to David Torn, but without a rock backdrop.

Klaus Schulze. *Irrlicht.* (Released 1972. Spalax import.)
—*Body Love.** (Released December 1976. Brain import.)
—*Body Love Vol. 2.** (Released December 1977. Brain import.)
—*Live.* (Released January 1980. Manikin import.)
—*Trancefer.* (Released November 1981. Brain import.)
—*Beyond Recall.* (Released 1991. Caroline.)

Grace Slick. *Dreams.** (Released January 1980. BMG.) Away from the FM rock/folk pop of Jefferson Airplane and Jefferson Starship, Slick was able to indulge her unique songwriting styles. While this recording is not a progressive album through and through, it does contain several songs (e.g., "Garden of Man," the title track) that are pure symphonic prog, not too far from the melodic, poetic visions of groups like Yes or Genesis. This is worth a second look from those who wouldn't normally listen to a title like this. *Dreams* is now coupled on CD with Slick's embarrrassing 1981 album *Welcome to the Wrecking Ball.*

Gilli Smyth. *Mother.* (Released January 1978. Spalax import.) As you would expect, this is exactly like the artist's material in Gong, only spread out over an entire album. Quite charming if quaint ethereal pieces emphasizing feminine and occult themes, with timid but atmospheric musical backing.

Soft Machine. *Volume Two.* (Released 1969. One Way.)
—*Third.* (Released April 1970. BGO import.)
—*Fourth.* (Released January 1971. One Way.)
—*5.* (Released 1972. One Way.)
—*Sixth.** (Released February 1973. One Way.) Although Soft Machine was an important group during progressive music's early years, the majority of their recorded titles are now fully absorbed into the mainstream of jazz, and can no longer be considered truly progressive. The production values of most of their releases are dreadful. Their best album is *Sixth,* a double album now on one CD; it has excellent sound, and all of the band's trademark elements are in peak form, especially the up-front drumming of John Marshall.

Solaris. *The Martian Chronicles.* (Released January 1985. Gong import.) Solaris are an all-instrumental band from Hungary, an unlikely place for progressive music, especially during the Cold War era. Combining symphonic rock with electronics, it only sometimes works, and the band's tendency toward empty guitar wailing is also a drawback. But this release works as a sci-fi concept album, and in that context is very entertaining.

The Spacious Mind. *Cosmic Minds at Play.* (Released 1994. Garageland import.)
—*Organic Mind Solution.* (Released January 1995. Garageland import.) This group is a Swedish band that explores psychedelic guitar rock, employing long, loud drones that mix Sonic Youth with David Torn or Robert Fripp. These releases also features some spacey acoustic guitar numbers with vocals and sound effects.

John Surman. *Upon Reflection.* (Released 1979. ECM.) Surman combines saxophones and synthesizers in various musical styles. This disc is perhaps his spaciest, but his other releases follow similar paths.

Tangerine Dream. *Cyclone.* (Released March 1978. Griffin.)
—*Tangram.** (Released May 1980. Caroline.)
—*Pergamon.* (Released January 1986. Sequel.)

Third Ear Band. *Live Ghosts.* (Released 1989. Materiali Sonori import.)
—*Magic Music.* (Released 1990. Materiali Sonori import.)
—*Brain Waves.* (Released 1993. Materiali Sonori import.)
—*Live.** (Released 1996. Voiceprint import.)

Throbbing Gristle. *Heathen Earth.** (Released 1980. Mute.)
—*Mission of Dead Souls.* (Released 1981. Mute.)
—*Throbbing Gristle Live Volumes 1-4.* (Released 1993. Mute import.)

Steve Tibbetts. *Exploded View.** (Released September 1986. ECM.)
—*Big Map Idea.** (Released 1989. ECM.)
—*The Fall of Us All.** (Released March 1994. ECM.)

Tiere der Nacht. *Hot Stuff.* (Released 1992. Rec Rec import.)
—*Wolpertinger.** (Released 1993. Rec Rec import.) Tiere der Nacht is the project of Guru Guru

drummer Mani Neumeier and guitarist Luigi Archetti. The two play mostly improvised, instrumental fragments of raw, over-the-top, adrenalin-charged bash-ups of drums, percussion, guitars, bass, and tape effects. *Wolpertinger* is the best of the two, with a meatier production. The overreliance on short vignettes and the inclusion of embarrassingly ridiculous vocal tracks distract from the duo's finer rhythmic jams.

Keith and Julie Tippett. *Couple in Spirit.* (Released 1988. Out of print.) This release is a series of improvisations from these two artists, with incredible vocal patterns and unusual keyboard work, and it achieves some great heights in terms of both sound and spirituality.

Keith Tippett and Andy Sheppard. *66 Shades of Lipstick.* (Released 1990. Out of print.) A collection of brief, jazzy, introspective and occasionally quite avant-garde duets for piano and sax, this release has an impressive intimacy.

Trilogy. *Here It Is.** (Released January 1980. Musea import.) This five-piece German symphonic group recorded their one and only album in 1978, but the release was delayed until 1980. All instrumental, their music is solidly in the vein of other keyboard-led classical rock groups like Collegium Musicum, ELP, Egg, and Trace. Their compositions and production are good, as is the bass player, but the guitarist is a disappointment, as is the reliance on dated organ soloing.

David Torn. *Tripping Over God.* (Released April 1995. CMP.)

The United States of America. *The United States of America.** (Released March 1968. Sony, or Edsel import.) This album is a classic slice of authentic psychedelia—similar to Fifty Foot Hose—led by very hip female lead vocalist Dorothy Moskowitz and electronics guru Joseph Byrd. The album is too vocal-heavy and pop to be progressive today, but it's a brilliant work, containing collage sections and blazing psych-rock-pop with bizarre interruptions from primitive synths, all relating a very intense counterculture political commentary. The Sony release has bonus tracks and a better band history in the booklet, while the Edsel import has sharper sound and reprints the lyrics.

Univers Aero. *Ceux du Dehors.* (Released 1981. Cuneiform.)

—*Heatwave.* (Released January 1987. Cuneiform.) This band has several releases, of which these are the most notable. Pioneers in the style of chamber rock, they are famous for creating very dense, dark, and lengthy instrumental compositions of great complexity. Later albums added synths. Their music is very much an acquired taste.

Marion Varga and Collegium Musicum. *Marion Varga and Collegium Musicum.* (Released 1975. Opus import.) A live album by the Czech symphonic band Collegium Musicum (why Varga's name is out in front is a mystery), this is an entertaining, well-recorded instrumental quartet workout, led by Varga's dated organ sound. Here an electric guitarist has been added, and the energy level of the playing is very good. This time, though, the material is not as strong as that of their 1973 live album (see review).

Cyrille Verdeaux and Bernard Xolotl. *Prophecy.* (Released 1981. Spalax import.) This album was recorded with only a Prophet synth and guitar synth on a Teac four-track. Despite this minimalist scale, the strength of the two composers' styles comes shining through. A minor, early gem of new age/space music, this has very sweet melodies and spacey drifts, and some nice cover art by Xolotl.

Vita Nova. *Vita Nova.* (Released May 1971. Penner import.) Notable for featuring Eddy Marron of Dzyan, this Austrian group was short-lived. This album is interesting because it's one of the earliest prog releases from Europe. Unlike the music of Dzyan, this is rather dated organ-driven prog, with some excruciatingly obnoxious Latin vocals. The disc is, however, mostly instrumental, and the sound quality is surprisingly good for an LP transcription.

Voice of Eye with Life Garden. *The Hungry Void Volume One: Fire.* (Released 1995. Cyclotron/Agni.)

Chad Wackerman. *The View.** (Released 1993. CMP.) This is a decent reassertion of the jazz/rock fusion genre, similar to the work of bands like Network, Xaal, the 1990s Brand X, and Bruford, but with a very polished, rhythmic, American sound. Composer/drummer Wackerman centers the mix around his powerful drum kit, and the production is immaculate. Guest Allan Holdsworth is the lead guitarist, giving the project a further boost.

Kazumi Watanabe. *The Spice of Life.* (Released 1987. Out of print.)

Weather Report. *Weather Report.* (Released May 1971. Columbia.)
—*I Sing the Body Electric.* (Released March 1972. *(Columbia.)*
—*Tale Spinnin'.* (Released 1975. Columbia.)
—*Heavy Weather.** (Released June 1977. Columbia.)
—*8:30.* (Released December 1978. Columbia.) One of the first fusion bands, Weather Report had a significant impact on several different musical quarters in the 1970s. Their early albums feature a softer, more poignant acoustic spaciness. The mid-to-late 1970s albums combine synths, world music, and a cracking rhythm section with their trademark sound. Weather Report are an important group, but really more in the category of jazz than progressive.

Eberhard Weber. *Chorus.* (Released February 1985. ECM import.)
—*Orchestra.* (Released December 1988. ECM.)
—*Pendulum.* (Released 1993. ECM.)

Werwolf. *Creation.** (Released 1984. Out of print.) This German prog rock band was similar to Curved Air or Renaissance in having a female vocalist (singing in English). The compositions on this recording are very enjoyable symphonic rock with both vocals and instrumentals. The sound is very good, as are the performances and album cover artwork, but the lyrics are howlingly bad. Nevertheless, it has to be recommended as an example of optimistic hippie prog during a low point for progressive music—the commercial 1980s.

Bernard Xolotl. *Procession.* (Released 1981. Erdenklang import.)
—*Mexecho.* (Released 1991. Erdenklang import.) A French keyboardist/composer similar to Clearlight's Cyrille Verdeaux, Xolotl creates new age–type synth instrumentals. While there is a distinct similarity to the pieces, some of the artist's song melodies are distinctly memorable.

Yes. *Time and a Word.* (Released July 1970. Atlantic.)
—*Going for the One.** (Released July 1977. Atlantic.)
—*Tormato.* (Released September 1978. Atlantic.)
—*Drama.** (Released August 1980. Atlantic.)
—*Yesshows.* (Released November 1980. Atlantic.)
—*The Keys to Ascension.* (Released 1996. BMG.)
—*Live in Philadelphia 1979* (video). (Released July 1997. Image laser disc.)

Michelle Young. *Song of the Siren.* (Released 1996. Naosha.) A surprisingly mature self-released disc by the promising composer/vocalist/instrumentalist Young, this is very solidly in the area of *Never for Ever*–era Kate Bush. Despite Young's much-too-obvious Bush influence, it's nice to see that this style of quirky, surreal vocal prog has penetrated into the unlikely region of Chattanooga, Tennessee, where this was recorded. Young's vocals, arrangements, and lyrics are of a very high standard, but the production and backing musicians are too pedestrian. The highlights are the unusual title track, and "Bamboo You," an instrumental that features flutes, pan pipes, wind chimes, synths, and nature sounds. The stunning cover photo of Young as a siren on a seashore is positively sumptuous.

Zao. *Akhenaten.* (Released 1993. Musea import.)

Frank Zappa. *Shut Up n'Play Yer Guitar.* (Released 1981. Rykodisc.)
—*Guitar.* (Released 1988. Rykodisc.) These two albums are lengthy sets of all-instrumental hard rock blowing from a big-band lineup, which were recorded live and then edited together in the studio. Most of Zappa's rock albums are so vocal-heavy that it puts the music in the background, so all that emerges is the occasional guitar solo in between the Mad magazine humor. Here, it's all balls-to-the-wall heavy metal jamming, focusing on rock/electric music as a pure form. The sound is great and the performances are exemplary, but the music is basically just a very powerful—and undeniably entertaining—way of proving that Zappa and band could really smoke in concert.

APPENDIX SIX

OBTAINING THE MUSIC

Mail-Order Importers

Imported recordings can often be difficult to track down. If your local music store doesn't make imports readily available, you'll have to resort to mail order to get the recordings you want. This isn't necessarily a bad thing, as often you'll get a better selection and price than you can get at most retail outlets. The following is a list of mail-order companies who specialize in carrying import titles, and many specialize in carrying the titles from this book. The addresses and telephone numbers were current at the time of writing, but may be out of date by the time you read this.

Eurock. *P.O. Box 13718, Portland, OR 97213. (503) 281-0247.* Imports by artists in this book: Agitation Free; Ash Ra Tempel; Lightwave; Shawn Pinchbeck and Marion Garver; Pekka Pohjola; Peter Schaefer; Klaus Schulze; and Cyrille Verdeaux.

Grand Rapids Compact Disc. *67 54th Street SW, Wyoming, MI 49548. (616) 531-1707.* Anekdoten; Anglagard; Atlas; Bonfire; Camel; Clearlight; Curved Air; Finch; Gong; Mike Oldfield; Ozric Tentacles; Renaissance; Klaus Schuize; Shylock; and Xaal.

Heartbeats. *418 Tamal Plaza, Corte Madera, CA 94925. (800) 767-4748.* Claire Hamill; Lightwave; Bill Nelson; Sally Oldfield; and Klaus Schulze.

Lakeshore Record Exchange. *905 Monroe Avenue, Rochester, NY 14620. (716) 244-6476.* Kate Bush; Camel; Chris and Cosey, Cosey Fanni Tutti; Danielle Dax; Gong; Mike Oldfield; and Throbbing Gristle.

Doug Larson. *62 Crane Street, Caldwell, NJ 07006. (201) 226-6332.* Anglagard; Luciano Basso; Camel; Egg; Finch; Führs and Fröhling; Gotic; Guru Guru; Lard Free; Popol Vuh; Renaissance; Shylock; and Zao.

Laser's Edge. *P.O. Box 2450, Cherry Hill, NJ 08034-0199. (609) 751-6444.* Anekdoten; Anglagard; Bonfire; Finch; Ragnarok; Renaissance; and Shylock.

M and M Music. *P.O. Box 63, Ashland, MA 01721. (508) 881-6737.* Anglagard; Atlas; Camel; Clearlight; Egg; Finch; Ozric Tentacles; and Popol Vuh.

Midnight Records. *P.O. Box 390, Old Chelsea Station, New York, NY 10113-0390. (212) 675-2768.* Agitation Free; Atlas; Bon fire; Clearlight; Curved Air; Finch; Gong; Guru Guru; Pekka Pohjola; Renaissance; and Third Ear Band.

Missing Link Records. *828 Broad Ripple Avenue, Indianapolis, IN 46220-1961. (317) 466-1967.* Agitation Free; Ash Ra Tempel; Chris and Cosey; Danielle Dax; Finch; Guru Guru; and Third Ear Band.

Of Sound Mind. *4134 E. Joppa Road, Suite 104, Baltimore, MD 21236. (410) 529-7082.* Agitation Free; Anekdoten; Anglagard; Camel; Clearlight; Dzyan; Finch; Führs and Fröhling; Gotic; Hugh Hopper; Lard Free; Lightwave; Mike Oldfield; Ozric Tentacles; Passport; Pekka Pohjola; Propeller Island; Klaus Schulze; Shylock; and Zao.

Seldom Seen Records. *P.O. Box 121, Villa Grande, CA 95486. (707) 632-5293.* Clearlight; Curved Air; Egg; Ron Geesin; Gong; Ozric Tentacles; and Passport.

Sound City 2000, Inc.. *P.O. Box 22149, Portland, OR 97222-0149. (503) 654-2196.* Jon Anderson; Bonfire; Kate Bush; Camel; Clear light; Curved Air; Dzyan; Finch; Führs and Fröhling; Gong; Mike Oldfield; Sally Oldfield; Ozric Tentacles; Passport; Annette Peacock; Annette Peacock and Paul Bley; Renaissance; Terje Rypdal; Klaus Schulze; and Eberhard Weber.

Syn-Phonic. *P.O. Box 2034, La Habra, CA 90631. (714) 894-9506.* Agitation Free; Algarnas Tradgard; Anekdoten; Anglagard; Ash Ra Tempel; Atlas; Luciano Basso; Bonfire; Clearlight; Curved Air; Dzyan; Finch; Führs and Fröhling; Gotic; Guru Guru; Lard Free; Ozric Tentacles; Pekka Pohjola; Popol Vuh; Ragnarok; Renaissance; Shylock; Terpandre; Xaal; and Zao.

Thoughtscape Sounds. *4801 South 31st #1, Fort Smith, AK 72901. (800) 435-6185.* Jon Anderson; Kate Bush; Camel; Curved Air; Bill Nelson; Mike Oldfield; Ozric Tentacles; Renaissance; Terje Rypdal; Klaus Schulze; Third Ear Band; and Throbbing Gristle. Also carries import laser discs.

Twist and Shout. *724 S. Pearl Street, Denver, CO 80209. (303) 722-9951.* Ash Ra Tempel; Danielle Dax; Führs and Fröhling; Gong; Guru Guru; Ozric Tentacles; Popol Vuh; Renaissance; Klaus Schulze; and Throbbing Gristle.

Vinyl Solution. *2035 28th Street SE, Kentwood, MI 49512. (616) 241-4040.* Jon Anderson; Anekdoten; Anglagard; Clearlight; Curved Air; Führs and Fröhling; Ron Geesin; Ozric Tentacles; Renaissance; and Klaus Schulze.

Wayside Music. *P.O. Box 8427, Silver Spring, MD 20907-8427.* Agitation Free; Algarnas Tradgard; Anekdoten; Anglagard; Atlas; Luciano Basso; Dzyan; Extensions; Finch; Isbin and deSutter; Bill Nelson; Pangee; Shawn Pinchbeck and Marion Garver; Pekka Pohjola; Popol Vuh; Shylock; and Marian Varga/Collegium Musicum.

The Wild Places. *P.O. Box 1461, Charlestown, RI 02813. (401) 364-7625.* Algarnas Tradgard; Anekdoten; Anglagard; Atlas; Lard Free; and Ragnarok.

Worldwide CD. *2501 N. Lincoln Avenue #289, Chicago, IL 60614. (312) 665-0030.* Jon Anderson; Camel; Curved Air; Gong; Mike Oldfield; and Renaissance. Also carries import laser discs.

Znr Records. *P.O. Box 58040, Louisville, KY 40268-0040. (502) 933-7078.* Jon Anderson; Anekdoten; Anglagard; Ash Ra Tempel; Atlas; Luciano Basso; Bonfire; Camel; Dzyan; Finch; Ozric Tentacles; Renaissance and Zao. Also carries import laser discs.

Independent Record Label Mail-Order Companies

Recordings from independent record labels, private labels, small labels, or simply labels which aren't carried by as are many music stores as major label titles can be obtained from the following list of mail-order companies.

Echodiscs. *P.O. Box 224, Eagle, PA 19480. (610) 458-1110.* Independent label artists reviewed in this book include: Constance Demby; Emerald Web; and Popol Vuh.

Heartbeats. *418 Tamal Plaza, Corte Madera, CA 94925. (800) 767-4748.* Dark; David Darling; Constance Demby; Deuter; Djam Karet; Emerald Web; Michael Harrison; Michael Hoenig; Lightwave; David Parsons; Popol Vuh; Robert Rich/B. Lustmord; Vicki Richards; Eberhard Schoener; and Kit Watkins.

Laser House. *P.O. Box 906, Sterling Heights, MI 48311-0906.* Dark; Emerald Web; Michael Hoenig; and Popol Vuh.

Laser's Edge. *P.O. Box 2450, Cherry Hill, NJ 08034-0199. (609) 751-6444.* Blue Motion; Finnforest; Happy Family; Heldon; Schicke, Führs and Fröhling; Steve Tibbetts; and White Willow.

M and M Music. *P.O. Box 63, Ashland, MA 01721. (508) 881-6737.* Blue Motion; Brand X; Djam Karet; Fire Merchants; Henry Cow; Solstice; and White Willow.

Of Sound Mind. *4134 E. Joppa Road, Suite 104, Baltimore, MD 21236. (410) 529-7082.* Blue Motion; Brand X; Djam Karet; Finnforest; Heldon; National Health; Network; Vicki Richards; Schicke, Führs and Fröhling; Solstice; Kit Watkins; and White Willow.

Syn-Phonic. *P.O. Box 2034, La Habra, CA 90631. (714) 894-9506.* Blue Motion; Boud Deun; Djam Karet; Finnforest; Fire Merchants; Gryphon; Happy Family; Heldon; Network; Schicke, Führs and Fröhling; Solstice; and White Willow.

Thoughtscape Sounds. *4801 South 31st #1, Fort Smith, AK 72901. (800) 435-6185.* Brand X; Fire Merchants; and Ron Geesin.

Vinyl Solution. *2035 28th Street SE, Kentwood, MI 49512. (616) 241-4040.* Djam Karet; Jack Lancaster and Robin Lumley; Solstice; and Kit Watkins.

Wayside Music. *P.O. Box 8427, Silver Spring, MD 20907-8427.* Djam Karet; Finnforest; Henry Cow; Annea Lockwood; the Lunch Factor; Massacre; National Health; Schicke, Führs and Fröhling; Kit Watkins; and White Willow.

The Wild Places. *P.O. Box 1461, Charlestown, RI 02813. (401) 364-7625.* Blue Motion; Constance Demby; Fifty Foot Hose; Finnforest; Fire Merchants; Bo Hansson; Henry Cow; Massacre; Melting Euphoria; Schicke, Führs and Fröhling; and White Willow.

ZNR Records. *P.O. Box 58040, Louisville, KY 40268-0040. (502) 933-7078.* Blue Motion; Boud Deun; Djam Karet; Fifty Foot Hose; Finnforest; Happy Family; Heldon; Henry Cow; National Health; Network; Renaissance; Solstice; Kit Watkins; and White Willow.

Record Label Addresses

If you cannot obtain specific recordings by ordering them from your local record store or through mail-order companies, you should be able to obtain them by writing to the labels directly. In addition, most artists can be contacted through their record label. Addresses for most of the labels whose recordings are reviewed in this book are listed below.

Ad Perpetuam Memoriam (A.P.M.). *P.O. Box 184, 3-78122 Borlaenge, Sweden.*

Admission to Music. *P.O. Box 54, D-28877 Grasberg, Germany.*

Art of Landscape. *Landscape Studios, Hye House, Crowhurst, Sussex TN33 9BX, U.K.*

Belle Antique. *404 SY Bldg. 3-15-18 Shimo-Ochiai, Shinjuku-ku Tokyo 161, Japan.*

Beat Goes On (BGO). *P.O. Box 22, Bury St. Edmonds, Suffolk 1P28 6XQ, U.K.*

BMG/ECM/Milan/RCA. *1540 Broadway, New York, NY 10036-4098.*

Brain. *Metronome Music GMBH, Uberseering 21, 2000 Hamburg 60, Germany.*

Brainworks. *18 The Crescent, Farnham, Surrey GU9 0LG, U.K.*

Capitol/EMI. *1750 N. Vine Street, Hollywood, CA 90028*

Caroline. *104 W. 29th Street, 4th Floor, New York, NY 10001.*

Castle. *Castle Communications, Colet Court, 100 Hammersmith Road, London W6 7JP, U.K.*

CBS/Columbia. *550 Madison Avenue, New York, NY 10022-3211.*

Celestial Harmonies/Fortuna/Kuckuck. *P.O. Box 30122, Tucson, AZ 65751.*

Cherry Red Records Ltd.. *Bishops Park House, 25-29 Fulham High Street, London 5W6 3JH, U.K.*

Cleopatra. *8726 S. Sepulveda, Suite D-82, Los Angeles, CA 90045.*

CMP. *530 N. Third Avenue, Minneapolis, MN 55401.*

Cuneiform. *P.O. Box 8427, Silver Spring, MD 20907-8427.*

Cyclotron Industries. *P.O. Box 66291, Houston, TX 77266.*

Demon. *Canal House, Transport Avenue, Brentford TW8 9HF, U.K.*

Digital Narcis/Touch. *Touch, 13 Oswald Road, London SW17 7SS, U.K.*

Discipline Global Mobile U.S. *P.O. Box 5282, Beverly Hills, CA 90209-5282.*

Dovetail. *P.O. Box 68, Brentford, Middlesex TW8 9BN, U.K.*

Dragnet. *Aureliusstr. 1-3, 5100 Aachen, Germany.*

East Side Digital (ESD). *530 N. Third Avenue, Minneapolis, MN 55401.*

ECM Records (Europe). *Postfach 600 331, 81203 Munchen, Germany.*

Emerald Web/Stargate. *P.O. Box 3156, N. Ft. Myers, FL 33918.*

Erdenklang. *In der Habbecke 16-18, 59889 Eslohe 3, Germany.*

EXT Records. *Oudstrijderslaan 18, B-8200 Brugge 2, Belgium FARN. Sandstrasse 24, D-72135 Dettenhausen, Germany.*

Fonomusic. *S.A. Garcia De Paredes, 12, 28010 Madrid, Spain.*

Garageland. *Box 343, 90107 Umea, Sweden.*

Great Expectations. *56 Standard Road, Park Royal, London NW10 6EX, U.K.*

Griffin. *P.O. Box 87587, Carol Stream, IL 87587.*

HC Productions. *P.O. Box 1421, Topanga, CA 90290.*

Headscope. *Street End Lane, Broadoak, Heathfield, East Sussex TN2T 8TU, U.K.*

Hearts of Space. *One Harbor Drive *201, Sausalito, CA 94965.*

Hybris. *Box 4301, S-10267 Stockholm, Sweden.*

Image Entertainment. *9333 Oso Avenue, Chatsworth, CA 91311.*

Innovative Communications. *P.O. Box 3, Little Sliver, NJ 07739.*

Ironic. *P.O. Box 58, Wokingharn, Berks RG11 7HN, U.K.*

IRS. *3520 Hayden Avenue, Culver City, CA 90232.*

Isildurs Bane. *Box 22, 310 42 Haverdal, Sweden.*

Island. *82 58th Avenue, New York, NY 10019.*

JMS. *12, rue Bouchut, 75015 Paris, France.*

King Biscuit Flower Hour. *P.O. Box 6700 FDR Station, New York, NY 10150.*

La Legende des Voix. *10 rue Versigny, 75018 Paris, France.*

Ladyslipper. *P.O. Box 3124, Durham, NC 27705.*

Laser's Edge. *P.O. Box 2450, Cherry Hill, NJ 08034-0199.*

Legend Music. *16 rue Deguerry, 75011 Paris, France.*

Linden Music. *P.O. Box 520, Linden, VA 22642.*

Lovely. *10 Beach Street, New York, NY 10013.*

Mantra. *Mantra/FGL, 45 rue Brancion, 75015 Paris, France.*

Mass and Fieber. *P.O. Box 1901, CH-8026 Zurich, Switzerland.*

MSI. *43, Avenue Rene Cassin, 47200 Marmande, France.*

Musea. *68 La Tinchote, 57115 Retonfey, France.*

Mute. *429 Harrow Road, London WTO 4RE, U.K.*

Mycophile. *30 Petten Grove, Orpington, Kent BR5 4PU, U.K.*

Naosha. *P.O. Box 21894, Chattanooga, TN 37424-0894.*

New Plastic Music. *Box 36B16, Los Angeles, CA 90036-1154.*

Nonsequitur. *P.O. Box 344, Albuquerque, NM 87103.*

NO CD. *Apdo. 329, 20100 Orereta-Renteria, Spain.*

O + A. *A-4061 Pasching, Wiener Bundesstr, 38, Austria.*

One Way Records. *P.O. Box 6429, Albany, NY 12206-0429.*

Opus. *Mlynske nivy 73, 827 99 Bratislava, Czechoslovakia.*

Ozone. *201 Engert Avenue, Greenpoint, NY 11222.*

Pangea. *230 Euclid Ave., Suite A, Long Beach, CA 90803.*

Paraiso. *Grabaciones Lejos del Paraiso, Tarnaulipas 125-23, Condensa 06140, Mexico.*

Pavian. *P.O. Box 193, 814 99 Bratislava, Czechoslovakia.*

Pinchbeck and Garver. *#2, 8403-189 Street, Edmonton, AB, Canada T5T 4Z2.*

Polygram. *625 8th Avenue, New York, NY.*

Progressive. *3180 Washington Boulevard, Suite 310, Ogden, UT 84401.*

Projekt. *218 S. Wabash #926, Chicago, IL 60604-2316.*

Pseudonym. *P.O. Box 2078, 3140 BB Maassluis, Holland.*

PSI-FI. *P.O. Box 248, Sevenoaks, Kent TN14 6WT, U.K.*

Rec Rec Genossenschaft. *P.O. Box 717, 8026 Zurich, Switzerland.*

Renaissance. *30 N. Raymond Avenue, Suite 212, Pasadena, CA 91103.*

Repertoire. *Gansemarkt 24, D-20354 Hamburg, Germany.*

Resource/Silence. *Box 44, S-670 41 Koppom, Sweden.*

Restless Retro/Medusa. *P.O. Box 6420, Los Angeles, CA 90028*

Resurgence. *P.O. Box 5, Derwentside, Co. Durham DH9 7HR, U.K.*

Rhino. *10635 Santa Monica Boulevard, Los Angeles, CA 90025-4900.*

RRR. *151 Paige Street, Lowell, MA 01852.*

Rykodisc. *Pickering Wharf, Building C, Salem, MA 01970.*

Sequel. *Castle Communications, 110 East 59th Street, 18th Floor, New York, NY 10022.*

Spalax. *10 rue des Feuillantines, 75005 Paris, France.*

Staalplat/Soleilmoon. *P.O. Box 83296, Portland, OR 97283.*

Tern. *Veldstraat 2, B-3051 Sint-Joris-Weert, Belgium.*

Themes International. *KPM Music Ltd., 21 Denmark Street, London WC2H 8NF, U.K.*

Third Stream. *7401 S.W. 63rd Court, Miami, FL 33143.*

Time Warner/Atlantic/Reprise. *75 Rockefeller Plaza, New York, NY 10019.*

Ventricle. *P.O. Box 19523, Seattle, WA 98109.*

Vinyl Magic. *Via Tibaldi, 29, 20136, Milano, Italy.*

Virgin. *338 N. Foothill Road, Beverly Hills, CA 90210.*

Virtalevy. *Akertegsgatan 7, 78465 Borlange, Sweden.*

WEA Records (Europe). *Warner Music, Germany GMBH, Postfach 76 12 60, D-22062 Hamburg, Germany.*

Weasel Disc. *1459 18th St. #140, San Francisco, CA 94107.*

Windham Hill. *P.O. Box 5501, Beverly Hills, CA 90211-2713.*

World Serpent. *Unit 7-1-7 Seager Buildings, Brookmill Road, London 5E8 4HI, U.K.*

Artist Contact Addresses.

A few of the artists in this book have contact addresses other than through their label addresses. These artists and their addresses are as follows:

Anekdoten. *Box 808, 10136 Stockholm, Sweden.*

Luigi Archetti. *Postfach 1312, Rote Fabrik, CH-8038 Zurich, Switzerland.*

Boud Deun. *EHP Productions, P.O. Box 1176, Warrenton, VA 20188.*

Chris and Cosey. *BM CTI, London WC1 3XX, U.K.*

Danielle Dax. *BCM SWARF, London WC1N 3XX, U.K.*

Constance Demby. *Sound Currents, P.O. Box 1044, Fairfax, CA 94978.*

Fire Merchants. *P.O. Box 5644, Santa Monica, CA 90409.*

Andy Glass (of Solstice). *#7 Augustus Road, Stony Stratford, Buckinghamshire NK11 IH5, U.K.*

Gong. *G.A.S., P.O. Box 871, Glastonbury, Somerset BA6 9FE, U.K.*

Manuel Gottsching (of Ash Ra Tempel). *Fuggerstr. 19, D-10777 Berlin, Germany.*

John Greaves (of Henry Cow/National Health). *Acousti Studios, 54 rue de la Seine, 75006 Paris, France.*

Michael Harrison. *256 Sixth Avenue, Suite A, Brooklyn, NY 11215.*

Steve Howe (of Yes). *44 Oswald Close, Leatherhead, Surrey KT22 9UT, U.K.*

Lightwave. *BP 10, 95620 Parmain, France.*

Annea Lockwood. *P.O. Box 16, Crompond, NY 10517.*

Melting Euphoria. *Summer of Love Music, 839 Divisadero #11, San Francisco, CA 94117.*

Phil Miller (of Hatfield and the North/National Health). *c/o Crescent Discs, 29a Colverstone Crescent, London B8 2LG, U.K.*

Mani Neumeier. *Auf Dem Berg 1, D-64757 Finkenbach, Switzerland.*

Hans Otte. *Einslebenersh 46, D-28329 Bremen, Germany.*

Ozric Tentacles. *No. 1 Woodman Hill, Berkeley, Frome, Somerset, U.K.*

David Parsons. *P.O. Box 24-113, Manners Street, Wellington, New Zealand.*

Pip Pyle (of Gong/Hatfield and the North/National Health). *c/o Gimini Music, 42 rue de la Republique, 94 430 Chenne-Vieres, France.*

Rapoon. *c/o Robin Storey, 15 Wiseton Court, Newcastle Upon Tyne, NE7 7NT, U.K.*

Richard Sinclair (of Hatfield and the North). *P.O. Box 326, Canterbury, Kent CT2 7GR, U.K.*

Dave Stewart (of Egg/Hatfield and the North/National Health). *c/o Broken Records, P.O. Box 4416, London SW19 8XR, U.K.*

Liz Story. *P.O. Box 9532, Madison, WI 53715.*

Tangerine Dream. *Tadream Production, P.O. Box 30 33 40, 10728 Berlin, Germany.*

Dr. Fiorella Terenzi. *P.O. Box 34182, Los Angeles, CA 90034-0182.*

David Torn. *c/o TEXTure, P.O. Box 465, Bearsville, NY 12409.*

Tuu. *Archive, P.O. Box 1035, Windsor SL4 3YP, U.K.*

White Willow. *Hulda Garborgsv. 32, 1364 Hvalstad, Norway.*

INDEX